World Music

World Music

A Global Journey

Fifth Edition

Terry E. Miller
Kent State University

and

Andrew Shahriari
Kent State University

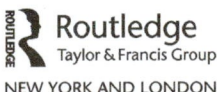

Routledge
Taylor & Francis Group

NEW YORK AND LONDON

Fifth edition published 2021
by Routledge
52 Vanderbilt Avenue, New York, NY 10017

and by Routledge
2 Park Square, Milton Park, Abingdon, Oxon OX14 4RN

Routledge is an imprint of the Taylor & Francis Group, an informa business

First edition published by Routledge 2006
Fourth edition published by Routledge 2016

Library of Congress Cataloging in Publication Data
Names: Miller, Terry E., author. | Shahriari, Andrew C., author.
Title: World music : a global journey / Terry E. Miller and Andrew Shahriari.
Description: Fifth edition. | New York : Routledge, 2020. |
Includes bibliographical references and index.
Identifiers: LCCN 2020020253 (print) | LCCN 2020020254 (ebook) |
ISBN 9780367423155 (hardback) | ISBN 9780367423148 (paperback) |
ISBN 9780367823498 (ebook)
Subjects: LCSH: World music–History and criticism.
Classification: LCC ML3545 .M54 2020 (print) |
LCC ML3545 (ebook) | DDC 780.9–dc23
LC record available at https://lccn.loc.gov/2020020253
LC ebook record available at https://lccn.loc.gov/2020020254

ISBN: 978-0-367-42314-8 (pbk)
ISBN: 978-0-367-42315-5 (hbk)
ISBN: 978-0-367-82349-8 (ebk)

DOI: 10.4324/9780367823498

Typeset in Melior
by Newgen Publishing UK

Senior Editor: Constance Ditzel
Senior Editorial Assistant: Peter Sheehy
Production Manager: Victoria Day
Marketing Manager: Alain Mentha
Text Design: Newgen Publishing UK
Copy Editor: Martin Noble
Proofreader: Victoria Chow
Cover Designer: Brian Alterio

Cover image, center: Photography by John Running, courtesy of Canyon Records.

Visit the companion website: www.routledge.com/miller

Contents

Preface

This textbook is inspired by a class we taught (and Andrew continues to teach) at Kent State University for many years, "Music as a World Phenomenon." In the mid-1990s, when the university established a requirement for cultural diversity classes, the course was a natural fit and enrollment exploded overnight. Fifty students a semester turned into over 500 within a few years. Dissatisfied with the introductory world music textbooks available at the time, we set out to write one that would serve this greater number of students, few of whom had formal music training. Its success has encouraged the class to grow to nearly 1500 students per semester and is one of the most popular courses on campus. Other universities have experienced similar growth in their world music surveys. The online version of the class at Kent State, which accommodates nearly 500 students, remains full, and the textbook with its accompanying interactive website has proven an invaluable resource, especially for those students. We hope this fifth edition of *World Music: A Global Journey* will encourage the same enthusiasm in both instructors and students for teaching and learning about the world and its music, as it has for us at Kent State.

Scope

Anyone who attempts a book such as this must settle on answers to a few questions:

- *Breadth* or *depth*? You cannot have both, unless you want a tome that could hold down your loose papers through a hurricane. We have chosen breadth. While we recognize the impossibility of doing justice to all the world's notable and interesting musics, we also feel that doing what you can is better than doing nothing. The second major question is:
- *Geographical* or *topical organization*? As ethnomusicologists we are tempted to organize our studies topically, in order to explore such issues as identity, gender, representation, meaning, globalization, and so on, but we have found that this approach leaves most students in a state of geographical disorientation. While such a plan would make it easier to discuss many of the issues at stake in "cultural diversity" courses, it would make it difficult to communicate a coherent view of the music of a given area. Thus, we have chosen a geographical organization, though certainly many of these musics are globally diffuse and can appeal to an international audience. A third question is:
- Should the concentration be on *music as sound* or *music as culture*? The study of world musics is the focus of a discipline known as *Ethnomusicology,* which seeks to understand both music and its cultural associations. This field of scholarly research has long had a fascination with the anthropological aspects of the music studied—what we used to call "the context"—but some of our field's critics have noted a growing reluctance to discuss musical sound at all, complaining that ethnomusicologists do "everything but the music." Others scoff at ethnomusicology as eth-NO-MUSIC-ology. We have striven for a balanced approach, choosing first to emphasize music as sound because we realize that many of the instructors using this book are situated in music departments and are naturally inclined to focus on music as sound. However, we also include important cultural aspects, allowing teachers using this book to choose which to emphasize.

Organization

Travel is the central metaphor of the book, in part because that is often how the authors experienced the music we present. After three introductory chapters in which we discuss the elements of music, we present ten chapters on specific geographical areas, be they a continent (e.g., Europe) or a subcontinent (e.g., South Asia). As with any major research trip, preparation is necessary before a specific area can be considered in depth.

"Background Preparation" provides the big picture giving the general lay of the land, some of an area's history, and raising certain issues related to music-making in the region. We then give an overview of music the region has to offer before landing in a particular country or area. Here we review the background information pertinent to this particular place and give the reader some feel for the locale's history and culture.

After this, we begin visiting our individual "Sites." These are the audio tracks and discussions we have chosen to represent the area—though you should always bear in mind that we have omitted many others of equal significance. As with travel, so with music: we simply cannot visit every interesting place. Hopefully, you can return to some areas later and experience more on your own. Each Site is explored in three steps.

1. "First Impressions"—In this section we attempt to convey the impressions and associations the music might inspire in a first-time listener. These are necessarily subjective and intended to encourage readers to consider their own first impressions in comparison to ours.
2. "Aural Analysis"—Here we focus on the site in terms of musical sound, discussing whatever is most relevant. This could include the medium (instruments and/or voices) and any of the prominent musical elements that distinguish an example.
3. "Cultural Considerations"—The final section is where relevant cultural matters are raised. These are the "contexts" and "issues" that have differentiated ethnomusicology from most other music disciplines.

This process can serve as a framework for exploring an infinite array of world music traditions. Instructors may wish to bring in some examples, based on their own focus and experience, as a supplement to the materials provided here.

The Fifth Edition

Following the release of the first edition in late 2005, we were gratified so many of our colleagues in schools of all sizes and missions adopted *World Music: A Global Journey* and found it useful. Although we feel fortunate that so many chose this book over the increasing number of other choices, we continually think about how we can improve it. Hopefully, the fifth edition offers many of the improvements suggested by users along with those originating with the authors.

*   **Streaming Online Music:** As technology updates around the world, old technology is becoming obsolete. Though CDs are still commonly sold, more and more people are accessing their music solely through online media. Many textbooks have already transitioned to downloadable supplementary materials, so we have opted to adapt to the times as well and offer the music examples discussed throughout the book as streaming media. While we know that some readers will be disappointed in this transition, the reality is that most students today have no means of playing CDs on their computers or other listening devices. Hopefully this will be a welcome change for them and acceptable to those needing to adjust to this new format.
*   **New Site**
    Georgian Choral Singing replaces the site on Bulgarian Women's Choir.

The former (fourth edition) site has been moved to the textbook website.

- **Musical Markers**: This new feature summarizing key musical features of each audio example is found at the end of each Listening Guide.
- **Updated "Inside Look" features**: Many of the musicians and scholars featured have revised their entries. While some of the earlier writers have been rotated off, we welcome a number of new and distinguished people to this feature: Patricia Shehan-Campbell (internationally renowned scholar of Music Education), Oleg Kruglyakov (Russian Balalaika virtuoso), Chan Park (scholar and performer of Korean P'ansori), Vivek Virani (scholar and performer of Indian classical music), and Mia Gormandy (scholar and performer of Trinidadian pan, i.e., steel drum).
- **New photos**: As we try to do with each new edition, there are many new photographs throughout the book drawn from our own field research and others in the field, as well as professional stock footage archives with an eye for fieldwork-oriented images that complement our original list of figures.
- **Additional Explore More box**: This essay focuses on Slovenian Polka.
- **Additional Resources**: These have been updated to include more recent publications and online resources.
- **Instructors' Resources**: These have been revisited to include new presentations, exam questions, class time activities, and a more integrated website that can be used to expand course coverage.
- **Interactive Listening Guides**: More of these have been incorporated on the website so that students can listen to streamed music at specific prompts.

Listening Guides

The purpose of the Listening Guides is to encourage *active listening*, rather than *passive listening*. Many students find they lack experience in listening actively to music. The music washes over them as a complete sound without much thought toward the details. Most everyone does this on a daily basis, such as listening to the car radio, walking through a mall, waiting in a doctor's office, or even while attending a concert. They passively "absorb" the sound without really thinking about it.

Active listening requires more than just your ears. You must focus on individual elements in the music in order to understand a variety of features, such as its organization or its rhythmic/melodic elements, its correlation to movement in dance/theater, the sound as a manifestation of emotional/spiritual expression, etc. Such intentional listening promotes a greater appreciation of the music, which will hopefully make it more appealing, if only from an intellectual perspective.

Each listening guide focuses on key features of the example that help you identify the timbre of different instruments, important melodic and/or rhythmic elements, as well as aspects of form and variations in dynamics, if applicable. Every guide begins with an introduction to the specific example, that is, title, chapter and site number, etc., followed by a description of the sound elements (vocal and instrumental) heard. The time outline indicates the minutes/seconds (0'00") of each "Listening Focus" item described. (These time codes may vary slightly according to the device you are using to play the example.) New to this edition is the inclusion of a "Musical Markers" section that focuses on the most prominent Fundamentals of Music heard in the example. You might think of these as "keywords" for the ears to help you quickly identify the example. (See Chapter 2 for further discussion of Musical Markers.) The guide concludes with the source for the example and an "Ethno-Challenge," (short for Ethnomusicology Challenge).

The Listening Guides will help you with the "Aural Analysis" section of the readings. Our recommendation is:

1. Listen first through the entire example *without* the guide, just to get a "First Impression" without concern over the details of the music. Compare your first impressions with those we have offered.
2. Read the "Aural Analysis" for the example.
3. Listen again *with* the guide and take note of each "Listening Focus" description. You may have to start/stop and rewind the example several times to hear each item. That's a good thing! It means you are actively listening to the music. If you get through the entire example without stopping once, this probably means you have returned to passive listening.
4. Listen through the entire example again after you feel confident that you have heard and understood all of the "Listening Focus" items. You will find you are hearing the music with a keener sense of its details. That gong sound missed before will now "jump out" at you, or you may find yourself humming the basic melody or tapping out the fundamental rhythm.
5. Note the "Musical Markers" at the end of the Listening Guide, which are what we consider the most prominent musical elements that can help you identify the style of music beyond the specific example.

To test your new perspective on the music, try playing the example for someone else and see if he or she notices the same details before you point them out.

We also hope that the Listening Guides will assist instructors in highlighting these key elements during lectures. To know the difference between the sound of a *tabla* and a *tambura*, for example, the instructor may have to highlight the distinction in the classroom. The time code references will help expedite searching for such "Listening Focus" items during class time.

Each guide ends with a feature called the "Ethno-Challenge." Some of these are quite simple, while others may be quite difficult. As ethnomusicologists ourselves, we tried to imagine an activity that would have benefited us in researching each music genre. This may involve library research, such as hunting down a rare manuscript or translating a foreign-language document on Beijing Opera; learning a performance technique, such as circular breathing; or even making a musical instrument, such as a mouth harp, etc. Instructors may have their own ideas for such challenges, but the end-goal remains to encourage more active participation and understanding of the music. The challenges are also meant to be fun projects for your own enjoyment or even to present to the rest of the class.

Finally, we encourage you to add your own "Listening Focus" points to these guides. We may have overlooked or intentionally omitted features due to their repetition within the example or other factors, such as space considerations for the page layouts. You will better develop your active listening skills by adding to these guides, which will ultimately make any music you hear a more meaningful experience.

Structure of Each Listening Guide

LISTENING GUIDE   0.0 (0'00")

Site 0.0
Country: Example Title

Instruments: *Trumpet* (aerophone), *Guitar* (chordophone), etc.
Voices: Male/Female

TIME   **LISTENING FOCUS**
0'00"   Example begins...

Source: *World Music: A Global Journey*

ETHNO-CHALLENGE (0.0): Listen to each audio example at least three times.

How Instructors Can Expand Course Coverage

"Teaching a textbook" is a widely and often effectively used method but also one that raises thorny issues. The problem with any world survey is that the authors must of necessity choose a certain set of examples and ideas based on their own thinking and experience—but course instructors may have a different view. We suggest therefore that teachers consider the following ideas when using this book:

Be selective. If you find that seventy music examples are too many for your class, then select those that suit your needs. We have attempted to provide reasonably good surveys of each area—considering the limitations of space—but for some instructors this will be too much and for others too little.

Use our plan as a model. Just as you can exclude specific sites, you can also add your own. These additions can be accomplished by either the professor or student. An excellent assignment would be for students to write about a music track not selected by us, using the three approaches employed in this book: first impressions, aural analysis, and cultural considerations. Such exercises could become class papers or presentations as well.

Research further on your own. Just as easily as additional sites can be researched and written about, those presented herein can be developed by students into class presentations that include audio examples, video/DVD clips, and even performances on substitute instruments or the real ones. Students and teachers may locate living representatives of a culture—or even musicians from the tradition under study—who can come to class to discuss the culture or perform the music live.

Consider utilizing additional resources in the neighborhood or university community. We have intentionally focused on pathways available via the Internet, but you might also consider some other areas of investigation, such as libraries and museums.

- **Libraries.** Most libraries, both public and those associated with colleges and universities, have collections of recordings and video materials. Anyone wishing to venture beyond this book might do so in places as diverse as one's local public library to world-class collections in places such as Indiana University's Archives of Traditional Music in Bloomington, Indiana, to the Library of Congress's American Folklife Center in Washington, DC. Similar collections can be found around the globe.

- **Museums.** Many large cities have excellent museums devoted to local history, culture, or general anthropology of the world. These often include displays of musical instruments, dioramas that include musical activity, and sometimes sound resources. A few have major collections of musical instruments, including the Metropolitan Museum of Art in New York City, The National Music Museum in Vermillion, South Dakota, and the Musical Instrument Museum in Phoenix, Arizona.
- **Internet.** The Internet offers virtually unlimited possibilities for exploration. Two sites relative to this book dominate: YouTube and iTunes. iTunes (and other similar sites) offer many kinds of music for paid download. These sites can be searched by genre, title, or artist; what kinds of music are offered will change constantly. YouTube similarly offers a nearly bottomless series of free video clips of most forms of music, dance, and theater known in the world. Searches of the Internet will also turn up many other kinds of information and resources. One of them is Wikipedia, a free, online encyclopedia. While many of the articles discovered (in numerous languages, too) are quite fine, users must remember that these entries are not always peer-reviewed, and their reliability varies widely since anyone (including you) can write and post entries.

Website – www.routledge.com/miller5e

The website is vital to *World Music: A Global Journey*. At Kent State, the book is used for an online course, so the website has been crafted to be adaptable for all kinds of teaching situations, with audio and visual elements and numerous teaching and learning tools:

For the student

- Flashcards of vocabulary words
- Additional articles and regional sites from previous editions of the textbook
- Practice quizzes
- Links to online videos
- Links to other suggested resources e.g., books, DVDs, websites, etc.
- Selected Listening Guides in an interactive listening guide application

For the instructor

- Downloadable classroom presentations
- Test banks, hosted in the Routledge QuestBank application
- Additional articles and Sites from previous editions of the textbook
- Suggested classroom activities and additional projects
- Select images from the book
- Author/Instructor Interactive Portal
- E-Package materials for online course development

Our Own Journey (Thus Far)

Neither author, of course, has been everywhere or heard every kind of music the world has to offer. Writing this book has been a humbling experience—only fools think they can cover the world's musics in a single volume. Regardless of our qualms, however, world music courses have become a normal part of the academic environment, and the need for such introductory courses will not go away because of philosophical reservations. If anything, the demand for them will grow. We have attempted to play to our strengths while recognizing our limitations. In the following pages of this Preface we engage in a kind of "truth in advertising," by revealing some of our own personal histories with regard to the musics of the world. Perhaps after having read of our experiences, which we present separately, you will better understand why we wrote what we wrote and perhaps see more clearly what your own trajectory might become in the future.

Terry E. Miller

My first experience hearing non-Western music came during my undergraduate years at the College of Wooster (Ohio), where I was majoring in organ performance. Ravi Shankar, India's most famous sitar player until his recent passing, came to the campus as part of the Community Music Series in 1964, several years before he became famous in his own right and as the teacher of George Harrison (member of the Beatles). After his performance, the music majors met with Shankar, but our attempts to understand the concept of raga were mostly unsuccessful. We simply had no conceptual framework for understanding modal improvisation. Further, we had never seen a musician perform seated on the floor, or encountered incense at a music event, and we also failed to understand the significance of the *tambura* lute player and *tabla* drummer accompanying Shankar. In those days there were virtually no world music courses anywhere, and recordings other than those on the Folkways label were rare.

My next encounter with an "exotic" music did not come until after I had been drafted into the U.S. Army in 1968 and sent to the Republic of Vietnam in 1969 to help fight the war from a swivel chair in front of a Remington typewriter. As a "chairborne" soldier working at a huge base about twenty miles from Saigon (now Ho Chi Minh City), I could have ignored Vietnam entirely. Instead, I decided to explore Vietnamese music. Doing so, however, required trips to Saigon. Having no official business there and no authorization, I had to go illegally on weekends. In Saigon, I attended theatrical performances, bought instruments and recordings, and visited the Saigon Conservatory of Music, where my language abilities were too limited for effective communication. A one-week leave to Bangkok, Thailand, in January 1970 brought me into contact with Thai music. During my visit, I purchased a long, bamboo mouth-organ instrument called the *khaen*, simply because its appearance reminded me of a pipe organ. I did not know how significant this instrument would become for my later life.

After returning to the United States, I enrolled in a Western Historical Musicology graduate degree program at Indiana University. In spite of the program I was in, I decided to write my master's thesis on an Ohio shape-note teacher and my doctoral dissertation on the music of northeast Thailand. With a

Co-author Terry Miller (on right) with fellow soldier while serving in the United States Army in Vietnam (1969)

Co-author Terry Miller (left) tries his hand at cutting the design into a giant Thai shadow puppet (*nang yai*) under the watchful eye of master Wira, in Singburi province, Thailand (2019)

generous grant in hand, I went with my family to northeast Thailand in late 1972, for a fourteen-month stay during which I researched that region's music. The resulting dissertation completed my Ph.D. and luckily I stumbled into a teaching position at Kent State University just as they were starting a graduate program in ethnomusicology. I taught at Kent State until my retirement in January 2005. Since that time I have remained actively engaged in research and writing, and I spend about two months a year in Thailand (wisely, during the American winter).

To make a long story short, I kept up my interest in Thailand during my tenure at Kent, but my interests also expanded in other directions. With the help of a succession of "native musician" graduate students, I started two ensembles, one to play traditional Thai music, the other to play Chinese music, and I played in both from 1979 and 1987 respectively until the ensembles were disbanded in May 2005. In 1998 the Thai Ensemble toured Thailand, performing in six cities and appearing on most television channels. The musics of mainland Southeast Asia—Thailand, Laos, Cambodia, Vietnam, Burma, and Malaysia—remain my core interest, with the greatest emphasis being on Thailand and Laos. I also developed a now long-standing interest in orally transmitted hymnody in the West, which has led to extensive and continuing fieldwork in the United States, Scotland, Jamaica, Trinidad, and St. Vincent, the latter three being part of the English-speaking Caribbean. My third area of interest has been Chinese music, and I have done fieldwork in China itself but much more in the overseas Chinese community of Thailand.

Lastly, I have collected material and experienced live music when possible in each country I've visited. In addition to Vietnam, Thailand, and China, these include the United Kingdom, Ireland, France, Germany, Spain, Hungary, Slovakia, Croatia, Greece, Israel, Nepal, Japan, Korea, Burma, Malaysia, Laos, and South Africa. All of these experiences have contributed to my bank of knowledge. Even so, they have exposed me to only a small percentage of the world's musics. The rest have thus far been experienced, if at all, only vicariously through audio and video recordings or at concerts given by resident or touring musicians. Naturally, knowledge gained through first-hand experience goes deeper than that gained from books and CDs, but even an introductory book like this and carefully listened-to recordings can shed some light on a corner of the world that would otherwise remain totally unfamiliar.

Co-author Andrew Shahriari (seated at piano) and friends perform in a jazz club with local university students in Moscow, Russia (1989)

Andrew Shahriari

My first recollection of an interest in "world music" is actually associated with a music that I knew quite well. As an undergraduate, I was fortunate to study abroad and to visit Russia on a two-week tour of Moscow and Leningrad (now St. Petersburg—again) in 1990, during the last days of the Soviet Union. My first revelation was that what I had previously believed about Russians was completely untrue: I had been misled all my life into thinking they were evil, American-hating Communists who would sooner spit on me than shake my hand. To the contrary, I found the people I met in Russia to be the most friendly, helpful people in Europe, with a great respect for Americans. My misconceptions were based on ignorance and on the stereotyping of people I did not know. Sadly, the negative propagandizing of other cultures by the media remains a problem today.

My second revelation came in a Moscow jazz club, where I realized that music can cross cultural barriers as effectively as speech. While music is not a "universal language," it nonetheless generally draws more on emotion than intellect. Music has the uncanny power to enable those who speak the same musical language to "connect" on a different level than is possible with the spoken word. Though conversations I had with Russians fluent in English were friendly, they were mostly superficial exchanges. In contrast, the twenty-minute "jam" my American friends and I played with the jazz club's Russian house band resulted in genuine laughter, bear hugs, and toasts in our honor for the rest of the night—without our ever even learning the names of our comrades. All of us knew we would never meet again, but for that night we were the best of friends because we spoke through music.

My Russian encounter inspired my interest in ethnomusicology and continues to motivate my core concerns as a scholar, educator, and musician. Cultural ignorance is the source of many stereotypes about other peoples. A primary goal of my own study and certainly of my teaching, as well as of this textbook, is to encourage an awareness of our cultural biases. You cannot learn about the world from only the nightly news and cable television. While the United States has "free" media, the stories that are presented are highly selective and strongly biased toward American interests. To think otherwise is naïve. This is true in other cultures as well. Politics and business influence the content of newspapers, books, television, movies, radio, even the Internet, all of which then shape our attitudes about others and ourselves. Recent revelations about such politcal influences via social media verify such far reaching concerns about the influence of

Co-author Andrew Shahriari (left) tries out a freshly made bamboo panpipe (*wot*) in northeast Thailand's Roi-et province, accompanied by student Charlie Occhipinti (2019)

media on psychological dispositions and consequent behaviors. We cannot avoid being culturally biased, but an awareness of this reality is important to keeping an open mind, which encourages understanding of other perspectives and fosters communication rather than conflict.

After college, I spent a couple of years pursuing a career in the music business, but quickly realized that the "business" of making music greatly overwhelmed the actual creation of it. Thankfully, a professor suggested I study ethnomusicology as a graduate student due to my interest in blues and jazz. I came to Kent State in 1992 and have never looked back. I explored my diverse interests in music and discovered many new and intriguing sounds that have spurred me to travel to many new countries, experience an array of new cultures, and to meet wonderful people from all over the world. Like Terry, I became fascinated with the music and culture of Thailand and focused my studies on the northern region (Lanna), an area that few had yet to explore in depth. I have since pursued other interests in music and spirituality, popular world music, and music therapy and traveled to numerous locales, including Mexico, China, India, Brazil, the Czech Republic, Portugal, Germany, Austria, France, Scotland, England, and throughout the United States.

But my exploration of world music is certainly not limited to only the places I have visited. Being part of a university culture allows for a great many opportunities to learn about world music on a first-hand basis by attending concerts, meeting international musicians and local residents, as well as learning from my many students who share their world music and culture experiences with me. By studying world music, I learn about people's passions. I learn what they value, and I learn how they think. Music can reveal the deepest emotions of a people, their philosophies of life, their conceptions of death, their hopes and fears, anger and affections, desires and dreams. Music says what cannot be put into words and often adds to words what cannot be merely spoken.

I hope that each person who reads this textbook will approach each site visited with an open mind and appreciate each tradition on its own terms. Remember that appreciation is not necessarily the same thing as enjoyment. Some music is like sugar, sweet to taste and easy to take from the start. Other music is an acquired taste, and may only ever be appreciated at an intellectual level. I myself do not find all music aurally appealing, yet I strive to keep an open mind and accept that all musics (or musical sounds) are worthwhile because they are significant to someone—otherwise they would not exist. If you have read this far, I am certain you will do the same.

Terry E. Miller
Andrew Shahriari
January 2020

Acknowledgments

None of us acquire knowledge in isolation, and all of us are indebted to the many people we have encountered during our lives. Certainly we are indebted to our own formal teachers at all levels, but our knowledge of the world's musics is only possible thanks to innumerable individuals, some known first-hand, others known through performances, some only known through the Internet, who have—wittingly or unwittingly—taught us what we know. But we, not they, are responsible for that which remains unknown or misunderstood.

In particular we are indebted to the many individuals who have made it possible to offer an unprecedented seventy tracks of music, especially those who did so without payment. Similarly, we are indebted to those who appear in our photographs and to the photographers who allowed us to use their photographs. Their names are to be found in the credits for each track and each photo.

We are also indebted to our many students, who over the years have made us increasingly aware of the challenges of teaching world musics. While some of our students have been music majors, the vast majority are "non-music majors" satisfying requirements for their Liberal Education Core and for Diversity courses. As such, few have had a special interest in the world's musics, so inspiring enthusiasm in the subject matter has been an exhilarating challenge. The insights brought from teaching students with a variety of majors and levels of interest in studying the world's musics and cultures have been our greatest resource. It is these students who inspired much of our writing throughout the book.

A great number of individuals offered special help, by recording tracks, offering detailed information on those tracks, supplying photos, and offering extensive corrections. For this fifth edition we are especially appreciative of the following: Paul Austerlitz, Mr. Balusubramaniam, Praphai Boomsermsuwong, Kelly Foreman, Eliot Grasso, Kathleen Joyce-Grendahl, Roderic Knight, Mary Lawson Burke, Marcia Loebeck, Scott Marcus, Sara Stone Miller, Priwan Nanongkham, Phong Nguyen, Adrienne Kaeppler, Dale Olsen, Anne Prescott, K.S. Resmi, N. Scott Robinson, Daniel Sheehy, Janine Tiffe, Eve McPherson, Amy Unruh, John Kolessar, Jennifer Johnstone, and Sunmin Yoon. Additionally, Andrew would like to thank several of his graduate students, especially Will Bulger, Alexis Hill, Anuthep Meelertsom, and Charlie Occhipinti, for their suggestions and contributions to this latest edition. If we have omitted your name—and you will know who you are—we apologize for our oversight.

Last but not least, we must thank our families for their forbearance and their tolerance of our long periods sitting before the computer writing and revising this book. Preceding that were many long and often demanding research trips to the field, usually with our spouses or with them left behind to "hold the fort" at home.

In addition, Terry would like to acknowledge the good humor shown by his children, Sonia and Esther, who, dragged along on numerous field trips, at least contributed their charms on his "research subjects." Esther in particular thought her family's trip to Trinidad in 1990 was to visit beaches but soon discovered that they were spending up to eight hours on Sunday in Spiritual Baptist churches. Andrew apologizes in advance, expecting that his children, Cyrus and Saffron, will have similar experiences in the future; but he promises to try to visit the beach at least once per field trip for the sake of his wife's sanity.

Finally, both of us would like to thank the professionals we have worked with at Routledge. These are especially Constance Ditzel, our Managing Editor, who has given special attention to this project, offered many excellent suggestions, and been especially supportive of our ideas by being flexible. Alain Mentha, our Marketing Manager, who has tirelessly promoted the book and offered great support in its dissemination throughout the globe. Peter Sheehy and Victoria Day have been consistently helpful, while keeping a low profile behind the scenes. We are especially indebted to Newgen Publishing UK who created the page layouts for this edition. It has been a pleasure working with everyone at Routledge since the inception of this book in 2002.

Map of the World

1 ALBANIA
2 AUSTRIA
3 BOSNIA
4 BULGARIA
5 CROATIA
6 CZECH
7 HUNGARY
8 MACEDONIA
9 MOLDOVA
10 ROMANIA
11 SLOVAKIA
12 SLOVENIA
13 SWITZERLAND
14 YUGOSLAVIA

Chapter 1

Before the Trip Begins

Fundamental Issues

Visitors arriving at Mingun, Myanmar (Burma), on the Irrawaddy River north of Mandalay, are offered "taxi" transport in a covered ox cart to see the base of a gigantic pagoda begun in 1790, left incomplete, and damaged by a great earthquake in 1839

What is Music?

Although virtually everyone listens to it and most libraries include books on it, music is notoriously difficult to define, describe, and discuss. While in a literal sense music is only a kind of sound vibration, it must be distinguished from other kinds of sound vibration such as speech or noise. This distinction is based not on observable acoustical differences but on the meanings we assign the sounds that become, in our minds, music. Music is thus a conceptual phenomenon that exists only in the mind; at least that is where the distinctions between "noise" and "music" occur. Graphic representations of music—notations of any sort—are only that, representations. A score is not "the music" because music is a series of sonic vibrations transmitted through the ears to the brain, where we begin the process of making sense of and finding meaning and order in these sounds. Music is also challenging in that it can only be observed in "real time," that is, over the course of its performance. Most other forms of art—paintings, sculptures, architecture—can be observed comprehensively at a glance.

We are normally surrounded by sounds—the sounds of nature, the sounds of man's inventions, of our own voices—but for most of us most of the time distinguishing "music" from the totality of ambient sounds around us comes "naturally." We recognize "noise" when we hear it; we recognize "music" when we hear it. Our sense of the difference between the two derives from a lifetime of conditioning. This conditioning is cultural in origin. Our own concept of what distinguishes music from noise is more or less the same as that of most everyone else within our "culture," as we were raised in an environment that conveyed to us general notions about the distinctions between the two. Therefore, definitions of "music" are of necessity culturally determined.

For example, some Americans make a distinction between music and singing; for them, the word *music* refers only to instrumental sounds. Some years ago we wrote to a Primitive Baptist elder (a church leader) in North Carolina regarding that denomination's orally transmitted hymn singing. We asked—naïvely—"when you sing, do you use music?" The answer was totally logical within the elder's own world: "We don't have any music in our church. All we do is sing." By *music* we meant *notation*, but for the elder music meant *instruments*. In this book, however, we use the term *music* more broadly to encompass both instrumental and vocal phenomena.

Within the vocal realm, one of the most intriguing distinctions is that between speech and song. At what point on the speech–song continuum does speech become song? The answers to this question vary widely from place to place. Listeners from one culture may easily misjudge sounds from another culture by assuming, based on their own experience, that this or that performance is "song," when the people performing consider it other than "song." A general term for such "in-between" phenomena is "heightened speech"; for example, chant. One is most likely to have trouble differentiating "speech" and "song" when experiencing the heightened speech of religious and ritual performances, especially those associated with religions that discourage or even ban the performance of "song."

In the Buddhist tradition of Thailand, for example, ordained monks are not permitted to perform song. But if you were to attend a "reading" of the great tale of Prince Wetsandawn (the Buddha's final incarnation before achieving *nirvana*), during which a robed monk intones a long poem describing the prince's life, you might, like most Westerners, describe the performance as "singing." After all, the monk performing the story clearly requires considerable vocal talents to negotiate such elaborate strings of pitches. From a Western perspective this performance sounds convincingly like song. From the monk's perspective, however—indeed, from that of most Thai—what he is performing cannot be song because monks are prohibited from singing. The monk's performance is described by the verb *thet*, which means "to preach." Why is this performance not considered song? Because there is consensus among Thai that it is not song but rather it is preaching. Thus, this chanted poetry is simultaneously "music" from our perspective and definitely "not music" from the perspective of the performer and his primary audience. Neither perspective is right or wrong in a universal sense; rather, each is "correct" according to respective cultural norms.

Thai Buddhist monks chant the afternoon service at Wat [temple] Suthat, Bangkok, Thailand

Music: Universal Language or Culturally Specific Activity?

It is frequently asserted that "music is a universal [or international] language," a "meta-language" that expresses universal human emotions and transcends the barriers of language and culture.

The problems with this metaphor are many. First, music is not a language, at least not in the sense of conveying specific meanings through specific symbols, in standard patterns analogous to syntax, and governed by rules of structure analogous to grammar. While attempts have been made to analyze music in linguistic terms, these ultimately failed because music is of a totally different realm. Second, it is questionable whether music really can transcend linguistic barriers and culturally determined behaviors, though some forms of emotional communication, such as crying, are so fundamentally human that virtually all perceive it the same way. In our journey we will come to see that particular musics do not support the notion that music is a universal language, and we do not believe such a concept to be useful in examining the world's musics.

As will become increasingly clear as you begin your exploration of the world's vast array of musics, musical expression is both culturally determined and culturally encoded with meaning. The field of *semiotics*, which deals with signs—systems of symbols and their meanings—offers an explanation of how music works. Although semiotics was not created specifically for music, it has been adapted by Canadian scholar Jean-Jacques Nattiez and others for this purpose.

A semiotic view of music asserts that the musical sound itself is a "neutral" symbol that has no inherent meaning. Music is thus thought of as a "text" or "trace" that has to be interpreted. In a process called the *poietic*, the creator of the music encodes meanings and emotions into the "neutral" composition or performance, which is then interpreted by anyone listening to the music, a process called the *esthesic*. Each individual listener's interpretation is entirely the result of

SEMIOTICS
The study of signs and systems of signs, including in music.

cultural conditioning and life experience. When a group of people sharing similar backgrounds encounters a work or performance of music, there is the possibility that all (or most) will interpret what they hear similarly—but it is also possible that there will be as many variant interpretations as there are listeners. In short, meaning is not passed from the creator through the music to the listener. Instead, the listener applies an interpretation that is independent of the creator. However, when both creator and listener share similar backgrounds, there is a greater likelihood that the listener's interpretation will be consistent with the creator's intended meaning.

When the creator and listener are from completely different backgrounds, miscommunication is almost inevitable. When, for example, an Indian musician performs what is called a *raga*, he or she is aware, by virtue of life experience and training, of certain emotional feelings or meanings associated with that *raga*. An audience of outsiders with little knowledge of Indian music or culture must necessarily interpret the music according to their own experience and by the norms of their society's music. They are unlikely to hear things as an Indian audience would, being unaware of culturally determined associations between, say, specific *ragas* and particular times of the day. Such miscommunication inevitably contributes to the problem of **ethnocentrism**: the assumption that one's own cultural patterns and understandings are normative and that those that differ are "strange," "exotic," or "abnormal."

ETHNOCENTRISM
The unconscious assumption that one's own cultural background is "normal," while that of others is "strange" or "exotic."

Whenever we encounter something new, we subconsciously compare it to all our previous experiences. We are strongly inclined to associate each new experience with the most similar thing we have encountered previously. People with a narrow range of life experience have less data in their memory bank, and when something is truly new, none of us has any direct way to compare it to a known experience. Misunderstandings easily occur at this point. We attempt to rationalize the unfamiliar in terms of our own experience and often "assume" the unknown is consistent with what we already know. Even if a newly encountered music sounds like something we recognize, we cannot be sure it is similar in any way. Perhaps a war song from another culture might sound like a lullaby in our culture. Knowing about this potential pitfall is the first step in avoiding the trapdoor of ethnocentrism.

Be Conscious of Labels

The German philosopher Ludwig Wittgenstein (1889–1951) famously warned, "labels terminate thinking." But because world music is such a vast subject, it must be broken down into manageable subcategories, which are labeled for the purpose of identification. While such labels are useful, they can also mislead. In teaching the musics of the world it is often tempting to use labels as shorthand. Unfortunately, not everyone understands their meanings and limitations; furthermore, these labels are employed in a variety of ways depending on the user's background. Thus, while we prefer not to employ such labels here, we recognize that they *are* difficult to avoid. When we do use them, we will attempt to limit them to particular circumstances.

Anyone who aspires to write a music survey, especially one covering the entire planet, cannot avoid using some labels. On the one hand, we recognize the problems with labels, especially the danger of stereotyping and over-generalized statements. On the other hand, a "phenomenological" perspective allowing no possibility for generalizations—emphasizing as it does the individuality of each experience—has no limitations. We recognize the dangers of labels and generalizations but find some of them unavoidable.

Terms that can cause trouble when studying the musics of the world include *folk*, *traditional*, *classical*, *art*, *popular*, and *neo-traditional*. For example, the term *folk* (from the German *volk*) carries with it a set of meanings and attitudes derived from the Romantic movement in literature, which flourished in Europe during the late eighteenth and early nineteenth centuries. During this period German scholars began exploring their own culture's roots in opposition to the dominant "classical" culture imported from France and Italy. Romanticism championed the common people over the elite, and in the early nineteenth century, writers such as the Grimm brothers and the

A large group of Dong minority men in China's Guizhou province play free-reed mouth organs of various sizes, but the resulting clusters of tones—without melody—challenges our definitions of "music"

pair Arnim von Achim and Clemens Brentano began collecting stories and song texts with subjects often centered on the "peasants," whose wisdom was seen as equal to that of learned scholars. As a result of its origin, then, the term *folk music* carries with it a lot of nineteenth-century European baggage that can clutter our thinking when it is applied to non-European musics.

Folk, classical, and *popular* are the trio of words most commonly used to categorize and distinguish among various types of music. Defining them individually is one issue; taken together they are problematic because they suggest a hierarchical value system in which *classical* is typically considered highest, *folk* of a much lower value, and *popular* at the lowest level. We would much prefer to have value-neutral terms with universally applicable definitions, but this is a difficult, if not impossible, goal within any single language. When we use terms such as *folk, classical,* and *popular* in this text, we mean to represent points on a continuum rather than distinct categories. We do not intend any hierarchical association, rather the terms are used merely as descriptors.

The term *classical* has several meanings and thus carries with it the potential for confusion. It may suggest connection with or influence from the styles of ancient Greece and Rome, though this usage is rarely associated with music. It also denotes a revered model or the epitome of a style or type. Thus we describe a 1956 Thunderbird as a "classic" car or certain films as "classics." In a sense many of the so-called classical musics of the world, be they European, Arabic, or Asian, conform to this second definition. A third definition, however, suggests value: it identifies *classical* as the highest form, that is, the best. Such a usage, particularly with reference to European "classical music," implies a problematic belief in a canon of "great works" created by a pantheon of "great composers"—a belief that has led to charges of cultural domination by "dead, white, European males." Finally, for commercial purposes and in the minds of many non-musicians, the word *classical* is used to refer to anything orchestral, even soundtracks and some Broadway shows.

Terence Liu

I had my new Ph.D. in ethnomusicology but was crew manager for the lunch rush at Arby's in Kent, Ohio, in December 1989 when Daniel Sheehy, then assistant director of folk arts at the National Endowment for the Arts (NEA), called to tell me I was hired as an arts grant specialist. I would be assisting him and Bess Lomax Hawes in the program they had shaped together to award federal grants to support folk and traditional artists around the country. After starting in January 1990, in 1996 I experienced a clash between the NEA and politics which resulted in me and about 90 other employees being part of a "reduction in force." After that I worked for three years as a folk arts coordinator in a local arts agency in California but returned to the NEA as an arts education specialist in 2000.

Today is a typical day. I will get documents ready for calls from a spring round of applicants who will be notified in a few days of their applications being rejected. Of the 150 Arts Education applications in that round, fewer than half were recommended for grants totaling $2.2 million. Interpreting what panel reviewers concluded about the proposals is actually valuable technical assistance for disappointed organizations. We have assembled experts from around the country and are currently reviewing another 150 applications from the summer deadline. New applicants looking toward next year's spring deadlines are also calling with their ideas. Grant making is an endless, labor-intensive cycle. I wish I had space to describe the excellent projects we fund, but you can visit the NEA website, www.arts.gov, to see for yourself.

Communication is central to my work. Today there is an email from the National Guild for Community Arts Education about my participation at the 2015 conference in Philadelphia next week. The Guild is a network of community schools of the arts, arts organizations, and arts education divisions of universities, museums, and other institutions collectively connecting more than 20,000 teaching artists and 2.5 million students each year. Two years ago at the conference held in Boston, the Guild membership worked together to define a new term, "Creative Youth Development," and pledged to support youth to study and create their own work in the arts and humanities as a pathway for personal, social, and intellectual growth.

At noon I meet Jonathan Dueck, ethnomusicologist at George Washington University, for lunch. We are leading the Local Arrangements Committee for the 2016 meeting of the Society for Ethnomusicology (SEM), which will take place in Washington, DC. Having no single university host presents an

Terence Liu (front)

unusual and challenging opportunity. We plan to collaborate with all universities in the area, including the Smithsonian Institution and American Folklife Center at the Library of Congress. As an NEA employee I am not allowed to participate in fundraising, so that whole task falls upon Jonathan. We are planning to get SEM members to experience local culture by getting on local transportation with designated ethnomusicology students as their guides. Our plans have approval from Stephen Stuempfle, executive director of SEM, and we are now preparing our presentation for the 2015 meeting in Austin.

When I retire, I will live in a culturally rich place to explore, share my experience for ethical world music education efforts, and keep playing violin and bass as I have all these years. Even as an Asian-American, I have participated in a Mexican mariachi, in Indian kirtan groups, and in both Celtic and Jimi Hendrix rock bands. I have used the training I had in conflict resolution during my work as collateral duty EEO counselor at the NEA, a job that somehow came natural to me as an ethnomusicologist trained in fieldwork and observation of human behavior and expression. I apply ethnomusicology to everything I do and will do so for the rest of my life.

Phong T. Nguyen

I was born in a rice-growing village deep in the Mekong River Delta of southern Vietnam. My family included many skilled traditional musicians. When I was five my father began teaching me music, and at age seven I began study with Tram Van Kien (Muoi Kien), a well-known regional master. I was trained in both instrumental and vocal music and performed music throughout the provinces. My music studies continued when my family sent me to a Buddhist temple in a nearby town where, at age ten, I became proficient in many chanting styles and also traditional music including instrumental, ritual, theatrical, folk songs, and art songs called *dòn ca tài tú'*.

Later as a student at the University of Saigon, I worked towards a Bachelor of Arts in Philosophy and Literature, which I received in 1972. To say there was uncertainty and stress during these years would be an understatement. Due to the war's increasing ferocity, my family's village was bombed and our home destroyed many times. Despite unspeakable devastation all around, I remember people continuing to do the things they did and striving to live as they did. During those years there was no time to lament the losses; there was only the energy to focus on surviving—for me, through music.

By the time the war ended in April 1975 and the country fell into complete chaos, I was working on a research project on Buddhist chant in Japan. Unable to return home, I sought acceptance from France—Vietnam's former colonial ruler—to emigrate. Fortunately, I was accepted, and in 1982, against all odds, I completed a Ph.D. in Ethno-Musicology with Distinction from the University of Paris (Sorbonne), writing my dissertation on the Buddhist music of Vietnam as viewed from a larger Mahayana perspective. These years of continued study and expansion were rewarding: I unexpectedly had the opportunity to do both research and performance in a European milieu.

By 1984 I moved to the United States and subsequently joined the faculties of the University of Washington, Kent State University, UCLA, and the University of Michigan along the way. It was during this period that I found time to refocus on my music in a way I hadn't been able to do for many years. Teaching and working with students brought peace and stability. That I could broaden the understanding of Vietnamese music in America was a personal milestone. In addition to classes, I organized and directed many Vietnamese music ensembles at the universities where I taught and through the years have worked with over 200 students.

Phong T. Nguyen (left)

I have been invited to play throughout the United States and around the world, including Canada, Norway, Netherlands, France, Germany, Switzerland, Italy, Korea, Japan, Singapore, Hong Kong, and Taiwan. Joining a much larger music community has been rewarding and energizing. In 1997, the National Endowment for the Arts awarded me a National Heritage Fellowship presented by First Lady Hilary Rodham Clinton. Later, in 2004–2005, supported by a Fulbright Grant, I had the honor of advising Hanoi's National Conservatory of Music in the creation and development of Vietnam's first Ethnomusicology Program. More recently, I again was tasked with designing Ethnomusicology courses for Mahasarakham University in Thailand where I was also taught for five years.

At present, I continue giving occasional performances and make field recordings. I also remain a scholar, writing books and articles and lecturing. My previous field research entailed interviewing and recording many masters, scholars, and performers within the various genres of traditional Vietnamese music whose work had stopped during the war and was slowly resuscitated thereafter. Many were quite elderly by the time I met them: some willing to have their stories and music documented; some suspiciously hesitant. Many introduced me to family members who continue their musical traditions to this day. At present, I have compiled over a thousand audio and video recordings and recorded a dozen compact discs from my own performance and field research, these now preserved at the Library of Congress' Folklife Center (The Phong Nguyen

Collection) and at Hobart and William Smith Colleges' Global Education Center (The Phong Nguyen Collection).

Music is a part of our humanness. I believe it can function subtly as a tool for finding common ground; it can also be a strong and reliable tool for mending and healing. Music can be a steadfast ally in overcoming the highest barrier; it can be a bridge to peace that safely leads into the future. As I continue my journey, I look forward to further findings and observations wherever I go.

Gypsy musicians entertain diners at an outdoor restaurant in Bugac, Hungary, a village near Kecskemet on the Great Plain (*Puszta*). From left to right: violin, *cimbalom* hammered dulcimer, string bass, viola

Perhaps the words *folk*, *classical*, and *popular* would be more useful if defined in economic terms. *Classical,* in that case, would denote music created in contexts where there is enough surplus wealth to release musicians from the necessity of providing their own food and shelter, so that they may spend their lives practicing their art and thinking up increasingly complex and technically challenging ways of creating and performing music. Competent performances of classical music produced under these conditions generally require specialized training and years of practice. *Folk* then denotes music created and performed by people of modest means whose main occupation leaves limited time for practice and whose limited income leaves little money for expensive instruments. Such music is usually simpler in process and technically less demanding because its practitioners cannot devote the time and energy to it that classical musicians devote to their type of music. As such, folk music usually requires less rehearsal to be performed proficiently and is usually learned through observation, recordings, and informal instruction.

Popular, a term that also means many things to different people, would, in economic terms, denote music that is widely disseminated by various types of media and supported by a broad base of relatively casual consumers, whose purchases make possible productions that may reach spectacular proportions. Popular music, therefore, needs to appeal to a broad spectrum of the population to achieve financial success. Critics of popular music may see it as merely reflecting current fashions in music, but we should remember that popular music, like all music, has the potential to express widely held feelings on subjects that are both peculiar to the time and place as well as universally felt (e.g., love). They may also be politically challenging when the sentiments expressed oppose the status quo, or unifying when the words express widely held feelings.

Finally, put these words—these labels—to the test. Take as an example Drum and Bugle Corps, an offshoot of military brass bands originally created in the United States but now found worldwide. Does "drum corps" exemplify folk, popular, or classical? The musicians are non-professionals and originally locally based but they perform as a large, complex ensemble after highly disciplined rehearsals playing carefully planned compositional routines. Stylistically their music is more likely to be popular in nature, though some corps play music from the Western classical tradition too. Can you realistically classify such groups under a single label?

Our discussion has to this point avoided the term *traditional*. Music that is spoken of as "traditional" is often contrasted with the individually innovative music of European classicism. It is also frequently contrasted with popular music or modernized music and is therefore considered synonymous with "folk." Traditional music is assumed to change little over time and to thereby preserve values long held by the community. Although the implication is that a special characteristic of "traditional" music is its emphasis on continuity over innovation, a great deal of music otherwise labeled as "classical" or "popular" is equally conservative or continuous in style. However, while we admit there are numerous problems with the term *traditional*, we doubt that any text on world musics can avoid its use entirely. At the very least, it can be said to be a more descriptive and less value-laden term than *folk*.

American Drum and Bugle Corps. Is it folk, popular, or classical?

Knowing the World's Musics

What can we know about the world's musics and how do we obtain this knowledge? These are basic questions in the field of **ethnomusicology**, but there is rarely a single answer to any question. If music is a part of the culture that produces it, and both the makers and the listeners of the music share similar lifetimes of experience that give the music meaning, then how can we as outsiders experience this music?

Obviously, upon first encounter with new sounds, our own personal life experience is all we have to draw on, and the ethnocentrism we referred to earlier may intrude. The sound quality of a singer may sound unpleasantly nasal compared to vocalists trained in a Western conservatory,

ETHNO MUSICOLOGY The scholarly study of any music within its contemporary cultural context.

while the performance of a Western orchestral symphony may sound bombastic and hideous to a rural farmer in Pakistan. One of the assumptions of those who study the musics of the world is that, with additional knowledge, we can gradually overcome our ethnocentrism and accept each music on its own terms. This is each individual student's challenge.

While several fields of scholarship have included music as part of their purview, such as anthropology, sociology, and **folklore**, the main field devoted to world musics is *ethnomusicology*. In its earlier days, at the end of the nineteenth century, the field was called *comparative musicology*, or in German, *Vergleichende Musikwissenschaft*. At the time, many European colonial powers sent researchers to their growing empires to gather materials for what became the great ethnographic museums of Europe. Early ethnomusicologists worked in these museums and in archives, using as their primary source materials, recordings and other artifacts brought back from the "field" by collectors. Sometimes, however, scholars were able to work directly with foreign musicians on tour, such as when Germans Carl Stumpf and Erich Moritz von Hornbostel recorded Siamese (Thai) musicians in Berlin in 1900 for the Phonogrammarchiv, the first international archive of recordings.

Early ethnomusicologists focused on description and classification, using the rapidly accumulating materials found in European museums. Germans Curt Sachs and the aforementioned E. M. von Hornbostel, for example, drew from earlier models to evolve a comprehensive system for classifying musical instruments based on *what* vibrates to make musical sound. (This system is discussed in Chapter 2.) Scholars throughout Europe transcribed recorded music into notation and attempted classifications based on genre, scale, and other observable characteristics. This was the era of the "armchair" scholar who practiced the "science" *(Wissenschaft)* of music.

Over time, scholars began doing their own **fieldwork**, during which they recorded music in the field on cylinder, disc, wire, and later magnetic acetate tape. Many of these scholars thought of themselves as ethnographers or anthropologists. Among the greatest of these was an American woman, Frances Densmore (1867–1957), who, working directly with Native American singers and instrumentalists, wrote fifteen books and numerous articles, and released seven commercial recordings, mostly through the Smithsonian Institution in Washington, DC.

FOLKLORE
The study of orally transmitted folk knowledge and culture.

FIELDWORK
The first-hand study of music in its original context, a technique derived from anthropology.

Modern digital recording devices make the field recording of music much simpler now. Although this recording of Lao *lam* repartee singing was being made in a remote private home outside Luang Phrabang in central Laos, the resulting sound is near studio quality

American ethnomusicology began changing dramatically in the 1960s, especially because of five men and the academic programs they influenced. Alan Merriam (1923–1980)—of Indiana University's Department of Anthropology—published in 1964 *The Anthropology of Music*, one of the most influential books ever written on the subject, in which he defined ethnomusicology as "the study of music in culture." Unlike the older school of Europeans who viewed music as sounds to be analyzed apart from their cultural context, Merriam saw music as a human behavior. Similarly, British anthropologist John Blacking (1928–1990) has defined music as "humanly organized sound."

Mantle Hood (1918–2005), originally a composer, provided a musicological alternative at the University of California, Los Angeles's Institute of Ethnomusicology, by emphasizing what he called *bi-musicality*. In this approach researchers combine learning to play the music under study with field observation. David Park McAllester (1916–2006) and others at Wesleyan University in Middletown, Connecticut, created a program in "world musics" that emphasized performance and composition taught by masters of musical traditions from around the world, especially India, Africa, and Indonesia. Finally, Bruno Nettl (1930–2020), a specialist in both Native American and Persian musics, influenced the course of ethnomusicology over the last fifty years, through his teaching at the University of Illinois and his numerous publications, and helped to guide the field through a period of increasing diversification. For many, Nettl's work represents both common sense and the mainstream of the profession.

Thus, ethnomusicology has long been pulled in two directions: the musicological and the anthropological, the first emphasizing the sonic artifacts of human music-making, the second centering on the study of human behavior and cultural context. Regardless of orientation, however, most ethnomusicology programs are found in college and university departments of music. Typical programs include courses for non-majors, especially world music surveys, and more specialized courses on both broad and specific areas of the world as well as courses in research methodology. Many schools offer opportunities to play in world music performance ensembles.

Ethnomusicology today, however, has been much influenced by new ways of thinking generally subsumed under the heading *postmodernism*. A reaction against *modernism* or *positivism*, in which the establishment of "truth" is based on verifiable "facts," postmodernism de-emphasizes description and the search for absolute truth in favor of interpretation and the acceptance of the relativity of truth. A great variety of intellectual approaches, mostly borrowed from other disciplines, offer ethnomusicologists new ways to interpret the meaning of music. These include gender studies and feminist theories; Marxist interpretations; semiotic approaches; cognitive studies; performance studies; attention to such issues as identity, post-colonialism, and the political ramifications of music; and, especially, popular music studies. The latter has risen rapidly since about 1980 under the influence of the "Manchester School" in England, and is associated with the term *cultural studies*, which denotes several postmodern theoretical approaches used to interpret popular culture. The study of popular music, however, has recently led to an apparent decrease of interest in first-hand fieldwork among ethnomusicologists and a parallel de-emphasis of the techniques appropriate to the study of "traditional" music, because popular musics are more easily studied through the media than are traditional musics.

Frances Densmore recording a Piegan Indian *c.*1916 (Library of Congress)

The Life of an Ethnomusicologist

What do ethnomusicologists actually do? How do they learn about the world's musics? We view the process as having **four basic phases**: (1) preparation; (2) fieldwork; (3) analysis; and (4) dissemination. Before going to the field, whether it be a faraway nation in Central Asia, a region

PHASES OF FIELD RESEARCH
(1) preparation
(2) fieldwork
(3) analysis
(4) dissemination

of Indonesia, or a nearby town in their own country, ethnomusicologists must *prepare* themselves by learning as much as they can about the area, the kinds of music they will encounter, and the conditions under which they will do their study. This is best accomplished through the use of library, media, and Internet resources and through interaction with others who know the area, especially people who grew up there or perhaps still live there. In many cases researchers must spend years studying the language of their area, which often is one that is rarely taught. Well-prepared field researchers will need not only high-quality recording equipment but also the wits and maturity to deal with all sorts of unexpected situations, both technical and social.

Besides doing research in the field, ethnomusicologists must also live and eat, and these necessities may present great challenges when unfamiliar food is on the menu or living conditions are radically different. In the course of their research, scholars may seek to acquire first-hand experience through participation in various rituals, festivals, and other events, and may need to create professional documents through still photography, videography, audio recording, and interviews. A detailed journal is important, not to mention the logs that retain the details of recordings and photographs. The *fieldwork phase* can last anywhere from a few days to several years. Based on our experience, we can say that the longer one stays in the field, the more one will know but the less one will understand. This apparent irony stems from the increasing perception of complexity that accompanies prolonged exposure to any culture: the more you experience it, the more you realize how much more there is to learn. First-hand experience teaches us that all cultures are deep and complex and that understanding a music is far more demanding than simply collecting it.

What do ethnomusicologists do with the material and knowledge they acquire? It is a standing joke among ethnomusicologists that we spend thousands of dollars and months of our lives, braving tough weather and unfamiliar foods, to bring back a few videos that we look at only once. The material collected in the field is considered "raw." After it is collected, ethnomusicologists must find ways to *analyze*, *interpret*, and *disseminate* what they have collected. This is done primarily through teaching, writing and reading "papers" at professional meetings, writing chapters, journal articles, and books and, perhaps, compiling CDs or DVDs for commercial release. As researchers acquire expertise in an area, they may be called upon to referee articles submitted to journals, write reviews of books, and CDs, or serve on state- or national-level panels that award grants to individuals and arts organizations. Many ethnomusicologists work as professors in colleges and universities, though some hold positions in publicly funded agencies such as the National Endowment for the Arts, while some work for museums, community programs, and art centers. Others work as freelance scholars and musicians. Few can afford to be just ethnomusicologists—that is, researchers—full time. Most must spend the majority of their time doing other kinds of work, e.g., teaching, performing, writing.

Co-author (TM) playing yang qin dulcimer (right) with an unknown musician playing yeh hu fiddle (left), Shantou, China (Sara Stone Miller)

Co-author (AS) blessed by a spirit dancer in northern Thailand (Christina Shahriari)

Representation: What Musics Does One Study?

A survey course on the musics of the world poses a challenge far different from that presented by a course covering the classical musics of Europe. In the latter case there is a rough consensus on who the "great composers" are and what the "great works" are. These make up what is called a *canon*—that is, a foundational list of core composers and works that every music student is expected to know. World music courses have no such canon, and certainly no list of great composers. The world is too large and there are too many choices for much consensus to form. Therefore, one must consider not only how to organize such a course but what to include. What should every world music student know? If the organization is geographical, such as this text, what genres and particular examples should "represent" a country or culture? Our choices reveal our biases and assumptions about what constitutes the music of a given place. Some might choose to emphasize contemporary culture by including a greater proportion of urban-based popular musics than "traditional" ones. Others would argue that the essence of a culture is in its traditional music. There is no way to resolve these questions except by agreeing that any world music course is only the beginning, the first few steps of a learning journey that can last a lifetime. In a way, it does not matter *how* one begins as much as it matters that one *actually* begins.

Resources for the Study of the World's Musics

Today's students are fortunate to live in a time when resources for the study of world musics are growing exponentially. The proliferation of publications, both print and recorded, has been astounding. We suggest the following as likely the most comprehensive and readily available resources for further study.

Reference Works

Two major reference works that introduce world music include the ten-volume *Garland Encyclopedia of World Music* and *The New Grove Dictionary of Music and Musicians*. The "Garland," as ethnomusicologists label the former, includes nine volumes which cover geographically defined areas of the world, with the tenth volume being a compilation of resources. Each volume is between 1,000 and 1,500 pages and includes both general and specific articles, hundreds of photos and musical examples, associated audio examples, and an extensive list of bibliographic and recorded resources. *The New Grove Dictionary of Music and Musicians*, second edition, in twenty-nine volumes offers extensive coverage of the world's musics, primarily through articles on specific countries. While the series emphasizes Western art music, there are numerous entries devoted to world music. Both the "Garland" and the "Grove" are also available online, but this will likely have to be accessed at a subscribing library, which your university/college/school may already do, or you can request that they consider it.

Video

The Internet is now also a valuable and easily accessed place for video of an unimaginable array of world musics. While the footage found on sites such as YouTube is generally of amateur quality, it allows free access to a vast arena of world music and culture that was barely imaginable even just a decade ago. The proliferation of such video through online delivery has unfortunately discouraged publishers from producing substantial hard-copy collections, though two still available deserve special mention. First is the *JVC/Smithsonian-Folkways Anthology of World Music and Dance*, a series of video clips with accompanying booklets. One drawback of this collection is that it was compiled in large part from pre-existing footage, and as a result in some areas the coverage is uneven or unrepresentative. Also worth mentioning is the *Beats of the Heart* documentary series, produced by Jeremy Marre for the world music label Shanachie, which includes narrated documentaries on such varied topics as Indian *filmi* songs, Jamaican *reggae*, and music in Thailand. Shanachie also produces a series of *World Music Portraits* focused on specific world music artists, such as Compay Segundo, Jimmy Cliff, and Salif Keita. Beyond these are a variety of documentary films that focus on world music, though they tend to be produced in limited number by different publishers. Utilizing streaming and delivery services such as Netflix can help world music enthusiasts to find films on subjects that are otherwise difficult to find.

Audio Recordings

A great variety of companies in the United States, Europe, and Japan have produced commercial world music CDs that are available internationally. Unfortunately, many of them were produced by non-specialists, and therefore the information provided in liner notes must be approached with caution. What is perhaps the most significant series of recordings was originally released on Moses Asch's Folkways label, and is now available online in expanded form by Smithsonian-Folkways in Washington, DC, along with new releases. Other important series have been produced by Lyrichord, Nonesuch, World Music Library, Pan, Rounder, Multicultural Media, and many other record companies around the globe. Regrettably, as consumers have turned to downloads and record stores have nearly vanished, the few remaining smaller companies are releasing little material now. A vast amount of world music can be found online today as well. Music access applications, such as iTunes, are popular around the world and provide an ever-increasing stream of music access to our global soundscape. Still, much music is only produced locally in hard copy, so be sure to investigate when your travels present such opportunities to explore the local music scene.

Journals

Most journals are produced by scholarly societies, and therefore the articles in them tend to be specialized, and at times obscure. Serious students, however, can gain much from such material. The most significant journals to consider include *Ethnomusicology*, *Yearbook for Traditional Music*, *American Music*, *Asian Music*, *Journal of African Music*, *Ethnomusicology Forum*, *The World of Music*, *The Journal of Popular Culture*, *The Journal of World Popular Music*, and a variety of other journals dedicated to specific areas of the world, such as *Chime* (focused on China).

Finally, it is worth restating that the Internet is now an invaluable resource with regards to the investigation of world music and culture. Many of the above mentioned resources have associated websites, and there are numerous online pathways to pursue when researching a topic. This textbook, for example, has an extensive website that can be used as a starting point for further exploration.

Questions to Consider

1. What do ethnomusicologists mean when they say, "Music is universal, but it is not a universal language"?

2. What are the potential problems in classifying music as "classical," "folk," or "popular"?

3. How might an ethnomusicologist approach the study of Western classical music differently from a musicologist?

4. What is "fieldwork"? What is its importance to the study of world music?

5. In what ways does world music study require an interdisciplinary approach?

6. What is ethnocentrism? Have you ever experienced it?

Chapter 2

Aural Analysis

1	ALBANIA
2	AUSTRIA
3	BOSNIA
4	BULGARIA
5	CROATIA
6	CZECH
7	HUNGARY
8	MACEDONIA
9	MOLDOVA
10	ROMANIA
11	SLOVAKIA
12	SLOVENIA
13	SWITZERLAND
14	YUGOSLAVIA

Listening to the World's Musics

A variety of drums (membranophones) and gongs (idiophones) from a shop in the drum making village of Mu Ban Tham Klawng in Ang Thong province, Thailand

How to Listen to World Music

The primary objective of this book is to expose you, the reader, to a generous variety of musical traditions from cultures around the globe. Learning something about the music of other people is like gaining a window into their world and is a chance to explore the creative power of humanity. The ability to recognize various musical traditions and express some knowledge about them is a good start toward crossing the cultural boundaries that often divide us. This book is not only about world music; it is about people, cultures, geography, and history as well. Some music traditions are easy to recognize, whereas others require you to develop a systematic method for identifying what you hear. Each person's method will undoubtedly be different, but here are some initial suggestions on how to listen to unfamiliar world music.

Begin by listening to the music examples included with this text before reading any of the material. Remember your initial gut feeling. Often your first impression of a musical sound helps you remember that sound in the future. Does the music sound familiar or completely alien? Do you like it, or does it make you want to skip to the next track? Does the music seem busy, cold, happy, relaxing, heavy? Does it sound like rain, whale calls, a screeching owl, a music box? Any image you can use later to help you recognize the music could be helpful.

Make the music samples part of your daily life, even if you don't like every example. Many new musical sounds require you to develop a taste for them before they can be appreciated. Listen in your car, before you go to bed, or while exercising, walking the dog, cooking, and so on.

Use the book to help you better understand the form and intent of each example. It is necessary to read each chapter to connect what you hear with what you know. If you don't know anything about the type of music you're listening to, what you hear won't mean much. You may enjoy the music, but you can't fully appreciate it unless you understand what is happening and why.

You will know you are "familiar" with a particular musical example when you can recognize it after just a few seconds of listening, and answer "yes" to the following questions:

- Do you know where the music originates (i.e., its geographical association)?
- Can you visualize the instruments, imitate the sound of the music, and anticipate melodic and/or rhythmic development?
- Are you knowledgeable of the example's cultural associations? Immediately knowing in what contexts the music is performed, or with which religion it is associated, are also indicators that you are becoming familiar with the tradition the example represents.

Don't limit yourself to the musical examples provided with this text. Find other recordings of the same types of music and compare them with the given ones. Identify the commonalities in musical sound so that you're able to recognize the tradition, not just the specific recordings from the book.

Remember, music is universal, but it is not a universal language. Understanding world music requires an open mind and a willingness to acknowledge that other perspectives, ideas, and attitudes are equally as valid as your own. Our world is "smaller" than it has ever been in history. You will likely have opportunities to meet people from many of the places discussed in this book. Knowing something about their music can help you communicate with them and may lead to cultural experiences you would never have anticipated. So, listen with both your mind and your emotions, as well as your ears.

"Talking" about Music

Every discipline, be it physics, economics, or art, has its own jargon, a vocabulary that must be learned. Music is no exception. Because music is conceptual, its components require names in order for discussion to occur. Music terms such as *melody* and *rhythm* are familiar to most readers, musician and non-musician alike. Other terms, such as *heterophony*, *idiophone*, or *rhythmic density* usually require some explanation. This chapter seeks to put all readers on an equal footing by explaining basic music concepts, as well as introducing certain terms peculiar to the discipline of ethnomusicology.

A musical sound has four basic components: timbre, pitch, rhythm and dynamics. ***Timbre***, or the quality of a musical sound, is inherently linked to a medium—that is, to the object or person producing the sound. ***Pitch*** is synonymously referred to in musical terms as *tone*. It is most often expressed with a letter name equating to a frequency; for example, the standard Western concert pitch of A = 440 Hertz (Hz). ***Rhythm*** depends on durations of sounds, which are often organized into regular patterns. Finally, ***dynamics*** denotes the volume, or relative loudness or softness, of a sound, and can be measured in decibels (dBs).

Timbre and Medium

The easiest way to learn to recognize a world music tradition is to become familiar with its media— that is, the sounds of its typical instruments and vocal qualities. In order to identify a specific medium, we must first become familiar with its characteristic timbre or "color." Most terms used to describe timbre are based on analogies between musical sound and everyday physical and sensory experience. Terms such as *nasal, dark, mellow, strained, rough, soothing, grating*, and so on, are highly subjective when applied to music but are nevertheless helpful in describing "aural color."

Just as we distinguish visually among red, blue, and green, so too we distinguish between aural "colors"—that is, among the characteristic qualities that define the sounds of, say, the trumpet, the violin, or the flute. (Compare Tibetan Buddhist Ritual—7.9; Cape Breton fiddling—13.1; Native American flute—13.12.) In the case of "visual color," determining the differences among red, yellow, and green is fairly easy. In order to differentiate among evergreen, lime, and emerald, however, one must possess a sharper and more experienced eye. Similarly, while it may be easy to hear the difference between a violin and a trumpet, learning to distinguish the similar sounds of a banjo, koto, and sitar from one another may take some time even for an attentive listener. (Compare Hindustani *Raga* (*sitar/tambura*)—5.1; *Guqin*—7.1; *Jali* with *kora*—10.7.) Fortunately, in addition to timbre there are other elements that can help you identify what you are hearing, such as pitch, rhythm, dynamics, style, and various extra-musical factors, i.e., cultural associations.

When listening to an example of an unfamiliar music tradition for the first time, you must determine whether you hear voices, instruments, or a combination. (Compare Steel band—11.4; Lined Hymn—13.3; Gospel Choir—13.7.) The next step is to identify how many voices or instruments you hear. Either you hear a soloist or a group, also called an *ensemble*. (Compare *Guqin*—7.1; Jiangnan *sizhu*—7.2.)

If what you hear is an ensemble, determine whether it is a small group, such as an instrumental trio or vocal duet, or a large ensemble, such as an orchestra or choir. (Compare *Mbira dza vadzimu*—10.5; Polyrhythmic ensemble—10.1.) The larger the ensemble, the more difficult it will be to distinguish specific media. However, this very difficulty may help you hear the ensemble as a whole rather than as individual performers leading you to a recognition of the tradition. In the instances where the ensemble is small enough that you can determine roughly how many performers there are, the next step is to try to identify each medium (instruments and/or voices) specifically.

Vocal Timbre

In the case of voices, you should be able to distinguish between male and female voices fairly easily, primarily based on their ranges. (Compare vocalists in Northeast Thai *lam klawn*, 6.4.) While range is a concept related to pitch, voices can also have timbral qualities that will help you to identify what you hear. Certain traditions—such as bluegrass and European opera—feature vocal timbres so distinctive that you can easily distinguish them.

TIMBRE
The tone quality or color of a musical sound.

PITCH
A tone's specific frequency level, measured in Hertz (Hz).

RHYTHM
The lengths, or durations, of sounds as patterns in time.

DYNAMICS
The volume of a musical sound.

Instrumental Timbre

In the case of instruments, timbre is closely related to instrument construction. The study of musical instruments is known as **organology**. Essential to organological study is the classification of instruments. In the European art music tradition, instruments are typically indentified using five basic categories: strings, winds, brass, percussion, and keyboards. This system, however, does not work well when applied to the rest of the world's musical instruments.

In the field of ethnomusicology, the **Sachs–Hornbostel (also, Hornbostel-Sachs)** system, developed by German musicologists Curt Sachs and Eric M. von Hornbostel early in the twentieth century, is the predominant system used to describe and classify instruments. The four primary categories are *aerophones*, *chordophones*, *idiophones*, and *membranophones*; *electrophones* have become a fifth category. An instrument is classified according to what part of it vibrates to set air molecules into motion and produce the sound. Each of these primary categories has several subcategories. Knowledge of only the more common subcategories is usually enough to help you perceive the timbre of a musical instrument and identify it. The more specifically you can subcategorize an instrument's construction, however, the more accurately you will understand how the construction affects the unique timbre of the instrument.

Aerophones: Flutes, Reeds, and Trumpets

Aerophones are defined as instruments producing sound through the direct vibration of air, rather than through the vibration of air by another medium, such as a string or membrane. Aerophones are typically subdivided into three categories: *flutes*, *reeds*, and *trumpets*. Flutes are defined as instruments in which a column of air is set in vibration when the air is split on an edge. (Listen to Native American flute—13.12.) Reed instruments have one or more small pieces of material, such as cane, bamboo, or metal, that vibrate(s) when air is blown over or through them and into a tube. (Listen to *Uilleann* bagpipes—9.5.) Trumpets require the performer's lips to vibrate rather than a reed, as they blow air into the instrument. (Listen to Australian Aborigine song with *didjeridu*—4.1.) Recognition of the characteristic timbres of flutes, reeds, and trumpets is an important first step toward becoming a discriminating listener. Keep in mind, however, that these terms refer to general categories, not specific instruments such as the European ("silver") flute or brass trumpet.

(left)
A Japanese *noh kan* horizontal flute

(right)
Double-reed aerophone (*pi*) from Thailand

The *ntahera* ivory horn ensemble of the Asantehene, Kumase, Ghana (Joseph S. Kaminski)

Chordophones: Lutes and Zithers

Chordophones are defined as having one or more strings stretched between two points. Sound is produced when a string vibrates. There are many chordophones in the world of music, but two basic types, *lutes* and *zithers*, comprise the majority. The shape of the instrument is the key feature that distinguishes a lute from a zither. The strings of a zither are stretched parallel to the entire sounding board, as with a piano. Thus nearly the whole instrument acts as a resonator. (Listen to *Dastgah* for santur and voice—8.3.) In addition to a resonating body, a lute has a neck, which allows a performer to vary the acoustical length of a string to produce different pitches, as with a guitar. Because its neck does not act as a resonator, a lute generally has less resonance than a zither of the same size, and its sound dissipates more quickly. (Listen to Country Blues—13.8.) Further, as the acoustical length of the strings on a zither are generally fixed, they tend to have more strings than lutes in order to produce a wider range of pitches.

The most common zithers are either hammered, as with the piano, or plucked, as with the Japanese *koto*, while lutes are generally either plucked, as with a guitar, or bowed, as with a violin. A hammered zither tends to have a more reverberant sound timbre than other types of chordophones. The resonance of a plucked lute will die away almost immediately as the vibration amplification of each note diminishes. (Listen to Arabic *Taqasim* (*buzuq* and *ud*)—8.2.) The sounds of a plucked lute or zither are further distinguishable by whether a plectrum or a finger plucks the string. The string vibration of a bowed lute is continuous for as long as the bow hairs are pulled across the string; thus, the sound does not immediately fade until the bowing stops. (Listen to Cape Breton fiddling—13.1.)

In addition to being plucked or bowed, lutes are either *fretted* or *fretless*. A **fret** is a straight bar of wood, bamboo, or metal placed on the neck of a lute perpendicular to the direction of the strings, as seen on a guitar. This enables a precise pitch to be played each time the performer presses the string against the fret. A fretless lute allows the performer to slide the finger between pitches, potentially sounding all of the frequencies between two distinct tones. (Listen to lute in Mongolion throat singing example—7.5.) Fretted lutes are more likely to be plucked than fretless lutes, which are more frequently bowed. This is due to the fact that plucked lutes sound tones of short duration, while bowed lutes can sustain for a longer period, allowing the sliding between pitches to be heard more readily.

Based on their construction, other major chordophone types fall into the *lyre* and *harp* categories. The strings of lyres and harps are suspended by an open frame and are most often plucked. The string plane of a harp, in particular, runs perpendicular to the resonating body, rather

CHORDOPHONE
Four types of stringed instruments: lutes, zithers, harps, lyres.

FRET
A bar or ridge found on chordophones that enables performers to produce different melodic pitches with consistent frequency levels.

The Finnish *kantele* zither

The Turkish *tanbur* lute

(Left to right)
Fretless lute (*sarod*) and fretted lute (*sitar*)
from India

West African spike harp (*bolon*) with
strings attached to a string holder
Ethiopian lyre (*kraar*)

than parallel to it as with lutes and zithers. The timbre of lyres and harps is generally difficult to distinguish from that of lutes and zithers, though visually the construction is quite distinct.

Idiophones: Plucked, Struck, and Shaken

Idiophones are defined as instruments that produce sound through the instrument itself vibrating (*idio* meaning "itself"). A strong sound can be easily produced on most idiophones. Practically anything can be considered an idiophone, from bottles to slamming doors, to change in your pocket or keys rattling on a key ring. Bells, rattles, and a variety of other percussion instruments are common idiophones in a musical context. Most idiophones fall into one of three categories: *plucked, struck,* or *shaken.*

Small, plucked idiophones are often a type of *lamellophone,* meaning that they have a *lamella* (tongue or prong) that is flexed, and then released, causing a brief sound before the vibration of the *lamella* ceases. (Listen to *Mbira dza vadzimu*—10.5.) A music box, with its comb-like metal prongs, is probably the most familiar example of a lamellophone, but the next most commonly encountered is the single, plucked lamella amplified by the mouth cavity, used for surrogate speech as much as for melody. Such instruments are known by many terms, such as "mouth harp," "jaw harp," and "jew's harp," the latter term probably a corruption of the French term *jeu* meaning "to play." (Note also that this type of lamellophone is not a harp, i.e., chordophone, despite the colloquial references.)

IDIOPHONE
Instruments that themselves vibrate to produce sound, such as rattles, bells, and various other kinds of percussion.

(left) Gourd rattle (*shekere*) from sub-Saharan Africa
(right) Three lamellophones from sub-Saharan Africa

Detail of four *khawng mon* (bossed gong circles) from Thailand

Struck idiophones comprise the most varied category and include gongs, bells, wood blocks, and just about anything else that can be struck. (Listen to Vietnamese bronze gong ensemble—6.1.) The great many timbres associated with such instruments are not easily generalized, though the sharp initial attack of the sound is a typical feature. Shaken idiophones are most often rattles. (Listen to *Mbira dza vadzimu* (*hosho* rattle)—10.5.) Most rattles have a hollowed center filled with small objects, such as pebbles, seeds, or sand. When the instrument is shaken, the particles bounce against the outer shell of the instrument causing it to vibrate. Other rattles are constructed so that the small particles are loosely fixed to the outside of the object, such as with a netted gourd rattle (e.g., *shekere*).

Membranophones

MEMBRANO-PHONE
Instruments, typically drums, that use a vibrating stretched membrane as the principal means of sound production.

Membranophones are defined as having a vibrating membrane, traditionally animal skin but often synthetic today, that is stretched over a frame. This category encompasses most drums found in the world. The different types of drums are further categorized on the basis of body shape—some, for example, are goblet-shaped, while others are barrel-shaped—and according to whether they are single- or double-headed. Most drums are struck with either the hand or some implement, usually a stick. (Compare Hindustani *Raga* (tabla)—5.1; Ghanaian talking drum—10.2.) There are too many kinds of drums throughout the world to make generalizations about timbre; however, smaller drums usually have a higher, tighter sound, while larger membranophones are deeper and earthier in character. Some drums can be tuned to specific pitches. Becoming familiar with the unique sounds of different drums takes time and effort. The essential first step is being able to distinguish between struck membranophones and struck idiophones. Not all membranophones are struck, however; those that are not—such as friction drums and "singing membranes" (e.g., kazoos)—are less common but particularly unique in timbre. (Listen to *Samba* (cuíca)—12.4.)

A group of drummers perform at the Elephant Festival at India's Tripunithura Temple (Martin Harvey/Getty)

Summary

Learning to distinguish among aerophones, chordophones, idiophones, and membranophones is the first step in training your ear to listen attentively to world music. Being able to recognize subcategories within these instrument groups greatly enhances your appreciation of sound and helps you identify the music you hear more quickly. You will encounter many similar types of instruments, such as the Japanese *shakuhachi* and the Native American flute, that are hard to distinguish from each other based on timbre alone. Fortunately, other aspects of musical performance such as pitch, rhythm, dynamics, and style can help you identify the tradition you hear. Differences in timbre, however, are most often what distinguish the sound of two instruments, even when all other aspects are identical. Familiarize yourself with the unique "aural colors" of each recorded example supplied with this text before trying to tackle the often more complicated issues associated with musical creation.

Pitch

Every sound can be described as having either a *definite* or *indefinite* **pitch**. A definite pitch is determined by the dominance of a specific frequency level, which is expressed as Hz (Hertz or formerly, cycles per second). For example, the Euro-American "concert pitch," A above middle C, has 440 Hz as its pillar frequency. Definite pitches are necessary to produce melody and harmony. An indefinite pitch consists of a cluster of frequency levels at more or less equal volume—that is, no one level dominates. Indefinite pitches, such as those produced by handclaps or rattles, are most often used in a rhythmic capacity. (Listen to Kiribati group song (vocal—definite pitches; handclaps—indefinite pitches)—4.4.) Some indefinite pitches are continuously variable, such as that of a siren. While indefinite pitches are regularly found in music traditions throughout the world, the varied uses of definite pitch are more often the primary focus of musical activity; therefore, the term *pitch* hereafter refers primarily to definite pitches.

PITCH
A tone's specific frequency level, measured in Hertz (Hz).

Tuning System

The term **tuning system** denotes the entire collection of pitch frequencies commonly used in a given music tradition. Tuning systems are culturally determined. Our ears become accustomed to the tuning system of the music we hear on a regular basis. When we hear an unfamiliar tuning system, some of its pitches may sound "out of tune" because we have been culturally conditioned to accept only certain frequency levels as "correct." Pitches with frequency levels significantly different from those in our familiar tuning system may sound strange.

TUNING SYSTEM
All the pitches common to a musical tradition.

The basis for most tuning systems around the world is the *octave*. An octave is produced when the frequency level or Hz of a specific pitch is either doubled or halved. Using 440 Hz (A) as the example, the octave above is 880 Hz and the octave below is 220 Hz. Pitches that are an octave apart (or a series of octaves apart) are considered to be the "same" pitch (i.e., they have the same pitch name) even though they have different frequencies. An easy way to understand this concept is to listen to a man with a "low" voice and a woman with a "high" voice sing the "same" pitch. Our ears sense that the two pitches are equivalent even though the man may sing at a frequency level of 220 Hz while the woman sings at 880 Hz, two octaves higher.

In the most commonly used European tuning system (called "equal-tempered tuning"), the octave is divided into twelve equal parts. In the Thai classical music tradition, however, the same octave is divided into only seven equal parts. (Compare Thai *Piphat*—6.3; Highland bagpipes—9.4.) Consequently, some of the pitches common to the European tuning system sound different from the pitches common to the Thai tuning system, whose intervals between pitches are wider. The tuning systems common to some traditions (e.g., in West Asia or India) may use more than thirty discrete pitches within a single octave. (Listen to Arabic *Taqasim*—8.2.)

Tuning pegs and micro-tone tuners of Turkish *kanun* zither

After extended exposure to a different tuning system, your ear will become accustomed to its standard frequencies. Even before this, however, the very "oddness" of an unfamiliar tuning system may help you recognize the musical tradition to which it belongs.

Scale

While a tuning system encompasses all of the pitches commonly used in a music tradition, a *scale* consists of a set of pitches (generally expressed in ascending order) used in particular performances. For example, a pentatonic scale (*penta* meaning "five," and *tonic* meaning "tone") uses only five tones from the greater tuning system. (Listen to Jiangnan *sizhu*—7.2.) Different pentatonic scales can be derived from a single tuning system, as long as the number of pitches available within a tuning system is greater than five. Thus, pitches 1, 2, 3, 5, and 6 from a particular tuning system may constitute the pentatonic scale for one composition, while pitches 1, 2, 4, 6, and 7 from that same system may form the pentatonic scale in a different composition. Scales in some music compositions are limited to as few as two or three pitches, while other pieces in the same tradition may use a greater number of pitches.

Interval

An *interval* is perhaps best thought of as the "distance" between two pitches. Intervals are described as either wide or narrow. A wide interval—such as that from A ascending to G (a seventh)—is one with a large difference in frequencies, while a narrow interval—such as that between A and B (a second)—has a relatively small difference. Likewise, the interval between the bottom and top pitches of an octave is wider than the interval distance of any two pitches within the octave. The difference between narrow and wide intervals can be both seen and heard. On a piano, for example, the size of an interval can be understood visually in terms of the distance between a pair of keys and aurally in terms of the frequency levels of the keys sounded, bearing in mind that Hz are expressed proportionally. A given tradition may be partially recognizable just based on its preference for wide or narrow intervals. (Compare the Classical Thai *piphat* music—6.11 to Japanese *Gagaku*—7.7.)

Range

Range refers to the span of pitches a given instrument or voice is capable of producing. It is described as being wide or narrow as well as high or low. An instrument with a narrow range is capable of producing fewer pitches than an instrument with a wide range. Instruments with wide ranges, such as the piano, are typically, though not always, physically larger than those with narrower ranges, such as the harmonica. Vocal ranges can vary substantially: trained professionals practice to extend their range, sometimes to more than three octaves, while an average person has a narrower vocal range of roughly two octaves or less.

Ranges are also characterized in terms of where they fall on the spectrum from very low-pitched sounds to very high-pitched sounds. An instrument or voice may have a relatively high or low range in comparison to other musical media. A female, for example, generally has a higher vocal range than a male. Instruments also often have characteristic ranges; for example, a violin uses a high range, while a tuba plays in a low range. (Compare Beijing Opera—7.3; Tibetan Buddhist ritual—7.9.)

Melody

A ***melody*** is defined as an organized succession of pitches forming a musical idea. These are the "phrases" and "tunes" that characterize a specific composition, such as "Twinkle, Twinkle Little Star." Because pitches exist in real time—that is, because each has a duration—rhythm also is always a necessary component of melody. If, for example, you play a descending C major scale on any instrument, this is generally not considered a melody. However, if you vary the duration of each pitch, that is, rhythm, to correspond to the tune "Joy to the World," those same pitches in combination with the new durations create a recognizable musical idea, or melody.

MELODY
An organized succession of pitches forming a musical idea.

Melodic Contour

A molody can be described in terms of its ***melodic contour***, or shape. "Joy to the World," for example, has a "descending" melodic contour as the pitches descend from high to low (see Figure 1). Melodic contours are typically drawn as a graph representing the direction of the melody. It is often useful to graph the contour of a melody to identify regularly occurring features characteristic of a music tradition. For example, our graph of a Native American Plains Indian chant reveals a characteristic "cascading" melodic contour, reflecting the Plains Indian practice

MELODIC CONTOUR
The general direction and shape of a melody.

Figure 1: Descending melodic contour

Figure 2: Cascading melodic contour

Figure 3: Irish bagpipe melodic contour

25

DRONE
A continuous or repeating sound.

of holding certain pitches longer than others in the course of an overall descending melodic line (see Figure 2; listen to Plains Indian Dance song—13.11). **Drone** pitches (pitches held or played continuously) can be represented as horizontal lines, while chords (several pitches played at once) are typically represented with vertical lines, as in our graph of Irish bagpipe performance (see Figure 3; listen to *Uilleann* bagpipes—9.5).

Ornamentation

Ornamentation consists of embellishments or decorations that are applied to a melody, and thus modify the original musical idea. This is often done when performers improvise on a melody. Improvisation is the art of spontaneously creating music as it is performed. Some traditions have elaborate systematic procedures for ornamenting a melody, while others place less emphasis on ornamentation or shun it altogether. Ornamentation can consist of just a few added notes or a long series of tones meant to display a performer's skills or make the basic melody more interesting. (Listen to *Kriti*—5.2.)

Text Setting

TEXT SETTING
The rhythmic relationship of words to melody; can be syllabic (one pitch per syllable) or melismatic (more than one pitch per syllable).

Text setting, a term limited to vocal performance, is the process of combining music and words. Settings can be one of two broad types, depending on the relationship they establish between syllables of text and individual sung pitches. If each syllable of a text corresponds to one pitch, the text setting is considered *syllabic*. If, however, several pitches are sounded for a single syllable of text, the setting is considered *melismatic*. It is perhaps best, however, to think of most text setting as being on a continuum between the purely syllabic and the purely melismatic. Most vocal performance falls somewhere on this continuum, more frequently toward the syllabic side. (Compare Islamic "Call to Prayer"—8.1; *Jali* with *kora*—10.7.) However, some traditions strongly emphasize either syllabic settings, as with rap vocal performance in hip-hop music, or melismatic settings, as with African-American spirituals.

Rhythm

RHYTHM
The lengths, or durations, of sounds as patterns in time.

Rhythm is essentially the relationship of sound durations. Some rhythms fall into regular patterns while others are less predictable.

Beat and Tempo

Beat is a regular pulsation of sound. The simplest example is your heartbeat, which pulsates at a relatively fixed rate. This rate, or speed, is called *tempo*. The tempo of your heartbeat increases when you become more physically active, whereas its speed decreases when you sleep. In the same way, musical tempo can be described as relatively fast or slow in relation to a basic beat. (Listen to Hurdy Gurdy—9.6.)

Accent and Meter

An *accent* is an emphasized beat. Accents frequently signal a particular kind of musical activity or a specific stage in a performance or piece. For example, the louder sound of accented beats may correspond to dance steps or signal the end of a performance. Accents are often used to indicate the underlying rhythmic structure of a musical performance. In many traditions, this structure is based on a system of grouping beats into regular units. Such grouping of beats is called *meter*.

Xylophones (*gyil*) from Ghana (Amy Unruh)

Most meters can be considered as either *duple* or *triple*. When groups of beats are divisible by two, the meter is duple; when the beats are divisible by three, it is triple. (Compare Russia *Balalaika*—9.3; *Mariachi*—12.6.) Meter may be articulated aurally by a single instrument, such as a woodblock sounding the basic beat. More typically, however, the meter is implied through the use of rhythms that elaborate on the basic beat to make the music more interesting. In some musical traditions meter can be asymmetrical (as in groupings of 2+3); in others, it is organized into closed cycles. Understanding these meters is important but hearing them is sometimes difficult. (Listen to *P'ansori*—7.6.) In other cases, such as often occurs in Africa, musicians do not think in terms of meter but rather in terms of how rhythms relate. Ascribing a meter to music from such traditions can detract from one's appreciation of the musician's approach to music-making.

The opposite of metered music is music in *free rhythm*. (Listen to Lined hymn—13.3.) Such music has no regular pulse, as is the case with speech. Without a regular beat to follow, a meter cannot be established. If you cannot easily snap your fingers to a piece of music, it may be in free rhythm. Such freely rhythmic music is usually highly ornamented and when performed vocally tends to have melismatic text settings.

Rhythmic Density

The term *rhythmic density* refers to the relative quantity of notes between periodic accents or within a specific unit of time. Rhythmic density can be described as a continuum between low and high (or thin and thick). Long sustained tones in free rhythm with little melodic activity have a low rhythmic density in contrast to music with a steady, usually quick, tempo and numerous notes of short duration. (Compare *Guqin*—7.1; *Akadinda*—10.6.) If the music sounds "busy," the rhythmic density is generally high (thick); if it sounds "relaxed," the density is more likely low (thin).

Phonic Structure

The term **phonic structure** (also *phonic music structure* and often described as *texture*) refers to the organizational relationship between or among musical sounds. A single line of music, whether performed by a soloist or in unison by an ensemble, is described as *monophonic* (adj.) or **monophony** (n.)—*mono* meaning "one"—as long as the performers play the same pitches with the same rhythms. (Listen to Ballad—13.2.) Music featuring melodic lines performed an octave apart, as when male and female voices sing the same line of music in different ranges, is still considered monophonic.

For the study of world music, we have adopted the principle that multiple lines of music (or parts) performed simultaneously are considered *polyphonic* (adj.) or *polyphony* (n.) (Please note that in discussions by Western music specialists, the term polyphony is typically limited to what we have called "independent polyphony.") **Polyphony**, therefore, has three primary subsets: *homophony*, *independent polyphony*, and *heterophony*. The term **homophony** refers to multiple lines of music expressing the same musical idea in the same meter, *homo* meaning "the same." Music that is homophonic requires the use of at least two pitches played simultaneously at an interval other than an octave. In Euro-American musical traditions such music is referred to as *harmonic*, a description that generally implies the use of *chords*, or combinations of three or more tones that are blended together simultaneously to produce *harmony*. Because harmony generally supports a melody, most homophony can be described as melody with chordal accompaniment. (Listen to Bluegrass—13.5.)

Independent polyphony consists of two or more lines of music expressing independent musical ideas. Each line of music is played or sung in relation to the others without any single line dominating. (Listen to Pygmy vocal ensemble—10.4.) This concept covers a variety of possibilities from European counterpoint to styles in which the voice and instrumental accompaniment are melodically independent. For example, having several singers perform "Row, Row, Row Your Boat" starting at different times results in a kind of independent polyphony called a "round."

The term **heterophony** refers to simultaneous variations of the same line of music, *hetero* meaning "different" or "variant." As such, heterophonic music requires more than one performer—each performing the same melody, but differently, either in terms of pitch, rhythm, or both. (Listen to Jiangnan *sizhu*—7.2.) Each manifestation of the melody in heterophony is shaped by the idiomatic characteristics associated with the performance style of each instrument or voice. A single melody played by two performers, only one of whom adds frequent ornaments to the melody, is considered heterophonic in structure. Complex heterophonic structures are especially common throughout much of Asia.

Dynamics

The term *dynamics* refers to the relative volume of a musical sound. The relative loudness or softness of a music can be a distinguishing characteristic of its performance. (Listen to Balinese *gamelan gong kebyar*—6.7.) A gradual increase in volume is known as a *crescendo*, while a gradual decrease in volume is called a *decrescendo*. These and other terms related to dynamics are mostly derived from the European art music tradition, which typically uses Italian terminology. Others, such as *forte* (loud) or *pianissimo* (very quiet), are rarely used in ethnomusicological writing.

Patricia Shehan Campbell

AN INSIDE LOOK

I've lived half my life in the Pacific Northwest, but my earliest memories take me back to my childhood on the east side of Cleveland. My father's family came from Ireland (Wexford and Mayo counties), and my mother's family was German-speaking Gotschee from the old Austro-Hungarian Empire. My earliest memories are of family meals where parents, grandparents, aunts, uncles and cousins, all fired up from their intake of calories, would shift from conversations to music-making. On Dad's side, we had cousin Jerry's accordion backing up the group-singing of popular Irish tunes like "Peg O' My Heart" and "The Rakes of Mallow," while Mom and her sisters washed dishes while singing German-language tunes and hit parade songs in triadic harmonies. I was drawn to the Irish-American tunes of my grandfather and his friends at their Friday night gatherings, and to the polka bands that played regularly at family weddings. I was enamored of the weekly "ethnic radio" programs devoted to Czech, Hungarian, Polish, and Slovenian music that I heard on the family Philco (radio), and was captivated by the high lonesome sounds that came crackling out of WWVA bluegrass programs in Wheeling, West Virginia.

I studied piano, sang in the church and school choirs, and leaped at every opportunity to dance and listen to music alone and with friends. In college, I majored in music and how to teach it. I became a school music teacher, honing my lessons to fit curricular standards of European art music that should be listened to, taught and learned, sung and played, in school. (I hid away my own musical roots, getting the message then that folk and popular music had no place in school.) It was not until I fell into a summer course in ethnomusicology that I realized that *my* music—all of that music of my earlier experiences—was as splendorous and real as I'd always thought, and that it met the mark for sharing in lessons intended for the children I was teaching.

Ethnomusicologists helped me to a new understanding about a wide span of "musical humanity," and I listened to their field recordings, watched their films, read their books, and started my own visits to various parts of Africa, Asia, the Americas, and Europe. I played in a Thai ensemble during my graduate studies at Kent State University, and I studied Japanese koto, Celtic harp, Karnatic Indian mridangam, and Bulgarian and Wagogo (Tanzanian) song and dance styles, over the years. My aim was to learn the music, even a little music,

Patricia Shehan Campbell

and then to work it into ways of teaching it—to children and youth in schools, and to university students. I became convinced that there was intrigue, brilliance, and great value in knowing more of the world's musical expressions, and that if I could learn to sing, play, and dance, then so could my students of various ages and experiences.

So, I learned and taught, taught and learned, and I wrote curricula for schools and then books that focused on the intersections of music, education, and culture. I sought to champion how diversity, equity, and inclusion can direct the content and curriculum of music in school curriculum and performance programs. *Lessons from the World* was my first book-length effort, in which I urged students to learn music by ear (rather than by note); it was at first panned by pre-publication reviewers who read it as heresy to school goals of notation literacy. Still, I pressed to make the point that if the Balinese and the Brazilians, and the Irish of Dublin, and the Indians of New Delhi, could acquire music through the oral tradition, then we could too. Later, I wrote *Teaching Music Globally*, recommending pathways of learning by listening—all the way from first exposure to the performance via the oral tradition. More recently, I worked up ideas on *Music, Education, and Diversity: Bridging Cultures and Communities* to show how students in schools can be enriched when teachers invite musicians living in local neighborhoods to "come, play" (and sing, and tell their stories). That theme came up again when my Singaporean friend, Chee-Hoo Lum, and I published *World Music Pedagogy: School-Community Intersections*, as we saw this kind of linkage to be a way forward to a more vibrant, relevant, and meaningful education in music.

It was important to me, as an educator, to venture from my university campus out into both local and distant communities with ideas for musically educating young people. Twenty years ago, I established a small program of musical education out at the Yakama Nation Tribal School in Washington state, and ventured also in developing the "First Band and First Place School", a start-up band for children of homeless and very low-income families. At the international level, I stitched together partnerships between the University of Washington and the University of Dar es Salaam (Tanzania), and also with Gitameit Academy (Myanmar), so that we might offer support on the design and delivery of courses to students on local and regional music practices. To my surprise, our efforts were noticed, and our model has been replicated here and there, leading to the 2012 Taiji Award (China) and the 2017 Koizumi Prize (Japan) for work on the preservation of traditional music through educational practice. I continue to teach at the University of Washington, offering courses at the interface of Music Education and Ethnomusicology. It was my privilege to serve as chair of the Advisory Board of Smithsonian Folkways for eleven years, and to continue to be engaged as an educational consultant in the repatriation of Alan Lomax recordings to the American South. So, music in all of its glorious splendors is the marvel of my life, and I continue to listen, to join in as I can with live musicians, and to learn further how remarkable we really are as members of a "musical humanity"!

Form

Another important feature of music is *form*. This term refers to the overall pattern or structure of a piece of music as it unfolds in time. Form may be likened to architectural design in that it provides the underlying structure over time that gives a musical performance a predictable or coherent shape. Some kinds of music follow a pre-existing form with, for example, an established beginning, middle, and ending section, while others have less obvious organization. The forms used in one world music tradition may vary greatly from those used in another tradition. Becoming familiar with some of these forms will help you recognize certain traditions and will also help you understand how particular performances are conceived of by performers and audiences alike.

Musical Markers

Over the years, students have generally found identifying a music style by ear is the most difficult aspect of their world music survey. There are so many unfamiliar sounds, instrument names, cultural associations, etc., that just recognizing a music seems a monumental task, especially for students with no musical background.

Our recommendation beyond the "three-fold" listening approach (First Impressions, Aural Analysis, Cultural Considerations) is to make a blank sheet of the Fundamentals of Music (see below) and then comment on each element, if you can. Often, students find that there are just one or two elements needed to help them discern a musical style. Most often, timbre of a distinctive instrument, e.g., didjeridu, is all that is needed for them to recognize the music immediately. Other times, three or four more music elements, e.g., harmony, can reinforce their initial guess.

The bottom-line is, if you cannot identify the music you are hearing, then it is impossible for you to say anything accurate about its cultural meaning or the people associated with the music you hear. By focusing on just a few key musical elements (i.e., "musical markers") that stand out to you, you will quickly discover that you are more literate in world music traditions than probably the majority of people you know.

Each of the listening guides in this edition of your book includes some suggested Musical Markers to get you started. Even though these suggestions are not applicable to every performance in a style, they are usually enough to get you "in the ballpark." The more you listen, the better you will get at recognizing themes of musical production, such as the use of harmony in European and European-influenced traditions. Distinguishing between Chinese Beijing Opera and Japanese Kabuki, for example, may seem daunting at first, but narrowing your focus to just a few prominent musical markers will help you to quickly identify the difference.

Fundamentals of Music   NEED TO **KNOW**

TIMBRE. The tone quality or "color" of a musical sound.

- **Medium.** An object which produces a sound—a voice, instrument, or both; solo or ensemble (duet, trio, choir, orchestra, etc.); one of various instrument types (aerophone, chordophone, idiophone, membranophone).

PITCH. A specific tone determined by its frequency level. Related concepts include:

- **Tuning system.** The pitches common to a particular musical tradition.
- **Scale.** The pitches used in a particular performance arranged in order.
- **Interval.** The difference between two pitches.
- **Range.** All the pitches that a voice or instrument can potentially produce.
- **Melody.** An organized succession of pitches forming a musical idea.
- **Melodic contour.** The general direction and shape of a melody.
- **Ornamentation.** An embellishment or decoration of a melody.
- **Text setting.** The correspondence of words to melody. Text settings can be *syllabic* (one pitch per syllable) or *melismatic* (several pitches per syllable).

RHYTHM. The relationship of sound durations. Related concepts include:

- **Beat.** A regular pulsation.
- **Tempo.** The relative rate of speed of the beat.
- **Accent.** An emphasized beat.
- **Meter.** A system of grouping beats into individual units.
- **Free rhythm.** Music with no regular pulsation.
- **Rhythmic density.** The quantity of notes between periodic accents or over a specific unit of time.

PHONIC STRUCTURE. The organizational relationship between or among musical sounds. Related concepts include:

- **Monophony.** A single line of music.
- **Polyphony.** Multiple lines of music. Related concepts include:

  - **Homophony.** Multiple lines of music expressing the same musical idea.
  - **Independent polyphony.** Two or more lines of music expressing independent musical ideas.
  - **Heterophony.** Multiple performers playing simultaneous variations of the same line of music.

DYNAMICS. The volume of a musical sound.
FORM. The underlying temporal structure of a musical performance.

Questions to Consider

1. **Which of the four basic components of music is most helpful in identifying a world music tradition? Why?**

2. **Name at least three examples from each instrument category in the Sachs–Hornbostel system. In which subcategories do these examples belong?**

3. **How does *pitch* differ from *tuning system*? How does *tuning system* differ from *scale*? How does scale differ from range?**

4. **How does *homophony* differ from *independent polyphony*? How does *independent polyphony* differ from *heterophony*?**

5. **What are some difficulties in using English terminology to describe the world's musics?**

6. **When music is represented graphically in notation, what are some of the limitations? How is Western staff notation limited in its ability to describe world music?**

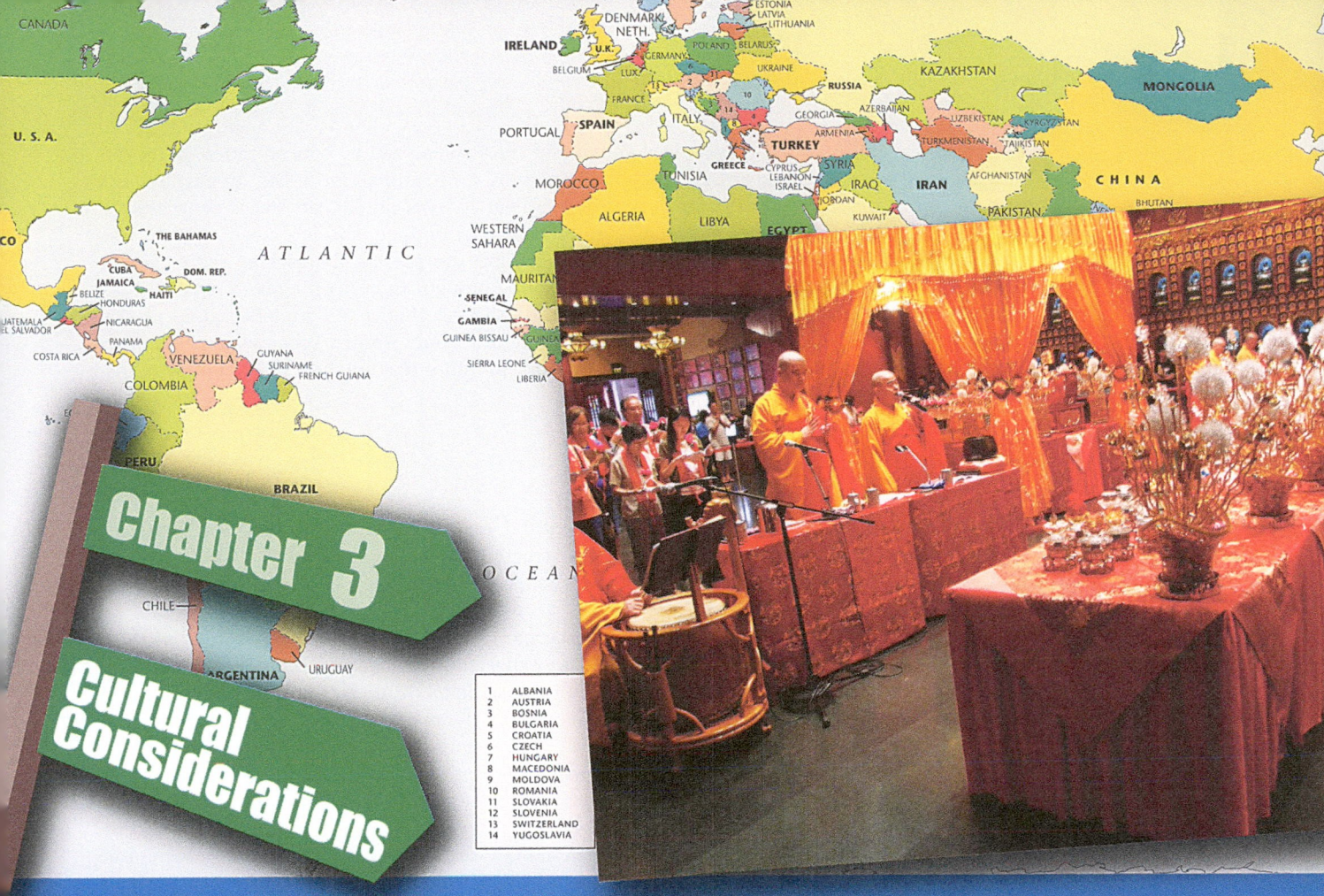

Beyond the Sounds Themselves

Monks conduct a service at the Buddha Tooth Relic Temple in Singapore

In a technical sense, music is organized sound and can be analyzed by concentrating on its elements alone, such as melody, rhythm, phonic structure, form, and so forth. But no music exists in a vacuum, free from social context, even if it primarily lives on concert stages or in recordings. All music manifests itself within a "culture," however defined, and has meanings for those who create, perform, or consume it that go far beyond the sounds themselves. This chapter briefly discusses some of the perspectives that may be brought to bear on a given musical type or style. These ideas, however incomplete, at least suggest that a full understanding of any music would require multiple approaches. Obviously, with only limited space we cannot apply all these concepts to every Site included in this book, but those that are most relevant will be discussed where appropriate.

Cultural Knowledge

Every individual absorbs a certain amount of cultural knowledge while growing up. Just being there makes you a member of a "cultural group," whether at the level of family, "tribe," community, nation, continent, or global cultural sphere (such as "the West"). Who you are depends on where you are and with whom you are living.

The experience of growing up within a given society creates a sense of normalcy; individuals develop expectations that the typical patterns they experience each day will continue. This sense that one's own culture is "normal," and that cultures which exhibit differences, both great and small, are "abnormal," "weird," or "exotic," is a natural perspective known as *ethnocentrism*.

Frederick Verney, Secretary to the Siamese (Thai) Legation in London in 1885, wrote that a great "stumbling-block" for many in the West when attempting to appreciate non-Western music is Western education, which "precludes the possibility of a full appreciation of music of a foreign and distinct school." In order for a Westerner to fully appreciate Asian music, it would be necessary "to forget all that one has experienced in the West." Ethnocentric reactions are natural and perhaps inevitable—but an awareness of ethnocentrism makes it more likely that one will come to accept and understand music that is "different." Scholars attempting to understand how music is experienced and "known" (i.e., "cognition") distinguish between "outsider" and "insider" knowledge. They have dubbed the "outsider" perspective *etic* (from "phonetic"), and the "insider" perspective *emic* (from "phonemic").

Insiders are assumed to react to their own culture's music in ways that draw on a lifetime of unconsciously absorbed cultural knowledge and attitudes. Outsiders, because they come to a given culture after their own perceptions were formed, are assumed not just to inject ethnocentrisms into their interpretations but also to prefer to dwell only on those aspects of music that are observable to outsiders, such as objects and sonic structures. The major drawback to this concept of "insider" and "outsider" is that it does not allow for a middle ground: there is no room conceptually for the sympathetic "outsider" who has acquired "insider" knowledge. Do we privilege the views of an insider, simply because he or she grew up in a given culture, over those of an outsider, no matter how knowledgeable that person is? Can individuals shift identities by living among a "foreign" people? If so, for how long must they live among them? These are questions that do not have simple answers.

Two cases in point. In 1982, I (TM) studied the precented (lined out) psalm singing done in the Scottish Gaelic language services primarily in the Hebrides Islands but also among island ex-pats living in Edinburgh and Glasgow. The small Gaelic-speaking congregation at Greyfriar's Kirk (church) in Edinburgh presented a challenge to the folklorists at the University of Edinburgh. Some years earlier, a young French woman had gone to live on the Hebridean island of North Uist, learned Gaelic, and had become exceptionally skilled in psalm singing. After moving to Edinburgh, she attended Greyfriar's and provided the strongest voice of the Gaelic-speaking congregation. Some of the folklorists contended that her singing was not "authentic" because she had come to Gael life as an adult—even though she was the group's best singer. In their view, an

ETIC
The perspective of a cultural outsider.

EMIC
The perspective of a cultural insider.

Ivory tusk horns in Ghana are essential to the Asante court in Kumase, but African elephants are endangered, and transporting such instruments across national boundaries is forbidden (Joseph S. Kaminski)

French ethnomusicologist Alain Weber performs with "The Musicians of the Nile" from upper Egypt

Judith Becker

My sojourn in the Shan States of Burma, from 1958 to 1961, eventually led me to the field of ethnomusicology. My husband was a Fulbright teacher in Taunggyi, Burma, and I was a newly married piano teacher. I found myself 400 miles from the nearest piano, and surrounded by music that I couldn't fathom. After studying the Burmese harp, *saung gauk*, and attending many festivals and dramas at which the Burmese percussion/gong ensemble, the *hsaing waing*, performed, I steadily grew to love Burmese traditional music. I had also come to appreciate how profound and how stimulating cultural differences and musical differences could be.

My husband and I and our three children returned to the United States in 1961 and took up residence in Ann Arbor, Michigan, where my husband began studying linguistics at the University of Michigan under Kenneth Pike (the emic/etic man). I discovered then that there was a discipline called "ethnomusicology." William Malm had recently been hired to teach world music courses and ethnomusicological theory at the university. When I took Professor Malm's world music course, I knew that I had found my calling. Hearing for the first time the music of the Shona *mbira*, the Persian *kamanche*, the Sundanese *kacapi/suling* ensemble, not to mention Central Javanese gamelan music, left me weak-kneed. At the same time, I was taking courses in anthropology and, with a certain astonishment, read the works of Edmund Leach, Clifford Geertz, Edward Sapir, Alfred Kroeber, and Franz Boas—seminal influences all.

In 1968, during the course of my protracted graduate study, William Malm arranged for the purchase of a large gamelan ensemble and asked me to direct it. (Remember, this was the 1960s and running ethnic ensembles was still a bootstrap operation.) After many listenings to the 1967 UCLA recording, "Music of the Venerable Dark Cloud," and reading *Music in Java*, by Jaap Kunst, I taught the students to play *Bubaran Udan Mas*, in slendro and in pelog. Later in that year, we were able to invite Hardjo Susilo from UCLA to come to Michigan to teach gamelan for two weeks. When he first arrived, my students and I met with him in the gamelan room. He asked us to play for him. We played my interpretation of what I thought I heard the instruments playing on the UCLA recording. After an excruciatingly long pause, Susilo good-humoredly quipped, "Well, . . . there's Yogya style, there's Solo style, and then . . . there's Ann Arbor style." So began the beginning of my education about gamelan performance.

Judith Becker

In 1972, I finally finished my Ph.D. and was hired as an assistant professor at the University of Michigan. For many years I directed the gamelan ensemble with help from visiting Javanese artists. Until the early 1990s, gamelan music, theory, and history were the focus of my research. This roughly twenty-year period resulted in many articles and the books, *Traditional Music in Modern Java: Gamelan in a Changing Society* (1980), *Gamelan Stories: Tantrism, Islam, and Aesthetics in Central Java* (1993/2004), and the three-volume set of translations of works on Javanese music by Javanese scholars, *Karawitan: Source Readings in Javanese Gamelan and Vocal Music* (1984,1987,1988).

Then, feeling that I had put into print all of the burning issues I had concerning gamelan music, I turned to a topic that had been simmering on the back burner of my mind for a long time—trance. Throughout the years in Burma and in Java I had witnessed many trance rituals, some of extraordinary beauty, all of which were compelling and mysterious. In 1996, I made a research trip specifically targeting three religious groups that included trancing as an integral part of their ceremonies, that is, Muslim Sufis in New Delhi, Buddhist *Yak-tovil* practitioners in southern Sri Lanka, and Balinese *bebuten* trancers in Indonesia. These three, plus Christian Pentecostals, formed the core of the ethnographic examples for my book on trance, *Deep Listeners: Music, Emotion, and Trancing* (2004). In that book I put forward the hypothesis that religious trancers and folks who are deeply moved by listening to music, whom I call "deep listeners," share a certain common physiology. It was clear that this intuition would remain in the realm of speculation unless I could devise an empirical methodology to test it. I was finally able to conduct a research project that involved measuring and comparing galvanic skin response of three groups, "deep listeners," Pentecostal trancers, and the control groups, while listening to music they loved. The results suggest that deep listeners and trancers do indeed share comparable lower-brain reactions to music they find moving. (See "Religious Ecstatics, 'Deep Listeners,' and Musical Emotions," *Empirical Musicology Review*, 4(2), 2009; "Ethnomusicology and Empiricism in the Twenty-First Century," *Ethnomusicology* 53(3), fall 2009.)

This venture into the realm of the science of music and the brain initiated my turn toward the biology and the neuroscience of the brain/body, an intellectual pursuit that I will not outlive, as I am now nearly 80.

I have so far written almost exclusively of my scholarly activities. But these interests were never pursued alone. Over the decades, my students, many now in leading positions all over the country in the discipline of ethnomusicology, have been both my first audience and my best critics. They have always been an integral part of my thinking-through scholarly questions about music. They have provided inspiration and, I hope, kept me honest. For me, teaching and scholarship have always been fused, and now, even in retirement, interaction with students continues to be a crucial aspect of my intellectual and musical life.

outsider could *never* attain insider status, even after many years of life among a new group, and they did not consider her singing to be "authentic" or "valid."

In contrast to that, growing up outside a musical system's home territory is not necessarily an impediment to its mastery. Audiences worldwide have no problem in respecting orchestral conductors and musicians who grew up outside Western culture—people such as Japan's Seiji Ozawa, India's Zubin Mehta, and New Zealand's Kiri Te Kanawa, the latter of the Maori ethnic minority. These artists, unlike the French psalm singer, however, were raised and trained in Western music from the beginning, even though the culture surrounding them was "non-Western."

Value Systems and Hierarchies

Within any given culture, people tend to evolve value systems that dictate what kinds of music, which performers, and which instrument-makers are considered "better" than others. Although in the West many accept and others assert that "classical" music is superior to "popular" music, such a ranking begs the question of *authority*—that is, the complex question of who gets to make such judgments. What, after all, are the criteria that make one music tradition superior to another? And who decides? Is it done by some kind of consensus, by appointed critics, or by *self*-appointed critics? What are the implications of such hierarchies?

Essentially, the question is whether expressions of value are to be taken as matters of truth, opinion, or perspective. In the United States, value systems and hierarchies are now understood more in political than aesthetic terms. Many ask whether a value system can be taken seriously when it asserts that the musical heritage of a dominant group, such as European-derived peoples, is inherently superior to that of, for example, African Americans. Music is necessarily part of the current debates in our society over *canons*, *diversity*, and *hegemony*. As with the canon of "great books," the canons of "great composers" and "great works" are essentially European. Calls for "diversity" challenge not just the canons but also hitherto accepted standards of greatness. Some feel threatened by these challenges to the hegemony of European tradition, others feel liberated. Courses in "world musics" (and textbooks like this one) have been part of this partially political process. Until relatively recently, the study of "music" in education at most levels focused almost exclusively on the Western "classics."

Courses on the musics of the rest of the world, which have now become common, still do not rock the boats of established music departments as long as they are restricted to studies of musical style and "exotic" instruments. But when you add scholarly assertions that all musics are potentially valid—or, as University of Michigan Japanese specialist William Malm often said, "different but equally logical"—those devoted entirely to "Western art music" can find these contentions unsettling.

Music and Identity

A person expresses his/her identity in a variety of ways. The clothes we wear, the foods we eat, and the language we speak are all outward projections of "who we are," or more accurately, "who we *think* we are" or "want to be." Biological factors, namely race and sex, are often cited as the source of a person's identity; however, cultural factors are equally, if not more, important determinants.

For example, what makes a person "African"? Must he or she have "black" skin? That can't be the case, because Africans come in an array of skin pigmentations, including "olive" and "white." Likewise, would it make sense to consider Australian Aborigines or the Trobrianders of Papua New Guinea "African" because many of them have a dark skin color? Certainly not. Rather, people are "African" because they think "African." And because they think this way, they behave as "Africans." While it is obviously naïve to think that "African" denotes any specific culture, it is equally naïve to think that "Western" is a culture as well, and yet this gigantic category of identity is often applied to anyone or anything associated with a Euro-American background.

How others interpret the behaviors of an individual or group is also important to the formation of identity. If, for example, a person's behaviors are considered by others to be representative of the qualities of being "African," then that person's self-perception as an "African" is reinforced. However, if others do not agree that the person's behaviors are typical of an "African," then a conflict arises in which either the individual must modify their behaviors, thereby altering the perception of them, or the atypical behaviors must be accepted by the others as properly

International tourists watch Cham musicians playing a double-reed aerophone and drums at a small cultural center at My Son, the site of ancient Cham ruins west of Hoi An in central Vietnam

"African." If the conflict is not resolved, then the "African" identity of our hypothetical person would be continually questioned. Obviously, discussions of identity easily run the risk of stereotyping.

Music plays a vital role in expressions of ethnic identity. Groups and individuals often use music as a way to assert their unique ethnic qualities in relation to others. Outside perceptions of particular musical activities as normative behavior for a group or an individual reinforce the sense of ethnic identity expressed through the music. Along with other cultural elements, such as language, religion, dress, diet, and so on, music shapes how people think about themselves and their role within a society.

In many cultures, the expression of ethnic identity through music is an essential aspect of daily life, so understanding and appreciating musical activities is an important part of getting to know how people from these cultures think. Even in cultures where music is considered a specialized activity, much is expressed and revealed through the types of music common to the culture. For example, the glitz and glamour of Super Bowl halftime shows reveals the emphasis American culture places on extravagant entertainment, even though these music performances are certainly not representative of all the music found in the United States.

Use versus Function

The anthropologist Alan Merriam spent an entire chapter of his landmark 1964 book *The Anthropology of Music* differentiating *use* from *function*. Whereas use, defined as "the ways in which music is employed in human society" (p. 210), can be easily observed, function requires much deeper inquiry into the meanings of music. Most studies of music's use are descriptive and are based on the observations of the researcher. The study of music's function, however, requires deep-level cultural knowledge and can entail much interpretation; for this reason, in answering questions of function, the perspectives of "insiders" are often privileged over those of "outsiders."

One of the most important contexts for music is its use in ritual. While the term ritual obviously encompasses religious services, it is more broadly applied to all situations in which formal patterns of behavior are repeated without question because they are seen to have meaning. Ritual behavior also occurs at sporting events, graduations, Memorial Day parades, Christmas dinners, and many other occasions when music is desired as part of the "pomp and circumstance." For example, the singing of the American national anthem occurs before virtually all sporting events in the United States. Superficially, this *use* is merely a step in a longer sequence of requisite events, but at a deeper level its *function* is to reaffirm national identity and solidarity.

When music's use in certain ritual contexts is considered, questions inevitably arise about the relationship between music and trance states. In rituals where trance occurs, such as those associated with the African-derived religious systems found in the Western hemisphere (e.g., Cuban *Santeria*), does music cause trance? Gilbert Rouget, in his seminal 1980 book *Music and Trance: A Theory of the Relations between Music and Possession*, demonstrates that seemingly trance-inducing music does not in fact cause trance, because if it did, it would automatically affect all who hear it, including the musicians and researchers. Music instead acts to stimulate, regulate, or end ritual trance states, which are not possible without training for and the expectation of altered states such as possession. Music may be *used* in a given possession ritual in order to "call the gods"—but its *function* is to regulate trance.

Music and Spirituality

The association of music with healing and spirituality goes beyond the "use" and "function" of music in ritual because it ascribes to music the power to affect beneficial change in human health, both physical and mental. In recent times, for example, many in the "New Age" movement have

Spiritual Baptists in the Caribbean nation of St. Vincent and the Grenadines sing a hymn in a trance state called "doption" (from the "adoption of the Holy Spirit")

asserted that music can heal, directly affect the mind and its many moods, or enhance contact with the spiritual world. Some believe in the so-called "Mozart effect"—an alleged increase in intelligence among infants exposed early on to the music of Wolfgang Amadeus Mozart—while others claim that listening to specific compositions will cure certain ailments.

Music and Ethics

Music has also been thought of in ethical terms. For Plato (428–328 B.C.E.), the ideal ruler was one shaped by an array of ethical forces, including music performed in the appropriate musical modes. Conversely, Plato also saw great ethical peril in music performed in the "wrong" modes. China's great philosopher Kong Fuzi (also known as Confucius) (551–479 B.C.E.) taught that the harmonious operation of the universe, down to the lives of individual humans, was directly affected by music. In his view, music must reflect the same order, balance, and restraint expected of human behavior. This kind of thinking persists in contemporary society where some believe in the aforementioned "Mozart effect," that playing Mozart's music for babies in the womb will have beneficial effects, or that heavy metal music potentially corrupts young people.

Music and the Environment

Music, it is often said, is "everywhere." One might conclude that this "every-whereness" means that modern societies place a high value on music. For many musicians, however, music's omnipresence may be more a curse than a blessing. Music is frequently the "auditory aspirin" of modern society. Especially with the development of media capable of delivering it anytime, anyplace, anywhere, music has come to be used more and more like a drug. People use music to get themselves going, to facilitate relaxation, to enter meditative states, to control the pace of work,

Plato's student, Aristotle, founded this school near Vergina, Greece, in about 338 B.C.E. where he tutored Alexander the Great and the other children of Philip of Macedonia

or to dispel boredom. The music business has developed the means to use music as a manipulative tool. Muzak, the company, promotes its "music product" as a means of achieving increased sales, moving people in and out of rapid-turnover restaurants (or keeping them there to buy more drinks), and maintaining productivity in the workplace by responding to the natural daily cycle of human energy. Some people drown their concerns in a tidal wave of sound, indeed, loud parties and booming cars have brought about "noise" laws in many cities, in an attempt to curb what many hear as "noise pollution."

Other forms of environmental degradation have also had an effect on music-making. As numerous plant and animal species have become endangered, many long-time musical practices have been lost or permanently altered. This is because traditionally many musical instruments were made of now-rare natural materials, such as hardwoods or ivory. Dancers used feathers from now-endangered birds, or instruments were made of skins from now-endangered mammals. As a result, many old instruments cannot be brought into countries that enforce international environmental laws, and in fact may be confiscated and destroyed. New materials have been developed to substitute for restricted substances; for example, plastic or bone are now often used in place of ivory. Some instruments, though, cannot be made of substitute materials, such as the ivory elephant-tusk horns used in West Africa. In certain situations, governments permit the hunting and use of certain endangered animals that are part of the ritual tradition of a given people.

New Theoretical Perspectives

Although we cannot offer an extensive history of recent scholarship, we believe that some discussion of it is required in any essay on holistic approaches to music. The original work of the Western classical musicologist was to create authoritative musical scores based on manuscripts or prints, as close to the original as possible. Musicologists also sought to write histories of music and musicians based on "primary sources," namely first-hand documents such as letters, as did ethnomusicologists whose "primary sources" were living musicians. Documenting and describing what musicians do was the field's original goal. This concern for "sticking to the facts" and "establishing verifiable truth" constitutes the core of what is called *modernist* scholarship.

Such work continues to be the focus of many musicologists and ethnomusicologists, but a counter-trend arose as a result of new kinds of scholarship in other fields, such as literature. Whereas modernism taught that (capital T) Truth could be established, what is now called *post-modernism* teaches that "truth" is relative and has little validity beyond the person attempting to establish it. Instead of "describing facts," postmodern scholars seek to "interpret texts," a text being any manifestation of culture, including a book, painting, sculpture, or a performance of music. There are other new directions in ethnomusicological scholarship as well, including those focusing on political and economic perspectives (e.g., Marxist interpretation); gender issues, such as feminism; and non-heterosexual perspectives (e.g., "Queer Theory," which examines music-making from varying perspectives of sexual identity. While some of this scholarship has proved to be provocative and stimulating, the specialized vocabularies common to such writing are often impenetrable to readers not familiar with the jargon or theories involved.

Music Technologies and Media

Technology has played a key role in the development of ethnomusicology. Wire recordings and the Edison wax cylinders of the late 1800s and early 1900s were important to the research of "comparative musicologists" who focused much of their attention on transcription and on the tuning systems of world music traditions. Throughout the twentieth century, technological advances enabled ethnomusicologists to record music in increasingly remote locations with greater and greater ease. While early field researchers traveled with heavy loads of equipment and numerous boxes of cylinders, later reel-to-reel tapes, and eventually cassettes and compact discs, today's ethnomusicologist can get studio-quality digital recordings with equipment that fits easily into a shirt pocket.

The media through which music is disseminated have also vastly changed over the last 100-plus years. They have evolved from radio and vinyl records to television and CDs to the Internet and MP3s—and each new development has made dissemination of the world's music easier and faster. This evolution has created greater opportunities for ethnomusicologists to disseminate their research in both academic and mass-market arenas.

The ease with which recording can be done today has resulted in a proliferation of world music recordings available to the general public, both as compact discs and Internet downloads. While many of these are well researched and come with scholarly liner notes, others are simply tourist trinkets slapped together to make a quick buck. Sometimes, however, what seems to be a poor-quality recording is actually an attempt to capture music in its original context, such as a crowded festival. Conversely, a studio recording with excellent sound quality may misrepresent a tradition, by, for example, leaving out instruments from an ensemble or incorporating inauthentic rhythms or melodies. With the virtual disappearance of "record stores," students can still obtain many fine releases from sources such as Smithsonian-Folkways or Multicultural Media, although sometimes even a carelessly compiled audio collection can provide an enjoyable listening experience. Streaming services, such as Apple Music or Spotify, also allow access to a seemingly infinite array of world music traditions.

Music and the Arts

The relationships between music and other arts—including dance, theater, the visual arts, and literature—are varied and complex. While there certainly is music that stands alone for its own sake, a surprisingly great part of the world's music exists in relation to other arts.

The relationship with dance is the most obvious. Dance without music is rare. Dance music provides far more than just a beat: it must also have a character appropriate to the kind of dance it accompanies, whether the dance occurs in the world of classical ballet, folk music, opera, an

Asian theater genre, or in a ballroom. A great deal of dance music may also be heard—indeed, normally is heard—separately from dance, causing us sometimes to forget that a particular song or piece was actually conceived to accompany movement.

Theater in the Western world is usually thought of as spoken drama, opera being a separate category of sung theater. The West also has theater types that include both speaking and singing such as the old German *Singspiel* of Mozart's time (the eighteenth century), the English ballad

A street performance of Chinese (Chaozhou) regional opera with percussion accompaniment in Shantou, Guangdong province, People's Republic of China

The elaborate altar for a Thai wai *khru* (teacher greeting ceremony)

opera (e.g., *The Beggar's Opera*), and the American outgrowth of the latter, the Broadway musical. But throughout the rest of the world, theater without music is mostly unthinkable. This is particularly true in Asia, which has some of the world's most distinctive theatrical traditions, including Indian *Kathakali* (masked dance), Thai *Khon* (masked drama), Indonesian *Wayang* (shadow puppet theater), and Chinese *Jingju* (Beijing Opera).

Music tends to have one of two relationships with the visual arts. The first is found in the field of *musical iconography*, the study of music history and practice—and particularly musical instruments—through pictures. The second occurs when a composer, especially in the Western classical tradition, creates a work that is allegedly inspired by or expresses a work of visual art. Perhaps the most obvious example is Russian composer Modest Mussorgsky's famous *Pictures at an Exhibition*, composed in 1874 and based on a series of paintings by Viktor Hartmann.

Music can also be related to literature—primarily by association—through title, text setting, or allusion. The general term for music of this type is *programmatic music*, meaning music that alludes to something outside itself, be it a story, a great literary work, a poem, a painting, or, even more broadly, an emotion or aspect of nature. Chinese music titles commonly allude to well-known stories from novels, "Chinese opera," natural phenomena, and famous poems. Most pieces in the Chinese repertoire have titles that suggest an image, emotion, or place—such as "Meditation at the Dressing Table," "Suzhou Scenery," or "Winter Ravens Sporting over the Water."

Transmission and Pedagogy

Musical knowledge can be acquired in various ways: intuitively by living in a given culture, directly from a teacher, from a book, or by observation. When teaching is involved, many issues arise—such as the nature of the student–teacher relationship and the question of what educational methodologies are employed. When technologies are used in instruction, questions concerning memory, notation, and recording also arise. Some cultures have developed formal institutions that transmit music to anyone willing to learn (the conservatory, for example) and others have created institutions for preserving it within a closed system (the Japanese Imperial Household, for example). In some societies, especially those of East, South, and Southeast Asia, the music teacher is a revered individual who offers knowledge as a privilege. The Indian *guru* (and by extension, the Thai, Cambodian, and Lao *khru*) dispenses knowledge in a somewhat unsystematic fashion over a long apprenticeship; in the past, students lived with teachers and acted as their servants. The process of transmission in these instances is most often by means of *oral tradition*, in which the musical knowledge is transmitted directly to the student through performance, rather than any form of written notation. In these Asian societies, rituals that honor the teacher and the teacher's lineage are often required before learning is permitted.

In contrast, music teachers in Europe have historically sometimes been seen as odd characters deserving of ridicule, as with the exaggerated eccentricities of Don Basilio in Rossini's often-performed opera *The Barber of Seville* (1816). As for students, many societies offer titles or other forms of recognition, such as certificates or degrees, when students attain certain levels of skill.

Notation Systems and the Creation of Music

Students of Western music are accustomed to thinking in terms of a "composition" and a "composer." Western classical music developed a division of labor between the creator/composer and the realizer/performer. Composers are assumed to have the "genius" that leads to a work's creation. In order to maintain control over all aspects of a work, the composer

The graphic notation for Tibetan Buddhist chant is enough to help informed practitioners remember the chants

represents his ideas through graphic symbols called musical notation—which must be played "as written" by subservient performers. Performers may add nuances but may not violate the composer's intentions. As a result, formal music education in the West tends to privilege "musical literacy," with the unspoken implication that cultures without notation suffer from "musical illiteracy." It is important to realize, however, that only certain aspects of music—such as pitch, melody, rhythm, meter, form, and texture—can be depicted in notation; aspects such as ornamental nuance, mood, timbre, and slight gradations of pitch and tempo cannot be written with much specificity.

Musical notation exists elsewhere in the world but most often only to preserve compositions for posterity or as a reminder to performers. Few cultures outside the West use music notation prescriptively, that is, as a guide to live performance. And even where there is notation, it is usually skeletal, because its function is to provide only what is necessary to cause performance. This type of notation is viewed as a point of departure, much as you find with jazz charts that provide the musical structure as a guide for subsequent improvisation.

Exchange and Adaptation

Although the existence of disparate musical categories such as *kabuki* and *bluegrass* suggests that musical systems are isolated from each other, the reality is much more complex. As distinctive as a given musical culture can be—and many are quite unique—none developed without outside influence. Some borrowed or loaned features travel better than others, however. Instruments, because they are objects, can be easily adopted by other cultures, though they are usually *adapted* as well to make them serve the aesthetic ideals of the borrower. On the other hand, even neighboring cultures can have dramatically differing musical concepts, timbre preferences, decorative styles, and tuning systems.

To give a specific example, Vietnam's musical culture is distinctive enough to be quickly recognized even by minimally experienced listeners. But it is also true that Vietnam was virtually a Chinese colony for nearly 1,000 years and adopted many aspects of Chinese music, especially its instruments. The Vietnamese transformed these Chinese instruments, however, to satisfy the requirements of their own sonic world. The most striking difference is the use of noticeably higher frets on the lutes, which also have loosely strung strings. While Chinese instruments were built primarily to produce fixed pitches, the Vietnamese system uses many "in-between" pitches and thus *requires* tone-bending created by pressing the strings downward between frets or sliding the fingers along the strings of fretless instruments. Though borrowed from Europe rather than China, the Vietnamese guitar, as an example, has an unusual neck with the wood between the frets scooped out to give the player the space in which to press the strings.

Notice the wood is carved out from between the frets of this "Vietnamized" guitar to allow for ornamentation by pressing the strings

Cultural Intersections

To the extent that the world ever had any isolated, unique cultures, the modern world in which we live has certainly breached most of the old walls. Culture contact between and among distinctly named cultural groups is the norm. Whereas in the past this contact occurred through personal interaction as people from one group visited, encountered, traded with, fought with, or expanded into the territory of other groups, today there are also pervasive media bringing music, film, and dance to almost anyone living anywhere.

In 1991, I (TM) visited a remote village in central Laos, then accessible by Landrover over miles of dirt roads through other pre-modern villages. As we approached our destination, we had to disembark from our vehicle and walk the last mile, because the bridge had been destroyed during the Vietnam War some twenty years earlier and had yet to be replaced. As we neared one of the larger houses, owned by the village headman, a group of traditionally dressed children, both ethnic Lao and upland minorities, emerged from the house to witness a rare visit by Westerners. After we climbed the ladder into the house, we noticed they had been watching a television powered by a car battery. On the TV were current popular music videos being broadcast from Khon Kaen, Thailand, hundreds of miles to the south. In this village seemingly 3 miles from the end of the earth, the young generation was fully aware of modern entertainments emanating from modernized Southeast Asian cities.

Throughout history, distinctive musics have resulted not from isolation but through contact. It is the unique mixing of peoples, events, and responses that generates the energy that leads to new and hybrid musical styles and instruments—and sometimes even to completely new genres. The United States offers many examples of this: jazz, blues, gospel, and salsa are four results of the energy produced when European- and African-derived peoples reacted to each other.

A remote village house in China's Fujian Province (Shouning County) now has electricity from a nearby hydro project and—seen in the photo's center—a satellite dish bringing state television

In Mandalay, Burma (Myanmar), the accompaniment to a local vaudeville show includes both Burmese percussion mixed with an electric keyboard and electrified guitars

47

A Case Study of Istanbul, Turkey: A Lesson in Geography, History, Religions, and Musical Exchange

We have chosen the modern city of Istanbul, Turkey, as a case study of cultural exchange. Situated in a strategic location straddling the Bosporus (a broad river connecting the Black Sea to the Mediterranean), it marks the boundary between Europe and Asia. A remarkable amount of history and culture passed through here, profoundly affecting vast areas from Europe to Central Asia and North Africa. Indeed, travelers to Istanbul today will encounter remains and monuments from each historical layer. Although now seen as an Islamic city—albeit in a secular Turkish state—Istanbul was once a major center of Christian European civilization. How Istanbul's status changed, and the musical implications of these changes, are the subjects of this case study.

The Early Islamic Empire (800 C.E.)

The story begins with the conquests of the Macedonian-Greek, Alexander the Great (356–323 B.C.E.), son of Philip of Macedonia (382–336 B.C.E.). Soon after being crowned in 336 B.C.E., Alexander set off to conquer a vast territory that eventually included northern Greece, much of Egypt, and lands across Western Asia into Central and South Asia, an expansion that continued until his death in 323 B.C.E. These conquests brought Macedonian-Greek (also called Hellenistic) civilization, including its architecture, language, sculpture, art, and most likely music as well, to the conquered peoples. The area around the Bosporus was well within the Greek world, and the small city founded on the European side was called Byzantium.

The Roman Empire expanded as Alexander's declined, and by the death of Emperor Trajan in C.E. 117, the Romans occupied much of western, central, and southeastern Europe, northern Africa, and most of the territory earlier conquered by Alexander. Within a few hundred years, Rome's unity would, however, crumble, and the humble village of Byzantium would grow to become one of the world's greatest cities. Because of the gradual decline of Rome and the defacto separation of the empire into western and eastern sectors, in 330 Roman Emperor Constantine I made Byzantium the capital of the [eastern] Roman Empire and renamed it Constantinople. His successor, Theodosius I, in 395 divided the empire into western and eastern halves, giving each of his sons dominion over one of the halves, though with the decline and fall of the western Roman Empire during the fifth century, the eastern half rose to greater prominence.

Whereas Rome was the center of what came to be called Roman Catholic Christianity, Constantinople was the center of the Eastern Rite, also called Byzantine Rite, the origin of a plethora of "Orthodox" faiths, each headed not by a pope, but a patriarch. With the fall of Rome to the Ostrogoths in 476, Constantinople assumed its place as both capital of what remained of the Roman Empire (the Eastern Empire) and center of the Eastern Church. The blending here of Greek and Middle Eastern civilizations brought about a culture, religious and otherwise, that was distinct from that of Rome. Emperor Justinian I (reigned 527–565) attempted to reform the Church, strengthened the Empire, and built one of the city's noblest churches, the Hagia (Saint) Sophia church.

The birth in 570 of Muhammad, the prophet and founder of Islam, in Mecca on the Arabian Peninsula was to change everything. By the time of his death in 632, Arabia had been converted to Islam, and by 656 parts of North Africa and most of the eastern expanses of the Eastern Roman Empire had been conquered as well. By 814 Islam had spread entirely across North Africa and into the Iberian Peninsula (Spain). At the same time, the Roman Catholic and Byzantine Churches continued to engage in disputes with each other even as both were also being torn apart by internal disputes. By 1054 a formal schism between East and West completed the separation.

As Islam conquered the "Holy Lands," a succession of events led to the Crusades, organized by various European emperors and kings to reclaim Jerusalem from those who were termed the "Infidels." There were seven crusades organized in Europe and originating from various points between 1096 and 1270. The great armies raised for these crusades spent months, if not years, marching (sometimes sailing) across vast lands, rivers, and mountains intending to reconquer Jerusalem and the Holy Land. Those that traversed the land had to fend for themselves, often resorting to raiding and destroying cities and killing their unlucky residents. Some sailed through the Mediterranean, but storms often reduced such navies to small bands of survivors. The ill-fated Fourth Crusade, organized in Venice in 1202, only reached Constantinople in 1204. Although the residents of the city were primarily Christian, the Crusaders plundered the capital of the Eastern Church, even establishing a line of weak Latin emperors, but failed to reach their goal, the Holy Land. Although there was a restoration of Eastern Emperors and a renewed flourishing of the Byzantine Church in the eleventh century, Constantinople remained under growing pressure from the Muslim Seljuq Turks, who were expanding their domain from the east.

The siege of Constantinople, begun in 1395, ended in 1453 when the city fell to the Ottoman Turks, and the city's name was changed to *Islambol* ("City of Islam"), romanized as *Istanbul*. The Turkish ruler, Mehmed II, repopulated the city with people brought from elsewhere in the rapidly expanding Ottoman Empire and converted the city's great churches into Islamic mosques. Not only were the great mosaics of these buildings covered in plaster, but towers, called *minarets*, were added around the buildings, both to indicate the importance of the mosque and to provide a tower from which a Muslim *muezzin* could call the faithful to prayer five times daily (see Chapter 8). Under Mehmed II and especially Süleyman the Magnificent (1520–1566), great mosques were constructed following the same basic cruciform (cross-like) pattern of the earlier eastern churches.

The Ottoman Empire continued to expand, especially into southeastern and central Europe, reaching its point of greatest expansion at the gates of Vienna in 1680, after which the empire began to recede and crumble. The Ottoman emperors, called caliphs, ruled from magnificent Topkap Saray Palace overlooking the Bosporus on the western side, accumulating

The great Cathedral of St. Sophia in Istanbul, Turkey, built in the sixth century, became an Islamic mosque, with minarets added after the conquest of Constantinople by the Ottoman Turks in 1453, then a museum in the twentieth century and again a mosque in 2020

great wealth—expressed in the arts, architecture, and music—by bleeding the subjugated areas dry of resources. Because the Ottoman Turks were exceptionally harsh masters, many rebellions arose, leading to great battles that make absorbing a full history of the Empire and southeastern Europe a daunting task.

Of special importance, because of its musical implications, is the *Janizary* (spelled *Yeniceri* in modern Turkish and *Janissary* is many Western writings), a corps of elite troops commanded by the Ottoman caliphs from the late fourteenth century until their destruction in 1826. Said to consist of Christian youths captured in the conquered Balkan provinces, these celibate (until the late sixteenth century) soldiers included bands of musicians who played martial music in parades. What made them distinctive was their use of double-reed aerophones (called *zurna*), metal trumpets, and a battery of percussion including bass drums, triangles, cymbals, and other percussion, including a pole with jingles, later called a "jingling johnny" in England. To Europeans these "exotic" instruments were later seen as quite attractive.

After 1680, as the Empire retreated from Europe, replaced by the now-growing House of Hapsburg (or at different times called the Holy Roman Empire or Austro-Hungarian Empire), the Ottoman government became increasingly corrupt and experienced various coups. After joining Germany as part of the Axis in World War I and being defeated, the Ottoman Empire was ripe for total reform. Mustafa Kemal (later given the title *Atatürk* [Father of the Turks]), disbanded the Empire in 1922 and reformed Turkey into a modern, European-oriented secular republic. Kemal also changed the writing system from Arabic to the Latin alphabet in the process. At this writing, Turkey is a member of NATO and aspires to membership in the European Union.

The modern traveler visiting Istanbul will be struck by the many layers of its history, manifested in a multitude of monuments all within walking distance of each other. There are Greek-style ruins, an Egyptian obelisk covered with hieroglyphics brought to Byzantium by conquering Romans, the incredible Roman cisterns—football field-sized chambers beneath

Istanbul supported by stone columns from dismantled government buildings and designed to store water for a city notoriously short of it—great Christian churches with their magnificent mosaics, and mosques that rival the great cathedrals of Europe.

The musical results are many, too. Among the more significant of these developments we should at least briefly mention the following:

1. Greek and Arabic music theories developed in closely related ways. They in turn became the basis for medieval European music theory, the foundation for the system used today.
2. Certain procedures and melodic styles from Turkey became fundamental in southeastern Europe. Likewise, various Arabic styles penetrated Spain, Portugal, and certain Mediterranean islands.
3. When Islam expanded into Europe, during the Ottoman period, it became a permanent part of many countries, including Albania, Bosnia-Herzegovina, Kosovo, Bulgaria, and Macedonia. The mosques throughout these lands practice typical Islamic forms of chant, including the Call to Prayer and the reading of the Koran, Islam's holy book.
4. Although the Byzantine Church once headquartered in Constantinople (now Istanbul) has long since disappeared, its direct descendant, the Greek Orthodox Church, even today retains many of Byzantium's musical practices.
5. Another group of people, the Romany (often called Gypsies), who came from India, migrated during the fourteenth to nineteenth centuries into northern Africa and Europe. They too brought with them much musical culture from western Asia. In some places the public music of the Romany became, or at least blended with, local traditional music, making conceptual separation nearly impossible.

Musical interchange occurred for many reasons:

1. The flow of culture from the Greek west to the conquered lands of the East (beginning with Alexander the Great), and the return flow of culture from these lands to the West as it was partially conquered by the Ottoman Turks.
2. The Crusaders, who no doubt brought aspects of European culture to the lands they crossed, and the souvenirs, mental and physical, they carried back if they were lucky enough to return home.
3. Intellectual, cultural, and material interchange within each of the great empires that successively occupied these lands. Because the Ottoman Turks were so hated in Europe, many people are still reluctant to admit the degree to which Turkish culture influenced the architecture, cuisine, dress, languages, lifestyles, and music of the conquered lands, but this influence is often quite obvious to an outsider lacking these age-old scars.

Even a casual comparison of Turkish instruments with many found in Greece, Albania, Romania, Bulgaria, and the former Yugoslav states will reveal obvious relationships. While the patterns of diffusion into both Asia and Europe are complex, we note some of the more obvious examples here:

1. *Fiddles or Bowed Lutes.* The distinctive shape of the Turkish *kemence* appears in the instruments of several southeastern European countries, including Greece (*lyra*) and Bulgaria (*gadulka*). We can speculate that these instruments are also related to such instruments as the medieval German *Scheitholt* and the French *rebec*. In some cases, the route of entry could also have been through Moorish Spain during the Muslim Arabic period.
2. *End-Blown Flutes.* The Turkish end-blown flute, called *ney*, also appears in southeastern Europe. Like the others, it is held obliquely.

Greek *lyra* (left) and Turkish *kemence* (right). Note the similarities to the medieval instruments played by angels depicted in a cathedral carving (below)

(far left)
The Turkish *ney*, an end blown and obliquely held flute

Persian (Iranian) *santur* (right) with the American "hammered dulcimer" (right bottom)

3. *Dulcimer/Hammered Zither.* Among the most widespread of instrumental types is the hammered zither (also called a dulcimer), which nearly always has a box resonator of trapezoidal shape. The origin is assumed to be the Persian *santur*. This instrument traveled west throughout Europe, transforming into, for example, the Greek *sandouri*, the Rom *cimbalom*, the German *Hackbrett*, and the French *doulcemelle*. It also traveled east to East Asia (China and Korea) and Southeast Asia, and west to North America, where it is called the "hammered dulcimer."

4. *Double Reeds.* Like the dulcimer, double-reed instruments have traveled east and west, though it does not seem probable that all are related to those from western Asia. The Turkish/Arabic *zurna* instruments are the likely predecessors of the Greek *zournas*, in a chain of instruments leading all the way to the French *bombarde* and even perhaps to the capped reeds, such as the medieval and renaissance *shawm* or *Schalmei*. It is also possible that all of these instruments, including the *zurna*, descended originally from the ancient Greek *aulos*, first developed in western Asia, then transmitted back to Europe.

5. *Pear-Shaped Lute.* The name for a pear-shaped lute in Arabic and Turkish is *al-'ud*, the root of the English word "lute." As the *al-'ud* traveled west, it evolved into folk instruments such as the Greek *lauto* and Romanian *cobza*, as well as the highly refined Renaissance instrument simply called *lute*. The Renaissance lute played in France, Germany, and England most likely entered from Arabic (Moorish) Spain. The *al-'ud* also traveled east, where it became the Chinese *pipa*, the Japanese *biwa*, and the Vietnamese *dan tyba*.

6. *Round-Bodied Lute.* Round-bodied lutes abound in western Asia and southeastern Europe under a variety of names, but they also occur in Europe outside the areas occupied by the Ottoman Turks. The Turkish *tanbur* (and related instruments called *bağlama* and *saz*) is made in various sizes with movable frets, and similar instruments, usually called *tambura* or a variant of this term, are found in, for example, Bulgaria, Croatia, and Serbia. Possibly even

Persians celebrate their New Year on March 21 with music played by a double-reed aerophone called zurna played with drums (Abedin Taherkenareh/Corbis)

The Malaysian serunai is similar to the *zurna*, though found thousands of miles to the east

Turkish *ud* lute (left) with Greek *lauto* (right)

Turkish *tanbur* (also spelled *tambur*) (left) with Greek *bouzouki* (right)

the Italian *mandolin* derives from these prototypes. Ironically, the best-known Greek instrument, the *bouzouki*, descends from the Turkish *buzuq*, and as a result some nationalistic Greeks refuse to listen to *bouzouki* music, since they consider the instrument a survival from the culture of their Turkish oppressors.

Our study of Turkish music shows how culture ebbs and flows between and among sometimes strikingly different civilizations over time and place. These processes are always complicated and can never be sorted out precisely, but it is clear that today's world results from a series of events that have been taking place over a long period of time. Without an awareness of these interactions, it is impossible to understand why things are the way they are today.

Questions to Consider

1. How might an "insider" to a musical tradition hear it differently from an "outsider"? Are both perspectives necessary for a complete picture?

2. What music best expresses your individual identity?

3. What distinguishes "modern" from "postmodern" scholarship in music?

4. What role does music play in your spiritual life?

5. How has technology changed the kinds of music we listen to and how we hear them?

6. Consider how a type of music familiar to you differs in its "use" from its "function."

Australia, Papua New Guinea, Hawai'i, Kiribati

Ayers Rock, known locally as Uluru, rises 2800 feet/863 meters above the central Australian plain southwest of Alice Springs (Max T. Miller)

Background Preparation

The area known as Oceania includes Australia and numerous island groups spread across a vast region in the Pacific Ocean. Whereas the land area of Australia is nearly three million square miles (more than 7.6 million square km), the total land area of the Pacific Islands is less than 500,000 square miles (just over 800,000 km), smaller than the state of Alaska. The islands of New Zealand, Papua New Guinea, and Hawai'i comprise over 90 percent of this land area, while the remaining islands, numbering almost 25,000, account for fewer square miles/km of land area than the country of Belgium. The Pacific Islands are divided into three subregions: **Melanesia** (meaning "dark islands,"), **Micronesia** (meaning "small islands"), and **Polynesia** (meaning "many islands").

Most of Oceania is considered tropical or subtropical. The Pacific Islands straddle the equator, with Micronesia in the northern hemisphere and most of Melanesia and Polynesia, as well as Australia and New Zealand, being part of the southern hemisphere. While Australia and larger islands such as New Zealand and Hawai'i are accessible by plane, many of the smaller islands and atolls of the Pacific are still quite isolated, with ships arriving on only a weekly or monthly basis. Tourism is a primary economic resource in the Pacific, but most indigenous groups continue to survive on subsistence farming or hunting and gathering. Some Australian Aboriginal communities keep their traditional practices fairly secluded, though many have adopted an urban lifestyle or rely on government support.

While European cultural influence is extensive throughout Oceania due to colonization, primarily by the British, the indigenous populations of Australia and the Pacific Islands maintain traditional cultural practices. These vary widely and are considered in many cases to be among the most ancient customs on the planet. A common denominator for all groups is a close relationship with nature. Complex animistic and totemistic spiritual systems have evolved throughout Oceania, in which practitioners call on animals and natural elements for guidance, protection, and subsistence. Rituals involving musical activity are most often associated with these beliefs, and many songs are believed to derive from ancestral spirits who are inevitably linked with spiritual forces of nature.

Along with these traditional beliefs one also finds much Christian influence, introduced by European and American missionaries during the nineteenth and twentieth centuries. Missionaries, along with colonial governments, drastically changed the cultural customs and social systems of many populations throughout Oceania. English or French are considered the "official" languages of most nations, though indigenous dialects continue to be spoken. Home to roughly 1,200 languages, Australia, Papua New Guinea, and the islands of the Pacific provide some of the world's most fertile soil for linguistic and anthropological studies.

The music of Oceania is primarily vocal, and thus effective research on music traditions often requires specialized linguistic study. With few exceptions, instruments tend to be small and portable, most being idiophones or membranophones. Slit drums are common, especially in Melanesia. The few aerophones found are primarily flutes, though the most famous instrument from the region is likely the Australian *didjeridu*, classified as a trumpet. Chordophones—namely the guitar or derivatives of it—are largely of European origin.

Myths and belief systems, along with practical knowledge and oral histories, pass from generation to generation through song and dance. Music is often considered a link to the spiritual plane, and specialists in ritual-associated music traditions are common. Subtle distinctions in vocal performance are considered vital to the identity of individual social groups; thus, music and dance are regarded as highly valued cultural property.

Planning the Itinerary

Our review of music traditions from Oceania begins with the mysterious sound of the *didjeridu*—an instrument found among the **Aborigines** of northern Australia, who maintain some of the

SUBREGIONS OF THE PACIFIC ISLANDS
Melanesia (meaning "dark islands").

Micronesia (meaning "small islands").

Polynesia (meaning "many islands").

DIDJERIDU
A long trumpet made from a hollowed tree branch and played by Aborigines from Australia. The sound is characterized by a low, rumbling drone.

ABORIGINES
A generic term for an indigenous population, often used to describe native peoples of Australia.

planet's most intriguing and ancient cultural practices. Next we introduce an example of one of the world's most common instrument types, the mouth harp, as we travel to Papua New Guinea, an area of major anthropological interest for several decades. While ethnomusicologists have been studying this region extensively, many music traditions remain largely unexplored due to the great cultural diversity of its indigenous populations. We then arrive on more familiar ground—Hawai'i—to examine indigenous vocal practices associated with the precolonial period of Polynesia, as well as more modern music, namely the Hawaiian slack-key guitar. Finally, we introduce the choral traditions of the Pacific through an example of Kiribati vocal performance, which reveals the influence of European musical creation over the last 200 years.

Arrival: Australia

The Australian wilderness is home to several unique species of animals. The koala, kangaroo, and platypus, just to name a few, are among the world's most intriguing animals. While many of the coastal areas have moderate vegetation that supports such species, the interior of the continent, known as the Outback or Bush, mainly consists of vast plains and large desert regions. The major cities—Sydney, Melbourne, and Perth—are located along the coast, while the few inhabitants of the interior are mostly members of Australia's well-known indigenous population, who are referred to as Aborigines.

While most of the nearly 800,000 aboriginal populations of Australia live in urban settings today, a government reserve in the Northern Territory, known as Arnhem Land, is home to roughly 9,000 Aborigines who maintain cultural practices that have existed for roughly 40,000 years. Though some of these Aborigines live in government-sponsored housing, many continue to follow a semi-nomadic lifestyle. These Aborigines acquire few material possessions, mostly related either to hunting (such as spears or boomerangs), or spiritual practices (musical instruments).

The close affinity such Australian Aborigines have with their environment is revealed in their totemistic belief system. Totemism centers on the relationship of an individual or group with animals or natural objects or elements, such as specific mountains or the ocean. *Animism*—the belief that all living things as well as natural phenomena, such as wind or fire, have a spirit—also plays an important role in the Aboriginal cosmology. Known as *The Dreaming* or **Dreamtime**, this cosmology is the focus of much artistic activity within the Aboriginal communities of Australia.

Aerial view of Sydney, Australia, and its iconic Sydney Opera House designed in 1973 (Harvey Lloyd/Getty Images)

ANIMISM
Belief systems in which natural phenomena as well as both animate and inanimate objects are considered to possess a spirit.

DREAMTIME
A term describing the Australian Aboriginal spiritual belief system and concept of creation.

Site 1: Australian Aboriginal Song with *Didjeridu*

First Impressions. The vocal exclamations in this example are accompanied by the steady pulse of wooden clapsticks and the low rumble of the *didjeridu*, an end-blown wooden trumpet that is the most distinctive feature of traditional music from Arnhem Land. The vocalist is like a storyteller shouting his words to all who would

An Aboriginal dance accompanied by clapsticks and a *didjeridu* (Axel Poignant, 1952)

An Aboriginal dance accompanied by clapsticks and a *didjeridu* (Axel Poignant, 1952)

listen, including ancestral spirits, while the constant drone of the *didjeridu* may suggest to the first-time listener a cloud of hornets swirling overhead or the rumbling sound of a large waterfall.

Aural Analysis. The *didjeridu* is traditionally made from a tree branch, typically eucalyptus, hollowed out by termites. Some *didjeridu* are made of bamboo, while modern instruments used in non-traditional contexts are sometimes made of plastic or even metal. Most *didjeridu* are between 3.5 and 7 feet long (106 cm to 213 cm), with a diameter of 1–3 inches (2.5 cm to 7.5 cm). The ring of the blowing end is covered with beeswax to protect the performer's mouth from the wood's ragged edge and to shape the blowing end to a preferred size, in order to create a secure seal for the player's mouth.

The guttural sound of the *didjeridu* is made by relaxing the lips and blowing air through the mouth to make the lips flap or buzz. This vibration echoes through the instrument producing a deep fundamental drone with a multitude of overtones. An adept performer can create different timbres and a rhythmically patterned drone by altering the airflow with his mouth and tongue. He may also force sudden bursts of air through the instrument to increase the volume or alter the pitch and timbre. Performers often add vocalizations, such as humming or growling, to change the sound of the instrument. This latter technique is especially important when performers attempt to imitate the sounds of birds, dingos, or other animals.

CIRCULAR BREATHING
A technique used to maintain a continuous exhaled airflow in aerophone performance.

Fundamental to playing the *didjeridu* is utilization of the **circular breathing** technique, which creates a continuous exhaled airflow, making it possible to produce a steady drone over long periods. Air is expelled through the lips by tongue and cheek muscles. As the performer exhales, he simultaneously inhales through his nose to replenish the air reserve stored in the cheeks. An easy way to try this technique is with a cup of water and a straw; a continuous airflow will maintain a steady stream of bubbles. While a beginner can soon do this with a small tube, the larger *didjeridu* is more difficult to master, because it requires much more air and pressure to produce a consistent and desired tone.

The clapsticks that are used to accompany *didjeridu* are generally made of hard woods and tend to be roughly a foot and a half (45 cm) in length and about an inch (2.5 cm) in diameter. Some Aboriginal groups use boomerangs as clapsticks, especially in ceremonies that prepare hunting parties for expeditions. The clapsticks provide a steady pulse, which the vocalist uses to frame his vocal phrases. The *didjeridu* performer may also correlate his rhythmic drone to the clapsticks by adding overtone bursts in conjunction with the pulse of the clapsticks. These bursts alter the pitch of the drone. In our example this pitch alteration, which raises the initial pitch by a semitone, occurs on roughly every other pulse shortly after the clapsticks enter. Often the clapsticks are played only during the *didjeridu* interludes and not during sung sections—though they do sound throughout both sung and instrumental sections of our example.

This performance consists of two parts: a presentation of the main text and a secondary section of vocables in which non-lexical (untranslatable) formulaic phrases are used. Though some overlapping of pitches occurs, the main text is generally sung in a higher range than the vocables section, which concludes in a comparatively lower range. Throughout the example, the melodic contour of the vocal line is typically descending. Here is a transcription of the words heard before the clapsticks enter (the main text is in boldface):

A *didjeridu* player in a remote area of Australia (Getty Images)

> *Dijan old jong, dijan iya—bushfire*
> (This one's an old song—bushfire)
> [*Didjeridu* enters]
> *ga* **andegarrana andegarran(a)**
> **andegarrana andegarran(a)**
> **andegarrana andegarrana** *ya*
> *a ga na ya ya ga ga*
> [Clapsticks enter]
> (*Bunggridj-bunggridj: Wangga Songs*, Alan Maralung; Northern Australia.
> SF 40430. Washington, DC: Smithsonian Folkways, 1993, p. 30)

The vocal timbre is nasal, and there is only one singer, which is typical among the Aborigines—though group vocal performances do occur. There is only one *didjeridu* player, as is almost always the case, because the fundamental pitches of different *didjeridu* are rarely the same. The instrumental dynamic level remains consistent throughout, while the secondary vocables section is at a slightly lower volume than the main text.

Cultural Considerations. The title of this example, "Bushfire," with its animistic reference to a natural phenomenon, is indicative of the strong association between musical performance and spiritual belief characteristic of Australian Aboriginal culture. Most traditional Aboriginal performances, whether in ritual contexts or for entertainment, have a sacred element that relates to *The Dreaming* (*Dreamtime*), the Aboriginal cosmology. *The Dreaming* tells of an ancient mythological past when the earth was merely a featureless swirl of creative energy. At that time, ancestral spirits (*wondjina*) roamed the planet creating life and shaping the topographical features of the earth. The spirits also created songs, known as "history songs," that provided the framework with which the Aborigines were able to maintain their society, the land, and totemistic

Village elders chant with accompaniment by *didjeridu* and clapsticks as well as clapping (Mark Crocombe)

LISTENING GUIDE

4.1 (1'52")

Site 4.1

Australia: Aboriginal Song with *Didjeridu*

Voice: Single male
Instruments: *Didjeridu* (aerophone), clapsticks (idiophone)

TIME	LISTENING FOCUS
0'00"	Spoken introduction.
(0'04")	("Bushfire" said by vocalist.)
0'07"	*Didjeridu* enters playing a drone (continuous sound). Listen for the dynamic "bursts" that initiate the cycle and provide a rhythmic pulsation.
0'12"	Vocalist enters. Listen for a descending melodic contour and a tendency toward syllabic text setting in the vocal line. The vocal timbre is quite "nasal" and has a declamatory style.
0'26"	Clapsticks enter with a steady pulse.
0'31"	Vocalist, second entry.
0'51"	*Didjeridu* and clapsticks alone.
0'54"	Vocalist, third entry.
1'05"	*Didjeridu* and clapsticks alone.
1'10"	Vocalist uses partial phrases with descending melodic contours to close the sung section.
1'33"	Vocalist imitates the drone of the *didjeridu*.

| 1'42" | *Didjeridu* stops. |
| 1'45" | Closing section of clapsticks and voice. |

Source: "Bushfire" by Alan Maralung, from the recording entitled *Bunggridj-bunggridj Wangga Songs, Northern Australia*, SF 40430. Recorded by Allan Marett and Linda Barwick; provided courtesy of Smithsonian Folkways Recordings. © 1993. Used by permission.

MUSICAL MARKERS: Timbre/Medium—Didjeridu drone has a unique tonal quality. Clapsticks are the only other instrument. Single male vocal. **Text Setting**—Mostly syllabic singing, as if telling a story.
ETHNO-CHALLENGE: Attempt to "circular breathe" (see Aural Analysis) by blowing bubbles in a cup of water through a straw continuously throughout the performance (1'51").

A night-time *corroboree* ritual performed by Aborigines from Goulburn Island, Arnhem Land, Australia (Axel Poignant, 1952)

relationships. Through the correct performance of these songs, the Aborigines are able to tap into this ancient and creative power left behind by the ancestral spirits. Aborigines believe that these history songs have remained unchanged since the beginning of time.

While history songs are regarded as the most important, songs related to totems or social activities also exist. New songs in the latter two categories are sometimes composed, though they usually are considered to have been inspired by an ancestral spirit or taught to an individual in a dream. Women do not usually perform songs along with men, and it is taboo for women to play the *didjeridu*. The sound of the *didjeridu* is considered the most sacred of all sounds and is regarded not only as symbolic of the creative powers of the ancestral spirits but also as an actual aural manifestation of their creative energy. Female performance on the *didjeridu* is taboo primarily because Aborigines believe that exposure to the instrument's spiritual power would make a woman more fertile, causing her to give birth to too many children for the community to support.

While tourists often have access to staged performances of aboriginal music, the most common contexts for traditional Aboriginal music performances are mortuary rites and boys' circumcision ceremonies. Songs are also performed on more informal occasions, most frequently during a *corroboree*, or night-time ritual. Most of these events are considered sacred and are closed to the uninitiated; thus, there is little documentation of them. Dance plays an important role in ritual contexts. White paint is applied to the dancer's dark-skinned body according to prescribed patterns associated with a clan's totems, the specific ritual, and other factors. At the night-time *corroboree*, this paint shines in the firelight, taking on spiritual significance. During these events, which are believed to connect participants with ancestral spirits, the hypnotic sound of the *didjeridu* helps create a feeling of disorientation from time and place.

Arrival: Papua New Guinea

While Papua New Guinea (often referred to as PNG) has a population of fewer than five million inhabitants, there are more than seven hundred languages spoken among its diverse cultural groups. Comprising the eastern half of the island of New Guinea (the western half being part of Indonesia), the region is the largest land area in Melanesia. Its precolonial history dates back roughly 50,000 years and is believed to be linked with that of the Aboriginal populations of Australia, based on several cultural and genetic similarities.

YariYari men play the *kundu* goblet drum and dance in Papua New Guinea (Michele Westmorland/ Corbis)

The major cities are found along the coast, while the highland interior is home to much of the population. Most indigenous groups practice subsistence farming—that is, they grow food and raise livestock for personal use rather than for commerce. While English is the official language due to years of British colonial influence, only a small portion of the population speaks it fluently. Indigenous languages predominate, along with Tok Pisin, a combination of pidgin English and Melanesian.

Christian missionaries, primarily from Europe, have had some influence on indigenous spiritual beliefs found in Papua New Guinea. Local traditions that missionaries considered pagan or erotic in nature were often prohibited by them, in particular traditional dancing that was targeted as an immoral activity thought to promote sexual promiscuity. As a result, many local customs, especially in lowland areas where missionaries have had the most influence, have been lost or modified.

Nevertheless, a wide array of traditional music and dance is still found in Papua New Guinea, and many customs have been reestablished since the country achieved independence in 1975. Tourists are visiting the island in increasing numbers, drawn by the elaborate dress and varied cultural activities of the many different ethnic groups. Probably the most visible of instruments found among the Papuans are the large slit drums called *garamut* and the hourglass-shaped drums known as *kundu*. These are used in many ceremonial contexts and have become a staple of tourist shows and government-sponsored festivals. Less popular at these events, but perhaps the most widespread instrument in the country, is the *susap*, a bamboo mouth harp commonly played for self-entertainment.

Site 2: *Susap* (lamellophone) from Papua New Guinea

First Impressions. The *susap* has a distinctive "twangy" timbre, as if the performer were talking through an electronic voice modulator. A first-time listener not seeing the instrument might imagine the performer is striking a metal spring or taut cable with a small screwdriver, creating a wobbly "boing" effect. This unique tone quality makes our example memorable even in the absence of a singable melody or repeatable rhythm.

Aural Analysis. Mouth harps, such as the *susap*, are one of the most common instruments found throughout the world. Most are made of either wood or bamboo, but some are made from metal, such as what used to be known as a "jew's harp" common to American folk music. Such mouth harps are not actually classified as harps (chordophones) but belong, rather, to a subcategory of idiophone known as *lamellophones* (or *linguaphones*). Lamellophones in general have multiple flexible tongues (each known as a lamella) that are typically plucked to produce sound. Most mouth-resonated lamellophones have a single *lamella* that is set or cut into a frame. The performer plucks the lamella so that it vibrates within the frame, producing a distinctive "twangy" timbre, whose quiet sound is amplified by the mouth cavity. The lamella must pass tightly within the frame to produce the desired effect. A small piece of wax is sometimes fixed to the end of the lamella to encourage its vibration or to change the instrument's timbre.

To play the *susap*, the performer holds its frame tightly within the lips, holding one end to maintain the proper angle while plucking an extension that is attached either to the frame or to the lamella. Often a small string is attached to the instrument and jerked to vibrate the lamella. The performer alters the sound by changing the size and shape of his oral cavity and vocal tract. While the fundamental pitch of the mouth harp does not change, the manipulation of overtones resonating in the mouth can produce recognizable melodic features, usually more closely related to speech than song.

In our example the performer maintains a steady plucking pattern but varies the rhythmic content through timbral changes. While the performance is likely improvised, the example can be segmented into four sections. The opening section includes twenty pulses without much

A Baruya man plays the *susap* mouth harp from the Eastern Highlands province of Papua New Guinea (Don Niles)

timbral variation. This is followed by a more rhythmically active section in which the player begins to "speak" with the instrument, producing an accented low tone echoed by a faint over-tone. The rhythmic emphasis shifts frequently: sometimes the fundamental tone is played twice before the echo is sounded, other times the player alternates evenly between the two timbres, producing one overtone for every low tone. This section is also marked by the frequent use of a long–short rhythmic pattern created by the performer using his tongue to silence the resonation just before plucking the instrument to produce the accented tone. One might express this rhythm as a short–long pattern, such as "du-duu, du-duu."

The third section occurs approximately ninety pulses into the performance and is character-ized by a less-prominent role for the lower, accented tone and a new emphasis on varying the timbre of the higher overtones. Variations in timbre are produced through manipulations of the size of the mouth cavity and by changes in the position of the player's tongue. This section is the most speech-like of the four sections. The final section commences at approximately 150 pulses and is marked by the "boing" effect already mentioned, which is created by fluttering the tongue inside the mouth cavity to produce a wavering, "wobbly" sound. This is perhaps the most unique timbral effect of the performance.

Cultural Considerations. In Papua New Guinea, as elsewhere, the mouth harp often acts as a "speech surrogate." Performers use it to imitate speech patterns and phonemes in order to create the illusion of speech in a musical context. The sounds of the mouth harp are often considered to be speech that is "disguised," in order that it not be understood by eavesdroppers.

Close-up showing details of a bamboo lamellophone from the southern Philippines. A toothpick has been inserted to display the vibrating tongue

LISTENING GUIDE

Site 4.2

Papua New Guinea: *Susap* (lamellophone)

Instruments: *Susap*

TIME	LISTENING FOCUS
0'00"	Opening pulse established. Timbre is consistent, with little variation.
0'07"	Second section, emphasizing a "short–long" (du-duu) rhythmic pattern.
0'24"	Section transition. High-frequency manipulation initiated.
0'28"	Third section, characterized by a "speaking" manipulation of the fundamental tone and emphasis on a single prominent overtone.
0'50"	Fourth section, characterized by "wobbly" overtone manipulation.
1'17"	Close of performance on the fundamental tone.

Source: "Badra from Buzi" ("Sounds of a *Susap*") performed by Amadu, recorded by Wolfgang Laade, Buji, Western Province, Papua New Guinea, 1964, from the recording *Music from South New Guinea,* Folkways 04216, provided courtesy of Smithsonian Folkways Recordings. © 1971. Used by permission.

MUSICAL MARKERS: Timbre—"Twangy" sound with unique "wah-wah" like fluctuations. No other instruments heard.
ETHNO-CHALLENGE: Make a "mouth harp." To do this, cut a "tongue" into a rectangular piece of plastic, metal, or wood. Experiment with different sizes and shapes.

Explore More

Singsings of Papua New Guinea

As with all of the destinations we visit, there is much more to the music of Papua New Guinea than covered in this book. While the *susap* is a common instrument, it is primarily played by children and is considered by most adults as a "toy" for those of courting age. Many other traditional forms of music have a much higher status for communities. These emphasize group vocal production, typically accompanied by communal dancing.

The most common instrument throughout PNG is the *kundu,* a small goblet-shaped drum with a face made of either lizard or snake skin. Many have anthropomorphic features, such as a crocodile shape and can exceed 9 feet (3 meters) in length. The largest drums (known as *diwaka*) are considered community property and played for important rituals and village gatherings. The smaller *kundu* are carried by the performers as they dance and sing. Other instruments include stamping tubes, a variety of flutes, and the well-known *garamut,* which are large hollow log idiophones struck with sticks that are used to communicate messages over large distances as well as accompany singing and dancing.

Singsings are among the most common contexts for musical performance among aboriginal populations in PNG. These events typically include participants from several villages, who perform clan dances and music throughout the day and often overnight. Singsings today are intended in part to celebrate the diverse ethnic makeup of the island communities and foster cultural exchange between groups that otherwise have little contact with each other. Participants adorn themselves in a colorful array of regalia, body paint, and sometimes face masks, attracting many outsiders to these social gatherings once considered a musical battleground between opposing clans, similar to the singing competitions found in other parts of Oceania (see Site 4: Kiribati).

While mouth harps are commonly used for self-entertainment, they are also frequently found in traditional courting rituals. In Papua New Guinea the *susap* is considered to possess love-controlling magic that men can use to attract a woman's affections. By using the instrument as a speech surrogate, the man is able to "say" things to the woman that might otherwise be considered inappropriate. The instrument also provides impunity from rejection. If the woman is attracted to her suitor, then the magic has worked; if not, the magic was either ineffective or not correctly utilized by the performer. An ignored suitor either has to improve his technique or use a different instrument to attract the woman's affections. This allows the woman more freedom to act on her feelings as well, as the instrument can be blamed for affecting her action or inaction with regards to her suitor. Thus, the *susap* functions to maintain social relationships between young men and women in small communities where daily interaction is necessary for subsistence.

Arrival: Hawai'i

The fiftieth state of the United States of America is geographically considered a part of Polynesia, a region including many other well-known islands such as Tahiti, Tonga, Samoa, Easter Island, the Cook Islands, and even New Zealand. The first inhabitants of Hawai'i most likely arrived from the Marquesas Islands and Tahiti, the largest of the Society Islands, sometime between the seventh and thirteenth centuries. These early settlers subsisted primarily on fish and *poi*, a pasty food made from taro root. Their social organization was essentially feudal and incorporated strict taboo systems, called *kapus*.

The first European visitor to Hawai'i was the Englishman Captain James Cook, one of the most famous explorers of the late 1700s. Arriving in 1778, Cook was initially welcomed by the islanders, but relations between the British and Hawaiians soon turned sour, and in 1779 Cook died in a skirmish on a return visit to the islands. Nonetheless, within a few years the islands became an important port for European and North American trade. Increasing contact with outsiders brought many changes to indigenous ways of life. The islands were politically unified in 1810 by King Kamehameha I, who encouraged foreign trade and successfully maintained Hawai'i's indepen-dence from colonial control. He also supported native cultural customs and the indigenous religion until his death in 1819.

Support for Hawaiian culture was, however, abandoned by Kamehameha's son and successor, Kamehameha II, who in less than a year destroyed the old system of *kapus* and abolished the ancient ritual practices. The temples and idols of the old religion, a complex form of animism, were ordered to be destroyed, and the king welcomed the arrival of Christian missionaries soon afterward. Visitors to the former palace in downtown Honolulu will note the strong central European influence adopted by the old monarchy. These events brought drastic changes to secular life as well, and the 1800s saw rapid changes in social organization, political power, and economic patterns. Sugarcane became a major export, and wealthy American businessmen began to acquire much power and land throughout the islands. The political power of the Hawaiian monarchy evaporated in the 1890s, and the country was eventually annexed by the United States.

The early 1900s saw an increased influx of immigrants from the United States, the Philippines, China, and Japan. Most came as laborers to work for the burgeoning pineapple and sugarcane plantations. The Japanese attack on Hawai'i's Pearl Harbor on December 7, 1941, precipitated U.S. entry into the Pacific theater of World War II and made the islands of vital strategic interest to the United States. Initially, Japanese-Americans in Hawai'i were distrusted, but their bravery in the ensuing war—they comprised some of the most decorated regimental military units in American history—diminished racial prejudice against them in the postwar years. Hawai'i acquired statehood in 1959 and quickly became one of the most popular tourist destinations in the United States.

Amy Ku'uleialoha Stillman

Hawaiian music is my birthright. My mother took me to hula lessons when I was five years old, and I had a ukulele in my hands by the time I was seven. After an adolescence hooked on Elvis and the Beatles, I returned to Hawaiian music in my high school years and have embraced it as my passion since. As an undergraduate at University of Hawai'i in the 1970s, I was shocked to read anthropological scholarship on Hawaiians that dismissed my parents' and my traditions of "modern" Hawaiian music as inauthentic because of its westernized character. I resolved then to get a Ph.D. in order to join the scholarly conversation at that level and be taken seriously.

A deliberate focus on research and writing precluded teaching hula performance for several decades, despite that I possessed the capacity to do so, because there were so few scholars with the aptitude for laborious archival research. My work has been devoted to exploring how contemporary Hawaiian performance retains indigenous Hawaiian aesthetics even as Hawaiian people embraced westernization and Christianity. I've reached back into archival resources and uncovered hundreds (if not thousands) of pieces of repertoire, only a fraction of which had been passed to the present in continuous performance. In the first edition of this book I wrote of my aspiration to bring the archival repertoire back to life by reuniting it with the performers who have maintained the skills of singing and dancing. Since then, I have

Amy Ku'uleialoha Stillman, music researcher, and scholar

done exactly that, by curating three concerts and producing three CDs of contemporary settings of archival repertoire. This experience led to an opportunity to collaborate with Grammy Award-winning producer Daniel Ho on writing new songs. Our very first CD of original material, 'ikena, received the Grammy Award for Best Hawaiian Album in 2009, and our second CD, He Nani, received a nomination in 2010. My career, initially devoted to documenting Hawaiian performance, has gone full circle to creating new repertoire, by adding to the stream of tradition.

Explore More

Hawaiian Steel Guitar and Ukulele

Although *hula* is the music and dance tradition most associated with the islands, steel guitar is also an important musical export of Hawai'i. The Hawaiian steel guitar style is distinctive for its characteristic "sliding tone" (i.e., portamento) produced by sliding a metal bar along the strings without pressing them down to the fretboard. This allows the performer to sound all the frequencies between two standard pitches, thus "sliding" into many pitches of the melody. Because of the emphasis on this pitch-bending effect, melodic lines tend to have a low rhythmic density and the overall tempo is moderate to slow. Wide vibrato and harmonic overtones are common to

Hawaiian steel guitar performances, particularly on electric instruments, which first became popular in the 1930s.

While the guitar is believed to have arrived in Hawai'i during the 1830s, the first appearance of the "sliding" performance technique is typically attributed to Joseph Kekuku in 1885, who as a young boy experimented for several years with this sound on his guitar using various materials, string tunings to produce a variety of chords, and timbral effects, such as harmonic overtones, that were to become standard to the Hawaiian steel guitar tradition. In 1904, Kekuku traveled to the United States (Hawai'i was not yet a state) and also toured Europe with his pioneering guitar style. Other performers who had adopted Kekuku's style followed, and

The Hawaiian ukulele (Shutterstock)

by the mid-1920s the Hawaiian steel guitar had become popular throughout the mainland and abroad, particularly with vaudeville troupes and Country & Western musicians who incorporated the instrument into their own music, leading to the development of the *dobro* and pedal steel guitar as the instruments are known today. African-American blues artists of the 1920s–1930s also utilized a similar sliding technique, creating a "bottle-neck" style of blues music that incorporated fingerpicking as well. Hawaiian steel guitar remained popular through the 1960s, particularly in association with Hollywood movies, such as Elvis Presley's *Blue Hawai'i* (1961).

Whereas the Hawaiian steel guitar tends toward a long, lilting melody, the *ukulele*, a small four-stringed Portuguese version of the guitar, often has a more rapid playing technique. Brought to the islands in the late nineteenth century, the ukulele was adopted by Hawaiians to accompany vocal performance and to be played as a solo instrument. The name translates as "flying flea," a reference to the fast plucking technique utilized by its early

performers. The standard (or soprano) ukulele is roughly 18–20 inches long (46–53 cm) with twelve to seventeen frets following the Western tuning system. The strings are tuned to G–C–E–A, such that the C is the lowest pitch, with the others above in the same octave. The instrument often appears in small ensembles that also include a guitar and string bass and has become popular to accompany modern *hula* dances.

Another important Hawaiian style of performance is known as the "slack-key guitar," which first appeared on commercial recordings during the 1940s. Played on a regular acoustic or electric guitar, this method requires the instrument strings be loosened ("slackened") to alter the standard tuning to sound a full chord, usually G, when the open (non-fretted) strings are played. Instrumental performances include a rapid fingerpicking style as well as hammer-on and pull-off techniques with the fretboard hand and "chime" effects produced by lightly touching a string at its harmonic node to sound an overtone. Vocalists often accompany themselves with this guitar style and pass on their songs through oral tradition. Among the most famous performers of the genre was Raymond Kane (1925–2008), a recipient of the National Heritage Fellowship in 1987, as well as Ledward Kaapana (b.1948) who is well-known today.

Site 3: Hawaiian Drum-Dance Chant

First Impressions. While chanting in most traditions is strongly speech-like, Hawaiian drum-dance chant is often more song-like. Each phrase rolls off the vocalist's tongue like the gentle lap of ocean waves on a white sand beach or the graceful, flowing arm movements of Hawai'i's famous *hula* dancers. The drums add a solid, but not overbearing, undercurrent that gives the performance an earthy feel, suggestive of a spiritual connection to nature.

Aural Analysis. Hawaiian drum-dance chant consists simply of a voice, one or two drums, and accompanying dance. Other rhythmic instruments, such as stamping tubes (*ka'eke'eke*) or gourd idiophones (*ipu heke*), can be added. The preferred vocal timbre is usually full, with a deep, resonant tone quality. Vocal ornamentation is important, as with all styles of Polynesian chant. A prominent feature of Hawaiian vocal performance is the use of *vibrato* (a wavering of tone). While vibrato is commonly used in many world traditions, it is generally applied to sustained pitches. Hawaiian vocalists, however, frequently apply vibrato to shorter tones as well. The text setting is primarily syllabic—that is, it employs only one pitch per syllable, utilizing only two tones at an interval of a minor third. The vocalist emphasizes the upper pitch but "falls" or "slides" to the lower pitch on sustained tones. This "sliding" technique is referred to as **portamento** and involves a continuous movement from one pitch to another, usually from high to low, with all of the frequencies between the two pitches being sounded. The singer in our example uses portamento occasionally at the beginning of the performance.

Another distinctive feature of Hawaiian vocal performance is inherent in the language itself. Most words end with open vowel sounds, such as *ah, oh, oo, ai,* and so on, rather than closed, hard consonants, such as *k, t,* or *p*. While hard consonants are found at the beginning of some words, they tend to be deemphasized. As such, the singing flows from one phrase to the next with smooth transitions, as in our example, which begins with the vocalist speaking the phrase "*(Ai) Kaulilua i ke anu Waì alé ale*" before singing it. The open vowel sounds facilitate the use of portamento as well as vibrato and help give the music its "flowing" feel.

The accompanying drums are known as the **pahu** and the **kilu** (also *puniu*). The *pahu* is a single-headed cylindrical membranophone that stands vertically on a carved footed base. The base and resonator are typically a single unit made from the wood of either a breadfruit or coconut tree. The *pahu* can be as short as around 9 inches (23 cm) or as tall as almost 4 feet (123 cm). Its face is traditionally made from sharkskin, or sometimes from manta ray skin, and is attached with twine made from the outer fibers of coconuts. The *kilu* is a smaller drum made from a gourd, wood, or a coconut shell and traditionally has a face made from fish skin. The *kilu* is sometimes attached to the performer's leg with a strap. It is played with a narrow strip of braided coconut fibers, creating a higher "slapping" sound relative to the *pahu*, which is played with the hand. The *pahu* is considered the more important of the two instruments, and its irregular rhythmic patterns correspond to important points in the song text and associated dance movements.

PORTAMENTO
A smooth, uninterrupted glide from one pitch to another.

PAHU
A single-headed cylindrical membranophone from Hawai'i that stands vertically on a carved footed base.

KILU
A small drum from Hawai'i, usually made from a coconut shell with a fish skin face.

LISTENING GUIDE

4.3 (1'52")

Site 4.3

Hawai'i: *Mele Hula Pahu* (Drum–Dance Chant)

Voice: Single female

Instruments: *Kilu* (high-pitched drum), *pahu* (low-pitched drum)

TIME	LISTENING FOCUS
0'00"	Spoken text: "(Ai) Kaulilua i ke anu Waì alé alé"
0'04"	Introductory four-pulse (duple meter) drum pattern, followed by basic pattern used throughout performance. Listen for variations in the basic drum pattern, such as at 0'28", 0'37", 0'54", etc.

Drum Introduction

Kilu (high)	- x x x	- x x x	- x x x	- - x -
Pahu (low)	x - - -	x - - -	x - - -	x - - -

Basic Pattern

Kilu (high)	- x x x	- x - -	- x x x	- x - -
Pahu (low)	x - - -	x - x -	x - - -	x - x -

0'09"	Vocalist enters. Spoken text (at 0'00") is now chanted (0'09"–0'13").
0'37"	Both drums sound simultaneously.
0'56"	Listen for extended vibrato in voice.
1'01"	Second verse begins.
1'44"	Extended vocal vibrato closes verse.

71

1'49"	Closing drum pattern.
1'55"	Closing spoken verse.
1'58"	*Kilu* drum closes the chant with three strikes.

Source: "Kau ka hali'a I ka Manawa," performed by Noenoe Lewis (drum, vocal) and Hau'oli Lewis (calls, dance); from the recording entitled *Hawaiian Drum Dance Chants: Sounds of Power in Time*, SF 40015, provided courtesy of Smithsonian Folkways Recording © 1989. Used by permission.

MUSICAL MARKERS: Melody—Vocal line emphasizes a single pitch with a fast "wavering" vibrato and falling pitch at the end of phrases. **Text Setting** – mostly syllabic, as if telling a story. **Rhythm**—Drum pattern is simple and repetitive at a moderate tempo.
ETHNO-CHALLENGE: Write out the drum patterns for the entire example and play along with the performance.

Cultural Considerations. The best-known examples of Hawaiian music today are heavily influenced by European musical traditions. Because Christian missionaries were often strict with regard to the vocal practices of converted islanders, much of the vocal music came to be based on European hymnody and utilizes conceptions of harmony that presumably did not exist prior to contact with Europeans. Popular instruments such as the Hawaiian "slack-key" steel guitar, which uses a steel slide to stop the strings, or the *ukulele*, a small chordophone modeled after the guitar, only appeared in Hawaiian music after the colonial period began. Thus, the "traditional" ensembles that tourists often see accompanying modern *hula* dancers or hear on popular recordings reveal much Western influence.

Hawaiian drum-dance chant, however, is considered free from outside influence and remains a vital aspect of Hawaiian musical identity. The songs play an important role in the maintenance of indigenous language, spiritual beliefs, history, and social customs. While the

A Hawaiian musician plays the *kilu* (left) and *pahu* (right) drums (George Bacon)

Near the edge of Hale Ma'uma'u Crater, dancers perform a *hula* in honor of Pele, the volcano goddess (Adrienne L. Kaeppler)

Male dancers perform a *hula kala'au* at Lanikuhonua in 2011 in a *mele* in honor of Kuali'i. (Photo by Janel Te'o and courtesy of La'akea Perry)

poetic text of these songs or chants is the primary focus, the musical delivery is also important, as it enhances the efficacy of the words. Poetry used in drum-dance chant is generally referred to as *mele*. There are several categories of *mele*, the most sacred of which, *mele pule*, consists of prayers dedicated to traditional gods, performed by ritual specialists known as *kahuna*. Lesser categories of *mele* trace genealogical histories, name and honor people, or signify specific ritual contexts, such as weddings or funerals.

Mele hula are songs specifically associated with dance. Some are purely vocal, while those called **hula pahu** are accompanied by the *pahu* drum. *Pahu* are highly valued ritual objects that hold much spiritual power (or *mana*). The sound produced is considered a voice and traditionally was believed to "speak" to the gods. Drums were typically the property of chiefs or priests and were symbolic of their authority and sacred power. As such, they were treasured items sought after by rival kingdoms. The *pahu* was used in many ritual contexts, such as important births or memorial services but today is primarily found accompanying dances and rituals promoting Hawaiian ethnic identity.

HULA PAHU
Hawaiian dance songs using drum accompaniment.

Dance: Tongan Dance
Concepts, genres, and movements

by Adrienne L. Kaeppler, Smithsonian Institution

The Kingdom of Tonga has been an independent member nation of the British Commonwealth since 1970. Comprised of about 150 islands and about 200,000 people, half of which live overseas, Tonga lies at the southern point of a triangle formed with its two important neighbors Fiji and Samoa. In these areas, and throughout Polynesia, dance is a visual extension and enhancement of sung poetry based on complex arm movements performed solo, in small or large groups, seated or standing in one or more rows facing an audience.

The audience-oriented movements project oral literature into visual form and are an artistic medium used to praise and honor the gods and chiefs, to formally recognize national or local events, to praise places and people, and to entertain.

Tongan dance, within this overall tradition, focuses on three parts of the body. Leg movements, in addition to bending the knees, are often a series of side steps executed nearly in place and are used primarily to keep the rhythmic pulse. A side

Lakalaka from the village of Kanokupolu at the Coronation festivities for King Tupou V, August 2, 2008. Princess Latufuipeka, the King's niece, is the central performer. (Adrienne L. Kaeppler)

head tilt known as *fakateki* is sometimes choreographed, but more often is added by a dancer to express an inner feeling of exhilaration called *māfana*. The most important movements are those of the hands and arms and include placement of the arms in space, flexions and extensions of the wrists and knuckles, palm facings, curling of the fingers, and the rotation of the lower arms. These arm and hand movements form a series of movement motifs which allude to selected words of the text or concepts arising from the poetry. The motifs also form beautiful movements that decorate the text, complete textual or musical phrases, and form "dividing motifs" that divide stanzas or sections of poetry.

Arm motifs are known by the general term *haka*, while a number of motifs have specific names, such as *milolua*, a movement which derives from the wringing of kava (a drink made from an infusion of the root of a pepper plant). Arm movements for women are soft and graceful while foot and leg movements are small in keeping with the stricture of always having the upper legs parallel and close together, even while seated. Men's movements are larger and more virile. Arm movements are delivered with stiffer wrists, steps are wider and legs may be more separated. There is more body movement, including moving to one knee, striking the ground with feet or hands, and lying or rolling on the ground.

The main dance forms in the current Tongan repertoire are the following:

- *Lakalaka*, a standing dance for men and women which adds the movement dimension to sung poetic speeches. *Lakalaka* are usually village based and often include 50, 100 or more people.
- *Ma`ulu`ulu*, a dance performed by boys/men and/or girls/women seated or in graduated tiers of sitting, kneeling, and standing. They are performed in conjunction with one or more *nafa*, skin drums, and a sung, poetic speech.
- *Me`etu`upaki*, a men's standing dance in which paddles, *paki*, are skillfully manipulated in conjunction with a *nafa*, slit gong, and sung poetry.
- *`Otuhaka* and *ula*, are the sitting and standing parts of an old dance also called *fa`ahiula*, performed by women or girls in conjunction with sung poetry and a rolled mat that is struck with two sticks (or some other form of percussion).
- *Tau`olunga*, a standing dance performed by one or more girls or women in conjunction with *hiva kakala* (sweet songs) and usually a string band. One or more secondary dancers (usually men) known as *tulafale* may join in to perform movements that contrast in various ways with those of the primary female dancers.
- *Kailao*, a standing dance performed by men or boys, based on the manipulation of wooden clubs in conjunction with the striking of a metal container. Unlike other Tongan dances the movements are not associated with a poetic text.

- *Soke*, performed usually by boys/men and/or girls/women in groups of four, which combine into eight, then 16, and so forth up to 100 or more people. In each group of four, two performers use 3-foot long parrying sticks and two performers use two, one-foot long striking sticks. The dancers jump to different positions, accompanied by rapid rhythms beaten on empty metal biscuit tins, in conjunction with a sung text.

Most important of these performance genres is *lakalaka*, a major art form in Tonga. *Lakalaka* was recognized by UNESCO in 2003 as a "Masterpiece of the Oral and Intangible Heritage of Humanity". For Tongans *lakalaka* is their distinctive dance and purveyor of their cultural identity. *Lakalaka* is one of the most important conveyors of two Tongan aesthetic concepts, *faiva* (skill) and *heliaki* (indirectness), which contribute to an understanding of Tongan ways of thinking about the arts. *Faiva* refers to any work, task, feat, trade, craft, or performance requiring skill or ability; *heliaki* means to say one thing but mean another and requires skill based on cultural knowledge to carry out. *Heliaki*, especially as conveyed in *lakalaka* is manifested in metaphor and layers of meaning and is developed by skirting a subject and approaching it from different points of view. Encoding hidden meanings and unravelling them layer by layer until they can be understood requires considerable creative skill, imagination, and knowledge for composers and audience members. *Lakalaka* and its meanings cannot be apprehended by simply viewing the product, but should be approached in relation to poetry as oratory, which incorporates social philosophy and is the basis of their aesthetic system. Visual and verbal arts elevate and honor individuals or chiefly lines and can be seen as frames for interpreting the politics of prestige and power and how they convey knowledge about social order through an aesthetic medium. Metaphorical associations with specific places, residences (or former residences), trees, flowers, and flower constructions are related to aristocrats of the past and present.

During presentation the dancers feel *māfana*, inwardly exhilarated, especially if they are led by individuals of high rank or prestige. The beholder prides him or herself on his or her historical and cultural knowledge and ability to recognize and understand the *heliaki* of the motifs and the essence of the overall design as well as the text and movements. Composers realize the importance of a well-presented performance as a political action. Although a presentation will exist primarily in memory, the imagery conveyed embeds historical and cultural values basic to kingdom identity and the philosophical and aesthetic concepts that underlay Tongan society.

Arrival: Kiribati

Kiribati (pronounced "Kiribas") is a collection of islands in Micronesia situated about 2,500 miles (4,000 km) southwest of Hawai'i. Its thirty-three coral islands, all but one of which are atolls (circular islands with a central lagoon), are divided into three groups: the Line Islands (east), the Phoenix Islands (central), and the Gilbert Islands (west), the latter being where most of the population resides. Kiritimati, also known as Christmas Island, is the largest coral atoll in the world and was among the many islands of the Pacific explored by Captain James Cook in 1777. Throughout the 1800s, British and American sailors visited the islands while hunting sperm whales and expanding trade routes. The British eventually claimed most of the islands of Kiribati as British protectorates; thus, English is widely spoken along with the native tongue, Gilbertese, an Austronesian language.

The first Protestant missionaries arrived in 1857, while the earliest Roman Catholics came in 1888. Much modern social life revolves around church activities. International sports, such as soccer and volleyball, are popular, along with traditional competitive activities, such as canoe racing. Many I-Kiribati, as the islanders are known, rely on fishing and subsistence farming for survival and live in traditional houses made of wood and coconut palms, though there are also a few urban areas where inhabitants live in modern houses and import much of their food and other necessities.

Site 4: Group Song for *bino* (sitting dance) from Kiribati

First Impressions. Vocal performance among Pacific islanders is often a communal activity. The choir in our example comprises both men and women and has a distinctive "childlike" tonal quality once the group begins to sing. The example may initially give the impression of a solemn occasion, but then transitions to a celebratory atmosphere with boisterous hand clapping and enthusiastic singing in a regular rhythm with harmony.

Aural Analysis. Vocal choirs are common throughout Micronesia and Polynesia. Because most traditional performances are sung in unison, the use of harmony in our example reflects European musical influences, primarily introduced by Christian missionaries. Indigenous songs tend to use fewer pitches than those associated with the church—normally no more than five. The "youthful" vocal timbre of primarily the female singers is somewhat nasal and strained, in contrast to the male voices that are forceful and full.

In the Kiribati islands, vocal performances influenced by the church sometimes start with a freely rhythmic section that is closer to indigenous traditions. These are most typical of sitting dances (*te bino*), where the majority of performers are seated on the ground. More recent music/dance genres (e.g., *te buki, te kaimatoa, te kateitei*) do not have an initial freely rhythmic section. These begin with the metered section often marked by the steady pulse of handclaps. During the metered section, the voices follow a call-and-response pattern, though the call is primarily just a shout that establishes pitch and signals the choir's entrance. The text setting is mostly syllabic. A whistle is sometimes used to signal the choir to close the performance with a brief series of handclaps.

As described by Mary Lawson Burke, the ethnomusicologist who recorded the site example:

This example of music for the bino sitting dance begins with the traditional freely rhythmic section, and then proceeds into the main body of the piece, which is characterized by a

Seated dancers during a *bino* ceremony in Kiribati (Mary Lawson Burke)

A Kiribati woman performs in a temporary performing space at an island festival wearing a thick grass skirt and flower-and-fiber adornments, with a conductor and a seated chorus in the background (Adrienne L. Kaeppler)

steady beat, clapping accompaniment, and alternation between "traditional" monophonic music and harmonized music. Prior to the beginning of the piece you can hear the call "akeia," which calls everyone to attention and provides the starting pitch, and then the song leader sings "au bino," or "my bino"—which is always done at the start of the sitting dance.

I picked this example because the text is rather interesting in that it deals with WWII. (The famous Battle of Betio was fought on Tarawa atoll.) After the initial rather ambiguous section, the words don't discuss the local battle, but instead describe the pitiable state of Hitler (Ai kawa ra, Hitler eee), in that he thinks he will triumph in the end, but won't. America is fighting against him, with the aid of Britain. And near the end . . . the flag of victory is flying. Hurray.

Except for the repeat of the last section, and some minor internal textual repeats, the text is through-composed. In performance, people would generally immediately repeat the whole thing again. The clapping patterns correspond with quick movements of the head, arms, and hands in the dance. The bino is one of over 10 dance genres, exact number depending on the island, that are distinguished by melodic style ("traditional" music genres), dance style, local vs. Polynesian-influenced, and whether the music incorporates Western harmony.

(Personal Communication, 2011)

Cultural Considerations. Choral traditions in Oceania predate the arrival of European colonialism. In Kiribati, music and dance were important symbols of social identity. All members of a performance ensemble were of the same descent group. Participation in performance was essential to community cohesion, and musical skills were regarded as valuable clan property. Song was considered a vital link to ancestral spirits and supernatural powers associated with natural elements, such as the wind or the ocean. Communities sang in communal meetinghouses called *maneaba* the night before a battle, in order to help protect warriors or weaken enemies.

In lieu of physical combat, battles between rival clans frequently took the form of music and dance contests. Contests could involve the whole community or consist of matches between

MANEABA
Term for a communal meetinghouse in Kiribati.

LISTENING GUIDE   4.4 (2'25")

Site 4.4
Kiribati: Group Song for *bino* (sitting dance)

Voices: Mixed male/female ensemble

TIME	LISTENING FOCUS
0'00"	Opening section in free rhythm. Two male vocalists establish tonal center and initiate the performance.
0'14"	Choir enters singing in free rhythm with a monophonic structure.
0'35"	Main body of performance begins with regular beat and handclaps. Note that slight variations of tempo occur throughout the performance. Singing continues with monophonic structure (A section).
0'43"	Singing shifts to homophony (B section).
0'56"	Monophonic singing (A).
1'06"	Homophonic singing (B).
1'18"	Monophonic singing (A section with variation).
1'40"	Homophonic singing (B section with variation).
1'59"	Previous section (B with variation) repeats.
2'16"	Closing calls.

Source: "Kai e titirou e matie," sung with clapping by men and women of Ititin Rotorua Dance Troupe, Betio Village, Tarawa Island, Kiribati; recorded by Mary Lawson Burke, 1981. Used by permission.

MUSICAL MARKERS: Timbre/Medium—Vocal group with handclaps. Very nasal, almost "child-like" vocal quality. **Phonic Structure**—Single melodic line (monophony) contrasting with simple harmonizing (homophony). **Rhythm**—Opens in "free rhythm," though everyone sings together. Beat is often irregular (difficult to count).
ETHNO-CHALLENGE: Listen repeatedly and sing along with each part of the homophonic structure (just the pitches will do). If you are able to, try to transcribe the music with Western staff notation.

individuals. Competitors drew upon their knowledge of song to empower themselves with offensive and defensive magic. A dancer might call on the wind to "knock over" his enemy or conjure up a wall of dark thunderclouds to hide himself from his opponent. Through song, powerful deities were called on for strength and disparaging insults were traded, wrapped in metaphorical phrases, intended to antagonize the rivals. For example, a deity might be called on to strike the "distant rocks" (i.e., the rival group), so that they would crumble into the ocean and be eaten by baby sharks—a request that obliquely insulted the strength of the competitors, because baby sharks were viewed as weak and harmless. Competitions could put the dancers into an ecstatic state in which the power of the spirits would seem to work through the performers. These states were marked by labored breathing, trembling, and occasional screaming, and performers generally fainted after the spiritual power had left them.

The colonial government and Christian missionaries found the dances and their associated spiritual beliefs to be irreligious, unhealthy, and unproductive. As a result, restrictions were placed on dance activity to subdue the potential for ecstatic physical states. At the same time, church-related groups and social clubs without lineal affiliation began participating in the competitions, which undermined their function as surrogate battles between lineages. The focus of the competitions shifted from an emphasis on descent groups and the supernatural powers of the participants to the artistic skills of the dancers and musicians.

Along with this shift in focus came changes in musical values. European musical practices, namely the use of harmony, became markers of superior musical performance and thus a common feature of song in Kiribati. Since achieving independence in 1979, however, Kiribati has experienced a revival of interest in traditional culture that has encouraged the performance of freely rhythmic unison singing along with the metered harmonic choral singing.

Questions to Consider

1. Why would vocal traditions predominate in Australia and Oceania?

2. How do you circular breathe? Why is this technique useful when playing certain musical instruments?

3. How do Hawaiians use music to express their unique identity within American culture?

4. Why is music important to the Australian Aborigine's cosmology, *The Dreaming*?

5. How might musical instruments be used in courting practices? Does your culture have any courting rituals? If so, does music play a role in them?

6. Name some ways in which Christian missionaries have influenced traditional music in Oceania.

Site 1

CHINA

UZBEKISTAN
TAJIKISTAN
TURKMENISTAN

Mazar-e Sharif

N.W. Frontier Province
GILGIT
Northern Areas
Disputed Border

KABUL ★
KHYBER PASS
PESHAWAR
Herat
ISLAMABAD ★
SRINAGAR
Jammu and Kashmir

AFGHANISTAN

TIBET

Disputed Border
JAMMU
Himachal Pradesh
THIMPHU
LAHORE
Punjab
SIMLA
Sikkim
Arunachal Pradesh

QUETTA
Punjab
CHANDIGARH
Haryana
ITANAGAR

PAKISTAN
DELHI
NEW DELHI
NEPAL
GANGTOK
BHUTAN ★
DISPUR
Assam
Nagaland

Balochistan
KATHMANDU ★
KOHIMA

IRAN
JAIPUR
Uttar Pradesh
Meghalaya
SHILLONG

Site 4
Sindh
Rajasthan
LUCKNOW
BANGLADESH
Manipur
IMPHAL

KARACHI
INDIA
PATNA
DHAKA ★
AGARTALA

GANDHINAGAR
Bihar
West Bengal
Tripura
AIZAWL

Gujarat
BHOPAL
Mizoram

Diu
Madhya Pradesh
BHUBANESHWAR
CALCUTTA
BURMA (MYANMAR)

Daman
Orissa

ARABIAN SEA
Maharashtra

BOMBAY
Bay of Bengal

Approximate divide between North (Sites 1 and 2) and South Indian (Site 3) musical regions.
HYDERABAD

PANAJI
Goa
Andhra Pradesh
ANDAMAN ISLANDS

Karnataka

LAKSHADWEEP ISLANDS
BANGALORE
MADRAS

Pondicherry

Kerala
Tamil Nadu
NICOBAR ISLANDS

TRIVANDRUM

COLOMBO ★
SRI LANKA

Site 2 + 3

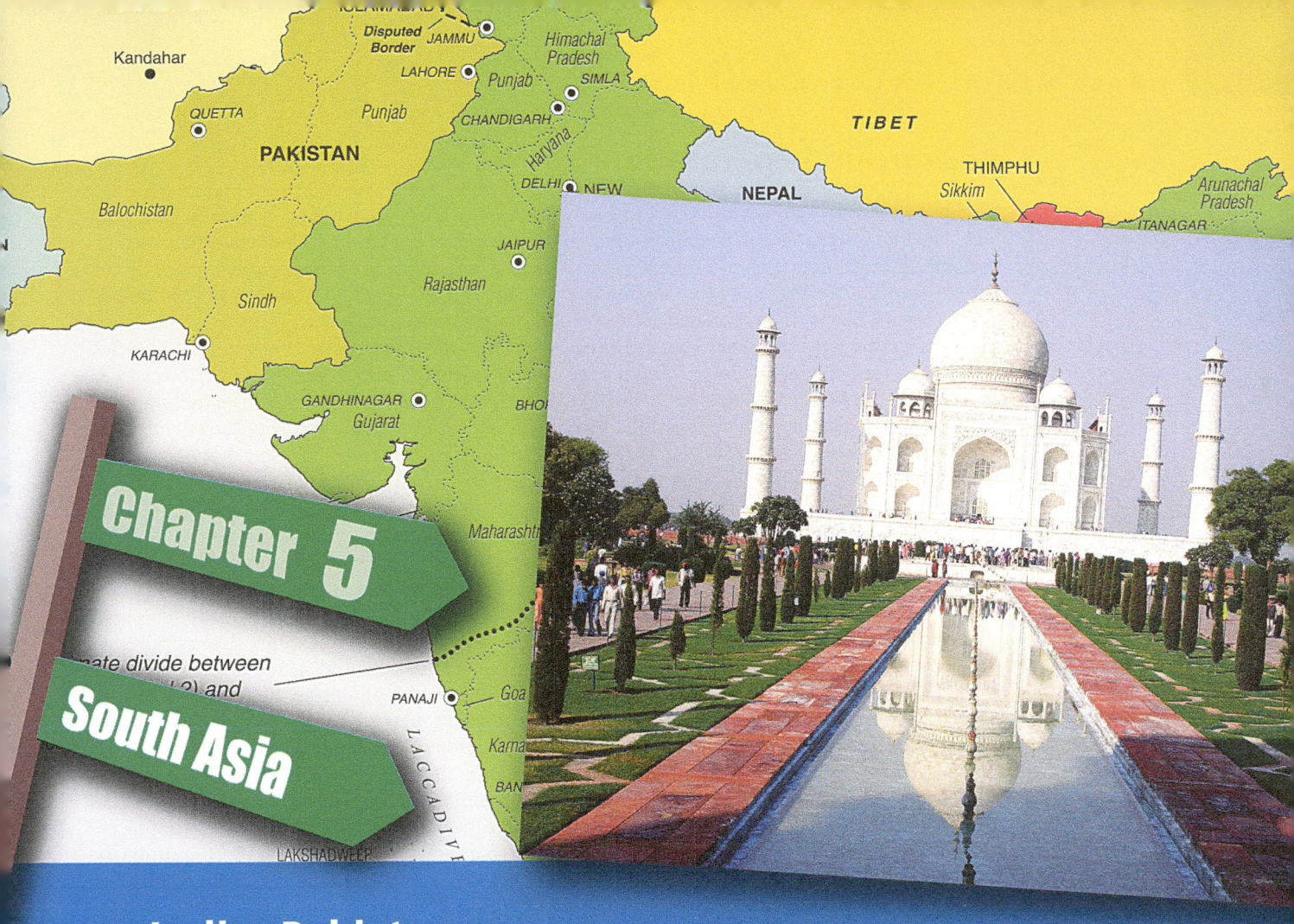

Chapter 5

South Asia

India, Pakistan

The Taj Mahal in Agra, Uttar Pradesh, the most famous tomb in the world, built by Shah Jahan and completed in 1652 (N. Scott Robinson)

Background Preparation

There are two areas of the world that can easily overwhelm someone wishing to explore their musics. The first is East Asia, where approximately one quarter of the world's people live. The second is South Asia, an area with 1.8 billion people, again nearly a quarter of the world's people. One nation—India—dominates South Asia demographically (population 1.3 billion) and in landmass, but the region also includes Bangladesh, Nepal, Bhutan, Pakistan, Sri Lanka, and even Afghanistan (in some groupings). India, Pakistan, and Bangladesh all have extensive coastlines stretching to the Arabian Sea and the Bay of Bengal, leaving the other countries landlocked; Sri Lanka, however, is an island to the southeast of India. In addition, a few island groups, though having slight populations, are also considered part of South Asia, including the Andaman and Nicobar Islands, the Maldives, and the Seychelles. Parts of Afghanistan and Pakistan and most of Nepal and Bhutan are mountainous, but unlucky Bangladesh is not only flat but also only a little above sea level, leaving it vulnerable to numerous typhoons each year during which up to half of the country may flood. In addition, Bangladesh and many neighboring islands are threatened by rising sea levels.

Much of the region experiences fairly harsh climates, varying from the intense heat of India to the tropical moisture of Bangladesh and Sri Lanka to the arid winters of the northern and upland areas. Temperatures in India can reach as high as 127° Fahrenheit/53° Celsius; conversely, temperatures in India's snowy northern mountains are frigid in winter. Numerous great rivers drain the Himalayas through India and Bangladesh, including the well-known and sacred Ganges (or Ganga), along with the Indus and Brahmaputra. Parts of Pakistan and Afghanistan, however, are desert. Populations tend to be the greatest and most concentrated where water is most plentiful; most great civilizations began and flourished along rivers, and this principle holds true for South Asia.

In South Asia, India is the country no one can ignore. It is a nation of striking contrasts. India has riches in the form of palaces, treasures, and temples that are beyond imagination, but it also has great poverty. Many in the West are familiar with the plight of the underclass in places like Kolkata (formerly Calcutta), where Mother Theresa worked to alleviate suffering. India is the world's largest democracy, but struggles to maintain a balance among competing religions and ethnic groups. It is a nation where hundreds of millions of farmers work in conditions that have changed little over the centuries, but which also is home to the world's largest computer programming industry, clustered around high-tech Bangalore. India is home to several of the

Village in the hills near Kathmandu, Nepal, from which could be seen the tops of the Himalaya Mountains

A sheep herder in Afghanistan (Shutterstock)

world's great religions, all having the common goal of peace—but it is also a place where tragic inter-ethnic and inter-religious conflicts have broken out.

While South Asia is dominated by a small number of large countries, these monolithic political groupings belie the diversity of the region's populations. During the colonial era prior to the independence of both India and Pakistan in 1947, the British collected together some 562 small states into a single Indian colony, which originally included Pakistan and Bangladesh. While modern-day India uses only two main languages—Hindi and English—the constitution recognizes sixteen official languages. Some 25 percent of the population, mostly in the South, speak a variety of Dravidian languages. In reality there are some 1,652 languages and dialects spoken in India today. In addition to India's many languages, Persian (Farsi) and several Turkic languages are spoken in Afghanistan, Urdu and English are officially spoken in Pakistan, and Nepali in Nepal. Most of these languages are part of the vast family of Indo-European languages.

Many different religions can be found throughout South Asia. Hinduism is the major religion of India (82 percent). Islam is also found within India (12 percent), principally in the north,

In Old Delhi, Jama Masjid Delhi or Masjid-i-Jahan Numa, the largest Muslim mosque in Asia (N. Scott Robinson)

83

and is the dominant religion of Bangladesh, Pakistan, and Afghanistan. When Britain granted independence to the Raj in 1947, Pakistan was formed as a separate Muslim state and originally consisted of eastern and western portions flanking India. In 1971 Pakistan's Eastern Province seceded to become Bangladesh. Theravada Buddhism is the primary religion of Sri Lanka, though the country has a Hindu minority as well. Mahayana Buddhism predominates in Nepal and Bhutan, but some Hinduism is also found in both countries. Finally, Jainism, Sikhism, the Baha'i Faith, and Christianity, not to mention a small community of Jews, are also found in India along with small congregations of animistic practitioners.

CASTE SYSTEM
A hierarchical system of social organization based on one's hereditary status at birth, found in India and associated with Hinduism.

Traditionally, social organization in South Asia was hierarchical. This was especially true in India, where the population was organized into **castes** or groupings—ranging from the highest or priestly class to the lowest or "untouchable" class—to which an individual was assigned based on their status at birth. This system, which is tenuously related to Hinduism, has now been abolished in India, though it still influences many spheres of life, such as marriages and occupational opportunities. Certain castes or sub-castes were closely associated with specific kinds of music. For example, only Brahmin priests are permitted to recite the highly sacred *Vedic* chant, while non-Brahmins normally specialize in the playing of instruments, particularly ones that involve skin (drums) or saliva (flutes and reeds). In addition, gender plays a major role in determining who can perform what kinds of music or play what kinds of instruments.

South Asia exhibits striking contrasts in terms of level of development. Afghanistan, a thinly populated and mountainous country with little infrastructure or internal unity, remains the least developed, while the urban areas of Pakistan and India are highly developed. Indeed, India and Pakistan have produced many of the world's greatest scientists and thinkers, and today India is a leader in the high-tech world. With its crushing population statistics, however, India must struggle to keep much of its population fed, clothed, housed, and employed. As in most developing countries, there are great contrasts between the wealth of the few and the poverty of the many. In Afghanistan and Sri Lanka, and sometimes in Pakistan as well, political instability has made modernization and development difficult to maintain. India, often described as the world's largest democracy, has remained stable even with one of the most diverse populations in the world.

One of many great temples on the sacred Ganges River in Varanasi (Benares), India (Max T. Miller)

Indian street musician "charms" two cobra snakes with his *puṅgī* (also called *bīn* or *murlī*), consisting of two pipes with single reeds (a drone pipe and a melody pipe with finger holes) inserted into a gourd windchest (Max T. Miller)

K. S. Resmi

AN INSIDE LOOK

My name is Resmi Kunjan Saraswathy, and I am from Kerala in the southwestern part of India. Typically in India, we have only one name (Resmi), but we also take the names of our father and mother (Kunjan and Saraswathy, respectively). We typically put those names as initials in front of our name, so in my case I am known as K. S. Resmi. I come from a family of musicians, martial artists, and teachers and have become a professional Carnatic vocalist and music teacher. I began learning music when I was just two years old. By the age of twelve, I began living with my teacher, Dr. K. Omanakutty, to enter the *gurukula* system. In this system, we live with our teachers and exchange helping around their home for intense daily music training. My lessons began at 4:00 a.m. every day for three hours. After that I would go to school, and when I returned each day, there would be music rehearsals in the evenings. In learning Carnatic music, we use our memory primarily. When our *guru* sings a phrase, we must memorize the lyrics, melody, *tala*, and *raga* quickly going over the material until it is mastered. We also must learn many different languages to perform Carnatic music. From

K. S. Resmi

Carnatic music studies, I had to learn compositions in Sanskrit, Tamil, Telugu, Malayalam, and Kannada. I also had to learn Hindi and English at school. I completed twenty-two years of this training and have studied with Lalitha Shivakumar since 2005. Indian musicians never stop learning from our *gurus* during our lifetime. In addition to Carnatic vocal music, I have also studied Carnatic *vina* from Kamala Lekshmi, Hindustani Khayal singing from Ramesh Narayan, and Dhrupad singing with Ramakant Gundecha of the Gundecha Brothers. My study of Kathakali vocal music was with Nelliyode Vasudevan Namboodiri.

After earning BA and MA degrees in South Indian Carnatic vocal music, I became a full-time tenure-track faculty member in the Department of Indian Music at the University of Madras in Chennai, Tamil Nadu, India, where I taught from 2004 to 2007. My career has involved performing on 19 CD and cassette recordings, numerous film/TV soundtracks, and performance tours in India, USA, Germany, Canada, and Scotland. I am the first woman in the world to be featured on a CD recording of Kathakali *padams*, entitled *Samyamakannorudyanam*, which are the songs for the traditional Kathakali music/dance/ theater of Kerala.

I met American ethnomusicologist and percussionist N. Scott Robinson in 2005. After we married in 2006, I moved to the USA, where I had to learn new ways to use my Carnatic music training. I have since begun an online Carnatic music school in the USA and have many students from different parts of the world. In my traditional training, we never used such technology in learning Carnatic music. With the use of current technology and the Internet, many students outside India are able to connect with their traditional culture and music with this methodology. I even use Internet technology to continue lessons with my *gurus* who remain in India.

While living in the USA, I also began to perform in new musical contexts, such as jazz, rock, and fusion, with many different types of musicians. If I had never left India, I would never have experienced performing with musicians in jazz, rock, and other types of music. Some of the musicians I have worked with outside Indian music include jazz artist Larry Coryell and former Doobie Brother Dale Ockerman. Carnatic music involves developing a mastery of improvisation, so with that skill I am able to adapt to these different musical situations while continuing to perform traditional Carnatic music in the USA. You can hear examples of my Carnatic and fusion music on my website at http://www.ksresmi.com.

Vivek Virani

Growing up in suburban New York, my first musical obsessions were Beethoven and Billy Joel. Even though my parents were from India, our family had no connection to traditional Indian music. I always wanted to learn more about it to connect to my heritage and because I had heard that Indian music was "spiritual." I did not know what that meant, but it intrigued me.

I first learned about Indian music and spirituality when my family began attending weekly "Sai *bhajans*," a form of musical worship in which people gather to sing together out of love for God. The musical format is based on Hindu tradition, but "God" is referred to using names from many religions. I learned to sing and play the accompanying instruments—*tabla* (hand drums) and *harmonium* (reed organ)—and bhajans became a central part of my life. This music is not only sung by Indians living in India and abroad, but also by people from diverse backgrounds all over the world—from Venezuela, to Slovenia, to Japan. As I grew older, I met people everywhere I traveled who knew the same songs. Singing together can provide deep joy and connection to people across cultures. Music creates a sense of community and belonging, not only among those singing together in a room but across global networks.

Vivek Virani

I wanted to develop a deeper understanding of Indian music, so after college I moved to India to become a full-time disciple of North Indian *tabla* master Suresh Talwalkar. Talwalkar, whom we called "Guruji" (revered teacher), taught in the traditional *guru-shishya* (master-disciple) paradigm that has almost disappeared in modern India. I was one of eight students who trained with Guruji for six to eight hours every day. He would play a single phrase or short composition a few times and we were expected to listen attentively until we could join in, playing it with him dozens or hundreds of times until we were dripping with sweat and our arms felt like jelly. Then, he would choose a new phrase and the process would repeat.

We were not to speak unless directly addressed. Guruji seldom spoke during lessons—unless one of us made a mistake, upon which we would be scolded mercilessly. I had never experienced such strict or intense training in America, but I quickly saw its value. My ears became sharper and my fingers more controlled; within two years, I could listen to almost anything just once and play it back at full speed. I began to understand nuances of rhythmic expression that cannot be explained verbally but may be discovered through hundreds of hours of focused listening and practice. Guruji taught us to approach musical practice as *sādhana*, a term used in Hinduism to describe forms of discipline used to attain self-mastery.

My experiences inspired me to pursue a Ph.D. in Ethnomusicology. During my dissertation research, I spent a year living and traveling with Indian villagers who performed folk music. These musicians had no formal training in classical music and had not spent eight hours a day practicing, yet music defined their lives. They sing poetry by a fifteenth-century mystic saint named Kabir that describes how divinity resides within all people. For Kabir and his followers, this is not just abstract philosophy, it is about real life; it means challenging all forms of inequality and oppression. Today, millions of villagers in India are listening to and singing Kabir's poetry as a form of social activism against persecution based on caste or religion.

In recent years, I have begun studying and performing *dhrupad*, the oldest form of North Indian vocal classical music. Until the twentieth century, *dhrupad* was transmitted in hereditary lineages, meaning performers would only teach their sons and nephews. But recently, as the art came close to extinction, families like the Dagars who had been performing *dhrupad* for many generations began to teach outside students. My teachers, the Gundecha brothers, learned from the Dagars. They eventually established their own school, which is now attended by students from all over the world. *Dhrupad* is considered not only a form of music but a form of meditation or "*nād-yoga*" (yoga of sound), in which practitioners try to merge their consciousness fully into each note they sing.

I am currently a professor of Ethnomusicology at the University of North Texas in Denton, Texas. I teach my students about music from India and other parts of the world and encourage them to think about the different ways music can be meaningful to people. I also continue to perform on several instruments and sing spiritual music in multiple styles and languages. Through my teaching and performances, I hope to share the artistic diversity that exists under the label of "Indian music" and the different ways that music can be "spiritual." Music may create bonds among a religious community; it may be used for individual discipline, meditation, or introspection; it may be a vehicle for social justice or resistance to oppression. I hope my research and performance continues to introduce me to new ways to understand music and to use music to understand ourselves.

Planning the Itinerary

Each of the nations that comprise South Asia offers exciting and distinctive musics, but it is the "classical" music of India that has gained most of the attention of outsiders. Culturally, India is divided into north and south, with the former comprising two-thirds and the latter one-third of the country. Northern culture is called **Hindustani** and southern culture is called **Carnatic** (also spelled Karnatak). The north of India was deeply influenced by Indo-European invaders who brought the Aryan civilization from the northwest between 2000 and 1500 B.C.E. No one religion dominates the north, a situation not only giving rise to many coexisting faiths (Hinduism, Jainism, Sikhism, the Baha'i Faith, Islam), but also resulting in a more secular society. Hindustani music reflects this diversity and has far fewer relationships to religion than Carnatic music. Most northern languages are related to Hindi, while southern languages are mainly Dravidian, having been derived from layers of people who preceded the Aryans. The South in general has experienced less outside influence, and as a consequence Hinduism predominates—leading to a society that makes little distinction between the sacred and the secular.

Not surprisingly, Carnatic music is closely tied to Hinduism, though it has little to do with temple activities per se. Classical music in both traditions can be vocal or instrumental. The North Indian classical instrumental music is well known to Western audiences, while its vocal music, though highly developed, remains less recognized outside India. Carnatic music, on the

HINDUSTANI
A term referring to the cultural traditions of North India.

CARNATIC (ALSO, KARNATAK)
A term referring to the cultural traditions of South India.

other hand, is primarily vocal. Indeed, much of the instrumental music of South India derives from pre-existing vocal compositions.

Indian classical music, unlike the communal music of Africa or the ensemble music of Southeast Asia, is individual and often virtuosic. One attends a concert to hear a particular artist, rather than specific compositions or ensemble types, because most Indian classical music, especially that of the north, is composed spontaneously during performance through a process called *improvisation*. These improvisations usually unfold at a very leisurely pace: a full performance of a single improvisation can last anywhere from thirty minutes to two hours, and Indian classical concerts can easily last four or more hours.

In spite of the fact that Indian classical music is widely disseminated both in and outside India, the majority of the Indian population prefers to sing or listen to other kinds of music. Hindu lay people often sing devotional songs called *bhajans*, which can be popular in style. Music written for and transmitted by the movies is widely popular; in fact, the term for much of India's popular music is ***filmi***. Because India's film industry produces more films per year than that of any other country, the number of *filmi* songs is understandably vast, in the tens of thousands. Beyond that is a great variety of popular styles collectively called "Indo-pop," while *bhangra*, a relatively new form of popular music and dance derived from traditional Punjabi sources, first flourished among the Indian community in the United Kingdom in the 1980s and 1990s.

A musical tour of South Asia might also lead us to eastern India—known as Bengal—and to Bangladesh as well as to the west, to Pakistan. Most striking in Bengal and Bangladesh are the Bauls, free spirits who comment in their songs on topics as diverse as society, philosophy, and the joys and pains of daily life—and who can perhaps be thought of as the equivalent of America's "singer-songwriters." Although Pakistan is an independent nation with a Muslim majority, no single type of music epitomizes its culture. Depending on the region, its music alternately reveals relationships with Afghanistan, Iran, or India. One kind of Pakistani music has, however, attracted a following outside Pakistan, a Sufi-Muslim devotional song genre called ***qawwali*** (sometimes spelled *kawwali*).

FILMI (ALSO, FILMI GIT)
Popular music taken from films in India.

QAWWALI (ALSO, KAWWALI)
Sufi-Muslim devotional songs.

Arrival: North India

India's northern cities—especially Mumbai, Pune, Delhi, Varanasi (Benares), and Lucknow—reflect the diversity of the peoples who together created modern Hindustani culture. What made North Indian culture distinctive were the many waves of people migrating or attacking from the Northwest, especially from Persia. Consequently most people in the north are described as Indo-Aryan. This influx eventually brought Islam to India. Northern India offers visitors many great mosques, along with Sikh and Jain temples, the sixteenth-century palaces of the Mughal emperors, and the many governmental and celebratory edifices left by the British colonials. The region's vast cities are also home to North India's complex and sophisticated classical music tradition.

Site 1: Hindustani (Instrumental) *Raga*

First Impressions. Hindustani instrumental improvisations, called *raga*, are normally quite long. Because a piece of an hour or more would not be practical to study here, we have chosen a shorter example that is nonetheless an accurate representation of *raga* performance. If you listen carefully to the very beginning, you will hear a buzzing timbre emanating from a plucked chordophone. Almost immediately, a more prominent and commanding stringed instrument asserts itself, while the first instrument continues in a slowly repetitious manner. The rather dreamy introduction music gradually grows more excited until there is a sudden deceleration, an exhale, if you will—followed by the entry of drums and return of the solo instruments. This new phase continues to the end.

Several elements stand out to the first-time listener: the "twangy" buzz of the introductory instrument, the constant ornamentation and pitch-bending of the main melodic instrument, and the

Manju Mehta (*sitar*), Arup Chattopadhyay (*tabla*), San Diego, 2016

steady tempo of the drums, one of which has a distinctive "scooping" sound. Noticeable changes in the level of relaxation and an increase in tension also occur as the performance proceeds.

Aural Analysis. Few other areas of the world's music require as much technical explanation as does Indian classical music. That is because an appreciation of this fascinating blend of fixed and improvised elements involves an understanding of several important musical aspects. Even as it employs a highly systematic compositional process, Indian classical music also allows for endless variation, and the genius of a performer is not in how well he or she follows established conventions but in how those conventions are manipulated for the purposes of individual expression.

The word ***raga*** (or *rag*, meaning "color" or "atmosphere") denotes a comprehensive system for the simultaneous composition and performance of music in both North and South India. Because the English word *improvisation* suggests a near total degree of spontaneity, it fails to capture the control, predictability, and bounded nature of *raga*. The creation of a *raga* is indeed a highly controlled compositional process, with established constructional boundaries—even if it allows for nearly unlimited individual variations within these boundaries. Western ethnomusicologists use the term ***mode*** to describe such systems. Think of them as *composition kits*; the elements of each *raga* provide the tools for the musician's performance. Whereas most Western music is notated on paper by "composers" before its performance, Indian classical music is unwritten, even though a *raga* unfolds in highly predictable ways. The length of a performance can vary from a few minutes to a couple of hours, depending on time constraints and the interest of the audience as sensed by the musicians.

Raga comprises several elements, the first being tonal material (what might be called a "scale"). These "scales" consist of a hierarchy of strong and weak notes, a set of typical melodic figures, and a set of extra-musical associations with such things as moods, times of the day, and magical powers. *Raga*s are sometimes represented pictorially as individual human beings or deities in miniature paintings called *ragamalas*.

The pitches of a *raga* are expressed in **solfège** syllables, a mnemonic system of names for each degree of the scale. The Indian equivalent to the West's *do-re-mi-fa-sol-la-ti-do* is *sa-re-ga-ma-pa-dha-ni-sa*, with which students of Indian *raga* can sing melody. As in the West, there are actually more pitches in the total tuning system than these seven because some pitches can be flatted or sharped; in India the total possibilities are usually said to be twenty-two, whereas only twelve pitches are used in the West. Several distinct *ragas* may use the same set of pitches, but identical pitch sets are differentiated in

RAGA
A mode or system of rules and procedures for composition and improvisation in Indian classical music.

MODE
A set of rules and customary procedures used to compose or improvise music in a particular tradition.

SOLFÈGE
Mnemonic syllables corresponding to individual pitches in a scale.

practice from *raga* to *raga* due to differences in pitch hierarchy, typical melodic units, and extra-musical aspects. The two most important pitches are *sa* and *pa*, always a fifth degree apart.

The "buzzing" pitches briefly heard at the beginning of our audio example are played on the **tambura**, a four-stringed, long-necked lute with a large gourd body. The buzz timbre is produced due to small threads being placed on the bridge under each string, causing them to vibrate against the bridge when played. The person who plays this instrument, often a young disciple or a spouse of the lead instrumentalist, simply plucks the four strings successively throughout the *raga*. The four pitches reinforce the two most important pitches of the *raga*, usually the fundamental or "home" pitch (*sa*/pitch I) and another an interval of a fifth above (*pa*/pitch V), and are generally played in the order V (upper), I (upper), I (upper), I (lower). This continuous sound of the *tambura* solidifies the tonal framework of the *raga* and can be likened to incense permeating a room, except through sound rather than smell.

TAMBURA
A round-bodied gourd lute used to provide the "drone" element in Indian classical music.

SAROD
A fretless plucked lute from northern India.

ALAP
The opening section of a *raga* performance in which the performer "explores" the *raga*.

JOR
A regularizing of the beat in the opening section of *raga* performance in Indian classical music.

Below the main strings of the *sitar*, and passing beneath the curved metal frets, are a large number of "sympathetic" strings that vibrate involuntarily when the main strings are played

The main melodic instrument in our example is the **sitar**, also a long-necked lute. The *sitar* is generally around 48 inches (approximately 1.2 meters) long and has a large gourd resonating body with a wooden front that is light weight, but sturdy. Its neck is wide and hollow with usually twenty arched moveable frets. The *sitar* typically has three or four main melodic strings as well as a few drone strings used primarily to accentuate the rhythm and tonal center. There are also eleven to fifteen "sympathetic" metal strings running from within the neck (out through small, ivory-lined holes) to a series of smaller pegs on the side of the neck. These latter strings are tuned to vibrate in acoustic "sympathy" with the main strings, and thereby provide a background of ethereal ringing. Sometimes the player will strum them briefly, mostly at the beginning of the piece, but otherwise they are not directly plucked in order to sound. Holding the instrument at an angle with the top passing the left shoulder, the musician usually wears a wire plectrum over each of their first two fingers of their right hand to pluck the main strings. The player can also pull (stretch) them to the side with the left hand to create the tone-bending and ornaments that practically define Indian *raga*.

The first portion of a *raga* is called the **alap** and could be described as a period of exploration of the *raga* and its characteristics. The principal melodic player begins with the lower pitches, approaching them in a leisurely and experimental manner; there is no regular beat because

The *tambura* above has an unfretted neck, four strings, and is played throughout a *raga* to produce drone pitches (N. Scott Robinson)

Pandit Manilal Nag (left, b. 1939) from West Bengal comes from a family of sitar players (Wikimedia Commons)

CHIKARI
Refers to a set of drone strings on Indian chordophones.

TABLA
A pair of drums found in Hindustani music from India.

TALA
Cyclic rhythmic framework that organizes a *raga* performance in India.

the melody is played in free rhythm. Consequently, the drum, which is primarily responsible for the rhythmic element of a *raga* performance, is not heard during this opening section.

An *alap* can last for a mere minute or so, or be extended to an hour or more, depending on the taste of the performer and the interest of the audience. As the *alap* progresses, the player explores more pitches and melodic units, moving from the lower range of the instrument—representing relaxation or repose—into the higher ranges, which increases tension. Gradually the rhythms become somewhat steadier, though they never become totally metered; the term ***jor*** denotes this tenuous regularizing of beat. As the tempo and excitement increase (along with the tension), the player begins a regular alternation between melodic pitches and a set of drone strings called the ***chikari***, as the form reaches its climactic section (known as *jhala*). Just as the playing reaches a feverish level of excitement, the "drive" suddenly slows as the player quickly descends through the scale back to the point of relaxation and the *alap* concludes.

At this point a pair of drums enters. These consist of a small cylindrical wooden drum with a single head called *tabla* and a larger, rounded metal drum with single head known as *baya*; together, the pair is also called ***tabla***. Most players strike the smaller drum with the right hand and the larger with the left. The *tabla* (i.e., the smaller of the pair) is tuned to the *raga*'s fundamental pitch by tightening or loosening leather straps attached to the face; their tension is controlled by moving cylindrically shaped pieces of wood wedged between the straps and the body of the drum. Each drum stroke has a name, and drummers memorize the stroke names as part of the learning process. Indeed, most drummers can *speak* the strokes, in a kind of "verbal drumming" (*bols*)—and many listeners are able to keep track of the cycle of strokes through patterns of handclaps and waves (see below).

The drummer plays a cycle of strokes called the ***tala***. A *tala* is considered a closed cycle, because it has a fixed number of beats; these are subdivided into three or four sections. In Hindustani music there are hundreds of possible *talas*, each with its own name and specific number of beats, theoretically ranging from 3 to 128. In practice far fewer are used, and *talas* using seven to sixteen beats predominate. Of these, the best known and most often encountered is *tintal*, a *tala* having

Tabla refers to both the pair of Hindustani drums and to the cylindrical drum (below) in particular, while the kettle drum (above) is called *baya*

BOLS
Mnemonic syllables corresponding to drum strokes in Indian drumming traditions.

THEKA
(pronounced *teh-kah*) The entire pattern or set of words (*bols*) for a given *tala* in classical Indian music.

sixteen beats divided into four groupings of four pulses each. While *talas* are played beginning on beat 1, they do not end on the last beat, that is, 16, but rather end on beat 1 of what would have been the next cycle. The audience can hear where they are in the cycle by listening for the deep tones of the *baya* drum; in *tintal*, the *baya* either drops out or is played quietly during the third group (beats 9–12), allowing listeners to anticipate the restatement of beat 1.

Each drum stroke—whether played on a single drum or on a combination of drums—has a name, such as *dha*. Totally there are more than a dozen named strokes, some involving one drum, some both, some closed, that is, dampened (the fingers stay on the head, deadening the tone), some open (the fingers spring away allowing the head to vibrate). Drum stroke names are called **bols**. The entire pattern or set of words for a given *tala* is called the **theka**. The most basic *theka* for *tintal* is: *dha, dhin, dhin, dha/ dha, dhin, dhin, dha/ dha, tin, tin, ta/ ta, dhin, dhin, dha. Talas* can be recited in syllables as well. Skilled drummers play patterns that go far beyond this basic set, including a great many elaborate "compositions," each based on the *tala*'s cycle of beats.

During the *tabla*'s performance, disciples and audience members may "keep the *tala*" in a pattern involving claps, counts, and waves. As mentioned, tintal has four sections with four beats each. For sections 1, 2, and 4, you clap on beat 1 and silently count beats 2, 3, and 4. In section 3, you turn over the right hand, giving a mini-wave (instead of clap) and then silently count the remaining three beats. When silently counting, you can either touch your right hand to the left or touch your thumb to three successive fingers.

When the drum enters, it normally starts in the middle of the *tala* cycle (beats 9–16), but exceptions occur frequently. In our example, the **gat** begins on beat 1 and the drum enters on beat 11. The *sitar* or *sarod*, now relaxed and calm, plays a short composition—a kind of tune—called the *gat* (in vocal music this is called *chiz*). The *gat* is the skeletal melody around which the player will improvise. When improvising, the player may fragment the *gat*, restate it in whole, or depart from it entirely. Some longer *raga* performances have more than one *gat*, perhaps a slow *gat* (*vilambit*) first that is longer in duration, a medium *gat* (*madhya*), then a fast *gat* (*drut*) that takes the shortest time to complete. The rhythmic density of the slow *gat* is the lowest, whereas the fast *gat* has the highest rhythmic density, contributing to the increasing tension of the music. The name of the *raga* remains the same regardless of the *gat* chosen, and although the *gat* is a composition, it does not usually have a "title" and the identity of its composer is regarded as insignificant.

The length of the *gat* matches the length of the *tala*; therefore, the use of *tintal* requires a sixteen-beat *gat*. In a sense, anything can happen during the overall *gat* section, which can last anywhere from a few minutes to an hour. As with the *alap*, the length of the *gat* depends on the audience's reaction, the performers' skill level and ability to cooperate or challenge each other in positive ways, and the context of the performance.

The instruments of India are numerous, and quite a few of them can be used as the lead melodic instrument in *raga*s. In the West, the instrument that has become most famous is the *sitar*, which for Westerners is virtually synonymous with Indian music. The *sitar* is a long-necked plucked lute, with a body made from a gourd and with seventeen arched metal frets running up the neck. Over these frets four main melodic strings and three *jhala* (rhythm/drone) strings and beneath them pass around twelve sympathetic strings (which vibrate (ring) in "acoustic sympathy"). *Ragas* can also be performed on many other stringed instruments, such as the *sarod*, the *santur* (hammered zither), or the *sarangi* (bowed lute), as well as on non-stringed instruments such as the *bansri* (flute) and several reed instruments, such as the *shehnai*. Among the most curious of instruments used in *raga*s is the *jal tarang*, a semicircular series of small china bowls each filled/tuned with different levels of water and struck with a small beater. *Raga*s are also sung. Vocal *raga*s are structured according to one of two formal patterns, both of which differ from patterns used in instrumental *raga*s. These patterns, called *Dhrupad* and *Khyal*, both require great endurance on the part of performers. Full appreciation of vocal *raga*s naturally requires knowledge of Indic languages, which is perhaps why instrumental performers tend to be more internationally recognized.

Now that we have run through some of the basic principles and characteristics of the *raga*, we will return to our musical example. It is *Raga ahir bhairav*, a type of *raga* appropriately performed at daybreak. The ascending and descending scale used in this performance consists of

GAT
The skeletal melody used as a basis for improvisation in a *raga* performance of classical Indian instrumental music.

a)

DHA	DHIN	DHIN	DHA	DHA	DHIN	DHIN	DHA
X				2			

DHA	TIN	TIN	TA	TA	DHIN	DHIN	DHA
o				3			

Schematic of the North Indian *tala* in a sixteen-beat cycle called *tintal* the pitches C♭, D♭, E, F, G, A, B♭, c—though in the ascending form the G is often avoided. The *tala* used is a fast *tintal* (16 beats).

Cultural Considerations. If you were to attend a *raga* performance, you would probably be amazed at the musicians' dexterity, creativity, and stage presence, and at the way that their music can involve an audience. These are some of the aspects that have long made Indian *raga* attractive to Western audiences and to a number of Western popular performers, such as George Harrison of the Beatles and John McLaughlin of Shakti and the Mahavishnu Orchestra.

While a *raga* performance may be relatively easy to follow on an aural and visual level, there is, however, much more involved than mere sound and sight. Important extra-musical cultural and philosophical matters come into play as well, encompassing the *raga*'s relationship to, and effect on, both the individual listeners and broadly on the smooth working of the universe.

The extra-musical aspects of *raga*, which may seem merely curious to outsiders, are essential to Indians. Each *raga* has an articulated mood, called **rasa**, which creates in performer and listener alike a state of mind, such as love, heroism, or anger. The *rasa* can become so pervasive that listeners begin to conceive of the *rasa* as a person. Personified *ragas* are frequently depicted in miniature paintings called *ragamala*, often showing humans performing music. Some *ragas* are believed to have magical powers. A *raga* performed correctly can heal, influence personality, and even bring the divine into both performer and listener. *Raga Dipak* is said to create fire when performed well, and the *Mallar ragas* can create rain. *Kedar ragas* will cure diseases and melt stones. Indian jailers, always ready to earn some extra money, were said to have taught *Raga Kedar* to prisoners who hoped to melt the stones of the prison and escape.

Each *raga* is to be performed at a proper time of day, and consequently there are *ragas* appropriate for specific times, from before dawn to after sunset. For Indians this is important because they believe there is a reciprocal relationship between the sound of music and a smoothly functioning universe. Walter Kaufmann, who researched *ragas* in India prior to World War II, reported that one great musician predicted the coming of that terrible war, which he claimed would result from the Western habit of playing music at the wrong times (as when funeral music is played when there is no funeral). He shouted to Kaufmann, "How long will the universe tolerate this abuse of music, music, mind you, a most sacred thing?" As a result of this negligence a great calamity would befall the West, he said—and indeed it did.

During the 1960s, many Westerners turned to the East—India in particular—in search of spiritual enlightenment. Because Indian music is overtly spiritual (though not religious per se), it soon became popular with Western audiences. Ravi Shankar, the late Hindustani sitar specialist, who also composed many film scores, toured the United States as early as 1964 and soon became a cultural icon. George Harrison of The Beatles studied sitar with Shankar, and Harrison's use of the sitar in several Beatles' songs, including "Love You Too" from *Revolver* (1966) and "Within You Without You" from *Sgt. Pepper's Lonely Hearts Club Band* (1967), brought about a rising interest in Indian music. Around the same time England's John McLaughlin, leader of both Shakti and the Mahavishnu Orchestra, also invoked Indian sounds and spirituality. These groups, and many others, added Indian drummers and sitarists, making the distinctive dry timbre of the tabla and the twangy sitar familiar to many Westerners. Today the sounds of the tabla and sitar can be easily imitated on synthesizers and have become commonly accepted in mainstream Western popular music.

Because Indian music is played by soloists, one finds both virtuosos and a "star" system associated with its performance. Ironically, Indian musicians can make more money touring in Europe and North America than in India. Ravi Shankar made a great success for himself doing this, and his daughter, Anoushka Shankar, has followed in his footsteps. A few Americans, such as Ken Zuckerman, have completely mastered Indian instruments and styles and have become professional Indian musicians, touring both here and in India. Even though Indian music no longer holds Western popular culture in its thrall, Indian concerts in the West continue to attract large audiences of both Indian expatriates and Westerners. Indeed, its popularity around the world makes it one of the most prominent classical traditions on the planet.

RASA
A mood or sentiment associated with artistic activity, such as *raga* performance, in India.

An Indian minature painting, or *ragamala*, titled "Krishna and Radha watching rain clouds," from India's Punjab Hills, *c.*1790 (Cleveland Museum of Art)

Ravi Shankar, India's most famous musician until his death in 2012, plays the *sitar*, a fretted North Indian lute with sympathetic strings (Jack Vartoogian/FrontRowPhotos)

LISTENING GUIDE   5.1 (4'38")

Site 5.1

India: Hindustani (Instrumental) *Raga*

Instruments: *Sarod* (fretless plucked lute), *tambura* (plucked lute), *tabla* (pair of hand drums)

TIME   **LISTENING FOCUS**

The duration of the initial *alap* section—the exploratory opening section of the overall form—is much shorter than normal in this performance, due to the recording's time limitations. Note the use of free rhythm and the absence of drum during the *alap* section.

0'00"   Tambura enters, followed immediately by the sitar musician sounding the sympathetic strings (*taraphs*, also *tarabs*) to highlight the pitches of the raga. Note the "buzzing" drone as the tambura continuously sounds.

0'05"   Sitar begins *alap* section with melodic improvisation.

0'11"   Listen for melodic phrase endings emphasizing the tonal center as the tambura drone continues.

1'50"	Notice the "bending" of pitches on the sitar (fretted lute). (You might compare this to other music examples featuring a *sarod* or *sarangi* [fretless lutes], which typically have "slides" between wider intervals than the sitar.)
2'42"	Alap section ends and a *gat* melody is introduced along with a regular meter (16 beats, *tintal*).
2'46"	Tabla enters solidifying a regular meter (*tal*).
2'51"	Listen for a repetition of the gat melody.
2'58"	Note the gat melody repeating again.
3'05"	Listen for the sitar musician adding variation to the main gat melody.
4'32"	Listen for the tabla establishing a regular rhythmic phrase (*theka*). The rhythmic pattern repeats periodically throughout the performance as a basis for variation.
5'02"	Focus on the regular pulsation of the meter and clap along.
5'38"	Listen as the tabla increases its rhythmic density in three "bursts" as it signals the end of the rhythmic cycle (*tal*).
5'45"	Note the appearance of a new melodic idea and try to "keep the tal" (16 beats).
5'59"	Hear how the melodic phrases are transposed to higher pitches as the tabla maintains the rhythmic cycle.
6'35"	Listen for new melodic material and improvisation.
6'57"	Listen for increased rhythmic density of melodic improvisation.
7'09"	Focus on the tabla as it "stretches" the beat within the rhythmic framework.
7'18"	Note how the tabla returns to the basic meter.
7'25"	Listen for increasing rhythmic density of melodic phrases.
7'51"	Note the triple repetition of a melodic motive.
8'13"	Listen for the melodic "bursts" of rhythmically dense phrases.
8'31"	Note the syncopated rhythm to signal the end of the rhythmic cycle.
8'35"	Listen for the longer melodic passages of rhythmically dense material as the sitar's rhythmic drone (*chikari*) strings become more prominent during the *jhala* section.
9'22"	Note the triple repetition of a melodic motive to signal the close of the performance.
9'34"	Listen for the increased rhythmic density of the tabla musician as the performance reaches its climax and final conclusion.

Source: "Khamaj" by Shamim Ahmed from the recording entitled *India's Great Shamim Ahmed: Three Ragas*, MON00489, courtesy of Smithsonian Folkways Recordings. © 1967. Used by permission.

MUSICAL MARKERS: Timbre/Medium—"Twangy" quality of the sitar. "Boing" sound of the baya drum coupled with higher pitched "patter" of the tabla drum is typical of Hindustani (North India) music. **Drone**—Continuous buzz of the tambura or Sruti box. **Form**—Begins in free rhythm and shifts to regular meter when drum enters. **Pitch**—Frequent tone bending.
ETHNO-CHALLENGE: "Keep the *tal*" (sixteen beats) during the *gat* section of the performance (clap on beats 1 and 5; wave on beat 9; clap on beat 13). Listen especially for how your "1" pulse corresponds to the melodic hook throughout the performance. Anticipate the final pulse of the performance and stop counting.

Fundamentals of Indian Classical (Hindustani) Music

Modal System. *Raga* denotes a comprehensive system governing the creation of melody—improvised or composed. Its elements include:

- Tone material (a limited number of pitches presented in both ascending and descending forms)
- Pitch hierarchy (strong and weak pitches that define the tonal center of the mode. The *vadi* is the strongest—and central—pitch followed by the *samvadi*; these are reinforced by the sounds of the drone instrument)
- Solfège (a system of syllables used to articulate pitches, called *sargam* and expressed in ascending order as *sa, re, ga, ma, pa, dha, ni, sa*)
- Magical powers (Indian musicians ascribe magical powers to some individual *ragas*)
- Mood or character (each *raga* has a *rasa* or mood/ feeling/personality that can be personified in small paintings called *ragamala*).

Rhythmic/Metric System. *Tala* denotes a comprehensive system governing the organization of the music in time. Its elements include:

- Fixed number of beats organized into a closed cycle
- Grouping of beats into units

- Visible means of "keeping the *tala*" with a clap followed by counts or a wave followed by counts
- Words to represent drum strokes (known as *bols*) used by drummers during learning or in demonstrations of drumming.

Form. Although partly improvised, *raga* performance follows expected patterns. These include:

- *Alap*, the beginning section of melody (vocal or instrumental) accompanied only by the drone instrument
- *Jor*, as the alap proceeds, it becomes faster and emphasizes the higher pitches of the *raga*. In the *jor* the music becomes somewhat steady, but not yet in tala
- *Jhala*, coming at the end of the *alap*, the music reaches maximum tempo and rhythmic density. It is mostly steady in beat, while the player repeatedly use drone strings (called *chikari* strings) in alternation with the melodic pitch
- *Gat*, the section that coincides with the entry of the drum(s). The *gat* is a relatively short composition that becomes the basis for further improvisation. *Gat* refers to instrumental *ragas*; the vocal equivalent is called the *chiz*.

Arrival: South India

South India has been less influenced by outside cultures over the centuries than the northern region, which was more affected by foreign peoples who invaded or established trade routes through the area. Primarily Hindu, southern India is thought to preserve what remains of India's earliest civilization, that of the Dravidians. The sophisticated music of South India, called Carnatic (also Karnatak) music, is closely associated with Hinduism, though not specifically with temple rituals. There is a greater emphasis on vocal performance, though many instruments, such as the Sarasvati vina, are distinctive to the region. Many Carnatic music enthusiasts claim that the music of the south is more "pure" than that of northern India due to its historical insulation from outside influence.

Site 2: Carnatic Classical (Vocal) *Kriti*

First Impressions. Our example begins with a sustained drone, after which a rich toned male vocalist begins to sing in free rhythm, as a drum is briefly heard warming up in the background. The opening section seems also to be a "warm-up" for the singer as he improvises on a few non-lexical syllables. As he improvises his phrases, another instrument—a bowed instrument that sounds like a violin—shadows him. After a brief pause, the vocalist initiates a metered section, that prompts the drummer to join the performance with accented pulses and short flourishes of rhythmic vibrancy. Listening closely, it is evident that the singer is repeating the same lyric with each vocal phrase, decorating his performance with a fascinating display of ornamentation and seeming improvisation. Compared to the previous track (Hindustani *raga*), the rhythm and meter are clearly articulated by strong drum beats, giving it an almost march-like feeling.

Aural Analysis. The most important difference between the classical music of North and South India is that whereas Hindustani music is mostly improvised, Carnatic music is based on fixed compositions. Improvisation occurs only after the composition has been fully presented, and even the highly patterned ornamentation performed by the singer is part of the composition. Carnatic music's most important compositional form is a type of devotional song called **kriti**, which is based on a genre of devotional Hindu poetry of the same name. While the lyrics could speak of devotion to God, they can also focus on religion, love, or historical stories. The composer of a *kriti* normally writes both the poetry and the melody, the former being written in one of several South Indian languages, each with its own script (e.g., Telugu, Kannada, Malayalam, and Tamil). Pitches are written in one of the many local notational systems; only the main pitches are indicated, ornamentation being determined by oral tradition, highly patterned, rather than freely improvised. Vocalists usually perform an improvised introduction called *alapana* before launching into the *kriti* itself, though these can be extremely brief in some cases. This serves to ready the vocalist for the more demanding vocal feats of the ensuing performance and helps to prepare the audience as well.

Our example is "Manasā! Etulorttune" ("O unworthy Mind!"), a *kriti* by Sri (usually translated as "saint") Tyāgarāja (1767–1847), South India's most famous composer. The language is Telegu but the title is Sanskrit. *Kriti* texts are typically in three sections. The first, called *pallavi*, consists of one or two lines of text which reappear throughout a performance, a kind of refrain. This *kriti*'s text begins with the words "O unworthy Mind! How long can I put up with you, if you do not listen to my counsel!" (translation by T. K. Govinda Rao, *Compositions of Tyāgarāja*. Chennai, Tamil Nadu: Gānamandir Publications, 2009, p. 136). The *pallavi* is followed by a second section, called *anupallavi*, which begins "Follow my advice. Spend your time in singing the glory of Srī Rāma,

KRITI
A South Indian genre of devotional songs using Hindu poetry.

A Carnatic (South Indian) classical singer performs a *kriti* devotional song, accompanied (left to right) by a *mridangam* drum, *kanjira* hand drum, *tambura* lute, and violin (N. Scott Robinson)

the jewel of the solar race with humility and devotion." The final section of the text, called *charanam*, is longer than the others and is followed by a repeat of the *pallavi* text, giving it a "rounded form." Improvisation, if present, follows the *charanam*, but the work will always conclude with a restatement of the *pallavi*. Regarding the overall form, where improvisation loosely based on the *pallavi* melody occurs, some describe the form as resembling "theme and variations."

South Indian *ragas*, whether they are *kritis* or other musical forms, operate on principles similar to the *ragas* of North India—but the specifics are quite different. The Carnatic system is, at least on the surface, unusually extensive because there are so many theoretically possible scales. If you allow for all possible arrangements of the seven pitches (some pitches are available in two variants as well), there are seventy-two possible scale forms. When you factor in other variables, such as ornamentation and pillar pitches, there are theoretically some 36,000 possible *ragas*. In practice, only a small number of *ragas* are commonly used. Our example is *Raga Malayamārutam*, whose pitches in ascending order are C♯, D, F, G♯, A♯, and B (if sounded on a Western instrument such as piano). Expressed in solfège, the *raga* is Sa, Ri, Ga, Pa Dha, Ni, Sa; the *raga* then has six tones, the fourth pitch (Ma) being omitted.

South Indian drum cycles, like those in the North, are also called *tala* but follow a different set of operating principles. As with the *raga* system, the Carnatic *tala* system also allows for far more cycles than are actually used. In practice, the system is actually fairly simple, but like so much of Indian music, it can be confusing to beginners because of its extensive terminology.

A Carnatic *tala* consists of three variable elements, called *anudrutam, drutam*, and *laghu*. As in the North, South Indian music uses a system of hand gestures to symbolize *tala* patterns. The *anudrutam* is signed as a one-beat clap; the *drutam* is a clap followed by a wave gesture of the right hand; the *laghu*, which consists of a variable number of beats, is signed as a clap followed by right-hand finger counts. South Indian audience members often "keep the *tala*" on their hands during a performance, and sometimes a singer will also use the gestures as s/he performs. Each *tala* has a name that combines two elements: a *tala* name and a *jati* name, with the latter representing a variable number of beats in the *laghu*. The most commonly used *tala* in Carnatic music is properly called *triputa* (*tala* name) *chaturasra* (*jati* name), consisting of a four-beat *laghu* (clap and three counts) and two *drutam* (each a clap and wave). The full cycle of eight beats, then, is "clap, count, count, count, clap, wave, clap, wave." Because the name *triputa caturasra* does not roll off the tongue so easily, the nickname *adi tala* ("ancient" tala) is commonly used. It is unlikely that you could ever attend a Carnatic music concert and not hear *adi tala*. The selected track, however, is an exception, using a much shorter *tala* called *rūpakam*, which consists of only three beats, consisting of an *anudrutam* and a *drutam*, with no *laghu*; it is signed as "clap, clap, wave." But because the cycle is so short, the performers play it as a group of four repetitions (that is, an overarching twelve beat cycle (3+3+3+3)).

The most commonly used drum in Carnatic music is called *mridangam*; it is a two-headed barrel drum with leather strap lacing, and heads that are weighted (tuned) with a mixture of cooked rice mixed with iron filings and perhaps ash; this pasty mixture adds weight to the drum head, thereby lowering the pitch. Players use their hands to strike each head. Many players also wrap the body of the drum in cloth. The recording also includes a *kanjira*, a small frame drum consisting of a jackfruit frame, a single head usually of monitor (lizard) skin, and a single hole in the frame into which three or four thin metal discs or old coins are placed to rattle when the drum is struck by the player's hand. The *kanjira* is essentially the same as what Westerners know as the "tambourine." This instrument only became common in classical playing in the 1930s.

The first sounds heard in our example, those of the drone, could be the *tambura*, the same drone chordophone found in Hindustani music, but in this performance the musicians employ a small "black box" called a *sruti box* that emits continuous drone pitches electronically. As in the North, the drone reinforces the basic pitches of the *raga*. The bowed instrument that shadows the singer is a European violin—but one that is held in a way that no Western violinist would ever employ: it is placed between the chest and right foot of a player seated on the floor. The violin, like the harmonium, was introduced into India by British colonialists but functionally transformed into an Indian instrument. Its use in Carnatic music is to closely follow and imitate the singer. Thanks to the way that the instrument is held, players can easily slide their left hand along the neck to create any of the twenty-three named ornaments found in both the instrumental and the vocal music of South India.

South Indian *mridangam* drummer plays during a concert surrounded by six more drums (N. Scott Robinson)

LISTENING GUIDE

5.2 (4'14")

Site 5.2

India: Carnatic Classical (Vocal) *Kriti*

Voice: Single male
Instruments: Violin (bowed lute), *sruti* box (electronic drone), *mridangam* (barrel-shaped drum)

TIME	LISTENING FOCUS
0'00"	*Sruti* box (drone) begins. (Tonal center = C♯). Note the violin tuning and *mridangam* (drum) warming up in background.
0'09"	[*Alapana*] Voice begins with highly melismatic improvisation in free rhythm.
0'14"	Listen for the violin "imitating" the melodic contour of the vocalist. Note this exchange of voice followed by violin throughout the opening section of the performance.
2'59"	Applause signals the end of the opening section.
3'04"	[*Pallavi* section] Vocalist begins the "composed" section of the performance. Note that the violin (3'06") no longer "imitates," but plays along with the same melody as the vocalist.
	Line 1 (first half): *Manasa! Etulorttune*
	("O Unworthy Mind! How long can I put up with you,")
	Repeats a total of five times before the second half of the line begins.
3'10"	*Mridangam* enters.
3'24"	Line 1 (second half): *Manavi Cekonave*
	("if you do not listen to my counsel.")
3'28	Return to beginning of line 1 and sung three times.

3'51"	Return to first half of line 1.
3'56"	Vocalist sings on syllable "O!"
4'04"	Drums signal end of the *pallavi* section.
4'07"	Second section [*anupallavi*] begins just before the excerpt fades. Though brief, listen for the change in text.
	Line 2: *Dinakarakula Bhushununi*
	("Follow my advice.")

Source: "Manasā! Etulörttunë" *Raga Malayamārutam, Rūpakam Tala*, composed by Sri Tyāgarāja and performed by Sri V. Ramachandran, vocal; Sri S. Varadharajan, violin; Ramnad Sri Raghavan, *mridangam*; Sri R. Balasubramaniam, *kanjira*; recorded at the 2002 St. Thyagaraja Festival by the Thyagaraja Aradhana Committee, Cleveland, Ohio, 2002. Used by permission.

MUSICAL MARKERS: Drone—Continuous "buzz" of the tambura or Sruti Box. **Melody/Text Setting**—Highly ornamented solo vocal melody (melisma) with "mimicking" violin. **Rhythm**—"Thud" sound of the mridangam (rather than "boing"), suggesting Carnatic (South India) music.
ETHNO-CHALLENGE: Mimic the vocal melody, along with the violin part, during the introduction (*alapana*). Also, sing along and memorize the melody of the composed section (*pallavi*) as if you were a student of this musician.

Cultural Considerations. Whereas Hindustani music is primarily improvised, albeit with a pre-composed *gat* or *chiz* serving as a skeletal framework in the metrical portion of the performance, Carnatic music is primarily composed in song form, though with the expectation that the performer will add typical (and codified) ornaments to the main notes. Consequently, South India has, like Europe, a small pantheon of saint-like composers, of whom Tyāgarāja (1767–1847) is the most famous. Other renowned composers include Muttusvami Diksitar (1776–1835), Syama Sastri (1762–1827), and Svati Tirunal (1813–1846), all contemporaries of Beethoven, Schubert, Chopin, and others from early nineteenth-century Europe. Tyāgarāja, a man who prophesied his own death and is therefore called "Saint" in English, is celebrated in an annual **aradhana** (festival), originally held in Tamil Nadu state but now observed in many parts of the world, including the United States. Since 1907 the festival has included, in addition to *puja* (worship), performances of Tyāgarāja's compositions by both amateurs and professionals. One of the largest festivals is held each year in Cleveland, Ohio, when the local community brings in major singers and instrumentalists from India.

While they predominate, *kriti* are not the only vocal form found in South Indian classical music. Vocalists sometimes improvise extensive *alapana*, together with a violinist who imitates entire phrases following the main performer's rendition. Carnatic repertory also includes other song genres, including the *varnam*, *ragamtanam-pallavi*, and *tillana*. Some are secular, even erotic, and may include extended melismatic passages in which the performer shows off his or her mastery of improvisatory techniques. Carnatic dance is typically accompanied by vocal performance, especially the widespread *Bharata Naatyam* dance tradition.

The instruments of South India are fewer than those of North India, but several are worthy of mention. The most important is a plucked lute called **sarasvati vina** (or *veena*). Held horizontally or even placed on the floor, this instrument has up to nine strings for playing melody and rhythm but generally no sympathetic strings. Players may use plectra or their bare fingertips. The most memorable South Indian instrument is a long, black double-reed called **nagasvaram**, usually played in pairs and enthusiastically accompanied by a pair of short barrel drums called **tavil**. One may also encounter performers using the *venu* (flute) or the *dilruba* (fretted bowed lute). In recent years, several new Western instruments have been adapted into Carnatic music, most prominently the mandolin, made famous by one player, the youthful U. Srinivas. Other

ARADHANA
A South Indian festival.

SARASVATI VINA
A plucked lute from South India, often associated with the Hindu goddess Sarasvati.

NAGASVARAM
A double-reed aerophone from South India.

TAVIL
A pair of drums from South India, often used to accompany the *nagasvaram*.

A South Indian violinist plays during a St. [Sri] Tyāgarāja Festival in Cleveland, Ohio. Note how he holds the instrument between his chest and right foot, making it easier to play the ornamentation required in this music

Sri Tyāgarāja (1767–1847) is South India's most famous composer, whose music is still celebrated in festivals throughout the world (Aradhana Committee, Cleveland, Ohio)

The *sarasvati vina* of South India (Andrew Shahriari)

Explore More

Kathakali

Kathakali performance: two drums on left, two actors in middle, two gong players on right

Attending a performance of Indian *Kathakali* dance drama, whether in India or a touring group, is an unforgettable experience. Perhaps you will not recall the musical accompaniment (drums, percussion, singing), but you cannot have ignored the actors' make-up or costumes. Going beyond the fascinating visual aspects, however, requires the detailed study of all the aspects appreciated by connoisseurs: gestures, make-up codes, facial expressions, dance movements, and the accompanying music, including the meaning of the sung words and their role in telling the story.

Although it originated in the extreme southern state of Kerala, *Kathakali* is considered particular to that state alone but has come to the notice of audiences not just throughout India but worldwide. But understanding the words, which are in a southern language called Malayalam, sometimes mixed with Sanskrit, is near impossible for people living elsewhere. Fortunately, most of the clips of *Kathakali* available on the Internet include subtitles.

None of the actors, whose facial colors indicate character (e.g., green indicates a noble character), speaks or sings, this being done by off-stage performers, because the actors' gestures, expressions, and dance are so complicated. But the musicians are clearly seen on stage: one or two drummers (a horizontal drum played with the hands (*maddalam*) and one vertical played with sticks (*chenda*)) on the viewer's left, and two players who strike small gongs with wooden beaters on the right.

Traditionally sacred in character, though never part of Hindu temple rituals, the 101 classical stories derive from many sources, especially the epic tale called the *Mahabharata*. In earlier times a performance lasted the entire night, but today's performances are shortened to three or four hours (although on-tour performances are much shorter). In addition to the old stories, writers have created new stories, such as from the Bible, from Shakespeare's dramas, and even from Goethe's *Faust*. Learning to perform *Kathakali* requires up to ten years just to appear on stage followed by a lifetime of continuing effort, including the study of Kerala-style martial arts. Because arts such as *Kathakali* are so "deep," serious connoisseurs also grow over time, coming to see and hear more with every new performance. This inherent allure to appeal to both novice and veteran audiences makes the *Kathakali* one of the most memorable of Indian theatrical genres.

Kathakali dancer (Wikimedia Commons)

Western imports include the violoncello (or 'cello), the viola, the alto saxophone, and the clarinet; the latter's reeds and mouthpiece are altered to allow for greater ornamentation and tone-bending. In South India, instrumental music consists primarily of vocal compositions performed without words, though the original melody is generally elaborated on through improvised passages requiring great virtuosity.

Site 3: Hindu *Bhajan* Devotional Song

BHAJAN
Hindu devotional songs from India.

First Impressions. Along with a reed instrument and pair of drums, a male vocalist sings a short line, which is answered by a group of singers, both male and female, who sound more like a congregation of ordinary people at worship than professional singers. The melody they sing is rather simple, repetitive, and easy to imitate with the melodic instrument providing the pitch outline of the vocal phrases. A metallic instrument joins the group, adding a steady rhythmic element like the sound of a model train chugging along to the beat.

Aural Analysis. The reedy sound of the melodic instrument is a *harmonium*, a free-reed pump organ originally from France. Full-sized harmoniums became popular parlor instruments in "better" American and European homes during the nineteenth century, and many families today still preserve one as a treasured heirloom. These domestic instruments were fairly large, often had extensive wood carvings as decorations, had a keyboard, a bank of pull stops, and were pumped using two pedals.

Portable versions of the harmonium became popular by mid-century and were quite compact with a small keyboard and a hand-pumped bellows at the rear of the case. This type of harmonium was originally designed for missionaries and other traveling religious leaders, who used them to accompany hymn singing. Many British missionaries went to India, taking the harmonium with them—though they certainly did not anticipate that Indians would embrace the instrument so enthusiastically and blend it into their traditional music. In *bhajans* today the harmonium player often provides just a steady drone, but he can also play the lead melody to support the vocal line, as with our audio example.

A man sings while playing a hand-pumped harmonium at a temple in Kathmandu, Nepal

In addition to a harmonium, a drum (or, more properly, two drums) is often heard in *bhajan* performance. The sound should seem familiar, as it is a *tabla*, an instrument heard earlier in the Hindustani *raga* (see above). Unlike the *tala* patterns heard in classical performances of Hindustani *raga*, the one rhythm here is simple and regular, alternating between a four- and an eight-beat cycle. The metallic instrument that is also heard is peculiar to the overseas Indian community in Trinidad and Tobago, called a *dandtal* (or *dental*), and consists of a steel rod struck from within a horseshoe-shaped beater. In this example, it plays a short–short–long pattern throughout.

Bhajan singing typically follows a call-and-response format in which a leader (in this case male) sings a phrase that is then sung by the group. This pattern differs from call-and-response performance in most traditions, because normally a group completes a vocal line sung by its leader, rather than simply repeating it. Therefore, *bhajan* practice is closer to antiphonal singing, in which leader and group alternate. Practically speaking, the leader in *bhajan* performances is also prompting the singers, who might not know the words otherwise. The vocal lines are very simple melodically and are repeated. In our example, there are basically two phrases, both of which use a pentatonic scale. The five tones could be described as 5, 6, 1, 2, 3, with 5 and 1 as the most important and 1 as the fundamental pitch. Because the term *bhajan* denotes a great range of devotional songs sung by members of virtually any of India's faiths (though they are most prominent in Hinduism), and because they are normally sung by lay people, the texts can be in whatever local or national language is preferred.

The text of our example was written for the Hindu sect that follows the great **guru** (teacher) Sai Baba, and begins (in translation) with these exhortations: "Lord Ganesha, son of mother Parvati and Lord Shiva. You are ever pure. Protect me O Blissful Lord. You confer auspiciousness."

GURU
A teacher or spiritual guide, primarily associated with Hindu traditions from India.

LISTENING GUIDE

5.3 (1'36")

Site 5.3

India: Hindu *Bhajan* Devotional Song

Voice: Male vocal lead and mixed-group response
Instruments: Harmonium (keyed aerophone), *tabla* (pair of hand drums), *dandtal* (idiophone)

TIME	LISTENING FOCUS
0'00"	*Tabla* and harmonium enter.
0'02"	Lead vocal enters with first verse.
	Line 1: *Parvati Nandana Gajanana*
	(Translation: Lord Ganesha, son of mother Parvati and Lord Shiva.)
0'07"	Congregation responds with repetition of the first line.
0'13"	Lead vocal, then congregation, repeats first line.
0'18"	*Dandtal* enters with a consistent short–short–long rhythm.
0'25"	Lead vocal enters with second verse.
	Line 2: *Pashupati Nandana Niranjana*
	(Translation: You are ever pure.)
0'31"	Congregation responds with repetition of the second line.

0'37"	Lead vocal, then congregation, repeats second line.
0'48"	Lead vocal, then congregation, sings first line again. (Repeated.)
1'11"	Lead vocal enters with third line.
	Line 3: *Pahi Prabho Mam Pahi Prasanna*
	(Translation: Protect me O Blissful Lord. You confer auspiciousness.)
1'16"	Congregation responds with repetition of the third line.
1'22"	Lead vocal, then congregation, repeats third line.

Source: "Parvati Nandana Gajanana," recorded by Terry E. Miller at the Sai Baba Temple, Longdenville, Trinidad, 1985. Used by permission.

MUSICAL MARKERS: Timbre/Medium—Small "organ" sound of the harmonium. Hi-pitched drum and metal "triangle-like" accompaniment. **Melody**—Lead vocal repeated by congregation. Minimal ornamentation. **Phonic Structure**—Monophonic. **Rhythm**—Steady pattern on a metal idiophone as the congregation claps the beat. **ETHNO-CHALLENGE:** Sing along, as if you were a member of the congregation. Additionally, clap the *dandtal* rhythmic pattern throughout the example. For an additional experience, watch one or more *bhajans* on YouTube and ascertain as much as you can about the visuals that accompany it.

Cultural Considerations. *Bhajans* are devotional songs sung by lay people for many occasions, both formal and informal, at home or in a temple, accompanied or unaccompanied. They can be traditional songs, homemade ones, or a blend of traditional and popular music styles. In a sense they parallel Protestant hymns in the Christian tradition. Indeed, some Indian Christians have adopted *bhajans* to their own faith. *Bhajan* meetings, predominantly associated with Hindus, are often held during the week, and anyone in the congregation can lead a song.

Swaminarayan Akshardham Temple in Delhi, the world's largest Hindu temple (N. Scott Robinson)

Bhajan performance at Hindu temple near Chaguanas, Trinidad, West Indies. Accompaniment is provided by drum, harmonium, and *dandtal*

The *dandtal* is a metal rod struck with a horseshoe-shaped metal beater used to accompany *bhajans*

If Hindu, services usually begin with the chanting of *om*, the fundamental sacred sound of Hinduism. *Bhajan* texts can be sung in any language and may consist of nothing more than a repetition of the names of God, because God is believed to have many incarnations. Other texts express the devotees' love for God, and offer praise and devotion.

Bhajans can be heard throughout India, Nepal, the Tamil parts of Sri Lanka, and anywhere else where there are Indian or Hindu communities, such as South America and the Caribbean, particularly Guyana and Trinidad and Tobago. Among the Hindu spiritual teachers who have attracted followings outside India is Sai Baba, originally from the Indian states of Andhra Pradesh and Karnataka. *Bhajan* singing typically takes place in Sai Baba temples on Thursday or Sunday. The *bhajan* selected for inclusion here was recorded in a Sai Baba temple in Chaguanas, a town in central Trinidad, where there is a concentration of Hindus. (Around 40 percent of Trinidadians are descendants of Indians brought to the country as indentured workers after slavery ended.) *Bhajan* singing is a major aspect of Sai Baba worship but is also found among Hare Krishna devotees, another sect that has also established congregations and temples worldwide.

BOLLYWOOD
An informal name for India's film industry, combining "Bombay" and "Hollywood."

Explore More

Indian *Filmi Git* (Film Song)

While Indian film songs, or *filmi*, are clearly not part of the classical *raga* tradition, many film directors and performers were trained in Indian classical music, and as a result *filmi* retains some classical characteristics. Most films are laden with musical productions that break away from the basic plot and encourage an escapist experience for the audience. Though atypical in modern cinema, historical film buffs will recall that many American films from the 1930s to the 1960s also included numerous songs. Just as *The Sound of Music* (1965) or *Singin' in the Rain* (1952) would be unremarkable without musical performance, so, too, would the hundreds of similarly produced film-musicals found in Indian cinemas

107

and abroad today. While the song-film format fell out of favor in the West long ago, it has not in India, a country where millions toil every day in the heat for little reward. Movies that help to transport people from the grinding poverty of their own lives into fantasies of love, adventure, or exceptional religious devotion are clearly valued by their primary audience.

The Indian film industry, colloquially referred to as "**Bollywood**" (a combination of the words "Bombay" and "Hollywood"), has become the world's number-one producer of films, releasing more than 2000 films per year. Hindustani artists traditionally dominated the Indian film industry, and as a result for many years mainstream *filmi git* were also generally Hindustani. Eventually, the South developed its own style of film songs, and in recent years these have gained popularity throughout India and abroad.

The first Indian "talkie" was released in 1931. Early films required the actors themselves to sing songs derived from "light classical" Indian music into a "single-system" camera. By the 1940s, however, when sound and image could be recorded separately, producers began using "playback singers," individuals who recorded the songs in a studio; the songs were then played back to the actors who lip-synched the words on the film set. Because of India's diverse population and languages, songs were frequently recorded in more than one of India's major languages. Film producers hired music directors who, with a team of writers and musicians, created, performed, and recorded all the music for a given film. To this end, studios had to retain a great many musicians playing primarily Western orchestral instruments plus a few Indian instruments, especially for "traditional" scenes.

Today's film music, however, makes greater use of synthesizers. Certain of the film music producers became major figures in their own right, and most of them were musicians themselves. The "playback" singers who have performed most songs since the late 1930s are far fewer in number than the actors and actresses they sing for, meaning that audi-

A dance scene typical of Indian film with actress singing a *filmi* song (Shutterstock)

ences often hear the same voices doing the songs in film after film, regardless of who is being seen on-screen.

Two figures have tended to dominate the genre, either personally or by setting the style. Male actor-singer Kundan Lal Saigal set the standard early on with his warm voice, which recorded well with the early microphones. But a single female singer, Lata Mangeshkar, has dominated the industry for six decades, since 1942; her light, "little girl" voice being virtually the signature sound of Indian *filmi*. Cited by the *Guinness Book of World Records* as having produced more recordings than any other singer, she has recorded thousands of film songs in numerous languages. Her younger sister, Asha Bhosle, is similarly an iconic figure of the *filmi* music industry. In recent years, the Indian film industry has become increasingly prominent on the global market with many films achieving critical acclaim and financial success rivaling the Hollywood film industry. The recent success of *Slumdog Millionaire* (2008), a British production that was filmed and set in India, has done much to heighten global attention to South Asian cinema. While the musical format is often absent from these newly released films, *filmi* remains a popular music style of the majority of Bollywood films.

Arrival: Pakistan

Pakistan, like many other nations formed out of colonial empires, took its form more as a result of external forces than around common culture or language. Unified geographically by the Indus River basin and by its religion, Islam, Pakistan was home to some of the world's earliest civilizations and a crossroads of numerous cultures arriving both through trade—it was on the "Silk Route"—and because of invasions. By the nineteenth century, Pakistan had become the western

Lahore, Pakistan, at sunset with minarets silhouetted in the fading sunlight (Shutterstock)

portion of the British Raj encompassing most of South Asia. Soon after the British granted independence to its Indian empire in 1947, disputes broke out between the Hindu majority and the Muslim minority which were resolved in the agony of one of history's greatest human migrations; millions of Hindus left the provinces of both the east and west for what became India and millions of Muslims left India for either the eastern or western provinces, which together became Pakistan later that year. Following numerous disputes with India over Kashmir and internally with East Pakistan, in 1971 the eastern province of Bengal broke away and became the nation of Bangladesh.

Pakistan, formerly just the western portion and whose area is slightly smaller than Texas, has a population of 187 million, making it the second most populous Muslim country after Indonesia. In addition to its two official languages—English and Urdu—there are more than sixty other languages spoken among the country's numerous ethnic groups, Punjabis being the largest (44 percent). The country's capital, Islamabad, with a population of only 700,000, is dwarfed by its largest city, Karachi, with a population of around fourteen million. Because of its ethnic diversity, Pakistan has long been stressed by ethnic division, and although the military has traditionally been the glue that held the country together, the country's territories along the Afghanistan border have remained notoriously difficult to govern.

Visitors to Pakistan would rightly ask, "what is 'Pakistani music'?" There is no easy answer because each of Pakistan's cultural regions has more in common with neighboring countries (Iran, Afghanistan, India) than with a national culture. Further, when the great migration occurred in 1947, a great number of people from India settled in West Pakistan, and yet the country's new identity was founded on being distinct from India. As a result, the most sophisticated form of Pakistani music (what some call its *raga*-based "classical music") is virtually the same as Hindustani (Indian) *raga*. After that there are nearly endless forms of regional and local music associated with particular ethnic groups. In the 1960s Pakistan's national radio attempted to use *qawwali* songs to represent the national culture. Unofficially this continues to hold true in that *qawwali* is Pakistan's most prominent music in the eyes of the rest of the world.

Site 4: *Qawwali* (Sufi Devotional Song)

Qawwali performance by Rizwan-Muazzam Qawwali during the WOMAD Festival, 2010 in Wiltshire, United Kingdom (David Corio/Getty Images)

First Impressions. The clustered tones of a reed instrument are immediately joined by one—or sometimes two—voice(s) in a seemingly improvisatory melody. Three quick raps on a drum allude to the coming main section in which drums help define the meter. Sometimes sounding subdued, sometimes not, the singers reach sudden points of intensity, suggesting this is more than mere poetry but perhaps a personal declaration.

Aural Analysis. Two elements constitute the sound of *qawwali* song: instruments and voices. The melodic instrument heard immediately is the harmonium, a small hand bellows-powered keyboard instrument whose sounds emanate from small cane free-reeds. This instrument was discussed more fully in the *bhajan* site (see above). The player, who is usually also the singer, parallels the sung melody. Typically, two kinds of drums participate: first, a pair of drums called *tabla* (see Chapter 5, Site 1), and second, a small two-headed barrel drum called *dholak*, better known for its widespread use in Indian film music, *bhajan* singing, and other "light" forms of South Asian music. *Dholak* can be tuned using metal turnbuckles or traditional rope lacing; the left head is "loaded" with a pasty mixture to tune it.

The lead singer or singers dominate the vocal element. In this case there are two: the world-famous Sabri Brothers, who sometimes alternate and sometimes sing together. Joining them now and then is a chorus of four or five men, who also provide clapping sounds on the strong beats. The chorus also repeats some of the lines sung by the soloists to emphasize their importance.

The song heard here makes use of a simple diatonic scale of seven tones, approximating the Western C major scale but theorized by *qawwali* musicians as a *raga* (see Chapter 5, Site 1). When the drums enter, the metrical pattern is a three-beat *tala* (rhythmic cycle), creating the feeling of triple meter. The sung text of this section, part of a much longer composition, begins "*Jamale kibriya main hoon*," meaning "Man is the light of God. Adam modeled in clay is made of divine transparence. Adam, the first of men, opens the way." Originally sung in Persia's main language, Farsi, most *qawwali* today are sung in Punjabi or Urdu, though songs exist in many other languages as well.

Qawwali songs typically last between fifteen and thirty minutes, too long to be reproduced here in full. Some, however, last more than an hour. During that time period the song changes mood, from the restrained emotion of the beginning—heard here—to increasing power and emotion.

Cultural Considerations. Associating *qawwali* music with Islam seems counter intuitive at first, because of Islam's traditional distrust of the sensuous art of music. *Qawwali*, however, is not part of mainstream Sunni or Shia Islam, rather it is expressive of the mystical Sufi sects of both Pakistan and India. Sufis are indeed Muslims but are considered heretical by many for their pursuit of spiritual and mystical experiences that bring them into communion with God. Music is an important element in most Sufi religious meetings (see Chapter 8, Site 5). The musicians (called *qawwal*) heard in this example traditionally performed at shrines for Sufi saints on their anniversaries, but sometimes weekly on Thursday or Friday as well for audiences of devotees. Revered for having achieved exceptional nearness to God, the saints are celebrated by modern Sufis wishing to achieve such spiritual elevation, which can be enhanced by hearing *qawwal* sing. As the song progresses from calm to agitation and exclamation, the listeners, too, can experience heightened spirituality to the point of achieving a trance state. As the song winds down, then, the participants are guided in gradually withdrawing from their trance back to normalcy.

For devotees, the most important element in *qawwali* is the poetry, for, although the music can reach great intensity, it is the text that affects their minds and arouses their spirituality up to and including a trance state. Much *qawwali* poetry, however, is strikingly earthy, speaking directly of human love. But this is the surface meaning, and devotees understand that all is metaphorical for the love and connection between humans and the divine. For this to happen, listeners must understand the language of the singer, suggesting that traditional performance was assumed to take place within a small community. This being so, it is somewhat surprising how *qawwali* has managed to become one of the most sought after of "world musics," for audiences who are neither Muslim nor speakers of the singer's language.

Two kinds of Pakistani drums: *naal* (left) and *dholak* (right), the latter the mainstay of *qawwali* singing (N. Scott Robinson)

111

LISTENING GUIDE

Site 5.4

Pakistan: *Qawwali* (Sufi Devotional Song)

Voices: Two male leads, male vocal group of four to five singers.
Instruments: Two harmoniums, *tabla*, *dholak*

TIME	LISTENING FOCUS
0'00"	Harmoniums enter in free rhythm, followed by lead vocalists and then vocal group in brief. The text setting is strongly melismatic, paralleling the ornamented melodic line of the harmoniums.
0'44"	*Tabla* and *dholak* (drums) sound briefly.
0'53"	Melodic performers pause, followed by a gutteral vocal utterance, "Allah."
0'54"	Male vocalists continue, exchanging the lead. Note that the text setting is less melismatic than the opening section.
1'18"	Both male vocalists sing together.
1'46"	Vocal group enters along with drums. The text setting tends toward syllabic singing.
2'06"	Lead vocalists return briefly.
2'12"	Vocal group returns with repeated refrain.
2'31"	Dynamic level diminishes as only a couple of male background vocalists continue.
2'37"	Audio example is edited to transition to next section.
2'39"	Example fades in during antiphonal chanted section between lead vocalists and vocal group. The text setting is strongly syllabic. A steady beat is emphasized with hand claps.
3'11"	Drums stop as the music shifts to free rhythm. Lead vocalists and harmonium continue in upper melodic range.
3'39"	Steady beat returns as drums and vocal group enter at a faster tempo.
4'03"	Music shifts again to free rhythm as vocal group and drums drop out.
4'04"	Gutteral vocal utterance, "Allah," is heard as example fades.

Source: "Jamale kibriya main hoon" performed by the Sabri Brothers, from *Musiciens Kawwali du Pakistan/Les Frères Sabri/ Musique Soufli, vol. 3*, Arion ARN 64147, 1991. Used by permission.

MUSICAL MARKERS: Timbre/Medium—Small "organ" sound of the harmonium. Male vocal timbre somewhat strained and "passionate." **Melody/Rhythm**—Harmonium imitates the vocal melody. Highly ornamented vocal line in free rhythm contrasts with metered sections marked by handclaps and drum with less ornamented vocal line. **Form**—Intermittent breaks of free rhythm with vocal soloists followed by group singing with a steady beat.
ETHNO-CHALLENGE: Accompany the vocal group throughout the performance. For a more difficult challenge, sing along with the lead vocalists.

Qawwali came to the notice of the non-Muslim world primarily as a result of the career of one of its greatest exponents, Nusrat Fateh Ali Khan (1948–1997), who became head of his family's *qawwali* group in 1971 at the age of 23. By the early 1980s he began touring in Europe and later participated in several of Peter Gabriel's WOMAD world music concerts in the early

Qawwali ensemble led by Farid Ayaz (Jack Vartoogian/ FrontRowPhotos)

1980s and appeared on numerous RealWorld label releases. From 1992 to 1993 he was a visiting artist at the University of Washington. Nusrat's untimely death in 1997 cut short a career that had nevertheless put *qawwali* on the world's stages. Our example was recorded by the Sabri Brothers, a family group headed by lead singers Haji Ghulam Farid Sabri and younger brother Maqbool Ahmed Sabri. Ghulam died in 1994 at the age of only 64. Both the Sabris and Nusrat went beyond traditional *qawwali*, participating in the soundtracks of numerous Pakistani films. In addition Nusrat (or his songs) were featured in two American films: *The Last Temptation of Christ* (1985) and *Dead Man Walking* (1995).

Explore More

Bhangra

Bhangra is a music style originally associated with the Punjabi populations of northern India and southern Pakistan. The music is common to group celebratory dances, particularly in association with harvest festivals and weddings. The major instruments heard in *bhangra* are the *dhol*, a large barrel drum played with two sticks on both ends, and the *tumbi*, a single-stringed plucked lute. Other instruments, such as the harmonium, are also common, but the *dhol* and *tumbi* provide the basic rhythm and tonal center for performances. A lead male vocalist with accompanying group response is typical in both folk and popular contexts.

During the late 1960s and 1970s, large numbers of Punjabis, primarily Sikhs, migrated to Great Britain and elsewhere around the world in search of economic prosperity. *Bhangra* accompanied them and remained an important cultural activity to remind these populations of their homeland. By the 1980s, however, Punjabi youth in London, England, began blending *bhangra* rhythms and vocal performance with modern music styles to create a new "pop" genre of *bhangra* that reflected their cultural identity in a diaspora community. The sound quickly spread throughout Punjabi populations around the world, making its way back to India and Pakistan where the music is commonplace alongside Bollywood *filmi* music and other forms of Indian popular music. *Bhangra* superstars, such as Malkit Singh and Daler Mehndi, perform internationally to huge audiences and frequently record for Hindi film soundtracks that have helped to promote *bhangra* to global audiences as well.

Questions to Consider

1. Why does the Indian classical tradition dominate the musical image of South Asia in the West?

2. Discuss the following terms important to a Hindustani classical music performance: *Raga, Alap, Gat, Tala, Rasa.*

3. Compare and contrast Hindustani and Carnatic music traditions.

4. How do *filmi* songs differ from *Qawwali* songs?

5. In what ways is Indian music spiritual?

6. What made India and Indian music attractive to the "world traveler" or "hippy" generation of the 1960s and 1970s?

Sites 4 & 5

Sites 1 & 2

CHINA

BURMA
(MYANMAR)

HANOI ★

LAOS

VIENTIANE

GULF OF
TONKIN

Hainan

TAIWAN

Hong
Kong

PHILIPPINE
SEA

RANGOON
(YANGON) ★

"ISAN"

Luzon

THAILAND

MANILA ★

BANGKOK
★

VIETNAM

PHILIPPINES

Site 3

ANDAMAN
SEA

CAMBODIA

PHNOM
PENH ★

GULF OF
THAILAND

SOUTH
CHINA
SEA

Mindanao

SULU SEA

MALAYSIA

BRUNEI

CELEBES SEA

PACIFIC
OCEAN

KUALA
LUMPUR
★

Strait of Malacca

Sarawak

SINGAPORE

Sumatra

Borneo

Kalimantan

Bangka

Makassar Strait

Sulawesi

Moluccas

Ceram

Irian Jaya

Strait

INDONESIA

JAVA   SEA

BANDA   SEA

INDIAN
OCEAN

Sunda

JAKARTA ★

Java

Lesser Sunda Islands

Bali

Flores

Timor

ARAFURA   SEA

Site 6

Site 7

Chapter 6
Southeast Asia

Vietnam, Thailand, Laos and Northeast Thailand, Indonesia (Java and Bali)

Thailand's Wat [Temple] Phra Kheo is part of the old Grand Palace in Bangkok and Thailand's most important Buddhist temple

Background Preparation

It is difficult to imagine a more colorful region of the world than Southeast Asia, a vast area split between the Asian mainland and some of the largest islands in the world. As a result of both internal histories and colonization, the region has developed into eleven independent states, seven on the mainland and four among the islands, of which all but Thailand were earlier colonized by European powers before gaining independence during the twentieth century. Prior to the colonial period, Southeast Asia consisted of both large and small kingdoms, the borders of which constantly expanded or retreated depending on a given power center's projection of influence. The names of some countries may be familiar, but others are understandably little known, including that of the region's newest nation, Timor-Leste (East Timor), which only gained independence from Indonesia in 1999. The nations on the mainland include Myanmar (pronounced "MiYA-ma," formerly known as Burma), Cambodia, Laos, Malaysia, Singapore, Thailand, and Vietnam, while the island nations are Brunei, Indonesia, the Philippines, and Timor-Leste.

There are many more ethnic groups than there are states, however, for mainland Southeast Asia alone is home to more than 140 named ethnic groups and the islands another sixty or more. Population densities throughout the region vary widely: both Vietnam and Indonesia (especially the main island, Java) have high-density and rapidly growing populations, while the populations of Myanmar and especially Laos are scattered and sparse. The largest urban areas grew rapidly during the last half of the twentieth century, especially as rural populations migrated to the cities seeking safety (during periods of war) or economic opportunities. The region's largest cities include Jakarta in Indonesia, Bangkok in Thailand, Ho Chi Minh City in Vietnam, Manila in the Philippines, and the city-state of Singapore at the tip of the Malaysian Peninsula. Some capital cities, however, remain relatively small and undeveloped; these include Vientiane in Laos and Phnom Penh in Cambodia. Myanmar, however, recently built an entirely new capital named Naypyidaw in an isolated area 500 miles/800 km north of the old capital in Yangon (formerly known as Rangoon). Because Southeast Asian cities exhibit the most modern aspects of life in each country, it is in the small towns and villages, where rice-growing and animal husbandry are the chief occupations, that "traditional" culture thrives.

Many aspects of Southeast Asian life—agricultural, ritual, and festive—are shaped by broad weather patterns called *monsoons* (winds). Life on the mainland is governed by alternating wet and dry monsoons; the former come from the sea and bring on the rainy season, and the latter

One of Bangkok, Thailand's venerable temples, Wat Pathumwanaram Ratchaworawihan, sits in stark contrast to all manner of modern buildings, including the gigantic Central World Plaza (mall), as seen from upscale Siam Paragon Mall next door

A typically timeless village near the banks of the mighty Maekhong River in southern Laos near the Khong waterfalls

The terraced rice paddies of Bali, Indonesia, effectively utilize every inch of available space

come from the Asian continent and bring dry weather, either cool or hot. During a given season, the weather tends to vary little from day to day. Island climates are generally more even throughout the year, because the humidity that produces rain is nearly always present. Overall, equator-straddling Southeast Asia is tropical and rather humid, but upland areas, especially on the mainland, can become quite cold during the cool, dry monsoon. Temperatures in northern Thailand and upland Laos can drop to freezing, and snow has been known to fall in the highlands of central Laos. Because most rice is grown in flooded paddy fields, rice agriculture is restricted to the rainy season except where irrigation systems have been constructed. Countries experiencing a dry monsoon period otherwise have only one harvest, while those with rain year-round may have two or more.

Poverty remains a major issue in parts of Southeast Asia, especially Myanmar and the Philippines. Economically, most of Southeast Asia is still considered "developing," though Malaysia, Thailand, and Singapore have achieved rapid growth and modernization in recent decades. In economically advanced countries such as these, one finds fully developed communication and sanitation infrastructures, but in the less developed areas, such as Laos, there are still few paved roads, no railroads, and little modern communication.

Planning the Itinerary

Because around 200 distinct, named ethnic groups are found throughout Southeast Asia, an exploration of the region's cornucopia of musics is as daunting as it is exciting. Each of the larger nations, with the exception of the Philippines, has or had wealthy aristocratic courts that were long-time patrons of the arts. Wherever these court systems thrived, highly sophisticated "classical" music developed, performed by relatively large instrumental ensembles in a variety of contexts, including dance, theater, and ritual. In one case, that of Bali in Indonesia, these ensembles were primarily associated with Hindu temples rather than with the royal court. Outside courts and temples, music largely flourishes in the rural areas, primarily in villages, because Southeast Asian farmers prefer to live in clusters. In these areas, music-making is necessarily simpler because few musicians are able to devote themselves to it full-time or afford expensive kinds of instruments. Many Southeast Asian nations also have large minority groups, usually living in remote uplands. Their music is often unrelated to that of the dominant lowland cultures.

In addition, most cities have large segments of Chinese or Chinese-descended people who are either well integrated, like those of Thailand, or remain more separate, as in Indonesia or Malaysia. Throughout Southeast Asia, though especially in urban areas, there is also a great variety of modernized popular music. In countries with developed media, this type of music reaches into the most remote areas, even if the televisions have to be powered by car batteries.

Southeast Asia is especially known for two materials used to make instruments—bronze and bamboo. Bronze is an alloy of the naturally occurring metals copper and tin. Bronze metallurgy is extremely old, going back to around 2000 B.C.E. For this reason, a great variety of bronze instruments are found throughout the region. Being rigid and heavy, bronze instruments are invariably idiophones. Most ensembles that feature bronze instruments also include non-idiophones, especially drums. A second key feature of this region's music is the widespread use of bamboo, although bamboo instruments are also commonly found in East Asia. In Southeast Asia's tropical climate, bamboo grows rapidly and easily, providing material not just for musical instruments but also for numerous everyday objects, such as bowls, knives, building materials, even textiles from the interior fibers.

Demographics must be considered when categorizing the music of the region. One basic division is between lowland and upland peoples. Lowlanders mostly live in villages and are generally wet rice farmers, though the people of the great lowland cities, who vary from wealthy businessmen and high-ranking government officials to unskilled laborers, live quite differently. Uplanders everywhere remain rural, with some practicing swidden agriculture, in which nomadic communities clear hillsides or mountaintops for temporary agricultural use by slashing and burning the trees and planting dry crops such as rice or maize. Besides its indigenous peoples, Southeast Asia also hosts great numbers of Chinese immigrants, most of whom came to the cities to engage in commerce during the nineteenth and early twentieth centuries, often retaining their distinct temple traditions, instrumental music, and opera. On a smaller scale, the same is true of immigrants from India.

The famous triple *chedi* in fourteenth-century Wat Sri Samphet in Thailand's former capital, Ayuthaya, which was destroyed by Burmese armies in 1767

Southeast Asia is a subcontinent known more for instrumental ensembles than for soloists. Vocal music also plays a strong role, because many traditional forms articulate narratives of great warriors, royalty, and religious men, as well as great women, comic characters, and superhuman heroes. Theater is exceptionally important as well, and virtually all Southeast Asian theater types combine instrumental music, song, and dance. Additionally, theater employing puppets of various sorts—especially flat, leather "shadow" puppets—is a major art form throughout the region. Vietnam's unique water-puppet theater, which takes place in a pond with the puppeteers behind a screen standing waist-deep in water, features amazingly agile wooden puppets placed at the ends of long, underwater complex mechanical arms.

All musics, whether traditional or modern, require a system of patronage in order to survive. While the courts and royal families of Vietnam, Laos, and Myanmar have long since disappeared, royal arts in those countries continue to a degree thanks to modest state support. Even in Thailand,

Constructed in the eighth and ninth centuries in Java, Indonesia, Borobudur is the world's largest Buddhist temple

Sumarsam

AN INSIDE LOOK

I was only seven years old when I began my interest in gamelan. Whenever there was a gamelan performance in my village in East Java, especially when accompanying *wayang* shadow puppet play, I could not resist watching it. Coincidently, my neighbor was a *dhalang* (puppeteer). He often invited me to see his performances and ask me to sit down behind him, on the stage. His musicians knew me as a young boy who often got together with friends to play gamelan in my neighbor's house. Once, one of the musicians playing for a *wayang* performance fell asleep. The leader of the group invited me to play the vacant instrument. That was my first public performance. Subsequently, the musicians asked me to join the group, playing with them in performances held in my village and its vicinity. But when I entered my teenage years, I stopped playing, trying to focus on my study at the junior high school. After graduating, I celebrated my interest

in gamelan by performing nightly for a month to accompany a *kethoprak* theatrical company. That was the best way for me to build up my musical competency and repertoire, which turned out to be a very useful experience in preparing myself for my next gamelan journey—as a student at the gamelan conservatory in Solo, Central Java. Moving from village to city, from informal learning to formal study with highly respected court musicians, from playing often rusty iron village gamelan to playing refined bronze instruments, from learning aurally to using notation, and learning new behaviors (e.g., not stepping over the instruments)—these were major transitions for me. In any event, after getting to know these new acquaintances (and them me) better, a group of us became good friends, involving more gamelan activities inside and outside school hours, including organizing a gamelan group led by our teachers, performing in different venues in Solo and surrounding areas. Up to this time I had learned the diversity and richness: (1) in the contents of the music (e.g., the court gamelan has a greatly expanded repertoire and performs with a higher degree of refinement than the village gamelan, but basically they share much repertoire and many performance practices), (2) in gamelan pedagogy (e.g., aural transmission versus formal learning with notation), and (3) in new performance contexts and meanings of the gamelan. Music is a sound structure that can offer aesthetic enjoyment, but musical meaning grows out from and is shaped by performance context. In gamelan, the contexts include marking and celebrating rites-of-passage, religious festivals, national and local events, and radio and television broadcasting.

Because of my noted musical activities and later my teaching position at the conservatory, more opportunities to perform opened up to me, including participating in government-sponsored performance events. In the mid-1960s, I was assigned for the possibility to perform gamelan abroad, but the political situation forced the government to cancel dispatching the group both to the 1965 New York World Fair and Romania. Performing gamelan at the 1970 Expo in Osaka, Japan, for seven months was my first experience to perform gamelan abroad. Returning home, I resumed teaching at the conservatory and studying at ASKI for one year. I was then invited to teach gamelan at the Indonesian Embassy in Canberra, Australia. Subsequently, in 1972, Wesleyan University in Middletown, Connecticut, invited me to teach gamelan there. Since then I have focused my gamelan teaching and performing in the context of liberal arts education. Concurrently, the academic environment inspired me to continue my education by enrolling myself in an MA program in music at Wesleyan (1974–1976) and the Ph.D. program at Cornell (1983–1992). In spite of my achievement of receiving the highest academic degree, I continue to teach gamelan performance, in addition to teaching courses in the history and theory of Indonesian performing arts. Indonesian gamelan teachers at the university must teach beginning students each semester, teaching them basic repertoire. The teacher must thus sacrifice the chance to perform gamelan with their colleagues in Java. However, if one believes in the value of educating non-Indonesian students about Indonesian music performance and musical culture, teaching and performing gamelan abroad are indeed honorable endeavors. It introduces students to the diversity of world music, exploring different kinds of aesthetic experiences, and encouraging comparative thinking.

Malaysia, and Cambodia, which retain kings and royal families, patronage has also been taken over by the state, which encourages the arts in various ways, especially through the educational system. Only in Indonesia, where Javanese sultans still hold court, does royalty actually help sustain the traditional arts. But even there, government-supported music conservatories can be found. Traditional music, theater, and dance at the local and regional levels, however, are mostly left to their own devices. Many music traditions have had a tough time surviving due to increased modernization and the spread of popular culture through globalization. Some forms have retained widespread support by modernizing, but many have simply become rare or extinct as people turn increasingly to various popular musics, both of local and of foreign origin. All Southeast Asian countries now have their own popular music, much of it originally stimulated by the importation of Anglo-British ballroom dance music from the 1930s and continuing to today with the latest releases from European, American, and Asian pop stars.

Arrival: Vietnam

Vietnam stretches dragon-like along the South China Sea for some 1,500 miles (2,400 km). Two major rivers create vast sandy deltas before they empty into the sea: the Red River in the north, which flows past the capital city, Hanoi, and the Maekhong River (sometimes spelled Mekong), which flows south from China and splits into nine branches in Vietnam—the "Nine Dragons" (*Cuu*

An upland Bahnar village near Kontum, Vietnam. Note the lightly framed houses with stucco walls and the steps carved into a log

Long in Vietnamese)—and flows through the endless rice fields of the southern delta. Vietnam's backbone is a chain of mountains that runs from south to north, spilling into neighboring Cambodia, Laos, and China. Vietnam's vast population of more than eighty-seven million people is predominantly Viet (or Kinh), a wet rice-growing people who live in the lowland plains between the mountains and the sea. In central Vietnam, the coastal plains are sometimes no more than a few miles or even a few hundred feet wide. Indeed, between Danang and the old imperial capital of Hue, "Sea and Cloud Pass" brings the mountains into the sea itself. The majority of Vietnam's people live in the lowlands, while some fifty-four minority groups, most unrelated to the Viet, live in the interior hills and mountains that border Cambodia and Laos to the west and China to the north.

Culturally speaking, Vietnam has three distinct regions: the north, the center, and the south. Each has a different history, a distinct accent, and different preferences for instruments and genres of music or theater. The north includes Hanoi, the country's ancient capital and the locale for several important kinds of music, including the music of the distinctive water-puppet theater. The center's heart is the old imperial city of Hue, seat of the Nguyen dynasty from the early nineteenth century until 1945, when Vietnam's last emperor, Bao Dai, abdicated. The south, centered on Ho Chi Minh City (formerly Saigon) and several major cities in the delta, has the youngest culture and is the least formal in behavior.

The people who live in the mountains are mostly different from the Viet and speak a variety of Austro-asiatic and Malayo-Polynesian languages. Living in isolated villages and often practicing "slash-and-burn" or "swidden" agriculture on the mountainsides, they relocate from time to time when the fields are depleted. Their musical cultures encompass both songs and instrumental music. Most instruments in the uplands are made of bamboo and other organic materials, but they are nonetheless incredibly varied. Perhaps most surprising are the large bronze gong sets played during year-round rituals and festivals.

For many in the West, "Vietnam" is known as a war, but, of course, it is actually a country—and *one* country, not two as during that war. The capital, Hanoi, formerly only known as a forbidding Communist city and the prime target of American bombers in "North Vietnam," is located along the broad Red River, whose delta forms a vast plain in the north. Hanoi's architecture reflects three eras: fascinating temples dating back to the eleventh century, French colonial architecture created during the later nineteenth and twentieth centuries, and the modern buildings of a capitalist-leaning and increasingly cosmopolitan Vietnam reborn in the 1990s.

Members of the Jarai ethnic group, the same ones heard in the track, perform on a set of flat bronze gongs and a drum in Vietnam's Central Highlands (Phong Nguyen)

Site 1: Vietnamese Central Highlands Bronze Gong Ensemble

First Impressions. The clanging sound of the gongs may remind you of church bells, albeit a very large set of them, in a small country church. This hypnotic music seems simple, using mainly metal gongs with somewhat "fuzzy" pitches for the short-repetitive melody. A careful listen reveals a mix of sound changes because the musicians are walking in a circle past a stationary microphone.

Aural Analysis. The ensemble heard in our example consists of approximately thirty members, all from the Jarai ethnic group, and was recorded in Pleiku in Vietnam's Central Highlands. Led by young female dancers, the male musicians walk counter-clockwise in a circle, each striking a single bronze gong. These vary in diameter from about 24 inches (61 cm) to around 12 inches (30 cm). Some have bosses (raised knobs), and others are flat; all are struck by padded beaters. In addition, the ensemble includes two horizontally played barrel drums and metal cymbals. A careful listen reveals six pitches in the octave, expressed as 1, 2, 3, 4, 5, and 7—but because the Jarai do not theorize about their music, this scale has no name. The range of the melody is relatively narrow, and the intervals between adjacent melodic pitches are no more than a fifth.

Because each musician has only one gong, each capable of producing only a single pitch, the sounds of the different gongs are "strung together" to produce melody. This is an example of *interlocking construction*, in which a succession of individual pitches played by different people creates the effect of a continuous melody. A Western music tradition that parallels this idea is a bell choir, often heard in churches during the winter holiday season. Considering that each musician only strikes one gong, it is not surprising that there is no ornamentation, as this would disrupt the continuity of the melodic line.

The rhythm follows a clear duple meter and sounds fairly simple except for a certain freedom displayed in the pitches' non-simultaneity. One senses that these performers cooperate but do not feel obligated to play in lockstep. The melodic units are relatively short and have a narrow range that falls toward the lowest pitch (1). This pitch is the tonal center, or "home" note that creates an aural feeling of rest and resolution. Although the music consists primarily of a single melodic line, making it monophonic, accompanying gong-players sound the "pillar" pitches of 1 and 5 from time to time, giving the music a strong tonal framework. Its form is iterative in that the melody is repeated for as long as necessary. There are no intentional dynamic shadings.

Cultural Considerations. Ensembles of gongs are typical among upland Vietnam's upland ethnic groups. They are associated with both festivals and religious rituals, including funerals and the annual buffalo sacrifice. Because they require a large number of musicians, no one of whom dominates, these ensembles reflect the communal nature of upland village life. In this music, as

LISTENING GUIDE

Site 6.1

Vietnam: Central Highlands Bronze Gong Ensemble

Instruments: Bronze gongs of various pitches, small cymbals, low- and high-pitched drums

TIME	LISTENING FOCUS
0'00"	Cymbals signal beginning of performance.
0'02"	Opening gong establishes the duple meter and central pitch. The cymbals also mark this regular pulsation, initially at half the rhythmic density of the opening gong and then with the same density (at 0'09").
0'05"	Melodic gongs enter and repeat the melody every sixteen beats. Listen for the primary melodic pitches of 1 and 5 in contrast to the interlocking melodic gongs. The drum also enters, but is not easily distinguished until roughly 0'10".
0'13"	The melodic line repeats.
0'14"	A low-pitched drum enters, adding a recurring "roll" throughout the performance.
0'21"	The melodic line repeats. Listen for further repetitions at 0'28", 0'36", etc.
0'48"	A syncopated "inner" melody is added to the performance.
1'01"	A very high-pitched gong adds an additional syncopated rhythm.

Source: Gong ensemble of the Jarai, Pleiku City, Pleiku province, recorded by Terry E. Miller and Phong Nguyen; from *Vietnam: Mother Mountain and Father Sea*, White Cliffs Media WCM 9991 (6 CDs and 47 pp. book), 2003. Used by permission.

MUSICAL MARKERS: Timbre/Medium—"Clanging" metallic sounds in a middle range with a short sustain.
Melody—Short and repetitive.
ETHNO-CHALLENGE: Walk along with the basic beat and then choose a prominent pitched gong heard in the recording (such as 1) and clap at the points in the melody where it sounds.

in the society, each person has a specific role to play: some reiterate the pillar-like pitches, some play melody, and some dance; overall, there is no apparent distinction between "musician" and "non-musician." Anyone in the community could expect to participate, if so inclined.

Gong ensembles typically play for funerals and thus have a strong association with the afterlife. But visitors are more likely to encounter them during public upland festivals now promoted by the government. Perhaps the most difficult event to witness is the buffalo sacrifice, during which several young men seem to become nearly hypnotized as they begin piercing the hide of a buffalo tied to a tree. Accompanied by the gongs, whose music lends itself to this hypnotic state, they continue stabbing the buffalo until it finally dies. For most visitors, this is not a pleasant experience—but for central highlanders the sacrifice is an important ritual that honors the spirits in order to assure the continuity of human life and successful harvests.

Many unanswered questions remain about the relationship between upland and lowland cultures. While bronze metallurgy has been dated to around 2000 B.C.E., it is unclear which culture developed it first. Are the upland peoples the remnants of the original inhabitants of Southeast Asia, whose ancestors were pushed from their lowland homes by advancing peoples (the early ancestors of the Viet) coming from the north? Because the lowland Viet make little use of bronze and play instruments that reflect Chinese influence, it is tempting to conclude that the upland peoples reflect the earliest layer of musical culture in Vietnam. Others argue, however, that upland cultures have always been at the margins of Vietnamese society and have absorbed and preserved aspects of lowland culture no longer prominent there. That would suggest that upland cultures reflect what is called "marginal survival," in which aspects of mainstream culture now lost are preserved in outlying areas, where culture changes more slowly. At present, however, there is no way to prove either theory. In 2005 the Central Highlands were designated as "The Space of Gong Culture" in the Third Proclamation of UNESCO's "Masterpieces of Oral and Intangible Heritage of Humanity" program.

Site 2: *Nhac Tai Tu* Amateur Chamber Music

NHAC TAI TU
(pronounced
ni-yak tai tuh)
A type of
chamber music
ensemble from
southern
Vietnam.

First Impressions. **Nhac tai tu** has a free and improvisatory feel in both melody and rhythm that includes much tone-bending and syncopation. While a prominent fiddle cuts through with a busy melodic line, lower stringed instruments complement with a cornucopia of timbres and rhythmic riffs. The music well reflects the casual setting where a group of friends meet to play favorite compositions, be it in a private village home or in a music club room in the market area of a town.

Aural Analysis. While many Vietnamese instruments were derived from Chinese instruments, they nearly always have been modified to allow for the tone-bending so preferred by Vietnamese musicians. Thus, to accommodate this fundamental aspect, Vietnamese stringed instruments have higher frets and looser strings than their Chinese equivalents. The decoration on Vietnamese instruments also tends to be unlike that found on Chinese instruments—generally, it features much intricate mother-of-pearl inlay. These refined decorations are in some ways analogous to the ornamentation that is so crucial in Vietnamese music.

A southern instrumental chamber genre, *nhac tai tu* is a gathering of amateur instrumentalists who play more for their own enjoyment than for others. In this way it is similar to the Chinese *sizhu* "silk and bamboo" chamber music from Shanghai (see Chapter 7). The recording features three melodic instruments—the *dan kim* lute, the *dan tranh* zither, and the *dan co* fiddle—plus the **song lang** "slit-drum" clapper. While this is a typical ensemble for this type of music, on some occasions other instruments may also join in such as a Vietnamese guitar (*dan ghi-ta*), a horizontal flute (*sao*), or a pear-shaped lute (*dan tyba*).

SONG LANG
(pronounced
shong long)
A "slit-drum"
clapper idiophone
from Vietnam.

Vietnamese music is generated from a complex modal system. Each mode has its own set of pitches (basically five), a hierarchy of strong and weak tones, required ornamentation, and associated extra-musical meanings. In this way, the Vietnamese system resembles the *raga* system of

At My Tho, along
one branch of
Vietnam's *Cuu
Long* ("Nine
Dragons") making
up the delta of
the Maekhong
(Mekong) River,
the area where
nhac tai tu
flourishes

A southern Vietnamese *nhac tai thu* group performs at a festival in Ho Chi Minh City. From left to right: *dan nhi* (fiddle), *dan nguyet* (lute), singer with guitar behind, and *dan tranh* (zither) (Phong Nguyen)

A Vietnamese *song lang* clapper/ slit drum. The small beater strikes the slit wooden gong to produce the "clicks" that articulate the rhythmic cycle in Vietnamese music (Phong Nguyen)

South Asia more than music processes found in East Asia, even though East Asia is the source of Vietnamese instruments. Certain pitches in each of the Vietnamese modes are outside the Western tempered tuning system, giving Vietnamese music a piquant feeling for those accustomed to Western tuning.

Another aspect of Vietnamese music that relates to India is the use of a closed cycle of beats similar to the Indian *tala*; in Vietnam, the clicks of the *song lang* clapper articulate points in these cycles. Unlike the Indian cycle, however, but similar to the Thai cycle, the *final* beat is the most accented. Our example is organized in a four-beat cycle called *nhip tu*, and the *song lang* is struck on beats 3 and 4. Because these main beats occur at a slow tempo, it may be easier to feel and hear this cycle in sixteen sub-beats instead of four, counting the clapper strikes on beats 12 and 16. Another distinctive feature of Vietnamese rhythm is its tendency toward rhythmic syncopation (i.e., toward shifting the accent to a weak beat in a measure).

The musicians in a *tai tu* ensemble all play the same fundamental melody but each adds ornamentation typical of his/her instrument, resulting in the phonic structure called *heterophony*. Before the group begins playing the tune, it is customary for each musician, in succession, to

---

LISTENING GUIDE
6.2 (1'37")

Site 6.2

Vietnam: *Nhac Tai Tu* Amateur Chamber Music

Instruments: *Dan Kim* (plucked lute), *dan tranh* (plucked zither), *dan co* (bowed lute, i.e., fiddle), *song lang* (clapper idiophone)

TIME	LISTENING FOCUS
0'00"	*Dan tranh* (zither) enters with a freely rhythmic improvisation.
0'05"	*Dan kim* (lute) enters.
0'09"	*Dan co* (fiddle) enters.
0'23"	*Song lang* (clapper) sounds to mark the transition to the composed/metered section of the performance.
0'24"	*Dan tranh* initiates composed section with a gradual increase in tempo.
0'26"	The *dan kim* and then the *dan co* reenter to affirm the basic pulse, but listen for the heavy use of syncopation.
0'28"	*Song lang* sounds on the third beat of the rhythmic cycle. Breaking the cycle down into sixteen subdivisions, the instrument marks the twelfth subdivision.
0'31"	*Song lang* sounds again on the fourth beat (sixteenth subdivision) to close the rhythmic cycle.
0'42"	Melodic instruments "close" the melody (i.e., reach a cadence) on the sixteenth beat of the cycle as the *song lang* sounds.
0'50"	*Song lang* sounds on the third beat (twelfth subdivision).
0'53"	*Song lang* sounds on the fourth beat (sixteenth subdivision).
1'03"	Melodic line reaches a closing cadence again.
1'25"	Closing cadence.
1'47"	Closing cadence.
1'55"	The example fades.

Source: "Xuan tinh (Spring Love)" performed by Nam Vinh, *dan kim*; Sau Xiu, *dan tranh*; and Muoi Phu, *dan co*; recorded by Terry E. Miller and Phong Nguyen. From *Vietnam: Mother Mountain and Father Sea*. White Cliffs Media WCM 1991 (6 CDs and 47 pp. book), 2003. Used by permission.

MUSICAL MARKERS: Timbre/Medium—Variety of stringed instruments (plucked "twangy" lute with lots of pitch bending; nasal-sounding fiddle; "harp-like" sound of the zither. Also, distinctive "click" sound of the song lang percussion.
Phonic Structure—Begins with seemingly random entrances, followed by strong heterophonic rendering of the melody.
ETHNO-CHALLENGE: Keep track of the *song lang* rhythmic cycle and clap on the beats where it sounds.

improvise a short introduction in free rhythm. Improvisation of this sort is atypical of the rest of Southeast or East Asia, lending further credence to the view that Vietnamese culture, while deeply influenced by East Asia, sometimes exhibits traits more typical of South Asia where a freely rhythmic introduction is common in classical music performance.

Cultural Considerations. Vietnam is, musically, an extremely complex country. The example used here, *tai tu*, is but one of many kinds of music that are essentially songs accompanied by a small instrumental ensemble. Some types of music were originally associated with court ceremonies in the former imperial capital, Hue; some are associated with rituals such as possession rites or funerals; and some, like *tai tu*, are still used simply for entertainment. Sophisticated poetry is much appreciated in Vietnam, and even though *tai tu* songs are "amateur," they are also refined.

It is difficult to divide Vietnamese music into categories such as "classical" and "folk," because the same repertory of tunes can be played in many different ways. A learned musician will most likely approach a given piece differently than a farmer would—but in fact many farmers are highly refined and skilled musicians. Within the span of a few days, the same musicians might be hired to play for a religious rite and a theater performance—and might also perform together for their own enjoyment. In fact, *tai tu* music was the basis for the music that accompanied the *cai luong* theater, a "popular" (i.e., commercial) genre created and cultivated in the south from around 1917 until its gradual decline in the 1990s in the face of competition from film and television.

The challenge for visitors to Vietnam today is finding genuine "traditional" music as opposed to what is normally offered as such, what the Vietnamese call *cai bien* music and which can be translated as "neo-traditional." During the communist period from the 1950s until the 1990s, many northern Vietnamese studied in eastern Europe where they learned about the propaganda value of "folkloric" state troupes that presented modernized forms of old music, fully composed and rehearsed, that conveyed ideas of national solidarity and identity. Most returned as professors at the Hanoi Conservatory of Music, and there they created Vietnam's response to these ideas. They combined "improved" (i.e., modernized) versions of lowland Viet instruments with similarly altered versions of instruments from the Central Highlands and composed elaborate compositions making use of harmony, full orchestration, and having politically loaded titles. Although the promoters claimed the music came from "the people," in fact it came from European ideas of "socialist realism," an aesthetic philosophy that uses music to influence people's political thinking. Conservatories came to teach this style almost exclusively, and the current generation of students tends to believe that this is indeed Vietnam's "traditional music."

Arrival: Thailand

Thailand has long been one of Southeast Asia's favorite tourist destinations. For many years travelers entered the country through Bangkok's Suvarnabhumi (pronounced *Suwannaphum*) Airport, but with the development of southern Thailand's beaches and island resorts, quite a few fly directly to Phuket (pronounced Poo-ket) Island and skip Bangkok altogether. As beautiful as these islands are, they provide visitors with little of the country's musical and artistic culture. Although going to Bangkok is obligatory for anyone wishing to experience Thai music, many visitors also travel to the northern region and its principal city, Chiangmai, where many tourist-oriented regional musical performances can be heard. Few travelers, however, make it to the northeast region, called Isan. Isan maintains a vibrant traditional culture, which, if somewhat modernized at times, remains an integral part of society and is not geared toward outsiders.

Bangkok is a busy, sprawling city famous for its gorgeous Buddhist temples, palaces, shopping, and, alas, world-class traffic jams. Tourists are still enticed to Thailand by colorful posters of small boats laden with produce and crafts on the *khlong* (canals), but if you want to see this "floating market" phenomenon, you will only find it southwest of Bangkok, where it is maintained both for tourists and for Thai. While old neighborhood open markets can still be found in

Priwan Nanongkham

AN INSIDE LOOK

I grew up in a rice-farming village in Northeast Thailand, a region that is culturally Lao and known locally as Isan. When I was in the seventh grade at the local secondary school, I joined a Thai music club. At that time people said that playing Thai classical music was not just for enjoyment but it also influenced people to be good human beings. There I began my first music lesson on the *ranat thum* (lower xylophone) and later *saw u* (two-stringed coconut fiddle), the first two instruments that brought music into my life. I really enjoyed playing music in our school's music club ensemble. We practiced and rehearsed after school and weekends and had chances to perform locally.

At the end of that academic year, I came to the conclusion that music was what I wanted to do for the rest of my life. Thus, I decided to switch schools and restarted seventh grade in Roi-et city at the local *Natasin*, a kind of high school for the arts that includes the first two years of college. There I majored in *piphat* ensemble, one of the classical genres from central Thailand. Classical was the only genre offered as a major program in academia in the mid-1980s.

As an Isan native, however, I felt that I should also know the music of my home region. My school also offered the study of local music as elective courses, but only for the fourth year-students and beyond, and I could not wait that long. In my second year, I began informally taking lessons on Isan music with an older friend at school. The first Isan instrument I studied was the *khaen,* a free-reed mouth organ that is the primary instrument in Lao culture. By the third year I was ready to join our school's "Isan traditional music" troupe (consisting of musicians and dancers) known today as *wong ponglang*. It was so named after the *ponglang*, a vertical log xylophone, the main instrument of an ensemble created during the 1980s to help preserve our tradition in the face of influences from modernization and globalization. Our school troupe rehearsed after school and during vacation periods. We were invited to

Priwan Nanongkham, Thai musician and teacher

perform throughout Thailand and even went to Germany and the Netherlands in the summer of 1989.

After having six years of intensive training as a performer at Natasin Roi-et, I decided to expand my work in music through the study of pedagogy at Chulalongkorn University in Bangkok, where I earned a Bachelor of Music Education degree in 1992. The following year I entered the masters program in Cultural Studies at Mahidol University near Bangkok where I began my graduate music study. Before finishing, however, I decided to pursue an opportunity to go to the United States to teach Thai music in 1994. Soon after I moved to New York where I taught Thai music in a Thai Buddhist temple. Following that I entered the graduate program in Musicology-Ethnomusicology at Kent State University and wrote an MA thesis on *ponglang* music from Isan. My dream, after completing my Ph.D., is to become a music professor, field researcher, scholar, and musician focused on the study of the music of my own regional culture, Thailand as a whole, and of the rest of Southeast Asia, if not the world.

many areas, the outlying and newer parts of Bangkok are served by gigantic malls and megastores that dwarf American Wal-Marts. Premiere shopping malls in central Bangkok attract throngs of shoppers, many from Japan, Korea, and China who visit Thailand specifically for this purpose.

The tourism authorities have in recent years promoted the slogan "Amazing Thailand." What we find most amazing about Thailand is that, no matter how modern it seems, beneath the apparent development, commercialization, and Westernization is a "Thainess" that triumphs over all things imported or imposed. As you walk through one of Central Corporation's many gigantic malls and observe thousands of ordinary Thai walking, shopping, eating, and generally relaxing in

Old-fashioned *khlong* (canal) at Bang Khen east of Bangkok in 1972. The same area now is fully developed with high rises, the small boats replaced by fast, modern boats

the air conditioning, understand that hidden within remains a Thai worldview that makes room for spirits alongside Toyotas, magic alongside the stock market, a faith in Buddhism alongside a job running computers, and a complex form of traditional "classical" Thai music alongside every imaginable form of popular music, both domestic and imported. Sometimes this clash can be maddening to a foreigner trying to figure out just what Thai culture is. While there is the appearance of modernization, democratization, and globalization through the Internet, there are also factors such as the monarchy, Buddhism, village life, and age-old rituals (such as the "teacher greeting ceremony"), which connect even the most forward-looking Thai to the past and his/her culture.

Traditionally, Thailand (or Siam, as it used to be called) was an absolute monarchy. Following the revolution in 1932, the monarchy lost political power, though it retains tremendous moral authority to this day. Thailand is now a constitutional monarchy with a revered royal family headed by King Bhumibol Adulyadej, Rama IX, who reigned for 66 years until his passing in 2016, succeeded by his son, Maha Vajiralongkorn, Rama X. Traditional music requires a context in which to thrive, and as much of that context (age-old rituals, old-style farming, close-knit villages, a slow pace of life, etc.) has diminished, some of the music and dance associated with it has disappeared or survived by moving to the stage. One thing that remains, however, is "classical" music. Though classical music was never popular with the masses, there is a general tendency to think of classical traditions, such as the *piphat* ensemble, as representing the essence of musical Thainess through music.

Site 3: Classical *Piphat* Ensemble

First Impressions. For many listeners new to world music, **piphat**, considered the main Thai classical court ensemble, may have to be appreciated as an acquired taste. The percussive timbre of the melodic instruments overlaid with a nasal aerophone play what seems to be a clamor of notes only held together by drums and some minimal percussion. After an initial listening, some elements will stand out, such as the regular ring of a small pair of cymbals and the predominance of a very active high-pitched xylophone. Several different melodies seem to overlap continuously in a sort of "organized chaos."

PIPHAT (pronounced *bee-paht*) A type of classical ensemble from Thailand characterized by the use of melodic and rhythmic percussion and a double-reed aerophone.

131

A student *piphat* ensemble performs for guests at a university in Udon Thani, Thailand. From left-front clockwise: *ranat thum* (lower xylophone), *ranat ek* (higher xylophone), *ranat ek lek* (higher metallophone), *pi* (double reed), *taphon* (horizontal drum), *khawng wong lek* (higher gong circle), and *khawng wong* yai (lower gong circle)

Aural Analysis. Called *piphat mai khaeng* ("hard-mallet *piphat*"), this ensemble produces what is perhaps the most characteristic sound of Thai traditional music. Central Thai instruments are quite varied. They may include prominent wooden- or bamboo-keyed instruments played with mallets (higher and lower xylophones), circular frames of tuned metal gongs, bowed and plucked strings, flutes, double reeds, drums, and small rhythmic percussion. Although some of these have solo repertories, Central Thai instruments are more characteristically found in ensembles. Three ensemble types predominate: (1) *piphat,* made up of melodic and rhythmic percussion and the double reed (heard in this track); (2) *mahori,* consisting of melodic and rhythmic percussion, strings, and flute; and (3) *khruang sai,* consisting of strings and flute with light rhythmic percussion. Whereas the *piphat* primarily plays theater, dance drama, and ritual music, the other ensembles ordinarily play lighter, more entertaining and tuneful music.

    Piphat ensembles require at least three melodic instruments and two rhythmic instruments but usually add to these. The lead instrument is a high-range xylophone (*ranat ek*) with twenty-one bars of either hardwood or bamboo suspended over a boat-shaped resonator. Although this instrument's performance is the most rhythmically dense, the lower circle of tuned gongs (*khawng wong yai*)—whose player sits in the middle of its round rattan frame—plays the fundamental form of the composition. In addition a full ensemble would include a lower-ranged xylophone (*ranat thum*) that plays a highly syncopated, even playful, version of the composition, plus a higher-ranged gong circle (*khawng wong lek*) that plays a highly embellished version of the main melody. The aerophone used in hard-mallet ensembles is a quadruple-reed oboe (aerophone) called **pi**, and its duty is to play a flexible, seemingly distinct, version of the same main melody. Although it works as a double reed, each half consists of a folded piece of bamboo, making it actually quadruple.

    The Thai tuning system has seven equidistant tones in an octave in contrast to the European system of twelve equidistant pitches, meaning that some Thai pitches can sound "out of tune" to non-Thai ears. This is not always obvious since within a given passage a melody will mostly

PI
(pronounced *bee*) A double reed aerophone found in the piphat classical ensemble of Thailand.

employ a pentatonic scale of only five tones, in the form of 1, 2, 3, 5, 6. Because this kind of music sometimes shifts from one tonal center to another, it is possible to hear a total of six or even seven pitches used in a given composition, including those heard here.

Virtually all Thai music is in duple meter, which means it operates with groupings of two, four, or eight beats. Certain strong beats are articulated by a pair of small cup-shaped bronze cymbals, called *ching*, that are attached to each other with a string. The **ching** plays two strokes, the undamped (open) "ching" and the damped (closed) "chap." Thai meter is organized cyclically, somewhat like an analog clock. The cycles of much of the repertory have four *ching* strokes ("ching-chap-ching-chap"), with the final stroke ("chap") being accented. This means that Thai music is actually *end*-accented, making it the opposite of Western music generally, which accents beat 1. There are three relative rates of ching strokes, the slowest (called "third level" or *sam chan*), a medium rate twice as fast (called "second level" or *sawng chan*), and a

CHING
A pair of cup-shaped cymbals from Thailand.

(top left) *Khawng wong* yai (large gong circle) and *ranat ek* (higher xylophone)

(left) Left to right: two sizes of *pi* (double-reed aerophones), three sizes of *khlui* (vertical flutes)

(top right) Left to right, rear: *thon* (goblet drum), *rammana* (frame drum). Left to right, front: *chap lek* (larger cymbals), *ching* (small cymbals), and *krap sepah* (wood clappers)

fast rate twice as fast again (called "first level" or *chan dio*). These relationships are relative to the rhythmic density and not the absolute tempo. The track included here consists of three separate compositions: the first (*Sathukan*) uses only "ching" strokes, the second (*Sathukan klawng*) alternates "ching" and "chap," and the final one (*Rua*) returns to "ching" alone. There are two drums: 1) the *taphon*, a two-headed drum mounted horizontally on a stand, and 2) the *klawng that*, a pair of large barrel drums tilted at an angle toward the player.

The lower gong circle (*khawng wong yai*) is key to the organization of *piphat* music. It plays the simplest and least dense form of a given composition; its part has fewer notes—a lower rhythmic density—than the other instruments. Although it can be hard to hear, all of the other melodic instruments play idiomatic variants of the lower gong circle's version. Thus, the phonic structure of Thai *piphat* music is best described as a kind of layered heterophony often referred to as *polyphonic stratification*—that is, a layering of simultaneous patterned variants of the same melody.

All Thai music is composed, and the names of the composers are known for most compositions created after about 1800. Unlike Western composition, however, the composer writes nothing, for even now only beginning students use rudimentary notations. The composer was also a musician and transmitted his creations to fellow ensemble members (or students) by playing the large gong circle version. The others then "realized" that structure into the particular idioms of their own instruments; all memorized the compositional structure.

The track included here presents the first two compositions of a much longer suite played during the "Teacher Greeting Ritual" (*Pithi wai* **khru**) explained below. All are classified as "action tunes" (*phleng naphat*) because in addition to appearing in several different ritual suites they also accompany the masked drama (*khon*), dance drama (*lakhon*), and the large shadow puppet theater (*nang yai*). The first piece, "Sathukan" (meaning "Greeting" and referring to the Thai custom of greeting each other with hands in "prayer position"), like most "action tunes" is too old to have a known composer but is the opening piece played for all ritual suites and for many theatrical performances. Motivic rather than melodic, this work flows continuously without obvious phrasing, and its rhythmic structure is marked by continuous "ching" strokes. "Sathukan klawng" (meaning "Greeting the drum") immediately follows. It is more clearly phrased, and the *ching* plays alternating "ching" and "chap" strokes. Completing the track is a short coda called "Rua" (referring to the tremolo technique used by the instruments to sustain pitches) which can be attached to many parts of the suite. It is non-metered, uses only "ching" strokes, and requires players to rapidly alternate the beaters to produce "tremolo."

KHRU
A Thai teacher; the term is linguistically associated with the word *guru* in the Hindi language.

LISTENING GUIDE
6.3 (4'48")

Site 6.3
Thailand: Classical *Piphat* Ensemble

Instruments: *Pi* (reed aerophone), *ranat ek* (high xylophone), *ranat thum* (low xylophone), *khawng wong yai* (gong circle), *daphon* (barrel drum)

TIME	LISTENING FOCUS
0'00"	*Daphon* (drum) initiates the performance. Listen for the contrasting high and low pitches of each drum face. Although it follows a cycle, the patterns played do not regularly repeat.
0'02"	*Ranat ek* (high xylophone) initiates the melodic content followed by the *pi* (reed aerophone) and remaining instruments. Listen for the higher range of pitches on the lead xylophone played in octaves and its busier rhythmic density in comparison to the other instruments. Also, note the "duck call" timbre of the *pi* that is quite prominent.

0'05"	Listen for the *ching* (small hand cymbals) entrance. Note there are no "chop" strokes during this section of the performance.
0'13"–0'14"	The heterophonic structure of Thai classical music makes it difficult to follow the melodic content. A good thing to focus on is the point at which the *khawng wong yai* reaches a cadence (closing phrase). Listen for the "ringing" timbre and thinner rhythmic density of this instrument, which provides the fundamental melody.
0'49"–0'55"	Listen for the *ranat thum* (low xylophone). This instrument is most difficult to hear, having a mellower timbre than the lead xylophone. Listen for its characteristic syncopations, broken octaves, and quick three-note ornamentations. Its melodic line frequently moves in a direction contrary to the other instruments.
1'16"–1'29"	Listen for the brief decrease in rhythmic density of the *pi* for twelve *ching* strokes as the ensemble moves toward a cadence point that quickly passes. Note how the *pi* (and other instruments) matches the ending pitch of the phrase at 1'29".
2'30"	Contrast the tempo at this point in the performance with the opening material. The tempo has increased significantly. (From roughly 84 beats per minute to about 104 by this point in the music.)
2'49"	Tempo slows dramatically at closing of opening section.
2'59"	Second section begins. Note the use of both "ching" and "chop" strokes with the *ching*. Also, note the increased activity of the *daphon* and clearer synchronization of the melodic instruments.
3'24"	Melody repeats.
3'45"	Tempo slows as ensemble reaches end of section.
3'51"	Third section begins. Note the ensemble plays in free rhythm to the end of the performance. Listen for the contrasting timbre and melodic style of each instrument.

Source: "Sathukan" and "Sathukan Klawng" from *Wai Khru/The Traditional Music of Siam*, produced by The Committee of the College of Music Project, Mahidol University, Bangkok, Thailand, 1994.

MUSICAL MARKERS: Timbre/Medium—"Ching" sound of timekeeper. "Duck-like" quality of the aerophone with various xylophones/metallic melodic gongs. **Rhythmic Density**—High-range xylophone is very thick and steady. **Phonic Structure**—"Controlled chaos" as the instruments play simultaneous variations of the same melody (i.e., heterophony). **ETHNO-CHALLENGE:** Match the basic rhythmic density of the *khawng wong yai* by tapping your hands on your book at each pitch. Listen again and match the rhythmic density of the *ranat ek* (lead xylophone), using both hands simultaneously from start to finish (as is the performance technique of the musician). An easier challenge is to listen to the example repeatedly following each instrument through the performance to note its unique realization of the fundamental melody.

Cultural Considerations. During the heyday of the Thai monarchy in the nineteenth and early twentieth centuries, classical music was generously patronized and played a major role in court ceremonies, both secular and Buddhist-related. As a consequence, Thai classical music is closely associated with the society's most important state occasions, festivals, and sacred rites of passage, such as ceremonies to honor teachers, ordinations, funerals, and certain Buddhist rituals. Perhaps we can say that Thai classical music as a sonic structure is mainly of interest to musicians; for others, it serves to engender positive feelings and to reaffirm Thai cultural identity. Although relatively few Thai choose classical music for general listening, there is a broad consensus that classical music best represents the country and its traditional culture.

A *piphat* ensemble using a pair of *klawng khaek* drums (in front) performs at a festival to honor a great teacher near Bangkok, Thailand

In Thai society, the acts of teaching and learning, of passing on and receiving knowledge, are considered near sacred, and one honors not just the present-day living teacher, but that person's entire lineage leading back to the ultimate sources of knowledge, the pantheon of gods drawn from animism, Hinduism, and Buddhism. Before a master can begin transmitting knowledge to a student, the latter must perform a ritual "teacher greeting ceremony" or *phithi* (pronounced *pee-tee*) *wai khru*, the last word being the Thai pronunciation of the well-known Indian term *guru*. Simple *wai khru* ceremonies are performed at schools in which students simply reaffirm their allegiance to all their teachers, but for classical musicians and other such artists the teacher greeting ceremony is one of the most important rituals of their life.

A *wai khru* ceremony requires an elaborate altar area containing tables covered with many kinds of food, finely crafted objects, theatrical masks of the deities, and a full set of musical instruments, many being newly made in order to receive blessing during the ritual. A male ritualist intones sacred words in a mix of Thai and Pali, the latter being the sacred language of Thai Buddhism. The *piphat* ensemble performs several pieces throughout the ceremony—which concludes when the ritualist marks the forehead of each student and musician with ashes and places a small cone made of banana leaf behind one of their ears. If a student has not studied before, they are given a ritual first lesson on the large gong circle or, for young children, a lesson on playing the small *ching* cymbals.

Although few non-musicians normally experience Thai classical music except in passing or as background to rituals and ceremonies, such as the *wai khru*, general attention to serious *piphat* music became more widespread after the release in 2004 of Itthisoontorn Vichailak's hit film titled *Homrong* (The Overture), now available with English subtitles. A partially fictional life story of Luang Phradit Phairoh (1881–1954), Thailand's most famous composer, the film includes extended footage of classical music performed both solo and in ensemble, climaxing with a dramatic contest between the protagonist and his chief rival, Khun In, the latter played by an actual master musician. Musically, it is accurate in most details and highly recommended as an introduction to Thai music and culture.

Dance: Thai Classical Dance   by Sara Stone Miller

palace solely by women. Originally, classical music and dance were under the patronage of the kings, royalty and nobles, and performances were given only in the palaces or aristocratic houses.

The *Ramayana* tells the story of the mythical Prince Rama, who is an incarnation of the Hindu god Vishnu. It combines art, entertainment, religion, and politics. Influences of the *Ramayana* in Thailand are found in bas-relief sculpture as early as the thirteenth century. The importance of the epic in Thai culture is also seen in other types of art works such as temple murals, most notably those found on the walls surrounding the temple compound of *Wat Phra Keow*, the Temple of the Emerald Buddha, in Bangkok.

The *Ramakien*, the uniquely Thai version of the *Ramayana*, was formally created in writing after the defeat of the Thai by the Burmese in 1767, partly to help achieve the goal of social and political unification. This version was completed in 1798 under the auspices of King Rama II. Performances were held only within the royal court until after the Revolution of 1932. The government then established the Department of Fine Arts (*Krom Silpakorn*) under the Ministry of Education. With the establishment of a constitutional monarchy in 1934,

Thai classical dance is closely associated with Thai culture and is very expressive of Thai artistic ideals. As in much of Asia, Thai classical dance is associated with drama and stories, and there are stylized gestures and movements which interpret the narrative. The movements are controlled, graceful, and rather angular. The classical styles developed from folk dances and later incorporated hand gestures as well as arm and leg movements of the classical Indian *Bharata Natayasastra*. Thai classical dance costumes are elaborate, colorful, and richly embroidered and include either masks or elaborate headdresses.

Classical dance in Thailand falls into two main theatrical categories, *khon* and *lakhon*. *Khon* is masked dance drama which portrays episodes from the Ramakien, the Thai version of the Indian epic Ramayana. *Lakhon* is dance-drama in various styles. Classical *khon* was originally performed by men, while a type of *lakhon* known as *lakhon nai* ("dance-drama of the inside" or "inner theater") was performed in the royal dance and music were transferred from the Bureau of the Royal Household to the Department of Fine Arts, which took over the training and production of dance and dance-drama.

The story of the *Ramakien* is known to Thai from their childhood years, through school, children's books, and even comic books. An important method of portrayal both in the past and present is in various forms of puppet theater. The performers wear war costumes and *Khon* masks, which are considered sacred objects possessing supernatural power. *Khon* masks are three-dimensional and cover the entire head. *Khon* is accompanied by *piphat* orchestra, consisting of *ranat* (xylophones), *pi* (oboe), *taphon* (drum), *khong wong* (gong circles), *ching* (finger cymbals) and *klong* (two drums). Several singers and narrators recite the story and dialogue in rhyme.

Lakhon, dance-drama originally performed only by women, now includes both men and women. *Lakhon* is romantic and social in its themes and portrays messages based in Buddhism. Instead of masks and war costumes, *Lakhon* dancers wear make-up and royal costumes. While *Khon* performers emphasize leg and body movements and martial steps, *Lakhon* dancers emphasize hand and arm movements. The major traditional genre of *Lakhon* is *Lakhon ram*, which includes not only a chorus and solo singers to provide the narrative but poetic dialogue spoken by the dancers. Stories performed in traditional *lakhon ram* are taken from *Jataka* tales (previous lives of the Buddha), usually about the adventures and romances of kings and princes in Buddha's previous lives. *Lakhon* is accompanied by *piphat* orchestra.

There are other forms of *Lakhon*, such as *Lakhon nora*, from the South, which tells the story of a *kinaree* (a supernatural half-bird half-human) princess and her escape from an evil king through her wit. *Lakhon nok* ("outer theater") uses elements of the classical tradition but is most likely to be performed in rural areas. Variants of *Lakhon* can take place in a ritual context, especially at the *Erawan* shrine or the City Pillar (*Luk Mueang*) in Bangkok. In this case, performances are sponsored by people making a wish or fulfilling a vow.

Thai dancers, in both folk and classical styles, hold their bodies straight from the neck to the hips and move up and down with knees bent and opening outwards. The arms and hands are kept in curves at different levels. Male and female characters have different styles of these curves and angles, with the male being wide and open and the female narrow and closed. Basic hand gestures include closed fingers (thumb and index) and opened fingers.

Thai dancers undergo rigorous training, usually starting from the age of eight or ten. The Department of Fine Arts oversees the education of students in dance and dance-drama. Classical dance, *Khon*, and *Lakhon*, as well as folk dance, music, and art are taught in fine arts schools (*Witthayalai Natasin*) in Bangkok and in branches in the four major regions of the country. Students study regular subjects in the morning followed by dance, music and art instruction in the afternoon. Students receive either a certificate of dance or a bachelor's degree depending on how far they pursue their studies.

Students begin their training with a foundation series of dance movements called "slow movements" (*phleng cha*) and "fast movements" (*phleng reo*). They repeat the onomatopoetic sounds of the *taphon* drum as they perform the basic movements. They then learn the basic patterns of dance for the type of character they will portray. Students studying *Khon* are taught to play the part of the character-type for which they are best suited: hero, heroine, demon, or monkey. Girls studying *Lakhon* specialize in either male or female roles, as the styles of movement and gesture differ.

Dancers must learn the language of hand gestures. There are fixed gestures which interpret the stories and express the characters' emotions. Though the dancers must follow strict patterns of movements and gestures, each dancer must practice how best to interpret the story and character. There is still room for individual interpretation and creativity of expression.

Dancers and musicians, and indeed all Thai students, must perform a ceremony known as *wai khru* ("paying respect to the teachers") before beginning their study. Students not only pay homage to their human teachers but to deceased masters in their teachers' lineage as well as spiritual teachers, including Buddhist, Hindu, and animist spirits. The Hindu spirits are represented by an altar of *Khon* masks. The *wai khru* takes place annually, by tradition always on a Thursday. In addition, dancers perform a brief ceremony paying respect to the deities residing in the *Khon* masks before all performances of *Ramakien* origin and other special occasions.

Performances of Thai classical dance and dance drama take place often at the National Theatre and other theaters as well as at temples, schools, and universities throughout the country. It is always included in performances representing Thai culture to visitors in cultural venues and restaurants. Finely crafted models of *Khon* masks and classical dancers are prized by Thai and visitors alike. Thai classical dance remains at the heart of Thai culture.

A teacher initiates new students of Thai music at the annual *wai khru* "teacher greeting" ceremony at Bangkok's Chulalongkorn University (Andrew Shahriari)

Arrival: Laos and Northeast Thailand

Various historical events, including the European colonization of much of Southeast Asia, led to the Lao people being separated into two areas. Currently, only about five million live in sparsely populated Laos north and east of the mighty Maekhong River, while approximately thirteen million live in the northeast region of Thailand. This resulted from a number of wars and invasions from about 1775 to 1830, when the Siamese Thai defeated the Lao and forcibly moved much of the population to sparsely settled northeast Thailand. The people of both countries share a common language, cuisine, literature, and traditional way of life, but the two populations are also now quite different due to their political separation. Until the 1970s both areas where the Lao people are concentrated were equally undeveloped: Laos was a French colony until 1949 with no modern infrastructure while the northeast of Thailand was that country's most neglected region. After 1975, when the Royal Lao government fell to the communist Pathet Lao, Laos went backward economically and is only now beginning to recover, whereas Northeast Thailand's level of development was raised dramatically by Thailand's booming economy and the government's new attention to the region after the 1970s. Indeed, the northeast now includes two of Thailand's largest cities—Khon Kaen and Nakhon Ratchasima (known also as Khorat).

Of the six million plus people in Laos, a significant number live in the uplands—which account for much of the country's terrain—and speak non-Lao languages. The ethnic Lao live in the lowland areas, primarily along the Maekhong and its tributaries. Because the Lao are primarily farmers, growing glutinous (also called sticky) rice in wet paddy fields, the cities are small and economically dominated by Vietnamese and Chinese. Vientiane, the capital and largest city, has only about 700,000 residents. With infrastructure being so underdeveloped, Lao culture has developed regionally, giving rise to more than a dozen local musical styles.

Northeast Thailand, commonly known as **Isan**, is primarily a flat plateau, and although subject to dramatic variations in weather—drought to flood—facilitates easier travel. With modern development has come the growth of the media and the rise of a vibrant popular music culture drawn from its traditional music. While the people of both Isan and Laos share the same cultural roots, those of Isan are strongly oriented toward Bangkok and the dominant culture. Since World War II great numbers of young Isan people have migrated to Bangkok seeking employment in factories, in construction, as maids, and as taxi drivers, bringing with them their musical culture.

ISAN (pronounced *ee-sahn*) A term referring to Northeast Thailand and its regional culture, including music.

Explore More

The *Ramayana*: An Indian Epic from a Southeast Asian Perspective

One of the great epics of world literature is the *Ramayana*, a story based on Hindu mythology and believed to be more than 3,000 years old. Originating in India, this tale spread throughout much of South and Southeast Asia and is fundamental to understanding many elements of the cultures of the region. The *Ramayana*'s influence has been profound. Social and moral codes exemplified in the stories and characters of the *Ramayana* shaped political structures, city planning, marriage customs, and basic human interaction for centuries. Indeed, the present king of Thailand is known as Rama IX, after the *Ramayana*'s main character.

Scenes found in the *Ramayana* inspire much artistic activity in Myanmar, Cambodia, Laos, and Indonesia, as well as Thailand, in the visual arts, dance, and music. In Thailand, where the story is called *Ramakian*, *Khon*, the most important classical genre of entertainment, is based on this work. Performed monthly at the National Theater in Bangkok, *khon* features masked dancers who enact a different scene from the epic with each performance to the accompaniment of a *piphat* ensemble. The dancers do not speak while on stage; rather, a vocalist chants/sings the story as the actors mime the epic's best-known scenes. *Khon* has become symbolic of the arts in Thailand; it is performed by students and professional performers in tourist

Scene from a *khon* masked dance performance of the *Ramakian*, Thailand's version of the Indian epic *Ramayana*, at the Siam Society. Rama (right) with the "good" demon Pipek (rear), Rama's brother, Lakshmana (left), and fallen monkey warrior, Sukreep

shows, school plays, and television broadcasts, as well as in festivals and other cultural programs overseas.

Although countless variations exist, the basic storyline of the *Ramayana* is as follows: Prince Rama, an incarnation of the Hindu god Vishnu, retreats to the forest at his father's request for several years accompanied by his wife, Sita, and brother, Lakshmana. During his exile, Sita is kidnapped by the evil demon Ravana (Totsakan in the Thai version) after the two brothers are lured from her protection by a golden deer. Ravana takes Sita to his island fortress, Lanka, where he tries to persuade her to marry him, but she refuses as she is loyal to her husband and confident in her rescue. During her capture, Sita dropped a clue for a watching band of monkeys who aid Rama in rescuing his wife. Key among these characters is Hanuman, the white monkey god who has many supernatural powers. Hanuman's adventures are numerous as he searches for Sita. He eventually discovers where Sita is imprisoned and returns to Rama to aid in a great battle with Ravana's demons. Allied with the monkeys and bears of the forest, Rama defeats Ravana's demon army, kills Ravana, and rescues the princess.

The conclusion of the story varies depending on the region. In the Indian version, Rama and Sita return to his kingdom together, but rumors casting doubt on Sita's fidelity while imprisoned force her to undergo a trial by fire to prove her loyalty. Although she passes the test, Rama still exiles her to prevent his rule from being undermined by rumors that continue to persist. In the Thai version, Rama and Sita are reunited after the trial by fire and live happily ever after.

Mural scene from the epic *Ramakian* at the Temple of the Emerald Buddha in Bangkok. The performance scene shows a *piphat* ensemble and the large shadow puppets that actually depict the *Ramakian* story

Mr. Ken Somjindah plays the northeastern Thai *khaen* with sixteen pipes in See-Kaeo village, Roi-et province, Thailand

Earlier looked down upon as inferior and rustic, Isan culture is now viewed positively, and its attractive music (along with its food) was a principal reason.

Music in Isan includes both old-fashioned forms and many newer ones—including pop songs featuring troupes of dancing women, a rock combo, and bright lights. Even the modern types often appear in a traditional context, however, such as a Buddhist or New Year's festival. Our audio example exemplifies the most important older form of traditional singing that was popular until the 1990s, when it was eclipsed by more modern styles, but people today continue to honor this style by showcasing it at cultural events and local festivals.

Site 4: *Lam Klawn* Repartee Singing

First Impressions. Many first-time listeners will find the sound of the instrument heard in *lam klawn*, known as the *khaen*, relatively familiar, likening it to a harmonica or a pump organ. The instrument seems to play harmony, a musical concept usually reserved for European-inspired traditions. The two vocalists—one male, one female—have a slightly nasal quality and often seem to be speaking their lyrics between extended melismatic phrases. As the music moves into a more regular rhythm, their performance seems more like a Southeast Asian "freestyle rap" than melodic singing.

141

KHAEN
A bamboo free-reed mouth organ from Northeast Thailand and Laos.

Aural Analysis. Playing **khaen** practically defines being Lao because it is the culture's most significant instrument. The *khaen* is a free-reed bamboo mouth organ ranging in length from about 23 inches (0.6 meter) to more than 3 feet (one meter). It has sixteen thin, hollow bamboo tubes fitted into a carved, hardwood windchest with the pipes wrapped at three points with a kind of wide, dried grass. Each bamboo tube has a small, rectangular hole cut into its wall fitted with a thin plate of copper-silver alloy into which is cut a three-sided tongue, the "reed" (technically, a "free reed") that produces the sound as it vibrates. With the reeds sealed into the windchest with a black insect wax, the reed tongue vibrates in its frame when the player either inhales or exhales through the windchest. Each tube has an open finger hole, but its reed only sounds when the finger hole is covered. Since many finger holes can be covered at once, the *khaen* is capable of clusters of pitches which form sounds analogous to Western chords, that is, harmony.

Both Lao and Isan singers perform *lam*, an age-old kind of singing in which the melody is generated according to a basic pattern coordinated with the lexical tones of the words. (Lao and Thai are tonal languages, meaning that each syllable has, in addition to consonants and vowels, a tonal inflection. Without this inflection, the word's meaning may be unclear or erroneous.) The language is Lao as spoken in Northeast Thailand, which has six tones. The term *maw* denotes someone with a skill, and thus a singer is a *mawlam* and a *khaen* player is a *mawkhaen*. There are numerous genres of *lam* among the Lao, both in Laos and in Isan; the one heard here is performed by a pair of singers—one male and one female—and is called **lam klawn** (poetry singing) or *lam khu* (pair singing). Although *lam klawn* has lost much of its popularity during the last twenty years as several modernized genres of *lam* have become the rage among the younger generation, it is still performed for special events and embodies Isan–Lao traditions better than any other form.

LAM KLAWN
(pronounced *lum glawn*)
Vocal repartee with *khaen* accompaniment from Northeast Thailand.

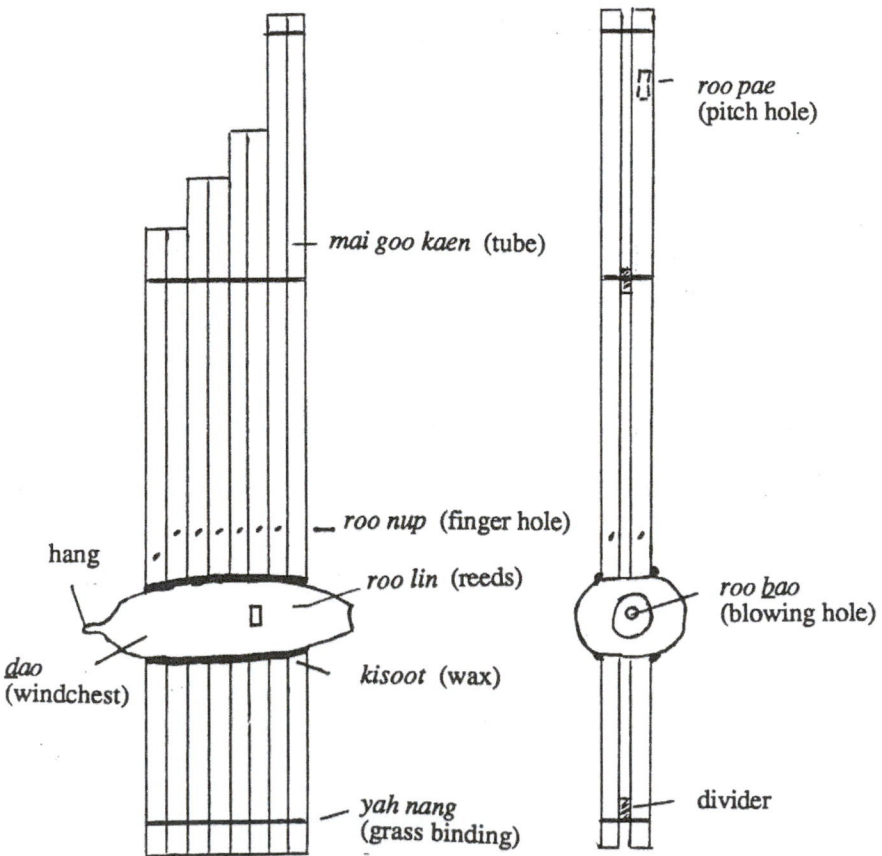

The *khaen* shown in side view and front view with parts labeled

As seen in this 1973 photo of old-fashioned *lam*, a female *mawlam* singer, accompanied by *khaen*, performs on a small temporary stage at a Northeast Thai Buddhist temple in Mahasarakham, Thailand. Her male counterpart dances next to her

Old-fashioned traditional performances of *lam* began around 9.00 p.m. and continued to nearly 6.00 a.m. The performance took place on a temporary stage, and the singers and *khaen*-players stood to perform. When the male sings, the female usually performs a simple but graceful dance, and vice versa. The performance proceeds in three sections, the first lasting most of the night. Called *lam thang san* (literally "short-way singing"), this first section consists of the male and female vocalists singing in alternation (known as a "repartee"), each beginning a section with an unmeasured introduction, usually on the phrase, "*O la naw*," followed by the main poem in meter. The scale is pentatonic and could be described as C, D, E, G, A (or 1, 2, 3, 5, 6), with C (1) as the "home" pitch. The meter is always duple. Singers memorize vast amounts of poetry, all written in four-line stanzas with a rhyme scheme peculiar to Lao poetry. The example here excerpts the beginnings of *lam thang san* for both male and female singers.

Site 6.4

Thailand: *Lam Klawn* Repartee Singing

Vocals: Single male, single female
Instruments: *Khaen* (free-reed aerophone, i.e., mouth organ)

TIME	LISTENING FOCUS
0'00"	*Khaen* enters with improvisatory free rhythm. Listen for the three musical elements of drone, chord accompaniment (polyphony), and melody.
0'04"	Male vocalist enters with improvisatory free rhythm on a single non-lexical syllable ("O"), using a three-pitch melodic line to establish the tonal center.
0'14"	Vocalist continues improvisation with extended melismatic phrase, "*O la naw*."
0'30"	Vocalist introduces some poetic verse while the *khaen* continues to play in free rhythm.
0'55"	Melismatic improvisation on the phrase "*O la naw*," again with a brief verse to close the phrase.
1'14"	Vocalist transitions to the metered section with poetic verse.
1'19"	*Khaen* follows the vocalist with duple-metered performance and regular melodic content.
1'46"	Example briefly fades. Normally, the male vocalist sings for several minutes before the female vocalist enters.
1'48"	*Khaen* enters with improvisatory free rhythm. Listen for the change in mode (i.e., the pitches utilized).
1'53"	Female vocalist enters with melismatic improvisation on the phrase "*O la naw*," sung in free rhythm.
2'07"	Vocalist introduces some poetic verse while the *khaen* continues to play in free rhythm.
2'27"	Melismatic improvisation on the words "*O la naw*," again with a brief verse to close the phrase.
2'44"	Vocalist transitions to the metered section with poetic verse.
2'48"	*Khaen* follows the vocalist with duple-metered performance and regular melodic content.
3'00"	Example fades, though the female vocal section would normally continue for several minutes.

Source: "Lam thang san" (excerpts), sung by Saman Hongsa (male) and Ubon Hongsa (female), and played by Thawi Sidamni, *khaen*; recorded by Terry E. Miller in Mahasarakham, Thailand, 1988.

MUSICAL MARKERS: Timbre/Medium—"Mellow, but peppy" harmonica-like timbre of the mouth organ. **Text Setting**—Each vocalist begins with freely rhythmic "Oh La Naw" melisma before transitioning to a syllabic sung poetry. **Phonic structure**—Mouth organ plays three parts—underlying drone, "chords" to accentuate rhythm, and higher ranged melody.
ETHNO-CHALLENGE: Learn the melismatic style of the vocalists by matching the introductory phrases ("*O la naw*"). Clap the beat during the metered sections of the performance.

Cultural Considerations. There is a saying about the Lao people: if a man lives in a house on stilts, eats sticky rice, and plays the *khaen*, he is a Lao. Traditionally, the Thai, Lao, Khmer, Burmese, and even Malay lived in houses built on stilts, partly for protection, partly to provide a shelter for their animals beneath. Sticky, or glutinous, rice, however, is peculiar to the Lao; the rest of Asia eats ordinary rice.

Lam klawn is not merely entertainment, even though it can be highly enjoyable. While a performance often takes the form of an imaginary courtship between the singers, and can involve earthy double entendres, it also addresses many essential aspects of Lao life. The vocalists often "discuss" or debate (in sung verse) matters of history, religion, literature, politics, geography, etiquette, and excerpts of famous stories, sometimes, but not always, offering listeners a model of approved thinking and behavior. Here is a typical example of love poetry, sung by a female:

> *O la naw* [introductory words without meaning] You are a handsome one. Please divorce your wife and then marry me. I will also divorce my husband and we will marry each other; can you? *O la naw*, you are a handsome man. One day I looked at the stars in the clear night and found the moon and many stars. But for myself, I could find no one.
>
> (Translation by Jarernchai Chonpairot)

As recently as the 1980s, *lam* was enjoyed by people of all ages throughout Northeast Thailand. Before Northeast Thai villages acquired electricity, entertainment was scarce, and everyone availed themselves of the chance to hear live music. In Laos the old days remain because there has been less development; the situation there remains much as it was in Isan thirty years ago. In Northeast Thailand, *lam* was most often heard during the cool or warm dry seasons (November to April), in conjunction with various events including monk ordinations, Buddhist festivals, the New Year (Western, Chinese, and Thai), an annual temple fair, and even funerals. People gathered and sat on the ground around the stage, which was open on four sides and the grounds were flanked by vendors selling snacks. As the *lam* performance progressed without breaks, audience members ate, slept, snacked, wandered off, flirted, or gossiped.

This form of *lam* lost popularity in the later 1980s as electricity—and thus radio and television—became widespread, and as a type of popular song called *luk thung* (see Site 5) became the rage. *Lam* singers fought back, creating a new fast-paced, popularized, brightly lit genre called **lam sing** (*sing* meaning "racing" or anything that is fast). *Lam sing* and other modernized genres have since swept Northeast Thailand, although they have barely penetrated Laos. Because there are so many Isan people living and working in Bangkok, *lam sing* and its related genres have also become well known there and throughout Thailand. As a result, Isan music in particular and Isan culture (and food) in general have become popular. Even McDonalds in Thailand for a period offered the now famous Isan green papaya salad called *somtam*.

LAM SING (pronounced *lum sing*) A popular music form from Northeast Thailand.

Site 5: *Luk Thung* Popular Song

First Impressions. As the song starts, it sounds vaguely like the *lam* poetic verse heard in the previous track. But with the addition of drums, other instruments, and harmony this suggests popular song with an attractive, danceable beat. Those who are accustomed to current forms of American popular music may find this style old-fashioned and folky, but it is among the most attractive of current pop styles in Thailand, especially among people living in or from the northeast region.

Aural Analysis. Melodically, the accompaniment stays close to the traditional style of the *khaen* mouth organ heard in the previous track but here it is played by an electric guitar. During the later 1980s, when this song first appeared, musicians had not yet adapted the traditional plucked lute of the northeast, the **phin**, into a useable electric form, but the guitar heard in this track clearly imitates the style of the *phin*. Accompaniment is provided by a basic rock combo that includes a keyboard synthesizer, electric bass, and drum set. The scale form heard is pentatonic but unlike that of the *lam* in the previous track. Here it sounds minor, having the pitches A, C, D, E, and G, with A as the "home" pitch; sometimes it also uses pitch B in passing.

PHIN (pronounced *pin*) A fretted, plucked lute from Northeast Thailand.

The song's title, "Sao Chan Kang Kop," translates as "Miss Chan's Broken Heart." It was released in 1986 by male singer Phawnsak Sawng-saeng (b. 1960) who was born and raised in Isan's Khon Kaen province. After 1981, with three albums of *luk thung isan* songs—country

The three most common musical instruments of Northeast Thailand, left to right: *saw pip* (fiddle), *phin* (lute), and *khaen* (free-reed mouth organ)

songs that used the Isan language but little of any local style—he switched to the new *mawlam* style for this album. Because *luk thung mawlam* remains immensely popular, Phawnsak's popularity has held over a long period as well, and this song retains its popularity today. While the title suggests a broken heart, *kangkop* literally means "to shade one's eyes," referring to the female protagonist constantly looking into the distance for her Bangkok lover, who broke his promises to follow her back to Isan. The lyrics imply that she was too easy in giving in to the demands of her selfish boyfriend who left her without saying "goodbye" after exploiting her. She constantly looks into the distance, searching for him. The singer, however, speaks as a local village boy who did his best to warn her of the dangers of Bangkok, of city people, and especially of central Thai. He says "I warned you but you never listened to me. Instead you got mad at me. Now, see! You deserve what happened."

Most of the lyrics are in northeast Thai/Isan dialect (Lao) and set to a flexible version of a traditional melody called *lam toei phama*, literally "Burmese toei." About halfway through, however, the style changes abruptly to a typical *luk thung* melody similar to such tunes found throughout Thailand. Even within the *toei* sections, however, the singer switches between central Thai and northeast Thai several times. After the pop melody, he returns to the *toei* melody before repeating both sections.

Cultural Considerations. Thai popular music developed out of the ballroom dance music that began to be created in the 1940s by the Suntaraphon Band. With their sophisticated poetic texts, these songs came to be called *luk krung*, literally "city children." During the 1950s some composers began creating songs with poetry that commented on the lives of the working people, both farmers and city people, using more direct and casual words. These were first called *phleng talat* ("market songs") but later came to be called *phleng luk thung* ("rice field children"). Today outsiders call these "country songs," and in many ways the allusion to Nashville is justified. But while country songs originated in central Thailand, especially in Bangkok, the present track comes from the northeast, culturally Lao and commonly called Isan. Because this song shows a clear

Two "classic" *luk thung* covers: (left) Four *luk thung* artists, one holding the *khaen* mouth organ as a reminder of *luk thung's* connections to traditional northeast Thai music; (right) scene of traditionally dressed singer with drawing of old fashioned village and water buffalos

Luk thung pop songs are part of the performance of *lam sing*, a modernized form of the traditional lam klawn repartee. This performance took place on a temporary village stage on New Year's Eve southwest of Mahasarakham, Thailand

relationship with traditional *mawlam*, it is a *luk thung mawlam*, the current favorite among both immigrants from Isan living in Bangkok and back home in the villages and towns of the northeast. Some of the artists singing these started in traditional *lam* but crossed over into *luk thung*.

    Luk thung songs have no clear point of origin, but their predecessors, found from the 1940s onward, were those Thai popular "market" songs (also called *phleng sakon*, "modern songs") that had unsophisticated texts and often commented on the lives of common working people, including farmers. Like the "city songs" with their sophisticated poetry, many were in ballroom dance tempo, especially cha-cha-cha and rumba. Others derived from the music for a central Thai couple dance called *ramwong* ("circle dance"), which had its origins in the 1940s. They differed in that *ramwong* songs were accompanied by small percussion only—principally a small clay drum—while *luk thung* used melodic instruments as well.

147

6 WORLD MUSIC: A GLOBAL JOURNEY

LISTENING GUIDE 6.5 (3'17")

Site 6.5
Thailand (Northeast): *Luk Thung* Popular Song

Voice: Single male
Instruments: Electric *phin* (plucked lute), keyboard synthesizer, electric bass, rock drum set with *klawng fifa* (electric drums), *chab lek* (cymbals)

TIME	LISTENING FOCUS
0'00"	(Intro section) Drum set, electric bass, and synthesizer begin with a steady beat in common meter. Listen for the melodic shift of the synthesizer (0'10").
0'17"	(A section, "*toei*") Electric *phin* enters followed by the vocalist who sings in the Central Thai language. The text setting is syllabic and the rhythmic density of the voice in this section is thick in comparison to the B section (below). Note also that the synthesizer sustains a single pitch to provide a strong tonal center.
0'40"	(A section) Section repeats with different lyrics sung in the Isan language.
1'12"	(B section, "*luk thung*") The rhythmic density of the voice lessens and is more melodic. The lyrics are again sung in the Central Thai language. Note the synthesizer plays a complementary melodic line.
1'40"	A section returns with the lyrics sung in the Isan language.
2'05"	B section returns with the lyrics sung in the Central Thai language.
2'32"	A section returns with the lyrics sung in the Isan language.
2'59"	(Outro section) Opening content returns to finish the performance.

Source: "Sao Jan Kang Kop" sung by Phawnsak Sawng-saeng, from *Sao Jan Kang Kop*, JKC Marketing Co., Ltd, JKC-CD 157 (nd), used by permission.

MUSICAL MARKERS: Timbre/Medium—"Popular music" instruments (synthesizer, electric "guitar," drum set) with a nasal lead vocalist. The distinctive "chwae" sound of the cymbals. **Text Setting**—Tends toward syllabic "poetry" singing, as with the lam klawn singing above. **Rhythm**—Simple duple meter. "Chwae-chwae-chwae" rhythmic pattern common to Thai folk and popular music.
ETHNO-CHALLENGE: Investigate *Luk Thung* artists and popular music from Thailand via the Internet to find the karaoke video associated with this example.

During the later 1960s and early 1970s singers took traditional regional styles from the north, south, and northeast and began infusing them into their pop songs. Besides the usual combo instruments—drums, electric guitar, and, later, keyboard—some added regional instruments; whether these were present or not, composers imitated the styles of local instruments. Many *luk thung* singers had a background in traditional genres and crossed over when it became apparent there was money to be made. *Luk thung* from the north and south, however, declined in popularity, while those from the northeast became increasingly favored, eventually coming to dominate the Thai media in the 1980s. This process snowballed because tens of thousands of northeasterners had been migrating to Bangkok over the years as Thailand developed into an "Asian Tiger" economy. These economic refugees, many of whom became relatively prosperous, became a natural market for all manner of *luk thung*-related media products and events. These included *luk thung* movies, live *luk thung* shows, and, of course, *luk thung* cassettes, CDs and VCDs. Get into most any taxi in Bangkok and you will hear northeast *luk thung* songs on the radio or on recording, because most taxi drivers come from the northeast. Go into the servants' quarters of an upper-class house or into factories and you will encounter them as well.

148

Each stanza of the song includes a switch from the Lao language of the Northeast (called *Isan*) to central Thai. When this song first appeared, the central Thai still looked down on Northeasterners, seeing them as country bumpkins. By singing part of the song in central Thai, the singer demonstrates that he is bilingual and therefore "respectable." By the advent of the twenty-first century attitudes had changed, and it is now "respectable" to sing in the Isan language alone.

Luk thung has given rise to star singers who, in spite of the sparseness in which they grew up, have become quite wealthy singing songs that express the feelings and humble lives of their compatriots. Early favorites who solidified the style in central Thailand include the late female singer Pompuang Duangjan and the late male singer Suraphon Sombatjalern. Today there are too many *luk thung* singers to mention, some making recordings and being heard throughout the land, others singing their songs in local restaurants and clubs in gritty upcountry towns. *Luk thung* shows nearly superseded traditional *mawlam* by the late 1980s, and traditional performers, because they receive little government support even as honored "culture carriers," had to change in order to stay in business. The traditional theater genres of Isan also adopted *luk thung* songs into their format, as did the *lam klawn* genre, with its alternating male and female singers. Because Isan was producing the most popular type of music in Thailand, many people in the other regions modified their stereotype of Isan as a backwater full of poor rice farmers and came to see it instead as a hotbed of stylish young musicians.

Arrival: Indonesia (Java and Bali)

Map of Indonesia. Note locale of Java and Bali

Indonesia, the largest archipelago in the world, consists of more than 13,000 islands created by centuries of volcanic activity, which continues to this day, sometimes resulting in devastating tsunamis that engulf coastal areas. Though many of these islands are uninhabited, the larger islands, especially Sumatra and Java, are densely populated, making Indonesia the world's largest Muslim nation with 240 million people. The first-time visitor will be struck immediately by the extreme heat and humidity, due to Indonesia's position on the equator and its sea-level elevation. Tropical rainforests, vast parts of which are burned each year, enveloping parts of Southeast Asia in dense smog, are found in many of the areas, along with mist-shrouded mountains and volcanoes, white sand beaches with spectacular offshore underwater reefs, colorful flowers, and

Dancers at the Akademi Seni Tari Indonesia (College of Indonesian Dance) in Yogyakarta, Java, Indonesia, perform a refined court dance (R. Anderson Sutton)

unique wildlife such as orangutans on less-populated islands. The heavy annual rainfall helps support an agricultural system largely based on wet rice cultivation, which together with seafaring activity provides the mainstays of Indonesian cuisine.

Indonesia recognizes several religions: Islam, Hinduism, Buddhism, Christianity, and a variety of animistic traditions, each with its own varied cultural activities. Throughout the main islands of Java and Sumatra, Islam gave rise to the courts of the sultans who were the traditional patrons of the arts. Bali, however, preserves an even richer tradition of music, dance, and theater associated with the Hinduism that makes the tiny island so distinctive. Though there are over 300 languages spoken throughout the islands, the national language is Bahasa Indonesia, an Austronesian language common throughout the region and essentially the same as Malay peninsula. English is widely spoken as well in areas frequented by tourists, but the colonial language, Dutch, has virtually disappeared.

The music of Indonesia, which is dominated by ensembles of bronze instruments, is perhaps the most studied and best known in academia of all world music traditions. Many pioneer ethnomusicologists, such as Jaap Kunst, Colin McPhee, and Mantle Hood, took an early interest in the music of Indonesia and spread knowledge of it through writings, teaching, and their own musical compositions. Various composers, including Claude Debussy, Benjamin Britten, Francis Poulenc, Philip Glass, and Steve Reich, have also acknowledged the influence of Indonesian music on their works. Indonesian music has therefore greatly affected the development of modern music in Europe and America, and its influence can still be heard in everything from orchestral music to television commercials.

GAMELAN
An ensemble from Indonesia comprised primarily of membranophones and metallophones.

Although there are hundreds of distinct musical traditions found throughout the numerous islands of Indonesia, the most recognized music is that of the **gamelan** ensemble. We will focus on two traditions, Javanese court gamelan and Balinese *gamelan gong kebyar*, in order to introduce this intricate and entrancing music.

Site 6: Javanese Court Gamelan

A Javanese gamelan accompanies a performance of shadow puppet theater (wayang kulit) for visitors to a museum in Yogyakarta (Getty Images)

Performers of Javanese dance drama, accompanied by gamelan, make nightly presentations for tourists in Yogyakarta, site of the Sultan's palace and center of cultural tourism in Java

An intimate and permanent stage offers nightly performances of Java's shadow theater (*wayang kulit*), in Yogyakarta. Visitors may view the action from both behind the screen and in front, the latter position showing only the shadows

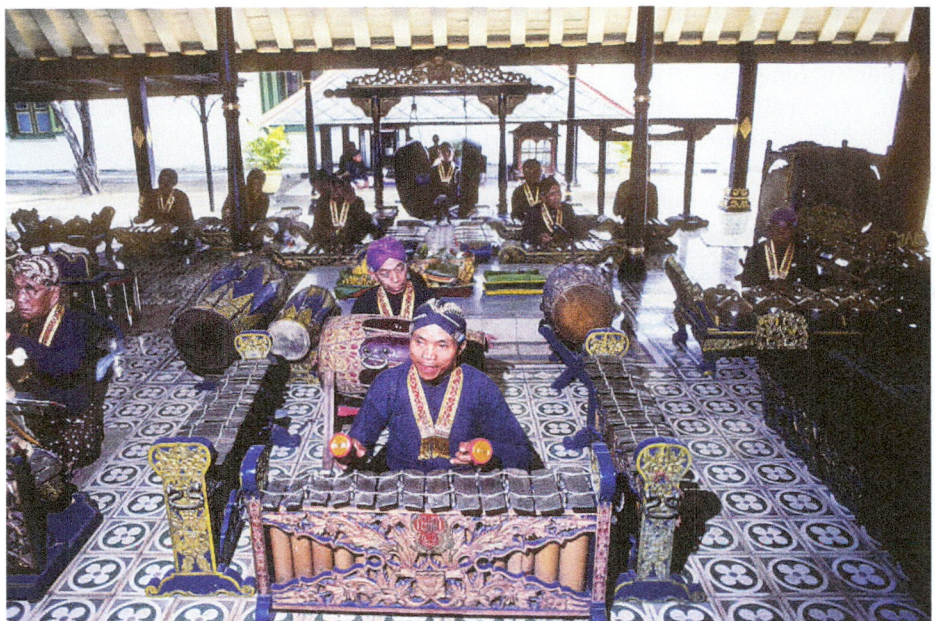

A Javanese gamelan at the *kraton* (palace) of the Sultan in Yogyakarta with a court musician seated at the *gender*, an instrument with bronze keys and tube resonators (Jack Vartoogian/ FrontRowPhotos)

First Impressions. A gamelan is an ensemble that primarily comprises idiophones made of either bronze or iron, including a variety of hanging gongs, rack gongs, and metal-keyed instruments. The ethereal sound of the instruments is hypnotic, as is the music's repeating cyclical structure. Other instruments, such as flutes, zithers, various drums, and a fiddle called the *rebab*, may also be present along with vocalists, both male and female. The voices, too, contribute an elegant air to the overall feel of the performance. The music of the Javanese court gamelan is divided into two basic styles, *soft* and *strong*. The soft style has a "misty" quality that is mellow and tranquil, reminiscent of an early morning fog lifting as the sun rises from the ocean. In contrast, the strong style is bold and loud; more reflective of the midday sun watching over hard-working rice farmers during a harvest.

Aural Analysis. Javanese court gamelan is based on a *colotomic structure*, meaning that its music is organized into cycles defined by periodic punctuation played by a specific instrument—in its case, hanging gongs. The principal melody is typically provided by either voices and/or melodic instruments, such as the rack gongs, metal-keyed instruments called metallophones, wooden-keyed instruments called xylophones, or non-idiophones such as the fiddle or bamboo flute. Other rack gongs, metallophones, and xylophones embellish this melody by filling in the aural space, giving the music its "misty" quality.

Javanese gamelan instruments must be built and tuned as a unit; interchanging instruments from one ensemble to another is not permitted due in large part to the individuality of the tuning. There are two primary tuning systems: *sléndro* (comprising five relatively equidistant pitches to an octave) and *pélog* (comprising seven pitches to an octave at non-equidistant intervals). Gamelan instruments tuned in one system cannot be played with a set tuned in the other. Furthermore, the fundamental frequencies of two different gamelan using the same system, for example, *pélog*, do not always match, so interchanging instruments even in this case is not possible. Indeed, individual gamelan sets have specific names (the one housed at UCLA in Los Angeles is "The Venerable Dark Cloud"), suggesting the instruments are to be thought of as part of one family. A complete ensemble includes a subset of instruments in both *sléndro* and *pélog* tunings,

153

which can be thought of as siblings in the same gamelan "family." The example here is in *sléndro* tuning—that is, it uses a five-tone pentatonic tuning/scale.

Our example includes two styles of Javanese court gamelan performance, described as *strong* and *soft*. Strong-style gamelan emphasizes the metallophones and bossed rack gongs, which carry the principal melody at a faster tempo and are struck powerfully. Although the soft-style gamelan, when the metal bars or gongs are struck with less force, often includes a female vocal soloist and a male chorus, this example does not. The non-idiophone instruments, namely the fiddle, zither, and bamboo flute, support the principal melody, and the tempo is slower than in the strong style.

After a brief introduction by a *bonang* (rack gong), the principal melody is loudly proclaimed. This melody can be simply notated using numbers to represent pitch. The full ensemble enters on the last pitch of the introduction, which is also the start/stop point of the cycle marked by the largest and deepest pitched hanging gong (*gong ageng*).

Principal Melody of Javanese Gamelan Audio Example

Introduction	- 1 1 1	5 6 1 2	2 1 6 5	6 1 6 5
A	6 5 3 2	6 5 3 2	2 3 5 3	6 5 3 2 (repeat)
punctuation		- * - -	- * - -	- * - +
B	1 5 6 1	5 6 1 2	2 1 6 5	6 1 6 5 (repeat)
punctuation		- * - -	- * - -	- * - +

* = upper hanging gong + = lower hanging gong

Each melodic line is repeated once before the entire melody is repeated (AA-BB-AA-BB-AA, etc.). Notice that the phrasing of the melody is symmetrical (there are two groups of four phrases with four beats each), exemplifying an emphasis on balance typical of Javanese music. Underlying this melody is the periodic punctuation provided by the hanging gongs (marked by * and +). These instruments punctuate specific points in the cycle to articulate the underlying aural framework of the piece. Falling between the pitches of the principal melody at twice the rhythmic density are the quiet embellishments of other metallophones and rack gongs. These three parts are most easily heard in the strong-style gamelan performance.

The soft-style section is signaled by the drums. The tempo slows and the quieter instruments become the aural focus, providing the principal melody along with the subdued sounds of the gongs. The colotomic structure and embellishing instruments are still present, but the shift in mood gives the music a haunting quality. The dynamic level diminishes with the slowed tempo and both increase again when the strong-style gamelan returns.

Cultural Considerations. Although the gamelan music of both Java and Bali uses similar instrumentation and is organized in structures governed by colotomic periods, the sharp contrast of musical characteristics between Javanese Court Gamelan and Balinese *gamelan gong kebyar* (see below) reveals strong differences in musical values. These values are in large part due to differences in the function and contextual associations of the two musics.

The population of Java is predominantly Muslim, though the Islam here is peculiar to Java. Javanese gamelan music is frequently associated with court ritual functions, usually presided over by a sultan. The sultan is regarded as a secular authority with divine powers, and his palace grounds are imbued with spiritual significance. The slow, stately sound of the court gamelan reflects the regal atmosphere of this environment, and the music is characteristically calm, to avoid distracting attention from the sultan or the ceremonial activity. The music serves the occasion rather than being the primary focus of the event.

Most often, gamelan performance accompanies dance and/or theatre. The *bedhaya* dance is among the most sacred, symbolizing the mythical union between an historical

LISTENING GUIDE

Site 6.6

Indonesia: Javanese Court Gamelan

Instruments: Full instrumental *gamelan* ensemble (metallophones, flutes/chordophones, drums)

TIME	LISTENING FOCUS
0'00"	*Bonang* (rack gongs) enter with a brief introduction.
0'05"	Full ensemble enters with principal melody (A), embellishments, and periodic punctuation. Listen for each of these musical elements during repeated listening. Use the table included in the Aural Analysis to follow the principal melody and periodic punctuation.
0'13"	Melodic phrase (A) repeats.
0'21"	Second phrase of principal melody (B).
0'28"	Melodic phrase (B) repeats.
0'35"	Melodic phrase (A) returns.
0'43"	Melody phrase (A) repeats.
0'51"	Melodic phrase (B) returns.
0'58"	Melodic phrase (B) repeats.
1'06"	Melodic phrase (A) returns.
1'14"	Melodic phrase (A) repeats. The tempo gradually slows in anticipation of the "soft-style" interlude.
1'27"	Melodic phrase (B) returns at a slower tempo.
1'31"	"Quieter" instruments, namely the *rebab* (fiddle), *celimpung* (plucked zither), and *suling* (flute), become the aural focus. The principal melody (B) continues, most easily identified by the low-pitched metallophones heard in the background. Listen for the *gong ageng* (lowest-pitched hanging gong) sounding the end of each phrase.
1'49"	Melodic phrase (B) repeats.
2'10"	Melodic phrase (A) returns.
2'32"	Melodic phrase (A) repeats.
2'54"	Melodic phrase (B) returns.
3'15"	Melodic phrase (B) repeats.
3'36"	Melodic phrase (A) returns.
3'56"	Melodic phrase (A) repeats. Drums quietly signal the reentrance of the louder metallophones.
4'02"	Drums play at a louder volume and the tempo increases as the metallophones gradually return as the aural focus (4'06").
4'11"	Melodic phrase (B) returns.
4'20"	Melodic phrase (B) repeats.
4'28"	Melodic phrase (A) returns.

4'36"	Melodic phrase (A) repeats.
4'45"	Melodic phrase (B) returns.
4'53"	Melodic phrase (B) repeats.
5'01"	Melodic phrase (A) returns.
5'09"	Melodic phrase (A) repeats at a lower dynamic level and slowing tempo to close the performance.

Source: "Udan Mas" ("Golden Rain"), from the recording titled *Music of the Venerable Dark Cloud: The Javanese Gamelan Khjai Mendung*. Institute of Ethnomusicology, UCLA, IER 7501, 1973. Used by permission.

MUSICAL MARKERS: Medium/Form—Gongs of varying sizes. Middle section includes quiet flutes and subtle "scratchy" strings.
Phonic Structure/Range—Layered heterophony. Busy "tinkie" of high-range metallophones, forceful "clang" of mid-range rack gongs, booming "Gong Ui" of low-range hanging gongs.
ETHNO-CHALLENGE: Imitate the upper and lower gongs utilized during the "periodic punctuation" heard throughout the example.

sultan and the goddess of the sea, an indication of pre-Islamic spiritual beliefs helping to legitimize Islamic secular authority. The slow-moving choreography and subtle gestures of the dancers express serenity and refinement, just as the gamelan itself demonstrates the tranquility and balance valued so highly in Javanese culture. Gamelan also accompanies shadow-puppet theatre, known as *wayang kulit*. The storylines for these productions often draw from the ancient Indian epics of the *Ramayana* (see above Explore More: The *Ramayana*) and the *Mahabharata*, similarly revealing the underlying Hindu influence on Javanese culture that pre-dates Islamic rule, which first appeared in Indonesia during the twelfth century.

Dancers at the Sultan's Kraton (palace) in Yogyakarta perform *bedhaya*, considered the "crown jewel" of Javanese court dances (Jack Vartgoogian/ FrontRowPhotos)

Site 7: Balinese *Gamelan Gong Kebyar*

First Impressions. Whereas the music of Java conveys a sense of tranquility, much music of Bali is filled with dynamic energy. Similar instruments are used, including bronze gongs, metallophones, flutes, and drums, but the character of the music continually shifts, with sudden bursts of brilliant virtuosity contrasting with airy melodic phrases. A feeling of continual agitation pervades the music as it accelerates, slows, crescendos, and relaxes. Then just when you think you have it figured out, the music again turns in an unanticipated direction.

Aural Analysis. Balinese **gamelan gong kebyar**, like the Javanese court gamelan, is organized according to a colotomic structure. However, this structure is not always as evident as with its Javanese counterpart. Many compositions are through-composed, meaning that the melody does not repeat in a series of continuous cycles. Also, *gamelan gong kebyar* frequently uses sectional solos in which different instruments, such as the drums and cymbals, flutes, metallophones, or rack gongs, are highlighted. This shifting orchestration emphasis, along with dynamic variation and sudden tempo changes, contributes to the sudden shifts of mood that characterize the Balinese gamelan style.

The high rhythmic density of Balinese *gamelan gong kebyar* is also a distinguishing characteristic. In many sections of a performance the musicians interlock their parts, so that multiple musicians playing identical instruments are required to produce a complete melodic line. For example, if Player X plays the odd-numbered pitches (1, 3, 5, 7) and Player Y plays the even-numbered pitches (2, 4, 6, 8), the players must interlock their pitches to play them in consecutive order from one to eight. This interlocking of melodic pitches, known as *kotekan*, enables the performers to create a high rhythmic density, so that the music sounds as if the melody is being played at a "superhuman speed"; indeed, it is often faster than a single player could perform. While this technique is used in Javanese gamelan as well, the super-thick rhythmic density is associated primarily with the Balinese style.

Another noticeable distinction of the Balinese *gamelan gong kebyar* is what might be described as the "shimmer effect." This shimmering sound is most evident in the wavering tones of the small metallophones on long sustained pitches. The effect is produced by the use of pairs of identical instruments tuned slightly apart. When the instruments are played simultaneously on the same pitch,

GAMELAN GONG KEBYAR
An ensemble type from Bali, Indonesia, primarily comprising metallophones and characterized by rhythmically dense performance technique.

Balinese gamelan at the "Full Moon Festival" in Bedulu village, Bali (Shutterstock)

Seated on the grass in an open field and dressed informally, a Balinese gamelan plays for activities at a public funeral for several individuals in a small town in Bali's southwest

the slight tuning difference in frequency produces a perceptible pulsation due to the minimal increase in volume as the pitch frequencies overlap. Therefore, a complete Balinese gamelan must include identical pairs of metallophones, with separate players on each instrument playing the same notes but with slightly different tuning. When coupled with the need for interlocking pitches, four or more musicians may be required to produce a complete melodic line.

A pair of *gendèr wayang* bronze-keyed idiophones with tube resonators used, with an identical pair (not shown) tuned slightly differently to produce shimmering sounds, to accompany the shadow play (*wayang kulit*)

At the Sidha Karya gamelan factory near Blahbutih, Bali, a master tuner fine tunes the "beats" heard when two bronze keys are of the same pitch but differ slightly to produce the ringing sound characteristic of Balinese gamelan

Cultural Considerations. While Java's population is chiefly Muslim, the island of Bali is predominantly Hindu. Temples are found throughout the island, each devoted to a particular Hindu deity. Most temples have a gamelan ensemble that is expected to perform for festivals or other events associated with the temple's deity or the Hindu faith. Frequently performances function as a musical offering, and the music is therefore intended to attract and entertain the deity as well as participants. The dynamic character and bright timbre of the Balinese *gamelan gong kebyar*, with its "superhuman speed" and bright, boisterous metallophones, becomes the center of attention. Dances accompanied by this and other Balinese gamelan styles, such as Gamelan semar pegulingan, are often vigorous and characteristically "angular," with quick movements of the head, arms, and legs. Such performances, too, are typically related to Hindu mythology and often involve spirit possession and demonstrations of supernatural power, particularly in masked drama performances, such as the *barong* dance.

159

LISTENING GUIDE

6.7 (4'01")

Site 6.7

Indonesia: Balinese *Gamelan Gong Kebyar*

Instruments: *Gangsa* (metallophones), *reyong* (rack gongs), *gong ageng* (pair of hanging gongs), *kempli* ("timekeeper" gong), *suling* (flute), and *kendang* (barrel-shaped drums)

TIME	LISTENING FOCUS
0'00"	*Gangsa* initiate performance.
0'04"	Double-interlocking technique (known as *kotekan*) on the *gangsa* first appears. A "timekeeper" gong is also heard providing a steady beat as lower-pitched metallophones enter.
0'10"	The largest of the *gong ageng* sounds, and the melodic instruments pause. Listen for the "shimmering" sustain of the metallophones.
0'14"	Melodic activity resumes.
0'20"	Another melodic pause and "shimmering" sustain. The *gangsa* become the aural focus, continuing with "start/stop" melodic activity.
0'53"	Lower metallophones and "timekeeper" gong return. The example continues, with frequent melodic pauses followed by "bursts" of melodic passages introduced by the *gangsa* and followed by the "timekeeper" gong and others.
2'00"	A new melodic section begins to anticipate entrance of full ensemble. A dancer often performs during this section of the music.
2'26"	Full ensemble enters, including *reyong* and drums.
2'38"	*Reyong* performs solo, utilizing the double-interlocking technique to achieve a thick rhythmic density.
2'58"	*Gong ageng* sounds briefly in the background.
3'00"	*Gangsa* return as aural focus. Tempo is slower.
3'07"	Drums sound to introduce return of full ensemble.
3'15"	Listen for the *suling* (flute) playing as the metal instruments play more quietly.
3'42"	Listen for the *gangsa's* more frequent use of syncopated rhythms, which generally corresponds to a dancer's movements.

Source: "Hudjan Mas," recorded in south Bali by a *gamelan gong kebyar* ensemble; from the recording titled *Gamelan Music of Bali*, Lyrichord CD 7179, n.d. Used by permission, Lyrichord Discs Inc.

MUSICAL MARKERS: Timbre/Medium—"Shimmering" metallophones and gongs. **Rhythmic Density**—"Super-human" speed sections contrasting with periods of silence. **Rhythm**—Steady gong "timekeeper" during the busier sections.
ETHNO-CHALLENGE: Try to perform the "superhuman" double-interlocking technique (*kotekan*) along with a friend by tapping your hands on a flat surface or by using a musical instrument, such as a piano or xylophone. Once successful, add another matching pair of performers.

Gamelan gong kebyar, which often accompanies dance performances, is a relatively recent musical style that first appeared in the early twentieth century. While numerous styles of gamelan exist on Bali, *kebyar*, translated as "to flare up" or "to flower," is by far the most prominent. The explosive character of the music and astounding displays of virtuosity by its musicians require hours and hours of practice to achieve precise performance. The music is carefully composed, though musical notation is not generally used, and rehearsals are intense, particularly in preparation for the frequent contests that attract ensembles from throughout the island. The high demand for this music encourages experimentation and continual creation of new music to the delight of tourists, locals, and academics alike. Many ensembles have found success touring internationally, presenting spectacular shows to audiences worldwide. The popularity of the *gamelan gong kebyar* has spread to academic institutions around the world as well, where student ensembles perform the music often with the assistance of a guest artist/composer direct from Bali who teaches the ensemble.

The respective styles of gamelan music from the islands of Java and Bali give listeners a strongly differing musical experience. Indeed, the contrast between the hypnotic serenity of the Javanese court gamelan and the entrancing dynamism of the Balinese *gamelan gong kebyar* is a testament to the creative power of Indonesian musicians, who have managed to create two very different musics out of similar resources.

The elaborate hand-carving at the center of a case for either a tromping or reyong/reong, the longest set of tuned bronze gongs requiring multiple players

In a valley of endless wood carving shops and factories, that founded by I Made Ada stands out. Each day a group of young performers assembles upstairs to practice gamelan. On this day two young students portrayed the revered barong, a mythological cat figure who is king of the gods and champions good over evil. In a full performance he is destined to fight Rangda, the demon queen

Behind the screen at a performance of wayang kulit, the shadow theater of Bali. Note the use of the old-fashioned oil lamp

KECAK
A Balinese theatrical performance of *The Ramayana*

Young dancers perform a Welcome Dance at the Full Moon Festival in Bedulu village, Bali (Shutterstock)

Explore More

Kecak: The Balinese "Monkey Chant"

The "Monkey Chant" has become one of the most popular tourist attractions on the island of Bali. Its performers, who are considered a kind of "human gamelan," act out scenes from the Indian epic the *Ramayana* (see Explore More box on p. 140) with minimal stage props and costumes. The name of the genre, **kecak**, is derived from the interlocking "cak" sounds of the performers as they imitate armies of monkey soldiers in a mythological battle of good versus evil. Other performers sound out the colotomic structure by imitating gongs of the gamelan ensemble. In addition to the monkey armies, whose performers are dressed merely with a black-and-white checkered sarong, there are costumed dancers who portray the major figures of the story. Such performances were originally intended as musical offerings to the Hindu

Kecak, the so-called "monkey chant" of Bali, is primarily performed for tourists. In this performance in Ubud, Hanuman, the famous white monkey general who defends Rama, is surrounded by men representing his monkey army.

deity Rama, a major character in the epic. This association, however, as well as the storyline, is typically unfamiliar to Bali's many visitors.

Questions to Consider

1. To what extent are the terms classical, folk, and popular appropriate labels for describing Southeast Asian musics?

2. What are some factors that help maintain traditional Southeast Asian music in the face of modernization?

3. Metrical cycles are characteristic of many Southeast Asian musics. How do they work in the sites reviewed?

4. How do the types of "heterophony" found in Vietnamese Tai Thu, Thai Piphat, and Javanese Gamelan differ?

5. Though Thailand and Vietnam are both part of Southeast Asia, what historical and cultural factors have determined the present musical differences?

6. Compare Javanese and Balinese Gamelan in terms of their function and use. How do their differing functions affect their respective musical styles?

Map of East Asia showing numbered study sites.

SEA OF OKHOTSK

Sakhalin Island

JAPAN

TOKYO

PACIFIC OCEAN

Sites 7 & 8

Site 6

Site 2

Site 4

Site 9

Site 3

Site 5

Site 1

Khabarovsk

Vladivostok

N. KOREA

S. KOREA

P'YONGYANG

SEOUL

BEIJING

Shanghai

T'AIPEI

TAIWAN

"FUJIAN"

Hong Kong

RYUKYU IS.

Irkutsk

Lake Baikal

ULAANBAATAR

MONGOLIA

Huang He

Chang Jiang

C H I N A

VIETNAM

LAOS

Mekong

BURMA (MYANMAR)

THAILAND

T I B E T

BHUTAN

BANGLADESH

Himalaya Mountains

NEPAL

KAZAKHSTAN

Lake Balkhash

KYRGYZSTAN

TAJIKISTAN

AFGHANISTAN

PAKISTAN

INDIA

China, Mongolia, Korea, Japan, Tibet

Beijing, China's "Forbidden City," constructed from 1406 to 1420, then served as the palace of the emperor and seat of government until 1912 with the fall of the final dynasty, the Qing. The "city" consists of nearly one thousand buildings covering 180 acres

Background Preparation

Culturally, East Asia incorporates not just the immense nation of China but also North and South Korea, Japan, and Mongolia. Although disputed, Tibet and Taiwan are also parts of China, the latter remaining independent as the Republic of China. Geographically, East Asia also encompasses the eastern half of Russia, including Siberia, which is considered Northeast Asia. East Asia is home to roughly one quarter of the earth's population: China has 1.38 billion people, the Koreas 77 million, Taiwan 23 million, and Japan 127 million, for a total of more than 1.5 billion. The other areas, including Mongolia and eastern Russia, have very slight populations spread over a vast territory. Tibet, an autonomous region of China, is often viewed by outsiders as a distinct nation under Chinese occupation while the Chinese government views it as an integral part of China.

The term *Chinese*, broadly speaking, can be applied to cultural activity found not only in the People's Republic of China and the Republic of China (Taiwan) but also in the self-governing city of Hong Kong and in other places where "Overseas Chinese" comprise important segments of the population. These places include Malaysia, where nearly one-third of the population is of Chinese ancestry, and the city-state of Singapore. Throughout the world there are cities with large Chinese populations, including Bangkok, Thailand; Manila, Philippines; Jakarta, Indonesia; Ho Chi Minh City, Vietnam; Toronto, Canada; New York, USA; London, UK, and in smaller concentrations throughout the world. Roughly ninety million people out of China's total population belong to some fifty-five non-Chinese minority groups, which are as diverse as the Hmong and Dai of the southwest and the Koreans of the northeast.

In spite of its immense size, East Asia is unified in numerous ways. Foremost among the factors that bind East Asian cultures together is an ideographic writing system developed by the Chinese millennia ago, in which icon-like "characters" have meaning rather than phonetic sound. At various times in history, each East Asian culture has adopted the Chinese writing system, allowing literate people in all areas to communicate even though the spoken languages (e.g., Japanese, Korean, Vietnamese, or Mongolian) were otherwise unrelated and mutually unintelligible. Over time, however, distinctive writing systems also developed in Japan, Korea, and Mongolia, while Vietnam romanized its writing system because of the influence of French and Portuguese missionaries.

潮州弦诗全集

국제민속음악학회 회의 및
국제민속음악제

一つとや

ひと夜あくれば賑かで　賑かで、

おかざり立てたる松飾り　松飾り。

From top to bottom, the scripts are from China (top), Korea (middle), and Japan (bottom)

Geography has played a major role in the development of East Asian culture. The original Chinese civilization, that of the "Han" Chinese, arose along the Yellow River in northern China forty centuries ago (*c.*2000 B.C.E.) and over time spread through the vast territory of East Asia, even into Southeast Asia. At the same time, Chinese civilization was profoundly influenced by outside cultures, especially those coming from Western and Central Asia along the "silk road." Many foreign elements, such as Buddhism, came to the Chinese first, were transformed into a Chinese form (a process called *sinicization*), and then absorbed and further modified by neighboring cultures. Within China, Han Chinese civilization spread mostly to the south and southeast, because much of eastern China is relatively flat, while the rest of the country consists of mountains, deserts, and high plateaus. Even today, in fact, the vast majority of China's billion-plus people live in the eastern third of the country. The Korean civilization developed on a peninsula to the northeast of China, and although Korea was profoundly influenced by China, its culture is otherwise distinct. Because the Korean peninsula is to the north and rather mountainous, Korea has limited arable land and harsh winters, and the Korean people have often had to struggle to survive. After the division of Korea into South and North Korea in 1945, the South has prospered and developed its own form of democracy, while the North has suffered immense ecological damage from industrialization and deforestation, which brings cycles of droughts and floods. In addition, its autocratic government has brought isolation to North Korea. The result is that many people in the North endure harsh lives and much of their culture has been completely politicized.

Japan's culture is also deeply affected by its geography. Japan is a chain of islands, stretching from cold and bleak Hokkaido in the north to the warm and lush Ryukyu Islands trailing southwest from Kyushu, Japan's southernmost major island. Although influenced by Chinese civilization, Japan was relatively isolated until the nineteenth century, which allowed it to develop a distinct culture. With most of Japan's population, nearly half that of the United States, crowded into the main islands of Honshu, Shikoku, and Kyushu—together smaller than the state of California—efficient land use is critical. The Japanese have developed an amazingly homogenous culture, though ethnic diversity certainly does exist, particularly in rural areas. The country's historical relative isolation from outside political and cultural influences until the mid-nineteenth century supports this mindset of the Japanese as a strongly nationalistic and unified entity.

Whereas Western histories are conceived in terms of centuries, Chinese history—and by extension Korean and Japanese history—are conceived in terms of dynasties, a **dynasty** being a succession of related rulers, such as the Sung or the Ming. The Chinese dynastic chart reveals a fairly consistent pattern of change. First, an energetic new Chinese dynasty forms and quickly unifies the country under newly effective rule; then, over time the dynasty's effectiveness erodes, enemies begin nibbling at China's borders, and public services and safety break down; finally, the dynasty crumbles, and following a period of instability, a new dynasty establishes itself. Between China's greatest, most stable, and longest-lasting dynasties were periods of disunity and chaos, such as the "Warring States" period (403–221 B.C.E.) and the "Six Dynasties" (222–581 C.E.). During certain dynasties, such as the Yuan (1260–1370) and Qing (1636–1911), foreign invaders—in these cases, the Mongols and Manchurians respectively—dominated China. Even though the rulers were foreigners, the vast Chinese bureaucracy maintained a control over Chinese institutions that insulated them from foreign cultural influence. Indeed, some foreign conquerors such as the Mongolians and Manchurians ended up being Sinicized to the extent that their own cultural distinctiveness eroded or disappeared.

The arts have long been elements of the political process in China. Seeing the arts as far more than mere entertainment, the government has often harnessed music and theater for their abilities to influence the thinking and behavior of the general population. Underlying this is a belief that music can have an influence on a person's ethical character. In ancient China—and by extension elsewhere in East Asia—the views of philosopher Kong Fuzi (551–479 B.C.E.; romanized as Confucius) had a profound influence on the role of music in the lives of the scholar class. In more recent times, Chairman Mao Zedong (1893–1976), China's communist leader from 1949 to 1976, not only believed that music and theater could influence people, but insisted the arts be harnessed by the state to create correct political thinking. Similarly, the government of North Korea has used music and related arts to influence its population.

DYNASTY
In China, a ruling family, like the Ming, and the era characterized by that family's dominance.

	CHINA		KOREA		JAPAN	
	ANTIQUITY					
	Xia	21st to 16th century				
B.C.E. 1200	Shang	c. 1600–1045				
1100	Zhou	1045–256				
1000						
900						
800					ANTIQUITY	
700	Spring and Autumn	770–476			Zyômon	to c. 200
600						
500						
400	Warring States	475–221				
300	DYNASTIES OF IMPERIAL CHINA					
200	Qin	221–206			Yayoi	c. 200 B.C.E.–250 C.E.
100	Han	202 B.C.E.–220 C.E.				
C.E. 0						
100						
200	Three Kingdoms	220–280				
300	Jin	265–420	THREE KINGDOMS		Kohun Culture	c. 300–400
			Koguryŏ	?–668		
400	Northern and Southern Dynasties	420–589	Paekche	?–660		
			Silla	?–668	IMPERIAL PERIOD	
500	Sui	581–618			Asuka	c. 550–710
600	Tang	618–907	DYNASTIES OF ROYAL KOREA			
700			Unified Silla	668–935	Nara	710–794
800					Heian	794–1192
900	Five Dynasties and Ten Kingdoms	902–979	Koryŏ	918–1392		
	Liao (Qidan [Khitan])	916–1125				
1000	Song	960–1279			MEDIEVAL PERIOD	
1100	Northern Song	960–1127			Kamakura	1192–1333
	Southern Song	1127–1279				
1200	Jin (Nüzhen [Jurchen])	1115–1234				
1300	Yuan (Mongol)	1279–1368			Muromati	1334–1573
	Ming	1368–1644	Chosŏn	1392–1910		
1400						
1500					PREMODERN PERIOD	
1600					Azuti–Momoyama	1573–1610
	Qing (Manchu)	1644–1911			Edo	1600–1867
1700						
1800			MODERN KOREA		MODERN JAPAN	
	MODERN CHINA		Japanese colonial period	1910–1945	Meizi	1868–1912
1900	Republic of China	1911–	Republic of Korea (South)	1948–	Taisyô	1912–1926
	People's Republic of China	1949–	Democratic People's		Syôwa	1926–1989
2000			Republic of Korea (North)	1948–	Heisei	1989–

Luo Qin

AN INSIDE LOOK

Although I am Chinese, as a musician and music student growing up in Hangzhou in eastern China, I was primarily a Western musician. As such I studied violin, composition, conducting, and Western music history, and I learned to lead an orchestra as concert-master. Fortunately, I also became familiar with Chinese music and instruments, though I did not emphasize this musical side. However, when I entered the graduate program at the Shanghai Conservatory of Music, where I majored in Chinese music history, my thoughts about music changed. After graduation I taught at the Conservatory for several years, but in 1991, still a young scholar and musician, I entered the ethnomusicology master's program at the University of Washington (Seattle, WA) and then continued doctoral study in musicology and ethnomusicology at Kent State University (OH). During my time in the States, I not only learned various musics from around the world but also came to understand the peoples, societies, and cultures related to these musics.

Through the study of the theories and practices of ethnomusicology, I feel I became a whole musician, scholar, and person who loves music, culture, people, and their lives. Now I specialize in two fields: the history of Chinese music and the urban music of Shanghai City and its people studied from an ethnomusicological perspective. I have done much fieldwork and published several works, including a *History of Chinese Musical Instruments*; *Kunju, a Chinese Classical Theater and Its Revival in Social, Economic, Political and Cultural Contexts*; *World Musical and Cultural Narration*; *Culture in Music and Music in Culture*; *The Narration of Shanghai Musical History*, and others. Based on my fascination with American music and knowing that Chinese students are curious, I also published *Street Music: An Epitome of American Society and Culture*. I also love to create music for those who enjoy playing music. For example, while directing Kent

Dr. Luo Qin, Professor of Musicology, Shanghai Conservatory of Music; president and editor-in-chief of Shanghai Conservatory Press

State's Chinese Ensemble, I revised a Chinese violin concerto called *The Butterfly Lovers* into a work combining violin solo and Chinese ensemble.

After receiving my Ph.D. degree, I returned to China. At present, I am a Professor of Musicology at the Shanghai Conservatory of Music, one of China's premier music institutions. In addition I am in charge of the Anthropology of Music Division E-Institutes of Shanghai Universities. After over twenty years of teaching, I have learned that I could and should do more if I want people to understand musics and their cultures. To reach that goal, I am also President and Editor-in-chief of the Shanghai Conservatory Press. Nonetheless, I still teach. I hope to continue making contributions to the society in which I live and working to help more people come to love music.

Planning the Itinerary

Our musical tour will encompass China, Mongolia, Korea, Japan, and Tibet. The music of each country is quite distinct in overall sound, timbre, character, and process. Yet all share certain traits that bind them together, making the concept of "East Asian" music a reasonable one. One way to explain these distinctions is by analogy using food. If you have had opportunities to visit both Chinese and Japanese restaurants outside Asia (Korean, Mongolian, and Tibetan restaurants are rarer), you have probably noticed striking differences. Those differences in the way food is prepared and presented and in overall atmosphere are analogous to some of the differences between the various countries' musics. Consider the décor: Chinese restaurants are usually highly decorated with colorful lanterns, dragons, and phoenixes (mythological birds) in strong shades of red, gold, blue, and green, whereas Japanese restaurants tend more toward plain white walls and natural wood, especially blond varieties. Whereas Chinese dishes, which feature colorful mixtures of many ingredients, are randomly placed on the table and shared by everyone, Japanese meals are often served individually on lacquered trays with many compartments for well-separated delicacies. The space separating the food in Japanese restaurants is analogous to the silence separating sounds in Japanese music. Whereas the behavior of both patrons and staff in a Chinese restaurant—especially in Chinese cities—is informal, enthusiastically loud and busy, behavior encountered in a Japanese restaurant is much more formal, quiet, and subtle. Once again, many of these distinctions also apply to Chinese and Japanese music.

A second analogy may perhaps help explain some of the major differences in East Asian attitudes toward "tradition," preservation, and change. Consider the following metaphor: a wonderful, ancient bridge (akin to traditional music) occupies a key position in a city. Because it is no longer adequate to handle modern traffic, the government calls for engineers to study the situation—one Chinese, one Korean, and one Japanese. After a thorough consideration, the Chinese engineer announces that the bridge will be "preserved" by bringing it up to modern standards. Workers will replace and widen the deck, put on new railings, add modern lampposts, rebuild the support system, and level the approaches. Thus, they claim, the old bridge will remain, but it will have been "improved" and "modernized." The Korean and Japanese engineers, however, conclude that the bridge is wonderful in its present form and should be preserved as it is. Recognizing the demands of modern travel, however, the engineers recommend both keeping the old bridge open for those who prefer to use it and building a new one nearby for those who need it.

Thus, in China most "traditional" music struggles to survive as best it can, while newly arranged and orchestrated music, considered "improved" and "modernized" by many Chinese officials, is commonly used to represent Chinese music to the outside world. In Korea and Japan, however, institutions both public and private preserve all surviving forms of traditional music and theater as living anachronisms in an otherwise modern world. As a result there is little difficulty in defining "tradition" in Korea and Japan. Within China there are widely differing views of what is traditional and what music should represent China, while foreign researchers often have views that contradict those of the Chinese. The state of traditional music in Mongolia resembles the Chinese situation, whereas traditional Tibetan music survives intact, including among exiles living in countries such as India, Nepal, and Bhutan.

The statue of China's greatest philosopher and teacher, Kong Fuzi (Confucius), in the Kong temple of Quanzhou, China

Arrival: China

As with all major civilizations, the Chinese developed their great cities and agricultural centers along rivers and around great lakes. Indeed, the names of many Chinese provinces reflect geographical features. For example, the name of Shandong province means "east of the mountains," while Shanxi means "west of the mountains." Similarly, Hubei is "north of the lake" and Hunan is "south of the lake." China's greatest threats in earlier times came from the northern border areas where non-Chinese invaders, including the Jürched, the Mongols (of Chinggis (also spelled Genghis) Khan fame), and the Manchu originated. China's Great Wall, stretching 1,400 miles over the northern mountains, was built to keep out the northern "barbarians."

Being a vast land, China has more than one gateway city. These include Beijing (the capital), Shanghai (China's largest city and commercial center), and Guangzhou (its most internationalized city). Beijing, a sprawling city of thirteen million built around the spacious Forbidden City (the former palace of the emperors), is the center of government and culture, whereas Shanghai and Guangzhou are centers of industry, commerce, and banking. The majority of the Chinese population lives in eastern China, an area with dozens of surprisingly large cities unknown to most foreigners. Though little known to outsiders, Shandong province in central China nonetheless produces products that are much appreciated by them. Owing to Shandong's earlier "colonization" by Germany, it is the center of Chinese beer-making, with Qingdao being the home of "Tsingtao" beer. But to the Chinese, Shandong is more important as the ancestral home of Kong Fuzi (Confucius) in the small city of Qufu near the sacred mountain called Tai Shan.

China has undergone an extreme makeover since the 1990s, and the construction crane is far more prominent than temples or red-tiled roofs. Skyscrapers, department stores, vast restaurants, and wide, traffic-clogged roads represent China today, and one cannot go far without stumbling on a McDonalds ("Mai dang lao"), Pizza Hut ("Pi shang ke"), KFC ("Ken de ji"), or Wal-Mart ("wo er ma"). In this din of modernity, traditional music is only one small voice.

In terms of culture, it is customary to distinguish between northern and southern China. One essential difference is that the northern Chinese prefer wheat (in the form of flatbreads, dumplings, and noodles), because it grows more readily in the relatively dry and temperate north, whereas southern Chinese, because the region is subtropical, prefer rice as the fundamental carbohydrate. Even within northern or southern China, there are numerous regional distinctions, often identified with specific provinces. As is widely known, there are regional styles of Chinese cuisine, such as Sichuan (Szechuan), Hunan, Guangdong (Cantonese), Shanghai, Beijing, and so forth. Language is also regional, because Chinese civilization developed in

The Great Wall of China north of Beijing at Badaling (Max T. Miller)

relatively isolated pockets. While all Chinese languages are related (as all the European Romance languages are), many are also mutually unintelligible, even though the writing system is the same for all. Even within a single province there may be several languages; in Guangdong, for example, these include Cantonese, Hakka, and Chaozhou. At the provincial level, languages may differ markedly from village to village because the mountainous terrain imposes such isolation. Today's national language, called *Mandarin* in English and *pu tong hua* in Chinese, originated in the north. Regional distinctions are also extremely important in Chinese music, especially in the narrative and theatrical genres.

Until the latter part of the twentieth century, most writing on Chinese music focused on ancient instruments, rituals, and aesthetic principles. The great Chinese music documents often took into account the living music of that time, but when Westerners began writing about Chinese music, they tended to omit living music. Earlier European scholars from the early twentieth century often viewed living music as unsophisticated and insignificant remnants of the glorious past. Ethnomusicological research into Chinese music only blossomed during the last three decades of the twentieth century, because, in earlier years, China had been off limits to most foreign researchers because of near continuous war from the 1920s until 1949 and the country's later political convulsions. This was particularly so during the **Cultural Revolution** (1966–1976), a top-down upheaval initiated by Chairman Mao Zedong and his influential wife, Jiang Qing, a former actress. After the end of the Cultural Revolution, a few foreign researchers came to China at a time when most Chinese scholars were still collecting "folk music" for use in compositions by conservatory-trained professionals. Much of the new research, however, was confined to urban phenomena because the government for some time rarely permitted research in rural areas and favored sending conservatory ensembles on foreign tours. Today the government no longer views music as a tool of propaganda and has allowed all kinds of music to flourish as best they can. But the question of what music best represents Chinese culture to the outside world remains a topic for discussion even today.

China has an incredibly diverse array of instruments, many of which had origins outside China but were Sinicized over time. Traditionally, the Chinese classified musical instruments into eight categories, known collectively as the ***bayin*** (or "eight materials")—namely, wood, bamboo, metal, stone, clay, skin, silk, and gourd. For the Chinese, the number "8" had a philosophical and aesthetic significance, and a philosophically complete ensemble would necessarily include instruments from all eight categories. Many ensemble types have names that refer to these material categories, including one studied here, the "silk and bamboo" ensemble (***sizhu***).

Chinese music is considered to be fundamentally vocal music. Besides a vast quantity of regional folk songs, there are many regional forms of narrative song and theater, the latter always having music. Because of the language problem, however, Western recording companies have preferred to release instrumental music, giving a skewed impression of the reality in China. Chinese music is primarily based on melodies that can exist in any number of guises and contexts, be they vocal or instrumental, solo or ensemble. Most have programmatic titles that allude to nature (e.g., "Autumn Moon and Lake Scenery"), literature or myth (e.g., "Su Wu the Shepherd"), a mood (e.g., "Joyous Feelings"), or even musical structure (e.g., "Old Six Beats"). Whether a composer's name is known or not—most are anonymous—the tune exists at an almost conceptual level, ready to be performed as an unaccompanied or accompanied instrumental solo, an ensemble piece, a song with or without accompaniment, an orchestral piece arranged for modern ensemble, or even as an operatic aria or modern popular song.

Besides this vast body of instrumental and vocal music, there is also the now rarely heard but once vibrant narrative tradition in which singers combined speaking and singing to tell long tales, accompanied by one or more instruments. More prevalent today are the nearly countless regional forms of theater, all of which have music and singing as integral parts. Beyond these one could also explore a variety of forms of instrumental and vocal music associated with Daoism and Buddhism, as well as the now revived music of Confucian ritual. The twentieth century also saw the development of many new forms of Chinese music reflecting "international" (read, "Western") influence, from violin-inspired *erhu* fiddle playing, to fully orchestrated arrangements of Chinese traditional melodies played by Western-style orchestras using "traditional"

CULTURAL REVOLUTION
A ten-year period in China's history, from 1966–1976, marked by severe social and political upheaval.

BAYIN
The Chinese organological system based on eight materials.

SIZHU
A "silk and bamboo" music ensemble, comprising Chinese stringed ("silk") instruments and flutes ("bamboo").

instruments, to all manner of Western-style classical music and popular song. Now experiencing a surprising revival are the politically influenced Revolutionary Operas and Revolutionary Ballets created during the Cultural Revolution (1966–1976) and imposed on the population to the exclusion of all else during that difficult time.

Site 1: The *Guqin* (Seven-String "Ancient" Zither)

First Impressions. The ***guqin*** represents Chinese culture at its most historical and refined. Many first-time listeners are struck by its sparseness, its lack of a clear beat, and its variety of odd timbres, including scraping sounds and ringing overtones. The character of the music is intimate and meditative, as if the performer were just playing for himself. Indeed, this quiet contemplation was for centuries a music particular to Chinese scholars and philosophers.

QIN/GUQIN
A bridgeless, plucked zither with seven strings.

Aural Analysis. The *guqin* (also spelled (*gu*) *ch'in*—pronounced "chin") is one of the most ancient instruments in the world to have remained in continuous use. The instrument is a roughly 51 inch (130 cm)-long rectangular board zither made of paulownia wood (top only) painted black, and has seven strings, traditionally of twisted silk, running lengthwise from end to end, without frets or bridges. There is also a series of eleven inlaid mother-of-pearl circles along one side marking the acoustical nodes or vibration points for each string. To the player's left, the strings pass over the end and are tied underneath to two small peg-like feet attached to the instrument's lower board. At the right end the strings run over a slight ridge that acts as a bridge, then pass through holes to the underside where each is tied to a small wooden peg. The instrument is tuned by twisting these pegs to loosen or tighten the string's tension. The player, seated on a chair with the instrument on a table or frame, plucks the strings with the fingers of the right hand and stops the strings with the fingers of the left hand.

The characteristic timbres of the *guqin* are many, as a typical performance includes plucked sounds produced either by the nail or the flesh of the finger, tone-bending created by the sliding movements of the left hand, and the use of harmonics (clear, hollow sounds produced by gently

The Chinese *guqin* (seven-string bridgeless zither), one of China's most ancient instruments, played here by respected scholar/performer Dr. Mei Han (Zheng Guanping; used by permission)

Guqin tablature notation

TABLATURE
Notation that indicates how to pluck, stop, or touch each string rather than indicating pitch.

touching the string at a node). Scraping sounds are produced when the player slides the left hand along the rough textured strings. Sometimes these sliding movements continue even after the string has stopped vibrating, expressing the view that music does not have to be heard to exist. Each string is tuned differently, but many of the same pitches can be produced at various nodes on different strings. Sometimes a pitch is repeated not on one string but on different strings or stopping points, which creates a series of slightly different timbres. While *guqin* music is fundamentally pentatonic (comprising five tones), other pitches may come into play, though all sound familiar enough to ears accustomed to the Western tuning system, because the Chinese system is similarly constructed.

Rhythmically, *guqin* music sounds fluid, improvisational, alternately halting or rushing, especially because often there is no clear beat to define a steady meter. *Guqin* notation is in a form called ***tablature***; more precisely, it consists of a chart that indicates how to pluck, stop, or touch each string, with minimal indications of pitch or rhythm. Thus, it is left up to each individual performer to express the meaning of a piece in his or her own idiosyncratic rendition.

Guqin music, like most traditional Chinese music, is basically monophonic, but is more often built of short motives rather than extended melodic lines. For this reason, *guqin* compositions may sound inconsistent at times because they can suddenly change style or mood. Perhaps this explains why the *guqin* is a connoisseur's instrument and its sound something of an acquired taste.

Our example, titled "Yangguan Sandie" (Parting at Yangguan—a mountain pass used as an outpost in ancient China), illustrates the most common *guqin* traits: a contemplative atmosphere, a rather changeable form, and a great variety of subtly different timbres. Much of the beginning is played with stopped tones, but there are brief passages of harmonics at 1'30." During some of the higher-range passages you can clearly hear the scraping sounds, produced as a finger or thumb of the left hand slides up or down to reach the next pitch.

LISTENING GUIDE

7.1 (2'04")

Site 7.1
China: *Guqin* ("Ancient Zither")

Instruments: *Guqin* (bridgeless plucked zither)

TIME	LISTENING FOCUS
0'00"	Melodic theme begins performance.
0'12"	Listen for tone-bending as the performer slides between pitches.
0'21"	Listen for "scratching" sounds that add timbral variation.
0'35"	Listen for subtle variations in timbre as the performer plays the same pitch on two different strings.
0'37"	Melodic variation of the opening theme.
1'29"	Melodic variation of the opening theme using harmonic overtones until 1'35".

Source: "Yangguang sandie," performed and recorded by Bell Yung, Pittsburgh, PA, 2002. Used by permission.

MUSICAL MARKERS: Timbre/Medium—Fretless zither. Note "scratchy" quality on some quieter passages.
Pitch—Occasional pitch-bending with "slides" between tones; also, use of overtones for some melodic content.
Rhythmic density—Low, not very busy.
ETHNO-CHALLENGE: Find a chordophone—for example, a guitar—and sound the overtones on a single string by lightly touching various harmonic nodes (at the mid-point, or a quarter or an eighth along the length of the string, for example) while plucking with your other hand.

Cultural Considerations. From ancient times and continuing at least into the nineteenth century, the *guqin* was closely associated with the *literati* or scholar class, from which the Chinese government chose its officials. Scholars were required to be knowledgeable in Confucian Chinese literature, poetry, calligraphy, divination, history, philosophy, and music. Music, rather than being a pleasurable or sensuous art, was a way of inculcating and expressing the ethical values of Confucianism, which include restraint, order, balance, subtlety, and hierarchy. Nonetheless, much *guqin* music is indeed quite sensuous. When scholars played a *guqin* composition, they had to flesh out and interpret the minimalist score by taking into account the meaning of the piece, its mood, and their own feelings in relation to it. In short, *guqin* music was a form of personal expression that aided in self-development and brought the player closer to China's highest ideals through a kind of sonic meditation.

Because *guqin* playing was part of a scholar's general cultivation of learning and of sensitivity to the arts, it is not surprising that "Parting at Yangguan" was inspired by a poem—specifically, a Tang Dynasty poem by Wang Wei (701–761) titled "Seeing Yuan Er Off to Anxi." Sometimes performers will sing this poem as they play "Parting at Yangguan" on the *guqin*, because the form of the composition closely parallels the poem's verse structure. The earliest tablature notation of

"Parting at Yangguan" appeared in 1491 in a collection titled *Zhiyin Shizi Qinpu*, although the version performed here is from an 1864 publication.

Guqin playing, because it was cultivated by a small elite, was probably always rare and little known to the general public. Today it is similarly rare, and the scholar class of bureaucrats who once practiced *guqin* playing along with their calligraphy and poetry has long been abandoned by Communist Party functionaries. Nonetheless, *guqin* players of many nationalities are still found throughout the world in small numbers, and in recent years, these scattered groups of musicians have been linked together by the Internet. In 2003, UNESCO designated *guqin* playing as an "Oral and Intangible Heritage of Humanity."

Site 2: *Jiangnan Sizhu* ("Silk and Bamboo") Ensemble from Shanghai

First Impressions. Most listeners find China's "silk and bamboo" ensemble music readily accessible. Compared to *guqin* music, one can more easily hear a tune, clear phrases, consistent rhythm, and repetition of certain musical ideas. The music is quite busy, as each instrument plays continuously throughout and makes frequent use of ornamentation. But, because most instruments play in a high range, the overall sound is "thin," due to the lack of low range instruments and absence of harmony.

Aural Analysis. Why the name *silk and bamboo* (*sizhu*)? Recall that the Chinese classified instruments according to eight materials. "Silk" instruments are those with strings, both plucked and bowed, because the original material used for strings was twisted silk. "Bamboo" instruments are flutes, both vertical and horizontal. Thus a "silk and bamboo" ensemble consists of fiddles, lutes, and flutes, with or without a few small percussion instruments. These ensembles play named compositions or tunes from a limited repertory, especially the "eight great compositions" that every musician must know.

Some *Jiangnan* compositions, like much Chinese music generally, have titles that suggest an emotion, allude to a poem, describe a scene, or reference something historical. Our example's title, "Huan Le Ge," means "Song of Joy" and suggests its character as a "happy" piece. But *Jiangnan* music also has a great many pieces whose titles suggest musical structure, such as "Lao Liu Ban" meaning "old six beats" and referring to the structure of the original notation. Another well-known piece in the repertory is "Zhong Hua Liu Ban," literally, "middle flowers, six beats," also describes technical aspects of the music's organization. The Chinese term *fangman jiahua* means "slowing down and adding flowers" (i.e., ornaments), and thus *zhonghua* refers to a "middle" degree of ornamentation (*zhong* is "middle" and *hua* is "flower"). This process of "adding flowers" suggests a traditional approach to embellishing melodies spontaneously but according to the idiomatic characteristics of each instrument.

The "silk" category includes a wide variety of bowed and plucked stringed instruments, including certain lower-range versions introduced during the twentieth century as part of China's drive to modernize. Four instruments, however, are essential: the *erhu* (fiddle), *yangqin* (hammered zither), *pipa* (pear-shaped lute), and *dizi* (horizontal bamboo flute). Other instruments can be used as well. Our track adds the *xiao* (vertical notch flute), *ruan* (round bodied long-neck lute), *san xian* (three-stringed lute), plus two small percussion instruments, a *ban* woodblock struck with a small beater in the right hand and a *gu-ban* clapper held by the left hand.

The *erhu* fiddle consists of a round or hexagonal wooden resonator with python skin covering one face. The scales of the snakeskin influence the timbre of the instrument: larger scales produce a deeper sound, while smaller scales encourage the preferred thin and grittier timbre of the *erhu*. A long stick serving as the neck pierces the body and has two rear tuning pegs at the top. Two strings, traditionally of silk but now often nylon, run the length of the instrument, although their acoustic

This amateur *Jiangnan sizhu* "silk and bamboo" music group meets each Sunday afternoon in a neighborhood school in Shanghai to play through favorite compositions

The Chinese *erhu* (two-stringed fiddle)

length is limited to the section between the string loop along the neck and the bridge in the middle of the resonator. The horsehairs of the bow pass between the two strings, and the player pulls or pushes the bow hairs against the appropriate string while touching the strings with the left hand to create specific pitches; unlike the violin, the strings are not pressed so as to touch the neck.

The *yangqin* dulcimer, formerly a small trapezoidal-shaped instrument with two rows of bridges, was modified during the twentieth century to increase its range and power, first to three bridge sets, then four, and most recently to five or six. Each "string" is actually a course of two or three strings, which the player strikes with two small bamboo beaters, one in each hand. The *yangqin* is often used as an accompanying instrument, much like the piano in Western music.

The *pipa* lute is one of China's quintessential instruments, as it has an extensive solo repertory in addition to appearing in ensembles. It has a hollow wooden pear-shaped body with four strings that pass over raised bamboo frets that allow for the use of all twelve tones of the Chinese tuning system. Earlier instruments had fewer frets because older Chinese music used only seven tones. The player, using fingernails or plectra covering the nails of the right hand, plucks the strings in an *outward* fashion (unlike finger-picking a guitar). The use of all five fingers in rapid-fire motion to sustain a pitch during some passages is a particularly distinctive stylistic feature of *pipa* performance.

The *dizi* is a bamboo tube ranging in length from about 16 inches (41 cm) to 2 feet (51 cm), with a blowing hole at the left end, a membrane hole, and six finger holes. The membrane hole must be covered with a thin membrane taken from the inside of a piece of bamboo. When properly attached and stretched, this skin vibrates to create a buzz that gives the *dizi* its particular timbre, somewhat like a subtle kazoo.

While some regional styles of Chinese music make use of pitches that sound out of tune to Western ears, "silk and bamboo" styles originating in the Shanghai region, such as our example, use pitches that sound quite familiar. Players need only instruments capable of playing the seven regular pitches of the D major scale. Seven pitches are required even though the music is essentially pentatonic, because the melodies expand to more than five pitches through shifts in tonal center or

The Chinese *yang-qin* (hammered zither)

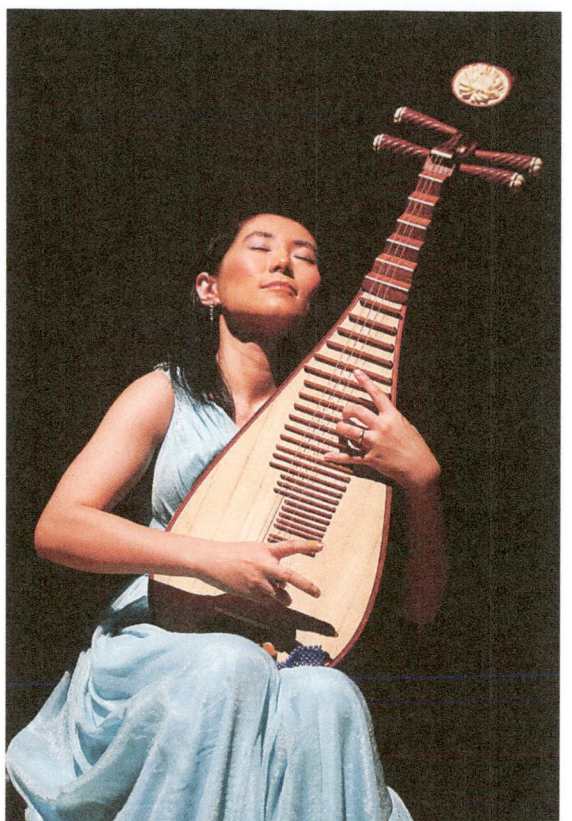

The Chinese *pipa* (pear-shaped lute) (Photo courtesy of Kent State University)

The Chinese *dizi* (bamboo flute)

conjunct passages. The two most common keys—called *diao* in Chinese—are D and G, especially in the Shanghai area. Unlike *guqin* music, the meter of which is often vague, "silk and bamboo" music has a clear duple meter, with obvious downbeats and upbeats. Rhythms tend to be relatively simple, with nothing more complex being found than a few syncopations and many dotted values.

What might strike you about our example, though, is that all the musicians are playing the same tune—but differently, resulting in a heterophonic structure. Heterophony is a fundamental phonic structure of most east and southeast Asian traditional music ensembles. Virtually all instruments in *sizhu* have a high range, giving the music a bright, busy quality. If you listen carefully, you can hear the timbres of individual instruments and differences in the way each plays a phrase. The *erhu* "slides" into some notes, the *dizi* "flutters," the *pipa* utilizes its tone-bending and "rapid-fire" plucking techniques, while the *yangqin* "bounces" along adding occasional ornamentations, primarily at the octave. Also notice that the instruments play all the time and that there is little or no shading of dynamics. This type of music is quite tuneful, so you may find yourself humming the catchier melodies, some of which are quite well known and are part of the foundational repertory of Chinese music. Even though such compositions are tuneful, the more advanced repertory—of which "Huan Le Ge" is an example—tends to be through-composed or continuously unfolding. What binds a piece together is the use of a number of short musical motives that reappear often, as well as the use of a single key and a consistent heterophonic structure. For the most part, this music is played at one dynamic level and with little more subtlety as far as tempo is concerned than a slowing down at the end. What makes the music fascinating, however, is the ever-evolving interplay of the different instruments, which makes each performance unique in its details.

LISTENING GUIDE
7.2 (5'32")

Site 7.2
China: *Jiangnan Sizhu* ("Silk and Bamboo") Ensemble

Instruments: *Erhu* (bowed lute), *gaohu* (bowed lute), *pipa* (plucked lute), *dizi* (flute), *yangqin* (hammered zither), *zhong ruan* (mid-range plucked lute), *ban* (woodblock idiophone) and *gu-ban* (hand-held clapper)

TIME	LISTENING FOCUS
0'00"	Wood block (*ban*) initiates the piece.
0'06"	All instruments enter following a heterophonic structure. Listen attentively for the timbre of each instrument and note the individual interpretations of the melodic line. The initial five pitches are noted as 3, 2 3, 5, 1.
0'29"	Listen for the brief sustain on the sixth scale degree (6) of the pentatonic scale (1, 2, 3, 5, 6). Note that an additional pitch (7) appears as a passing tone periodically throughout the performance (e.g., 0'33", 1'18", 1'54", etc.).
0'48"	Melodic resolution on first scale degree (1).
1'07"	Brief sustain on sixth scale degree (6). Listen for such sustains on this pitch throughout the performance (e.g., 1'44", 3'04", etc.).
1'27"	Melodic resolution on the first scale degree and again at 2'03".
2'44"	Brief sustain on third scale degree (3). Listen for such sustains on this pitch throughout the performance (e.g., 3'13", 3'32", etc.).
2'50"	Brief tonal shift to second scale degree (2).

3'39"	Melodic resolution on the first scale degree and again at 4'25".
4'28"	Musicians pause and then transition to faster tempo section.
5'16"	Tempo slows to final resolution on the first scale degree (1).

Source: "Huan Le Ge" recorded in Shanghai, PR China by Terry E. Miller, 2007.

MUSICAL MARKERS: Medium—Minimal percussion with woodblocks keeping time. Different kinds of stringed instruments with "buzzy" flute. **Phonic Structure**—Heterophonic (same melody with variations for each instrument's style). **Rhythm**—Duple meter with some changes in tempo.
ETHNO-CHALLENGE: Using the pitches indicated in the Listening Guide, notate the basic outline of the melody using cipher (numeral) notation.

Cultural Considerations. As with Chinese cuisine, "silk and bamboo" music is regional, and there are at least four prominent and distinct traditions. Our example, as we have already noted, represents the tradition found in and around Shanghai. Because the mile-wide Yangtze River, the more southern of China's two major rivers, reaches the ocean at Shanghai, it forms a major geographical marker for the region. For this reason, the region is known as *Jiangnan* ("south of the river"), and the "silk and bamboo" music from the area is called *Jiangnan sizhu* or the "silk and bamboo music south of the river." Other distinct regional types include *Cantonese* (from Guangdong province in the south), *Chaozhou* (from eastern Guangdong province), and *Nanguan* (from Xiamen and Quanzhou in southern Fujian province).

"Silk and bamboo" music is best described as an amateur music because it is typically played by non-professionals in a casual clubhouse setting for their own pleasure, rather than on a stage for an audience. Originally, however, Jiangnan music was more widely heard in other settings, including weddings, and was also used to accompany one of the operatic genres of Shanghai as well as a local narrative singing tradition. As in many Asian cultures, professional musicians in China traditionally had a low social status, especially those who played for opera performances, weddings, and above all funerals. "Silk and bamboo" ensembles allowed ordinary working people the opportunity to be artistic without being tainted as "professional musicians." While all regional styles are typically played in a private clubhouse or meeting room situations, the *Jiangnan* style can also be heard by visitors to the Mid-Lake Pavilion Teahouse in Shanghai's historical district, where the sounds of the music mingle with the chatter of patrons and the clatter of dishes. In addition, music conservatories now teach students to play this music but from refined, fully written-out arrangements.

Experienced Chinese musicians play without notation from a knowledge of the tune's basic structure plus the idiomatic characteristics of the instrument. Less experienced musicians may prefer to read notation using *jianpu*, a form of Chinese notation using Arabic numerals (referred to as cipher notation in English). Probably adopted originally from Western missionaries, most likely from France, who brought hymnals printed in numeral notation, *jianpu* is quite practical and easy to read. Regardless of key, the "home" pitch (tonic or keynote) is 1. In "D diao" (key of D), 1 is D, 3 is F♯, and 5 is A, but in "G diao" pitch 1 is G, 3 is B, and 5 is D.

Though Chinese melodies are mostly diatonic and remain in a single key, this notation can also be used to notate more complex compositions using additional signs from Western staff notation, such as sharps (♯) or flats (♭) and other graphic signs. Much traditional music is played in D and G *diao*, though other keys are possible. Dots above or below a number indicate octaves above and below the main octave, respectively. Rhythm/duration is indicated with horizontal lines below the numbers, while measures are marked with vertical lines.

Jiangnan sizhu meeting: three lutes (from left to right) small *san xian* (three-stringed lute), *ruan* (round lute), and *pipa* (pear-shaped lute)

Measures 1-3 of "Huan Le Ge" in *jianpu* (numeral) notation. Pitch 1 is Western pitch D or do. Order of instruments from top to bottom: *dizi* (horizontal flute), *sheng* (mouth organ), *pipa* (lute), *san xian* (three-stringed lute), *yangqin* (dulcimer), *erhu* (fiddle), *zhong hu* (middle-range fiddle), and *ban/gu* (clapper and drum). Ed. Ma Sheng-Long and published in Shanghai in 1986/2000

A *Jiangnan sizhu* ("silk and bamboo") ensemble playing informally in its meeting room, Shanghai, China (Phong Nguyen)

Site 3: Beijing Opera (*Jingju*)

First Impressions. On listening to our recorded example, you probably cannot help but notice the clangor of the percussion, particularly the "rising" and "falling" sound of the gongs. The prominent fiddle is quite nasal-sounding and some of the pitches it plays probably strike you as out of tune. The vocal quality is piercing compared to most world music traditions, particularly in comparison to opera traditions from the West. The music of the Beijing Opera is often challenging for first-time listeners to appreciate, although the chance to see a live performance would no doubt win some new fans with its visual spectacle: the vivid costumes, the striking painted faces of some of the performers, and the stage action—especially the acrobatics, which are inspired by Chinese martial arts.

Aural Analysis. With many musics from around the world, timbre is the aspect that most challenges the first-time listener due to unfamiliarity with the instrument sounds and vocal styles. This is certainly true of Beijing Opera, called ***jingju*** (meaning "capital city opera") in Chinese. For most listeners, even in China, the vocal quality of *jingju* is decidedly different from what is normally encountered. All roles are sung with little or no vibrato, and many sound rather nasal and quite high in range. Men playing female roles, a common practice in *jingju,* use the falsetto (or "head") voice. The *jing* (painted-face characters) tend to sing in a rough, declamatory style.

The instrumental accompaniment is a combination of melodic and percussion instruments that play as two groups. The melodic group is divided into "civil" and "military" sections, the former led by the genre's distinctive short, two-stringed bamboo fiddle, called *jinghu*, the latter by the loud double-reed called *suona*. Other melodic instruments include an *erhu* fiddle, the moon-shaped *yue qin* lute, and sometimes other lutes, but rarely the *pipa*. The military group, comprised entirely of percussion, is led by a "conductor" who plays a clapper (*gu-ban*) held in the left hand, and uses a stick held in the right hand to beat on a distinctive small drum (*ban gu*). He is accompanied by musicians playing both large and small gongs and cymbals. The conductor's drum has a dry, hollow timbre, while the tone of the large gong (*daluo*) decays downward (i.e., its pitch drops as its volume falls), and that of the small gong (*xiaoluo*) decays upward

JINGJU
Literally "capital city opera," known as "Beijing" or "Peking" Opera.

Jingxi (Beijing Opera) performance: a red-faced general is flanked by a painted face (*jing*) to his left and a young man (*xiao sheng*) to his right

The *jing hu* (fiddle), the main instrument of the *jingju* opera

Student musicians accompany a rehearsal performance of *jingxi* (Beijing Opera) at the Shandong Opera School, Jinan, China

(its pitch rises as the volume falls). Besides marking beats, these percussion instruments also provide sound effects that symbolize actions, emotions, or objects.

Singers have to work closely with both the "conductor" and the *jinghu* player, because singing is improvised according to a host of variables, which comprise what is called a "modal system." This practice is quite unlike that of many other regional opera traditions, which require lyricists simply to write poetry to fit pre-existing, named tunes. Simply put, the "modal system" that governs the creation of melody here consists of several variables that allow for a kind of composition simultaneous with performance. Among these are: (1) role type; (2) melodic mode; (3) metrical/rhythmic pattern; and (4) linguistic tone.

Our example features an aria from the opera *Mu Kezhai* (named after the main character), which is sung by a female warrior, Mu Guiying, the daughter of an infamous outlaw from the Sung Dynasty. After an introductory section performed by the percussion, during which she performs militaristic stage actions, the female warrior begins singing in speech-like rhythms, accompanied by the melodic instruments. After another percussion interlude, she begins a section in a regular duple meter during which the conductor's clapper is clearly heard.

Cultural Considerations. Typically, Asian theater traditions strive for symbolic rather than re-alistic action, depict individual characters as universal types, make music an integral part of the performance, and generally stylize all aspects of performance. *Jingju* perhaps develops these tendencies to a greater degree than any of the other local theater traditions found throughout China. Most of those use realistic, if stylized, scenery, but *jingju* does not. The props are minimal, normally only a table and two chairs. As in most Chinese theater traditions, *jingju* actors use a special stage language, though the comedians speak in Beijing dialect to indicate their low class status. Although many of the local types of theater were—and continue to be—performed in a ritual context on a temporary stage within a temple facing the main god's altar, *jingju* is mostly performed in formal theaters, the other context for Chinese opera. In most local operas, players receive informal training within a troupe, but *jingju* can be studied formally in government-sup-ported schools. Indeed, *jingju* has come to be the preferred way to represent traditional Chinese culture to the outside world; other kinds of Chinese theater are rarely encountered outside of China except within the confines of an overseas Chinese community, such as Cantonese opera in New York City or San Francisco.

LISTENING GUIDE

Site 7.3
China: Beijing Opera (*Jingju*)

Vocal: Single female (*Dan*)
Instruments: *Ban gu* (wood clapper/drum), *xiaoluo* (small, high-pitched gong), *da luo* (large, low-pitched gong), cymbals, *jinghu* (high-range bowed lute), *erhu* (middle-range bowed lute), *yue qin* (plucked lute)

TIME	LISTENING FOCUS
0'00"	Percussion introduction begins with the *ban gu*, followed by the gongs and cymbals.
0'01"	Listen for the "rising" pitch of the small gong compared with the "falling" pitch of the larger gong.
0'21"	Short percussion break. Instruments resume in anticipation of the vocal solo.
0'32"	Melodic ensemble enters. Note that the music is in free rhythm.
0'55"	Vocalist enters. Listen for the *jinghu* (high-range bowed lute) supporting the vocal line. The music continues in free rhythm.
1'57"	Percussion returns.
2'23"	Melodic ensemble returns. Note that the music follows a regular beat.
2'47"	Vocalist returns as music continues with a regular beat.
2'57"	The tempo gradually decreases.
3'14"	Vocalist drops out and the melodic ensemble returns to a faster tempo with a regular beat.

Source: "Tao Ma Tan (role), aria from *Mu Kezhai* (opera)," from the recording titled *The Chinese Opera: Arias from Eight Peking Opera*, Lyrichord LLST 7212, n.d. Used by permission, Lyrichord Discs Inc.

MUSICAL MARKERS: Timbre/Medium—Distinctive "rising" and "falling" pitched gongs. Shrill (female role) or gruff (male role) vocal timbre. Lead fiddle has piercing timbre, accompanied by small string ensemble and minimal percussion during melodic sections. **Form**—Alternates between vibrant percussion sections and melodic ensemble accompanying vocalist. **Rhythm**—Rhythmic density is thick during "military" (percussion) sections. Tempo fluctuates to follow vocalist and movements of actors on stage.
ETHNO-CHALLENGE: For theatrical performance such as this example, it is important to see the on stage activity. Watch a video recording of a Beijing Opera (*Mu Kezhai*, if possible) in its entirety.

The typical *jingju* performance places the music ensemble on stage left (the audience's right). Actors and actresses enter and exit from and to the left or right, using the table and two chairs to represent everything from a throne scene to a mountain battle site. An actor holding a stick with a simulated mane is understood to be riding a horse, and an official flanked by young actors holding cloth flags with wheels painted on them is understood to be riding in a chariot. For many years, men had to play women's roles, singing in falsetto (head) voice, because women were often banned from the stage as theater was seen as morally corrupting. Today, with such bans long gone, women not only play female roles but sometimes play men's roles as well, while some men continue to impersonate women. Regardless of his or her gender, each performer specializes in a role type. There are four major role types with numerous subdivisions: (1) *sheng* (male roles), subdivided into young man, old man, and military male; (2) *dan* (female roles), which are similarly subdivided; (3) *jing* (painted face roles), which feature a facial pattern that

A performance of a
military style play in
Taipei's Military Theater
as seen from the
lighting booth

Military *jing* painted face character

Imprisoned *dan* (female) character with
chou (comedian) keeper

Dan (female) preparing make-up in dressing
room

Military scene
with numerous
generals

symbolizes the person's character; and (4) *chou* (comedians), who are easily identified by the white patch in the middle of their faces.

If you see a performance given in North America by a visiting troupe, chances are the singing portions will be shortened and the acrobatic sections lengthened, because it is commonly believed that Western audiences cannot tolerate the musical aspects of *jingju* well. But within North America there are also *jingju* clubs that give performances for connoisseurs who do not need rapid stage action to maintain interest.

Site 4: *Chuida* Wind and Percussion Ensemble from Quanzhou, Fujian, China

First Impressions. Reedy wind players and a loud drum, joined later by a small bell and clattering cymbals, seem to roam aimlessly, following a melody that does not quite become a tune. The music sounds slightly raucous, perhaps because it is played outside, perhaps as part of a procession. The sustained melodic pitches give way to a more active melody following a more regular beat. The intensity of the music attracts listeners to discover what is happening, even as the somewhat challenging timbres and loud volume may prompt children and those unfamiliar with the sound to cover their ears.

Aural Analysis. Although it is true that the music has no discernible "tune" and may sound almost improvisatory, likely the greater challenge to appreciation of *chuida* is the distinct and unblended timbres of the instruments. The melody is realized by two rather strident sounding wind instruments playing more or less in unison. These are called *suona*, China's distinctive "oboe" or double-reed aerophone consisting of a conical wooden tube with eight finger holes, a detachable flared metal bell, and a tiny double reed mounted at the upper tip of a metal holder (called a *bocal* in the West). The reeds, tied onto a narrow metal tube with a piece of string, are entirely within the player's mouth. Players maintain a continuous sound through "circular breathing," a technique that requires the player to maintain both high-pressured exhalation while inhaling air through the nose (see Chapter 4, Site 1).

A battery of widely used Chinese percussion provides the percussive sounds. The deep drum sounds come from a large wooden barrel drum (*gu*) with two leather heads nailed to the

At Beijing's world renowned Zhihua Temple, built in 1443 during the Ming Dynasty, a group of five musicians, members of the 27th generation, play ritual *chuida* music several times daily. From left to right: *yunluo* (gong set), *dizi* (horizontal flute), *guanzi* (double reed), *sheng* (free-reed mouth organ), and *dagu* (large drum)

A suona (double reed aerophone) player accompanies a funeral at a Chinese temple in Bangkok, Thailand

189

Two *suona* players lead a funeral procession in a village in Qingyuan county, Zhejiang province, China

Two *suona* players lead a funeral procession in a village in Qingyuan county, Zhejiang province, China

body. The upper head is struck with two wooden beaters. Such drums come in a variety of sizes and shapes, some suspended from frames. The metallic sounds come from:

1) A pair of thin cymbals (*naobo*) struck or rubbed together horizontally or sometimes with the upper one at a 90-degree vertical angle. The sound of such Chinese cymbals is more damped then the Western marching band style of "crashing cymbals" played vertically.
2) A large bronze gong struck with a padded beater (*daluo*). When struck just slightly off-center, the sound decays rapidly as a falling tone.
3) A small gong with a square, flat face struck with a thin wooden stick (*xiaoluo*). When struck with the corner of the stick slightly off center, the sound decays quickly as a rising tone.
4) A small high-pitched gong in a frame struck with a small wooden mallet (*xiang*). More commonly found as a temple instrument than in ensembles, the clear, flat tones of the gong sound above everyone else in this recording.

The composition, "Taizi you Shimen," which literally means "The Prince visits the four gates," evokes the story of Prince Siddharta (the future Buddha) going out from his palace. It is a "labeled tune" (*qupai*) used in a local opera genre known as *Puxian xi* (associated with the city of Putian and the district of Xianyou) from the area surrounding Quanzhou city on the coast of Fujian province in southern China.

A "labeled tune" is one that has a name but does not have lyrics. In many local Chinese opera genres constructed using such tunes, the librettist specifies the tune by name in the score and writes lyrics that fit the tune. In more familiar Western terms, the librettist/composer would write verses and mark them "sung to the tune 'Amazing Grace.'" Thus, generic tunes can be used in many different opera productions but with different words to fit different situations.

With the hope of developing Chinese tourism, Yueshan village in Zhejiang province's Qingyuan county offers visitors a cultural show in the village auditorium. Preceding a performance, both "wind and percussion" musicians and lion dancers warm up in a nearby school yard. (Photos by Terry E. Miller, 2019)

Cultural Considerations. There is a basic dichotomy between softer-sounding ensembles, one of which is heard in Site 2 (see above *Jiangnan sizhu*), and louder ensembles as heard here. The former usually play indoors, are seated, and are considered "civil" (*wen*) in Chinese thinking. The loud ensembles are more likely heard outdoors, commonly stand or march, and are classified as "military" (*wu*). This site explores one type of "wind and percussion" ensemble generally known as *chuida* (blowing and hitting) and *guchui* (drumming and blowing). In some areas these ensembles may include plucked and bowed strings, requiring the ensembles to sit. Ensembles including only percussion are called *daluogu* (hitting gongs and drums). Recalling that Chinese traditionally classified instruments into eight materials (such as "silk and bamboo," as seen in Site 2), *chuida* ensembles typically include instruments from multiple categories: 1) wood (*suona*, double-reed pipe with bell), 2) bamboo (*guan*, short, double-reed pipe), 3) gourd

Drums, gongs, and cymbals constituting a *daluogu* ensemble ("hitting gongs and drums") accompanies Lion Dance for the opening of a new restaurant in New York's Chinatown

(*sheng*, free-reed mouth organ—gourd because the windchest was originally a gourd), 4) skin (all drums), and 5) metal (gongs and cymbals).

As with the silk and bamboo tradition, wind and percussion ensembles exist in both the traditional context of a local community and in the highly controlled context of the music conservatory. The former learn and play everything from oral tradition passed from one generation to the next within the community, while the latter learn and play in the conservatory from elaborate written scores under the tutelage of teachers. The form heard on this track represents the local "traditional" form. Where non-conservatory "silk and bamboo" musicians (Site 2) are amateurs and represent the Confucian ideal of people edifying themselves by playing refined music, non-conservatory wind and percussion players usually play for money and are thus placed at the lower end of the social scale. The Chinese aphorism that says "let your daughter marry anyone, but never a wind player for funerals and weddings" suggests this social stigma.

Chuida ensembles continue to have an important function in contemporary Chinese society, both within cities and far away in remote mountain villages over much of China. They play chiefly for funerals, weddings, and a variety of festivals, both agricultural and temple-based. Although temples may have private rooms reserved for funerals, many take place on the street in front of the deceased's home or shop. The family usually hires a full funeral troupe that includes ritualists, musicians, setup assistants, costumes, food, and all ritual objects. The musicians may be seated around a long table in front of the coffin, all in full view of the passing public. Following these rituals, there is often a procession through the streets led by the musicians that draw attention to the event. The procession terminates at a site where large, elaborate paper objects representing houses, cars, electronics, food, and money, are burned. Thus, the family assures their loved one will be well provided for in "heaven." Weddings also may result in public processions that include a *chuida* ensemble. Similar customs may still be seen among the overseas Chinese throughout Southeast Asia, in the various "Chinatowns" of the West, and in cultures strongly influenced by Chinese customs, such as Vietnam.

Perhaps the most prominent occasion for purely percussion ensembles (*daluogu*) is accompanying the "Lion Dance." For many festive occasions and parades, a group of men line up under a long cloth representing the body of a mythological lion or perhaps a dragon with the lead player manipulating a large, fanciful head. The dancing "lion" weaves through the street, sometimes turning to acrobatics when the dancers stand on each other's shoulders. Usually two comic figures wearing large clown heads are added to "herd" or "control" the lion. In the United States, lion dance troupes are often associated with martial arts centers and perform annually for Chinese New Year celebrations. In cities with large "Chinatowns," the troupes may be employed to open a new shop or restaurant.

Additionally, *chuida* musicians make up the "military" section of the ensemble that accompanies opera in China, including Beijing opera. They play an especially prominent role in opera stories full of splendidly dressed military warriors, massed armies, and battles, both between opposing armies and rival generals. Indeed, the ensemble heard in our example includes members of the *Liyuan Xi*, that is, the Peartree Orchard Opera Troupe.

LISTENING GUIDE
7.4 (2'53")

Site 7.4
China: *Chuida* Wind and Percussion Ensemble

Instruments: Two *suona* (reed aerophone), *gu* (barrel drum), *naobo* (pair of hand cymbals), *daluo* (large "falling" gong), *xiang* (high-pitched gong), *muyu* (wood block)

TIME	LISTENING FOCUS
0'00"	*Suona* initiates the piece, playing extended pitches with slight fluctuation. Initial scale only includes three pitches.
0'02"	*Gu* (barrel drum) immediately follows with short triplet pattern, then speeds up with a higher rhythmic density.
0'08"	*Xiang* (high-pitched gong) enters with irregular pattern.
0'12"	*Naobo* (cymbals) joins, as *suona* continues. *Gu* varies its rhythmic patterns, as featured soloist.
0'45"	Listen for the *daluo* ("falling" gong) as the *gu* solo ends.
0'52"	*Suona* gradually move into more active melodic line, as the tempo and rhythm instruments become more regular.
1'16"	*Suona* melody returns to original extended pitches, as tempo slows and rhythmic density lessens.
1'22"	Percussion pattern changes and tempo increases, emphasizing a single melodic pitch and climaxing rhythm.
1'35"	Note the *gu* drops in volume to highlight the metallic percussion and *suona*.
1'42"	*Gu* signals loudly to start a new section.
1'53"	Note the *suona* melody becomes more active again.
2'09"	Listen for the drop in rhythmic density and entrance of the low-pitched woodblock.
2'21"	Note the absence of *gu*, as the high-pitched woodblock enters.
2'28"	Feel the tempo accelerating.
2'31"	The *gu* returns, as the music reaches a climax.
2'38"	Feel the tempo slow as the performance concludes.

Source: *Chuida* Wind and percussion ensemble, "Taizi You," from the recording entitled *China: Chuida Wind and Percussive Instrumental Ensembles*, AUVIDIS-UNESCO D8209, 1992. Used by permission.

MUSICAL MARKERS: Medium/Dynamics—Loud pairs of reed aerophones and variety of vibrant percussion. **Rhythm**—Opening tends to be irregular, moving into a steady beat. **Pitch**—Often emphasizes single pitches for an extended period transitioning into brief melodies.
ETHNO-CHALLENGE: Analyze the form of this performance, noting in particular the changes in instrumentation and rhythmic elements. This example also presents an opportunity to try circular breathing (see Chapter 4, Site 1).

Arrival: Mongolia

If there's a place that deserves the title "Big Sky Country," it would be landlocked Mongolia, tucked between China to the south and Russia to the north. Its open grassland landscapes—called *steppe*—and the great Gobi Desert, plus most days being cloudless, give visitors a feeling of great openness. With little arable land, sparse rainfall, and a short growing season, the Mongolians long ago learned to co-exist with their harsh climate, hot in the summer and extremely cold and windy in the winter. Originally a nomadic people dependent on their beloved horses, today only 30 per cent of the population of only 2.9 million maintain this lifestyle. In spite of this tiny population, Mongolia is a country of great diversity, of numerous if little-known ethnic groups, and of religious complexity. While many Mongolians continue to practice their ancient form of shamanism—shamans being specialists who "travel" to the land of the spirits—they long ago also embraced the Tibetan form of Buddhism, as seen in magnificent temples in urban areas.

A first-time visitor will be struck by Mongolia's apparent emptiness. Although the capital city, Ulaanbaatar (also spelled Ulan Bator), appears large, its population is only 1.34

Explore More

Popular Music in East Asia

Popular music in East Asia is steadily growing in its influence around the world. While few specific artists are known to most people outside the region, pop culture generally has embraced many innovations from the region, such as Karaoke, Japanese *anime*, and martial arts films from Hong Kong, which have inspired modern-day action films in the United States and abroad. Teenagers and young adults from this region are as familiar with the icons of Western mainstream pop, such as Lady Gaga, as their Western counterparts, but add to their iPods music from indigenous superstars, such as Hikaru Utada, Namie Amuro, Gackt, Ayu, Anita Mui, Faye Wong, and Jackie Chan, the latter being best known as an international movie star but also a pop music icon in East Asia. The majority of pop stars from East Asia are from Japan and Hong Kong, though others from Taiwan and Korea, such as hip-hop artist PSY, find regional and international fame as well.

Mainland China, however, has produced very few popular music stars due primarily to the communist political climate of the last half century, which largely discouraged popular styles as having a negative influence on society. The irony is that popular music throughout much of East Asia is considered to have originated in Shanghai during the 1920s as a mix of Chinese traditional music and American jazz called *shidaiqu* ("contemporary songs"). The most famous figure associated with this early style was Zhou Xuan (1918–1957), a singer and movie actress who became popular during the late 1930s. After the Chinese Civil War (1945–1949), however, the new communist government restricted this music as well as other outside influences coming from the West. Famous popular artists, such as Elvis Presley and The Beatles, were largely unknown on mainland China until the end of the Cultural Revolution (1966–1976). Elsewhere, however, the popularity of American and European music idols thrived, inspiring the various modern music styles of J-Pop (Japanese Pop), K-Pop (Korean Pop), M-Pop (Mando (Mandarin)-Pop), and C-Pop (Canto-Pop), as well as other East and Southeast Asian styles, including *Luk Thung* (Thailand) and *Dangdut* (Indonesia).

Mongolian round canvas homes (*yurt*) (Shutterstock)

million—nonetheless, the city is home to nearly 40 per cent of the country's population. With a land area nearly four times that of California and equal to that of Iran, Mongolia has one of the lowest density populations in the world. Mongolia's neighbors include Chinese Turks to the southwest, Russia to the northeast, and the Republic of Tuva (properly, Tyva) to the northwest; the latter, a member of the Russian Federation, is home to thriving musical traditions similar to those found in Mongolia. Despite Mongolia's historically small population, in the twelfth century the Mongol civilization became extremely powerful, and the armies of the Khans (emperors), particularly Chinggis (Genghis) Khan (d. 1227), subdued not only China during the Yuan Dynasty (1260–1227), but a vast area stretching from Korea to the Black Sea and including parts of Southeast Asia. When Italian adventurer Marco Polo visited China in the late thirteenth century, his host was the Mongol emperor Kublai Khan, grandson of Chinggis.

The capital city of Mongolia is hardly a haven for traditional culture; instead, it reflects the Soviet influence Mongolia came under after achieving independence from China in 1921. The city's architecture looks far more Soviet than Mongolian, and it was under Soviet influence that Mongolians developed their "folkloric troupes" to represent Mongolian culture to the outside world, as well as visitors.

Originally, much of Mongolia's music had spiritual and religious significance, because music was often considered a form of communication between the worlds of humans and spirits. Under communism, however, most musical traditions were secularized and put on the stage. Music that had been—and mostly continues to be—passed down orally has also been harnessed by the European-style music conservatories. It is "**overtone** singing" that has brought Mongolian music to world attention. While overtone singing is both important and distinctive, the country's most typical form of music is actually the *urtïn duu*, the "long songs" accompanied by Mongolia's most distinctive instrument, a trapezoid-bodied, long-necked bowed lute called the *morin khuur*. Where the overtone singing lacks lyrics, the long songs retell the culture's great stories and history as well as describe the natural environment; some say that these "sing the landscape."

OVERTONE
One of the ascending group of tones that form the harmonic series derived from the fundamental pitch.

Site 5: Mongolian *Urtyn Duu* (Long Song) with *Khöömei* (Overtone or "Throat" Singing)

First Impressions. It is not the instrument that attracts our attention—that is clearly a bowed lute—or the female's singing but rather the other performer's singing, if that is the right term. Some listeners describe these sounds as unearthly and find them "haunting." Some observers say it resembles whistling and wonder how such sounds are produced. Additionally many ask what might have inspired a culture to produce such sounds.

Aural Analysis. Traditional Mongolian life was and, for many, continues to be lived in nature and among one's flocks of sheep and goats. Without horses, Mongolians would have no way to travel or herd their flocks, and thus it is not surprising that they would enshrine the horse on their principal bowed lute, the *morin khuur* which, because of the carved horse-head at the top is translated as "horse-head fiddle." This long-necked fiddle, with two silk strings and a separate bow, is normally played by a seated male, with the body of the instrument resting on his knee and the neck resting against his shoulder. The song they are performing, *Sünder Agula* (Sünder Mountain), alludes to the sacred nature of mountains in old Mongolian society. It comes from a song genre called *Urtyn duu* or "long songs" and originated in western Mongolia. In addition to the "normal" singing by a female, a male performs regular singing while another sings in a manner that sounds like whistling. It is this kind of vocal production that has attracted so much attention to Mongolia over the past thirty or so years.

KHÖÖMEI
Throat or overtone singing from Mongolia.

The Mongolian term for this type of singing is ***khöömei*** (also romanized as *höömii*), while in English it is called *throat-singing* (a somewhat odd label, because all singing takes place in the throat) or *overtone singing*. What makes this singing so distinctive is the way in which the singer manipulates what are called *overtones*. Any tone or pitch, except perhaps one generated electronically, consists of a fundamental vibration and a series of harmonics, called *overtones* or *partials*. The timbre of a given tone is determined by which overtones are emphasized—a function of how the fundamental vibration was produced (e.g., by a double reed, a vibrating string, buzzing lips, etc.)—and by the relative weakness or strength of the various overtones. A tone in which the lower overtones are emphasized will likely sound "warm," whereas one in which the upper overtones are more prominent will sound "bright," "harsh," or perhaps "hollow."

In overtone singing, the performer—formerly only male, now female as well—produces, usually with significant pressure on the glottis (a part of the vocal cords), a fundamental and, by shaping the mouth cavity, brings out different patterns of overtones. A series of well-controlled, changing overtones produces an actual melody over a drone. Highly skilled singers can even produce both the lower melody and the overtone melody simultaneously, as heard in this track.

Mongolian "throat" singer, Ts. Sengedorj, performs in full costume (Jack Vartoogian/ FrontRowPhotos)

Cultural Considerations. Among "world music" enthusiasts few styles have garnered as much attention in recent years as "throat-singing," also called "overtone singing." While a similar form of this singing found in the nearby Republic of Tuva has perhaps attracted a greater following in the West in recent years, Mongolian overtone singing is certainly just as striking. Singers in other areas of the world, including Altai, Khakassia, the Chukchi Peninsula, Tibet, Japan's Hokkaido (where it is extinct), Sardinia in the Mediterranean as well as the Inuit of Alaska, practice various forms of overtone singing, but less prominently

Two Mongolian musicians play the *morin khuur* (two-stringed, "horse-head" fiddle) (Shutterstock)

LISTENING GUIDE
7.5 (2'39")

Site 7.5

Mongolia: *Urtyn duu* (Long song) with *khöömei* (overtone or throat singing)

Voices: Single female, single male, male also performing overtone singing
Instrument: *Morin khuur* (horse-head fiddle)

TIME	LISTENING FOCUS
0'00"	*Morin khuur* begins.
0'07"	*Khöömei* vocalist enters. Listen for the deep fundamental drone tone along with the overtone singing. Note that the overtone melody follows the melodic line of the fiddle.
0'20"	Female vocalist enters as *khöömei* vocalist stops. Note that the singer and instrumentalist follow the same melodic line.
1'16"	*Khöömei* vocalist joins the singer and instrumentalist.
1'30"	Male vocalist enters as the *khöömei* and female vocalists stop. Note again the singer and instrumentalist follow the same melodic line.
2'27"	*Khöömei* vocalist joins the singer and instrumentalist.

Source: "Urtïn duu Sïnder Mountain" from *Mongolia: Living Music of the Steppes/ Instrumental Music and Song of Mongolia*, Multicultural Media, MCM 3001 (1997). Used by permission.

> **MUSICAL MARKERS: Pitch**—High-pitched "whistle" sound, i.e., overtone, as vocalist sings. **Melody**—"Plaintive" fiddle echoes the vocalists.
> **ETHNO-CHALLENGE:** Sing a deep drone pitch and change the shape of your mouth to create different timbres. Listen for the subtle changes in overtones and try to amplify these over the fundamental sung pitch.

than in Mongolia. Few outsiders will have the opportunity to hear Mongolian overtone singing in its original context—performed in a *yurt* (round tent) with singers surrounded by family and friends. Nonetheless, many recordings of overtone singing exist, sometimes even combining it with various forms of art and popular music. American musician Bela Fleck, for example, has collaborated with Mongolian throat singer Kongar-Ol Ondar. In 1968 during a period of sonic exploration in the West, German avant-garde composer Karlheinz Stockhausen, created an extended work titled *Stimmung* in 1968, which featured overtone singing.

In Mongolia this unique style of singing is closely tied to the shamanistic/animistic beliefs still held by many Mongolians. The voice is meant to imitate the sounds of nature, attempting to duplicate the rich timbres of natural phenomena such as the swirling wind or rushing water. Mountains, rivers, and animals are believed to contain a spiritual energy that is manifested not only physically but sonically as well. Echoes reflected from a cliff, for example, are said to be infused with spiritual power. Overtone singers believe they can assimilate this power by recreating such sounds. Some speculate that overtone singing originated from the efforts of herders to imitate animal sounds when trying to rescue newborn animals when unable to nurse or when rejected by the mother. Sometimes herders soothed or coaxed their animals with their overtone singing. From these functions it is believed that herders honed their abilities until this form of singing became part of the musical traditions of Mongolia.

Arrival: Korea

Although the Korean language is unrelated to the languages of its closest neighbors, China and Japan, the fact that it is partially written in Chinese characters shows that early in its history Korea absorbed many aspects of China's civilization. Korea also accepted Confucian teachings and philosophy, the emperor system, Chinese Buddhism and Daoism, and many of China's instruments and musical types.

Sandwiched between China and Japan, Korea has suffered repeatedly as each of these kingdoms expanded. From 1910 to 1945 Korea was a colony of Japan. Following World War II, Korea found itself as the battleground in a struggle between China and the West; this led to a kind of internationalized civil war, which ended with an armistice in 1952. Today, the Korean peninsula remains divided into two countries—North Korea and South Korea.

Altogether, the Korean peninsula is only the size of the United Kingdom. While North Korea is the larger of the two countries, it has less than half of South Korea's population. The two nations are unequal in many other ways as well: the South is a modern, developed, democratic nation that manufactures goods for the entire world, whereas in the North, currently under the strict control of a quixotic ruler Kim Jong-Un, malnutrition and starvation stemming both from government policies and natural disasters remain problems, especially in rural areas, while the cities have a surprisingly modern and developed look. Culturally speaking, both countries have departed from the old Korean traditions, the North because of its peculiar form of communism, the South because of modernization. Nonetheless, in some major cities, such as Seoul, the capital of South Korea, "traditional" culture continues to flourish in the "musical museums" of certain government-sponsored institutions.

Just as Korean cuisine has attained little prominence in the West, Korean music has also struggled to be appreciated, even within Korea; for many Westerners both the food and the music can be described as "acquired tastes," the spiciness of Korean food being likened to the sonic spiciness of Korean music. From the first century onward Korea absorbed much Chinese musical culture, especially the ancient court and ritual musics. Much of this has been essentially preserved in Korea, even as music in China continued to change, and the old ritual traditions abandoned. As a consequence, Korea maintains one of the oldest continuously living music traditions in the world, the Confucian ritual music called *a-ak*. These hymns to the ancient Chinese philosopher, Confucius, are still sung once a year on his birthday (September 27). The Chinese originals first underwent change to accommodate Korean tastes. Similarly, Korean court music, preserved today by several cultural institutions, remains extremely archaic.

In the face of the politically induced stresses of the last century, particularly the Japanese occupation (1910–1945), World War II, the Korean War, and the Korean Peninsula's division into north and south, traditional forms of music have struggled to survive. South Korea has preserved some forms in educational and cultural institutions, where they are still taught and performed as museum pieces, while North Korea has discarded most vestiges of tradition in favor of newly created and highly politicized forms of music inspired by the old Soviet "Socialist Realism," an approach that requires all art to have political ramifications and inspire the people to uphold state policies.

South Korea nonetheless retains a rich repertory consisting of solo, semi-improvised instrumental music (called *sanjo*), ensemble music, narrative and lyrical song, theatrical music, "farmer's band music," and the now widely known folk-derived percussion music called *samul-nori*. Although there are exceptions, China's instrumental timbres tend to be bright and clear, while those of Korea might be described as "rough," "fuzzy," and "wavering" because of the strong use of vibrato. While China's music is clearly based on tunes, Korea's does not generally sound tuneful to foreign ears; indeed, when Korean ensembles play together, some listeners have trouble hearing the instrumental parts as even being related to each other. Finally, ornamentation in Korean music tends to come unevenly in sudden spurts.

Site 6: *P'ansori* Narrative

First Impressions. **P'ansori** is a passionate music. The vocalist begins with a cathartic wail, so powerful that it strains the limits of the recording equipment. Accompanied by seemingly random drumbeats, she employs a great variety of vocal techniques, from near whispers to speaking to singing and raspy shouting. A noticeable wide vibrato heightens the emotion, encouraging a highly evocative and dramatic performance. Even while the language is a barrier to non-native speakers, the fierceness with which *p'ansori* performers display their craft attracts loyal followers around the world.

Aural Analysis. *P'ansori* is one of Asia's greatest narrative forms and certainly among the most dramatic. Although considered a form of "folk" music, *p'ansori* requires extensive training, a prodigious memory, and incredible physical strength and vocal endurance. Today singers perform only five stories, each potentially lasting several hours, but in the distant past there were as many as twelve. Our example provides an excerpt from one of the five, *Ch'un-Hyang-Ka*, the story of a young woman whose name means "Spring Fragrance." As with many classical stories from East Asia, the plot revolves around a young student and his lover; in this case, the student is named Li Mongnyong and his lover is called Ch'un-Hyang. Her mother is a *kisaeng*—that is, a professional singer and entertainer—but she does not want her daughter to follow in her footsteps. The two lovers are secretly married before Li Mongnyong departs for Seoul to begin the classical studies that will hopefully lead to a position of authority in the government. After many years as an official, he returns to his hometown disguised as a beggar to check on his wife and discovers that she and her mother have suffered greatly during his absence. He then reveals his true identity. Some have interpreted the story as a critique of feudalism and its abuses.

The story is realized by two performers, a vocalist—in this case a respected and elderly female master—and a drummer. The drum used is the *puk*, a shallow barrel drum with two tacked

P'ANSORI
Korean narrative vocal performance style, featuring epic-length stories.

Korean *p'ansori* (narrative) performers, the singer on the left, the *puk* barrel drummer on the right (Embassy of Korea)

Drummer playing *puk* drum to accompany *p'ansori* (narrative) (Embassy of Korea)

heads. Held vertically by the drummer, he strikes the right head with a stick and the left head with his hand, occasionally calling out praise or encouragement to the singer. Both performers have a degree of freedom to improvise, limited within strict conventions. The vocalist's performance is governed by a modal system that provides an appropriate scale, melodic motives, and conventional ways to express emotions. The drummer's part is based on fixed cyclic patterns of drumbeats, but because the cycle is rather long in duration and the drumbeats are not continuous, the cycle may have a random feel to non-connoisseurs.

The range of vocal timbres is exceptionally rich, as the vocalist varies from speaking to declamation to song, to raspy, tense bursts of sound. The vocal range is unusually wide. Different pitches (depending on the particular scale/mode) have different degrees and kinds of vibrato, a distinctive feature of *p'ansori* performance. Connoisseurs of this music recognize the distinctions in vibrato, which gives them a greater appreciation of the performer's ability. The intensity of expression throughout a performance parallels the emotional intensity of the story. Indeed, emotional intensity is characteristic of *p'ansori* and of Korean music in general, despite the restraint and balance otherwise demanded by Confucian aesthetics.

LISTENING GUIDE
7.6 (2'11")

Site 7.6
Korea: *P'ansori* Narrative

Vocal: Single female
Instruments: *Puk* (shallow barrel drum)

TIME	LISTENING FOCUS
0'00"	Example fades in with vocalist and accompanying drum.
0'08"	Listen for the quiet declamations of the percussionist.
0'16"	Note how the descending melodic contour of the vocalist includes little vibrato in this phrase.
0'22"	Now listen for the heavy use of vibrato in the voice to contrast with the preceding phrase. Pay attention to such variations in the vibrato throughout the performance.
0'39"	Listen for the strong, raspy quality of the vocal timbre at the start of this phrase.
0'49"	Listen for the timbre heard when the stick strikes the drum's face, and compare this with the sound made when it strikes the drum's side (0'55") or strikes simultaneously with the hand (1'04").
1'08"	Vocalist sings with falsetto.
1'27"	Vocalist shifts to spoken dialogue.
1'57"	Vocalist transitions back to sung text.

Source: "P'ansori, Ch'un-Hyang-Ka, Song of Spring Fragrance," sung by Mme. Pak Chowol with drum accompaniment by Han Ilsup, and recorded by John Levy; from the recording titled *Korean Social and Folk Music*, Lyrichord LLST 7211, n.d. Used by permission, Lyrichord Discs Inc.

MUSICAL MARKERS: Medium/Timbre—"Passionate" vocalist with small drum accompaniment. **Form**—Vocal style frequently shifts between strong "wailing" vocals to rhythmic singing and spoken word. **Pitch**—Frequent use of "wide" vocal vibrato.
ETHNO-CHALLENGE: Sing a comfortable pitch and attempt to vary the level of vibrato from none to very wide and back again.

Cultural Considerations. Before 1910, when Korea was still a kingdom, certain music traditions were maintained by the court while others were practiced by ordinary people of the villages. A tremendous variety of instrumental and vocal music existed, performed in ritual contexts, on official occasions, during calendric festivals, and for entertainment. Many traditions were prohibited or lost during the twentieth century, because of the Japanese occupation and especially because of the Korean War and the consequent division of Korea. After 1952, as South Korea modernized into one of the "Asian Tigers" and North Korea slid into despair under Kim Il-Sung's "cult of personality"-style rule, traditional music struggled to survive. In the North, music was harnessed for state purposes under the banner of "socialist realism," and was both "modernized" and turned into propaganda. In the South, the government made the decision to preserve rapidly dying cultural traditions by keeping them in living aural museums. Traditional ways of life were "preserved"—really reconstructed—in designated "ethnographic" villages where time stands still both politically and technologically. Music, dance, and theater are similarly preserved in rather rigid forms within certain government-sponsored cultural institutions and the educational system. Independently, however, modern Korean artists have created completely new forms of expression derived from tradition, but for the most part, the traditional and the modern are kept separated.

P'ansori is one of the types of music that has been preserved through government support. Its storytellers were once found amidst festival events, where their voices had to compete with other activities. These wandering bards traveled the countryside telling their tales. Some found favor with aristocratic audiences, who continually debated over the artistic value of these talented but lower-class performers. *P'ansori* performers were an "endangered species" by the middle years of the twentieth century, until 1964, when the Ministry of Culture and Information designated several performers as "holders of artistry of intangible cultural assets." Since that time *p'ansori* has been found primarily on concert stages in institutionalized settings along with other traditional Korean arts, such as *sanjo*.

A visitor to South Korea can still hear and see the most formal of ritual musics, the most refined of vocal and instrumental genres, and even "folk song," all alive but now unchanging. These are studied in many cases with designated masters—living national treasures—the nation's most valued culture-bearers. Unusual as this practice of keeping archaic forms of music alive artificially may seem from a Western viewpoint, it reflects a decision that traditional Korean music is worth preserving as an expression of what is most essential and defining in the Korean soul.

While much of Korean musical culture came originally from China, most of this imported Chinese culture was modified to suit the nature and personality of Korea. For example, the Chinese zither (*zheng*), formerly having sixteen strings but now expanded to twenty-one, is played with plectra (originally finger nails), giving it a crisp, clean timbre. The Korean equivalent, the *kayagum*, has only twelve strings, but they are thicker and played with the fleshy part of the fingers, giving the music a more diffused timbre. There are also, however, aspects of Korean musical practice that are not derived from China, such as the Korean preference for 6/8 and 9/8 meters, this being exceptional not just in East Asia but in all of Asia. These meters give Korean music a lilting rhythmic quality not heard elsewhere.

Korean musicians have built new kinds of music while keeping the old alive. Today one finds orchestras of traditional instruments, the mixing of Korean and Western instruments, and various kinds of popular music that sound more or less Korean. Most striking of all, however, is a new genre that has received worldwide attention, *samul-nori*. Derived from the old-time "farmer's band music," *samul-nori*, which means "four instruments playing," was created in 1978 by four musicians in Seoul who played large and small gongs (*ching* and *kwaenggwari*), an hourglass-shaped drum (*changgo*), and a barrel drum (*puk*), performing mostly fixed compositions with amazing agility and passion. During the 1980s and especially the 1990s, other groups expanded *samul-nori* to include more and larger drums, creating one of the most dramatic, energetic, and appealing new genres in the world. Because *samul-nori* has grabbed the attention of foreigners as no other Korean music had before, even the government is now promoting it as an expression of Korean identity in spite of the music's newness.

Chaneung Park

I was a geo-cultural alien when I stepped into the exclusively inherited world of *gugak*, traditional Korean musical performance: I neither was from Jeollado, the hotbed of *pansori* singing, nor did I have a kinship easing me into the Korean traditional music community network. I received rigorous academic training outside the tradition and excelled in foreign languages and humanities and chose a scholarly career as my father and most of the male clan ancestors before him had. I was an avid listener of American pop and folk tunes of the Vietnam War era and at one point almost decided to become a singer-songwriter. Like many Koreans I accepted the reality of the cultural hierarchy that marginalized Korean traditional musical performance in the nation's drive toward modernity. During my college years as an English major, I participated in the English-language musical productions the program annually hosted. This was my initial training in the reflexive probing of the deeper truth about self that occurs in the process called performance. It guided me to grow as an independent thinker making choices often against the precepts of convention. Performance reveals painful truths about our world as well, perhaps the reason why Plato and Confucius similarly left cautionary warnings against poetry and music. When in 1974 an opportunity to learn pansori singing opened for me, I could no longer resist. Pansori singing builds on the sustained strength of your gut voice, and it liberated mine suffering from a physiological structural inability to project the falsetto essential to our standard music curriculum. As a graduate student in a prominent Asian theater program, I witnessed the systemic absence of Korean theater. The realization added urgency to my determination to prove Korean theater was alive and well. I took another baby step toward adopting pansori as my lifelong discovery under the tutelage of my late teacher, Chung Kwonjin (1927–1986), Preserver of the Important Intangible Cultural Asset No. 5, 1963. That was 44 years ago.

How could I make this Korean-language story singing attractive to English-language audiences? After due trial and error I brought onto stage a bilingual interpretive pansori alternating the singing with English spoken summaries. Buoyed by the cheering reception at the Storytelling Festival, Honolulu Museum of Art, 1993, my work progressed to a kind of seated and self-accompanied pansori monodrama without the separate drummer who is typically unavailable and unaffordable outside Korea. Thanks to the heartwarming reception of the local audiences of Honolulu, my bilingual seated pansori yielded the first

Chaneung Park

harvest and future promise. It has been maturing with new possibilities in the American Heartland where I relocated to join the faculty at The Ohio State University in 1995. The old-fashioned noisy slide projector is now replaced with a PowerPoint. The bilingual subtitles projected above the centerstage singer-drum seat add literary substance and highlight the esthetics of minimalist mise en scène of a seated pansori. The English is for the audience; the Korean is for the readers of Korean and the slide-changer, whose job is to know when to change slides. I have rarely been in places where there was not a single Korean or Korean language reader available for the task.

Aside from the lecture/performances for academic audiences, I have premiered or helped premiere several experimental pansori productions for general audiences. They include: *In 1903, Pak Hungbo Went to Hawaii*, a monodramatic storytelling about the Korean immigration to Hawaii (Honolulu, January 13, 2003); *When Tiger Smoked His Pipe*, a pansori-like folktale theater for children (Honolulu, 2003); *Shim Chong: Korean Folk Tale*, a postmodernist retelling of the story of Shim Chong with pansori narrator (Getty Museum & National Theatre in Seoul, 2003); *Klanott and the Land Otter People, the Southeast Alaskan p'ansori*, experimentation in the Western classical music register (Alaska, 2005); *In 1937 Pak Hungbo Went to Almati* (Almati, 2007) dedicated to the seventy years of Korean settlement in Kazakhstan; *Fox Hunt and the Death of a Queen* (2012), pansori-puppetry retelling of Empress Myeongseong's assassination, which occurred in 1895.

As a mother of three growing biracial children, I had my share of answering their existential question: "Am I Korean or American? Are we *hapa* (Hawaiian for half Caucasian) because only 50% of our blood is *haole* (Hawaiian for Caucasian)?" One of my answers that did not add up mathematically but was most truthful was that they are 100% Korean and 100% American, totaling 100%! Situated in language and literature outside music, dance, and theater programs institutionally sanctioned as "arts," how did I do with the hyphenated responsibilities intrinsic to performance and scholarship? Over time, the labors of performance and scholarship more often than not came to be welded to my professional career as one entity weighing 100%!

Insofar as teaching is a main offshoot of research, the students in my Korean performance and dramatic tradition courses also receive their education in a theoretic-somatic hyphenated manner. Since 2014, I have been directing the newly inaugurated Chris Sungkyu Lee Korean Performance Research Program at Ohio State University (u.osu.edu/kprp), a self-funded program promoting the understanding of Korean history, culture and society reflected in the performative expressions from the past. Last year, the program hosted the 6th *Annual Korean Wind and Stream* performance event, bringing together professionals of international visibilities and Korean music lovers and learners including students. (See on YouTube: *osukoreanperformance*) *The Korean Wind and Stream* is being recognized as a rare venue of interdisciplinary education and networking between our American higher education community and the world. Looking back from this point in my fifth decade of discovery of pansori, this discursive path has brought me here to continue my journey as learner, teacher, and promoter.

Arrival: Japan

Because Japan is an island nation, consisting of four main islands (from north to south, Hokkaido, Honshu, Shikoku, and Kyushu), plus the Ryukyu chain, land and resources are severely limited. With nearly 80 percent of the land being too steep for housing and difficult for farming, the Japanese have been forced to use their land to extreme efficiency. In a country slightly smaller than California but with a population nearly four times as large, the Japanese also have to be tolerant of each other due to such crowded conditions. Additionally, Japan's position on major geological faults brings devastating earthquakes. These the Japanese have learned to defeat structurally, but as the 9.0 earthquake of March 2011 showed, any resulting tsunamis can be far more devastating. Although profoundly influenced by Chinese civilization, Japan (like Korea) modified the culture imported from China to suit its own needs and to express its individualism. Also like Korea, Japan has tended to preserve its traditional music, theater, and dance separately from new developments, offering visitors the opportunity to experience archaic forms much as they were hundreds of years ago.

GAGAKU
A Confucian-derived ritual court ensemble from Japan; literally, "elegant music."

SANKYOKU
A Japanese chamber ensemble, consisting of voice, *koto* (zither), *shakuhachi* (flute), and *shamisen* (lute).

Just as Japan itself is compact, its traditional arts are few and well defined. Japan's court music and court dance, called **gagaku** and *bugaku* respectively, are among the oldest continuously living musical genres on the earth; to be appreciated properly, they are best experienced live and in their original context. Three forms of traditional theater are particularly striking: the ancient *noh*, the more recent *kabuki*, and the incredible puppet theater known as *bunraku* with each puppet's three human manipulators dressed in black but in plain sight. Three instruments—the *koto* (zither), the *shakuhachi* (flute), and *shamisen* (plucked lute)—are essential in Japanese music. When they play together with a vocalist, they comprise Japan's best-known chamber music, called **sankyoku**, meaning "three instruments." Other essential types of traditional music include folk song, festival and dance music, and Buddhist chant, as well as the globally popular *taiko* drum ensembles originally associated with Shinto ritual practices.

Japan's music, like its arts generally, is best understood in terms of Japanese specialist William Malm's well-known aphorism, "maximum effect from minimum means." Whereas much Chinese and some Korean musics can sound continuously "busy," Japanese music prefers minimal activity and makes silence an integral part of the soundscape. This sparseness, together with

Undecorated space, nature, and earth tones are characteristic of the Japanese aesthetic. Here a sand and rock garden sits next to a traditional building in the Hama-rikyu Garden, a place of refuge from the city of Tokyo located on the grounds of a former seventeenth-century Shogun palace (Anne Prescott)

the use of strongly articulated notes, requires calm and attentive listening on the listener's part. In Japan, musical instruments are treated as extremely refined, artistic objects and remain unusually expensive, even student models. Indeed, most kinds of Japanese performance, including performances of folk songs or music for *bon* (festive) dancing, are quite formal, even ritualized.

Whereas Chinese tunes are continually rearranged and are embellished freely, Japanese music tends to be played with greater consistency. Musical spontaneity is not characteristic; in fact, some Japanese instrumental music is notated exactly, even down to the ornamentation. In short, whereas flexibility and casualness are characteristic of Chinese music, Japanese music is characterized more by fixedness and great refinement of detail.

Site 7: *Gagaku* Court Music

First Impressions. If any music embodies the idea of timelessness or suspended time, it would be *gagaku* ("elegant music"). What makes an immediate impression is the way the piece seems to be constructed of clearly differentiated elements, with each instrumental timbre apparently having a separate function: melody, punctuation, background. As with much Japanese art and music in particular where sparseness is preferred, there is relatively little activity, with much aural space separating the musical elements. If you were to witness a *gagaku* performance at a temple or palace, you would see how the architecture and its decoration (or lack thereof) have elements that echo the character of this music: patches of empty white space, stark contrasts of colors and material, and a rugged, almost four-square quality created by massive wood beams and large pieces of cut stone. "Entenraku" sounds massive and timeless and seemingly transports us into another plane of existence.

In Tokyo, Japan, a colorful sound truck advertises the Kanda Matsuri (festival) centered at the Kanda Shinto Shrine but celebrated with parades throughout Tokyo (Anne Prescott)

A single drummer in a raised pavilion pounds out the rhythms for a Japanese bon dance. Bon dancing is part of the larger Obon Festival held annually to honor one's ancestors, though it is loosely associated with Buddhism as well

Aural Analysis. The first sound heard in our example is that of the *ryuteki*, a small horizontal bamboo flute (called the "dragon flute") that plays an unadorned melody; some of the pitches it plays are outside the Western tuning system and thus may strike inexperienced listeners as "out of tune." A drum accompanies the flute, but its patterns do not create an obvious metrical structure. Suddenly a mewling double reed called the *hichiriki* joins the flute; both now play over a foundation of dense tone clusters created by a group of *sho*, small free-reed mouth organs with seventeen pipes. As the melody unfolds in its own time-stretched world, certain sustained pitches are punctuated by alternating instruments playing a single plucked note followed by a brief, rising three-note motive; the first one heard is the *biwa*, a pear-shaped four-stringed lute derived from the Chinese *pipa*, and the arpeggio is played by the *koto*, a long board zither with thirteen strings.

The tension rises as the flute and reed rise to ever-higher pitches. The music seems to ebb and flow between states of tension and relaxation even without the use of harmony—the West's way of creating these effects. Even though the meter may not be easily heard, it does underlie the

A Japanese *gagaku* ensemble plays in a concert hall. Back, left to right: (horizontal flute), *hichiriki* (double reed aerophone), *sho* (free-reed mouth organ). Front: gong, *koto* (zither), drum, *biwa* (lute), and drum

Part of a *gagaku* ensemble performs on stage. (Hiroyuki Ito/Getty)

Gagaku musicians from left to right: drum, *biwa* (lute), and *sho* (free-reed mouth organ). (Hiroyuki Ito/Getty)

A *sho* (mouth organ) player warms up backstage for a concert in Taipei, Taiwan

music; some sense of beat is created through the punctuation of drums and the three-note motives played by the *koto* and *biwa*. Not only is the music's sound stately, but *gagaku* is performed with extreme formality by expressionless musicians who hold and play their instruments in ritualistic ways.

Cultural Considerations. Originally a specific kind of court music imported from China in the sixth century, *gagaku* grew into a complex of ensembles and functions that have come to symbolize both the imperial court and certain non-court ritual functions. Our example, "Entenraku," is just one composition out of many but perhaps the best-known. It comes as no surprise that the title translates as "music of divinity." What does surprise though, is the thought that its melody is said to have been a "popular" song during the Heian period (794–1184).

Gagaku is one of the products of Japanese culture that has fascinated the West the most, along with *haiku* (Japan's extraordinarily succinct poetry), *bonsai* trees, *origami* paper folding, tea ceremony, and *sumo* wrestling. There have been at least a few attempts to capture the sound world of *gagaku* in a Western context. French composer Olivier Messiaen's 1962 piece

LISTENING GUIDE 7.7 (2'17")

Site 7.7

Japan: *Gagaku* Court Music

Instruments: *Ryuteki* (flute), *kakko* (two-headed drum), *taiko* (large barrel drum), *sho* (free-reed mouth organ), *hichiriki* (double-reed aerophone), *biwa* (plucked lute), *koto* (plucked zither)

TIME	LISTENING FOCUS
0'00"	*Ryuteki* (flute) begins performance.
0'07"	*Kakko* (two-headed drum) enters.
0'13"	*Taiko* (large barrel drum) sounds a single stroke, and again at 0'18". *Ryuteki*, *kakko*, and *taiko* continue until other instruments enter.
0'51"	*Sho* (free-reed mouth organ) enters followed by the *hichiriki* (double-reed aerophone). Listen for this entrance pattern throughout the example.
1'11"	Listen for a single pitch plucked on the *biwa* (plucked lute). The *kakka* anticipates the sound. It appears a few times, such as at 1'20" and 1'29".
1'31"	*Koto* plays a three-note melodic motive and sounds again at 1'46" and 2'03".

Source: "Entenraku," from the recording entitled *Gagaku: The Imperial Court Music of Japan.* Performed by the Kyoto Imperial Court Music Orchestra, Lyrichord LYRCD 7126, n.d. Used by permission.

MUSICAL MARKERS: Timbre/Medium—Distinctive "tone cluster" sounds and "squawking" wide-reed aerophone. **Pitch**—Deliberate isolation of single pitches. **Rhythmic Density**—Extremely long sustained tones. **Tempo**—Very slow moving.

ETHNO-CHALLENGE: Create a graphic notation system to follow all the parts of this examples.

for chamber orchestra, *Sept Haïkaï*, Movement IV, entitled "Gagaku," reproduces the sound of the Japanese ensemble by using trumpet, oboe, and English horn for the melody and eight violins for the *sho* clusters.

One of the non-musical influences on *sankyoku*, as well as most Japanese music, is *Zen* Buddhism, a form of Buddhism derived from the Chinese *Chan* and brought to Japan in the twelfth century. Where some Buddhist sects emphasized the study of the scriptures, resulting in much intellectualizing, Chan/Zen emphasized clearing one's mind through meditation in order to reach enlightenment. Thus, in the Zen aesthetic, emptiness is valued over busyness, plain white space over decorated space, and in music, silence over continuous sound. Zen Buddhism and the music influenced by it were the inspirations for the so-called "Minimalist" movement in Western art, which rose to prominence during the late 1960s and early 1970s. During that time many European and American artists had a fascination for Japanese art and music, one aspect of a period filled with a broad range of interests in the non-Western world.

Site 8: *Kabuki* Theater

First Impressions. In comparison to Western theatrical genres, the sound of *kabuki* is much more subdued. Twangy plucked lutes, a single flute, and a collection of small drums accompany a solitary storyteller as the action unfolds on stage. No fiddles or brash trumpets or reeds, no crashing

Explore More

Komuso

Even in Japan the sight of someone wandering around town dressed in robes, wearing a basket over his head, and playing *shakuhachi* flute had to attract notice. That this person was a *spy* justifiably gives rise to an obvious question: how secret can a spy be with a basket over his head? Delving into the history of the *komuso* only deepens the mystery, starting with their oxymoronic descriptor as "lay-priest." Far from being religious men, they were former *samurai* warriors who had lost their masters during the upheavals and civil wars of the late sixteenth century. Their duty was to roam the streets to observe what the citizens were doing and saying and report back to the authorities, but because their headquarters was at a former Buddhist temple, many believed they were somehow priests; hence, the idea of the "lay-priest." The *shakuhachi* was not just a large tube of sturdy bamboo but its lower end was thick and rough from being part of the bamboo root. If need be, the *komuso* could defend themselves by striking opponents with the instrument's lower end. When not having to fight however—most of the time—they actually played the *shakuhachi*, developing a growing body of compositions. After being disbanded in the mid-nineteenth century, when the stigma of violence was separated from the instrument, the *komu-*

A Japanese Komuso playing the *shakuhachi* (Thomas Holton/Getty Images)

so promoted what came to be one of Japan's most treasured repertoires. After that the *shakuhachi* was embraced by *sankyoku* musicians and came to replace the *kokyu* bowed lute.

Dance: Japanese Music and Dance   by Kelly Foreman

Japanese traditional music historically shared a close relationship to dance in contexts ranging from sacred Shinto and Buddhist ritual, the Imperial court, the theaters, and chamber performance settings. The term *nihon buyo* today refers to classical Japanese dance, but this term was only adopted during the beginning of the twentieth century. The three terms—*mai, odori,* and *furi*—describe the three main types of Japanese dance seen in traditional dance genres. *Mai* describes the smooth, stately style of dance seen in *kagura, bugaku,* and *noh,* where dancers slide the feet and keep them low to the stage. In contrast, the energetic o*dori*-style dance is associated with outdoor festivals such as *Obon* and is characterized by energetic steps and faster movements, while *furi* describes the characteristic of mime and embodied story-telling.

The oldest dance is sacred Shinto ritual dance (and music) called *kagura*. The *Kojiki* (Records of Ancient Matters)

and *Nihongi* (Chronicles of Japan) describe a sacred dance performed by the goddess Ame-no-Uzume-no-Mikoto, who lured the hiding sun goddess Amaterasu out of her cave by climbing on top of an upended barrel and stomping her feet in an ecstatic trance. *Kagura* continues in Shinto ritual and outdoor festivals, ranging from the stately shrine dances performed by *miko* (shrine priestesses) to dramatic lion dances.

The arrival of Chinese officials brought Chinese imperial court dance, and these blended with *kagura* within the Japanese Imperial court setting to produce *bugaku* (accompanied by *gagaku* music). *Bugaku* retains the slow, restrained movements of *kagura,* keeping the feet in close contact with the stage. The dancers perform short, repetitive phrases toward the four directions of the stage, with the focus on the large and dramatic gestures articulated by the upper body.

The smooth, ethereal movements of *bugaku* were then incorporated into dance for the *noh* theater. *Noh* dance, or *noh-mai*, is elegant, slow, and circular, symbolizing the unhurried movements of court nobility (as well as the supernatural). It is transmitted by the guild-headmaster system, through stylised movement patterns or forms called "*kata*" (practiced also in Japanese martial arts) that tie together to form larger works. Specific characters in the play are conveyed through the actor/dancer's symbolic gestural vocabulary, as well as through masks.

In the early 1600s, a wandering Shinto shrine priestess named Izumo no Okuni combined the elegant *noh* dance with energetic *odori*-style dance, storytelling/mime, and comic interludes, and staged this as an all-female production on a Kyoto riverbed stage. For musical accompaniment, she combined the music of *noh* with the exotic *shamisen*, newly imported from the Ryûkyû islands. Dressed as a man and wearing a Christian cross, this unconventional theater was as popular as it was controversial, and it was soon banned. The *kabuki* then shifted to an all-male performance tradition in 1629, and incorporated highly-skilled female impersonation, several musical genres, stories of the puppet theater, and puppet-like poses within *kabuki* dances. Women—though banned from official positions within the theater—nevertheless learned and performed *kabuki* dances within private contexts, most notably as geisha. Formal guilds led by headmasters were established in order to transmit and manage dance training; accomplished dancers (including both *kabuki* actors and geisha) adopted (and continue to adopt) the family name of the headmaster as they do for music. In Kyoto, the Inoue dance guild chose to highlight certain aspects of the older *noh* dance, and the unique style of the Inoue guild is referred to as *Kyô-mai*, maintained amongst the Kyoto Gion geisha community. The use of the term *mai* in *Kyô-mai* positions this style somewhat apart from the dances of the *kabuki*, and underscores the subtleties in terminology for traditional dance in Japan.

After World War II, other styles of dance took root in Japan. In 1959, Hijikata Tatsumi and Ohno Kazuo gave a performance of uniquely Japanese contemporary choreography/performance art called *butoh*, and in 1964 the Tokyo Ballet was established based on classical Russian ballet models and repertoire. In addition to the many styles of traditional dance, there are studios and training centers in Japan for ballroom, contemporary, flamenco, hula, hip hop, samba, and others. As in North America, students and amateurs comprise the majority of dancers in these places, and serve an important role in maintaining their financial health and continuation.

Lastly, any discussion about dance/music relationships in Japan must include mention of embodiment in drum performance. Students learning Japanese drums—whether the *ko-tsuzumi*, *ô-tsuzumi*, or *shime-daiko* drums of the *noh* and *kabuki* theaters, the collection of drums performed within *taiko* ensembles, or the drums of the *gagaku* court ensembles—learn patterns focusing on choreography. The movements the musicians create with their bodies are as integral to the art as is the sound, recognizing an essential body-sound connection and perhaps connecting in some small symbolic way to Ame-no Uzume-no-Mikoto's sacred stomping dance performed on what could be seen to be, in fact, an early drum.

Two leading actors in a Japanese Kabuki play

cymbals or heavy drums—this music is refined and deliberate. Perhaps most easy to recognize are the "yo" and "ho" calls of the drummers at the transition from vocal to instrumental sections, a distinctive feature of *kabuki* and Japanese *noh* drama.

KABUKI
Popular music theater form developed for Japan's middle class in the seventeenth and eighteenth century.

Aural Analysis. When listening to an audio recording of a music theater work, it can be difficult to make sense of the music because one cannot see how it relates to the dramatic action. ***Kabuki***, a theater type developed in Japan during the late seventeenth and early eighteenth centuries as a newly rising middle class of business people coalesced in the city of Edo (now called Tokyo), has considerably more action and visual interest than Japan's earlier and more reserved theater, *noh*. *Noh* features slow-moving actors behind masks playing eternal human types to the minimalist accompaniment of three drums and a horizontal flute. *Kabuki* kept the instruments used in *noh* but added plucked lutes, sound-effects instruments (such as wood blocks, cymbals, and scrapers), and a greater variety of vocal sounds.

Our example features various forms of theatrical speech, and several types of instruments. First among the instruments heard is a group of long-necked plucked lutes called *shamisen*. The *shamisen*'s square resonator body is covered with catskin that supports a bridge carrying three strings from the bottom up the fretless neck to the top end. Because players use a large ivory (or plastic) pick, the resonator skin has an additional patch around the area where strings are plucked for its protection. The large picks give the instrument its strongly percussive timbre. Three drums then begin to punctuate the *shamisen*'s sound: an hourglass-shaped drum called *o-tuzumi*, which is held at the hip; a smaller version of the same drum, called *ko-tuzumi*, which is held on the shoulder; and a small barrel-shaped drum called *taiko*, which is played with two sticks. Next, a horizontal bamboo flute called *nokan* joins the ensemble. Lastly, one of the sound-effects instruments, a small metal gong, joins in. Throughout you hear occasional calls of "yo" and "ho." These surprising elements are drummers' calls and are considered part of the audible pattern of drumming. The total effect is one of diverse, unblended sounds that together make *kabuki* a unique sonic world.

As with much Japanese music, tonal subtleties abound, especially because of the frequent tone-bending heard in the *shamisen* and *nokan* to a lesser degree. Although each part seems to operate in its own world, all work together to achieve a continually changing flow of tension, relaxation, movement, and meaning. Underpinning this are the standard drum patterns, but their minimal number of beats makes perception of a regular downbeat or meter a challenge, though in most performances a regular duple meter can be felt.

Fighting scene in a Japanese *kabuki* performance

(left) *Kabuki* star Shoroki displaying his "mie" glance in the role of "The Spirit of the Earth Spider" in the *kabuki* play *Tsuchigumo* at the Metropolitan Opera House (Jack Vartoogian/ FrontRowPhotos)

(right) Famed *onnagata kabuki* star Bando Tamasaburo V dancing "Kanegamisaki" ("The Cape of the Temple Bell") during a solo performance at the Japan Society, New York City (Jack Vartoogian/ FrontRowPhotos)

In the village of Hinomata, Fukushima Prefecture, Japan, amateur *kabuki* actors perform each year for the entertainment of their neighbors (Koichi Kamoshida/ Getty)

Cultural Considerations. Kabuki theater, like Japan's other "classic" arts, is preserved in a living, but museum-like setting. In the heart of Tokyo's fashionable shopping district, the Ginza, sits a major theater, the Kabuki-za, which is dedicated entirely to twice-daily performances of *kabuki*. Inside this otherwise modern building is a wide proscenium stage. Two aspects are exceptional, however. First, there is a long walkway leading

Kabuki musicians who accompany *nagauta* songs: (back row left to right) singers, *shamisen* (lute) players; (front row) *taiko* (drum), *o-tsuzumi* (side-held drum), *ko-tsuzumi* (shoulder-held drum), and *nokan* (transverse flute) (Jack Vartoogian/FrontRowPhotos)

Chōbo narrators (left) and *shamisen* players accompany the story in a Japanese *kabuki* performance (Jack Vartoogian/FrontRowPhotos)

through the audience to the front of the stage area over which actors enter and exit when required. Second, most of the musicians are plainly visible on stage (positioned at stage left). Most of the singing and all of the narration are performed by a single vocalist accompanied by a *shamisen* player; this pair is known as *chōbo*. Unlike the *noh* stage, which has no props and only a painted pine tree as a backdrop, the *kabuki* stage has realistic scenery and props, including building facades.

Performances begin in the morning and continue in the afternoon following a lunch break, which may be taken within the theater itself (patrons may bring box lunches and eat them in their seats). Because of this schedule, there tend to be more women, some drawn to their favorite actors, than men in attendance, because most men work during the day. Women actresses have been banned from public *kabuki* performance for centuries, and some of *kabuki*'s most famous actors actually specialize in women's roles. Geisha (female dancers and musicians) perform large, staged productions that look like *kabuki* (newly created each year) at public theaters, while performances of dance and music pieces excerpted from the *kabuki* repertoire sometimes occur in private settings for patrons. The stories depict the lives of imaginary people from Japan's feudal age, the age of the *samurai* warrior. The example here is taken from a play titled *Dozyozi* or *Dojoji*, about a Buddhist monk who refuses the advances of a beautiful woman who later turns herself into a monster. As with virtually all Asian theater traditions, the goal is not realism but a highly stylized depiction of archetypical human scenarios, behaviors, characters, and emotions.

LISTENING GUIDE   7.8 (1'42")

Site 7.8

Japan: *Kabuki* Theater

Vocals: Single male vocal lead, briefly heard male vocal ensemble
Instruments: *Shamisen* (plucked lute), *nokan* (flute), *o-tsuzumi* (hourglass-shaped drum), *ko-tsuzumi* (smaller hourglass-shaped shoulder drum), *taiko* (barrel-shaped drum), *atari-gane* (small gong)

TIME	LISTENING FOCUS
0'00"	*Shamisen* (plucked lute) begins performance, followed by male vocalist.
0'19"	Vocal group utters non-lexical declamation to anticipate instrumental section.
0'21"	Remaining instruments enter. The *nokan* (flute) is the aural focus as the other instruments play supporting melody and rhythm.
1'02"	*Shamisen* briefly becomes the aural focus.
1'12"	*Nokan* reappears.
1'20"	Vocalist returns. Note how the *shamisen* and voice follow the same melodic line.
1'22"	Small gong enters.

Source: "Excerpt from *Dozyozi [Dojoji]*," performed by the Kyoto Kabuki Orchestra and recorded by Jacob Feuerring; from the recording titled *Japanese Kabuki Nagauta Music*, Lyrichord LLST 7134, n.d. Used by permission, Lyrichord Discs Inc.

MUSICAL MARKERS: Timbre/Medium—"Yo" and "Ho" vocal calls. Vocal timbre is nasal. "Twangy, banjo-like" timbre of the lute. Flute and small drum accompaniment. **Melody**—Seems to move "point to point," rather than "flowing."
ETHNO-CHALLENGE: With theatrical performances such as this, it is important to see the on stage activity. Locate and watch a video recording of a Kabuki performance in its entirety (*Dozyozi*, if possible).

Arrival: Tibet

Tibet is often referred to as "The Rooftop of the World" because it has the highest elevation of any inhabited region on the planet. The southern border of Tibet is formed by the Himalayas, which includes Mount Everest, the tallest mountain in the world at over 29,000 feet (8,800 meters). The northern and western borders are also surrounded by mountains, making the Tibetan plateau one of the world's most isolated areas.

Most Tibetans live between 4,000 and 17,000 feet (1,200 and 5,100 meters) above sea level. Generally, they live in rural areas practicing subsistence farming or raising small herds of Tibetan yaks, which provide milk and meat for nourishment as well as fur and leather for clothing and shelter. While nights in Tibet are typically bitter cold, daily temperatures vary widely. Early morning hours are often below freezing, while by midday the temperature can rise to more than 80 degrees Fahrenheit (26.6 Celsius).

Sudden storms are common, and travelers must always be prepared to find shelter should a sudden dust or snow storm occur. The high elevation and lack of vegetation result in low oxygen levels. While outsiders visiting Tibet may find it difficult to breathe, centuries of living in the region have enabled Tibetans to develop increased lung capacity. Still, Tibetans are cautious not to sleep at high elevations while traveling for fear of death from lack of oxygen. Tibetans cope with such survival difficulties through a strong spiritual life.

Explore More

Taiko

Taiko (meaning "big drum" in Japanese) references one of the most popular world music genres to draw international audiences in the past several decades. More correctly referred to as *kumi-daiko*, the first taiko drum ensemble was created in 1951 by Daihachi Oguchi (1924–2008), a Japanese musician with a love for American jazz. He gathered a variety of taiko drums associated individually with other traditions and combined them into a single ensemble. His early compositions were rooted in the drumming patterns of *Shinto* ritual music, but the organization was inspired by the structure of a jazz drum kit. Large, low-pitched taiko (e.g., *odaiko*) emulated the kick drum, while high-pitched taiko (e.g., *shime-daiko*) played more complex rhythms as would a snare drum. Other taiko (e.g., *nagado-daiko*) along with cymbals and other percussion paralleled the remainder of the kit. The result was an ensemble with a strongly traditional sound but a distinctly modern style.

Oguchi's idea was quickly appealing, and soon other *kumi-daiko* troupes formed. New compositions and performance techniques were incorporated, inspired by Japanese traditional arts. Choreography, drawn from martial arts movements, became an essential feature of performance. By 1964, this new style of taiko performance was popular enough to be featured in the opening ceremonies of the Summer Olympics in Tokyo. By the end of the decade, *taiko* troupes were traveling and performing for audiences throughout Europe and the United States. The San Francisco Taiko Dojo (est. 1968) helped spawn amateur and professional ensembles throughout the United States, which have flourished since the 1980s. *Kumi-daiko* ensembles are now a fixture of many music education programs in Japan and are commonly found throughout the world in association with Cherry Blossom Festivals, an annual Japanese celebration of flowers and the coming of Spring. Professional troupes, such as Kodo, are heralded by international audiences and have performed at many prestigious venues, such as Carnegie Hall (New York City, USA) and the Greek Acropolis. Taiko music is also often featured in Hollywood films and television commercials, as the style continues to thrive as part of a growing public interest in world music traditions.

Japanese *taiko* drummer (Shutterstock)

Tibetan Buddhism is practiced by the majority of the population, despite the region being considered a part of the People's Republic of China. While Tibet's relationship with China has ebbed and flowed for many centuries, Tibetans lived with relative autonomy under a theocratic government until 1959, when the communist Chinese government asserted its authority over the region and invaded. The Chinese placed severe restrictions on religious practice and in general attempted to Sinicize the region. The Dalai Lama, considered by most Tibetans to be a "living Buddha" as well as their secular and spiritual leader, fled to India to escape capture. Many monasteries were pillaged and numerous monks and other Tibetans were killed defending sacred sites and the Tibetan way of life.

Relations remain strained between Tibetans and the Chinese authorities. The Dalai Lama remains in exile but has helped to establish many Tibetan communities in India, Nepal, Bhutan, and even in the United States. While restrictions against religious practices in Tibet have eased, many of the monasteries are today considered museums and are more frequented by visiting tourists than occupied by monks. Tibetan secular culture continues to survive, but the centuries-old spiritual practices of the Tibetans are best examined in monasteries and Tibetan communities outside of the region.

Site 9: Tibetan Buddhist Ritual

First Impressions. For most outsiders, Tibetan ritual music has a mysterious and eerie sound. Alternately blaring and foghorn-like sounds produced by trumpets come in slow waves, supported by the rumble of drums and punctuated by the sound of a single cymbal. The guttural chants of Buddhist monks seem to summon centuries of sacred spirits, pressing listeners in the modern era to expand our definitions of music.

Aural Analysis. The music of Tibetan Buddhist ritual involves a limited number of instruments. The *kang dung* trumpet, traditionally made from a human thighbone but today made of metal, is most prominent with its widely wavering blare. *Dung kar* conch shell trumpets are played with a similar technique and are difficult to distinguish from the *kang dung* based on timbre alone. The *kang dung* and *dung kar* are played in pairs, with one performer overlapping his sound with the other so that a continuous sound is produced. In our example the *kang dung* sounds first with a slightly brighter timbre and a higher pitch, while the *dung kar* echoes at almost a semitone lower. The other distinctive instrument is the ***dung chen***, a metal trumpet that is usually between 5 and 12 feet (1.5 and 3.5 meters) long; the longer of these are usually played outdoors. *Dung chen* produce very low pitches and are also frequently played in pairs.

> **DUNG CHEN**
> A long metal trumpet with low tones blown during Tibetan ritual.

The percussion instruments found in Tibetan Buddhist rituals usually include drums and cymbals. The most common drums, *nga bom*, are double-faced frame membranophones that hang vertically in a stand and are struck by a hook-shaped stick. They have a deep timbre and are struck with slow, solitary pulses that usually correspond to either the trumpets or chanting. Large cymbals, called *rom*, are common as well and are most often played to accompany chant. While our example includes only one cymbal, which is struck lightly with a wooden stick, the *rom* are usually quite loud and are used to punctuate the ends of chanted phrases.

Throughout our example, the upper trumpets waver on their respective pitches a mere semitone apart, creating a very dissonant, unsettling sound. The *dung chen* begins with a low straight tone before rising to the pitch produced by the *kang dung*, which is the interval of a tritone (flatted fifth) above—an interval that Western theorists historically considered "uncomfortable." The percussion instruments are heard as well, seemingly in free rhythm, but actually following a long metric cycle articulated primarily by the drum. After the opening instrumental section, the drum provides a steady pulsation that accompanies the chanting monks, who dwell on a single low pitch. The instruments then interrupt before the *dung chen* sounds with percussion accompaniment.

Cultural Considerations. In Tibet, the chants and instrumental performances that appear in Buddhist ritual are regarded more as spiritual sounds than as music. The primary intended audience for such performances is the various deities and spirits associated with Tibetan Buddhism.

Buddhism is thought to have come to Tibet during the mid-eighth century with the arrival of Padmasambhava (717–762 C.E.), a legendary monk who was believed to have great magical powers that could drive away demons. Padmasambhava practiced a unique form of Buddhism known as Tantrism, which emphasized the use of symbols, ritual objects, and yoga practices in the quest for enlightenment. A primary goal of Tantric Buddhism, as Tibetan Buddhism is often called, is to overcome the fear of death and thus make death powerless to prevent a person from attaining enlightenment.

Tibetans have long been preoccupied with death. The fragility of life in the harsh environment of the Tibetan plateau led, before the arrival of Buddhism, to the development of a spiritual belief system known as *Bonism*, which was centered on a group of dangerous and fearful demons. Because these demons could control the elements and take life unexpectedly, Bonist priests performed rituals and gave offerings in order to appease them. Many of these priests were feared, as human sacrifices were among the methods used to win the demons' favor.

Tibetan Buddhist monks of the Gyuto sect performing the *dung-chen* (long trumpets) (Jack Vartoogian/FrontRowPhotos)

Tibetan Buddhist monk plays the *gyaling* (double-reed aerophone)

When Padmasambhava arrived with the assurance that Buddhism could overcome death and drive away such demons, most Tibetans embraced the new religion and its non-sacrificial rites.

One of the more interesting customs found in Tibetan Buddhism is the use of prayer wheels. While the ultimate goal of all Buddhists is to attain enlightenment, most accept that attaining a higher rebirth in the next life is a more practical spiritual goal. Chanting prayers is considered a way to earn spiritual merit, which in turn helps boost one's chances of a higher rebirth. Prayer wheels can help with this accumulation of merit. Each wheel has a prayer written on the outside, as well as a prayer written on parchment inside. Tibetan Buddhists believe that each time the wheel is spun, the words are "written on the wind."

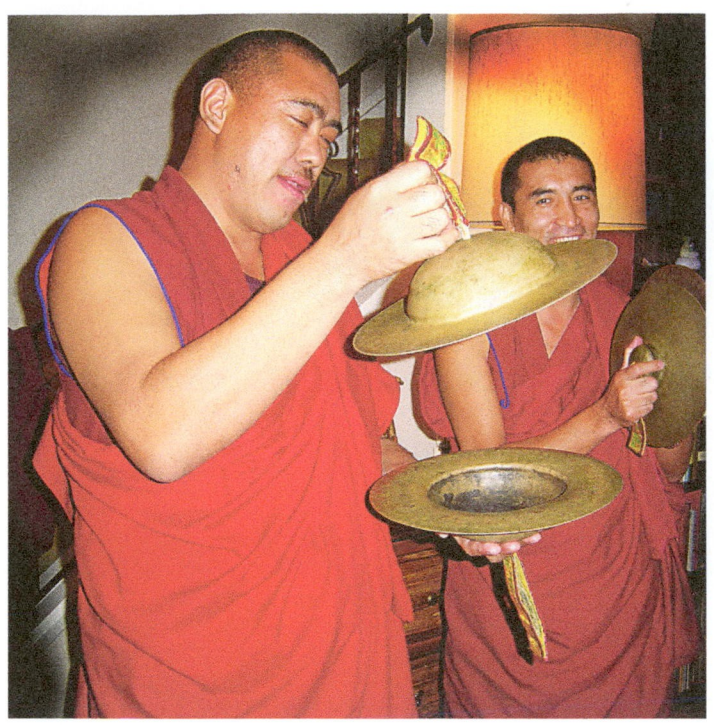

Tibetan Buddhist monks play a *rom* (pair of large cymbals)

Bodhnath Stupa, a temple frequented by Tibetans living in exile near Kathmandu, Nepal. A man chants on the left while another turns a prayer wheel on the right

LISTENING GUIDE

7.9 (2'03")

Site 7.9

Tibet: Buddhist Ritual

Vocals: Male vocal ensemble
Instruments: *Dribu* (bell), *dung chen* (low-range trumpets), *kang dung* (mid-range trumpets), *nga bom* (drum), *rom* (cymbals) and woodblock

TIME	LISTENING FOCUS
0'00"	*Dribu* (bell) sounds at start of example, followed by a *kang dung* (trumpet) and then a second *kang dung*. Listen for the "wavering" timbre and overlapping technique of the two trumpets.
0'02"	*Rom* (cymbals), which play throughout the performance, enter.
0'04"	*Dung chen* (long trumpets) enter.
0'07"	*Nga bom* (drum) enters.
0'10"	The *dung chen* sounds a higher pitch.
0'31"	Brief pause in the trumpet performance.
0'48"	*Kang dung* stop.

219

0′50″	Congregation of male vocalists chants along with more active performance on the *nga bom* and a woodblock.
0′55″	*Dung chen* stop.
1′07″	*Dribu* sounds again, followed by the *kang dung, rom,* and *dung chen.*
1′35″	The *kang dung* stop and the *dung chen* play a series of low bursts along with the *rom* and *nga bom.*
1′54″	Congregation of vocalists returns, accompanied by the *nga bom* and woodblock as the example fades.

Source: "Genyen gi topa ('In praise of Ge-nyen')," performed by the monks of Thimphu and nuns of Punakha and recorded by John Levy; from the recording titled *Tibetan Buddhist Rites from the Monasteries of Bhutan, Volume 1: Rituals of the Drukpa Order,* Lyrichord LYRCD 7255, n.d. Used by permission, Lyrichord Discs Inc.

MUSICAL MARKERS: Timbre/Medium—"Fog horn-like" deep trumpets and wavering mid-range trumpet pairs. Low guttural chanting marked by a bell. **Pitch**—Trumpets overlap at times to maintain a continuous pitch. **Form**—Alternates between blaring instruments and group chant.
ETHNO-CHALLENGE: Make a necklace of prayer beads—that is, a rosary (known as *mâla*) of 108 beads. Chant the sacred mantra, "*Om Mani Peme Hung*" (Om, Jewel of the Lotus) 108 times or, for a real challenge, one million times, as many Tibetans do for purification and to acquire spiritual merit.

Musical performances are most important to rituals involving groups rather than individuals. The blaring sounds of the trumpets are meant either to drive away evil deities or to call benevolent ones. The deep sound of the *dung chen* is said to imitate the trumpeting of the elephant, which is considered a powerful animal. The *dung kar*, which are highly valued instruments because conch shells are rarely found so far from the sea, can call spirits as well but are also frequently used to make announcements or to sound warnings. The *kang dung* is ideally made from a human thighbone, to remind believers that physical life is impermanent. These trumpets often play a prominent role in calling the faithful, be they living or ancestral spirits. The percussion instruments function primarily to emphasize structural points, by marking the ends of both instrumental and chanted phrases.

Chanting the *sutras*, or Buddhist prayers, is a primary activity among Tibetan Buddhist monks. The deep guttural utterances are said to represent the fundamental sound of the human body when all else is in complete silence. Complete awareness of one's physical self is an important aspect of preparing for the body's eventual demise. The body is, however, merely the cup that holds the spiritual nectar. When the body dies, the spirit is released and is housed in a new form. This consciousness of the impermanence of all things is fundamental to Tibetan theology.

Certain Tibetan Buddhist sects practice a unique form of chant in which they sound two tones at once, a low fundamental tone and a high frequency overtone. This technique is believed to enable a monk's spirit to travel to the spiritual plane. By visiting the spiritual plane, the monk is able to achieve "death without dying," and he thereby gains knowledge of the afterlife, thus robbing death of some of its fearful sting. During this chanting, a monk's heartbeat can slow dramatically and his breathing may become almost imperceptible. While only Tibetan monks perform these spiritual practices, the spiritual life of all Tibetan Buddhists is focused on overcoming their fear of death.

Questions to Consider

1. How do attitudes toward traditionality and modernization affect music differently in China than they do in Japan and South Korea?

2. How are music and the arts used in East Asian cultures to reinforce cultural identity, nationalism, and notions of authenticity?

3. How are the aesthetics of music in Japan shaped by both Confucianism and Buddhism?

4. How are the types of East Asian theater different from theater and opera in the West?

5. What spiritual role does music play in Tibetan Buddhist ritual?

6. How do East Asian attitudes toward professional musicians and actors contrast with the status of amateur music making?

Chapter 8
The Middle East

Islam and the Arab World, Iran, Egypt, Turkey, Israel

Istanbul's Sultan Ahmed Mosque, commonly called the "Blue Mosque," was built from 1609 to 1616 by the Ottoman Turks and today is the nation's primary mosque, with five great domes and six minarets.

Background Preparation

Geographically, the area covered in this chapter defies easy description. The designation *Middle East* is conventional and convenient—but it is also ethnocentric, as are *Near East* and *Far East*. After all, the regions these terms describe are only "near" or "far" from the perspective of the West. On the other hand, referring to the "Middle East" as "West Asia and North Africa" is clumsy, though geographically more specific. For this reason, we have chosen to adhere to the conventional term, whatever its drawbacks.

A second problem is that the boundaries of this region are less clear cut than those of most other areas: potentially, they encompass everything from Morocco in the west (directly south of Europe) to China's westernmost province, Xinjiang. The nations that can be said to comprise this area straddle three continents: part of Turkey is in Europe; five of the Middle Eastern nations are in Africa; and the rest are in Asia. However, some consider the former republics of the Soviet Union, such as Turkmenistan, Uzbekistan, and Kazakhstan, to be part of "Central Asia" rather than of the Middle East, but few books, including this one, can afford the luxury of a Central Asian chapter.

It has been customary to subdivide the Middle East into sectors. The major units are: (1) the *Maghrib* or North Africa, consisting of Morocco, Algeria, Tunisia, and Libya; (2) the *Mashriq*, consisting of Egypt, Israel, Jordan, Lebanon, Syria, and Iraq; and (3) the Arabian Peninsula, consisting of Saudi Arabia, Yemen, Oman, and the various smaller nations on the Persian Gulf. Turkey, Iran, and Central Asia are usually treated as separate areas, and culturally speaking Israel and Armenia are considered as special cases.

It is tempting to describe this vast region as the "world of Islam" because its nations and peoples are predominantly Muslim, but there are important exceptions such as Christian Armenia and Georgia, and Jewish Israel, as well as significant numbers of Zorastrians and believers in the Baha'i Faith. Islam, while certainly the predominant faith, is no more a unified monolith than, say, Christianity is in the West, or Buddhism is in Asia. Linguistically, while several mutually unintelligible language families are present, a certain unity has been created through the use of classical written **Arabic**, allowing learned people over a vast area to communicate, much as Latin once unified Europe and Sanskrit (or Pali) parts of Asia. Arabic belongs to the Afro-Asiatic family of languages, which includes all Semitic languages, Hebrew and Egyptian among them. The Indo-European languages are represented in the region by the Indo-Iranian subfamily, which includes Persian (Farsi) and Kurdish. Armenian is a stand-alone language, while Turkic

MAGHRIB
Literally, "the time or place of the sunset." The Arabic name designating the region from present-day Libya west through Morocco.

MASHRIQ
Literally, "the time or place of sunrise—the east." The Arabic name designating the parts of Asia (and Egypt) conquered and populated by the Arabs.

ARABIC
A Semitic language originating with the Arab ethnic group; also, the holy language of Islam, and a musical tradition whose history is intricately linked with the spread of the language.

Egypt's great temple of Ramses II at Abu Simbel moved to its present location when the Aswan High Dam was built in 1970 (Max T. Miller)

The exquisite Patio de los Leones (Courtyard of the Lions) is the most famous place in Granada's fourteenth-century Moorish palace, the Alhambra

languages, which stretch from Turkey to China's Xinjiang, are part of the Altaic family and are related both to Mongolian in the east and to Hungarian in the west. While language similarity might be expected to create greater unity, that is not always the case; for example, Arabs and Hebrew-speaking Jews have related languages but have been at odds for decades. Similarly, while Islam would seem to unify the region, it is also the basis for division and strife, because Islam has numerous factions that can be as different from one another as Christianity's multitude of sects.

When the Middle East is mentioned, many outside the region likely envision deserts, camels, nomads, pyramids, and simple villages where people are surviving at a subsistence level. While it is true that much of the Middle East is desert, other parts are quite lush, especially along the Nile, Tigris, and Euphrates rivers and there are regions filled with green fields, forests, and mountain streams. Parts of the Middle East also get quite cold and experience snow in the winter. While some Middle Eastern nations have major oil deposits, others have none and must import all the oil they use.

The Middle East is home to some of the world's earliest and most important civilizations. Indeed, the valley of the Tigris and Euphrates rivers, once called Mesopotamia and now largely within Iraq, is sometimes called the "Cradle of Civilization." The ancient Egyptians developed a great civilization along the Nile, leaving the world with incredible monuments, the pyramids among them. And Alexander the Great, a Greek-Macedonian, conquered much of the Middle East, leaving a strong imprint of Hellenic civilization throughout the region. The Middle East is dotted with extensive Greek and Roman ruins, testaments to the early spread of Greek learning and culture and the development of sophisticated urban areas.

During Europe's Middle Ages following the dissolution of the Western Roman Empire and the splintering of Europe into small, disorganized entities, classical learning flourished among the Arabs. Alexandria, Egypt, was home to what was perhaps the world's greatest library until 642, when its contents were burned on the orders of the city's conqueror, Omar, Caliph of Baghdad. Arabic music scholars, such as al-Kindi (790–874) and al-Farabi (872–950), preserved and developed Ancient Greek music theory, which later influenced European theory. Today's Middle East continues to produce highly sophisticated music, often in combination with some of the world's most fluid and sensuous poetry. In the midst of war and internecine violence, the Middle East remains home to unusually attractive music in spite of much of Islam's traditional distaste for such a sensuous art.

George Dimitri Sawa

AN INSIDE LOOK

I was born in Alexandria, Egypt. For socio-economic and political reasons, my music career began with Western rather than Arabic music. Before European colonization, an *ud* (lute) was often part of an Egyptian bridal dowry, but afterward middle-class wealth combined with the Arab inferiority complex toward the West caused us to replace it with the more expensive and "technologically advanced" piano. My father, who provided for his yet unmarried sister, and who always planned ahead, bought a piano as part of her dowry. My aunt never married, and lived with us, so the piano became part of our household.

I began my musical career by playing Egyptian popular songs by ear on the piano. My father, eager for me to develop good technical habits, took me at the age of ten to a private teacher, the eccentric and highly talented violinist and pianist Madame Irene Drakides. She had been a student of Alfred Cortot and had many stories to tell about her acquaintances with famous French composers Maurice Ravel and Gabriel Fauré, some of whose works she had premiered. She trained me well, and I later contemplated a career as a concert pianist. However, when I was in Sweden as an exchange student in electrical engineering, and played both Arabic and Western music on the piano to my hosts, they asked me the obvious question that I had never asked myself: "Why don't you play an Arabic instrument?" So I resolved to learn the *qanun* (zither), an instrument that had fascinated me from early childhood.

At the Higher Institute for Arabic Music in Alexandria, the teachers were all touched that an Egyptian skilled at the piano would turn to the *qanun*! I had a lot to learn, such as oral learning and the art of improvisation, but more to unlearn, because Arabic pre-composed pieces were not frozen entities, but instead improvised ornaments, tastefully executed, that made every performance unique.

George Dimitri Sawa, Egyptian musician and historian

After completing degrees in piano, *qanun*, and yes, electrical engineering, I emigrated to Canada to study musicology and ethnomusicology. Arabic music was to be my career, and there was no turning away from it. I was most interested in its performance history, which led me to research the medieval sources on theory and ethnography. No music program in North America could provide the training for this type of work, so I created my own program by doing a Ph.D. in two departments, Music and Middle Eastern studies. The latter gave me the necessary training in socio-cultural history and the bibliographical tools to research my subject. The medieval Arabic world that unraveled before my eyes was stunning. There was a fusion of musical styles, Arabic, Persian, and Byzantine; court patronage that generously maintained practitioners and scholars; a scholarship that combined the writings of the practitioners with Greek music theory and Middle Eastern humanities. In short, it was a discipline that predates modern ethnomusicology by a thousand years. I was hooked for life.

OTTOMAN EMPIRE
A powerful Turkish dynasty that ruled over various parts of West Asia, Eastern Europe, and northern Africa from the thirteenth to the early twentieth century.

    Arabic influence on Europe goes far beyond the ancient Greco-Arabic music theory that formed the theoretical systems of Europe's first millennium. The city known consecutively as Byzantium, Constantinople, and Istanbul served a historic role as a bridge between Asia and Europe over which culture passed in both directions. The vast **Ottoman Empire** that incorporated much of Southeast Europe for hundreds of years—in some places even into the early twentieth century—left those areas with many Turkish instruments and musical influences. In fact, most of Europe's instruments can ultimately be traced to Arabic sources. These instruments entered Europe both through Turkey and from North Africa, especially via Spain. For a thousand years or more before the expulsion of the Moors and Jews from Spain in 1492, both North Africa and Southern Europe were part of a unified Mediterranean and mostly Muslim culture. Europe—and European music in particular—would be unthinkable without Middle Eastern influence.

Planning the Itinerary

For readers whose curiosity remains unsatisfied by this necessarily brief survey, there are still more areas to explore. This is especially so of the Central Asian nations, whose music remains little known in the West. Beyond that is distant Xinjiang, the westernmost province of China, where Turkic peoples create music with close ties to the music of Turkey itself. At the other end of the Middle East, there is Morocco, where the remnants of Moorish-Andalusian music survive from Spain's Middle Ages.

While three major language groups are found in the Middle East—Arabic, Turkic, and Persian—Turkic and Arabic musical traditions are similar enough that we can combine them and discuss Middle Eastern music through two broad traditions: Arabic and Persian music.

Because Islam is of central importance throughout the entire region, we must of necessity give some consideration to the relationship between music and mosque. But because Israel is the world center of Judaism, we must also consider the role of music in the synagogue. Finally, our introduction to the music of Turkey keeps with a focus on religious traditions, namely the Sufi Dhikr Ceremony of the Mevlevi Order, though certainly there are numerous secular traditions throughout all these regions that could be presented.

Arrival: Islam and the Arab World

With more than 1.8 billion adherents, or 24 percent of the world's population, Islam is not just a major religion but a profound influence on culture—both generally and musically—around the globe. Though there is a close connection between the Middle East and Islam, both historically and demographically, Islam is also a major force in numerous countries beyond the Middle East, especially in Africa, South Asia, and Southeast Asia. Looking eastward, northern India is predominantly Muslim along with Pakistan and Bangladesh. Afghanistan, straddling both South Asia and the Middle East, is Muslim. In Southeast Asia two countries are predominantly Muslim: Malaysia and Indonesia, the latter being the most populous Muslim country in the world. In addition, the southern Philippines is Muslim. Muslims are also found in Thailand, Vietnam, Myanmar, and in smaller numbers in most countries of Southeast Asia. Western China, especially Xinjiang province, is Muslim, and most nations of Central Asia (Azerbaijan, Kazakhstan, Kyrgyzstan, Tajikistan, Turkmenistan, and Uzbekistan) are predominantly Muslim. In Africa, besides the northern tier countries—considered part of the Middle East at least culturally—Islam is prevalent in many countries, especially Nigeria. Because of the earlier expansion of the Ottoman Empire into Europe, much of Southeast Europe includes Muslim communities, while three nations—Kosovo, Albania, and Bosnia-Herzegovina—are predominantly Muslim. In the rest of Europe there are increasing numbers of Muslims stemming from the many "guest workers" and refugees brought to places such as Germany, the United Kingdom and France, as well as from refugees and political dissidents. Islam also flourishes in the United States, with the greatest concentration found in Dearborn, Michigan.

Most Muslims—estimated at 80–90 percent—belong to the Sunni branch. What sets Sunnis apart is their adherence to the *Qur'an* (also Koran), Islam's most sacred writings, and the *Sunnah*, which is the record of Muhammad's life. Sunni believe that Muhammad specified no particular leaders to follow after him, and therefore Sunni Muslims have no hierarchy of ecclesiastical leaders. The Shia, however, believe that Muhammad's cousin and son-in-law, Ali ibn Abi Talib, was his designated successor, and they consider Ali to have been the first *imam*, they being the religious leaders of Shia Islam. The Shia constitute only about 10–20 percent of the world's Muslims, but they have been exceptionally prominent politically because of conflicts in Iraq with Sunnis and because Iran is primarily Shia. Beyond these two major branches, there are numerous smaller branches, the most prominent being the Sufis, who are discussed in detail in Site 5, as well as previously introduced in Chapter 5 (Qawwali music, 5.4).

Site 1: Islamic *Adhan*, "Call to Prayer"

First Impressions. In our example, which features a man calling the faithful to prayer, the vocalist performs a single melodic line, adding fairly extensive and technically demanding ornamentation. This performance seems to meet most definitions of "music," as it has definite pitch, rhythm, and contour. Yet, in an Islamic context, this would not be considered as "singing"; it would be thought of, rather, as heightened speech or "holy" speech, delivered in a style requiring both declamation and the spinning out of syllables.

Aural Analysis. Anyone who has visited a Muslim nation has likely heard the "Call to Prayer"—in Arabic, the **adhan**—which is uttered five times daily. In most places today, considering the size of modern cities and the amount of noise from traffic, *adhan* are now transmitted through loudspeakers mounted on a tower at a local mosque, but in the recent past they were still performed acoustically. Because the purpose of the call is to communicate a specific message and because Islam discourages the use of the sensual arts, the call consists essentially of spoken words, but the manner of delivery takes on characteristics of melody. Indeed, some versions of the *adhan* are highly virtuosic and melismatic. The set of pitches used is normally characteristic of a musical *mode*, a term denoting not just a scale but typical melodic patterns as well. *Adhan* are melodically improvised to a certain degree and are also in free rhythm, being a series of declaimed phrases each separated by a pause. The words used are declaimed in classical Arabic and are virtually the same throughout Islam—the only exceptions being that the line "Prayer is better than sleep" is only chanted during the predawn call, and that Shia Muslims add the line "Ali is his successor" after affirming that **Muhammad** is the prophet of God:

ADHAN
The Islamic Call to Prayer.

MUHAMMAD
Muslim prophet and Arab leader who during his lifetime (570–632 C.E.) spread the religion of Islam and unified a great deal of the Arabian Peninsula.

Allahu akbar, Allahu akbar	God is great, God is great,
Ashhadu an lail aha illa ll ah	I testify that there is no god but God.
Ashhadu anna Muhammadan	I testify that Muhammad is the prophet of God.
ras ul Allah	
Hayya 'al a'l-sal at	Come to prayer.
Hayya 'al a 'l-fal ah	Come to salvation.
(Al-Salat khayr min al-nawn)	(Prayer is better than sleep.)
Allahu akbar, Allahu akbar	God is great, God is great.
Lail aha ill all ah	There is no god but God.

LISTENING GUIDE

8.1 (1'49")

Site 8.1

Islam: "Call to Prayer"

Vocals: Single male (*muezzin*)

TIME	LISTENING FOCUS
0'00"	Vocalist calls in free rhythm. The text setting is syllabic. Note that throughout the example, each initial line is primarily syllabic and then repeated with increased melisma.
	Line 1: *Allahu akbar, Allahu akbar* ("God is great, God is great").
0'07"	Line 1 is repeated with increased melisma.

0'17"	Line 2: *Ashhadu an lail aha illa ll ah* ("I testify that there is no god but God").
0'25"	Line 2 repeated with increased melisma.
0'35"	Line 3: *Ashhadu anna Muhammadan ras ul Allah* ("I testify that Muhammad is the prophet of God").
0'45"	Line 3 repeated with increased melisma.
0'58"	Line 4: *Hayya 'al a'l-sal at* ("Come to prayer").
1'05"	Line 4 repeated with increased melisma.
1'14"	Line 5: *Hayya 'al a 'l-fal ah* ("Come to salvation").
1'22"	Line 5 repeated with increased melisma.
	Note line 6 (see above) is not heard in this example.
1'30"	Line 7: *Allahu akbar, Allahu akbar* ("God is great, God is great").
1'40"	Line 8: *Lail aha ill all ah* ("There is no god but God").

Source: Islamic "Azan" ("Call to Prayer") by Saifullajan Musaev from the recording *Bukhara, Musical Crossroads of Asia*. Recorded, compiled and annotated by Ted Levin and Otanazar Matykubov, provided courtesy of Smithsonian Folkways Recordings, Smithsonian/Folkways CD SF40050, © 1991. Used by permission.

MUSICAL MARKERS: Medium—Solo male voice. **Rhythm**—Site 8.1 Free rhythm. Long pauses between vocal phrases. **Other**—Site 8.1 Listen for "Allah" reference throughout.

ETHNO-CHALLENGE: Visit a local mosque (with permission) and observe a service such as Friday prayers.

Cultural Considerations. Islam has a great deal in common with Judaism and Christianity, despite the misunderstandings and conflicts that have arisen among adherents of these three religions. All three are monotheistic—in fact, they worship the same god, who is called Allah by Muslims, Yahweh or Jehovah (also known as Adonai, meaning "Lord") by Jews, and God by (English-speaking) Christians. All trace their lineage to Abraham and recognize the biblical prophets. While Jesus of Nazareth, the man who is the basis of Christianity, is considered by many to have

The Beyazit Camii (Mosque), built in 1504, is Istanbul's oldest standing mosque

been a prophet as well as messiah, most Jews see Jesus as a "false messiah" or pay little heed to his presence, since Judaism does not place individual humans at the center of their faith.

For Muslims, Muhammad (570–632) was not just a prophet, but the central prophet. Born in the Arabian Peninsula, Muhammad lived in Mecca and Medina and founded Islam in the latter. While all Muslims accept the teaching of Muhammad, divisions arose after Muhammad's death. As a consequence, there are "denominational" differences in Islam, especially between the more dominant **Sunni** and the minority **Shia** branches of the religion. (Note, however, that Shia Muslims are the majority in Iran.) Shia Muslims differ from Sunni because of their belief that Muhammad's cousin and son-in-law, Ali, was the rightful successor, in contrast to the Sunni who do not accept Ali's legitimacy. Also, Shia designate spiritual leaders as *imam*, Ali having been the first of them. In addition to these main sects, there are many smaller sects, including the **Sufi**. Because Sufis seek union with God through trance, often induced through a variety of ritual activity accompanied by music, such as the whirling dance of the Mevlevi Order in Turkey (see below, site 5), some Muslims view Sufis as being so unorthodox that they are not considered mainstream Muslims.

Muhammad designated Mecca as Islam's holy city and built a great mosque there containing Islam's holiest shrine, the *Ka'ba*. Since that time, every Muslim capable of doing so is expected to make a pilgrimage (*hajj*) to Mecca; pilgrims are honored as *hajji* upon their return home. Muslims are also expected to pray five times a day, facing in the direction of Mecca. The Call to Prayer developed as a reminder to the faithful to fulfill this obligation. In English the term *mosque* denotes any building used for Islamic worship but the Arabic term is *masjid*. There is no typical architectural form associated with mosques; indeed, many early mosques were converted Christian churches. In Istanbul the oldest mosques, those built in the sixteenth century, follow the same

SUNNI
The mainstream or majority branch of Islam.

SHIA
The minority branch of Islam that follows Muhammad's cousin, Ali.

SUFI
The mystical branch of Islam.

Two minarets of Istanbul's famous Sultanahmet Camii, better known as the "Blue Mosque," built in 1616. A *muezzin* calls the faithful to prayer from the *minaret* five times a day

basic design as the city's much older Byzantine churches: both feature a central dome surrounded by smaller half-domes. Each mosque, however, has a *mihrab*, a semi-circular niche in a wall that orients worshippers toward Mecca for their daily prayers. Mosques are relatively empty compared to churches, because worshippers pray on the (usually carpeted) floor. While Friday is the day for hearing sermons in the mosque, Muslims are expected to pray seven days a week.

One architectural feature that distinguishes all but the earliest mosques from churches is the presence of one or more tall, thin towers called *minarets*. An essential function of the minaret is to provide a place from which to sound the Call to Prayer. The person who gives the call is commonly called a *muezzin* (properly a *mu'adhdhin* in Arabic). When Muslims hear the call, they are expected to stop what they are doing and either pray or be still and silent. This applies to traffic as well as to television programs in many countries, although this degree of observance occurs more frequently in the less secular states, such as Yemen or Iran, than in secular states such as Turkey and Egypt.

Although Islam is primarily associated with the Middle East, it is a major religion in other areas as well, including much of the central third of Africa, northern India, parts of southeastern Europe (especially Albania and Bosnia), and parts of Southeast Asia, especially Malaysia, Indonesia, and the southern Philippines; indeed, Indonesia has a greater population of Muslims than any other country. Consequently, one hears the Call to Prayer in places outside the Middle East such as Singapore; Bangkok, Thailand; Manila, The Philippines; New Delhi, India; and Lagos, Nigeria, not to mention the United States. For overseas Muslims out of hearing range of a mosque, two substitute methods have been devised. Some believers tune into a radio station that broadcasts the Call to Prayer, while others rely on computer applications, mobile phone apps, and battery-operated clocks programmed to emit a recorded Call to Prayer five times a day.

Most branches of Islam are suspicious of music, which they view as overly sensual. In Islamic aesthetic theory, expressions that combine pitch and rhythm—all of which would usually be classified as "music" in Western culture—are divided into a higher-level category called *non-musiqa* (non-music) and a lower-level category called *musiqa* (music). All categories of *non-musiqa*, including the Call to Prayer, are considered "legitimate." These include readings from Islam's holy book, the Qur'an (or Koran), which are delivered in heightened speech, as well as chanted poetry. Some *musiqa* is also legitimate, including familial and celebratory songs, occupational songs, and military band music, but the classical genres of *musiqa* as well as local types of "folk music" are considered "controversial," meaning that more fundamentalist Muslims generally discourage these traditions. At the bottom of this hierarchical scale is "sensuous music," such as American popular music, which is branded "illegitimate," though many liberally-minded Muslims throughout the world still listen to it. However melodic, musical, or sensuous you may find the Call to Prayer, it is considered by Muslims to be "non-music" and unsensuous, and therefore legitimate. These views clearly illustrate that definitions of "music" are culture-based and not universal.

Site 2: Arabic *Taqasim* for *Ud* and *Buzuq*

First Impressions. The timbre of the opening instrument sounds very much like a guitar. The timbre of the following lute has a much brighter quality, the two together suggesting perhaps "belly dance" music, though with a much dreamier atmosphere. The melodic line seems spontaneous without a regular rhythm, the two instruments alternating the lead role. This kind of music is heard throughout the Arab world, including Turkey. We could be in Beirut (Lebanon), Damascus (Syria), Baghdad (Iraq), Cairo (Egypt), Tripoli (Libya), Amman (Jordan), Istanbul (Turkey), or any number of other places throughout the Middle East.

UD (Also, AL 'UD)
A fretless, plucked pear-shaped lute that is found in Arabic music traditions and is the origin of certain lutes of Africa, Asia, and Europe.

Aural Analysis. The deeper sounding instrument first heard in the example is the **ud**, a large pear-shaped lute with a short fretless neck. The *ud* is found throughout much of the Middle East and is associated mostly with the "classical" tradition rather than village styles. With a history going back to the eighth century C.E., the *ud* has undergone numerous changes over time in terms of size and number of strings. Today the instrument most typically has five "courses" of strings, a course being a pair tuned in unison, but *ud* with four, six, or even seven courses exist today. The musician can stop the strings anywhere on the neck, because there are no frets; this allows for fine gradations of intonation. The player uses a plectrum, or sometimes the fingers or fingernails of the right hand, to pluck the strings over the middle of the instrument's body. The Middle Eastern *ud* is considered the original form of an instrument that traveled to Asia—where it became the Chinese *pipa*, the Japanese *biwa*, and the Vietnamese *tyba*—and to Europe, where it became the European *lute*, which reached its greatest popularity during the Renaissance, then gradually fell from favor during the eighteenth century. Indeed, the word lute derives from the word *ud*, typically referred to as "*al'ud*," that is, the *ud*.

The brighter sounding instrument that appears second in the example is called the *buzuq* and is different in many ways from the *ud*. It is used in both classical and non-classical music and has

Ali Jihad Racy, originally from Lebanon and now of the United States, plays the Arab *buzuq* (lute) (Linda Vartoogian/ FrontRowPhotos)

Close-up of the face of an *ud* (lute). See full picture in Chapter 3

a rounded body, nylon frets wrapped around its neck, and three double courses of strings played with a plectrum. One of the three double courses is played melodically, while the other two are primarily strummed to create intermittent drones. The *buzuq* probably derives from a similar instrument that the Turks call *saz*, and a form of it is found in Greece where it is known as the *bouzouki*.

The music in our example may sound improvised, because it is unmetered and the melodic line seems to spin out spontaneously. Middle Eastern "improvisation," however, should not be understood as a license for the players to do whatever they want. Rather, it provides an opportunity for the performer to compose, within strict boundaries, while playing. The usual Arabic term for the system within which improvisation occurs is **maqam** (*makam* in Turkish), a word loosely translated as "mode." As with the broad sense of the term *mode* (e.g., as when it is applied to the Indian *raga*), each *maqam* (pl., *maqamat*) consists not only of a scale but also of specific melodic forms, moods, and other non-musical associations; they are perhaps best viewed as "composition kits." In fact, there are many fully written ensemble compositions that include no improvisation but still follow the conventions of *maqam*.

Each *maqam* has a name and is characterized by a specific starting and ending note—as well as a set of specific pitches organized into two groups of four pitches, each called a *tetrachord* in English. Describing these pitches is difficult, however, because many differ in intonation from all twelve pitches of the Western equal-tempered chromatic scale. Arabic theorists have devised a system—which may vary slightly in actual practice—of twenty-four pitches in an octave, with each measuring fifty **cents** (i.e., a half semitone or quartertone). The basic seven steps of individual scales consist of combinations of two, three, four, or six quartertones. Two of these quartertones equal one Western semitone and four equal a Western whole tone, but three comprise an interval that is between a Western semitone and whole tone and six form an augmented (raised) second interval. If that sounds complex, indeed, it is.

To add to the complexity, a given performance may shift from one *maqam* to another. The complete track from which our excerpt comes begins in *maqam kurd*, with the pitches D, E♭, F, G, A♭, B♭ and octave C, but then shifts to *maqam rast* (F, G, A♭, B♭, C, D, E♭), to *maqam 'ajam* (F, G, A, B♭, C, D, E), to *maqam nahawand* (F, G, A♭, B♭, C, D♭, E♭), and, finally, to *maqam bayyati* (C, D♭, E♭,

MAQAM (Also, MAKAM) Arabic/Turkish mode or system of rules and expectations for composition and improvisation.

CENTS A way to measure sound intervals with 1200 cents in an octave and a semitone measuring 100 cents.

233

LISTENING GUIDE

Site 8.2
Arabic *Taqasim* Improvisation for *Ud* and *Buzuq*

Instruments: *Ud* (fretless plucked lute), *buzuq* (fretted plucked lute)

TIME	LISTENING FOCUS
0'00"	The *ud* begins the performance. Listen for the mellower timbre and lower range of this instrument compared with the brighter timbre of the *buzuq*. Also, note that the performance is in free rhythm throughout.
0'02"	The tonality of the improvisation is established with this sustained pitch.
0'31"	*Buzuq* enters, overlapping with the concluding phrases of the *ud*. Listen for the *ud* returning to the tonal center, but an octave lower than what was originally established. Note also that the *ud* does not drop out entirely, but just lowers its volume and melodic activity as the aural focus shifts to the *buzuq*.
0'51"	The aural focus shifts again to the *ud*. Note that the *buzuq* continues to play at a quieter volume and with less melodic activity.
1'15"	The aural focus shifts yet again to the *buzuq*. New tonalities are briefly established, but the phrase returns to the original tonal center at its conclusion.

Source: "Maqam Kurd," performed by Ali Jihad Racy, *buzuq*, and Simon Shaheen, *ud*, from *Taqasim: Improvisation in Arab Music*, Lyrichord LYRCD 7374, n.d. Used by permission, Lyrichord Discs Inc.

MUSICAL MARKERS: Timbre/Medium—"Dueling" plucked lutes (chordophones). *Ud* has a darker quality due to use of nylon strings. *Buzuq* has a brighter quality due to use of metal strings. **Rhythm**—Free rhythm. **Pitch**—Uses modal improvisation with frequent ornamentation. Scale often utilizes a minor second. Frequent tremolo (rapid repetition of a pitch) is heard.
ETHNO-CHALLENGE: The first phrase of this example (played on the *ud*) makes heavy use of a *tremolo* plucking technique (very fast on a single string). If not a musician yourself, locate a guitarist to show you the plucking technique and match the rhythmic density of this tremolo. Note how Western-trained musicians tend to pluck lutes by moving their forearm up and down, while Asian musicians pluck the instrument by rotating their forearm with a bent wrist.

F, G, A♭, B♭). Theorists disagree on the number of *maqamat*: some claim there are up to seventy or more. There is also disagreement on the categorization of *maqamat*, which are divided into three families by some theorists. In our excerpted example, two musicians realize the *maqam* through improvisation—that is, they explore the characteristic intervals and melodic fragments gradually and spontaneously, alternating between *ud* and *buzuq*. When one musician is prominent, the other strums lightly, playing drone effects or modestly mimicking the phrases of the other. Any resulting simultaneity of notes is incidental and does not constitute harmony of any sort because the music is conceived monophonically. These improvisations may occur alone or as part of a longer suite that also includes fixed compositions in meter. An unmetered movement featuring improvisation is called a *taqasim* (or *taqsim*) when performed by instrumentalists, and *layali* or *mawwal* when performed by vocalists. Whereas musicians of nearly any skill level can play metered compositions, only the most skilled can play *taqasim* with any authority.

Cultural Considerations. In addition to being suspicious of the sensual aspects of music, Islamic aesthetics frowns on realistic representation in art, especially of the human form, to avoid the temptation toward idol worship. But as with sound, it may not always be obvious to outsiders what is considered art and what is not. Important mosques boast interiors covered with beautiful

Though not considered to be artwork, the intense decoration of a mosque is analogous to the ornamentation of Arabic music. The recess in the center (*mihrab*) orients worshippers toward Mecca, Saudi Arabia, as seen in Istanbul's Beyazit Cammii (Mosque) of 1504

ceramic tiles, which certainly appear "artistic" to the Western eye, even if their designs are non-representational. Indeed, even Arabic calligraphy lends itself to incorporation into decorative design and can be considered artistic. Such designs are appreciated as expressions of spirituality and respect toward Allah, rather than secular indulgences in artistic splendor.

Within various cultures, an apparent correlation often exists between the degree of decoration found in art and architecture on the one hand and music on the other. In the case of Arabic music, this correlation is fairly compelling. Mosques characteristically have little undecorated space within them, and this is paralleled by the busy character of much Arabic music, in which the distinction between main notes and ornamentation is frequently blurred. Interestingly, whereas the ornamentation of classical *musiqa* is clearly categorized as "controversial," the same thing in a Call to Prayer is "legitimate" because the *adhan* is *non-musiqa*.

From the eighteenth century onward, Arabic decoration made a strong impression on Europeans. The French term *arabesque* came to denote European architectural embellishments featuring floral or curling patterns. In music the term denotes elaborately embellished melodies or counter-melodies, such as Claude Debussy's *Deux arabesques* for piano. Few of these compositions, however, have any further relationship to Arabic music per se. Some composers and musicians, particularly pianists, at Middle Eastern conservatories otherwise devoted to European music have sought to assert something of their roots by composing or improvising their own "arabesques" as well.

Arrival: Iran

Little visited these days by Western travelers, Iran, a country the size of Alaska or Quebec, is home to nearly seventy million people. Because much of the country is mountainous and rainfall is scanty except along the Gulf of Oman coast, Iran's large population often has to cope with difficult and dangerous conditions. Earthquakes are a constant concern in many areas, and when one occurs, typically large numbers of people die.

Iran, known as Persia until the twentieth century, is different from most of its neighbors on several accounts. The vast majority of its inhabitants share a non-Arab origin and speak Farsi, an Indo-European language related to that of the Kurds, who live at the juncture of Iran, Turkey, and Iraq. Most of Iran's population is Shia Muslim, Shia being the division of Islam that in many places is associated with the lower economic classes and that tends to express itself more emotionally than Sunni Islam, which has become the so-called mainstream form of Islam in most Middle Eastern countries. Shia Islam has a more developed clergy, the lower-ranking members being called *mullahs* and the higher-ranking ones *ayatollahs*. At various times, the more radical manifestations of the group's fundamentalist tendencies, such as the 1979 Iranian hostage crisis, have strained political relations between people and governments not only in the West but also among non-Shia Muslims and neighboring countries as well.

Persia has a long history, from its first flourishing in the sixth century B.C.E. under Cyrus the Great, through its periods of subjugation by Alexander the Great, the Parthians, the Turks, and the Mongols, to independence in the eighteenth century. Some consider its greatest period to have been during the rule of the Sasanian dynasty (third to seventh centuries C.E.). Modern Iran was created in the early twentieth century, along with a hereditary line of rulers called *shahs*, the last being Shah Muhammad Reza Pahlevi, who ruled until deposed by a revolution in 1979. Since 1979 Iran has been a theocratic democracy, ruled by an uneasy union of semi-official *ayatollahs* and official secular leaders.

Dome of mosque and two minarets in Isfahan, Iran, one of the country's centers of Islam (Rex Shahriari)

Site 3: *Dastgah* for *Santur* and Voice

First Impressions. Iranian classical music often has a melancholy mood. Both the instrumentalist and vocalist in this example express this quality through pitch, rhythm, and dynamics. Even the vocal timbre is heartfelt, encouraging an intimate atmosphere that is typical of Persian classical performance. On first hearing, this Iranian example may sound rather similar to the Arabic example heard earlier. It begins with a stringed instrument playing a rhythmically free melody in an improvisatory manner. This section then gives way to a section featuring an unaccompanied female singer, who continues the rhythmically free approach. Despite the apparent similarities between Arabic and Iranian music (or, more properly, Persian music), however, the two systems are conceptually quite different.

Aural Analysis. Although the instrument that introduces our example is a chordophone, a careful listener will detect a percussiveness that distinguishes it from the plucked instruments heard earlier in the Arabic *ud* and *buzuq* duet. Indeed, the player is using two small wooden hammers to strike the strings. Organologically, such an instrument is called a "dulcimer" or a "hammered zither," because the strings are parallel to a trapezoid-shaped soundboard without a neck, and struck by mallets. The instrument is a Persian **santur**, Iran's most distinctive and centrally important instrument. It is also considered by academics as the predecessor of the rest of the world's dulcimers, which are distributed as far as China and Korea in the east, Thailand and Vietnam in Southeast Asia, and Europe and the United States in the West. Indeed, some scholars even consider the European piano to have been inspired in part by the *santur*, because pianos work on the same principle of sound production, except that keys flip mechanical, hinged hammers against the strings.

SANTUR
A hammered zither from the Persian classical tradition.

The *santur* is constructed of a hardwood, trapezoidal-shaped body with a lower side around 3 feet (91 cm) in length and an upper side only around 14 inches (35 cm) across. Courses— groups—of four strings each stretch from tuning pins on the right over two rows of moveable bridges, in rows of thirteen and twelve respectively, to tunable anchor pins on the left. Players hammer the strings near the bridges on either side of the left row and on the left side only of the right row of bridges. If plain wooden hammers are used, the tone is more percussive than when players cover the mallet tips with felt or cloth, as is the case in our example. The *santur*, in slightly different forms, is also played in other Middle Eastern countries, though elsewhere it is not the centrally important instrument it is in Iran. Iconographical evidence dates the *santur* at least to the Babylonian period (1600–911 B.C.E.).

The vocal soloist who enters following the introductory section sings verses from the *Masnavi*, a book of mystical poetry written by the thirteenth-century poet Jalal al-Din Muhammad Rumi, who also founded the Mevlevi Order of Sufi Islam, famed for its "whirling dervishes" (see Chapter 8, Site 5). Written in rhythmically free verse, the sung text begins with the following lines: "The grieving of the heart announces the state of love / And there is no illness like that of the heart." Persian music, like Arabic music, is based on an elaborate modal system (recall that the term *mode* refers to a "composition kit" used in improvisation), which in Persian music is called **dastgah** (plural, *dastgah-ha*). Officially there are twelve *dastgah*, each having seven pitches, plus a number of sub-modes called *avaz*. The track heard here is in *Dastgah shur* (also spelled *shour*), which uses the pitches C, D♭ (flat one quarter step), E♭, F, G, A♭, B♭, and C.

DASTGAH
Persian mode or system of rules and expectations for composition and improvisation.

There are, however, essential differences between the Arabic *maqam* and Persian *dastgah* systems. Unlike Arab musicians, who rely on an oral tradition of melodic phrases appropriate to a specific mode, Persian musicians have created a vast body of "composed" melodic phrases that amount to short compositions; these are called *gusheh*. Each *dastgah*, then, is learned by memorizing a variable number of these short *gusheh* compositions that can then be strung together to create a longer and more complete performance/composition. Groups of *gusheh* are organized around specific pitches of the *dastgah*, allowing the player to progress from the lowest (or home) note, called the *ist*, to higher pitches, where the musical tension becomes greater. The number of *gusheh* employed in any particular performance depends on the performer's knowledge and needs, while the specifics of the *gusheh* used vary according to the player's "school" (or tradition). For pedagogical purposes, as well as to set a kind of national standard, scholars have

The Persian
santur (dulcimer)

collected and printed all the *gusheh* for all the *dastgah* in a book called the *radif*. Therefore, a student can memorize as many *gusheh* as might be needed for performance, but the *radif* itself differs from "school" to "school" ("school" being the tradition of a single master), as different music masters altered the original melodies to their unique style preferences.

A complete performance of a *dastgah* typically unfolds in several sections and requires a substantial amount of time, because the sections can be quite different from each other. A typical performance's opening movement, called the *daramad*, is rhythmically free and emphasizes the lower-pitched *gusheh*. Following this is the *tahrir*, another section in free rhythm emphasizing melismatic melodic work. Then follow two metered pieces called *kereshmeh* and *chahar-mez-rab* respectively, which are followed in turn by a repetition of the rhythmically free *daramad*.

Cultural Considerations. The classical *dastgah-ha* of Iran form a vast and flexible system, which allows musicians to create both fixed compositions and improvisations by stringing together numerous short compositional blocks. Naturally, this system also calls for an element of individual creativity, because Persian music-making is about far more than building Lego-like performances.

LISTENING GUIDE 8.3 (2'58")

Site 8.3

Iran: *Dastgah* for *Santur* and Voice

Vocals: Single female
Instruments: *Santur* (hammered zither)

TIME	LISTENING FOCUS
0'00"	*Santur* begins in free rhythm. Listen for the creative use of variations in volume. Also, note the free-flowing tonality, challenging the listener to hear a tonal center, which is only finally solidified on the last pitch in octaves heard just before the voice enters (0'59").

0'04"	Tonality focuses on G (fourth scale degree).
0'13"	Tonality focuses on F (third scale degree).
0'24"	Tonality focuses on D (tonal center).
0'50"	Tonality focuses on C (seventh scale degree).
0'59"	Tonality centers on D (tonal center) to anticipate the entrance of the vocalist.
1'02"	Vocalist enters, confirming the tonal center. Listen for her melismatic ornamentations that diverge from the tonal center briefly and then return.
1'38"	*Santur* plays solo break.
2'11"	Vocalist returns. Listen for the *santur* reinforcing the basic pitches of the melodic line.

Source: "Dastgah of Shour" by Mohamed Heydari, *santour*, and Khatereh Parvaneh, voice, from the recording entitled *Classical Music of Iran: The Dastgah Systems,* SF 40039, provided courtesy of Smithsonian Folkways Recordings. © 1991. Used by permission.

MUSICAL MARKERS: Timbre/Medium—Bright hammered zither (*santur*). Vocal quality is "melancholy." **Rhythm**—Free rhythm. **Pitch**—Frequent use of melisma in vocal line. Note the "rolling" (like a drum roll) on extended pitches. **Form**—Alternates between instrumental solo and vocal with accompaniment.
ETHNO-CHALLENGE: Use an electronic tuner to determine how many cents "flat" the named scale degrees (C, D, F, and G) are in this example compared with standard Western tuning (A = 440 Hz). Sing the fundamental pitch (D—quarter tone) throughout the vocal section to hear how the singer ornaments around this pitch.

The Persian *tar*, a distinctively shaped lute with six strings

The art comes in how the *gusheh* are joined to each other and in how they are subtly changed and elaborated. Because musicians belong to various "schools" and consequently have learned different approaches to the *dastgah*, specific *gusheh* generally sound different from one performance to another. The use of measured rhythm in metrical cycles is no longer as significant in Persian music as it once was, and the metered pieces found in suites, such as the *chahar-mezrab*, employ fairly simple rhythmic patterns. While foreign audiences generally prefer the metered compositions because of their use of one or more drums and their steady beat, Persian musicians and connoisseurs value rhythmically free improvisations most highly for the display of refined musicianship they allow.

Although the *santur* is probably Iran's most iconic instrument, other kinds of instruments are important as well. These include two plucked lutes, the *sehtar* and the *tar*. The latter's skin-covered body has a distinctive shape, resembling the number "8." Also important is the round-bodied bowed lute called *kemancheh*. One aerophone, the *ney*, an end-blown notch flute found throughout the Middle East, is commonly heard. The main percussion instrument is a goblet-shaped, single-headed drum called the *dombak* or *zarb*, which resembles the Arabic *darabuka*.

Arrival: Egypt

If any nation typifies the Middle East, it is Egypt. Her ancient civilization, nearly as old as civilization itself, seems to live on through incredible relics—the pyramids, the Sphinx, great temples, hieroglyphics, wall paintings, and mummies—and is symbolized by the River Nile, which flows thousands of miles northward out of Africa to the Mediterranean Sea. This nation, which constitutes the northeast corner of Africa, is smaller than Canada's Ontario province, but has a population of eighty-three million. That the land can support so many is surprising considering how much of Egypt is desert. Most of the fertile land is found along the Nile, where many crops, including great quantities of cotton, are grown. The Suez Canal, opened in 1869, connects the Red Sea to the Mediterranean Sea and separates the main part of Egypt from the Sinai Peninsula.

Although ancient paintings depict musicians playing harps, lyres, lutes, flutes, double reeds, and other kinds of instruments, little is known about the sound of Egyptian music until long after contact with Islam. However, coastal Egypt, particularly Alexandria, was part of the ancient Mediterranean civilization, where Islamic-period Arab music theory was brought to an intellectual zenith during the first millennium of the Christian era. Music in modern-day Egypt reflects a welter of more recent influences, including European art music, which has made Egypt—at least urban Egypt—a center of European musical culture outside Europe. For example, Italian composer Giuseppe Verdi's opera *Aida*, whose music is European but whose locale is set in Egypt, was commissioned by Khedive Ismail of Egypt in 1869 for the opening of the Cairo Opera House.

Site 4: *Takht* Instrumental Ensemble

First Impressions. With its catchy beat and sinuous melody, this piece may bring to mind the image of a veiled belly dancer swaying gracefully before an audience. Some of the instruments might seem familiar, including one that sounds like a tambourine, but the tuning of a number of the intervals heard among the melodic instruments sounds "off," one in particular.

Egypt's Great Sphinx of Giza, which along with the pyramids, is a symbol of ancient Egypt (Denise A. Seachrist)

Aural Analysis. Songs accompanied by instrumental ensembles pervade Egyptian musical life. They run the gamut from religious songs—as heard in this case—to folk songs, wedding songs, and love songs. Egyptian instrumental ensembles may also, however, perform on their own, without a vocalist. The musical systems found among Egyptians generally contrast slower-paced and unmetered music played by a single musician with clearly metered music played by a group, with or without a vocalist. In contrast to the improvisatory approach that is such an important part of solo performance, instrumental groups play fixed compositions. In Egypt the typical ensemble is called a **takht** and consists of three to five players, though more are possible. In modern times these ensembles have often been enlarged through the addition of new instruments, some borrowed from Europe, a region some Middle Easterners jokingly call the "Near North."

Most of the melodic instruments found in *takht* ensembles are chordophones, such as bowed lutes, plucked lutes, and zithers, but at least one aerophone, the end-blown cane flute (*ney*), is nearly always present as well. Among the most prominent of the plucked lutes is a pear-shaped *ud* lute. Of the bowed lutes, the *kemanja*, an unfretted spike fiddle, is most prevalent, but today *takht* ensembles may also incorporate violins, 'cellos, and even string basses. The most important zither is the **qanun**, a four-sided instrument resembling an autoharp that has an amazing number of tuning mechanisms to allow for various tunings (see photo below). Our recorded example features *ud* (plucked lute), violin (bowed lute), *ney* (end-blown flute), *qanun* (plucked zither), *riqq* (tambourine), and *tablah* (goblet drum). The melodic instruments perform the same melody but with slight variations, resulting in a slightly heterophonic structure.

Three types of drums may be found in *takht* ensembles: the *duff*, the *riqq*, and the *tabla*. The *duff* is a small, single-headed drum sometimes having snares; the *riqq* is similar but has pairs of small cymbals inserted into the frame that jingle when the head is struck (i.e., it is a tambourine). The *tabla* is a small, goblet-shaped single-headed drum similar to others with different names found throughout the Middle East but is not related to the Indian pair of drums of the same name.

TAKHT
An Arabic music ensemble including zithers, bowed and plucked lutes, drums, aerophones, and sometimes non-traditional instruments.

QANUN (ALSO, KANUN)
A plucked zither used in Turkish and Arabic music traditions, prominent in *takht* ensembles.

A small *tahkt* ensemble (front row) and two belly dancers (back row). Front row, left to right: *ud* lute, *kanun* zither, *darabukka* drum (George Sawa)

Collection of Middle Eastern hand drums: (left) Moroccan *bendir* with snares inside, (lower) Arabic *riqq* or *def*, (above) Persian *daf* with internal ring chains, (right) Nubian *tar* from southern Egypt and northern Sudan, and (middle) Egyptian *tabla* goblet drum, called *darabukka* in Turkey (N. Scott Robinson)

Arabic drumming is highly organized, and much of it is conceived as being in closed cycles of beats. The standard, named patterns realized by drummers are known in Arabic as *iqa* (plural, *iqa-at*), best translated as *rhythmic modes* in English. Using named drum strokes, drummers continuously play a given mode or cycle, with greater or lesser degrees of elaboration and ornamentation, to reinforce the metrical organization of a composition's melodic parts. Even when Egyptian composers create fixed pieces, they work within the Arab modal system called *maqam*, which governs the choice of pitches and intervals and offers standard melodic patterns as well. Compositions are also divided into certain well-known set forms, with names such as *dulab*, *tahmlla*, and *bashraf*.

During the mid-twentieth century, an orchestra-sized variant of the *takht* ensemble appeared. Known as *firqa*, these larger ensembles sometimes include a chorus in addition to the principal vocalist. As with the smaller ensembles, the instruments used are mostly chordophones and aerophones, the former including most Arab possibilities plus members of the Western violin family, and the latter being mostly end-blown flutes of the *ney* variety. While traditional ensembles play heterophonically, performances by modernized *firqa* ensembles are usually highly arranged, with varied orchestration and occasional harmony.

Cultural Considerations. In addition to accompanying singers, *takht* ensembles also accompany dance. From the perspective of most Westerners, Middle Eastern dance is synonymous with "belly dance," which is often assumed to be erotic because of the undulating pelvic movements that are so stereotypical. In fact, this dancing is a highly skilled activity that is often appreciated for its technical merits. Traditionally, the dancers who mastered the most rapid hip movements were called *ghawazi*, a term derived from the name of the Ottoman coins that adorned their costumes. The nearest equivalent to the Western conception of belly dance is the **raqs sharqi**, which varies from performances by fully clothed artistic dancers to stripteases. Interestingly, the latter were historically performed by foreigners rather than Arab women, because Arab women could never hope to be married if they had been associated with erotic displays. Another

RAQS SHARQI
The Arabic name for what is commonly referred to by outsiders as "belly dance."

distinctive form is the *sham'idan* (candelabrum dance), so called because the dancer performs with a large, heavy candelabrum with lighted candles balanced on her head. Some theorize that these dances once symbolized fertility for Egyptians, but others claim that they came from the Halab and the Ghajar, two Rom tribes from India who entered Egypt most likely with the Ottoman Turkish armies in 1517.

LISTENING GUIDE

8.4 (9'41")

Site 8.4

Egypt: *Takht* Instrumental Ensemble

Note: The below description was contributed by Scott Marcus, the lead member of the ensemble in this recording.

Instruments: *ud* (plucked lute), violin (bowed lute), *ney* (end-blown flute), *qanun* (plucked zither), *riqq* (tambourine), and *tablah* (goblet drum)

TIME	LISTENING FOCUS
0'00"	The set starts (with *ud*) in *maqam nahawand* on G, similar to the Western minor (G A B♭ c d e♭ f♯ g) except that the minor third is significantly lower in pitch than the piano's equal-tempered minor third. Many (theorists) understand this third to be a Pythagorean minor third (294 cents as opposed to 300 cents), although performers do not think in terms of cents.
0'58"	Next, we play a *dulab* in *maqam nahawand* on G. *Dulab* is an instrumental genre. The compositions are very short. *Dulab*s serve to set the *maqam* of the following pieces; in this sense, they serve the function of a prelude, although note that 'prelude' is a Western term that is not used in Arab music. *Dulab*s are generally older compositions, understood to come from an unknown past: no known composer, they were part of the tradition in the late nineteenth century, but we do not know when the genre or these specific compositions appeared. As in our example, *dulab*s commonly move between two different rhythmic modes, the first called *wahdah*, and the second called *maqsum*.
	The pattern for *wahdah* is D – MT – KT – (i.e., dum – ma tak – ka takk –).
	The pattern for *maqsum* is DT – TD – T – (dumm takk – takk dumm – takk –). Both of these patterns take the same amount of time. In staff notation, they are written as 4/4. In our *dulab*, there are six repetitions (six measures) of *wahdah*, then seven repetitions of *maqsum*, then a return to *wahdah*.
1'40"	Next we have a violin *taqasim* on a *wahdah* ostinato in *maqam nahawand* on G.
2'42"	Full ensemble returns.
3'23"	Next a *ney* (end-blown reed flute) *taqasim* in *maqam nahawand* on G on a G drone (no ostinato).
4'28"	Then a *qanun* (plucked zither) *taqasim* on a ciftetelli ostinato. This ostinato is twice as long as the *wahdah* or *maqsum* rhythms, and thus could be understood as an 8/4: (D – MT – K T – D – D – T –). The first half is similar to the *wahdah* pattern. The *qanun* includes a modulation to *maqam nawa athar* on G: G A B♭ c♯ d e♭ f♯ g.
5'37"	(Pause) Then we play a high energy instrumental composition composed by Muhammad 'Abd al-Wahhab (*c*.1900–1991). This composition occurs in the middle of a lengthy song that 'Abd al-Wahhab composed for the singer Umm Kulthum (*c*.1900–1975). The song is called "Fakkaruni." (Note each instrument is highlighted with brief solo passages.)

7'38"   In the middle of this instrumental piece, we feature a drum solo. The drum, called tablah, in Egypt, is metal with a plastic head (the norm since the old-style clay drums with skin heads lost out in the mid- to late 1980s).

8'36"   We conclude after the drum solo by returning briefly to the Fakkaruni composition.

Source: A short *waslah* performance in *maqam nahawand* and *maqam nawa athar*, performed by members of the University of California, Santa Barbara Middle East Ensemble, Dr. Scott Marcus, director, 2011. Used by permission.

MUSICAL MARKER: Medium/Rhythm—Opens with a solo plucked lute (*ud*) in free rhythm. Ensemble enters in a regular meter. **Form**—Mostly follows a similar pattern of a solo instrument in free rhythm followed by an ensemble break in a regular meter. **Pitch**—Tuning system is not "Western." Scale sounds "minor" through use of "Pythagorean minor third." **ETHNO-CHALLENGE:** Find and record a song by a local musician or group. Play the recording back to them and ask for a description of the piece from an "insider" view. Create a Listening Guide, such as that above, based on their commentary.

Dance in Egypt is also closely associated with religious expression, particularly among members of the more mystically inclined sects. Dance in a religious context can bring participants to great spiritual heights, including states of ecstasy and even possession.

Ali Jihad Racy, a noted scholar and performer of Arabic music, asserts that the essential difference between European music and Middle Eastern music is that the former strives for the representation of images and concepts (including structural patterns), and the latter strives to evoke intense emotions in both the performers and the listeners. These emotions can affect people in both positive and negative ways, a concept known as *ethos* to the Greeks and *ta'thir* to the Arabs. Indeed, for Arabs, music has the power to heal and to bring people closer to union with God. As Racy remarks in his book *Making Music in the Arab World*, "In Arab culture, the merger between music and emotional transformation is epitomized by the Arab concept of **tarab**" (p. 5). Although much Arabic music can be described in purely technical terms (e.g., the modal system), the goal of Arab music-making is not so much to create clever structures as to bring listeners into a state of ecstasy. Although this ecstasy can have a religious dimension—by bringing the

TARAB
Arabic word for a state of emotional transformation or ecstasy achieved through music.

An artistic depiction of belly dance drawn by Richard Bong for the art magazine *Moderne Kunst* (Modern Art), Year VII, No. 22 published in Berlin in 1892–93. (Photo by DeAgostini/ Getty Images)

hearer into spiritually heightened states—music's sensual aspect is still viewed as suspicious by Islamic theologians, and consequently, as we have read, *musiqa* is proscribed from the mosque.

Arrival: Turkey

Sufism is frequently described as the "mystical" branch of Islam. While Sufis regard themselves as being part of the Sunni tradition and as having the same core religious values as all branches of Islam—namely, belief in Muhammad as the last prophet of Allah—their interpretation of the Qur'an allows for activities, especially with regards to music, that are discouraged or prohibited by most other Muslims. A fundamental philosophy of Sufism is that a person can become one with Allah through the elimination of the ego, a belief rejected by orthodox Islam. This controversial belief results in a variety of opinions, both negative and positive, of Sufi practices. Many Muslims consider Sufis devoted followers of Allah, but others view them as heretics whose ritual practices are sacrilegious. In Turkey, Sufis have been held in high esteem for centuries. The Mevlevi sect, one of the best-known Sufi orders, was founded there in the thirteenth century and exerted great influence on rulers of the region for several centuries.

The term *Sufi* is derived from the Arabic word *suf*, meaning "wool," in reference to the woolen robes worn by devotees. Sufi brotherhoods are numerous, each having its own rules and rituals. Many Sufis seclude themselves in monasteries, called *tekke* or *khanegah*, in order to focus exclusively on their spiritual quest to know Allah. Others practice trades in the secular world and perform the sacred rites of their brotherhood only on specific occasions. Still others commit themselves to an itinerant existence. This latter lifestyle earned Sufis a secondary title, *dervish*, which loosely translates as "beggar," as the wandering clerics rely on alms from the general public for their survival. *Dervish* is the term most frequently used in the Western world for those Sufi orders that present public performances of sacred music and dance as a means of disseminating knowledge about their religion. The term, however, is perhaps better thought of as applicable to those Sufi practitioners accepting material poverty in pursuit of their spiritual path.

Site 5: Sufi *Dhikr* Ceremony of the Turkish Mevlevi Order

DHIKR (Also, ZIKR)
A Sufi devotional act in which believers chant the name of God with the goal of entering an ecstatic state.

First Impressions. Unlike most Islamic worship, with its solemn mood, Sufi music is often upbeat, though with an undertone of seriousness. This performance, a hymn recorded in Turkey, is almost like a spinning top: it seems repeatedly to slip and then straighten itself, until it finally slows and comes to rest. Accompanied by several instruments, the voices swirl round and round and up and down. This exuberant celebration of devotion to Allah then gives way to a more solemn mood as a single voice cries out over the hearty chant of fellow worshippers.

Aural Analysis. Sufi music of the Turkish Mevlevi Order varies in mood and instrumentation. The *ud*, *qanun*, *kamance* (also spelled *kemanja* and *kamence*; a spiked bowed fiddle), *ney*, and *bandir* (a frame drum) are the most common instruments, although the *tanbur* (a fretted plucked lute), *riqq* (tambourine), and occasionally the *kudum* (a kettle drum) and *halile* (cymbals) are sometimes included as well. The *ney* is particularly important in Sufi ceremonies of the Mevlevi Order and is often used for extended solos.

Vocal performance in Sufi music of the Mevlevi Order belongs to one of three categories. The most prominent type is associated with the male vocal specialists known as *zakirler*, who perform metered passages in unison. This type of singing is heard in the first section of the track. The melodic contour of this vocal performance continually rises and falls, supported by the melodic instruments, while the *bandir* provides a steady duple-metered pulse. The tonal center shifts frequently, keeping the music always slightly off-balance. While the text setting is primarily syllabic, melismatic descents occur at the peaks of concluding phrases.

After this "swirling" singing, the tempo slows and the other two vocal categories are heard simultaneously. In the foreground, the vocal soloist chants rhythmically free melismatic passages akin to the *muezzin*'s Call to Prayer. This style of singing is known as *kaside*. Some instruments accompany the voice, providing key melodic pitches for the vocalist's reference rather than complete melodic passages. This allows the vocalist to improvise his melodic phrases without being bound to a specific melody or rhythm. Other instruments do, however, follow a pulse, which is articulated by the remaining *dervishes*, whose performance is an example of the third vocal category. The chorus sings a deep, raspy chant, consisting of repetitions of the phrase "*Hu, hu,*" meaning "It is He" ("He" being Allah).

JALAL AL-DIN MUHAMMAD RUMI
Sufi saint of Islamic mysticism known for his poems and as the founder of the Mevlevi religious order.

Cultural Considerations. For Sufis, chants provide the believer with the opportunity to attain union with Allah. Indeed, they believe that music is a primary way of reaching this ultimate goal. Sound is thought to be a vital link between the spiritual and physical realms. Whereas orthodox Islam, as we have seen, generally discourages musical performance, especially in the context of worship, Sufis emphasize its use as a means of heightening spirituality. Rather than believing that music tempts the soul away from Allah, Sufis assert that music merely strengthens a person's inclinations and temperament. Thus, music performed in religious contexts with the intention of uplifting the soul is acceptable and often necessary, whereas music played in the context of sensual indulgence only reinforces the sinful nature of the flesh.

One of the most important contexts for Sufi musical performances is the *sema* ritual, where the devotional act known as *dhikr* (also called *zikr*), a name that translates as "remembrance," is performed. The practice of *dhikr* differs among Sufi orders, but the best-known form of the ceremony is associated with the Mevlevi sect founded by **Jalal al-Din Muhammad Rumi** (1207–1273 C.E.).

LISTENING GUIDE

8.5 (1'57")

Site 8.5

Turkey: Sufi *Dhikr* Ceremony of the Mevlevi Order

Vocals: Male vocal ensemble. Single male vocal with male group chant.
Instruments: *Ney* (end-blown flute), *kemanja* (bowed lute), *ud* (plucked lute), *kanun* (plucked zither), *bandir* (frame drum).

TIME	LISTENING FOCUS
0'00"	Listen for the "swirling" ascending–descending vocal line and matching melodic instruments following a steady duple meter. Note the reference to "Allah" in the text that corresponds to an ascending melodic contour.
0'06"	Text changes and several voices drop out.
0'21"	Tonality shifts, but note the continued use of a "swirling" melodic line that now emphasizes a descending contour.
0'35"	Tonality shifts again, but continues with the descending melodic phrases.
0'50"	"Allah, Allah" refrain returns.
1'05"	Vocal ensemble drops out and tempo slows.
1'09"	Listen for the regular pulsation of the ensemble's hearty chanting. The instruments continue to be heard, but the melodic instruments are minimally active.
1'16"	A single male vocalist chants a freely rhythmic and melismatic text setting.

1'28" The *ney* (flute) can be heard briefly, supporting the lead vocalist's melodic line.

Source: "Sufi Hymn (Turkish)," performed by the Jarrahi Dervishes and recorded by J. During, Konya, Turkey, 1982, from the recording entitled *The Silk Road: A Musical Caravan*, SF 40438, provided courtesy of Smithsonian Folkways Recordings. © 2002. Used by permission.

MUSICAL MARKERS: Timbre/Medium—Group of male vocals with accompanying ensemble. Flute (*ney*) is most prominent melodic instrument. **Melodic Contour**—Vocal line "swirls" with ascending and descending phrases in opening section. **Form/Rhythm**—Second section features a vocal lead in free rhythm contrasting wtih "raspy" rhythmic chanting of the group at a slow tempo.
ETHNO-CHALLENGE: Perform the "whirling" dance of the Sufis by spinning continuously throughout this example. As you spin, experiment with moving your hands away from your body and tilting your head to the side. Note what body positions encourage a "disconnected" feeling more quickly.

In this version of the ceremony—which is particularly associated with the December 17 memorial celebrations held in Rumi's honor in Konya, Turkey—music and dance are often performed for the public. The Western notion of Sufis as "Whirling Dervishes" is derived from this and similar ceremonies because the dances require performers to spin in a circle on one foot for an extended period at varying speeds. When a dancer is spinning at his fastest, his white robes become a blur, much like an ice skater doing a final spin at the Olympics.

A Sufi devotee uses music and dance in these ceremonies to progress through the evolutionary stages of the soul toward the ultimate goal of experiencing the absolute reality of Allah. By chanting the names of the ninety-nine divine attributes of Allah while performing specific ritualistic movements, Sufis enter a trance-like state in which they become spiritually ecstatic. Sufis describe this feeling as "soaring." Many Sufi ritual performances are hidden from the public and involve such amazing feats as piercing the body with swords, chewing on glass, or walking on hot coals to demonstrate the power of Allah working through the individual believer. Our recorded example is typical of the music found in private ceremonies.

The "whirling" dances of the Mevlevi sect are also intended to help believers achieve a spiritually ecstatic state. As the musicians play, the dancer rises and removes his black outer garment, which symbolizes the darkness of the secular world. Beneath this outer garment are

Sufi Muslims of the Mevlevi ("Whirling") sect, perform the *sema* ritual on stage in New York (Jack Vartoogian/FrontRowPhotos)

inner white robes that symbolize the purity of Allah. As the dancer spins, he raises his right hand toward the sky and lowers his left hand toward the earth. This action represents Allah handing down his divine grace to all humanity. The spinning motion symbolizes the movement of the heavenly bodies—that is, the earth and moon—and helps the dancer to detach himself from the material plane and achieve a heightened sense of spiritual awareness.

Arrival: Israel

While Judaism is practiced by more than fifteen million adherents throughout North Africa, Western Asia, Europe, and the Americas, its "homeland," the state of Israel, is in the Middle East. A nation half the size of Switzerland, Israel was created on May 14, 1948, from an area formerly known as Palestine. Sometimes called "The Holy Land," Israel is of great religious significance for Jews, Christians, and Muslims, as it has what are perhaps the most revered historical sites or monuments for each group: the Wailing Wall for the Jews, as well as the Al Aqsa mosque for Muslims, the Church of the Nativity for Christians, and the Dome of the Rock mosque for both Muslims and Jews. As a result this land has been fought over for more than one thousand years, going back to the time before the medieval Crusades. Traditionally, people of all three religions lived together in the region—and they still do to some extent—but since 1948 there has been continuous tension over land, water, and religious and political rights and privileges.

Israel is a nation with both "traditional" (i.e., Asian/North African) and immigrant populations (European, American, Asian, and African). Historically, most Jews lived in the "Diaspora"—that is, the countries outside the Middle East to which they migrated—often suffering discrimination and marginalization. In Europe, Jews were long kept at arm's length from the mainstream populations but allowed to establish themselves in certain occupations, music being one of them. Over the centuries, in many times and places, Jews were made scapegoats for Europe's problems. Following the rise of Adolf Hitler in the 1930s, the Nazi Germans began a policy designed to exterminate the Jewish population, not just in Germany but also throughout Europe, and during the 1940s, before the liberation in 1945 by the Allies, the Nazis murdered some six million Jews in what came to be called The Holocaust. In reaction to this history of oppression, Zionism, a Jewish political movement begun in central Europe in 1897, advocated the founding of a Jewish state that would be a refuge for Jews worldwide. The establishment of Israel in 1948 realized that goal, though European Jews had already been migrating to Palestine for many years.

The Temple Mount in Jerusalem, including the Western Wall and the Dome of the Rock (Shutterstock)

Jerusalem's Dome of the Rock, called *Qubbat As-Sakhrah* in Arabic and built between 687 and 691, is a revered shrine (*mashhad*) for Muslims

Jews in the Diaspora belong to several distinct communities. The term *Sephardic* originally referred to Jews forced out of Spain by King Ferdinand and Queen Isabella at the end of the fifteenth century but has come to be applied to any Jew of North African or Asian origin. Jews from Europe are called Ashkenazi Jews, and because they were the primary advocates for the establishment of Israel, they tend to dominate modern Israeli politics. The musical traditions of the two communities are quite different, and among Sephardic Jews there are many distinct local traditions, such as that of Jews from Yemen.

The terms *Jewish music* and *Israeli music* are difficult to define. The former refers not only to music (both chanting and singing) heard in tabernacle ritual but also to non-liturgical songs of many sorts having Jewish content. Israeli music can only be defined as the sum of its parts, because Israeli society is partially secular and comprises people from all over the world. Perhaps the best-known representative of "Israeli music" is **klezmer**, a kind of European-derived dance music mostly developed in the United States and influenced by jazz and other non-Jewish styles. We have chosen to represent the religious side of Jewish identity through a genre from the synagogue, liturgical cantillation, as well as a brief blowing of a *shofar*, a unique instrument associated with Jewish ritual.

KLEZMER
A European-derived dance music commonly associated with Jewish celebrations, influenced by jazz and other non-Jewish styles

Site 6: *Shofar* and Jewish Liturgical Cantillation

First Impressions. First we hear the sounds of a trumpet-like instrument, the *shofar*. The unaccompanied male singing that follows seems rather random and hardly tuneful, suggesting that the text itself might be more important than the performance's musical qualities. Not being able to understand the words is a serious obstacle in this case.

Aural Analysis. Preceding the cantillation is a short segment of *shofar* blowing. Referenced in the scriptures, including the Torah, the shofar is a hollow horn of an animal, usually a ram, blown by an approved male to mark many auspicious occasions in the Jewish cycle of festivals, especially Rosh Hashanah and to mark the end of Yom Kippur. But it is also blown during services to mark divisions. Since there are no finger holes or other devices to control pitch, the player must "lip" specific overtones produced on this trumpet-type instrument. The example heard here uses only two pitches an interval of a fourth apart.

The musical elements present in our example are mostly functional, that is, they serve primarily to give the text prominence. If you listen carefully, you'll detect eight pitches spanning slightly more than one octave. In notation, from low to high, they are D, E, F, G♯, A, B, C, E. Two of them seem more important than the others, the A and lower E. These are the reciting pitches, with E being the resting point that gives a feeling of finality. The G♯ is what gives the chant its Middle Eastern flavor, because G♯ down to F natural is an augmented second. Descending from G♯ to F also produces an incomplete feeling only relieved by hitting the lower E. There is no regular meter; rather, the words are delivered in "speech rhythm." While the text setting is generally syllabic, there are also some melismas present.

Jewish cantillation, called *nusach*, is an oral tradition, though some scholars have attempted to notate the chants of particular singers. We say "attempted" because notating a freely sung text is an inexact science. The version performed here is attributed to a European singer named Zev Weinman and has been notated in a collection of service music in transcription. Tabernacle singers (called *cantors*) construct melodies from a body of traditional modes and melodic formulas that can be freely interpreted. The text chanted in the audio example is "L'dor vador nagid godlecha" and is sung in Hebrew, the sacred language of Judaism as well as the national language of Israel. The words, taken from a Sabbath morning service, are:

L'dor vador nagid godlecha	From generation to generation we will declare Thy greatness,
u l'neitzach n'tzachim	and to all eternity
k'dushatcha nakdish.	we will proclaim Thy holiness.
V'shivchacha, eloheinu,	And Thy praise, O our God,
mipinu lo yamush l'olam va'ed,	shall never depart from our mouths,
Ki el melekh gadol v'kadosh ata.	Because Thou art a great and holy God and King.
Baruch atah adonai,	Blessed art Thou, O Lord,
ha-el hakadosh.	our holy God.

Toledo, Spain, once the home for a large Jewish community, preserves the Synagogue of Santa Maria la Blanca, a twelfth-century building with Moorish arches. It was later converted into a church in 1411 when the Jews were driven from Toledo

While the above text is exactly as printed in the prayer book, the performer, Dr. Peter Laki, added the following comments:

1. I sang using an Ashkenazi pronunciation, which is like an Eastern European dialect. The transliteration follows official Israeli Hebrew, which is the Sephardic pronunciation.
2. Twice I sang "kel" instead of "el" (third line from bottom and last line). This is because "El" is the name of G-d, which the Orthodox don't pronounce unless they are actually at the synagogue. They add a "K" to "disguise" the name.

Cultural Considerations. The term *cantillation* is used to denote a kind of heightened speech that is between speaking and singing. Most religions of the world employ some kind of cantillation, because full-fledged singing is often forbidden or discouraged for various reasons, its sensuality being the common objection. In some cases, religious ritualists are forbidden to sing; thus, even if the cantillation they perform is quite melodic, it is still not referred to as "singing." It appears to be true throughout the world that sacred texts or holy words are thought to have more authority and mystery, and to be more clearly understood, if delivered in some form of heightened speech. The human relationship with the spirit or spiritual world requires an extraordinary form of dialogue, one that takes it outside the realm of ordinary speech or song.

Jews worship the same supreme god as that of Christians and Muslims, but Judaism traces continuous communication with that god during their more than 4,000-year history through a line of prophets beginning with Abraham. Judaism is especially distinguished by its careful attention to sacred law, which requires Jews to observe greater or lesser numbers of specific requirements depending on their position in the continuum from Ultra-Orthodox to Reformed. The audio example comes from the Orthodox tradition, though Conservative and Reformed Jews may also chant in this style.

The sacred texts of Judaism, written in Hebrew, constitute what is called the Old Testament by Christians. Of these books, the first five, called the **Torah** or *Pentateuch*, are most important. Sacred writings, both biblical and non-biblical (as in the present example) are read in heightened speech, or cantillation. Such readings may occur either in a synagogue or in a home. The term *service* describes liturgical rituals that can be held several times each day, though those held at

TORAH
In Judaism the first five books (*Pentateuch*) of the Bible or more generally, all sacred literature.

LISTENING GUIDE 8.6 (1'01")

Site 8.6
Israel: *Shofar* and Jewish Liturgical Cantillation

Vocal: Single male
Instrument: *Shofar* (trumpet)

TIME	LISTENING FOCUS
0'00"	*Shofar* sounds on two pitches followed by cantor.
0'27"	*L'dor vador nagid godlecha* ("From generation to generation we will declare Thy greatness,")
0'31"	*u l'neitzach n'tzachim k'dushatcha nakdish* ("and to all eternity we will proclaim Thy holiness").
0'36"	*V'shivchacha, eloheinu, mipinu lo yamush l'olam va'ed* ("And Thy praise, O our God, shall never depart from our mouths,")

0'42"	*Ki el melekh gadol v'kadosh ata.* ("Because Thou art a great and holy God and King").
0'46"	*Baruch atah adonai,* ("Blessed art Thou, O Lord,")
0'51"	*ha-el hakadosh.* ("our holy God").

Source: "Cycle of 10 Calls During Additional Service" by David Hausdorff, from the recording entitled *Kol Háshofar (Call of the Shofar),* Folkways Records FW8922, provided courtesy of Smithsonian Folkways Recordings, 1957. Used by permission. "L'dor vador" sung by Dr. Peter Laki, recorded by Terry E. Miller, Kent, Ohio, 2005. Used by permission.

MUSICAL MARKERS: Timbre/Medium—Two-tone trumpet blasts characterize the shofar. Male vocal recitation ("speech-like") with no accompaniment. **Pitch**—Each vocal phrase follows a melodic formula. **Melodic contour**— End of each phrase typically descends.
ETHNO-CHALLENGE: Visit a local synagogue and observe a service.

SHOFAR
A Jewish ritual trumpet made of a ram's horn.

the beginning of the Sabbath (also called Shabbat, Friday evening after sundown) and during the Sabbath (Saturday, before sundown) are most important. Jews also celebrate their religion through an annual cycle of festivals, as well as through more private rites of passage such as circumcision, *bar mitzvah* or *bat mitzvah* (held when, respectively, a young man or woman comes of age), and marriage. In Orthodox Judaism only males may recite the scriptures and liturgy. The use of musical instruments is generally avoided, but there are exceptions. Jews traditionally have used a ram's horn, called a ***shofar***, as a ritual trumpet blown during the High Holy Days (such as Rosh Hashanah and Yom Kippur) and to mark divisions in a service.

After the Jews failed in their revolt against their Roman conquerors in 70 C.E., the great temple at Jerusalem was destroyed, leaving only the "Wailing Wall," and the Jews were dispersed to many parts of the world. Jewish congregations today tend to be either Sephardic or Ashkenazi, though mixed tabernacles exist. Sephardic congregations preserve musical practices derived from

A Jewish ram's horn trumpet or *shofar* played by a rabbi in Yemen (Shutterstock)

the *maqamat* tradition of Arabic modal music. Ashkenazi congregations practice what is called the "Jerusalem-Lithuanian" style characteristic of Eastern European Jews. The audio example represents the tradition common to Eastern Europe, especially Poland, Germany, and Hungary. In Ashkenazi tabernacles the main ritualist who intones the sacred texts—the cantor—sings in a European style and may be accompanied by an organ in contexts where instruments are permitted, especially in Reformed congregations. While cantors in both traditions are not considered singers per se because what they do is technically "cantillation," many cantors are in fact fine singers and have turned their cantillation into a performance art rather than merely a way to declaim texts. Indeed, some, such as Robert Merrill, were also renowned opera virtuosi.

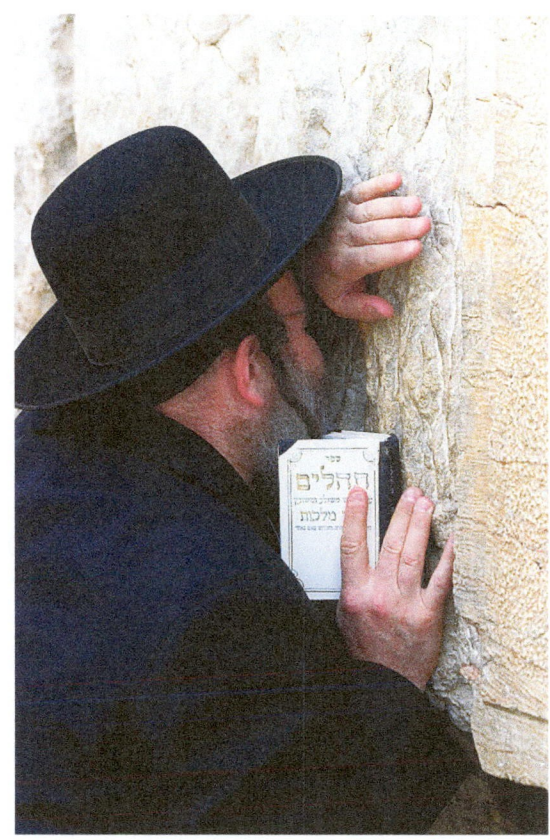

An Orthodox Jew praying at the Western (or Wailing) Wall in Jerusalem (Shutterstock)

Questions to Consider

1. How has Islam shaped conceptions of music for the peoples of the Middle East?

2. What is modal improvisation? Is it primarily a compositional or a freely expressive form of performance?

3. Because the Islamic Call to Prayer and Jewish biblical cantillation clearly have musical characteristics, why are they not considered "music" or "singing"?

4. What are the key factors that make Persian classical music different from Arabic music?

5. How do Sufi attitudes toward music differ from attitudes found in the other branches of Islam?

6. Taking into consideration the material discussed in Chapters 3 and 9, what are some of the musical relationships between the Middle East and Europe, especially in terms of instruments and musical styles?

Chapter 9

Europe

Greece, Spain, Russia, Scotland, Ireland, Hungary, Georgia

The Altes Rathaus, or "old city hall," in Bamberg, Germany, sits on an island in the Regnitz River

Background Preparation

Exactly what do we mean when we say "Europe"? If a friend were to tell you, "I'm going to Europe this summer," he or she would probably mean "Western" Europe, especially the United Kingdom (casually called Britain), France, Germany, Italy, Spain, and perhaps Switzerland and Austria. When a news reporter uses the term *European Union*, he or she refers not to all European nations but to a specific group of countries (which could theoretically come to include Turkey, a country not considered geographically part of Europe). In music history courses, when we refer to "European music," we mostly mean the "classical" tradition of "Western Europe." What, then, is Europe: a political entity, a geographical unit, a cultural area, or all of these things?

There are today some forty-one nation-states that constitute Europe, ranging from Russia, the world's largest country, to miniature city-states such as Monaco and Luxembourg. While forty-one may seem like a high number, before many of the modern nations such as Germany and Italy were unified in the nineteenth century, Europe consisted of scores, if not hundreds, of tiny states headed variously by kings, princes, dukes, and so forth. Many of the territories that are now part of nation-states were also successively part of the Roman, Holy Roman, and Austro-Hungarian Empires—though the "unity" of these empires was tenuous at best. During the nineteenth and early twentieth centuries, many nation-states were cobbled together out of linguistically, culturally, and ethnically distinct regions, mostly as a result of war (e.g., World War I). This process has recently begun to reverse itself: over the past twenty-five years or so, many small nations, particularly in central and southeast Europe, have formed after breaking away from larger ones. Even so, there are numerous other ethnic groups that would claim their own nations if they could, including the Basque, the Russyns, and the Vlachs.

Europe is also home to several groups who are not associated with any one region but are spread throughout the continent. One such group is the Rom—commonly known as "Gypsies"—a traditionally migrant people who originated in India. In those countries where the Rom have settled, whether they live in their own communities or are integrated into the mainstream, they have become an important part of the indigenous musical culture. Historically at least, the position of Jews in European society was similar; like the Rom, they were simultaneously insiders and outsiders but were nonetheless important to Europe's musical life.

Lübeck, center of the fourteenth-century Hanseatic League, is traditionally entered through the Holstentor, a mid-fifteenth-century double tower

In Telgart, Slovakia, the musicians are of Romani (Gypsy) descent, but they continue to play local music similar to that collected by Béla Bartók in the early twentieth century

The town band in Wenns (Tyrol), Austria, marches through town on their way to play an outdoor concert. Such wind ensembles, with their distinctive costumes, are a staple of small-town Austrian life

Sorting out Europe's peoples is challenging, but one possible way to group them is by language family. While most Europeans speak languages that belong to the overarching Indo-European family, some, such as the Finns, Hungarians, and Estonians (members of the Altaic family) and the Basque as well, speak non-Indo-European languages. Most Indo-European languages are members of one of four families: Germanic, Italic (or Romance), Balto-Slavic, and Celtic. In addition, there are at least three Indo-European languages that do not belong to any of these families: Greek, Albanian, and Rom. The table opposite classifies nations according to their primary language; some nations, such as Switzerland and Belgium, have more than one official language, however.

Both Roman and Orthodox Christianity along with Islam co-existed in Mostar, Bosnia and Herzegovina, once part of unified Yugoslavia, until the Balkan Wars of the early 1990s, when the famous Turkish bridge (*Stari Most*) over the Neretva River was destroyed; now it is rebuilt

While Ireland is listed in the Celtic category, relatively few Irish people still speak Gaelic. Celtic languages are also spoken (or were until recently) in the highlands and islands of Scotland, French Brittany, Wales, Cornwall in England, and in small pockets elsewhere.

While categorizing European peoples into language groups does help us to understand certain broad strands in European music, it is also essential to understand that none of these strands is isolated. As Hungarian composer and ethnomusicologist Béla Bartók (1881–1945) discovered early in the twentieth century, national musics cannot realistically be considered self-contained and unique unto themselves. Bartók, an ethnomusicologist before he became a composer, came to understand that Hungarian music, though distinctive, only existed in relationship to the musics of rival neighbors such as the Serbs, Romanians, Bulgarians, and even the Turks, with whom Hungary had long-standing hostilities. National boundaries within Europe have changed so many times over the years that it is all but impossible to think of any area as culturally consistent. On the other hand, it is also difficult to think of all these overlapping regions as comprising one "culture." Bearing this in mind, is it ever reasonable to use the term "European music"? The short answer is, probably not.

A Croat musician in the historic walled city of Dubrovnik plays the *lirica* (fiddle), an instrument type found throughout the former Ottoman Empire in southeastern Europe as well as in modern Turkey

A Croatian villager living in the highlands above Split plays the typical bagpipe of the region, the *diple*, with a double pipe providing both melody and drone

Table 9.1   Indo-European Language Groups of Europe

Germanic	Italic (Romance)	Slavic	Slavic (continued)	Celtic	Independent
Germany	France	Russia	Macedonia	Ireland	Greece
Austria	Belgium	Latvia	Serbia	(in part)	Albania
Switzerland	Italy	Lithuania	Montenegro	Wales (UK)	Armenia
Denmark	Spain	Belarus	Slovenia	Scotland (UK,	
Sweden	Portugal	Poland	Croatia	in part)	
Norway	Romania	Czech Republic	Bosnia-	Cornwall (UK)	
United Kingdom	Andorra	Slovakia	Herzegovina		
Netherlands	Monaco	Moldova			
Iceland	Switzerland	Ukraine			
Luxembourg		Bulgaria			

Table 9.2   Non-Indo-European Languages of Europe

Basque	Georgian	Uralic	North Caucasian	Hebrew	Turkic
Spain	Georgia	Estonia	Russia (North	Throughout	Cyprus
France		Finland	Caucasian	Europe in	Kosovo
		Hungary	regions)	diasporic	Azerbaijan
				communities	Greece
					Russia

"Classical" versus "Folk"

As with music everywhere else in the world, music in Europe is closely connected with notions of nation, region, ethnicity, and social class. The all-too-freely used terms *classical*, *folk*, and *popular* derive from European conceptions of how music exists in society. It is important to realize that these categories exist only in peoples' minds and may imply value judgments and hierarchical ways of thinking. The term *classical* refers to what is considered the highest class of music. This music is judged by standards that privilege complexity, individuality, and "sophistication," and that usually rate a long composition for a large ensemble as a "greater" achievement than a short piece for a small ensemble. Because music scholarship has primarily focused on "classical" music, and music scholars primarily work in universities, music students in universities, colleges, and conservatories worldwide study "classical" music almost exclusively. Consequently, for them "classical music" *is* European music—and, by the same token, European music *is* "classical music." Because classical music only flourished where there were wealthy patrons, courts, and aristocracies, relatively little classical music originated in southeastern Europe or much of eastern Europe or in other places where such support systems and contexts were often missing, such as Ireland, most Slavic states, Portugal, and Greece. The areas formerly under Ottoman Turkish control, some until the early twentieth century, naturally could not develop a "classical" music in the European tradition until they had established their independence.

What the field of ethnomusicology adds to the study of European music is a focus on what is usually designated "folk music," as well as an "outside" perspective on classical music. *Folk* is a demographic concept based on the assumption that there are "folk" and "non-folk." What is implicit is an evaluative hierarchy that places "folk music" in a humble position relative to "classical music." The notion of a "folk"—and by extension of "folk music"—is an outgrowth of Romanticism, an aesthetic orientation that flourished in the latter part of the eighteenth century and throughout much of the nineteenth century. Romanticism originated in the northern sectors of Europe, especially German-speaking areas, and was viewed as an antidote to the domination of "classical" French and Italian culture. Most spoken drama at the time, for example, was in French and most opera was in Italian, even in places such as England and "Germany" (in quotes because Germany as a unified nation did not yet exist). Germanic peoples were made to feel that their culture and languages were inferior to Mediterranean culture and languages—but with the rise of Romanticism they began to assert their cultural independence.

The term *folk song* (*Volkslied* in the original German) was coined by the philosopher Johann Gottfried Herder (1744–1803), who believed that the essence of a culture was in its peasants—whose pure souls were uncorrupted by the Industrial Revolution that had created poverty, pollution, and the destruction of traditional patterns of life. The "folk" were the antidote to the ills of the modern world. This notion stimulated a great deal of field research into northern roots, especially seen in the collecting of folk tales and

France's Chartres Cathedral, built by an unknown architect between 1194 and 1260, has mismatched towers folk songs. Many of these tales and songs were published in influential collections, such as *Grimm's Fairy Tales* and *Des Knaben Wunderhorn* (The Youth's Magic Horn), the latter a compilation of songs collected from the "folk" by Arnim von Achim and Clemens Brentano early in the nineteenth century. *Folk*, then, is a category that existed only in the minds of "non-folk" advocates such as Herder.

Our view, however, is that European music cannot really be divided into discrete "folk" and "non-folk" categories—there is, rather, a continuum from the music of the "lowliest" villager in Slovakia, for example, to the most sophisticated music of the aristocracy in Paris. Indeed, some of the historical music studied in music history classes as part of the "classical" evolution was originally the music of non-aristocrats. Likewise, in Europe much "classical music" was everyone's music: reed bands organized by factory workers played excerpts from symphonies, amateur choruses sang excerpts from operas, and player pianos and other automated musical instruments included classical excerpts on their rolls and barrels.

When its regions are considered together and all layers of its music are explored, the musics of Europe are revealed to be incredibly rich. Extensive as the classical orchestral instruments are, their number pales in comparison to the variety of instruments seen at the village level, from medieval survivals to the many exotic instruments that came to Europe from the Middle East via the Ottoman Empire and Moorish Spain. Collectively, the various vocal styles found throughout Europe feature most of the sounds humans are capable of uttering. "European music," then, encompasses everything from lullabies to operas, and its sounds range from the plaintive melody of a shepherd's flute to the power of a massed orchestra or pipe organ.

Planning the Itinerary

Europe consists of so many individual nations—many of which are home to several distinct peoples—that it is impossible in this brief survey to explore more than a few examples of European music. Of necessity, our itinerary must be highly selective.

Though Judaism exists in parts of Europe and Islam is important in the southeast, particularly Bosnia and Albania, and is increasingly significant in France and Germany, Europe is otherwise predominantly Christian. Thus, we include some music that is related to Christianity—Greek Orthodox (Byzantine) chant. From Europe's vast array of attractive and sometimes unique instruments, we have chosen two that allow exploration of several broad issues: the Russian *balalaika* and a representative of the *hurdy gurdy* family. Because bagpipes are pervasive throughout Europe—and not just a Scottish phenomenon—including bagpipes is a must. We have chosen two types—Irish and Scottish—in order to contrast two methods of operation. Caucasian Georgia's choral singing has been widely noticed outside Georgia, as has the Flamenco tradition from Spain, so we have chosen to include discussions of these as well.

Arrival: Greece

Greece can be considered in two ways: (1) as one of the classical cultures that forms the foundation of Europe; and (2) as a modern nation that shows much influence from its centuries under Ottoman Turkish rule. Classical Greek civilization centered on Athens from about 800 to 300 B.C.E., then spread throughout the Macedonian-Greek Empire of Philip of Macedonia and his son, Alexander the Great, the latter having been responsible for spreading "Hellenistic" culture over a vast area of Central Asia and North Africa. When the succeeding Roman Empire divided into West and East, Greece became part of the latter. After 1453, when it came under Ottoman Turkish rule, Greece was profoundly influenced by its conqueror, and modern Greece, especially in the north; this is displayed in its cuisine, architecture, and musical instruments. While urban Greece is clearly European, the countryside preserves distinctive patterns of architecture, cuisine, lifestyle, animal husbandry, and music-making that reflects a complex history and much earlier traditions.

Site 1: Greek Orthodox (Byzantine) Chant

First Impressions. If you were expecting something like the music from movies such as *Zorba the Greek* or *My Big Fat Greek Wedding*, then Byzantine Chant, an austere form of Eastern religious music, might come as a surprise. It is typical of the religious singing of the Greek Orthodox Church, also called the Byzantine Rite, as practiced in Greece. Sung by voices alone, the low drone underscores the higher melodic line that carries the text. Together they call up visions of bearded, robed men solemnly singing in an ancient church bathed in the colored light of stained glass windows.

Aural Analysis. In churches where a formal order of service is observed—what is called the *liturgy*—the spoken and sung texts are regulated year round according to church season and feast. Among the most important seasons is Christmas, celebrating the birth of Jesus of Nazareth. The present example is a Greek Orthodox Christmas hymn, the text of which begins "Come, faithful, let us see where Christ was born" and continues saying (paraphrased) "Let us see the manger, let us regard the three wise men who came to honor Him, the shepherds who came to pay homage to the one born of a virgin." In church perhaps as few as two men perform the hymn. Our track was recorded by a small choir organized by the Society for the Dissemination of National Music in Athens consisting of males, the upper octave being performed, not by women (who customarily do not sing in a religious service) but by boys.

The first sound heard—let's call it E for simplicity's sake—continues to be held as the second (and upper) part begins the melody. The lower held part is called a drone. While drones can sound above or below the melody, low drones such as this are a typical feature of Byzantine chant. The melodic part ascends using pitches E, F, G♯, A, B, C, D, and the upper octave, E, thus restricting the melodic range of the chant to one octave. Rhythmically, the chant is simple, with

Modeled after early Christian churches in the Eastern Roman Empire, this modern Greek Orthodox church is in downtown Athens

only two durations, the longer one being twice the length of the shorter one, creating an overall feeling of duple time, though not rigidly so. About three-quarters of the way through there is a brief passage in which the C becomes a C♯, giving the chant a "major" feel—but almost immediately C♯ begins alternating with C natural, and in the last part of the chant the scale returns to its original form.

The scale heard here does not conform to any standard scale form known elsewhere in Europe. It is neither major nor minor, nor any variant of them. Byzantine chant theory centers around a complex system of modes that provides both scales and a broader basis for melodic composition, a system somewhat like that of the Indian *raga* or Arabic *maqam*. These modes are called *echoi* (singular, *echos*). The scale of the present example is described as *kathisma*, chromatic fourth mode. It is believed that over time the chant became more and more complex melodically, to the point that church goers could not understand the words. At some point the chant was reformed through simplification, which the reformers assert is more like its early form.

Cultural Considerations. Note that only male voices are heard. Following a strict interpretation of Paul's admonition to the Corinthians, "Let your women keep silence in the churches; for it is not permitted unto them to speak" (I Corinthians, 14:34), the early churches forbade women from speaking, singing, or preaching; this is still true in some denominations today. In the Greek Orthodox Church, the leadership is exclusively male.

Today's Greek Orthodox Church represents the survival of the old Byzantine Church, originally centered in Byzantium (later called Constantinople), in modern Turkey. For centuries, the Byzantine (or Eastern) Church was more or less unified with the Western Church under the leadership of the Pope in Rome. In 1054, however, the Eastern Church split off, and from then on a Patriarch based in Constantinople oversaw it. After the fall of Constantinople to the Ottoman Turks in 1453, Eastern Christianity retreated back into Europe, and as the Turks expanded into southeastern Europe bringing Islam with them, the center of the Eastern Church retreated further to a mountainous peninsula off northern Greece called Mount Athos. Isolated from the Turks and

High above the sea on a sheer cliff, the fourteenth-century Monastery of Simonopetra (Simon and Peter) is one of dozens scattered throughout the mountainous Athos peninsula, technically the Monastic Republic of Athos, a roadless enclave belonging to the Greek Orthodox Church

LISTENING GUIDE

9.1 (1'43")

Site 9.1

Greece: Greek Orthodox (Byzantine) Chant

Vocals: Mixed male/female ensemble

TIME	LISTENING FOCUS
0'00"	Vocal drone is established on a pitch slightly below E♭. The upper voices rise to A♭.
0'08"	First verse begins. Listen for the continuous drone on E♭. Note that the melodic line establishes a regular pulsation at a tempo of roughly 104 beats per minute. Observe that the number of pulses for each line is inconsistent. The first phrase consists of ten pulses.
0'13"	Observe that the number of pulses for this phrase consists of nine pulses.
0'18"	Observe that the number of pulses for this phrase consists of eleven pulses. Continue to monitor the number of pulses for each phrase of the text.
1'02"	Listen for the unstable shift to a "major" sounding pitch (B), which then quickly returns to the original mode.
1'16"	The drone pitch drops to an A♭. Listen for the change in melodic pitches as well.
1'28"	The drone pitch returns to an E♭.

1'38"   Chant concludes with the drone pitch and melodic voices on A♭ (an octave apart).

Source: "Come, Faithful," from the recording entitled *Byzantine Hymns of Christmas.* Society for the Dissemination of National Music SDNM 101, n.d. Used by permission.

MUSICAL MARKERS: Timbre/Medium—Mixed vocal group. Strongly reverberant, as if performed in a church (a typical setting). **Phonic Structure**—Monophonic with a drone. **Rhythm**—Regular pulsation, but inconsistent meter. **ETHNO-CHALLENGE:** Keep track of the number of pulses used for each line of text. Also, try singing the drone pitches throughout the performance.

Islam, thousands of monks built marvelous monasteries, many high above the sea and accessible only by dangerous mountain trails. Today the Athos peninsula remains a technically independent religious entity, the Monastic Republic of Athos, administered by the Greek Church; it is mostly lacking roads and other forms of development and is strictly off limits to women. There, a much-diminished number of monks preserve the Church's oldest traditions, including its chant.

This chant is also heard throughout Greece in numerous "Greek Orthodox" churches and in some overseas churches. Byzantine chant, therefore, is one of the oldest continuously living song traditions in the world, linking us directly to the splendor of the old Byzantine churches still seen in modern Istanbul and in other areas of Turkey. The church buildings in which it is heard may be of great interest too. In the northern city of Thessaloniki (to whom the Apostle Paul addressed his epistles to the Thessalonians in the Greek Bible's New Testament), chant is still heard in mosaic-filled churches that date back to the fifth and sixth centuries, as well as in exotic-looking churches from the thirteenth century built in Byzantine style. During services, a small male choir stands near the front around a large wooden lectern reading from a large chant book. The congregation takes no part in the chanting, because in this ancient tradition, mass is said *for* the congregants, not by them.

Arrival: Spain

The beaches and bullfights of sunny Spain attract more than forty million visitors per year. The many holy days of the Roman Catholic calendar present numerous opportunities for *fiestas* throughout the country. Perhaps the best known of these includes the "Running of the Bulls" during the Feast of San Fermín celebrations in July in the northern city of Pamplona, reflecting the zest for life that permeates Spanish culture. Olive groves and vineyards are plentiful, especially in Andalusia in the south, where *cantaoras* sing late into the night to the accompaniment of a flamenco guitarist, and *tapas* bars serve wine and piquant delicacies until dawn.

Separated from the rest of Western Europe by the Pyrenees Mountains that form the border between the Iberian Peninsula and France, Spain exhibits a unique blend of European and North African cultural characteristics. The Romans occupied the peninsula for roughly seven hundred years (second century B.C.E. until the sixth century C.E.) before the Christian Visigoths (Germanic peoples) spread into the region, reducing it to a nominal vassal state of Rome. In addition, most cities had a Jewish quarter after the destruction of the great Temple in Jerusalem in 70 C.E. The Moors (Muslims) invaded from North Africa in the eighth century C.E. and occupied much of the peninsula for more than seven hundred years (711–1492), diminishing Roman Catholic influence in Spain and establishing the western front of the Islamic realm.

Arabic dominance began to recede in the eleventh century as the few remaining Christian rulers, encouraged by the Crusades, began to reestablish control of the peninsula. While Muslims, Christians, and Jews had lived in relative peace under Moorish rule, religious fervor came with the re-conquest of Spain, resulting in the infamous Inquisitions (1478), the expulsion of the Jews

An architectural gem in World Heritage city Toledo, Spain, the thirteenth-century Church of Santiago del Arrabal is described as Mudejar, a blend of Visigothic Christian (Mozarabic) architecture and Arabic decoration

and Moors (1492), and the aggressive conversion practices of the Roman Catholic missionaries who followed Spanish Conquistadors to the Americas beginning in the sixteenth century. The Spanish kings soon established Spain as a colonial world power dominating much of the "newly discovered" Western hemisphere.

Until recently Spain, along with Portugal, was the most isolated region of Western Europe. Long years of internal conflict and dictatorial leadership slowed its modernization and political development. Only after the death of General Francisco Franco in 1975 did Spain begin to catch up with the rest of Western Europe, a process hastened by the country's gradual integration into the European Union. As a result, Spain still retains a strong "Old World" sensibility that is felt less and less in other parts of the continent.

Site 2: *Flamenco*

FLAMENCO
A Spanish musical tradition featuring vocals with guitar accompaniment, characterized by passionate singing and vibrant rhythm.

First Impressions. **Flamenco** is a vibrant music. The powerful voice of the singer, the percussive performance of the guitarist, and the rhythmic clapping and heel-stomping of the dancers as onlookers shout "olé!" create a synergetic experience that propels the participants to heights and depths of emotion that can bring tears of both sadness and joy within the span of a single song. To feel this passion is to understand flamenco, no matter if you hail from Spain or elsewhere.

Flamenco dancers and guitarists perform in a club in Cadiz, Spain (Robert Garfias)

Aural Analysis. *Flamenco* includes one of the world's most virtuosic of guitar styles. Guitarists must have incredible dexterity with both hands in order to convey the power and delicacy the style demands. Performers use the fleshy part of the fingers for some sounds, while the characteristic strummed "flourishes" of flamenco and much of the solo work are produced using the fingernails. Percussive accents are commonly added by slapping the face of the guitar to emphasize a melodic passage or articulate a specific rhythm.

The guitar accompanies the *cantaora* (vocalist). The singer can be either male or female, though male performers predominate. The singer frequently sings in the higher reaches of his vocal range. This creates a strained timbre that encourages the sense that he is "giving it his all" by singing to the point where his voice nearly breaks. The heavy use of melisma is also a key feature of the flamenco singing style. The intricately ornamented melismas are intended to have an emotional effect, by making the singer sound as if he is crying, almost wailing, as he empties his soul into song. The lyrical content of flamenco is deeply personal, with death and devotional love, either accepted or rejected, being common themes.

Handclapping (*palmas*) as well as finger-snapping (*palillos* or *pitos*) are common in traditional flamenco performance. These gestures articulate the basic beat, though frequently the onlookers interlock their claps to create a thick rhythmic density that heightens the tension of the music. The dancers also add a rhythmic vibrancy through their toe- and heel-stamping choreography and/or use of castanets, a wooden clapper held in each hand.

Flamenco music generally emphasizes minor keys, and triple meters are more common. Our example follows a twelve-beat pattern divided into two six-beat phrases, which can be heard from the opening guitar chords. The home chord changes on beat 3 and returns on beat 9. The handclaps add syncopation before slipping into an interlocking pattern. The vocalist enters on the ninth repetition of the twelve-beat pattern and sings through three measures. Soon the tempo picks up dramatically as the dancers infuse their own energy into the music. While this particular example does not do so, many *flamenco* performances shift the meter from triple to duple and back to triple frequently within a single song. Rhythmically free passages may be interspersed within a performance.

Improvisation is a key element of *flamenco*, on the part of the guitarist, vocalist, and dancers. While the vocalist generally leads a performance, any of these three elements—voice, guitar, or dance—can change the mood of a performance through shifts in meter, tempo, dynamics, or rhythmic complexity. This stark change in mood is best illustrated in our example by a passage that occurs shortly after the dancers increase their tempo and rhythmic density. In this section, the guitarist plays alone, with the dancers adding occasional foot-stomps and finger-snaps to accent the rhythm. This quieter passage uses a different harmonic progression with a slightly fluctuating tempo. After a solo dance interlude, the performance then slips back to its initial energy level as the tempo increases, the original guitar accompaniment returns, the *cantaora* sings, and the dancers increase their intensity.

LISTENING GUIDE

9.2 (3'50")

Site 9.2

Spain: *Flamenco*

Vocals: Single male lead, as well as mixed male/female voices adding commentary
Instruments: Pair of guitars, handclaps, and foot-stomps

TIME	LISTENING FOCUS
0'00"	Listen for the exhortations of the onlookers and participants.
0'01"	Guitars enter using chords (i.e., harmony). Listen with headphones to hear the clear separation of the two instruments (lead guitar in the left channel and the supporting guitar in the right channel). Note that they begin with a loose adherence to a triple meter with six pulses.
0'06"	Listen for the handclaps, presumably contributed by one of the dancers, and the continued encouragement of the onlookers.
0'13"	Listen for the lead guitar playing a melodic line while the supporting guitar continues to play chords.
0'17"	Listen for the interlocking handclaps as other participants join the performance. Note that the guitarists now play with a more consistent attention to the meter.
0'39"	Vocalist enters. Listen for the extended use of a melismatic text setting.
0'54"	Focus returns to the guitars (and the dancers) as the handclaps continue.
1'02"	Listen for the vocalists' shout, *"Arriba!"* ("Take it up!" i.e., "faster").
1'04"	The tempo accelerates. Also, listen for the inclusion of foot-stomping by the dancers and the return of interlocking handclaps.
1'24"	Music pauses. Listen for the encouragement of the onlookers and the lead vocalist's praise of the dancers.
1'26"	The tempo slows as the lead guitar performs a solo passage emphasizing a single melodic line in a triple meter. Listen also for the declamations of the onlookers, indicating a new dancer is featured.
1'38"	Finger-snaps are briefly heard.
1'43"	Listen for the foot-stomps, finger-snaps, and handclaps of the featured dancer.
2'05"	Tempo accelerates as the rhythmic density of the dancer's foot stamping increases.
2'11"	Second guitar returns. Guitars now emphasize chords over melodic lines.
2'12"	Vocalist returns.
2'33"	Guitarists stop. Listen for the onlookers' declamations.
2'35"	Listen for the foot-stomping and occasional finger-snaps of the featured dancer.

2'37"	Note the vocalist's announcement of a "solo" section for the dancers.
3'00"	Lead guitars returns. Listen for the acceleration of tempo.
3'04"	Supporting guitar returns.
3'06"	Listen for the increase in the rhythmic density of the interlocking foot-stomping as more dancers appear.
3'15"	Listen for the climactic "wailing" of the vocalist and shouts of encouragement from the onlookers.
3'43"	Performance concludes, followed by applause and cheers from the onlookers.

Source: "Alegrias," performed by Carlos Lomas and Pepe De Malaga, from the recording entitled *Andalusian Flamenco Song and Dance*, Lyrichord LYRCD 7388, n.d. Used by permission, Lyrichord Discs Inc.

MUSICAL MARKERS: Timbre/Medium—Virtuosic guitar, passionate "strained" vocals, interlocking handclaps (*palmas*) and foot stomps. Shouts of "olé" and encouragment are common. **Rhythm**—Tempo fluctuations and variations in rhythmic density often leading to musical climaxes. **Pitch**—Strong use of melisma.
ETHNO-CHALLENGE: Perform the interlocking handclapping and foot-stomping with a friend. If possible, find a flamenco dance class in your local area and take a few lessons.

Cultural Considerations. Many Spanish musicians would likely assert that flamenco is the most passionate music on the planet. While a high degree of musicianship is essential, successful performances are judged according to the level of emotional intensity, or **duende**. Vocalists are expected to pour every bit of their emotion into a performance, whether the intent is to express extreme sorrow or exultation, and the goal is to achieve a state of catharsis for themselves and their listeners.

DUENDE
A Spanish word meaning "passion," which refers to an emotional quality considered essential in performances by Spanish *Flamenco* singers.

Flamenco was born in Andalusia, the southern region of Spain. Originally, flamenco featured the voice alone, in a song form known as *cante*. This traditional Spanish style of singing incorporates the strained timbre and heavy use of melisma typical of Arabic vocal traditions, reflecting the more than seven hundred years of Arabic influence in the region. Arabic influence is also reflected in the style's generally vibrant rhythmic activity. *Cante* is typically divided into three forms—deep, intermediate, and light—determined by the subject matter and rhythmic structure. *Cante* performances frequently feature audience participation in the form of handclapping, dance, and vocal interjections.

The earliest evidence of *flamenco* in its modern form dates from the early nineteenth century, when Gypsy (*gitano*) musicians were observed singing the *cante* forms with instrumental accompaniment. The private "jam sessions" of the Gypsy musicians in the bars and brothels of some of the larger cities, such as Seville and Madrid, caught the attention of upper-class clientele. By the 1840s *Cafés cantantes*, clubs devoted specifically to *flamenco* performance, became popular throughout the country. The guitar became the standard accompanying instrument, a choice reflecting both the Arabic emphasis on intricate melodic passages and the European taste for harmony.

While modern *flamenco* is frequently performed on a concert stage, traditional contexts for *flamenco* are much more intimate. The ideal setting is a *juerga*, an informal event in which the separation between musicians and audience is blurred. Everyone participates, if only with clapping and shouts of encouragement known as *jaleo*. These gatherings can happen almost anywhere, on a side street, in a *tapas* bar, at a musician's home, and so on. They usually last late into the night, often until dawn, and are characterized by much laughter and a family feeling.

Dance: Flamenco Dance by La Romera

The Role of the Dancer

In recent years, flamenco dance has become immensely popular. Leading flamenco dance troupes perform worldwide to sold-out audiences. Dance studios on every continent are packed with aspiring flamenco dancers.

It is universally recognized as the passionate, fiery dance of Spain. The word "flamenco dancer" invokes cliché images of seductive women in ruffled polka dot dresses, virile men in tight pants, proud carriage, fierce countenance, rapid-fire footwork, and castanets.

Most flamenco scholars concur that flamenco dance traces its roots to the ancient dances of the Indian Hindus, the Moors, and the Gypsies who came from Northern India. The percussive use of feet in classical Indian Kathak dance is the predecessor of flamenco footwork. It is easy to see in flamenco dance the kindred attributes of the fluid upper body, arm, and hand movement of classical Indian dance.

Photo of dance essay author, La Romera

The Gypsies of Andalucía have had significant impact on flamenco. Their unique style, rich musical heritage, and gift for improvisation have formed the character of flamenco. Like the blues, flamenco was conceived of an outcast people. The air of defiance and Gypsy pride is a strong theme in flamenco dance and song.

Flamenco dance footwork (*taconeo*) uses different parts of the feet as a percussive instrument, the flat foot (*golpe*), toe (*punta*), heel (*tacón*) and ball of the foot (*planta*) create contrasting sounds. The heavy accents, counter time, and syncopations are executed with athletic stamina and speed that builds to a dramatic stop. Commercially, footwork is often overused and the uninitiated spectator thinks that the best dancer is the one with the fastest footwork.

To reach a level of proficiency requires daily hours of rigorous training. The dancer must master the technique of arm and hand movement, footwork, and complex coordination. The dancer is likewise a percussionist and must develop the skill of handclapping (*palmas*).

Above all, the dancer must achieve intensive comprehension of the *compás* (rhythm) with emotional understanding of the music and song. Otherwise, a dance becomes nothing more than an empty showcase of memorized dance steps.

The dancer must be willing to reveal the deepest corners of their soul and dance with authenticity that is guided by instinct and heart. It is one thing to "learn a flamenco dance" and totally another to "learn to dance flamenco."

Owing to the number of years it takes to become a masterful flamenco dancer, it is quite common that great dancers hit their peak in their fifties or beyond. Fortunately, a dancer's age or weight is not an issue amongst genuine flamenco aficionados.

There is a notable distinction between flamenco dance and other types of dance. In most forms of dance, the dancer follows the music. In flamenco, the dancer takes the lead and the guitarist and singer follow the dancer's lead. The dancer establishes the tempo and length of the dance. Dances can be strictly choreographed, completely improvised, or a combination of the two, which results in a structured improvisation. Unless the dancer adheres to the same choreography every night, no two performances will be the same. It is that spontaneity between dancer, singer, and guitarist that makes the dance exciting.

For those who are involved in flamenco, it is the quest to unleash the mysterious spirit or *duende*. It is a profoundly spiritual moment and an incredible high.

The presence of the *duende* is felt amongst all and can rivet the onlooker to their seat and move them to tears.

Many people are attracted to flamenco dance because it is so powerful and expressive. Those who want to learn it for "fun and recreation" soon realize that it requires commitment in order to make even the smallest amount of progress. Therefore, there is a high dropout rate in flamenco dance classes.

The opportunity to dance is not just limited to studio and stage. Initially not performed for the general public, flamenco is at its most authentic when done in a non-commercial setting. Flamenco is pervasive at festive occasions such as Gypsy weddings and baptisms. And, there is nothing more delightful than to dance in a spontaneous session amongst flamencos who simply must sing and dance because the mood hits them.

For the dancer, singer, musician or aficionado, flamenco is a way of life.

It is what feeds the soul, and a life without flamenco is simply unimaginable.

La Romera is an American born flamenco dancer whose dancing career spans four decades of performing and teaching flamenco dance in Spain and the United States.

Flamenco has continued to develop in new ways. Theatrical productions of *flamenco* dance and song are common, and *flamenco* troupes are frequently found on international tours. Since the 1960s some artists have fused *flamenco* with other music forms, such as jazz and rock, to create popular sounds with a global appeal. Artists such as Paco de Lucía and the Gipsy Kings have helped to widen the audience of flamenco through their innovative compositions, while remaining true to the roots of the music and the spirit of *duende*.

Arrival: Russia

Russia is the largest country on the planet. While more than 80 percent of its territory is in Asia, it is European Russia, the part west of the Ural Mountains, that represents Russia's political and cultural identity to the outside world. The two largest cities, Moscow and St. Petersburg, are the destinations for most tourists, who discover a unique juxtaposition of the architecture of Czarist Russia, with its pastel-colored Baroque-like palaces and onion-domed Russian Orthodox churches, and Soviet Russia (1917–1991), which exchanged color for monumental concrete buildings and statues of steel. Since the dissolution of the Soviet Union in 1991, Russia, still a world power, has striven to transform itself from a totalitarian communist regime to a democratic free market society. This transition has not been easy or consistent, but the Russian people are resilient, having dealt with many dramatic political changes in their history.

During the nineteenth and twentieth centuries, Russian nationalism inspired much artistic development, especially in music. Many Russian "art music" composers, such as Nikolai Rimsky-Korsakov (1844–1908), Pyotr Ilich Tchaikovsky (1840–1893), and Igor Stravinsky (1882–1971), are counted among the greatest composers of the last two centuries. While many urbanites of modern Russia would rather consider these composers and their music as the essence of Russian musical identity, the work songs, *chastushki* (playful songs), and dance tunes of the Russian countryside inspired many of the most revered Russian composers and are in fact more indicative of Russia's distinctive musical culture.

Oleg Kruglyakov

AN INSIDE LOOK

I was born in 1966 in Omsk, Siberia, Soviet Union. When I was a child, we sang together in the village style during gatherings and after meals. My mother knew many Cossack songs, as well as traditional Russian, Belorussian, and Ukrainian folk songs, and I often sang with her spontaneously. As a child I was tested and identified as "musical." My mother wanted me to play piano or violin but I had heard the balalaika on radio and liked the sound of it so I chose to play that. At fifteen I went to study for four years at the Tumen College of Arts. After that I attended Urals State Conservatory in Yekaterinburg, studying balalaika with Shaukat Sabirovich Amirov and then later with Yevgeny Grigorievich Blinov, the foremost proponent of balalaika in the Soviet Union, who traveled around the world representing Soviet culture. I also studied pedagogy, conducting, and ethnic singing. The balalaika that I perform on was made in 1937, belonged to a member of the Moiseyev Ballet orchestra, and found its way to my professor who sold it to me when he retired.

After a two-year mandatory service in the Soviet army, where I was trained as an engineer, I started performing in many different ensembles. I taught at the Irkutsk School of Music, Perm College of Music and the Perm Institute of Culture, and still teach balalaika.

From 1989 to 1991 I toured Moscow, St. Petersburg, Siberia, and Ukraine with the Urals State Folk Choir. For three years I played with "Siberian Mosaic" touring the Irkutsk region of Siberia. Between 1993 and 1998 I traveled with the Urals Folk Ensemble "Prikamie" performing in France, Belgium, Denmark, Germany, Malta, and Turkmenistan. I concertized with the Russian folk instrument quartet "Golden Russia" (balalaika prima, domra, bayan, and contrabass balalaika). When I first came to the United States I had the honor of performing at the United Nations.

The balalaika, a true embodiment of Russian folk culture, is a good medium for performing all genres of music. I learned to appreciate classical, ethnic, world music, and contemporary composition. Traveling in different countries, learning music

Oleg Kruglyakov

from many traditions, working with others is my passion. I am trained as a virtuoso soloist but my musical philosophy has always been about collaboration. There are pieces written for balalaika solo; it also pairs well with guitar (I occasionally perform with the seven-stringed gypsy virtuoso Vadim Kolpakov), other Russian folk instruments and often accompanies Russian "chastushki."

I came to Cleveland to create the folk group "Moscow Nights" in which I had a successful eight-year career touring all over North America. In 2007, I started "Russian Duo" with American pianist Terry Boyarsky. This international, cultural collaboration has developed new potential for the art and repertoire of the balalaika. We perform classical music, original repertoire composed for balalaika-piano duo, virtuoso variations, romances, film music, tango, bluegrass, and sing folk songs. We create our own arrangements of ragtime music and are working with a living ragtime composer to expand the repertoire. We give participatory assemblies and workshops with Russian percussion and folk dance as part of our mission to share Russian culture and demonstrate the art of collaboration, all through the musical and historical lens of the balalaika.

Site 3: *Balalaika* Ensemble

BALALAIKA
A triangle-shaped, fretted plucked-lute from Russia.

First Impressions. The "chattering," high-pitched sound of the *prima balalaika* is apparent even in a full **balalaika** orchestra, as is heard in our example. This music may remind you of a German Oktoberfest as it has a "polka" feel, but it is distinctly Russian. Though the instrumentation is certainly different, such dance genres are also a staple of Russian folk music.

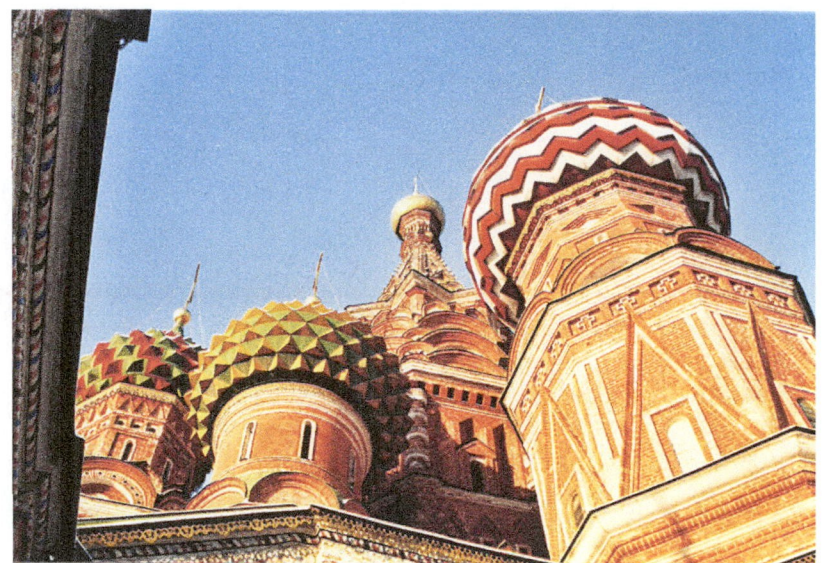

Aural Analysis. As is typical of musical performance in Europe, harmony is the key musical element. In this case, the major instrument heard is the *balalaika*, the most popular folk instrument in Russia. The *balalaika*'s most distinctive feature is its triangular-shaped resonating body. The instrument can be found in varying sizes, but the most common type is the *prima balalaika*, which has a wooden sound box a little more than 1 foot (30 centimeters) long on each side and a fretted neck that extends the instrument to nearly 3 feet (91 cm). Most *balalaika* have just three strings. Two strings are tuned to the same pitch or an octave apart, while the third string is tuned to a fourth above the root. The strings are usually made of steel, nylon, or gut and are played with the fingers, though sometimes a leather plectrum may be used.

The *balalaika* was most commonly used as a courting instrument, but also was found among court musicians. Its popularity waned during the early nineteenth century with the introduction of the harmonica, until its cause was picked up by a Russian nobleman, Vasily Vasilyevich Andreyev (1861–1918), who is today called the "Father of the Balalaika." Andreyev first became intrigued by the instrument after hearing one of his workers play it. In the spirit of Russian nationalism, he promoted the *balalaika* as the distinctive musical instrument of Russia and succeeded in modernizing the instrument so that it could play a classical repertoire. Andreyev had five different-sized *balalaika* created, the largest being the size of a double bass. His ensemble had its debut in 1888 to great acclaim and by 1892 had won the support of the Russian royalty. Afterward his Russian Balalaika Orchestra toured Europe and even visited America.

As is typical of European folk music, the melody is relatively short and repetitive. The double bass *balalaika* plods along with the basic harmonic structure as smaller-sized *balalaika* and *domra* "chatter" out the melody. An accordion helps to fill in the harmony and adds another timbre to the overall sound. Of note is the near absence of "percussion" instruments other than the occasional rattling of a tambourine.

Cultural Considerations. Though polyphonic vocal ensembles are more characteristic of Russian folk music, the *balalaika* has become the distinctive visual symbol of Russian musical identity. The predecessor of the *balalaika* is a similar lute, known as a *domra*, which has a round resonator. The earliest records of the *domra* date to the seventeenth century. The primary performers on the instrument were wandering minstrels and jugglers who performed for weddings, festivals, and other celebratory activities. These entertainers, known as *skomorokhi* ("jesters"), commonly appeared in costume, dressed up as, for example, an animal or a witch, in order to attract an audience.

Members of the St. Nicholas Russian Orthodox Church Balalaika Orchestra of Mogadore, Ohio, use instruments in several sizes. In the front row are seen the typical *prima balalaika* in triangular shape and the *domra* with a round body

The bass *balalaika* performed by a Russian street musician (Rex Shahriari)

LISTENING GUIDE

Site 9.3

Russia: *Balalaika* Ensemble

Instruments: *Balalaika* (high- and mid-range plucked lute), *bass balalaika* (low-range plucked lute), *domra* (high-range plucked lute), accordion (reed aerophone), tambourine, gourd rattle

TIME	LISTENING FOCUS
0'00"	Listen for the steady duple meter and absence of percussion instruments. Note that the bass *balalaika* is primarily responsible for articulating the basic pulse as well as the harmonic root.
0'06"	First melodic phrase repeats.
0'12"	Second melodic phrase with repetition.
0'25"	Accordion enters. Listen for a third melodic phrase.
0'38"	First melodic phrase returns.
0'52"	Second melodic phrase returns. Listen for the syncopated "upbeat" rhythm of some of the chordophones as the performers dampen strings to add an additional timbre.
1'04"	Third melodic phrase returns.
1'17"	First melodic phrase returns. Listen for the tambourine adding an additional rhythmic element.
1'30"	Second melodic phrase returns. Note that the tambourine stops.
1'43"	Third melodic phrase returns.
1'55"	Note the gourd rattle entering to emphasize the end of the piece.

Source: "Yablochka," from the recording entitled *Eastern European Folk Heritage Concert: St. Nicholas Balalaika Orchestra*, private issue, 2003. Used by permission.

MUSICAL MARKERS: Timbre/Medium—"Chattering" lutes with supporting bass line and accordion. **Rhythm**—Fast duple meter "polka" feel. **Melody/Phonic Structure**—Tuneful melodic phrases with supporting harmony.
ETHNO-CHALLENGE: Using numeral or staff notation, write out the pitches and rhythm of the three melodic phrases.

Unfortunately, the ruling powers of the time issued decrees that put strict restraints on various peasant activities, including the performance of music. In 1648 the czar ordered that all music instruments be burned and decreed that anyone who dared to play music would be flogged and exiled to the outer reaches of the kingdom. The *balalaika* likely developed as a consequence: because it was easier to make a triangular-shaped body than a round one, it could be more quickly made if a musician had been forced to abandon his original instrument for fear of persecution. After the harassment of Russian musicians subsided in the eighteenth century, the instrument became quite popular for its distinctive look and characteristic "chatter-like" sound. The *balalaika*'s name is derived from the Russian word meaning "to chat," and its sound is intended to contrast with the violin, which is considered to "sing."

Andreyev encouraged the dissemination of the *balalaika* among the populace by teaching soldiers and common folk to play the instruments, often giving them free instruments. Under Soviet rule, the *balalaika* continued to play a vital role in promoting Russian nationalism, and by the end of the twentieth century, it had regained its prominence as the most popular instrument in the country. Today it is frequently sought after by tourists and is used by *balalaika* "combos," which are popular in major cities throughout Europe. In addition, Russian music conservatories embraced the instrument as suitable for virtuosic use in performing both arrangements of classical music and the composition of new music, often accompanied by piano. The film *Dr. Zhivago* (1965), which featured the *balalaika* in its soundtrack, helped to familiarize Western audiences with the instrument.

Our example is performed by an ensemble based in the United States, the Balalaika Orchestra of St. Nicholas Church in Mogadore, Ohio, just east of Akron. Founded in 1985, this group of skilled amateurs performs a variety of folk music from Russia. Russian communities can be found throughout the United States, but that of northeast Ohio is one of the oldest. Indeed, Cleveland is also home to St. Theodosius Cathedral, the oldest Russian Orthodox church in the United States and the church featured in the 1978 film *The Deer Hunter*, which examined the experience of the Vietnam War in the lives of small town Americans. Balalaika orchestras, such as the St. Nicholas Balalaika Orchestra, have become an important means of expressing Russian identity for people in the Russian Diaspora, especially in the United States.

Arrival: Scotland

Although Scotland is often thought of as a country, in reality it has not been one since 1707; rather, it is a constituent part of the United Kingdom (or Great Britain), along with England, Wales, and Ulster (Northern Ireland). During the Roman occupation of Britain—from the mid-first century until the fourth century—what is now Scotland was inhabited by the much-feared but little-known Picts and was considered a fearsome land. To keep the Picts at bay, the Romans built a stone wall from sea to sea across northern England during the 120s C.E.; remnants of this construction, known as Hadrian's Wall, can still be seen today, though it barely keeps sheep from crossing now because people reused much of the stone for houses.

Scotland was a hardscrabble land for most of its inhabitants, especially those trying to eke out a living in the rocky highlands or the bleak, peat-covered plains of the Hebrides Islands, the areas of "traditional" Scottish Gaelic-speaking highland culture to the west and northwest. People working the land for a subsistence living were sheltered in "blackhouses"—sod or stone huts with thatched roofs and little light but much smoke. At the end of the eighteenth century, the English gentry, who owned most land in Scotland, decided that raising sheep was more profitable than renting land to small farmers and forced the Scots from their land in what is called The Clearances (1790–1845). Some of the Scots removed from their land died, while many others were forced to migrate. A segment of these Scottish immigrants settled permanently in northern Ireland, while others remained in Ireland for a time, then went on to North America to start a new life. Indeed, the "Scots-Irish" provided much of the backbone of Appalachian culture in the United States, while other waves of migration brought Scottish culture to eastern Canada as well.

Modern Scotland, home of two great cities—industrial Glasgow and learned Edinburgh—is now as prosperous as England. Thanks to "devolution," the political process by which the United Kingdom's four regions have obtained local governance, Scotland has been able to redefine itself to a far greater degree than it could in the eighteenth century while under the English yoke. Though many assume that Scots speak Gaelic (pronounced "gao-lick"), a Celtic language, today few do—mostly in the Outer Hebrides—the rest speak English or remnants of an earlier form of Scottish English seen in the poems of Robert Burns.

Site 4: Highland Bagpipes

BAGPIPES
A reed aerophone consisting of an airbag (bellows), *chanter* (melody pipe), and drone pipes.

First Impressions. Most North Americans have heard the Scottish highland **bagpipes** (called "pipes" for short), perhaps at a funeral, or at a festival, and certainly on television. Scotland's highland pipes have become commonplace for public funerals in the United States, especially those for police and other public officials. If you've ever been around someone playing these

Mick Moloney

Mick Moloney

I was born the eldest of seven children in 1944 in Limerick City in the southwest of Ireland and grew up in Castletroy, just about two miles outside the city. There was music in my family but it was of the popular sort. My father's party piece was "Frankie and Johnny" and my mother's "Ciribibin." They typically sang them at evening get-togethers at the seaside resort of Kilkee, where the family went for its annual monthly holiday. I was often pressed into singing my own party piece, "The Grand Coulee Dam," which I first heard on Radio Luxemburg, which at that time was the gateway to the musical world for young Irish people. I also sang that song at the age of fifteen during my first semi-professional appearances with the Michael Ryan show, one of the last of the old-style traveling variety shows in Ireland.

My initial exposure to live traditional Irish music was on O'Connell Street in Limerick, where two short-sighted brothers, Christy and Micky Dunne, played the tenor banjo and fiddle for donations every Saturday. They were travelers and played at fairs and sporting events all over the country. The first time I heard the wild sound of the banjo I knew for certain that I wanted to play that instrument. Already I was playing the guitar in a very rudimentary way and my first banjo was of the six-string variety. It did not take me long to figure out that it was going to be very hard to play jigs and reels with that guitar tuning. When I heard Barney McKenna playing tenor banjo on the radio I was really hooked and bought a four-string Framus banjo. Barney had figured out that the easiest way to play Irish music on the tenor banjo was to tune it GDAE—one fifth down from the standard tuning and a full octave below the fiddle.

When I went to Dublin to study political economy and economics at University College Dublin, I played several nights a week in the "ballad pubs" and earned about one pound, fifty pence per gig (6 dollars), which was pretty big money then. I played with a group called the Emmet Group with Donal Lunney and Brian Bolger, and we worked out nice original harmonies for our songs. A family group called the Johnstons from County Meath had a number-one hit with a Ewan McCall song called "The Travelling People," and they asked me, and later Paul Brady, to join the group. I became a professional musician, and we moved to England where we toured and made six LPs between 1967 and 1971, when I left the group.

Professor Kenneth Goldstein was instrumental in getting me a scholarship to the University of Pennsylvania, where I obtained a Ph.D. in Folklore and Folklife. He also introduced me to Ralph Rinzler at the Smithsonian Institution, and he appointed me fieldworker for the 1976 Bicentennial Festival of American Folklife. This helped open the door for me to the rich world of Irish traditional music in America, and the wonderful musicians I met all over the United States helped me learn my trade.

The 1976 Festival coincided with a major new national interest in American cultural heritage and that environment was to enable me over the next forty years to work as a musician, teacher, recording artist, record producer, arts panelist, arts presenter, and cultural activist. I performed with Eugene O'Donnell for close to twenty years, Robbie O'Connell and Jimmy Keane for over fifteen years and with scores of other brilliant musicians and dancers often with the Green Fields of America founded in 1978. Over that time I have made scores of recordings with many musicians. They included many fieldwork projects recorded in musicians' homes issued on a variety of labels.

I play guitar, mandolin, octave mandolin, and of course tenor banjo, which is still my first love. Indeed my primary identity is "banjo driver." Currently I teach Irish Studies and Music at New York University and play in and outside the U.S., mostly these days with the gifted fiddler Athena Tergis and the brilliant button accordion player Billy McComiskey. We are often accompanied by the great step dancer Niall O'Leary. I was honored to receive the National Heritage Award in 1999, the Irish Presidential Distinguished Service Award in 2013, and the Gradam Ceoil award in 2014.

Walter Mahovlich

I was born in Cleveland in 1952. My Hungarian and Croatian grandparents had settled in the thriving community of Eastern European immigrants in the mining and industrial Ohio Valley before World War I. The music played at weddings and picnics was central to their lives and sense of identity, then as now. My American born Hungarian mother and Croatian father spoke their parents' languages and taught me traditional songs as I grew up in Cleveland. The region in which I grew up was home to many people with roots in Eastern Europe; our languages and cultures were similar, and we felt a strong sense of kinship.

Far from home during my freshman college year, I longed for familiar cultures. I returned to Cleveland, became very active in Croatian and other ethnic affairs, learned my father's language, took up the *tamburica* [a plucked lute] and joined a Croatian folklore group. I soon began playing for parties and weddings. Concurrently, I was recruited to play clarinet by a group from the Lake Prespa region of Macedonia living in Lorain, Ohio. I quickly learned the traditional repertoire and customs, regional styles, and music representing different periods of immigration and regions. In another group, the traditional accordion style of my Serbian bandleader, Rade Simoviç, inspired me to take up accordion. These experiences, together with visits to Yugolavia and Bulgaria, internalized for me the music of the old homeland.

I frequented East European events while attending university in Cleveland, respecting immigrant musicians' playing as true expressions of their heritage, though it differed from contemporary folk music recordings. Discovering klezmer [east European Jewish music] clarinet player, Dave Tarras, I heard commonality with the music I already played, and learned these melodies. Jewish friends were thrilled, and soon I played my first bar mitzvah – with two other Croatian-Americans. I continue to play this music. After college I played accordion and sang with Croatian and Serbian friends in the Krajani Tamburica Orchestra.

In the mid 1980s, work in polymer science took me to New York, where I met and played with many fine East European musicians: Romanian, Albanian, Greek, Bulgarian, while continuing to play with Croatians, Serbs, and Macedonians. I also met and played with Michael Alpert and other leading exponents of the klezmer revival.

Walter Mahovlich (second from left)

Returning home in 1988, I resumed playing for my community. I met a young violinist who shared my love of East European music, klezmer, and Hungarian Gypsy music, which although I heard and loved it growing up, I hadn't yet played professionally. By chance I encountered Iosif Varga, a Hungarian speaking Rom ("Gypsy") from Nagyvarad (Oradea Mare), Romania, a truly outstanding traditional and classical musician. Iosif mentored me in Hungarian music, which led me to found my band, Harmonia. Our trio played frequently for Hungarian, Slovak, and Carpatho-Rusyn events.

The fall of the Berlin Wall in the early 1990s saw first-rate traditional musicians emigrating to the United States from Eastern Europe. Gheorghe Trambitas, taragot [single reed aerophone] player, and his band, came together from Transylvania. Gheorghe played with Harmonia and taught me about Romanian music. Shortly after I purchased a cimbalom [hammered zither], Iosif showed up with a young Gypsy, Elemer Mezei, who played cimbalom with us. After a year, Elemer left Cleveland and sold me his excellent concert cimbalom. I met Alexander Fedoriouk, a superb young cimbalom player from Ukraine, who shared my musical interests. Within months he joined Harmonia, becoming a key member, and we swiftly progressed. We added other Eastern Europeans: a vocalist, a folk flute player, violinists and, once Iosif became unable to play, bassists. We have performed at major festivals and large concert venues across the country, and I still love performing for the ethnic weddings and picnics where I began.

pipes, you know they are more appropriately played outdoors, because their strident tones can be deafening indoors. As with most bagpipe performances, our example features a highly ornamented melody together with sustained drone pitches. For American events, pipers customarily play "Scotland the Brave" or "Amazing Grace." Singly or as a band, they stand or march proudly, dressed in colorful kilts, with a *skean dhu* (knife) in their sock and greater or lesser amounts of regalia, depending on whether or not they are connected with the military or police.

Aural Analysis. The Scottish highland pipes, called *a' phìob-mhór* (pronounced "Uh feep vore") in Gaelic, are just one of dozens of types of bagpipes found throughout Europe, North Africa, and Turkey, though they are the most widely known. European bagpipes can be of two kinds: lung-driven or bellows-driven. The highland pipes are the former and the Irish *uilleann* pipes (see Chapter 9, Site 5) are the latter.

Bagpipes illustrate well the concept of a "folk instrument," in that all their parts (melodic chanter, drone pipes, and bag windchest) can be made or obtained in both urban and rural areas. The melody line is created on a *chanter*, a wooden pipe with finger holes given voice by a double reed made of cane, which is set in vibration when air passes through it. European double reeds, unlike many of those found in Asia, are not particularly loud, making them difficult to hear in outdoor situations. The pressure necessary to increase volume requires a good bit of lung power. The bagpipe solves these problems with a reservoir of air that is driven through the double-reed pipe and through additional drone pipes having single reeds by arm pressure. The air is stored in a bag traditionally made from the skin, stomach, or bladder of various common farm animals, especially goats and sheep. Cloth—usually a tartan—covers the animal-skin bag to hide its "unpleasant," if natural, appearance. The apertures—that is, the leg holes—into which the chanter and the three drone pipes are placed were natural to the animal. To fill the bag with air, the player blows into a fifth pipe, which incorporates a non-return valve to prevent the air from escaping when the piper is drawing more breath. When the player inflates the bag through the blowing pipe and squeezes the bag with his left arm, air is driven through the drone pipes and *chanter*, producing the exciting din of highland bagpipe music.

The medieval stronghold of the Macraes, Eilean Donan Castle in Dornie, Scotland, was reduced to rubble in 1719 by the English and only restored in the twentieth century to become Scotland's most photographed castle

To operate the bagpipes, the player must first fill the bag with air and begin pressing on it. The three drone pipes—one bass and two tenors—are the first part of the instrument to sound, often coming to life with a grumpy-sounding groan. These use single reeds comparable to those used with the clarinet or saxophone, and the pipes are built in sections, allowing the player to tune by lengthening or shortening them (lengthening lowers the pitch, shortening raises the pitch). Once a full, steady drone is achieved, the performer begins playing melody on the chanter, which is a double reed, giving it a different and more penetrating timbre.

The most familiar bagpipe music consists of tunes, such as "Scotland the Brave," "Mull of Kintyre," and "Amazing Grace" (which is not known to have had a Scottish origin). There is also much dance music for bagpipes, including jigs, reels, marches, waltzes, and even polkas, as well as the famous "sword dance." Little known but highly developed is the **pibroch** (*piobairèachd* in Gaelic), an elaborate form of theme and variations, in which the "theme" is actually a "ground" (a sort of bass line) rather than a tune. In all cases, the piper embellishes the melody extensively with quick ornamental notes made possible by the motions of the fingers on the chanter. This suggests that ornamenting a melody is as much a physical act as it is a melodic one, since the typical ornaments are remembered more in the muscles than in the brain. Our track includes two polkas, both duple meter dance-like tunes. "The Royal Scots Polka," heard first, was composed by Pipe Major Willie Denholm of the First Battalion, The Royal Scots, a military pipe band. The second one, called "The Black Watch Polka," is considered "traditional," meaning the composer is unknown. The pipe band heard is the multiple world championship City of Glasgow Police Pipe Band, which

PIBROCH
(pronounced *pee-brohk*) A form of Scottish bagpipe music with an extended theme-and-variations structure.

An "exploded" display of Scottish bagpipe parts in the Pipe Museum on the Isle of Skye off the northwest coast of Scotland

was formed in 1912 by combining bands from nearby Govan Burgh with that of Glasgow. After 1975 this band was reorganized as the Strathclyde Police Pipe Band, which remains active today.

Virtually all Scottish bagpipe music, including that heard here, is in meter. In some *pibroch* compositions, the tempo may be so slow with such extensive ornamentation that ascertaining the basic pulse is difficult. Individual pipers or, more likely, marching pipe bands are usually accompanied by bass and snare drums. Nearly all highland piping is done outdoors because it is associated with outdoor events, not to mention being quite loud. Some have called the highland pipes the "war pipes," and claim that pipers led clan troops into battle. Whether this is true or not, the term "war pipes" comes from a misunderstanding of *mhór* (pronounced "vore"), a Gaelic word that sounds like war but means "great."

Cultural Considerations. The old Gaelic language and culture, part of the larger Celtic culture and family of languages, is typically used to represent Scotland to the outside world. But Scotland also includes the lowlands where a form of English has always been spoken, the English of poet Robert Burns that is so difficult for outsiders to understand. Gaelic culture, to the extent that it survives today, is found in the north and northwest of the "mainland" and in the Hebrides Islands off the northwest coast, including Skye, Lewis, Harris, North and South Uist, and Barra. The health of Gaelic culture depends on the survival of the language, and in recent years, despite efforts to reverse the trend, there has been a steady decline in the number of native speakers. Much of the classic Gaelic culture is now seen only on special ceremonial occasions and in tourist shows.

LISTENING GUIDE
9.4 (3'01")

Site 9.4

Scotland: Highland Pipes

Instruments: Highland (Scottish) bagpipes, snare drums, bass drums

TIME	LISTENING FOCUS
0'00"	Snare drum rolls begin the performance.
0'03"	Drones sound just before the main melody begins.
0'06"	Opening theme ("Royal Scots Polka") begins (A). Each melodic phrase is four beats with four full measures for the complete melodic line (sixteen beats total).
0'16"	Opening theme repeats (A).
0'27"	Second line begins and repeats (B).
0'37"	Second line repeats with minimal variation (B).
0'48"	Variation of main theme begins (A').
0'58"	Variation of main theme repeats (A').
1'08"	Second line with variation begins (B').
1'19"	Second line with variation repeats (B').
1'30"	New theme begins (C). ("The Black Watch Polka")
1'41"	New theme repeats (C).
1'52"	Second line of new theme begins (D).

2'02"	Second line repeats (D).
2'13"	Third line of new theme begins (E).
2'24"	Second half of third line (E cont.)
2'34"	Final line begins (F).
2'45"	Final line repeats (F).

Source: Highland bagpipes by the City of Glasgow Police Pipe Band, "The Royal Scots Polka" and "The Black Watch Polka" from *All the Best from Scotland/ 35 Great Favorites*, vol.2, CLUC CD 77, n.d.

MUSICAL MARKERS: Timbre/Medium—Snare drum (buzzy timbre) rolls with strident-powerful bagpipe ensemble. **Rhythm**—steady "marching" beat. **Pitch/Phonic Structure**—Steady drone supporting "danceable" melody with frequent use of couplets.
ETHNO-CHALLENGE: Research and observe bagpipe performers in your local area. For a real challenge, try constructing your own bagpipe.

Scottish highland pipers march for visitors in Portree, Skye, in the Hebrides Islands off the northwest coast of Scotland

Inextricably linked to Scotland, the highland pipes serve as a symbol of Scottish identity, both visually and aurally. While it is true that piping was associated with clans and with both martial and festive occasions, the original Scottish musical instrument was not the pipes but the Celtic harp. In early times Scottish culture was an extension of Irish culture, and the harp was the basic instrument of both. Bagpipes are no more intrinsically Scottish than Scotland's other major instrument, the fiddle (or violin). Indeed, the highland pipes can be dated back only to the sixteenth century.

As much as pipes, tartans, and kilts are markers of Scottish identity, it was not always so. Hugh Trevor-Roper has written a fascinating study of the "invention" of Scottish cultural icons published in *The Invention of Tradition*, a collection of chapters edited by Eric Hobsbawm (Cambridge University Press, 1983). There Trevor-Roper traces the history of how all of these now deeply embedded "traditions" came about, including the outright creation of Ossian, allegedly Scotland's greatest poet of the past. While this scholarship challenges deeply held notions of Scottish identity—and there's no doubt this *is* Scotland's identity now—it also suggests that similar processes have happened elsewhere in the world as well.

In North America the highland pipes have come to be linked with funerals, particularly those of public officials and policemen killed in the line of duty. Pipers and pipe bands routinely play "Amazing Grace," a melody that originated in North America and is not known to be Scottish. Highland pipes have also become associated in North America with St. Patrick's Day, a celebration of Ireland's patron saint. While it is true that Irish police bands have used the highland pipes since the nineteenth century, this association is a stretch. Contemporary popular culture in the United States prefers to blend all Celtic areas together, so that pipes from Scotland can now symbolize Ireland as well. In fact, Ireland has its own pipes, but they are less commonly encountered and cannot be used for marching.

Arrival: Ireland

Ireland, often called the "Emerald Isle," is a mostly rural island generously speckled with castles, monasteries, and great houses, many in ruins. It also boasts the rugged beauty of the western seacoast, including the unforgettable Cliffs of Moher. One of Ireland's most enduring cultural attractions is its music, spanning everything from that played in local pubs by amateurs to sophisticated versions of traditional tunes presented by groups such as The Chieftains and the Riverdance theatrical dance troupe, both internationally renowned. Indeed, there has been an explosion of new types of Irish-based music generally labeled "Celtic."

But Ireland was not always a placid locale for music and sheep herding. Over the centuries Ireland endured successive waves of invasions, as the many ruined "round towers," roofless, ruined priories, and other fortifications attest. In spite of this fate, Ireland was long one of the most developed and cultured places in medieval Europe, with many great centers of learning, religion, and the arts.

While the Republic of Ireland has been independent from the United Kingdom since 1922 (technically, it was formally formed in 1949), one of its original four counties, Ulster (or Northern Ireland), remains a constituent part of the United Kingdom, a testament to an incomplete

Celebrated in song as well as visited by thousands of tourists each year, the Cliffs of Moher in western Ireland are among Europe's most dramatic sites (Sean Williams)

revolution. It is nonetheless important to recall that until the twentieth century Ireland itself was not independent and that English speakers far outnumber the fabled Gaelic speakers, who are mostly found in the west of the country. The population of Ireland, around four million today, suffered many sudden declines over its history, caused by disease, war, and famine, to mass migrations, especially to the United States, where there are far more people of Irish ancestry than in Ireland itself.

Site 5: *Uilleann* Bagpipes

First Impressions. Compared to the Scottish bagpipes, the Irish pipes sound mellower and much fuller with a warmer tone quality. Along with the expected melody and drone, one hears occasional "chords," groups of consonant notes sounded together. If this instrument sounds less martial, it is because the Irish pipes are played indoors for domestic occasions. In fact, you are just as likely to encounter these pipes playing with other instruments, such as the fiddle, banjo, wooden transverse flute, and perhaps even spoons, as to hear them solo.

UILLEANN BAGPIPES
The bellows-driven pipes of Ireland.

Aural Analysis. The Irish pipes, known in Gaelic as **uilleann** (pronounced *ill*-en) and erroneously in English as "union," are bellows-driven, meaning they have less power than mouth-driven pipes and as a result are played indoors. After the Siege of Limerick (1689– 1691), the Irish *Piob Mor*, or warpipe, fell out of practical use. Historically, it was no longer heard of after the Battle of Fontenoy (May 11, 1745) in which the French army overcame the Anglo-Dutch-Hanoverian army in the War of Austrian succession. It is possible that the decline of the warpipes in Ireland in the eighteenth century caused a rise in popularity of the non-martial, quieter *uilleann* pipes. The *uilleann* pipes are thought to have originated in Ireland in the mid-eighteenth century and have been played by both men and women. *Uilleann* piping was widespread in Ireland during the

(left)
Eliot Grasso (the piper heard in the music track) playing the Irish *uilleann* pipes (Ivor Vong)

(right)
Close-up of *uilleann* pipes showing chanter (right) and drone pipes with regulator levers

years prior to the Great Potato Famine of the 1840s. Pipers stricken with disease and starvation either perished or emigrated, thus causing a decline in *uilleann* piping in Ireland.

An *uilleann* pipe player sits with the bellows on the right hip secured with a belt, the drone pipes lying across his lap. The word *uilleann* is the genitive singular/plural form of the Irish-Gaelic word *uillinn*, meaning elbow, corner, or angle, and was perhaps named so because of the use of both elbows in the playing of the instrument. In pre-Famine contexts, the *uilleann* pipes were not built to any standardized pitch. However, the kind of concert pitch 'D' instrument heard in the audio example was first pioneered in Philadelphia around 1875 by the Drogheda-born Taylor brothers, William and Charles, to accommodate the instrument's use with pianos, accordions, and other fixed-pitch instruments. In 1893, the Gaelic League was founded and strove to revive and "promote values of the Irish folk" by reinstituting the Gaelic language and other aspects of indigenous culture including the playing of the *uilleann* pipes. The heated enthusiasm of this movement slowly cooled until the founding of Na Píobairí Uilleann ("The Uilleann Pipers") in Dublin in 1968, an organization whose primary goal is the promotion of the instrument and its music.

Disassembled for storage, the *uilleann* pipes consist of the bag, the bellows and strap, a chanter pipe, three drone pipes, and—in full sets—an additional three pipes fitted with a series of large metal keys. These additional pipes, called "regulators," allow the player to produce the chords that are the *uilleann* pipes' most distinctive feature. There can be anywhere from one to four regulators on a set of *uilleann* pipes. The chanter, drones, and regulators are powered by air sucked in through a bellows under the piper's right arm, forced through a tube across the piper's waist, and into a leather bag under the piper's left arm. Thus, a player must be exceptionally coordinated, having to pump the bellows with the right arm, press the bag with the left arm, play the melody on the chanter with the fingers of both hands, and sometimes press the regulator keys with the side of the right hand. Without doubt, the *uilleann* pipes in their fully developed form are the most complex bagpipes in the world.

Irish music is one of the world's most developed melodic traditions. The repertory is vast, though numerous individual tunes may be variants of other tunes. Sometimes the same tune is known by different names depending on the region, and sometimes tunes with the same name are musically distinct. Those that are not lyric songs with texts are likely to be one of the several types of dances tunes found in Ireland: namely, the jig (quick 6/8 or 12/8 time), the reel (quick 2/4), the hornpipe (6/8 or 12/8 time), and the polka (quick 2/4 time). Some tunes fall into the major–minor tonality system, but there is a tendency for them to be structurally pentatonic (i.e., to employ a five-tone scale) with the possibility of additional passing notes.

Because Irish traditional instrumental music is often played for dancers, it is typical to play two or more tunes consecutively. The two tunes played on this track, titled "Lilies of the Field" and "Fairhaired Boy," are *reels*. A reel is a dance tune genre in duple meter with two parts of equal length, each part typically consisting of eight measures. Each of the reels on this track, however, is a *single reel*, meaning that there are only four instead of eight measures per A and B part. Because the Irish instrumental tradition is largely an oral one in which tune authorship is not always known, these two reels remain anonymous.

In Irish traditional music, there is both a downbeat (where your foot would normally tap) and an upbeat (subtler and not necessarily acknowledged by all instrumentalists with the same attention). When playing the *uilleann* pipes, grace notes are often incorporated before eighth notes on beats 1, 3, 5, and 7 to communicate the dance rhythm clearly, indicating to a dancer when his or her foot ought to hit the floor.

Cultural Considerations. If much Irish music seems sad or sentimental, Irish history has provided many reasons for such emotions. Although blessed with natural beauty and generous rainfall, Ireland has experienced more than its share of violence over the course of history, from the Anglo-Norman invasions of the twelfth century, to English Protestant Oliver Cromwell's scorched-earth policy of the seventeenth century. Between invasions there were numerous intertribal battles, as

LISTENING GUIDE

9.5 (1'58")

Site 9.5
Ireland: *Uilleann* Bagpipes

Instruments: *Uilleann* Bagpipes

TIME	LISTENING FOCUS
0'00"	Chanter sounds two introductory pitches followed by the main melody of Reel 1 ("Lillies of the Field") and entrance of the drone pitches (A1).
0'06"	Main melody repeats with variation (A2).
0'11"	Second melodic line begins and repeats with variation (B1, B2).
0'20"	Main melody returns and repeats with variation (A1, A2). Listen for the "tapping" versus "sustain" sound of the regulators, as well as changes in chords.
0'30"	Second melodic line returns and repeats with variation (B1, B2).
0'39"	Main melody returns and repeats with variation (A1, A2).
0'48"	Second melodic line returns and repeats with variation (B1, B2). Note the regulators stop during this section.
0'58"	Main melody of Reel 2 ("The Fairhaired Boy") begins and repeats with variation (C1, C2). Note the regulators return.
1'07"	Second line of Reel 2 enters and repeats with variation (D1, D2).
1'17"	Main melody of Reel 2 returns and repeats with variation (C1, C2).
1'26"	Second line of Reel 2 enters and repeats with variation (D1, D2).
1'36"	Main melody of Reel 2 returns and repeats with variation (C1, C2). Note the regulators stop during this section.
1'45"	Second line of Reel 2 enters and repeats with variation (D1, D2). Note the regulators return. Example ends on sustained chord.

Source: "The Lilies of the Field" and "The Fairhaired Boy," private studio recording by Eliot Grasso, 2011. Used by permission.

MUSICAL MARKERS: Timbre/Medium—Mellower melodic timbre in comparison to strident quality of Highland Pipes. **Phonic Structure**—Drone with changing harmony in mid-range and "busy" upper melodic line. **Rhythm**—"Bouncing" duple meter and quick tempo.
ETHNO-CHALLENGE: Listen through the example and note the timecode reference for each of the "variation" melodic phrases (A2, B2, C2, D2).

various peoples and clans tried to gain dominance over one another and fought over land and religion. All of this has provided Irish songwriters with more than ample subject matter. The Great Famine that lasted through much of the 1840s not only starved many to death but also drove much of the population—reduced from 8.5 million to around four million in less than five years—from the island to the New World. The Irish population in North America, particularly in places such as Boston, New York, and Chicago, then struggled as a Roman Catholic underclass in a predominantly Protestant nation before eventually rising to prominence and power.

Donegal musicians gathered outside for a late afternoon session. From left to right: pennywhistle, *bodhran*, accordion, guitar (Sean Williams)

In 2015 cosmopolitan Bangkok, Thailand, had three genuine Irish pubs. Here five musicians play a "session" at Molly Malone's Irish Pub: (from left to right) Mick Moloney (banjo), Sharon Graf (fiddle), Brenda Castles (concertina), Bo Ratiwat (fiddle), and Michael O'Dwyer on tin whistle

While the Irish are widely associated with police work, many of them had to labor in the most menial of jobs before harvesting the fruits of upward mobility. Nonetheless, they were luckier than their compatriots overseas, because Ireland remained impoverished until the late twentieth century, when it became a fast-growing, technologically savvy success story in the European Union. That explosion of wealth, however, was short lived, but Ireland is again on the rise.

As already mentioned, the original Irish instrument was the courtly harp, but this fell into oblivion by around 1800. In the twentieth century, there has been a revival of the harp, which was reconstructed on the basis of pictures and written descriptions and inaccurately portrayed as a folk instrument. Besides this and the *uilleann* pipes, there are several other prominent Irish instruments: the fiddle (really just an inexpensive violin), the vertical tin whistle (a kind of metal recorder), the "timber" flute (a wooden transverse flute), and a variety of bellows-driven free-reed instruments with keyboards such as the melodeon, concertina, and accordion. Over time several foreign instruments have been adopted, including the Italian mandolin, the American tenor banjo, the guitar, and a hybrid lute derived from the mandolin called *bouzouki* after the Greco-Turkish lute. Percussion is limited to the well-known but recently introduced *bodhran*, a goatskin-covered frame drum played by the right hand using a wooden beater, and a pair of wooden "bones" (possibly borrowed from America along with the banjo), or spoons.

Traditionally, Irish music was played communally for family and friends in various settings, many private. Visitors are most likely to encounter Irish music in a public house (pub), where local musicians gather in their reserved corner in the evening to play for each other, the rest of the pub patrons being casual listeners rather than a formal audience. These gatherings are called "sessions" (*seisiún ceoil*). Because they are informal and ad hoc, the instrumental makeup varies greatly. The Irish pipes are one of the possible instruments found and blend well with the quieter sounds of other indoor type instruments. When an evening event features dancing and a named band, the group is called a *céilí* ("kay-lee") band; these events are also the most likely context for Irish music in North America today.

Music has become an important element of Ireland's tourist industry, and in areas where tourists tend to congregate, especially in the west, there is a conscious effort to have music every evening during the summer. Nowhere is this more so than in the village of Doolin in County Clare, where enormous, standing-room crowds gather nightly. Visiting musicians may join a session, though there are unwritten rules for participating. Outside the tourist pubs, visitors should request permission before taping or photographing musicians.

With the rise in popularity of all things "Celtic," another kind of music has also arisen that is better described as "pan-Celtic," meaning it sounds vaguely Irish but in fact reflects a variety of influences. This includes such phenomena as varied as Michael Flatley's popular Riverdance shows and the *cha-cha-cha* version of "Sleepy Maggie."

Arrival: Hungary

Like Hungary itself, the Hungarian people stand astride both West and East. Descended from the semi-nomadic Magyars who originated in the Ural Mountains of present-day central Russia, the Hungarians arrived in the Danube Valley and the Great Plain in the late ninth century. Over time they mixed with Germanic and Slavic peoples, and during the late tenth century they settled into a stable agricultural life under their first king, Stephen. But their location at the crossroads of Europe left them vulnerable to competing armies and subject to invasions. These invaders included the Mongols in the thirteenth century, the Ottoman Turks in the fifteenth, and finally, through marriage and other alliances, the Hapsburgs of Austria in the sixteenth. As a consequence, Hungary remained more oriented toward Central and Western Europe than to the East. Independence was achieved in 1919, but for much of the twentieth century Hungary was dominated first by Nazi Germany and then the Soviet Union. Rural Hungary preserves a lively folk music culture. Budapest is also home to a mature, European classical music establishment, and throughout the country the **Rom** (Gypsies) practice their own forms of music.

ROM (ALSO, ROMANI)
An ethnic group originating in India characterized by a semi-nomadic lifestyle; commonly known as Gypsies.

Site 6: *Tekerölant* (Hurdy Gurdy)

First Impressions. With its nasal tone and constant drones, the *tekerölant* (or **hurdy gurdy**) might strike some as sounding like bagpipes. If you saw a hurdy gurdy player—perhaps one of the well-known but little understood "organ grinders"—you would note that he was turning a crank with the right hand and pushing keys with the left. The sheer volume of sound can be deceiving; only one player is required to play this seeming "symphony in a box." Indeed, a medieval name for the instrument was *symphonia*.

Aural Analysis. The *hurdy gurdy* is classified as a chordophone because its sound emanates from three or four strings. Specifically it is a lute, with a slightly differentiated body and neck, the latter being very short and thick. The *hurdy gurdy*'s continuous tone suggests that it is a bowed, rather than plucked, lute. Indeed, it is, but its creators have also solved the two biggest problems associated with playing such instruments: bowing smoothly and accurately stopping the strings. The result is the ultimate "user-friendly" instrument, a foolproof fiddle with the added bonus of drones to eliminate the need for an ensemble. Such instruments have a long history in Europe dating back to medieval times, when they were even used in church, but by the eighteenth century they had begun to die out, except for two prominent forms: the French and the Hungarian versions. To some extent both forms have been in continuous use as traditional instruments right up to the present time, and both also played a prominent part in twentieth-century folk music revivals in their respective countries.

To allow for smooth and continuous bowing, the makers of the *hurdy gurdy* installed a resin-coated wheel turned by a crank held in the right hand. The strings are tensioned against the wheel and sound continuously, though some models allow for the disengagement of the drone strings. The melody string is stopped, not by the player's fingers, but by a series of wooden *tangents* (or keys) placed along the bottom side of the instrument so that gravity causes them to fall back after being pressed against the string. Consequently, the *hurdy gurdy* produces both melody and drone as a continuous sound. In addition the player can produce accents by moving into place a "buzzing bridge" that lifts one drone string enough for a buzzing sound to be created when the crank is "jogged" (jerked) as it is turned.

Much of the traditional instrumental music of the Hungarian Great Plain is intended to accompany dance, but players often begin by playing a section that lacks a regular beat before beginning the metrical dance section. The Hungarian ethnomusicologist and composer Béla Bartók referred to the unmeasured section as being *parlando-rubato*, that is, "in speech rhythm," and to the measured or metrical section as being in *tempo giusto*, meaning "precise tempo," a phrase suggesting that a regular beat is present.

HURDY GURDY
A chordophone common in France and Hungary that uses a wheel turned by a crank to vibrate the strings.

A typical Hungarian village house in Oskü, north of Lake Balaton in central Hungary

289

(left) Sean Folsom, plays the Hungarian *tekerölant* (hurdy gurdy), a cranked chordophone

(right) With the cover lifted, you can clearly see the parts of the Hungarian *tekerölant* (hurdy gurdy)

The example heard here consists of a series of tunes played on an instrument with one melody string and three drone strings, with the drones tuned A, e, a (the A being the tonic). Most of the melodies heard use the scale A, B, c♯, d, e, f♯, g, a, which is equivalent to the medieval Mixolydian "church mode," but in some passages the c♯ changes to c, producing the scale A, B, c, d, e, f♯, g, a, which has no church mode equivalent.

The track consists of five short melodies played without break, beginning with a *parlando-rubato* "song air." A second "song air" begins when the "buzzing bridge" is activated at 0'25." As the tempo picks up, you hear three "jumping dances" (at 0'58," 1'13," and 1'27"), with the repeat of the last one slowing down slightly. Completing the set is a "fast *czardas*" beginning at 1'59." The *czardas*, with its simple side steps, is Hungary's best-known "popular" dance. The meter is duple, but the phrasing of the fast *czardas* breaks the monotony of 4/4 time. The initial descending phrase, played twice, has four beats. Then follow three phrases of two beats each, producing a phrase with six beats. Thus, the dance shifts phrase groupings from four to six and back.

Cultural Considerations. Although traditional Hungarian music possesses certain distinct instruments and styles, it is better understood as part of a larger central and southeast European cultural sphere. When Béla Bartók began serious field research into Hungarian folk music in 1907, his goal was to isolate those elements that were quintessentially Hungarian. Inspired by Hungarian nationalism, his research was colored by the Hungarian antipathy toward non-Hungarian neighbors, especially the Romanians and Slovaks. To his surprise, however, Bartók discovered that Hungarian music had to be seen in a context that encompassed not only the music of Hungary's immediate neighbors but also the music of central and southeastern Europe as a whole. Owing to the Ottoman Turk influence on Hungarian music, he also conducted further work in Turkey and North Africa.

Bartók's research into "true" Hungarian village music did, however, reveal a side of Hungary that had been hitherto ignored; namely, traditional Hungarian folk music that was distinct from the music of the Rom (Gypsies). During the nineteenth century a number of composers, especially those working in Vienna, had a certain fascination with exotic sounds and styles they considered "Hungarian"; most turned out to be of Rom origin. Franz Liszt, for example, sometimes wrote music in "Hungarian style," such as the *Mélodies hongroises* (1838–1839) and *Ungarische Rhapsodien* (1846–1847)—but most of the sounds he understood to be "Hungarian" were actually Rom. Likewise, German composer Johannes Brahms's "Hungarian Dances" (1880) were really Rom in style. The same was true for most other "Hungarian" compositions of the time, because their encounters with the Rom were entirely in the sphere of urban public music-making where "Gypsies" predominated.

LISTENING GUIDE

Site 9.6

Hungary: *Tekerölant* (Hurdy Gurdy)

Instruments: *Hurdy gurdy*

TIME	LISTENING FOCUS
0'00"	Drone pitches begin on pitches A–E–a. Listen for the melodic pitches establishing the basic harmony (an A chord, A–C#–E–a) as they move into the melody, using a fluctuating tempo (i.e., *parlando-rubato*). Also, note the brief sounding of the "buzz" timbre that will be used later to add a rhythmic element.
0'13"	Opening melody repeats.
0'25"	Listen for the change in melody, increased rhythmic density, and faster tempo at a steady rate of pulsation. Also, note the addition of the "buzzing bridge."
0'36"	Second melody repeats.
0'46"	Second melody repeats a third time.
0'57"	Listen for the change in melody, increased rhythmic density, and faster tempo.
1'13"	Third melody is repeated with variation.
1'27"	Third melody is repeated with variation. Listen for the introduction of new pitches in the scale at 1'31."
1'57"	Final section. Listen for the change in melody, increased rhythmic density, and faster tempo.
2'06"	Example fades. Note that the drone pitches have sounded throughout the entire example.

Source: Medley of traditional tunes performed by Sean Folsom, 2003 (private studio recording). Used by permission.

MUSICAL MARKERS: Timbre/Medium—"Buzzing" crank box chordophone. **Phonic Structure**—Drone with single melodic line. **Rhythm**—Tempo fluctuations and varying rhythmic density.
ETHNO-CHALLENGE: Clap the basic meter throughout to note the use of *parlando-rubato* and changes in tempo.

The old "folk" world that Bartók revealed has largely disappeared because of the tremendous disruption and displacements of World Wars I and II, changes in national borders, the rise and fall of communism, and, more recently, the modernization that has resulted from Hungary's joining the European Union. While there are undoubtedly rural areas where ordinary local people continue to play folk music, much of Hungary's "traditional" music is now revivalist in nature. Young musicians have sought to reenact the old culture of their grandparents by forming strictly old-fashioned ensembles specializing in music that might have been transcribed from Bartók's field recordings. These ensembles may employ a number of fascinating instruments—some of which are otherwise obsolete—including bagpipes (*duda*), friction drums whose head vibrates when a wet stick is drawn through the membrane (*köcsög*), a zither (*citera*), a large hammered dulcimer (**cimbalom**) played both by Hungarians and by Rom, a struck lute (*gardon*), and long end-blown flutes (*hosszú furulya*).

CIMBALOM
A hammered zither from Eastern Europe, commonly associated with Rom (Gypsy) music. Also, the national instrument of Hungary.

Collecting songs in the village of Darázs (now Dražovce), Slovakia, in 1907, Hungarian ethnomusicologist-composer Béla Bartók has the singers project directly into the horn of a cylinder recording device (Archivo Iconografico, S. A./Corbis)

Local musicians playing the *citera* zither (left) and *köcsög* friction drum (right) in Bugac, Hungary, a village near Kecskemet on the Great Plain (*Puszta*)

Arrival: Georgia

Little known to Western tourists and difficult to enter, the tiny nation of Georgia—slightly smaller than the state of South Carolina—lies at the junction of Europe and Western Asia, a region called the Caucasus after a high mountain range that separates the region into north and south. Situated just south of the range with the Black Sea to the west, Russia to the north, and Turkey, Armenia, and Azerbaijan to the south and east, Georgia lies in the center of what has long been

Explore More

by Will Bulger

Slovenian Polka

Between 1899 and 1924, over a half million citizens each of Polish, Slovenian, Hungarian, Slovakian, and other Eastern European countries immigrated to the United States. People of these European groups tended to cluster in particular geographic areas, initially maintaining strong identities and ties to the cultural traditions of the mother country, including music. Over time, such traditions transformed into uniquely American conventions, the American polka band being a premier example. Each American ethnic group that developed a polka band style did so in a manner that was unique from the other styles. The principal styles include Slavic (Polish and Slovenian), Germanic (German, Czech, and Bavarian) and Southwestern (Mexican with elements of German and Czech influences) polka.

A couple dressed in Gorenjska national costumes performing a polka in Bled (Shutterstock)

The primary role of the polka band is to provide accompanying music to a dance that evolved in the early nineteenth century, i.e., the polka. Its origin is subject to speculation and perhaps even some myth involving a Czech servant girl believed to have created the "half-step" dance. By the mid-1800s, it had become an urban dance popular among working-class residents throughout Europe. The polka joined the waltz as a popular couple's dance, replacing the group and line dances of the rural populations of the period.

In the United States, the American polka band first appeared in Cleveland, Ohio, during the 1920s and was most strongly influenced by a son of Slovenian immigrants. William Lausche was a practicing dentist and trained pianist interested in tra-

ditional Slovenian folk music. Contemporary music, including jazz and ragtime, influenced his polka style with the addition of syncopation, more sophisticated harmonies, and faster tempos than the folk tunes, which became the basis for Slovenian polka in America. He served as a mentor for a generation of Cleveland area polka musicians of varying ethnicities, leading to several recordings by Lausche, his sister Josephine, and Mary Udovich on the national Victor label in the 1920s. During this same period, Cleveland accordionist, Matt Hoyer of The Hoyer Trio, recorded for the Victor, Columbia, and Okeh record labels. The Trio introduced innovations, such as the use of two accordions and sometimes the banjo to their recordings, an instrumentation copied by many subsequent polka bands.

After World War II, Slovenian-style polka reached its heyday of popularity. The song *Just Because*, as recorded by Frankie Yankovic (1915–1998), reached top ten status in the Billboard popular music chart, selling more than 2.5 million copies. It became an anthem of Slovenian polka bands and many other styles as well, helping Yankovic's popularity to soar. Over the next several years, he appeared with such legends as Lawrence Welk, Duke Ellington, Patti Page, Jackie Gleason, and Arthur Godfrey. Of his most memorable appearances was a performance on the Tonight Show with Johnny Carson in 1964. His accomplishments were recognized by the recording industry with his being awarded a Grammy in 1986. His many recordings spanned a twenty-six-year partnership with Columbia Records.

Though emergence of rock 'n' roll displaced polkas (and many other popular styles) on the national scene starting in the mid-1950s, Slovenian-style polka bands remained a vibrant tradition in western Pennsylvania, northern Ohio, southern Michigan, and Milwaukee. This is still true today. These bands are small with usually between four and six instrumentalists, many of whom also provide vocals. All polka bands include an accordion and, in the tradition of the Hoyer Trio, often two with one providing the melody and the other offering fills. The rhythm section, borrowed from jazz and ragtime ensembles, can consist of a banjo, a bass, and a drum set. Unlike Polish, Czech, or German polka bands, brass instruments (such as trumpet or trombone) are seldom included, although a saxophone does occasionally appear as melody instrument. The original button-box accordions common to the tradition are today replaced by modern piano keyboard style accordions, because these instruments can play a full chromatic scale.

Few Slovenian polka band members are full-time musicians. Most hold "other" full-time jobs with their music gigs providing additional income that allows them to maintain their music hobby. The bands usually have an alternate repertoire beyond polka and waltz music.

The alternate book can include country and western music, pop music, 1950s and 1960s rock and roll, and alternate dances (the hokey pokey or line dances). Such adaptations to changing circumstances give polka bands access to a wider audience, which promotes the familiarity of polka music in new cultural settings. As with so many music traditions around the world, polka, with its many styles and cultural associations, maintains a deep connection with the heritage of its community of performers and listeners, who reinforce its continuity with each generation.

contested territory. Consequently, Georgia has been invaded repeatedly over its long history. Conquered earlier by the Ottoman Turks, Georgians sought protection by the Russians but ended up as a republic in the former Soviet Union. Georgia seceded in 1991 but remained contested territory until the Rose Revolution in 2008 established a shaky independence. Two small regions within—Abkhazia and South Ossetia—remain officially as Russian territory, however.

Even with a population of less than 4 million, one quarter of whom live in the capital city, Tbilisi, Georgian culture, including its music, is made complex by many regional distinctions often dictated by geographical barriers. While all speak the Georgian language—unrelated to any other language—there are numerous local dialects even among such a small population. Their writing system is a unique alphabet. Excavations suggest that early humans arrived in Georgia from Africa 1.8 million years ago. Georgians claim to have created wine 3000 years ago, and indeed eastern Georgia specializes in wine production. They also claim to have been the first culture to embrace Christianity outside its point of origin in modern Israel, founding the Georgian Orthodox Church in the early fourth century, though Armenia also claims to have been first.

In spite of the many invasions and occupations over the centuries, Georgian music remains distinctive, if not downright surprising. Although Georgia is technically a European culture, its music stands in stark contrast to what most understand to be "European music." The Caucasus includes many other ethnic groups with distinctive musical idioms, few researched by ethnomusicologists and little known outside the region. Forming a crossroads between Europe and Asia, the region's mix of cultures includes both Christian/European groups as well as Muslim/Asian groups.

The village of Lenjeri in Svaneti, Republic of Georgia (Photo by Brian Fairley, used with permission)

Site 7: Georgian Choral Singing

First Impressions. Knowing how hard Georgians have fought for their cultural and political freedom over the centuries, including even recently, it does not surprise that their singing exudes strength and determination. Unaccompanied male voices combine to produce striking sonorities—a form of harmony—quite unlike those of Western Europe. What many listeners might describe as dissonance gives the music a spicy flavor only enhanced by a kind of yodeling in the upper voice. Perhaps the power of the singing reflects Georgians' determination to preserve their cultural individuality as distinct from those of their neighbors.

Aural Analysis. Although Georgia is part of the European world, its music sounds little like what we expect in "European music," a term that mostly implies Western and Central Europe. In this latter world, one expects melody based on a diatonic scale and harmony built from "triads," that is, three-note sonorities built on intervals of a third, e.g., C, E, G or 1, 3, 5. Georgian music also has melody and harmony, but its sound is strikingly different.

It is difficult to speak of Georgian composers. Although songs do indeed have melodies created at some point by a singer/composer, with there being no notation, such "compositions" are anonymous; they are remembered and passed on aurally and are flexible in their details. Since a form of tightly controlled improvisation informs Georgian music, different singing groups are likely to render the same song differently. Most vocal music is performed by a small group of singers, male or female (rarely mixed) without accompaniment.

Most Georgian songs consist of three vocal ranges, i.e., parts, with soloists performing the upper and middle parts and a small group the bass part. Songs in four parts might add a lower drone pitch. The middle part (called "to say") is the main melody, that which is the most fixed element, while the upper voice ("follower") often parallels the main voice. The bass voice ("bass") is typically the most active of the three. Thus, Georgian song is both contrapuntal ("linear") and harmonic ("vertical"). Listen for each voice as a distinct part but also listen to them simultaneously in harmony.

Indeed, such close listening will help you understand how Georgian music is so different from Western European music. Where, say, Germans find thirds and triads to be consonant and intervals such as the second or seventh to be dissonant, Georgians find the latter intervals to be at least normal if not consonant. Western European harmony forbids voices from moving in parallel fashion, especially at the interval of the fifth, but Georgians revel in parallel movement at

The town of Signagi in Kakheti, Republic of Georgia, with St. Stephen's church overlooking the Alazani Valley (Photo by Brian Fairley, used with permission)

various intervals including the fifth but even the seventh. Non-Georgian listeners may hear these intervals as intriguing, spicy, pungent, or perhaps even unpleasant, all reactions likely similar to those possible when sampling Georgian foods, a cuisine also little known in the West.

The unique phrasing of the three vocal parts in this example also helps to define this distinctive type of choral singing. The opening section (A) is sixteen beats in a duple meter for all of the vocal parts. However, while the upper and middle parts divide the melodic material symmetrically into two phrases of eight beats (8+8), the bass part follows an asymmetrical phrasing of ten beats followed by six beats (10+6). Thus, all the vocal parts begin and end together, but the incongruity of the melodic phrasing between the parts, as well as strong use of syncopation, provides a hearty rhythmic flavor. This may not be readily apparent on the first listen, but careful attention to the rhythm of the individual parts will reveal this characteristic feature common to Georgian choral singing. The second section (B) transitions into more predictable symmetrical phrasing in all the vocal parts (4+4). The overall melodic material is comprised of just eight beats, rather than sixteen, and is marked also by a noticeable increase in tempo, which happens again as handclaps enter to encourage a faster pace.

The track provided here is a kind of wedding song called *makruli* from the west Georgian province of Guria and having only nonsense syllables as text. It is performed by two antiphonal groups totaling about twenty singers, though it is difficult to tell when one ends and the other begins. In addition to the bass, middle, and upper parts, an additional high part featuring yodels gives the song an unexpected piquancy. Following the slower beginning section, the music turns into a dance song, though it does not accompany actual dancing.

Cultural Considerations. Though having been a constituent part of the Soviet Union from 1921 to 1991, the Republic of Georgia largely escaped Soviet state policies that sought to harness "folk music" to suit state purposes, especially in highlighting political themes. Such "state folkloric song and dance troupes" permeated most areas under Soviet or Chinese Communist control, resulting in highly choreographed stage productions that used folk elements only to suggest "tradition." Thus, it is surprising that music in Georgia has remained so close to its roots, to its old traditions. Because few musicians or singers identify as "professional," most music making is amateur and thus open to all. For such music to remain viable, however, it requires a context other than stage performance. Fortunately, many of these remain intact, resulting in a vigorous, living tradition of mostly vocal music in Georgia.

According to Joseph Jordania, the premier authority on Georgian music, the most important song contexts are calendric rituals (related to the annual cycle of festivals and holidays), life-cycle rituals (related to life events such as birth, weddings, and funerals), and religious music of the Georgian Orthodox Church. Although all of these continue to exist, it is also common for such songs to be sung informally around a large dinner table after a meal by family or a group of friends. Since everyone is assumed to have enough musical talent to participate, all feel free to join in.

Although none are heard in this audio example, Georgians also play numerous instruments, especially for dance and sometimes to accompany song. While vocal music has features that make Georgian music unique, most instruments are of types having broad distribution. It has always been easy to borrow instruments from one's cultural neighbors, though the music played does not transfer. Georgian membranophones include the *daira*, a frame drum with jingles, and the *daphdaphi* or *doli*, a large, two-headed drum. Among the chordophones are both bowed and plucked lutes, but most surprising is the *changi*, a triangular-shaped harp also found in Iran. Among the aerophones is a cane flute, a set of panpipes, and a variety of bagpipes.

The distinctive style and energy of Georgian singing and dance have such appeal that the government has sent groups to tour internationally as well as entertain visitors/tourists at home. Nonetheless, Georgian music flies mainly under the radar of most international audiences, the individualistic expression of a small but highly creative society who proudly preserves its musical traditions.

LISTENING GUIDE 9.7 (1'34")

Site 9.7

Georgia: Choral Singing

Voices: Two groups of men (smaller "lead" group and larger "following" group)

TIME	LISTENING FOCUS
0'00"	Part A opens with a single male voice—the middle "main" part.
0'02"	Upper "yodel" part and a single "bass" harmony part enter.
0'10"	Listen for the second vocal group entrance, which includes more bass voices.
0'21"	Note the return to the first vocal group and begin counting the number of pulses (sixteen) before the next vocal group transition.
0'31"	As the second vocal group returns, focus on either the upper or middle vocal parts to note the symmetrical phrasing (8+8).
0'42"	Now focus on the bass part and count the pulses of each phrase. Note the "pause" comes on pulse 10, followed by six more beats to the end of the section.
0'52"	Reflect on the differences in rhythmic density between the upper "busy yodel" part with its wide intervals, the less dense middle "main" part, and least dense lower "bass" part.
1'02"	Consider the phonic structure of the "linear" upper voice in relation to the homophonic movement of the lower voices.
1'22"	Part B begins with a shift to symmetrical phrasing (4+4) with all the vocal parts and a faster tempo (105 bpm).
1'40"	Handclaps enter and signal another increase in tempo (120 bpm).
2'15"	Listen for both vocal groups singing simultaneously as the performance draws to a close.

MUSICAL MARKER: Timbre/Medium—All-male vocal group. **Phonic Structure**—"Yodeling" upper voice. Main "middle" voice. Lower "bass" harmony voices with parallel motion. **Rhythm**—Asymmetrical phrasing between voices. Most "busy" in the upper voice. Moderately busy in the middle voice. Lower voice is the least dense, but closely parallels the middle voice.
ETHNO-CHALLENGE: With one or more partners, sing a familiar tune such as Happy Birthday in parallel intervals (thirds, fifths, sevenths), with or without a bass drone.

Questions to Consider

1. How is the history of European and Arabic cultural contact revealed through musical characteristics in places such as Spain and Georgia?

2. What defines a music as "classical" as opposed to "folk" in the European context? How has "classical" music influenced "folk" music style and performance and vice versa?

3. Drone is especially prominent in many European music traditions. What are some specific manifestations and how does drone relate to the overall sound?

4. Some "folk" instruments are designed to be easy to play but others require advanced techniques. Discuss examples of European instruments that typify both ends of the spectrum.

5. How are music and musical instruments used to express national identity in Europe?

6. Is language a reliable demarcation of musical style in Europe? Why or why not?

Chapter 10

Sub-Saharan Africa

Ghana, Nigeria, Central Africa, Zimbabwe, Uganda, Senegal, South Africa

An Asante paramount chief with his Ntahera ivory horn blowers passing the tradition through the generations (Joseph S. Kaminski, Ejisu, Ghana, 2001)

Background Preparation

Africa, the world's second-largest continent, is home to nearly 3,000 separate ethnic groups spread across 11.7 million square miles (30.3 million square km). While Africa boasts many densely populated urban areas, most other areas remain rural with limited infrastructure. Farming is the primary occupation of most Africans, although many people living in areas rich in natural resources, such as diamonds and coal, are employed by large mining companies and related industries.

The continent is customarily divided into three cultural zones: the pan-Arabic zone in the north, including the countries bordering the Mediterranean Sea; the Sahel zone, including those areas dominated by the vast Sahara desert; and sub-Saharan Africa, the rest of the continent south of the Sahara desert; the latter is the focus of this chapter. Western, eastern, and central Africa are equatorial and therefore quite hot and humid. Rainforests dominate the central interior, whereas the red-soiled Kalahari Desert typifies the arid landscape of southern Africa. Few mountain ranges exist, though several dormant volcanoes, the most famous being snow-capped Mount Kilimanjaro in northeastern Tanzania, provide a contrast to the vast rolling plains seen throughout most of sub-Saharan Africa. Wildlife preserves are scattered throughout much of the continent, which are home to such well-known animals as the African elephant, lion, zebra, giraffe, and rhinoceros.

While the ancient Egyptian pharaohs ruled the most famous kingdoms of North Africa, the kings of sub-Saharan Africa also held dominion over vast territories for numerous generations. In western Africa, the earliest known kingdom was the Kingdom of Ghana, which controlled the trade routes of West Africa from roughly the fifth to the eleventh century C.E., when Muslim militants from present-day Mauritania overtook it. Other important empires prior to the colonial era included the Mali kingdom (mid-thirteenth to late fourteenth century), and the Songhai kingdom (fifteenth to late sixteenth century), both Islamic. In southern Africa, the Zulu King Shaka (1787–1828) is best known, having organized a powerful military machine that conquered many peoples throughout South Africa and as far north as Tanzania. Historical warriors and royal lineages continue to play a vital role in the cultural identity of modern Africa.

The political borders of present-day Africa, however, resulted from European colonial occupation. Throughout much of the nineteenth century and into the early twentieth century, vast regions of Africa were claimed as colonies by several European powers. The 1884–1885 Berlin Conference is often cited as a decisive moment in Africa's political history, particularly for the Congo region. At this meeting, German, Belgian, French, British, and Portuguese officials, along with representatives

Zebras in a South African game reserve, one of Africa's visual icons (Max T. Miller)

of governments that had no colonial stake in the region, such as the United States, allocated territorial rights to most of central and southern Africa without the presence of a single African. Thereafter, based on these colonial entities, newly independent African nations were later formed with little regard for the cultural differences of the various peoples living within their borders. Consequently, many different ethnic populations, with diverse cultural traditions, often live in close proximity within a single country, while their brethren are separated from them in neighboring countries.

Decades of European colonial rule left strong marks on African religious life, governmental structures, and languages. Travelers to Africa will encounter multilingual speakers who may speak multiple indigenous languages (of which there are nearly 800 in sub-Saharan Africa alone), as well as one or two European languages, the most common being English, French, and Portuguese. Though colonialism affected many of the cultural activities of African peoples, often oppressively, traditional practices still thrive throughout the continent, especially in rural areas. Islam and Christianity have long co-existed in sub-Saharan Africa, though aspects of earlier animistic traditions have often been reinterpreted into the ritual activities of the mainstream institutionalized religions.

An emphasis on the collective community remains an overarching principle essential to the social organization and cultural identity of many African populations. Social identity is valued over individual identity, as expressed by the common proverb, "I am because we are." Each person serves a function within the overall group. In smaller villages, everyone is considered part of the same family, whether or not they are related by blood. A person's possessions are frequently "shared" with other members of the community, as if everyone lived in the same house. Furthermore, these "extended families" comprise not only living members of the community but also the spirits of ancestors. Even when a person is physically "alone," he is accompanied by one or more ancestor spirits who act as guardians and confidants.

Music is a vital aspect of the daily lives of people throughout sub-Saharan Africa. Even the most mundane tasks, such as canceling stamps at the post office, pounding millet, or walking are made enjoyable by putting them into the rhythms of music. Dance and singing are equally essential; indeed, music, dance, and singing, conceptualized as distinct from one another in the West, are described in many places throughout Africa with the same terminology, because they are considered inseparable. The importance of the collective community that characterizes

Kete dancer at an Asante funeral in Kumase, Ghana (Joseph S. Kaminski)

traditional African life is reflected in three main activities associated with music: communal dance, call-and-response singing, and the use of **polyrhythm** in instrumental performance. Informal dance activity often takes place when large groups of people are gathered. An individual may spontaneously step out from the crowd to dance in conjunction with a musical performance. The crowd may respond with cheers, and others may be inspired to dance as well. Spontaneous dance participation, however, is generally brief, and the dancer will fall back into the group to make way for others. The individual thereby demonstrates deference to the community by only briefly asserting an individual identity within the context of a larger social scheme. Formal dance activity also tends to emphasize group participation, though dance in ritual contexts, such as trance dancing, often involves only a few specialized performers. In these instances, the performance requires a specific knowledge of tradition or that the individual dancers are of a specific social status, such as performers with royal patronage. The set choreography of these dances differs from dancing in informal contexts and may not include opportunities for individual expression. Formal dance activities are performed with some social function in mind, such as honoring royalty or inviting ancestral spirits to participate in community events.

Vocal performance can occur as part of religious ceremonies or other ritual activities, in the context of storytelling, dance, or royal functions, or merely as entertainment. Though many solo vocal traditions can be found, the majority of vocal performances involve group singing, generally with a call-and-response organization. In call-and-response, an individual sings a "call" and the group "responds" appropriately. (A familiar American example: *Call*: Give me a G . . ., *Response:* G!; *Call*: Give me an 'O . . .', *Response:* 'O!'; *Call*: What's that spell?!, *Response*: Go!!!) This organization may also be thought of as a "question" by the caller and an "answer" by the group and is therefore clearly different from "prompting," in which the leader cues the group, which responds with the same words (as, for example, in the lined hymn to be studied in Site 13.3).

Polyrhythm is the predominant structure for organizing instrumental (as well as some vocal) musical performance in sub-Saharan Africa. For centuries, the polyrhythmic music traditions of sub-Saharan Africa were largely incomprehensible to outsiders. Missionaries and foreign explorers often characterized the rhythmically dense drumming traditions of western Africa as "chaotic." Colonial governments suppressed these musical practices and often labeled the "wild" playing associated with "pagan" rituals as evil music that corrupted the soul. Ignorance of how the complex polyrhythmic music organization worked was a primary factor behind these negative attitudes. Since the 1950s, however, ethnomusicologists, both foreign and African, have developed a better understanding of the inner musical workings of these traditions, which are some of the most complex on the planet, and helped to disseminate this knowledge to others. The old ethnocentric discrimination against African music has given way to great enthusiasm for these many vibrant musical traditions.

While drumming is assumed by many Westerners to be the primary African musical activity, much other music occurs involving aerophones and chordophones, either with or without accompanying idiophones and membranophones. Unique vocal traditions, many of them polyphonic, are common, and both storytelling and recounting the histories and genealogies of many of Africa's ethnic groups are passed from generation to generation via oral tradition.

Planning the Itinerary

Our survey of musical performance in sub-Saharan Africa is of necessity brief and highly selective but seeks to illuminate some of the key elements of African music-making. An examination of drumming traditions from Ghana, the type of African music perhaps most familiar to the outside world, begins our tour. We then make a stop in Nigeria to hear the popular music genre known as *jùjú*. Our visit to Senegal–Gambia will introduce the renowned poet/praise-singers/oral historians of the Mandinka, called *jali*. We will then consider the music of the Mbuti Pygmies of Central Africa, a xylophone tradition from Uganda, and lamellophone performance in Zimbabwe. Finally,

Adesanya Adeyeye

My maternal grandmother was an Osun priestess (Osun is the Yoruba goddess of the river). During the usual Osun ceremonies at Ilesa, Osun State, normally held three or four times a year, children like myself were encouraged to partake in the ceremonies especially in dancing and playing musical instruments. I was about five years then, in 1957. Elders play the Lukorigi drums, an ensemble comprising three cylindrical double headed drums of varying sizes with two *agogo* (iron bells) of different sizes to accompany chants and songs in praise of Osun, who is believed to cure barrenness in women. The overwhelming atmosphere created by the festivities had a greater influence on my musical perception and interest and later served as an impetus in my taking up music and music technology as a profession. But even as a child I was part of the usual village children's use of pawpaw stems and bamboo pallets in making musical toy whistles. That was in my father's village, via Ilesa.

My exposure to formal musical learning only began when I left secondary school, after 1971 through 1981 in Lagos. After enrolling at the Nigeria Institute of Music headed by Taiwo Ogunade and Chris Ajilo in 1978, I passed the Grade 8 Associated Board of the Royal Schools of Music theory examination. During these ten years in Lagos I also got musical training by playing guitar in *jùjú* and *highlife* bands. As a choir member of the Regina Mundi Catholic Church, Mushin, Lagos, I discovered that I was naturally gifted in playing the *sekere* (gourd shaker). Even though I had a keen interest in playing the *konga* drums (*agbamole* and *ogido*), choir master Mr. Joseph Osho was so much fascinated by the way I played the *sekere* that he would not allow me to play the drum but only the *sekere*. Thus seven years as a church choir member playing only sekere had a very strong influence in my musical life including later as a *sekere* maker. In 1981 I began undergraduate music studies at Kent State University, Ohio, United States.

After graduation from Kent State I went to Los Angeles for nine months (January to September 1986) and became involved in instrument making. I turned to *sekere* making, and this was my starting point into music technology. I became financially secure and gained cultural recognition in Los Angeles and the suburbs, like Pasadena and Hollywood. I went on to exhibit my *sekere* in various black cultural festivals in Los Angeles where they were highly admired. I lived very comfortably on sales of *sekere* in Los Angeles during the last six months of my stay. After that I returned to Nigeria in June 1987.

Adesanya Adeyeye, professional musician

In Nigeria I embarked into research on the construction of musical instruments. Since my knowledge of the construction of *sekere* was limited to the *sekere ikanyere* (the type using plastic beads), I decided to learn the art of making *sekere aje*, which use cowrie shells.

That same year my father-in-law, a traditional Chief of Kajola in the Atakumosa local government of Osun state, introduced me and my wife to Pa Jimoh Omoleke, the leader of the *sekere aje* players in Osogbo, and he taught us the art of constructing *sekere aje*. Pa Omoleke also provided us with the historical origin of *aje*, which he linked with the Iba Ologbo compound in Oyo Alaafin.

Between 1989 and 1992 while I was also researching the *Ifa eerindinlogun* divination corpus in the cult of Osun in Ijebu-Jesa,

I was able to learn how to construct *Lukorigi* and *Ukoko* drums. As noted earlier, *Lukorigi* are ritual drums in the worship of Osun. *Ukoko* is a set of clay pot drums used socially in various Ijesa traditional festivals. The art of making *Lukorigi* and *Ukoko* drums was passed on to me by Pa Sunday Akunmudan, a close relation on my mother's side at Ijebu-Jesa.

I have also learned the construction of other musical instruments by disassembling and then re-assembling them. They include the Western classical guitar, the *bata, sakara, samba, konga, oja, atentenben,* and many more. I have also carried out innovative construction of instruments through inspiration from fellow music technologists. Such instruments include the Western descant recorder and flageolets. Between 1988 and 2000 while I was a lecturer and researcher at the Music Technology department of the Polytechnic, I was also able to learn the construction of yet more instruments from traditional instrument makers who came to instruct my students. Such instruments include *agogo ide* (brass gong) and *saworo ide* (brass bell). In addition I have been able over the years to carry out my own original design of tools and machines used in the fabrication of innovative musical instruments, including circular saws, turning machines, and wood rolling machines.

Habib Iddrisu

AN INSIDE LOOK

I was born into the Dagomba/Dagbamba family of court historians and musicians in Gukpegu/Tamale in northern Ghana. There I was brought up under the tutelage of my grandfather, Manguli-Lana Adam Alhassan, chief drummer in Tamale, and was inspired by my great uncles, many of whom were famous Dagbon musicians, especially Jabling (Fuseini Alhassan).

Like many of my cousins, I started playing both the *lung-a* (talking drum) and *gungong* (supporting drum) at age six. By age eight, I was renowned throughout the region for my dancing and drumming in styles such as Takai, Bamaya, and Atikatika. As a young man I studied traditional Dagbamba music and dance as well as other genres from across Ghana and West Africa. The wealth of expressive styles that I encountered sparked my interest in sharing and teaching this material to as broad an audience as possible. Soon I was coaching in Ghana's largest cities, especially in Accra where I taught and performed with some of the city's finest cultural groups. Then I traveled extensively around the world to perform, and I won Ghana's Best Dancer Award in 1992.

Between 1999 and 2004, I studied at Bowling Green State University where I received undergraduate and graduate degrees in African Studies and History, respectively. I also coached a variety of African music and dance classes. In 2002, my choreography was selected and presented at the National American Dance College Festival at the Kennedy Center in Washington, DC. My studies have significantly enriched and broadened my artistic and analytical thinking. The music of Dagbamba *Lung-si* (drummers) is completely filled

Habib Iddrisu, Dagbon drummer and dancer

with language. Its rhythmic nature may lead an outsider to think the music is entirely improvised, but the reality is that almost every drum phrase represents Dagbamba spoken language (Dagbanli).

The music of my tradition is very intricate, yet easy to understand. It is intricate in that performance depends entirely on a person's ability to listen and memorize all the drum language that accompanies each occasion. Because drummers are storytellers, they must be able to talk (on their drums, of course) about the history, politics, and economic lives of the people. The drum language dictates the mood of not only the listeners but also the musician. When we drum in weddings, naming ceremonies, for the enskinment of a new chief, or just for a commoner in the marketplace, the atmosphere at the time is quickly absorbed by the *Lung-si*. For instance, when we drum during funerals, we react to the mood around, not like actors or actresses taking roles but as those whose heartbeats are attached to the messages the *lung-a* is sending at the time. The *Lung-si* role is quite versatile within the context of the community's needs. At any occasion when we drum, someone may fall into trance. When this happens, we assume the role of the "healer" who controls the mediums responsible for trance, thereby subduing the spirits and leading the person out of the trance at the appropriate time. Our main role in the community is to keep the history of our people alive and exciting, and this is what makes us *Lung-si*.

we will examine a Zulu choral tradition from South Africa known as *mbube*, which has a musical organization that contrasts with that of much music found in the rest of sub-Saharan Africa.

Arrival: Ghana

The Western world is perhaps most familiar with the cultural activities of West African populations because this region is geographically closer to both Europe and the Americas than is any other area of sub-Saharan Africa. The bulk of Africans forced into slavery by Europeans and sent to the Americas during the colonial period (roughly early 1500s to late 1800s) were taken from this region, and as a result the cultural traditions of West Africa were disseminated throughout the Caribbean and the Americas. The spiritual traditions of the Dahomey people from Benin and of the Yoruba from Nigeria, for example, are found throughout the "New World" in various permutations, namely as *vodou* (voodoo) in Haiti, *candomblé* in Brazil, and *santeria* in the United States and Cuba. Textiles and clothing used by African Americans to represent their African heritage frequently draw on the stylistic features of West African formal attire, and characteristics particular to music traditions from western Africa, especially the prominent use of drumming, have come to represent—incorrectly—all music from the sub-Saharan region. The reductive Euro-American characterization of African music as "drumming," while not accurate for the continent as a whole, is thus understandable, as drumming is so prominent in West Africa. Ghana (officially, the Republic of Ghana), a former British colony (with English as its official language) and nearly equal to the United Kingdom in size, was one of several colonies—most others being French—on Africa's "Gold Coast." Its twenty-four million people speak around seventy-five different African languages along with English.

Site 1: Polyrhythmic Recreational Ensemble

First Impressions. Polyrhythmic music can seem bewildering on first listening. The music does not follow "a beat" in the Western sense of the term; that is, no consistent pulsation seems to articulate an easily identifiable meter. The complexity of the interwoven rhythmic patterns creates a dense sound that agitates some listeners while hypnotizing others. High-pitched and low-pitched drums, rattles, bells, and voices all combine to create a multifaceted kaleidoscope of sound that continuously spins the same musical elements into an energetic torrent of "rhythmic melody." While these polyrhythms are difficult to grasp analytically, their effect can be powerful and immediate. Even many novice listeners will be inspired to dance along with this vibrant music.

Aural Analysis. Polyrhythm is a system of musical organization that may be challenging to those steeped only in European harmonic musical creation, where rhythm is organized into simple units of 2, 3, 4, or 6 beats most of the time. In the African polyrhythmic tradition no conductor articulates the basic beat for everyone to follow, and there is no need for notation telling the musician what to play. Each participant plays a rhythmic pattern that in and of itself is generally not difficult. Each pattern follows its own time—or what some scholars refer to as a timeline— without respect to the kind of underlying meter found in Western music.

The simplest example of polyrhythm is the "two against three" cross-rhythm. In this example, one pattern follows a timeline pattern of two pulses while another pattern provides three pulses within the same time span. You can try this yourself or with a friend. Pat your left hand on your knee with an even duple pulse, "1-2-, 1-2-, 1-2-. . . ." Now, tap on a book with your right hand to an even triple pulse, "1-2-3-, 1-2-3-, 1-2-3- . . .," making sure to sound the "1" beats of both pulses simultaneously. As you will quickly discover, while each pattern is simple in and of itself, combining the two becomes a significant challenge.

When these two patterns are combined, they form a *rhythmic melody* that can be articulated as one idea, namely as a "1–2&3–, 1–2&3–, 1–2&3- . . ." pattern, in which the "&" falls between the last two pulses of the triplet. Try the cross-rhythm again by starting with the right-hand triple meter tap, and just pat your left hand on the "&." This should be easier. Once you've gotten that down, add a pat on the "1" beat as well. The resulting rhythm is the same as the "two against three" pattern you initially tried, but the difference is that you are no longer thinking in terms of separate rhythms (duple vs. triple), but in terms of a unified whole (see Table 10.1). This latter conception is more in line with the way African musicians approach performance: for them, each individual musical element is part of the collective whole. Of course, however Africans themselves perceive of polyrhythmic music, understanding the intricacies of individual timeline patterns leads to a greater appreciation of the music's complexity.

Oftentimes it is easier to recognize the individual timeline patterns when the musicians can be seen. In our cross-rhythm example, you can say the phrase "Look to the left" in rhythm as you play. Seeing your left hand play the duple pattern will help you to hear it more clearly. Now say,

The Nsuase *kete* drum group performing at an Asante funeral in Kumase, Ghana (Joseph S. Kaminski)

Table 10.1 Two against Three Cross-Rhythm

Left Hand	1			&		
Right Hand	1		2		2	

"Look to the right" in rhythm and watch your right hand sound the triple pattern. Your ears will focus on that pattern more clearly. The absence of visual references requires that you listen for different timbres—for example, drums versus bells.

Our example of an Akan recreational band from Ghana features voices and several instruments: the **donno**, a double-headed hourglass variable-pressure drum played with a hooked stick and capable of producing more than one pitch; the *tom-tom*, a pair of tall, single-headed hand drums; the *afirikyiwa*, an iron clapper bell; and the *axatse* (pronounced "a-ha-che"), a gourd rattle with external beaded netting. Together, the musicians create complex polyrhythms, far more difficult to perform than our cross-rhythm example. In order for the musicians to collectively play the correct rhythmic melody, each individual musician must interlock his particular pattern very precisely with the other musicians' patterns.

A helpful analogy can be made to a bicycle wheel. One rhythm typically functions as a density referent, a pattern that is like the center of a bicycle wheel. Because drumming ensembles tend to be loud, a louder instrument with a distinctive timbre, such as a bell or a rattle, usually plays this part. Once the central rhythm is established, the other musicians play their parts in relation to it; held together by this central reference point, these other parts are like the spokes of the wheel. (Complicating our analogy, however, is the fact that musicians often use more than one reference rhythm to play their part, and thus interlock their pattern with multiple instruments at once, so it might visually look more like the inner-workings of a clock.)

Once all the patterns are added together, forming the collective analogous to the rim of the wheel, the music spins along without trouble. If, however, one of the patterns falls out of sync, then the wheel might start to wobble. The music starts to feel unbalanced, and if the troublesome part does not drop out and reenter correctly, the entire ensemble is in danger of "crashing." This frequently happens when amateur ensembles in the United States attempt to play African music. The music may spin easily for a while, but a slight distraction may cause one musician to lose concentration and fail to play his or her simple pattern in sync with the complex whole. As a result, the music falls apart like a house of cards, and the musicians must start over, typically by reestablishing the density referent and then gradually adding the other patterns until the music flows again.

The musicians in our recorded example are obviously quite skilled. The vocal parts follow a call-and-response pattern, while the instruments perform polyrhythm. It is not necessary to know what the specific rhythms are to appreciate the music as a whole. Representing all the parts of the music in metrical notation, as is frequently done by Western musicians, will mask the way African musicians generally perceive a rhythm as a timeline pattern. Nonetheless, focusing on specific instruments and parts can be a helpful way of explaining how polyrhythm works in a complex example such as this.

Turning to the bell (*afirikyiwa*) part first, we hear a rhythm that could be written as "1–2–3–(4), 1–2–3–(4), 1–2–3–(4). . . ." This three-pulse pattern with a silent fourth pulse can be heard as a reference point for the handclaps, which sound only once in the course of the bell pattern. When is the clap heard? The clap follows its own timeline, which is just one clap per cycle. If you think in terms of meter, then the clap in isolation can be considered to follow a duple meter, "1–(2)–, 1–(2)–, 1–(2)–. . . .," in which the second pulse is silent.

Alternatively, you can consider the clapping as falling slightly ahead of the "&" after the third bell pulse. But the tempo of the music is moving very quickly. Trying to count "1&2&3&4&, 1&2&3&4&, 1&2&3&4& . . ." in order to clap in the correct place is difficult and quite unnecessary. If you forget counting and just listen to the bell, you can "fit" your part in much more easily. Sometimes it also helps if you think of a phrase that suggests the rhythm as a whole. For example, try thinking of the rhythm as the phrase, "What do you think?" with the bell part sounding on "What do you" and the clap falling on "think." Easier? It should be, because when you do this you are hearing the rhythmic melody created by the combination of bell and handclaps.

DONNO

A double-headed hourglass-shaped drum found in Ghana and elsewhere in West Africa.

While this discussion places the bell pattern as the reference point in order to more easily hear how the handclaps work in relation to it, the central density referent in our audio example is *actually* the handclaps themselves. The bell pattern, as well as the rattle's three-note pattern, anticipates the claps, leaving space for them to sound and thus be heard clearly. The call-and-response form of the voices also references the handclaps to fit their "timeline" into the performance correctly, by emphasizing the third syllable of the vocal phrase in conjunction with the handclaps. The drums (*donno* and *tom tom*) alternate between high-pitched and low-pitched sounds in a duple pattern, with the lower drum corresponding to the handclaps. The alternating drum sounds may either be created by a single drummer, or by two drummers in tandem. Without seeing the performers, it's hard to know which is the case in our example.

Throughout the performance, the drummers slightly alter their patterns to make the performance more dynamic but then return to their initial pattern. The music spins like a bicycle wheel, or perhaps the aural equivalent of a kaleidoscope: it uses the same "pieces" but changes them just enough to make the music different each time the cycle repeats. Once you can identify each part individually, try listening to the whole ensemble again as a collective performance.

LISTENING GUIDE

10.1 (1'45")

Site 10.1

Ghana: Polyrhythmic Recreational Ensemble

Vocals: A single male lead and a single female lead. Also, a mixed male/female ensemble response
Instruments: Drums (*donno*, *apenteng*, *pate*), metal bells (*afirikyiwa*, *dawuruta*, *aggre*), rattle (*akasaa*). Also, handclaps

TIME	LISTENING FOCUS
0'00"	Example fades in with instrumental activity. Listen for the varying timbre of the drums, rattles, and bells. Refer to above discussion for more complete discussion of individual rhythms.
0'02"	Male lead vocalist enters.
0'19"	Group response, repeating the verse of the lead vocalist.
0'36"	Female lead vocalist enters.
0'41"	Male lead vocalist returns.
0'46"	Female lead vocalist returns.
0'52"	Group response.
1'08"	Male lead vocalist returns.
1'25"	Group response.

Source: "Fante Area: Vocal Band" performed by the Odo ye few korye kuw Vocal Band, recorded by Roger Vetter, Abura Tuakwa, Ghana, 1984, from the recording entitled *Rhythms of Life, Songs of Wisdom: Akan Music from Ghana, West Africa*, SF 40463, provided courtesy of Smithsonian Folkways Recordings. © 1996. Used by permission.

MUSICAL MARKERS: Timbre/Medium—Various percussion, including drums, shakers, and bells. **Form**—Vocal lead with group response. **Rhythm**—Polyrhythmic structure. "Simple" individual rhythmic patterns weave into a "complex" whole. **Rhythmic Density**—Thick/Hi.
ETHNO-CHALLENGE: Choose a rhythmic pattern, such as that made by the bell or the handclaps, and play it throughout, singing along with the group response.

Cultural Considerations. Polyrhythm is the basis for musical creation throughout much of sub-Saharan Africa. For those who grow up in cultures where polyrhythmic music is common, understanding comes "naturally" because these insiders are surrounded by it in various contexts, such as festivals, funerals, marketplaces, and so on. For outsiders, however, polyrhythm is one of the least penetrable forms of musical organization found anywhere in the world.

Our example is typical of music performance among the Akan—whose language is part of a family of languages that includes such ethnic groups as the Asante (Ashanti), Fante, and Denkyira—as well as among non-Akan speaking peoples of Ghana, such as the Ewe and the Igbo. Even though the performers are ordinary villagers from a small farming community, the musicians nonetheless display a high degree of musical skill. Such "recreational bands," as they are often called, play at wakes, funerals, and for annual festivals, as well as for social clubs, special community events such as weddings, and purely for entertainment.

Polyrhythmic ensembles often have a master drummer who oversees all aspects of a performance, including vocal performance and dance. The master drummer knows a multitude of rhythms that work within the performance and is responsible for helping each musician to "fit" within the group. He may briefly play specific "timeline" patterns that correspond to those of other instruments, establish a new pattern that someone will then follow, or play within the overall polyrhythmic activity, frequently "speaking" with his drum to communicate with the other musicians, dancers, or audience.

The majority of musicians who play in polyrhythmic ensembles learn their craft in an informal manner. Continual exposure to polyrhythmic music throughout childhood gives most an intuitive sense of rhythm and timing, though only a few become specialists capable of leading an ensemble.

Dance: West Africa by Janine Tiffe

There are perhaps few places in the world where drumming and dancing are more closely related than in West Africa. In fact, one way of perceiving this inseparable relationship would be to regard the drum as a choreographer because in many traditional dances, the lead drum dictates when and which movements dancers will perform for a particular piece. Dancers must be well versed in a wide range of rhythms and rhythmic cues, each specific to a particular dance, and be able to decipher these patterns amidst a cacophony of other beats to successfully participate in a dance. The intimate relationship between music and dance` is further illustrated by the fact that many dialects do not have separate words for music and dance; philosophically, they cannot be separated. There are prescribed dances to accompany every notable life event and circumstance, including, but not limited to, birth, religious worship, healing, weddings, war, harvest, rites of passage, socialization, and funerals.

While a tall and upright body posture takes precedence in many European-based forms of dance, West African dance emphasizes a posture that values being grounded and utilizes a relaxed spine. Bent knees and an arched back are also common stances. Dance steps and the magnitude of gestures may also vary in response to the audience. For example, if the "audience" is comprised of fellow community member participants, dancers need only worry about interacting in a relatively small physical space. However, when dances became staged events in the mid-twentieth century, village community traditions needed to be adapted to a formalized and larger space. In as much, many movements and gestures have become exaggerated so they may be seen more clearly from afar. Henceforth, these added elements of increased visual dramatics and pre-determined choreography have also become a part of numerous West African performance traditions.

There are a multitude of dances and dance styles across the region of West Africa. Within Ghanaian dance traditions, hand gestures can be very significant and convey highly specific messages or help tell a story. Audience members in Ghana express appreciation and support for a dancer's efforts by raising the index and middle fingers on one hand, (similar to a narrow peace sign), wiping sweat from a dancer's forehead, or pressing paper money to the dancer's brow. In the last few years, a dance called the Azonto has become widely popular across Ghana and been performed for a multitude of Afro-pop music videos.

Nigerian Yoruba religious dance is utilized as a form of honoring and communicating with a pantheon of *orishas*, or deities, including, but not limited to, Elegua, Ogun, Oshun, Oya, Shango, Yemoja, and Obàtálá. Each orisha has movements, artifacts, and colors that are specifically associated with him or her, which typically represent or imitate aspects of his or her character such as strength, femininity, air, water, metal, or lightning. In a more traditional context, dancers may be executing moves while being controlled by an orisha during a state spirit possession, known as being "ridden." Henceforth, the knowledge of corresponding movements allows other worshippers to know which orisha has descended to communicate through the dancer.

Adzewa group performing at a funeral at the Asante court in Kumase, Ghana (Joseph S. Kaminski)

Site 2: "Talking Drums"

First Impressions. This example alternates short sections of a text spoken by a young woman with drum passages that seem to mimic the girl's words, both tonally and rhythmically. What we are hearing are the famous "talking drums" (which usually are not coupled with spoken word passages; we have chosen this example because it makes the drumming's relationship to speech particularly clear). This is not music for dancing but for listening. In fact, it is not considered music at all but is rather a speech-substitute (also called "surrogate speech") in the context of a music performance.

Aural Analysis. Language is an integral part of music performance in Africa. Many African languages are "tonal," meaning that the intonation of the voice (for example, high/low tones or rising/falling tones) is as important to the meaning as the phonemes used.

Although tonal languages are encountered in many cultures, such as China and Nigeria, no European languages are tonal. One way to understand how intonation can change the meaning of a word is to listen to the different ways the word "yes" is pronounced, depending on whether it is used as a question or an answer. When it is used as a question, the speaker's inflection (i.e., prosody) has a rising tone, whereas when it is used as an answer the tone is level or slightly falling. Unlike inflected languages, however, tonal languages make the contoured or level inflection an integral part of the word regardless of context.

In Ghana, a drum capable of tone-bending is used to imitate the rising and falling inflections of the voice, in order to communicate words through music. Double-headed hourglass pressure drums, such as the *donno*, are especially equipped to accomplish tonal variation. When the player squeezes the strings that secure the heads (or faces), he changes the tension of the drumheads, which alters the pitch. For drums producing only a single fixed pitch, two drums of differing pitches can be used to imitate the direction in inflection; for example, a low pitch followed by a high pitch would convey a rising tone. Additionally, drummers replicate the "speech rhythm" of the words they imitate. By coupling the tones and rhythms of specific phrases, drummers can create surrogate speech comprehensible to native speakers of the language who are additionally familiar with the conventions of drum language.

A non-native speaker will not always recognize when linguistic meaning is being conveyed through musical performance. Musicians may do this in a variety of contexts: while praise-singing a chief or king, announcing the passing of a royal family member, recounting historical events, and so on. These performances may be solo or occur in the context of ensemble playing.

The "talking drums" played in this example are *atumpan*, a pair of large, goblet-shaped hollow logs with heads of tightly stretched animal skin, typically antelope. The particular piece praises a king and may be performed with or without the vocalist. In this case, the musician speaks in Twi, a common tonal language found throughout Ghana, before playing each phrase on the drums. The novice listener may perhaps be better able to appreciate the musical relationship between the language and music by first listening for the drummer's imitation of the speech's tonal aspect. Keep in mind that rising and falling pitches require two consecutive drum strokes, going from low to high or high to low, respectively.

The *mpintin* drum group of the Asantehene, Kumase, Ghana. The *mpintin* consists of several *donno* (hourglass pressure drums) (left), *mpintintoa* (membranophone with gourd resonator) (right), and other drums (not pictured) (Joseph S. Kaminski)

LISTENING GUIDE

10.2 (1'54")

Site 10.2

Ghana: "Talking Drums"

Vocals: Single female
Instruments: *Atumpan* (pair of drums played with wooden angled-sticks)

TIME   **LISTENING FOCUS**

The complete translation for this example is included in the site discussion. This guide refers to some key points to note.

0'00"   Example begins with the vocalist speaking the text, followed by the mimicking *atumpan*.

0'26"   Start of the section featuring drum language glorifying the king of Denkyira. Listen for the drum's manifestation of the spoken phrase "Adawu, Adawu."

0'34"	The phrase "*Ma wo ho me ne so*" ("Come forth in thy light") is used ●several times throughout this example. Listen for the manifestation of this phrase on the drum at 0'38" and try to identify it each time without referencing the text.
0'38"	Drum manifestation of the phrase "*Ma wo ho me ne so.*"
0'44"	Listen for the drum's manifestation of the spoken phrase "*Kronkron, kronkron, kronkron.*" Note that the drum sounds four times per word, indicating that the speech rhythm in performance is determined by more than merely the syllables of a word. (Two syllables, yet four drum strokes.)
1'47"	Final drum manifestation of the phrase "*Ma wo ho me ne so.*"

Source: "Talking Drum" by Elizabeth Kumi, and Joseph Manu from the recording entitled *Rhythms of Life, Songs of Wisdom: Akan Music from Ghana*, SF 40463, provided courtesy of Smithsonian Folkways Recordings. ©1996. Used by Permission.

MUSICAL MARKERS: Timbre/Medium—Spoken vocal with pair of differently pitched drums. **Rhythm**—Rhythmic patterns on drums mimic the speech rhythm and tonal contour of the vocalist.
ETHNO-CHALLENGE: Imitate your own speech rhythm and tonal inflections using a drum or other instrument that has a high or low sound.

Cultural Considerations. In Ghana drums are used as a surrogate for speech to give the words more power and to enable the praise-singing to be heard by ancestral spirits as well as the living. "Talking drum" performances often occur to honor someone of royal lineage or to praise a powerful ancestral spirit. Because royalty may be considered descendants of powerful spirits, praise-singing or praise-drumming frequently accomplishes both objectives simultaneously. Prior to the colonial period, chiefs customarily included in their entourage musicians capable of rendering poetic performances in honor of the chiefs and their lineage. This practice has diminished considerably but is still found among some groups, especially the Asante.

Here is a transcription and translation of the words in our example, first recited in honor of the king of the Denkyira people and then echoed by the *atumpan*:

Greetings to Those Present

Me ma mo atena ase, Nana ne ne mpaninfoo	I welcome you, Nana and his elders
Owura dwamtenani, *Enanom ne agyanom* *ne anuanom a yeahyia ha,* *yegye me asona*	Mr. Chairman, mothers, fathers and brethren here gathered, the response to my greeting is "asona"
Saa atweneka yi fa Odeefoo Boa Amponsem, Denkyira hene ho	This drum language is about Odeefuo Boa Amponsem, King of Denkyir
Odomankoma kyerema, ma no nko!	Creator's drummer, let it go!

Actual Drum Language Glorifying the King of Denkyira

Adawu, Adawu, Denkyira mene sono.

Adawu, Adawu, Denkyira the devourer of the elephant.

Adawu, Adawu, Denkyira pentenprem, Omene sono, ma wo ho mene so

Adawu, Adawu, Denkyira the quicksand, devourer of the elephant, come forth in thy light, exert yourself

313

Pentenprem, ma wo homene so,	Quicksand, come forth in thy light,
Ma wo ho me ne so	Exert yourself, in glory
Kronkron, Kronkron, Kronkron;	Your holiness, holiness, holiness;
Amponsem Koyirifa, ma wo ho me ne so	Amponsem Koyirifa, come forth in thy light in glory
Ako nana ma wo ho mene so	Grandsons of the Parrot, come forth in thy light
Ako nana a ho a ne mframa mene boo, ma wo ho me ne so	Grandsons of the Parrot whose winds sweep and devour even the stones, come forth in thy light
Wo a wofiri dodoo mu,	you who came from many,
Wo a wutu a ewiemu den se asamando, ma wo ho me ne so	You who fly and the skies become still like the cemetery come forth in thy light
Amponsem nana a "odi sika to," atomprada, ma wo ho me ne so	Amponsem's grandson who "eats mashed gold dust," and uses only freshly mined gold in his daily transactions, come forth in thy light
Agona adegyekan nana Wo a wode osee ye oyo	First grandson of the Agona line, You promise and you fulfill it
De nkoden akyekyere Denkyiraman, de ape no sibre, ma wo ho me ne so	Having fought hard to establish the Denkyira state, and having found it a place among the nations, come forth in thy light
Ayekra Adebo nana	Grandson of Ayekra Adebo [first ruler, fetish priestess of Denkyira]
Ahihi Ahaha nono	Grandson of Ahihi Ahaha
Wirempi Ampem nana a owo ntam na yenka, ma wo ho me ne so	Grandson of Wirempi Ampem whose oath is not to be sworn, come forth in thy light
Otibu Kwadwo nana	Grandson of great King Kwadwo Otibu, [accompanying audio ends here]
Wo a wode Denkyiraman firii Abankesieso baa Jukwaa, ma wo ho me ne so	who led the Denkyira people in their great migration from Abankesieso to settle in Jukwa, come forth in thy light
Odeefoo, ma wo ho me ne so	Benefactor, come forth in thy light
Ma wo ho me ne so Agona,	The Agona clan,
Denkyiraman da wo ase,	The Denkyira state,
Yeda wo ase a ensa,	Expresses its endless,
Esie ne kagya nni aseda	Gratitude to you

(Text and translation from *Rhythms of Life, Songs of Wisdom: Akan Music from Ghana, West Africa*. Smithsonian Folkways SF 40463, 1996, pp. 17–18.)

This translation provides the literal meaning of the message conveyed by the "talking drum"—but these words also have a deeper level of symbolic meaning that is unintelligible to cultural outsiders. Understanding the extra-musical aspects of musical performance is one of the most fascinating challenges of ethnomusicology, and of linguistics and anthropology as well.

Arrival: Nigeria

Nigeria (officially, the Federal Republic of Nigeria), smaller than Egypt, is Africa's most populous country with nearly 160 million inhabitants, twice that of Egypt. Nearly half of this population lives in urban areas such as Lagos, the nation's largest city. With massive deposits of oil, the country has been a promising prospect for investors at the start of the twenty-first century despite the political challenges faced by its budding democracy over the past decade. Nigeria has more than 250 ethnic groups with the dominant ones being the Fulani, Hausa, Yoruba, and Igbo. Nigeria's linguistic and musical tapestry is therefore quite diverse, leading to an incredible array of vocal and instrumental music traditions. The "talking drum" is also a common feature of music from this region where there are many types of hourglass pressure drums, such as *gan gan*, *dun dun*, and *kalangu*. These drums are heard in a variety of rural and urban contexts, particularly in association with festive and royal events, as well as the popular music style known as *jùjú*.

Site 3: *Jùjú* Popular Music

First Impressions. *Jùjú* blends the traditional foundation of polyrhythmic percussion and storytelling with modern elements of instrumentation and concert performance. The music has immediate appeal for its easily discernable "beat" but also an undercurrent of complex rhythm that requires a deeper appreciation of the music's Yoruba roots.

Aural Analysis. *Jùjú* music flows like a river with many ripples and eddies to attract the attention of even the novice listener for several minutes and beyond. Holding interest in an unfamiliar music is often a challenge when exploring world music. Modern audiences are accustomed to three-minute pop songs, a supra-cultural conditioning due to the early limits of recording technology that have continued to dominate the popular music soundscape. Music outside the popular music sphere, however, is typically not bound by such time limitations; for example, an Indian *raga* performance or a Western symphony. By and large, however, popular music around the world still follows this expectation of short performance. Not so with *jùjú* music, where a single song performance can easily last over an hour.

Jùjú music first appeared during the 1920s and is considered to be an innovation of Tunde King (Abdulrafiu Babatunde King). This early style utilized an acoustic guitar or banjo with a drum, gourd rattle, and tambourine as rhythmic accompaniment. Vocals were presented in a call-and-response pattern with a repetitive refrain and vocal harmony. Short instrumental solos were interspersed between verses, which included lyrics typically rooted in Yoruba proverbs and poetry, as well as praise-singing. This basic structure continues to be the primary form for modern *jùjú* music, even though the use of polyrhythmic percussion has become a more essential element.

Rhythm, as with most music from sub-Saharan Africa, is fundamental to *jùjú* and a primary reason a performance can hold the listener's attention for so long. While melody and harmony are more central in popular music in other parts of the world, the continuous undercurrent of complex polyrhythms drives this music. The duple meter provides a central, almost hypnotic, pulse surrounded with complex and subtle variations of rhythm and a multitude of percussive timbres.

Atop this polyrhythmic canvas are the vocal and melodic instruments, which punctuate, rather than dominate the *jùjú* sound: electric guitars, synthesizers, pedal steel guitars, sometimes saxophones or other melodic instruments mixing with local instruments, such as "talking drums," known as *gan gan* (hourglass pressure drums), *sakara* (frame drums), and *shekere* (gourd rattles) as well as a plethora of other percussion common to Western popular music idioms. The vocal parts similarly enhance the atmosphere with short phrases rather than extended melodic lines. Weaving its way through these musical elements is the lead electric guitar, or sometimes the *gan gan* or *iya ilu* (also an hourglass pressure drum), again sounding succinct passages that accentuate, rather than distract from the focus of the underlying rhythmic foundation.

LISTENING GUIDE

10.3 (3'58")

Site 10.3

Nigeria: *Jùjú* Popular Music

Vocals: Single male lead (King Sunny Adé, aka KSA), male vocal group
Instruments: Electric guitars, electric bass, Hammond B-3 organ, drum set, *gan gan* ("talking" drum), *sakara* (frame drum), *shekere* (shaken idiophone)

TIME	LISTENING FOCUS
0'00"	KSA establishes tempo with a four beat count, followed by instrumental introduction. Note the undercurrent of polyrhythmic percussion sounding throughout the example.
0'20"	KSA then male chorus enter on title refrain, "Oro Yi Bale." Melody instruments stop during this opening phrase. *Gan gan* is also heard leading into vamp phrase.
0'27"	Organ and guitars play the primary "vamp" phrase.
0'36"	Vocal refrain.
0'43"	Instrumental vamp. The *gan gan* features more prominently in this section.
0'51"	Vocal refrain.
0'58"	Instrumental vamp. The lead electric guitar features more prominently in this section.
1'07"	Vocal refrain.
1'14"	Instrumental vamp.
1'25"	*Gan gan* leads into new vocal lyric.
1'34"	Instrumental vamp.
1'43"	Extended vocal verse.
2'09"	Instrumental vamp. The *gan gan* features prominently before crossfade.
2'20"	Example edited to crossfade into organ solo. Lead electric guitar plays in background.
2'56"	Lead guitar becomes aural focus. Organ plays in background.
3'50"	*Gan gan* sounds just before the example fades.

Source: "Oro Yi Bale" from *Bábá mo Túndé*, composed and arranged by King Sunny Adé and his African Beats. © 2010 Mesa/Blue Moon Recordings/IndigeDisc. Used by permission.

MUSICAL MARKERS: Timbre/Medium—Electric guitars, electric organ, drum set (snare, cymbas, etc.). Hourglass pressure drum often prominent. Other complementing drums. Vocal lead and group response. **Rhythm**—Polyrhythmic "undercurrent" of percussion, but readily discernable "duple" feel. **Melody**—Short melodic phrases from vocalists and guitars/organ. Pressure drum featured between melodic phrases. Extended solos on guitar and organ.
ETHNO-CHALLENGE: Listen to King Sunny Adé's recordings via the Internet (iTunes) to hear how his style develops over time. Compare his music to that of other popular artists from West Africa.

Cultural Considerations. After World War II, musicians in Nigeria began incorporating electric instruments into their *jùjú* recordings. Innovators such as Ebenzer Obey and I. K. Dairo expanded the musical elements further by adding other instruments, such as the accordion, and introducing a greater variety of Yoruba percussion, the "talking drum" in particular. Nationalism was at its peak during the late 1950s and early 1960s when Nigeria achieved independence from the

United Kingdom. *Jùjú* was an important musical means of expressing Nigerian cultural identity, especially for the Yoruba population.

As rock music became increasingly popular around the globe throughout the 1960s, *jùjú* incorporated musical elements from various Western genres. By the 1970s, funk and reggae were also important musical influences on *jùjú* musicians, such as King Sunny Adé (b. 1946), the reigning monarch of modern *jùjú* music. Modeling his early performances on those of I.K. Dairo, KSA (as he is known in Nigeria) made his first local recording of *jùjú* in 1967. By the mid-1970s, he had become one of the primary figures in the style's development, highlighting the use of the "talking drum" as a soloist, dropping the accordion in the instrument line-up, and featuring the pedal steel guitar, synthesizers, and electronic effects, such as "wah-wah" pedals. KSA was highly acclaimed for his guitar skills and on stage performances.

KSA also achieved prominence in part due to his royal lineage, which created some controversy due to his career path as a professional musician, traditionally regarded as a low status occupation. In many ways, this enhanced his popularity among the masses, who admired his willingness to resist social convention in order to pursue his passion for music. His fans also lauded the moral themes prevalent in his music, which encouraged people to live with high ideals and respect their cultural roots. Many of his lyrics are based on traditional Yoruba poetry and storytelling, as with our listening example, which deals with the subject of female infidelity, a "heavy topic" (*Oro Yi Bale*) in Yoruba culture.

KSA achieved international recognition with his seminal recording, *Jùjú Music*, released in 1982 on Island Records, founded by Chris Blackwell in Jamaica. Blackwell was betting on KSA to become a successor to the deceased Bob Marley (1945–1981), who had elevated Jamaican reggae music into a fixture of the mainstream music market. KSA toured the United States and Europe, fueling interest in Afropop, which until then had achieved limited interest. While this exposure established KSA as a world music icon, *jùjú* music itself did not achieve the popularity Blackwell had hoped for, and he was soon dropped from the label. Nevertheless, KSA continued to record for local and other international labels, producing more than 100 albums over the

Nigerian musician and singer King Sunny Adé and his band (Al Pereira/WireImage/ GettyImages)

course of his career. The listening example, "Oro Yi Bale" is from his recent release, the highly acclaimed *Bábá mo Túndé* (2010), an homage to the founder of *jùjú* music. KSA continues to be the watermark for *jùjú* musicians from Nigeria and is rivaled in stature only by Fela Kuti, the founder of *Afrobeat*, another of Nigeria's most successful popular music styles.

Arrival: Central Africa

Modernization's spread to Central Africa beginning in the twentieth century has led to the destruction of much wildlife, most notably the endangered silver-backed gorilla, probably the best-known animal inhabiting the Congo basin rainforests. Even so, this region still maintains some of the most pristine areas of tropical vegetation on the planet and is home to one of the most intriguing and talked-about peoples of Africa, the Pygmies.

The total Pygmy population is unknown. Whatever their true numbers—estimates range from as few as 40,000 to nearly 600,000—they are spread across several countries in Central Africa, including The Congo, the Democratic Republic of the Congo (DRC), Gabon, Cameroon, and the Central African Republic (CAR). *Pygmy* is a generic term for a diverse population of forest-dwellers who are short by Western standards, being on average less than 5 feet tall. Contrary to popular belief, many Pygmies live in villages and farms, interacting with surrounding ethnic groups on a daily basis. Some **Pygmy** cultural groups, however, still live within the forest and maintain a nomadic lifestyle. Our focus is on a specific cultural group known as Mbuti.

Some Western anthropologists, including Colin Turnbull, have been intensely interested in the typical social structure of nomadic Pygmy groups, which provides one of the few examples of an egalitarian society. An egalitarian society is one in which every member of the community is considered equal. Certain individuals may take a leadership role depending on the context—for example, a strong young man may lead a hunting party—but there is no formal hierarchy. Cooperation rather than competition guides the social interaction within a Pygmy community, because each person is dependent on the others for his or her survival.

PYGMIES
A general term describing the many ethnic groups of forest-dwellers in the rainforests of Central Africa.

Site 4: Mbuti Pygmy Music from the Democratic Republic of the Congo

First Impressions. The aspect of Mbuti Pygmy music that generally strikes the listener first is the intricacy of the vocal performance. The "hoots and hollers" swirl around the listener as the vocalists sing, yodel, and clap. Few instruments are heard in Mbuti music, usually only flutes, an occasional rattle, a pair of clapsticks, or small drums.

Aural Analysis. Mbuti Pygmy music is dominated by vocal performance. Although Mbuti singing frequently employs a call-and-response organization like many other African traditions, it also features a unique polyrhythmic vocal style that makes it quite distinctive. As with other African traditions, polyrhythm is central to the structure and creation of Mbuti music. Since few instruments are used, the voice creates the basic timeline patterns that would otherwise be produced instrumentally among non-Pygmy ethnic groups in sub-Saharan Africa.

In our example, performed by a group of Mbuti Pygmies from the Democratic Republic of the Congo (DRC), a set of clapsticks plays a repetitive rhythm with minor variation that acts as the aural referent. If you consider it to be in a duple meter (though the musicians by no means think in terms of meter) with eight pulses, the basic clapsticks rhythm would be 1 2-4-6 7-. A lead vocalist provides the essential lyrical content necessary for the ritual, while the rest of the singers interweave their voices to create a complex polyrhythmic structure. As with instrumental performance elsewhere in Africa, each person performs a short repeating melodic pattern. Some

Performance of the Wunga dance by Pygmies of the Bangombe ethnic group in the forests of southwestern Central African Republic (Gerhard Kubik)

performers may sing a basic theme, while others sing variations. Each pattern interlocks with and overlaps those of the other performers, resulting in the unique rhythmically dense layering of melodic lines typical of Mbuti vocal performance. Handclaps or instruments may function as a density referent, as in our example, but often the basic theme acts as the aural center for the performers. Though soloists are not always set apart, call-and-response singing often occurs in addition to the polyrhythmic singing.

Cultural Considerations. The nomadic lifestyle and egalitarian social structure characteristic of Mbuti Pygmies are reflected in their musical performances, which are considered community activities. Each person plays an "equal" role, contributing his or her individual talents to the collective performance. The creation of complete melodic lines and thick rhythmic density requires the interlocking of parts and thus a dependency on other performers. The Mbuti's nomadic lifestyle is also reflected in the music's emphasis on the voice; after all, large instruments are not easily transported, but the voice can travel anywhere.

Communal performances among the Mbuti usually include dance as well as music, especially circle dances. These dances may be performed for ritual occasions, such as puberty ceremonies, or in anticipation of an important event, such as a hunt. Because animism predominates in the Mbuti spiritual belief system, music is often sung in conjunction with related ritual activity.

Arrival: Zimbabwe

Much of Zimbabwe (officially, the Republic of Zimbabwe), located in east Africa and being the size of Japan, consists of vast grasslands inhabited by a variety of animals, such as impalas, hippopotamuses, crocodiles, hyenas, and baboons. The rainy season occurs from November to March, creating an average annual rainfall of between 23 and 33 inches (58 and 84 cm). Mining is a major industry, though most people earn a living as farmers, growing tobacco and various

LISTENING GUIDE   10.4 (1'39")

Site 10.4

Democratic Republic of the Congo: Pygmy Music

Vocals: Single male lead and mixed male/female ensemble
Instruments: Clapsticks

TIME	LISTENING FOCUS
0'00"	Listen for the "duple meter" with eight-pulse subdivisions of the clapsticks. Note the varying accented rhythms, loosely emphasizing a 1 2-4-6 7- pattern.
0'04"	Note the rumbling thunder in the background. This performance is part of an animistic ritual intended to bring rain.
0'06"	Listen for the lead male vocal declamation.
0'11"	Lead male vocal returns. Listen for his reappearance throughout the performance.
0'14"	Listen carefully to the varying parts of the vocal melodic–polyrhythm. A prominent upper female voice is briefly heard at this point.
0'22"	Note the return of the upper female voice.
0'33"	Lead male transitions to speaking.
1'03"	Clapsticks rhythm noticeably shifts to a new rhythmic pattern loosely emphasizing a 1-3 4-6- rhythmic pattern.
1'32"	Loud thunderclap ends the musical activity. Exclamations by the performers are heard as the example fades.

Source: "Elephant Song" performed by Mbuti Pygmies from the recording entitled *Music of the Rain Forest Pygmies: The Historic Recordings Made by Colin M. Turnbull*, Lyrichord LYRCD 7157 (original recording, 1961). Used by permission, Lyrichord Discs Inc.

MUSICAL MARKERS: Timbre/Medium—"Hooting" interwoven vocal lines as lead vocalist performs in a declamatory style. Wood sticks provide additional rhythm. **Rhythm**—Polyrhythmic structure using primarily voices, rather than instruments.
ETHNO-CHALLENGE: Choose a recognizable vocal timbre and sing their part throughout the performance.

foodstuffs. The great Victoria Falls is found in Zimbabwe's western region bordering Zambia and is one of the most attractive tourist destinations anywhere in Africa.

Known as Rhodesia until achieving independence in 1980, Zimbabwe had been a colony of the British. Consequently, the official language is English, though many native languages are spoken as well. The predominant indigenous languages include Ndebele and Shona. The Shona ethnic group, who constitute more than 80 percent, has been of particular interest to ethnomusicologists due to a distinctive musical instrument they play known as the *mbira dza vadzimu*.

Site 5: *Mbira Dza Vadzimu*

First Impressions. The gentle sound of the *mbira dza vadzimu* (often simply referred to as **mbira**) is much like that of a child's music box. The music seems to float in an endless cycle, punctuated by an occasional somber cry from the performer. The sound of a small rattle helps maintain a

MBIRA
A general reference to lamellophones found throughout Africa, in particular those common to the Shona and other ethnic groups from Zimbabwe.

Victoria Falls
on the border
between Zambia
and Zimbabwe
(Max T. Miller)

steady pulse, while a distinctive "buzzing" sounds throughout the performance. This is hypnotically soothing music that might make you feel as if you were rocking in a chair on the front porch watching and listening to heavy raindrops fall from the eaves to puddles of water below.

Aural Analysis. It is accurate to describe the *mbira dza vadzimu* as a music box. As with a Western music box, tones are produced through the plucking of flat metal strips of various lengths. Such instruments are known as lamellophones, a subclassification of the idiophone family. Similar instruments are found among many other ethnic groups throughout sub-Saharan Africa and are called by various names, such as *likembe* or *kalimba*. The term *mbira* has become generalized in the Western world to denote all African lamellophones.

Performers pluck the long, narrow tongs of the *mbira dza vadzimu* with their thumbs and forefingers. A large, resonating gourd with one portion removed amplifies the quiet tones, making them audible to a small circle of listeners. Small seashells or pieces of metal, such as bottle caps, are usually affixed to the resonator to create the "buzzing" timbre, a characteristic sound of many instruments found throughout the continent. Often bottle caps are also found on a metal bridge attached to the keyboard of the *mbira*. The percussion instrument that enters shortly after our example begins is the *hosho*, a gourd rattle with internal beads. Usually, two *hosho* are used to maintain a steady cross-rhythm (two against three) throughout a performance.

Mbira dza vadzimu music has a minimum of two parts. The lead part, known as the *kushaura*, is most often played in the higher range of the instrument and is more easily heard. The *kutsinhira*, or "following" part, is typically played on the lower-pitched keys of the instrument. These two parts interlock and overlap to create polyrhythm. In our example, the higher *kushaura* pattern plays with a triple pulse, while the lower *kutsinhira* pattern follows a duple pulse. The accents of the *hosho* fall on the duple pulse with a deemphasized interlocking pulse.

The *hosho* reinforces the "following" part, and thus helps clarify the underlying harmonic rhythm of the piece. Harmony is a term most commonly associated with European music traditions (see Chapter 9), but a kind of African harmonic movement can be perceived in *mbira dza vadzimu* music as well. A *mbira dza vadzimu* piece often has four harmonic segments that repeat with seemingly endless variations. In our example, each segment has four beats articulated by the lower *kutsinhira* pattern and the *hosho* accents.

Try to hear the four four-beat segments of this *mbira dza vadzimu* song. Tap the duple pulse of the *hosho* with your right hand. Once you have established this reference point, listen closely to the upper *kushaura* melodic pattern. The melodic pattern starts in the high end of the instrument's range and then switches to slightly lower pitches. When you hear the melodic line of the lead part lower in pitch, start counting to four with your right-hand fingers. This change in the melody of the *kushaura* part marks the middle point of the four segments. The theme begins when the melodic line rises again. When you hear the melody return to higher pitches, use your left hand to count each segment as your right hand counts the "1" pulse again. The first two four-beat segments of the song use higher notes, while the second two segments use lower notes before the entire theme is repeated.

The *kushaura* and *kutsinhira* parts provide the basic structure of the music. Variations are often added, especially to the lead part. A single musician may even add a third "middle" part to increase the rhythmic density of the music. The ability to add variations and rhythms is the sign of a skilled performer. A second *mbira dza vadzimu* performer may also add variations and interlocking rhythmic patterns to the basic theme, as is heard in the background of this example.

The musicians may also sing. In our example, the musicians' voices enter just after the second pulse of the first harmonic segment and drop out at the end of the four-segment theme. In

Mbira dza vadzimu (lamellophone) from Zimbabwe

Close-up of
lamellae (springy
metal tongues)
(Shutterstock)

Three types of
lamellophones
(top, left to right)
*mbira dza
vadzimu* and
karimba, (lower)
matepe
(N. Scott
Robinson)

most *mbira dza vadzimu* performance contexts, the singer, not the *mbira*, is the primary focus. Call-and-response is common in group singing, but solo vocal performances are frequent as well.

LISTENING GUIDE

10.5 (1'41")

Site 10.5
Zimbabwe: *Mbira Dza Vadzimu*

Vocals: Single male. Secondary vocalizations also appear
Instruments: Pair of *mbira dza vadzimu* (lamellophone), pair of *hosho* (gourd rattle)

TIME	LISTENING FOCUS
0'00"	A single *mbira* enters to establish the referent melodic–rhythmic pattern. Listen for the contrasting range of high pitches interlocking with the lower pitches. Also note the buzzing timbre that accompanies each plucked tone.
0'04"	A single *hosho* (rattle) enters, marking the basic pulse twice before the second *hosho* is added to complete the rhythm (0'06"). A second *mbira* enters at this point as well. Note that the melody is halfway through its content and that the tempo increases.
0'09"	The overall melodic content repeats at this point. Listen for the division of the melodic content into four equal sections of four pulses each.
0'10"	Listen for the high-range descending melodic scale of the second *mbira*.
0'16"	Overall melodic content repeats again.
0'20"	Vocalist enters.
0'24"	Overall melodic content repeats again. Listen for this repetition with subtle variations throughout the performance.
0'36"	Secondary vocal declamation.
1'09"	Ululation is heard in the distance.
1'20"	A faint percussive timbre (wood tapping) is heard in the background, contributing to the polyrhythmic structure.
1'24"	Listen for the high-range descending melodic contour of the second *mbira*.

Source: Shona ancestral spirit song, "*Nyama musango*," performed by Elias Kunaka and Kidwell Mudzimirema (Mharadzirwa); recorded by John E. Kaemmer, Jirira, Zimbabwe, 1973. Used by permission.

MUSICAL MARKERS: Timbre/Medium—"Polyrhythmic music box." Lamellophone (mbira) has a "rain-like" timbre. Rattles help provide a rhythmic center. Vocalist has a declamatory vocal style. **Rhythm/Form**—Melodic cross-rhythm motives in pairs. Melodic content organized with a symmetrical form (AA-BB). **Melodic Contour**—Vocalist sings with a "yelping" descending contour.
ETHNO-CHALLENGE: Play the *hosho* pattern heard throughout this example using a pair of gourd rattles or similar-sounding idiophones. For a real challenge, construct your own *mbira*.

BIRA
A spirit
possession
ceremony of the
Shona ethnic
group from
Zimbabwe.

Cultural Considerations. The Shona use the *mbira dza vadzimu* in a variety of contexts, such as storytelling, entertainment, and rituals. The most important ritual context is the Shona spirit possession ceremony known as **bira**. The example heard here is from a *bira* ceremony in which ancestral sprits are invited to appear to the community through the body of a spirit medium. These spirits are believed to guide and protect the community members in their day-to-day activities.

Perhaps because of this association with spirit possession, the Shona consider the *mbira dza vadzimu* a specialists' instrument, one that requires a high level of skill for performance in ritual contexts. Many *mbira dza vadzimu* musicians are "called" to learn the instrument by an ancestral spirit and thus feel obligated to become proficient at performance to help facilitate possession during these rituals. Certain pieces are only to be played for these ceremonies and are prohibited from performance in other contexts.

Arrival: Uganda

Uganda (officially, the Republic of Uganda), along with Kenya and Tanzania, borders Lake Victoria, the second-largest freshwater lake in the world. The country has an exceptionally diverse population, with numerous languages spoken in addition to English. Chimpanzees roam through its jungles, and leopards hunt in its grassland regions. Most inhabitants are agriculturists, though fishing provides a significant income for those along the lake. Thatched huts can still be found in rural areas, though as the country develops they are becoming increasingly rare.

Uganda's known history dates to the fourth century C.E., when it was a major crossroads connecting northern Nilotic cattle herders and southern Bantu agriculturists via the Nile River, which flows from Lake Victoria through the region. The kingdom of Bunyoro became a powerful unifying force in the late fifteenth century but was eventually overshadowed by the kingdom of Buganda, which became the region's major power in the early nineteenth century. The kings of Buganda (known as *kabaka*) soon confronted British colonialists, who arrived on the heels of the Christian missionaries who had begun proselytizing throughout the region during the middle

Karamojong
women dancing
in northeastern
Uganda
(Shutterstock)

of the nineteenth century. By 1890 the kingdom and the areas around it had become a British protectorate, and Uganda's present boundaries were set.

After achieving independence in 1962, the country survived some rather notorious political and economic misdirection. Idi Amin, a brutal ruler, seized control of the government in 1971 and orchestrated a reign of terror that abolished the former kingdoms, ousted more than 70,000 "Asians," and massacred more than 300,000 Ugandan citizens. By the end of the decade, he was at war with neighboring Tanzania, whose forces, allied with Ugandan rebels, drove him from power. Since then, Uganda has struggled to regain stability and its footing as a regional power and trade partner.

Site 6: *Akadinda*

First Impressions. This music is like a sped-up film of a busy New York City street corner during rush hour. Looking for "space" in this continuous welter of sounds is futile. It is crowded and unrelenting. This is, perhaps ironically, one of the types of music that inspired "minimalist" composers such as Steve Reich, Philip Glass, and Terry Riley, who in the 1970s and 1980s created music that wove simple, repetitive phrases into intricate, interlocking, densely textured patterns of sound.

Aural Analysis. The **akadinda** is a large, heavy log xylophone with between seventeen and twenty-two bars. The wooden bars are arranged over banana tree trunks that rest on the ground set at a 90-degree angle to the logs. Long sticks driven into the ground separate the bars and keep them from shifting sideways during performance. The largest bars can be more than 2 feet (61 cm) long, and the instrument itself is nearly 7 feet (2.13 meters) long. *Akadinda* are also found in sets, in which case each instrument produces pitches in different ranges, so that altogether they cover between four and five octaves. The lowest ranged *akadinda* is often placed in a shallow pit, which serves as a resonator and gives the instrument a deeper sound.

While most xylophones in sub-Saharan Africa have bars with a flat surface, *akadinda* bars frequently have a carved "dip" in the center, and *akadinda* performers may strike the center of the bar at the "dip," which gives the instrument its unique "hollow" timbre. Mallets are either made of straight pieces of soft wood or have a "hook" shape to better strike the center of the bars. *Akadinda* performance requires substantial interlocking of parts. Two groups of three men each sit opposite each other with the xylophone between them. The first group plays a repetitive rhythmic pattern, typically in octaves, while the second group fills in an interlocking pattern to create a thick polyrhythmic structure. *Akadinda* performance usually also involves a third group of performers playing yet another interlocking pattern, and consequently the resultant tempos of such music can approach nearly 600 strikes per minute. This triple-interlocking technique is unique to *akadinda* performance; other African xylophone traditions have fewer performers and are limited to double-interlocking of rhythmic patterns.

It is nearly impossible to decipher this fast-moving music merely by listening to it. To unravel the intricacies of the interlocking parts would require seeing the performers in action. Nevertheless, as with all polyrhythmic music, just by listening you can begin to hear some of the subtleties. The music may initially strike you as chaotic, but if you focus on just one or two distinct sounds, you can start to hear how they work within the whole.

In our example, the highest-pitch strand is played with a steady pulsation on just one pitch in what can be thought of as a duple meter. While this pulse is part of a larger pattern, following it is a first step toward hearing individual parts. In the low-pitched patterns, a longer cycle can be heard that can be articulated as a pattern of high (H), center (C), and low (L) pitches, and can be rendered as: HC-HC-HL-HC-HCCC-. To put it in "Western" terms,

AKADINDA
A large, heavy log xylophone from Uganda that uses interlocking patterns that can approach nearly 600 beats per minute.

Performers on the *akadinda* xylophone of Uganda (Moya A. Malamusi)

A full set of *akadinda* keys from an instrument made by the Nakibembe Xylophone Group in the area of Busoga near the city of Jinja (Mark Stone)

Members of the Nakibembe Xylophone Group seated around an *akadinda* of their own making along with researcher Mark Stone (Nakibembe Xyophone Group; used by permission)

the high pitch anticipates the main beat, which corresponds to the earlier single-pitch pattern in duple meter. This "beat" falls on the center pitches of the first two pairs, the low pitch of the next, the center of the following pair, and the first and third center pitches of the four-beat finish. You might sound this out as "&1-&1-&Low-&1-&123," with the main beat on the ones and three.

Again, keep in mind that this way of singling out particular patterns is not how the African musician thinks about musical creation. A Ugandan musician is concerned with how the patterns fit together rather than with how they can be pulled apart.

LISTENING GUIDE
10.6 (1'52")

Site 10.6
Uganda: *Akadinda*

Instruments: *Akadinda* (log xylophone)

TIME	LISTENING FOCUS
0'00"	As mentioned in the reading, the triple-interlocking technique of *akadinda* performance is especially challenging to follow using your ears only. To begin, listen for the different ranges of pitch rhythms: high, middle, and low.
0'16"	Listen for the low-range melodic–rhythmic pattern. This is described in the reading as: HC-HC-HL-HC-HCCC- (H = high pitch, C = center pitch. L = low pitch).
	Expressing the rhythm with minimal reference to pitch level helps to indicate where the basic pulse is: &1-&1-&Low-&1-&123-. The 1, Low, and 3 mark the basic pulse, indicating a six-beat cycle at a tempo of approximately 126 beats per minute.
0'19"	The cycle at 0'16" repeats. Listen throughout the performance for this melodic–rhythmic pattern, which repeats after roughly every three seconds.
0'30"	Listen for the high-range pitches played between two alternating pitches. You might express the basic pattern as "Up/Up-Down, Up-Down, Up-Down, Up-Down. Up-Down, Up-Down." The double "Up" falls on the first pulse of the melodic–rhythmic pattern described above. The remaining "Up" strokes reinforce the basic pulse.

Source: Buganda *akadinda* song "*Gganga aluwa*" ("Gganga escaped with his life"), performed by Sheikh Burukan Kiwuuwa and his group of royal *akadinda* musicians; recorded by Peter Cooke, Kidinda Village. Mpigi, Buganda, Uganda, 1987. Used by permission.

MUSICAL MARKER: Timbre/Medium—Wood xylophones. **Rhythmic Density**—Triple interlocking melodic patterns create a super-dense "rush hour" feel. **Rhythm**—Polyrhythm. Individual patterns are difficult to discern because of similar timbre on one instrument.
ETHNO-CHALLENGE: Attempt the triple-interlocking pattern with two friends, labeling each person A, B, and C. Start slowly, alternating hands as you play. Each person should play on the following beats respectively: A (1, 4), B (2, 5), C (3, 6). Gradually increase your tempo and maintain the numerical order between players.

Cultural Considerations. Xylophones are among the instruments most common to sub-Saharan Africa. Many, such as the *balafon* found in West Africa, are small enough to be carried and played as solo instruments. Others, such as the *timbila* of Mozambique, exist in a variety of sizes and are typically played in larger ensembles. The polyrhythmic nature of xylophone performance combines with the use of melodic pitches to create exceptionally complex music.

Uganda is home to many xylophone traditions, but the *akadinda* is perhaps the most challenging and highly respected of them. Before the colonial period, *akadinda* musicians were part of the musical entourage that accompanied the *kabaka* (king) of Buganda. Their music was considered "royal" and was not played outside courtly functions. The melodies played on the *akadinda* are believed to be derived from vocal music; thus, through their association with specific texts, *akadinda* performances could convey a story or offer praise to the *kabaka* without needing a singer. Our example would be understood by Ugandans to have a specific meaning, despite being purely instrumental; according to the Africa volume of the *Garland Encyclopedia of World Music,* it "celebrates the rough justice meted out to Gganga, a young page of the palace who was caught sexually molesting the Princess Nassolo" (p. 824). The *akadinda* is closely related, both physically and in its performance practices, to the *amadinda,* another xylophone found in Uganda and other nearby regions, though usually in less formal contexts. Whereas the *akadinda* has seventeen or twenty-two individual keys, usually played with three distinct interlocking parts, the *amadinda* has only twelve individual keys and is played with two interlocking parts and a third resultant pattern that includes elements of the first two parts.

Arrival: Senegal–Gambia

The Gambia (officially, the Republic of the Gambia), about the size of Connecticut or Jamaica, is a sliver of a country embedded into the southern portion of the much larger Senegal (officially, the Republic of Senegal) at the western edge of the African mainland. Approximately 200 miles (320 km) from east to west and only 30 miles (50 km) wide from north to south, the country runs along the mouth of the Gambia River, which flows into the Atlantic Ocean. Most Gambians are agriculturists, the primary crop being peanuts. Because the country was formerly a British protectorate, English is common, as is French, the national language of Senegal, the nation that surrounds The Gambia on three sides. Indigenous languages are commonly spoken as well, especially Wolof, Jola, and Mandinka, the languages of the predominant ethnic groups of the Senegal–Gambia region.

Of particular musical interest in this region is the tradition of the *jali* (or *jeli*), a specialized musician associated with the Mandinka populations. In Mandinka society, the *jali* (pl., *jalolu*) serves as an oral historian, a role held by similar artisans throughout many parts of Western Africa. The history of most African populations is passed from generation to generation through oral tradition rather than through writing or other forms of empirical evidence. Though members of the community are usually familiar with the major events of their ethnic group's history, the responsibility of maintaining both this history and individual family genealogies is hereditary, usually falling on one particular family. In some societies, such as the Mandinkas, this activity is considered a family trade involving skills and knowledge passed down just as a blacksmith might pass on his skills to the next generation.

Site 7: *Jali* with *Kora*

JALI (Also, JELI; pl. JALOLU)
A poet/praise-singer and oral historian from the Mandinka of Western Africa.

KORA
A harp-lute or bridge harp played by a *jali* during his poetic recitation.

First Impressions. The music of the **jali** offers proof of the diversity of African music, which is frequently stereotyped by outsiders as revolving around drumming. No percussion is heard, merely a vocalist and his instrument, a plucked chordophone known as the **kora**. The opening flourishes on this instrument lead to a steadily repetitive melodic "groove." This churning, repeated pattern underlies the rapid-fire delivery of the vocalist. He has something important to tell you and displays his virtuosity with words rather than melody. His shouted praises for the group's VIPs are meant for everyone to hear.

Aural Analysis. *Jalolu* play a variety of other instruments as well, especially the *balafon,* a small xylophone, or the *koni,* a lute, depending on their geographic location and preference. The *kora,* the most distinctive of *jali* instruments, is a type of bridge harp unique to West Africa. The *kora* (left) Malick Pathe Sow of Senegal plays the *kora* (Shutterstock)

(right) *Kora* bridge

is constructed of a large resonating calabash (a type of gourd), which is cut so that the face of the instrument can be covered with cowhide. The neck pierces the body and forms the tailpiece at the base of the instrument. The strings, now made of nylon fishing line but formerly from thin strips of twisted antelope hide, are stretched between rawhide collars on the neck and an iron ring in the tailpiece. Instead of ending in the string holder, they pass over a tall bridge standing upright in its place on the resonator.

As on all harps, the strings of the *kora* lie in a plane perpendicular to the face of the instrument, but on the *kora* there is an additional feature. Since the strings pass over notches on either side of the bridge, there are two planes, both perpendicular to the face or sound table (and approximately parallel to each other). A typical *kora* has twenty-one strings, ten on the right, eleven on the left, though players today often add others. The player holds the instrument upright, grasping two tall handgrips embedded into the calabash and flanking the neck, and plucks with forefingers and thumbs. At first glance, it appears that the playing technique would involve a right-hand part and a left-hand part, but this is not the case, for the ascending scale is distributed alternately on the right and left sides of the bridge, meaning that scalar passages are played by alternate plucking of right and left. This allows for rapid virtuoso passages. Some pieces include an additional sound—a flick of the forefinger against the right-hand grip, and if a second person is available, he may tap the back of the *kora* in a rhythm tied to the piece being played. An accessory consisting of a thin metal plate with wire loops threaded around the edge is sometimes mounted atop the bridge. Known as *nyenyemo*, this leaf-life plate vibrates in sympathy with the strings, adding a buzzing or sizzling-like sound, something typical of many African instruments. Today it has largely been replaced with an amplifier pickup instead.

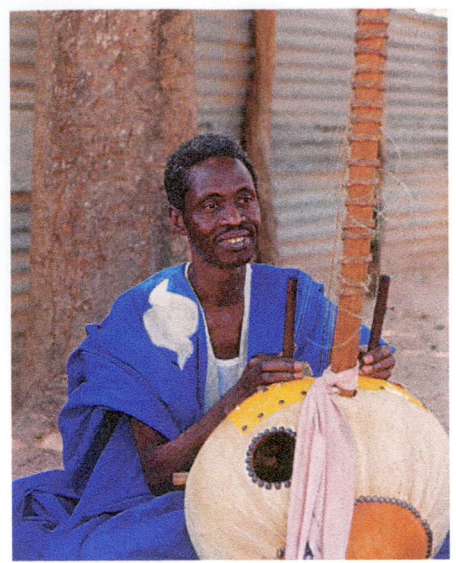

Kora (bridge-harp) performed by the late *jali* (praise singer) Bai Konte, from Brikama, The Gambia (Roderic Knight)

The performer ideally sits on the ground to play, with the instrument resting on the ground for increased resonance. A performance has two distinct sections—referred to as *birimintingo* and *kumbengo*—that allow the performer to show his skills both as a musician and as a praise-singer. The *birimintingo* sections are marked by flourishing solo runs on the *kora*. A performer may solo for an extended period of time in order to collect his thoughts, to survey the audience, or merely for his own enjoyment.

During the *kumbengo* sections, the performer plays a steady repeated pattern on the *kora* while singing praises that relate the history of the Mandinka or of individual family lineages. The steady rhythm of the *kumbengo* is maintained throughout the performance and underlies both the *birimintingo* solos and the vocalist's melodic passages. The *kumbengo* rhythm is yet another demonstration of the tendency of African musicians to use polyrhythm in performance.

In our example, the *kumbengo* is established after a short introductory *birimintingo* "flourish." A low and high part can be heard. The lower part provides a root rhythmic pattern while the upper part interlocks with it to produce a cross-rhythm. The repetitive nature of the *kumbengo* allows the performer to focus on his singing without thinking much about his *kora* performance. During *birimintingo* sections, the *kumbengo* is usually maintained in the lower part by the thumbs while the fingers play the upper melodic runs.

The melodic contour of the vocal part can generally be described as descending. The *jali*'s praises start high and fall to a long sustained tone at the end of the phrase. The performer does not sing continuously; rather, the vocal phrases are separated by instrumental sections that allow the musician to collect his thoughts before the next bout of praise-singing. The text setting tends to be syllabic with little or no melisma. A performance usually ends with a final *birimintingo* section.

LISTENING GUIDE

10.7 (2'57")

Site 10.7

Senegal: *Jali* with *Kora*

Vocals: Single male
Instruments: *Kora* (bridge harp)

TIME	LISTENING FOCUS
0'00"	Opening starts with *birimintingo*, a freely rhythmic improvisation. Note the absence of the underlying *kumbengo* rhythm.
0'32"	Vocalist quietly hums along with his instrumental melody until the *kumbengo* begins.
0'38"	*Kumbengo* rhythm begins. Listen for the contrasting low, middle, and high pitch ranges and the interweaving rhythmic patterns these produce. The low melodic–rhythm has a three-pitch ascending melodic contour, while the middle and high melodic–rhythms provide complementary motives.
1'06"	Vocalist enters. Note the declamatory singing style that utilizes a syllabic text setting, as well as the overall descending melodic contour.
1'19"	Second phrase of opening verse.

1'32"	Extended instrumental *kumbengo* break.
1'50"	Vocalist returns, connecting two melodic phrases (the second at 1'59") with a generally descending melodic contour.
2'12"	Text setting becomes more strongly syllabic, nearing speech, until the example fades.

Source: "Kuruntu Kallafa," performed by Salieu Suso with *kora*; from the recording entitled *Griot: Salieu Suso*, Lyrichord LYRCD 7418, n.d. Used by permission, Lyrichord Discs Inc.

MUSICAL MARKERS: Timbre/Medium—"Churning" underlying "harp" with declamatory male vocal. **Rhythm**—Polyrhythmic melodic lines. Vocal line structured in freely rhythmic phrases. **Form**—Steady "kumbengo" rhythm highlighted with rapid "birimintingo" flourishes on the chordophone.
ETHNO-CHALLENGE: Write a "praise" poem/song about an ancestor of your own. Trace your family history as far back as possible and note how many generations separate you from your most distant ancestor.

Cultural Considerations. Among the Mandinka, a person's surname will often indicate the nature of his family trade; Kouyate or Suso are well-known names for *jali*. Even if a person chooses another occupation, his family name indicates a link to ancestors who at one time practiced that trade. Once a *jali* learns the name of an individual, he can extemporize a musical performance that praises the contributions to the community of that individual, his family, and his ancestors. For example, Smith is a common surname in the United States. The name indicates a lineal connection to metal workers, e.g., "Blacksmith," a common occupation among English-speaking settlers in North America. A present-day "Smith" is not likely to be a metal worker (though entirely possible), but it is likely that his or her ancestors pursued such an occupation.

The texts of praise-songs are extemporaneously drawn from a pool of generic poetic verses learned over the course of a lifetime that can be customized for particular families and individuals. Praise-songs are most often reserved for members of royal lineages or, in modern times, for wealthy patrons, though almost anyone can be praised in this fashion. The person praised responds with gifts, usually money, which enables a *jali* to earn a living.

As already mentioned, the texts of *jali* praise-songs may relate to a specific individual, but frequently they deal more generally with the great deeds of the Mandinka people and with Mandinka history. In our example, Salieu Suso, the *jali*, sings of a Mandinka warrior who battled against the Fulani, another ethnic group in West Africa. The warrior, Kallafa (or Kelefa), captures many prisoners, who refuse to return to the Mandinka stronghold. Kallafa ties the prisoners together and has to "pull" them back home, and in so doing causes great dust clouds on his approach to the kingdom. The people mistake the dust clouds for smoke from fire until Kallafa is within sight. After recounting this episode, the *jali* then sings of the great deeds Kallafa performs as he enters the city. While the *jali*'s praises are improvised, they are based on a stock set of phrases and images known as "Kuruntu Kallafa" (or "Kelefa") ("Kallafa Pulling"), passed down through generations.

Through such stories, the *jali* is able to pass on knowledge of historical events to future generations and enhance community pride in the accomplishments of the Mandinka peoples. More specifically, however, since it is the descendants of Kallafa who are especially honored in this song, the song's performance obligates those descendants to reward the musician for his gracious praises. This is done by "spraying" him, either by placing money on his forehead, usually after a performance, or by putting money in his instrument through the resonator hole.

"Spraying" is important not only for the economic subsistence of the musician but also for the well-being of the community. A common belief throughout sub-Saharan Africa is that ancestral spirits can be brought into the presence of the community by invoking their names. These spirits have the power to help the community by keeping people healthy, maintaining good crops, warding off natural disasters, and so on. If, however, the spirits are not respected properly, they may become malevolent and cause disease, drought, or harmful accidents. The *jali*'s ability to praise the names of so many hundreds of ancestors is viewed by the Mandinka populations as a kind of supernatural power. A great warrior spirit, such as Kallafa, can protect the community from outside evils, or, if not respected properly, reveal his anger by, for example, making community members sick or causing a fire to spread throughout the village. Thus, the *jali* must be appropriately compensated for his services as a praise-singer in order to help ensure the security of the community.

Arrival: South Africa

South Africa (officially, the Republic of South Africa) is the southernmost country on the African continent. Equal in size to Texas, New Mexico, and Arizona combined, and larger than Egypt in north Africa and having a population of fifty million, the country has a diverse landscape marked by tall mountain ranges that separate its high interior plateaus from its extensive shoreline. As with much of sub-Saharan Africa, wildlife, including unique small black rhinoceroses, ostriches, and baboons, are found in several large game reserves, such as the more than 7,500 square mile (2,900 square km) Kruger National Park along the Mozambique border. Parts of the Western Cape (north and northeast of Cape Town) so resemble the wine country of Europe that visitors often cannot believe they are in Africa. Indeed, much of South Africa belies any stereotypes anyone might have about Africa, including its temperate climate.

South Africa is home to diverse ethnic groups representing a variety of racial families. The main ethnic groups that comprise more than three-quarters of the population include the Zulu, Xhosa, Sotho (North and South), Tswana, Tsonga, Venda, and Ndebele. White South Africans are primarily of British and Dutch descent. In addition, the country is home to more than a million people of Asian-Indian ancestry.

Archaeological evidence dates South Africa's earliest inhabitants, *Australopithecus africanus*, one of mankind's earliest ancestors, back more than three million years. More recent historical evidence indicates that hunter-and-gatherer groups, such as the San and Khoikhoi, inhabited the region along with Bantu-speaking peoples from West Central Africa, who settled

Traditional round house as seen in South Africa and elsewhere in Africa (Shutterstock)

as agriculturists and are believed to be the ancestors of the modern Nguni peoples, who include the Zulu, Xhosa, and other ethnic groups. Though explorers passed through the region in the late fifteenth century, the first colonialists to settle there arrived only in 1652. These settlers were Dutch and are known as the Boers, meaning "farmers." They landed at the Cape of Good Hope where they established a fort and a provision station for the many trading ships on their way to and from Asia. In 1814 the British bought the Dutch territories, and within a decade thousands of British colonialists arrived, soon demanding that English law govern the region's affairs. Many of the descendants of the Boers, known as **Afrikaners**, refused to accept the new government's authority and began migrating north during the 1830s, shortly after the British abolition of slavery in 1833, with plans to reestablish their own colony. By this time, indigenous peoples had asserted their dominion over the northern territories, and thus the migrating Afrikaners became embroiled in conflicts with various African groups.

The best known of the African kings who held sway in the northern regions was the Zulu warrior **Shaka** (1787–1828), who had uprooted many indigenous groups in the process of establishing one of the area's most powerful kingdoms. Shaka's repressive ruling tactics and impressive war machine have made him one of the most important historical figures in South Africa's history. Though viewed as a cultural hero by many, for others he is a tyrant whose remembered brutality still influences spiritual and social matters. The Afrikaners, who soon established their own independent territory where they maintained strict segregation of blacks and whites, defeated his successors.

Following the discovery of diamonds in 1867 and of gold deposits by 1886, the Afrikaner and British communities were continually at odds. By 1902 the British had overwhelmed the Afrikaner armies by pursuing a "scorched-earth" policy that destroyed Afrikaner farms and forced many women and children into concentration camps, where an estimated 20,000 Afrikaners and roughly 14,000 indigenous Africans died. To help end the war with the Afrikaners, the British agreed to allow the Afrikaners to continue their practice of strict segregation. By the middle of the twentieth century, this social separation had been instituted as a set of laws, referred to as *Apartheid* (Afrikaans for "separation"), which resulted in the segregation not only of blacks and whites, but also of "Asians" (i.e., East Indians) and "Coloureds" (people of mixed racial descent). Many Afrikaners attained positions of political power and succeeded in promoting governmental support of apartheid legislation.

Apartheid policies were maintained for the next few decades in the face of increasing disapproval from the international community. During this time, several anti-apartheid organizations struggled to find ways to end the oppression by South Africa's white minority of the rest of its population. The African National Congress (ANC), in particular, began seeking non-violent means for ending racial and social discrimination in South Africa after its inception in 1912. Opposition to the apartheid government finally reached its peak in the mid-1980s after half-hearted reforms resulted in numerous riots and hundreds of deaths. The government found itself in a perpetual state of emergency as it tried to maintain order and eventually lost the support of nearly all its foreign investors.

Nearly bankrupt, unable to maintain civil order, and finding itself increasingly isolated from the international community, the apartheid government finally became untenable. In 1989 Frederick Willem De Klerk, soon after accepting the South African presidency, began serious reforms that eventually led to an end of apartheid in 1992. He and newly freed ANC leader Nelson Mandela received a joint Nobel Peace Prize in 1993 for their cooperation in ending racial segregation and apartheid rule. Mandela became the first truly democratically elected president of South Africa the following year.

Site 8: *Mbube*

First Impressions. The lush harmonies of Zulu choral singing are immediately attractive to most Western audiences. No instruments are heard, just an all-male choir with a dominant lead vocalist and bass-heavy backing vocals. The performance is obviously well-rehearsed, with precise attention paid to tone, timbre, and rhythm. Though these are amateur vocalists, they have a professional sound. This is music for the stage, not an informal communal event.

AFRIKANERS
The descendants of Dutch colonialists in South Africa.

SHAKA ZULU
Zulu warrior king of the late eighteenth and early nineteenth centuries who reigned over much of South Africa.

APARTHEID
A policy of racial segregation and political and economic discrimination against non-Europeans in South Africa.

Aural Analysis. Though some female vocal groups exist, most *mbube* is performed by all-male vocal groups. A solo voice (referred to as the "controller") leads the group (called the "chord"), following the call-and-response organization typical of sub-Saharan African vocal performance. In this case, however, the responding group may also sing backing harmonies as the lead singer "tells his story." This is heard throughout this example, in which the lead vocalist laments the suffering of black people in apartheid South Africa.

By varying the interaction between the lead vocalist and the group, the performers are able to create definite changes in mood. In our example, the opening verse follows a call-and-response format, with the group responding to the leader's call in harmony. This section is then repeated. In the next section, the lead vocalist is featured, as supporting group harmonies establish a beat behind him. The third section models the first: the group responds to the lead vocalist, then blends with his voice in the concluding harmonies. This section is also repeated. In the final section, the lead vocalist makes his final declaration before the "bombing" harmonies of the group carry the music to its conclusion.

While Zulu choral singing existed prior to the colonial period, its harmonies and strong cadences (closing phrases) as currently heard reveal European musical influence. A distinctive feature of the *mbube* sound, however, is an emphasis on the lower vocal range. (The vocal ranges are described using European musical terminology; namely, *soprano*, *alto*, *tenor*, and *bass*.) The lead vocalist generally sings in a middle or upper register, though bass leads are found as well. One or two voices in the choir will represent the other upper parts, while the rest of the performers sing bass. For every one of the upper parts, there are often five or six bass voices giving the music its rich harmonic foundation. This distinctive emphasis on the lower range of voices is considered to be a characteristic of Zulu choral performance that predates the colonial period.

The *mbube* style is also distinctive for its frequent changes in tempo. The lead singer commonly begins his phrases in a "loose" manner approximating speech, that is, he does not emphasize a definite beat. The ends of vocal phrases often feature a slight slowing of the tempo and a short pause afterward that does not follow the established beat. The closing repeated refrain follows a tempo different than the rest of the performance, especially in competition pieces when the performers walk off stage (the footsteps of the exiting vocalists can be heard toward the end of our example).

LISTENING GUIDE

Site 10.8
South Africa: *Mbube*

Vocals: Single male lead with supporting male ensemble

TIME	LISTENING FOCUS
0'00"	Lead vocal ("Controller") enters and the group responds, followed by a second line with a call-and-response form and a closing call-and-response line. Listen for the use of harmony in the group responses and the emphasis on a low range of pitches.
0'09"	Listen for the harmonic tension–resolution of the closing cadence. Also, note that the tempo (approximately 104 beats per minute) slows at the end of the phrase.
0'13"	Opening verse is repeated, continuing in free-rhythm.
0'27"	Lead vocal is featured.
0'31"	Backing vocals return, articulating a regular beat (approximately 104 beats per minute).
0'41"	Closing harmonic cadence returns.
0'48"	Repetition of featured lead vocal part, supported by rhythmically regular backing vocals and followed by closing harmonic cadence.
1'10"	Return to call-and-response ("Controller" and "Chord") organization. Listen for the increased emphasis on the lower range of the group response at 1'20".
1'31"	Call-and-response section repeats.
1'51"	Lead vocal solo is featured in free rhythm.
2'00"	Lead vocal initiates the "bombing" section characterized by the "swooping" harmonies of the group response. Listen for the decrease in tempo (to approximately 84 beats per minute). Note that a second high voice adds another vocal line to contrast with the lead vocal and ensemble parts.
2'16"	Group harmony moves back to consistent pitch levels. Listen for the lead vocal initiating each repetition of the group response.
2'29"	Listen for the footsteps of the performers as the example fades.

Source: "Phesheya Mama" ("Mama, they are overseas") sung by the Utrecht Zulu Singing Competition and recorded by Gary Gardner and Helen Kivnick, 1984; from the recording entitled *Let Their Voices Be Heard: Traditional Singing in South Africa*, Rounder 5024, 1987. Used by permission.

MUSICAL MARKERS: Timbre/Medium—Male vocal choir with full voices contrasting with a somewhat "nasal" lead vocal. **Pitch/Phonic Structure**—Harmony with an emphasis on the low range. **Melodic Contour**—"Bombing" vocal sweeps common, particularly toward the end of a performance. **Form**—Lead/chorus contrast suggests a type of call and response. **Dynamics**—"Hushed" vocal lead with quiet backing vocals contrasts with loud full voices of chorus sections.
ETHNO-CHALLENGE: Research the music of South Africa in relation to the politics of the apartheid period. Search for music in your own culture that addresses political circumstances related to your own nation's history—for example, American music about the Vietnam War.

Cultural Considerations. As with much of Zulu traditional culture, the roots of *mbube* are thought to have originated during the lifetime of Shaka. Whether this belief is accurate, it is an indication of the degree to which Zulu people identify themselves with this great king. Shaka was regarded not only as a powerful warrior but also as a great dancer and strong singer. Much of the Zulu traditional repertoire is attributed to him, as he was said to have composed many songs to help keep morale high among his soldiers.

More recent influences on the sound of *mbube* are traceable to the 1920s, when migrant workers began holding evening singing competitions as a form of entertainment after long arduous days of hard labor in the gold and diamond mines found throughout South Africa. Many unique music traditions came from the labor camps, known as townships, in which most blacks were forced to live during the years of apartheid. The segregation was so strict that armed guards were often found at the gates leading to the townships. The townships were also divided into black and "coloured" (Indian or mixed descent) encampments. Soweto, meaning "Southwestern Townships," is a vast area near Johannesburg where millions of people still live in housing that varies from cardboard shacks to mansions. This area was home to Nelson Mandela before his imprisonment in 1962, as it still is to Archbishop Desmond Tutu.

By the late 1930s, nighttime *mbube* singing competitions had become characteristic of the Zulu encampments and hostels. One of the earliest recordings of this style of singing, "Mbube," was made by Solomon Linda and his Evening Birds vocal group. The single became very popular and later inspired two American hits, "Wimoweh" by the Weavers (1951) and "The Lion Sleeps Tonight" by the Tokens (1961). The song's title became the name for the "bombing" vocal style (so-called for its frequent descending melodic contour) exemplified by Solomon's group, with its deep four-part harmonies and soprano lead voice.

The best-known derivative of the *mbube* style is *isicathamiya* (a tongue "click" occurs on the romanized *c*, ISI-"click"-A-THA-MEE-YA), popularized by Ladysmith Black Mambazo, a vocal group from Ladysmith, South Africa, which gained international prominence after their collaboration with American artist Paul Simon on his highly successful *Graceland* album (1986), and soon after they won a Grammy for their own album, *Shaka Zulu* (1988). The name *isicathamiya* means "to walk like a cat" (i.e., stealthily), and is derived from a description of the dance that accompanies the singing. This style of dancing uses "tiptoeing" choreography and flowing gestures, in contrast to traditional Zulu dancing which frequently features hard stamping and vigorous "warrior" movements. The *isicathamiya* sound reflects this subdued dance style and tends to be "softer" and "smoother" than *mbube*.

Explore More

Ladysmith Black Mambazo

Ladysmith Black Mambazo (LSBM), South Africa's iconic choral group, has remained one of the most popular of world music artists around the world. While their members often change, Joseph Shabalala (b.1941), the group's founder, has remained the driving force behind the group's success. Shabalala formed his first group of *mbube* singers in 1960, following the conventions of the genre as exemplified in the audio site example. While successful, their performance was not otherwise unique among their contemporaries. In 1964, he writes that he had a dream that prompted him to create a new vocal group that would "cut down" his rivals in the local *mbube* "nightsong" competitions. At the time, *mbube* groups emphasized loud dynamic levels as a show of their strength and power over the other groups. Shabalala, however, took the opposite approach, creating the quiet *isicathamiya* style.

His new group, Ladysmith (the name of his hometown) Black (a reference to the black ox—a symbol of strength) Mambazo (meaning "axe" with the implication of "cutting down" the competition) found rapid success throughout Durban and Johannesburg. Soon the group was able to travel as professional musicians and was frequently featured at nightsong events as non-competitors to help draw audiences; they had become so dominant in winning the competitions the other groups would refuse to participate.

In 1973, LSBM made their first recording on Gallo Africa, the nation's largest record and broadcasting company. The recording, *Amabutho*, was historic as it was the first gold record (selling more than 25,000 copies) made by all-black musicians in South Africa to earn this award. The group continued to record throughout the decade and became particularly popular with religious community groups after their conversion to

Christianity in 1976. Many of their songs then came to emphasize this spiritual orientation or have a moralistic theme. By the early 1980s, LSBM had accepted invitations to perform in Europe, and their recordings made their way overseas to the American world music market as well. By the time they appeared on Paul Simon's *Graceland* (1986) album, they were already one of the best-known artists in world music circles. The tremendous success of that album, however, catapulted them into the mainstream for several years. They have since earned numerous awards and performed for many famous international figures, such as Pope John Paul II (1920–2005), Queen Elizabeth II (b.1926), and fellow-South African, Nelson Mandela (b.1918), a Nobel Peace Prize laureate. LSBM continues to record and perform internationally, though today they primarily focus on teaching others about South Africa and its culture. We have included a "bonus" track of their music, "Because I Love You" from their grammy-winning release, *Raise Your Spirit Higher* (2004), to present the contrasting styles of *isicathamiya* and *mbube*.

The well-known South African vocal group Ladysmith Black Mambazo performing on stage in New York City (Jack Vartoogian/FrontRowPhotos)

Questions to Consider

1. **How do the principal musical manifestations found in sub-Saharan Africa reflect the collective community and encourage group participation?**

2. **How is polyrhythmic music created in sub-Saharan Africa?**

3. **What linguistic elements are required to make a drum "talk"?**

4. **In what ways do *jùjú* and other types of popular music in sub-Saharan Africa draw on traditional music for inspiration?**

5. **What role does music play in maintaining oral histories and legitimizing royalty?**

6. **In what ways has music in South Africa reflected the particular history of the country?**

Chapter 11

The Caribbean

Haiti, Jamaica, Trinidad and Tobago, Puerto Rico, Cuba, The Dominican Republic

From the seventeenth century onwards Europeans brought African slaves and later, indentured workers, to the islands of the Caribbean to work vast sugar cane plantations. Near the coast of Tobago in the former British West Indies one encounters the remains of an old sugar mill with its iron wheels used to mash cane for its liquid

Background Preparation

The Caribbean represents many things to different people: white sandy beaches with clear blue water, dreadlocks and reggae music, cruise ships, Cuban communism and Fidel Castro, sugarcane, steel bands, or perhaps even offshore financial havens. For Americans, none of it is geographically very far away and yet most of it remains little known. There is much material poverty, but the region is a cornucopia of colorful and dynamic cultures. Despite a history of colonial brutality against the native population and of slaves being forcibly brought from Africa, the mixing of different peoples occurs more easily there today than practically anywhere else in the world, and this mixing has produced tremendous cultural and artistic energy. Tiny islands have developed stentorian cultural voices, producing music appreciated worldwide. Thus most readers likely will have heard steel band music, calypso, soca, reggae, and some form of Afro-Cuban music.

A map of the Caribbean shows a curving string of islands running from the Bahamas off the coast of Florida down to Venezuela. The largest islands—Cuba, Jamaica, Hispaniola (comprising Haiti and the Dominican Republic), and Puerto Rico—are in the center. The pre-contact population consisted of several indigenous groups, including the Arawak and Carib, but attempts to enslave them only led to their deaths or deportation. Today there are still black Caribs—a mixture resulting from contact with Africans—in a few places such as Honduras and St. Vincent. Contact with Europeans resulted first from the four voyages of Christopher Columbus, who between 1492 and 1503 "discovered" not "America" (meaning North America) but the Caribbean islands, Central America, and a bit of South America. After that, Spain claimed virtually all of the New World, though over time its rivals, the English, Dutch, and French, took possession of certain islands. Today, the Caribbean remains one of the world's last bastions of colonialism; Martinique and Guadeloupe remain French possessions and the Dutch **Antilles** (Curacao, Aruba, and Bonaire) belong to the Netherlands.

ANTILLES
Two chains of islands in the Caribbean, the Lesser and Greater Antilles.

The diversity of languages spoken in the Caribbean reflects the region's complex and colorful history. The main language currently spoken in any given place is the language of that country's most recent colonial ruler, but in many places a layering of languages can be heard; for example, in Trinidad and Tobago everyone speaks English normally, but one finds many Spanish place names and some Spanish terms have infiltrated the English spoken there. Spanish predominates in Cuba, Puerto Rico, and the Dominican Republic, whereas French predominates in Haiti, Martinique, and Guadeloupe. English is the main language of most of the remaining islands, including the Bahamas, Jamaica, the Virgin Islands, Dominica, St. Lucia, Barbados, Grenada, St. Vincent and the Grenadines, and Trinidad and Tobago, to name only the better known ones. Dutch and English predominate in the Dutch Antilles. In many islands one also finds linguistic blends, often called Creole or Patois, or old forms of English or French impenetrable to outsiders. Anyone who has listened to reggae "dub" or "dancehall" will know how difficult it can be to understand some forms of island English.

Most Caribbean islands have predominately African-derived populations. After their failure to enslave the Arawak and Carib, Spanish colonialists attempting to continue tobacco and sugar plantations and goldmines began importing African slaves in the early sixteenth century. This practice became pervasive by around 1650, as part of a trading triangle. Europeans exported manufactured goods to Africa in exchange for human cargo that was shipped primarily to South America and the Caribbean, after which sugar and rum produced by slave labor were exported back to Europe. Slave trading reached its peak during the eighteenth century. Periodically there were violent slave rebellions, and many Caribbean slaves escaped into the hills, mountains, or other remote areas; escaped slaves were called by the Spanish term *cimarron*, anglicized as *maroon*.

The English abolished slave trading in 1807, the French in 1818, and the Spanish in 1820, but Brazil allowed it to continue until 1852 and the United States until 1862. The English abolished slavery in 1834 in their colonies and the French in 1848 in their possessions, but it lingered until 1865 in the United States, 1873 in Puerto Rico, 1886 in Cuba, and 1888 in Brazil. Amazingly, the number of slaves emancipated in the United States (some four million) was greater than the combined total for the rest of the Americas. Following the end of slavery, the English brought indentured laborers from other parts of the world, especially India and China, while the Dutch brought them from Java, Indonesia. Indentured workers were only a step above slaves but could work their way to freedom. As a result, there are significant populations of people from India in Trinidad and Guyana (in South America), from China in Trinidad and Jamaica, and from Java in Suriname.

The Caribbean, with its incredible mix of peoples, also retains aspects of old cultures from Europe, Africa, and India. In the Bahamas and other nearby English-speaking islands, people of African descent sing old English traditional ballads and perform English **mummer** plays during Christmas. In Trinidad, also during Christmas, people still sing *parang* songs from Spain and Portugal. African traditional religions, surviving intact or in part, flourish in such places as Trinidad, Grenada, Jamaica, Haiti, the Dominican Republic, and Cuba. Aspects of eighteenth-century English hymn singing and some early "Negro spirituals" survive in the Bahamas, because during the Revolutionary War British loyalists left the rebellious colonies and settled in the Bahamas, taking their slaves with them. Many kinds of Spanish-derived music survived in Cuba, the Dominican Republic, and Puerto Rico.

MUMMER
A type of street theater actor, usually in English-derived performances staged during the Christmas season.

Planning the Itinerary

While the Caribbean is home to numerous little-known, though fascinating, kinds of music, it is also a wellspring of some of the world's best-known music genres. Steel band music, calypso, soca, reggae, and merengue all originated there and exemplify the idea that small countries can have big voices. Latin-based ballroom dance music, long fashionable around the world—*cha-cha-cha, mambo, rumba* (or *rhumba*), *merengue, bolero,* and *salsa*—derives from Cuban, Puerto Rican, and Dominican styles. Granted, some of these musics are better described as "popular" rather than "traditional," but reggae and calypso, to name only two, are thoroughly embedded in the cultures of their homelands, Jamaica and Trinidad respectively. We therefore survey a number of these well-known musics.

Arrival: Haiti

Haiti, a nation of around seven million people, occupies the western end of Hispaniola. Originally Spanish, it was ceded to France in 1697. Following a slave-led revolution that lasted more than ten years, Haiti became the first independent nation in the Caribbean in 1804. While the official language is French, most Haitians speak Creole, a blend of French, Spanish, Portuguese, English, and various African languages that is incomprehensible to outsiders. Today Haiti remains one of the world's most impoverished nations, in part because of frequent natural disasters, such as earthquakes, floods, and hurricanes, and the low value of its main crop, sugarcane; its population has also suffered through a series of brutal or ineffective political regimes. The 7.0 magnitude earthquake of January 12, 2010, resulted in the deaths of possibly 316,000 people and the destruction of much of the capital, Port-au-Prince. Virtually all Haitians are of African descent, but class differences based on skin color remain, and as a result Haitians with lighter skin (from mixing with Europeans) tend to hold more wealth and power than the rest of the population. Nonetheless, Haiti is alive with music and dance.

Site 1: *Vodou* Ritual from Haiti

First Impressions. *Vodou* (or *Voodoo*) is often stereotyped by outsiders as a dark religion with malevolent "black magic" rituals where pins are placed in dolls to hurt someone, or a mysterious powder is sprinkled on someone's doorstep to turn them into zombies. These characterizations are unfortunate and highly inaccurate. As for our recorded example, if you listen to it superficially, you will no doubt be struck by its similarity to West African music—which it essentially is—emphasizing polyrhythmic percussion and call-and-response singing. Even close listening, however, will not cause you to enter trance.

Aural Analysis. The audio example consists of two sections: the first includes vocal with drums, the second vocal with bamboo wind instruments. There are two main musical elements in the first part of the example: the rhythmic accompaniment played on drums and other percussion, and the vocal parts, which in this case contrast a male soloist and a group made up mostly of women. The structure of the vocal parts is responsorial—that is, it is based on a call-and-response pattern in which the soloist begins a sentence or thought that the group then completes. These songs are passed on through oral tradition, making them vary somewhat from one group to another, even as certain elements that maintain the song's identity are preserved.

The language is a combination of Creole and *langaj*, the latter being a ceremonial language derived from several West African and Central African religions. The accompaniment in *Vodou* rituals typically consists of three *rada* drums, sometimes along with an African iron bell or similar object, and some kind of shaken rattle, usually with the shells or seeds fastened to an external net, for example, the *shekere*. The largest drum is the leader, the middle drum provides additional rhythms, and the smallest provides a steady reference beat for the other instruments. As with other types of West African music, these polyrhythmic patterns result from short units known to scholars as "timeline patterns," rather than being thought as a continuous meter (see Chapter 10). Individual accompaniments and songs are specific to particular deities, and are played to invite those deities to a ritual. In a typical *Vodou* ritual, a succession of deities will be invited, each with its own music. Participants seek to be possessed by the deities they are invoking, and when this happens their dancing incorporates gestures and actions that express the character of that deity. The audio example features a song for Legba and part of a dance for Ogoun.

The second part of the audio track again has responsorial voices, but there are no drums. Instead a group of bamboo "trumpets" called *banbou* (also, *vaksin*) is heard, each instrument playing just a single note. However, because each instrument has a different pitch, a melody results from the interlocking patterns of these single pitches when played together as a group. The performance occasion is called *Rara*; processions of singers and players who go from one sacred spot (e.g., a cemetery) to another during the period between Carnival (the period preceding Ash Wednesday, the beginning of Lent, see Chapter 12, Explore More: Carnival) and the onset of Easter.

Cultural Considerations. *Vodou* is an African-derived religious system incorporating newly encountered and adapted influences from Roman Catholicism. Although at least 10 percent of the Africans brought to the New World were originally Muslims, the vast majority practiced traditional African religions. Some of these systems involved interaction with the spirits of ancestors, whereas others focused on a pantheon of personified natural forces, called *orisha* in the more

Haitians dance, offer food, sacrifice animals, and ask the *vodou* saints for help on the Day of the Dead in November, a festival devoted to the god Gede (Dario Mitdieri/ Getty)

A display of various drums used in Haitian *Vodou* ritual

LISTENING GUIDE 11.1 (1'37")

Site 11.1

Haiti: *Vodou* Ritual

Voices: Parts 1 and 2—single male lead and mixed male/female ensemble
Instruments: Part 1—*Rada* drums, *bas* (frame drum), *klòch* (bell), *ason* (gourd rattle); Part 2—*banbou* (bamboo trumpet aerophones, also called *vaksin*), shakers and wooden sticks (idiophones)

TIME	LISTENING FOCUS
0'00"	Part 1: Listen for the lead male vocalist followed by the group response throughout the performance.
0'01"	Listen for the tapping beat on the lead drum, which establishes the basic pulse.
0'05"	Listen for the rattle matching the basic pulse. Note that the tempo gradually increases throughout the performance.
0'07"	Listen for the first entrance of the *rada* drum, which is followed by the bell and the remaining instruments.
0'21"	Listen for the lead drum improvisations within the overall polyrhythmic organization of the ensemble.
0'43"	Part 1 fades out.

0'45"	Part 2 fades in. Listen for the continued use of call-and-response vocal organization, but the difference in lyrical content.
	Note the absence of drums. Listen for a steady pulse provided by a low shaker (idiophone), along with a pair of wooden sticks that contributes additional rhythms.
	Listen for the interlocking melodic pattern of the *banbou* (aerophones).
1'08"	Listen for the appearance of a high-pitched trumpet.
1'12"	Listen for the lead vocal's change in text and the consequent change in group response at 1'17".
1'31"	Example fades out.

Source: Excerpts from "Bosou Djo Eya (Mayi rhythm)" performed by Société Jour M'alongé Fòc Nan Point Dieu Devant, recorded by David Yih, Carrefour, Haiti, 1987, and "Guantanamo Song (Rara Rhythm, Southern Style)," recorded by Elizabeth McAlister, Port-au-Prince, Haiti, 1993. From the recording entitled *Rhythms of Rapture: Sacred Musics of Haitian Vodou.* SF 40464, provided courtesy of Smithsonian Folkways Recordings. © 1995. Used by permission.

MUSICAL MARKERS: Timbre/Medium—Mid-range drums, rattle, bells. Second section has "breathy" horns. Vocal lead with group response singing. **Rhythm**—Polyrhythmic with call and response vocals. Horn section is largely absent of percussion. **Rhythmic Density**—Thick. **Text Setting**—Mostly syllabic. **Other**—Many similarities to Ghanaian/Nigerian polyrhythmic ensemble traditions.
ETHNO-CHALLENGE: Find musical examples from other African-derived traditions similar to *Vodou* (e.g., *Santeria, Candomblé,* etc.) and compare ritual musical performance dedicated to the same deities.

SHANGO
A Yoruba name for the god of thunder and lightning in the West African pantheon. Consequently, also the name for a West African-derived religion found primarily in Trinidad.

widely known Yoruba language but called *loa* in Haiti. For example, in the Yoruba tradition found in present-day Nigeria, thunder and lightning are personified into a single god, **Shango**. In predominantly Roman Catholic colonies (which comprised most of South and Central America and much of the Caribbean), African slaves vastly outnumbered their European masters, because great numbers of workers were required to farm the sugar plantations. As a result, the Africans in these colonies were able to retain a fair amount of their African heritage, including their religions. More precisely, while many Africans appeared to profess Catholic Christianity, most saw Christ, the Virgin, and the Saints and Apostles as equivalents to African gods—an example of a process called *syncretism.* For instance, in some traditions Shango is equivalent to John the Baptist. Thus, the *Vodou* practioners considered there to be no contradiction between attending Mass in a church and participating in African rituals at an African ritual site.

Haitian *Vodou,* which blends the spiritual tradition focusing on ancestors with the one focusing on a pantheon of nature gods, derives mostly from Benin (formerly Dahomey) and nearby areas of West Africa. The two gods invoked in our example, both *loa* in the *Vodou* tradition, are Legba and Ogoun. Both are also well-known Yoruba-derived deities but classified into the "Rada" group in *Vodou.* Legba, the guardian of crossroads and barriers, is artistically depicted as a handsome old man with a flowing beard who limps while walking with a cane and likes meat and alcoholic drinks.

Ogoun, the god of iron, is often depicted with a sword, and can be quite fierce and active. While it is true that most African religions include some aspect of destructive power, they are actually predominantly positive in focus, as the principal goals are good health and healing, social cohesion, successful harvests, and the like. Participants reaffirm the power of the gods in rituals that involve dancing, singing, drumming, and possession. During possession a person's essence temporarily leaves the body, allowing the *loa* (deity) to "mount" the believer, who is considered to be the "horse." The possessed person acts out the personality of the god and demonstrates the god's traits in dance and gesture. At the conclusion of a possession, the "horse" may suddenly fall to the ground, after which s/he is given time to reunite with his/ her human essence.

Each deity is associated with a particular drumming pattern and song. Performing that music invites a named god to appear and hopefully to possess one or more lucky "horses." Despite myths to the contrary, *Vodou* music itself does not cause possession, because, if it did, anyone

A public celebration of *vodou* in the village of Souvenance in the Gonaives region on Easter Sunday using homemade bamboo trumpets called *banbou* or *vaksin*, as heard in the recording (Thony Belizaire/ Getty)

hearing it would be possessed. Indeed, the percussionists—almost always male—stay outside the ritual circle and are not subject to possession. *Vodou* ritual music *regulates* possession—that is, it makes the process of possession more even and efficient. Before a person can be possessed, he or she must learn how to become possessed; otherwise the experience of a *Vodou* ritual can be useless or even dangerous. A full ritual must begin with a song to Legba, the guardian of crossroads and gatekeeper to the spirit world. This is followed by a series of songs for other deities, presented in a prescribed order. These deities can be either nature gods or ancestors; some are violent or energetic, while others are calm. During possession, the "horse" may receive healing energy. Others nearby may also benefit or may ask the deity questions about life and the future. Extraordinary ritual acts, such as walking through fire, can occur at such a ritual, but these feats are intended to demonstrate the power of the deity and verify his/her presence. Such rituals are often sensationalized by outsiders, particularly in the movie industry, without understanding or conveying the purpose behind the actions. For followers of *Vodou*, however, they

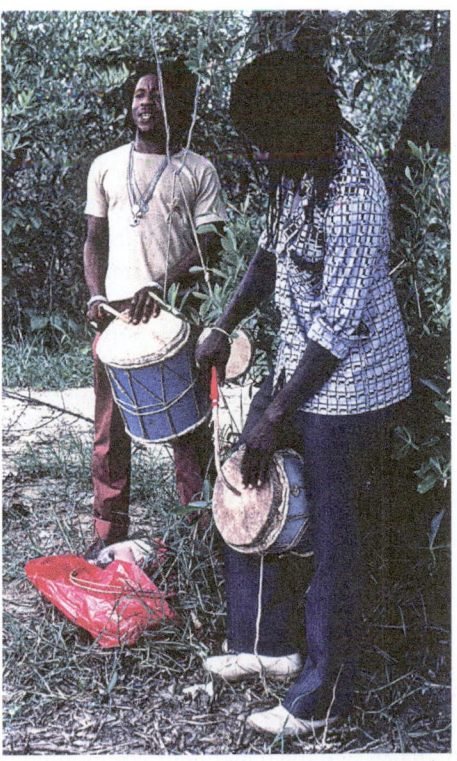

In Trinidad, two musicians play African-derived drums and sing for a Shango ceremony, a syncretistic religious tradition related to Haiti's *Vodou*

At the seacoast of Trinidad, six leaders of the African-derived Shango religion bow before ritual offerings about to be floated into the sea for Oshun, the goddess of the sea

are recognized as a confirmation of their faith and considered an essential element of their spiritual belief system.

There are a great many African-derived religions in the New World, though admittedly *Vodou* is the best known and most notorious because of negative stereotyping. Other African-derived religions include *Santeria* and *Abakwa* in Cuba, *Batuque, Umbanda,* and *Candomblé* in Brazil, *Shango* in Trinidad, and *Cumina* in Jamaica. Caribbean immigrants have transplanted some of these, including Vodou, to the United States, Canada, and England. Although not advertised, rituals associated with these religions may be found in cities such as New York, Miami, Toronto, and Los Angeles, as well as in many smaller cities.

Arrival: Jamaica

Jamaica is widely known for its white sand beaches along the north coast at Montego Bay, Ocho Rios, or Negril, classy resort hotels, and welcoming local musicians playing gentle calypsos and limbo dance music. For many Jamaicans, however, life is a different reality, one of hardscrabble poverty and crime. The population of this Connecticut-sized island is 2.5 million, of which fully one-third live in the greater Kingston area. In Jamaica, as in Haiti, there is a stark contrast between the very wealthy and the very poor. The country's colonial past, the low prices fetched by its principal exports (sugarcane and bauxite), and overpopulation in the Kingston area are all partly responsible for this situation and together comprise a recipe for tension and violence. Kingston can, unfortunately, be a dangerous city for foreign visitors. Nonetheless, it was in Kingston's slums that Jamaica's most vibrant music—reggae—originated.

The majority of Jamaica's population is of African descent, their forebears having come shackled in slavery. Spanish colonialists controlled Jamaica until the mid-seventeenth century, when English pirates drove them away. The country then became a British colony in 1670. Throughout Jamaica's history there were occasional slave rebellions, and many slaves escaped into the Blue Mountains in the east and into the uncharted "Cockpit Country" in Trelawny Parish in the west. In these regions, they were able to re-establish an African way of life, including what remained of their ancestral religion, called *Cumina*. Since achieving independence in 1962, Jamaica has struggled politically, going through—among other things—a disastrous experiment with socialism under Michael Manley. Not surprisingly, a great number of Jamaicans have left the island seeking a better life, principally in Miami, New York, Toronto, and London.

Site 2: Reggae

First Impressions. Many world music enthusiasts enjoy the easygoing "walking" feel of **reggae** music. Its characteristic "offbeat" emphasis (beats 2 and 4, instead of 1 and 3) helps distinguish it for even the novice listener. Several major reggae artists, such as Bob Marley and Jimmy Cliff, have achieved international recognition in the mainstream music business, bringing attention with it to some of the island's other musical creations, such as *ska* and *rock steady*. But while the sound of reggae may be familiar, the cultural context out of which the music was born and the meaning its lyrics hold for many Jamaicans are less well known.

Reggae is much more than a form of pop music. Those who enjoy the music purely as entertainment often overlook the politically and socially conscious lyrics that are the essence of the genre. The long, twisted hair (called *dreadlocks*) often worn by reggae musicians, the prevalence of the colors red, green, and gold, the frequent references to "Jah," even the celebration of *ganja* (marijuana), are not merely fashion statements or fads—they are part of a spiritual system of beliefs and way of life that infuses much reggae music.

REGGAE
A popular music from Jamaica characterized by a rhythmic emphasis on the offbeat and by politically and socially conscious lyrics.

Reggae's most famous artist, Bob Marley, as seen on the cover of his album, *Legend*

Painted house in downtown Kingston, Jamaica (Wikimedia Commons, Ralf Steinberger)

Aural Analysis. While the majority of instruments introduced throughout our study are unfamiliar to students new to world music, reggae music typically includes routine rock/pop instruments, such as electric guitars and bass, drum set, and electric keyboards. Some aspects of timbre distinguish their use in reggae performance. The tone quality of the electric guitar, for example, is usually set to emphasize the "treble" or high-end frequencies in order to contrast with the deep, low-end frequencies of the electric bass. The snare drum is often "tight" with the snare wires disengaged. European trumpets and saxophones are often heard, and the use of "back-up" singers is common for emphasizing the lyric refrain. Most important, however, is the lead vocalist, whose lyrics are intended to convey a message to the audience, whether of peace or protest. While much music with a "reggae sound" today lacks the socially conscious lyrics of classic reggae artists such as Bob Marley, these themes are expected of musicians who identify themselves with the genre.

LISTENING GUIDE
11.2 (3'42")

Site 11.2

Jamaica: Reggae

Voices: Single male lead, backing female ensemble
Instruments: Electric guitars, electric bass, electric keyboard, drum set (snare, toms, bass, cymbals, etc.), bongo drums, shaker

TIME	LISTENING FOCUS
0'00"	Electric guitar begins the performance.
0'02"	Listen for the focus on snare drum, leading into the start of a regular pulsation and the entrance of the remaining instruments at 0'06".
0'06"	Listen for the "upbeat" emphasis on the second and fourth pulses of the four-beat phrase.
0'08"	Lead vocalist enters with spoken dialogue. Listen for the reference to Bob Marley. Note the use of electronic "echo" on the voice at 0'10," 0'14," and 0'19".
0'24"	Listen for the lead vocalist transitioning to a singing voice.
0'27"	Listen for the backing vocals and first appearance of the "Torchbearer" refrain.
0'39"	Listen for the reference to "Jah."
0'58"	Listen for the reference to "I and I."
1'06"	First verse begins. Note the various examples of *rasta* terminology, references to Bob Marley's influence on the lead vocalist, and the review of Marley's personal history.
2'17"	Listen for the *Nyabinghi* reference.
2'26"	Listen for the "Yeah, yeah, yeah" lyric, used to close the first verse.
2'33"	Listen for a melodic–harmonic change as the lead vocalist continues the verse, with female vocalists singing in the background.
3'00"	"Torchbearer" refrain returns.
3'37"	Example fades.

Source: "Torchbearer," performed by Carlos Jones and the PLUS Band; from the recording entitled *Roots with Culture*, Little Fish Records LF02912, 2004. Used by permission.

Cultural Considerations. Reggae is different from most other types of music featured in this book, first because it has been commercially successful, and second because songs usually come from known, individual creators who infuse their life experiences into their work. Reggae musicians often view their music as having the power to prompt people into action against political and social injustice on behalf of those who are oppressed or marginalized in society. Reggae artists regularly regard their position on stage as an opportunity to educate their audience about these issues or other important associations with their music and culture. Our example, "Torchbearer," is such a song. Written by Carlos Jones, a reggae musician in Cleveland, Ohio, the song pays homage to Bob Marley, the most famous figure associated with reggae music.

Bob Marley (a.k.a. Tuff Gong), born Robert Nesta Marley on February 6, 1945, is considered the most important of reggae's many stars, especially for the quality of his lyrics and his articulation of fundamental Rastafarian concepts (see below). His career began in 1960 after he joined with a childhood friend, Bunny Wailer (born Neville O'Riley Livingston), to form The Wailers. Later joined by Peter Tosh (born Winston Hubert McIntosh), they recorded songs that encapsulated their life experiences in Kingston's most notorious slum, Trench Town. Through international tours, including one to North America called "Babylon By Bus," they spread their music to non-Jamaican audiences. Marley's 1981 death from cancer at the age of thirty-six was a devastating blow to both reggae and Jamaica, because, although establishment Jamaica shunned the Rastafarian "rude boys," the public had embraced Marley. Eventually a statue in honor of him was placed outside the National Stadium in Kingston.

Although some might view reggae as simply a Jamaican popular music, it is steeped in very particular aspects of Jamaican history and culture. Reggae is often challenging on several fronts, including the spiritual and the political. Many lyrics combine elements of Jamaican vernacular English with the peculiar vocabulary of the Rastafari religion that informs reggae. Reggae's roots are complex and tangled, as it draws on many contradictory styles, including American rock and rhythm & blues, evangelistic hymns and choruses, and African drumming and singing.

A full understanding of reggae requires a discussion of Marcus Garvey and the roots of the Rastafari spiritual tradition. Garvey (1887–1940), a major force for West Indian nationalism and a promoter of black social pride, founded the Universal Negro Improvement Association (UNIA) in Kingston in 1914. In 1916 he traveled to New York City where he founded a branch of the UNIA and started a number of businesses (such as the Black Star Shipping Company), a newspaper (*Negro World*), and a church (the African Orthodox Church). His arrest in 1925 on fraud charges led to his being deported back to Jamaica in 1927. It is reported that after returning home he proclaimed, "Look to Africa, where a black king shall be crowned." Indeed, Garvey's teachings led to the beginning of a "back to Africa" movement in Jamaica and beyond.

Many in Jamaica thought Garvey's words had been fulfilled when, in 1930, they read that an Ethiopian tribal chieftain named Ras Tafari Mekonnen had been crowned **Haile Selassie I**, the King of Kings, the Lord of Lords, Conquering Lion of the Tribe of Judah, the Emperor of Ethiopia. Many came to believe that Haile Selassie (meaning "Power of the Holy Trinity") was the black reincarnated Christ and that the black peoples of the Diaspora were the lost children of Israel held captive in Babylon, awaiting deliverance by Jah (God) and their return back to Zion—in this case Ethiopia, the spiritual home of all black African-descended populations. The colors red, green, and gold became associated with Zion, because they are Ethiopia's national colors.

HAILE SELASSIE I, An Ethiopian emperor considered by Jamaican Rastafarians to be a black incarnation of Jesus Christ.

Ethiopian Emperor Haile Selassie I, "Lion of Judah," born Lij Tafari in 1892, crowned emperor in 1930 until his death in 1970 (Rastafari Archive and Ras Adam Simeon)

Those who embraced this loosely organized faith were called Rastafarians. In addition to their core beliefs, they adopted a lifestyle that included the wearing of dreadlocks and the smoking of *ganja* (the Hindi term for marijuana). *Ganja*, or "herb," was already a traditional medicine in Jamaica but was brewed as a tea or eaten with food. Rastafarians believed, however, that smoking "herb" would put adherents into a more prayerful state and bring them closer to Jah. Rastas justify their use of *ganja* with passages from the Bible, such as Revelation 22:2, which states "The leaves of the tree were for the healing of the nation."

The audio example uses several instances of the language peculiar to Rastafarians, or *Rastas* as they are called for short. The phrase "I and I" serves as both a singular and a plural pronoun, its use signifying that Jah (the Rastafarian term for God) is always present with the speaker. In plural form it refers to the mystical relationships within a group and between the group and Jah. A *Nyabinghi* (referred to in the line "Nyabinghi shakes the ground") is a Rasta ritual convention at which chanting and drumming occur. The term, which is derived from the name of an earlier anti-colonial movement in Rwanda, also refers to dreadlocked Rastas and may be shortened to "Nya-man," as heard in the example. References to "vibration" in the song highlight the metaphysical goals of peace, brotherhood, and love espoused by Rastas generally. Jones also mentions Marley's bi-racial background (Marley had a white father and a black mother), and refers to Peter Tosh using his original surname, McIntosh.

In Jamaica, Rastas are often scorned by the establishment. Their close association with reggae, due in large part to Marley's adherence to the spiritual tradition, has prompted much of the music to express challenges to the social order. Because Rastas consider the white world to be "Babylon" (referring to the captivity of God's chosen people) and Africa their true home, reggae

Reggae artist Carlos Jones, composer and performer of "Torchbearer," of Cleveland, Ohio (Larry Koval)

lyrics also often challenge white hegemony. While not every reggae musician is necessarily a practicing Rastafarian, virtually all are sympathetic to this spiritual system.

Because live performances of reggae were long prohibited in Jamaica, the music was a phenomenon of Kingston's many small recording studios. There the musicians, using both acoustic and electric instruments, laid down tracks that were mixed to the liking of the audio engineer. Reggae music was then disseminated on vinyl recordings. Many party venues and dancehalls hired soundmen to bring sound trucks to provide reggae music for dancing. By the 1980s these DJs had discovered that by turning down the melody track and boosting the bass and rhythm track, they could "talk" over the music through a microphone. Eventually recordings without the vocals—or so-called "dub" versions—were made specifically for such improvised speech. This led to the creation of "dub" poetry, later evolving into a style called "dancehall." Some DJs became virtual reggae poets, creating long, complex poems that commented on life. Reggae "**dub**" also has a close relationship with the origin and rise of African-American rap and "toasting."

Reggae music derives in part from a number of earlier styles that were not associated with Rastafarians and rarely had political lyrics. The oldest style was *mento*, a creolized form of ballroom dance music that was popular in the 1940s. With independence in 1962 and the increasing concentration of the population in Kingston's burgeoning slums came *ska*, a Jamaican response to American rhythm and blues and rock and roll. By the mid-1960s *ska* was slowing down and incorporating more politically charged lyrics; these changes led to a new style called *rock steady*. Reggae, the name of which is attributed to Toots Hibbert, emerged around 1968. It incorporated not only these older styles but also new forms of blues, Latin American music, and Jamaican religious music. Reggae was also influenced by the music of Rastafarian religious gatherings, which blended the choral style of Christian revival meetings with *Cumina*, African-derived drumming and singing.

DUB (ALSO, DANCEHALL) Recorded music that emphasizes the bass and rhythm tracks so that a DJ can "talk" over the music through a microphone.

Arrival: Trinidad and Tobago

Trinidad and Tobago, one-fifth the size of Hawaii but with the same population, 1.3 million, has more than made up for its small size by contributing three of the world's favorite musics—steel band, calypso, and soca. The nation consists of two islands: Trinidad, the larger, is only about 50 miles by 30 miles (80 by 50 km), and Tobago is a mere 25 miles by 8 miles (40 by 13 km). The name of the capital, Port-of-Spain, suggests something of the island's history. "Discovered" by Christopher Columbus during his third voyage in 1498, Trinidad was held by Spain until the English wrested it away in 1797, holding it as a colony until 1962. The native population, the Carib, disappeared after the first Spanish colonists brought their slaves to Trinidad to establish sugar plantations. Even after the end of slave trading, Britain brought more than 134,000 East Indians, 8,000 Africans, and 1,000 Chinese as indentured laborers to work the land. As a result, today's population is around 40 percent East Indian. The range of religions found is quite varied as well: the country boasts a colorful landscape of Christian churches, Muslim mosques, and Hindu temples, along with many African ritual centers.

Most visitors to Trinidad come for Carnival, a festival preceding Lent, when Port-of-Spain comes alive with near non-stop music and dancing. Because the beautiful beaches on the north coast of Trinidad remain little known and under-developed, Tobago's easy to reach beaches have been the main destination for swimmers and surf lovers. Trinidad's Great Pitch Lake is perhaps the world's largest pitch (tar) deposit and has been the source of material for paving roads in both Europe and the Americas.

CALYPSO A popular music from Trinidad characterized by improvised lyrics on topical and broadly humorous subject matter.

Site 3: Calypso

First Impressions. Our example of classic **calypso** opens with the sounds of a small dance band dominated by winds. Soon a male vocalist is introduced, who speaks as much as he sings; in a simple but direct manner, he gives his personal view of money and its corrosive influence on people. The repetitive music behind him sounds almost incidental, more a vehicle for the singer to convey the words than an attempt to charm the listener with a sophisticated melody.

Aural Analysis. Studio-recorded in New York City in 1979, using an eclectic group of pan-Caribbean musicians, our example opens with a simple melodic line consisting of four short instrumental phrases; this melody returns periodically during brief interludes and also serves as a coda to the song. While the trumpet and clarinet dominate the purely instrumental sections, quieter instruments, including violin, piano, guitar, and electric bass, are heard accompanying the singing. Throughout, a **conga** drum reinforces the beat.

The singer's stage name is The Growling Tiger, but he was born Neville Marcano in Siparia in southern Trinidad. A prizefighter and sugarcane worker in the early 1930s, he was inspired to become a calypso singer ("calypsonian") in 1934 during a trip to San Fernando, the largest city in the south. Within a short time, his talents as a lyricist and singer had become apparent, and in 1935 he and other singers were sent to New York City to record for Decca Records. Among these early recordings, now considered classics, is Tiger's calypso "Money is King." The present track is a re-recording of this song done some forty-four years later when Tiger was at least in his sixties.

"Money is King" is a Depression-era commentary on the lives of the haves and the have-nots, with the calypsonian, of course, speaking for the latter. Organized into five stanzas, the lines of the song are not consistent in length or in rhyme pattern, and do not fit neatly with the music; the singer forces some lines into the allotted time by rushing the words in speech rhythm. Each stanza has eight lines, and thus the melody consists of eight phrases. The first four melodic phrases, however, are the same, whereas each of the second four is different, leading to a melodic structure that can be expressed as A, A, A, A, B, C, D, E.

In the first stanza Tiger declares that if you have money, you can get away with murder, and people will not even care if you have the disease *kokobe* (yaws)—but if you are poor, you are little more than a dog. The latter theme reappears in the third, fourth, and fifth stanzas. In stanza two Tiger asserts that if you have money, the storeowner will treat you like a king and will even go as far as sending your goods to your house on a motorbike. The third stanza declares that even a college-educated man with no money will not be given credit at a Chinese restaurant ("'Me no trust-am,' bawl out the Chinee [sic] man"). In the fourth stanza Tiger says that even a dog can find scraps of food around, and if it's a good breed, people will take it in as a pet—but a "hungry man" will be treated worse than a dog. Finally, without money a man cannot attract a woman, buy her gifts, or show affection. His conclusion: "If you haven't money, dog is better than you." (These lyrics are quoted in Hill 1993, pp. 259–260.)

Port-of-Spain, Trinidad from the west. (Wikimedia Commons, Christian Welsh)

LISTENING GUIDE

Site 11.3
Trinidad: Calypso

Voices: Single male
Instruments: Guitar, bass guitar, piano, clarinet, trumpet, violin, conga drums

TIME	LISTENING FOCUS
0'00"	Listen for the instrumental "hook," a refrain that highlights the trumpet, violin, and clarinet parts. Note that the bass, guitar, piano, and drums play a supporting role throughout the performance.
0'03"	Vocalist enters. Listen for the violin imitating the melodic contour of the vocalist and adding supporting harmony.
0'14"	Listen for the change in melody and supporting harmony.
0'23"	Listen for the lyrics "dog is better than you," which conclude the verse.
0'24"	Listen for the instrumental refrain.
0'35"	Second verse.
0'55"	Listen for the lyrics "money is king," which conclude the verse.
0'57"	Instrumental refrain.
1'08"	Third verse.
1'27"	Listen for the lyrics "dog is better than me," which conclude the verse.
1'29"	Instrumental refrain.
1'39"	Fourth verse. Listen for the explanation of why a "dog" is better than a poor man.
1'58"	Listen for the phrase "dog is better than you," which concludes the verse.
2'00"	Instrumental refrain as the example fades.

Source: "Money is King," performed by Growling Tiger and the Trans-Caribbean All-Star Orchestra; from the recording entitled *Growling Tiger: High Priest of Mi Minor—Knockdown Calypsos*, Rounder 5006, 1979. Used by permission.

MUSICAL MARKERS: Timbre/Medium—Popular music "dance" band with "talking" vocalist. Steel drum often included in modern ensembles. **Text Setting**—Strongly syllabic. Lyrics include witty social commentary, often poking fun at contemporary issues.
ETHNO-CHALLENGE: Transcribe the lyrical content of this example. Write your own "calypso" verse to add to the present song.

Cultural Considerations. Trinidad's particular history of "kinder and gentler" colonialism helped create the more relaxed attitude reflected in its arts, quite unlike Jamaica, where an oppressed underclass continues to seethe with anger against the wrongs of both today and the past. Although Spain originally claimed the islands of Trinidad and Tobago, few Spanish actually settled there. After the English drove the French out of certain islands of the Lesser Antilles group during the mid-eighteenth century, some French and their slaves resettled in Trinidad, bringing Roman Catholicism with them. The French had a relatively laissez-faire attitude toward their slaves, but tolerance of slave customs declined after the Protestant English took control of the island in 1797. Slavery was abolished in Trinidad in 1843, after which great numbers of indentured laborers, especially from British India, were brought to the country. Thus, the population of nineteenth-century Trinidad consisted of freed slaves, indentured workers (free or still under contract), and a small number of French and English colonials.

Carnival, the period of celebration before Lent begins—called Mardi Gras in New Orleans—is widely celebrated in Roman Catholic countries, and although Trinidad became English, its Spanish-French heritage remained strong. Early Carnivals were polite affairs celebrated publicly by the upper classes, while the working classes were left to their own devices. By the mid-nineteenth century, however, the "rowdy" classes had taken over Carnival, now celebrated through street dancing, the singing of songs that often mocked the upper classes, stick fighting, and a great parade of costumed revelers. The British authorities attempted to bring this growing chaos under control by passing and enforcing laws against excessive noise. In 1883 the government passed a "music bill" that permitted "drums, tambours, and chac-chacs [rattles]" to be played only under license and forbade all such music at night. The prohibitions on drumming led to protests, riots, and the singing of increasingly critical songs. Not to be outwitted by the British, Trinidadians denied drums began beating or stamping on bamboo tubes, creating the "tamboo bamboo" band—the term *tamboo* being derived from the word *tambor*, meaning drum.

During the latter part of the nineteenth century, government officials, especially Norman LeBlanc, began a process of both co-opting and civilizing Carnival activities. By creating competitions among singers (called *chantwells*) and bands, held in tents during Carnival, he simultaneously harnessed what came to be called calypso song and provided an acceptable place for its expression. At the same time, the language of the songs was changed from *patois* to English. Eventually, these now tamed topical songs became one of Trinidad's national musics.

Thus, a "calypso" is a topical song or musical commentary on current events, the foibles of the upper classes, recent scandals, or odd fashions. As such they have a short shelf life, but during their brief existence they often sting. Yet calypso is rarely an angry music like reggae; parody, satire, and ridicule are its methods, though, as is often pointed out in the lyrics, these are used *sans humanité* ("without mercy"). Because calypso songs were created in response to particular events close to home, they also did not export well, and calypso recordings have not had the wide distribution that recordings of steel band have. However, when the Andrews Sisters

CARNIVAL
A pre-Lent festival celebrated in predominantly Roman Catholic cultures, primarily in Europe and the Caribbean. Known as Mardi Gras in the United States.

Calypso monarch The Mighty Sparrow (aka Slinger Francisco) performing at the Lincoln Center Out of Doors "Caribbean Cultural Center: 30 Years of Carnival" concert in New York City (Jack Vartoogian/FrontRowPhotos)

His costume more than 12 feet high and 10 feet wide, Anthony Paul portrayed the "Splendour of Moonlight" during Trinidad's annual Carnival parade (Unknown)

rerecorded Lord Invader's "Rum and Coca Cola" in the United States in 1945 and sold millions of copies, they showed that some songs could appeal to a broad market. (Lord Invader, who had not received any royalties, later sued and won a settlement.) Jamaican-born Harry Belafonte has also made a career of singing watered-down calypso music for a mass audience in North America.

Many calypsonians took on bombastic names, to match their sometimes bombastic lyrics. Major figures have included Attila the Hun (Raymond Quevedo, a labor leader and politician), The Mighty Sparrow (Slinger Francisco), Lord Protector (Patrick Jones), The Mighty Chalkdust (Hollis Liverpool, a school teacher), Lord Kitchener (famous for his "Pan in A"), and others with names such as Roaring Lion, Cro Cro, Lord Superior, Lord Executioner, Houdini, Calypso Rose (a rare female singer), and Immortal Spoiler. Because they were considered thoughtful commentators rather than popular stars, many continued to perform into old age. Among the new generation of calypsonians are Brian London, Kizzie Ruiz, and Superblue.

Trinidad, however, has not been immune to other musical currents, and calypso has faced stiff competition from North American rock, soul, and jazz, as well as reggae, Afro-Cuban music, and *zouk* (from the French Lesser Antilles). In the late 1970s some singers began blending calypso with aspects of rock and reggae, creating *soca* (soul-calypso), a more danceable style with

Calypso Rose, Trinidad's most famous female calypsonian

Lord Kitchener (né Aldwyn Roberts, 1922–2000) from Trinidad performing at the Caribbean All-Star Calypso Festival at Radio City Music Hall, New York City (Jack Vartoogian/ FrontRowPhotos)

less consequential words. New blends of calypso and other genres continue to be produced, but because the calypsonians retain a significant place in Trinidadian society as commentators, the pure calypso tradition continues. However, since calypso is mostly performed during Carnival, the singers can rarely make a year-round living through their art. Many work in other sectors the rest of the year, and some live abroad, returning to Trinidad only for Carnival.

Site 4: Steel Band (Pan)

First Impressions. Uninitiated listeners could easily mistake the sounds of a steel band for a steam calliope, a theater organ, or some sort of automatic pipe organ contraption. In fact, the steel band is an unlikely orchestra, made up, in part or entirely, of 55-gallon oil drums, whose heads have been beaten into a series of circular concave dents or depressions. Steel band music is usually energetic, highly rhythmic, and pop music flavored—but it can also be serene, even "classical." In existence now for more than fifty years, steel band has soared in popularity in North America recently, resulting in an increasing number of schools, colleges, and universities that sponsor steel band ensembles. This music is tiny Trinidad's most famous gift to the rest of the world.

PAN
A musical instrument from Trinidad made from a steel oil drum.

Explore More

Soca

While calypso is considered a popular music, its success in recent years has been limited mainly to local audiences. The tremendous international interest in Caribbean folk and popular music during the 1950s and early 1960s subsided as rock music and its many strands of styles took over the radio airwaves throughout the world. Calypso, as with so many other local popular world music traditions, absorbed some of these influences in order to maintain its popular appeal. By the 1970s, these influences were taking calypso farther and farther away from its traditional roots as an outlet for social commentary. Many calypso artists and fans criticized the new developments, stating that the music had lost its "soul."

Among these critics was calypsonian Lord Shorty (born Garfield Blackman (1941–2000)), who is today regarded as the Father of Soca music. His style fused calypso with rock music, as well as Indian *filmi*, which was hugely popular among Trinidad's large Indian population. Though these musical elements broadened the music's appeal, Shorty maintained the social commentary of his lyrics, describing this as the "soul of calypso," which was abbreviated to "soca" as a way of describing the new style. The peppy new sound did indeed appeal to audiences and musicians alike, but Shorty's hope to maintain the focus on the lyrics came to be overshadowed by an increasing number of soca dance hits emphasizing more universal "party" themes; for example, drinking, dancing, and casual love affairs, particularly in association with the Carnival festivities that attract thousands of tourists to the island each year.

Soca artist Alison Hinds performs in 2016 on the stage of New York's HOT 97s On Da Reggae & Soca Tip (Photo by Johnny Nunez/WireImage)

Soca received huge international recognition with the global success of "Hot, Hot, Hot" recorded by Arrow (Alphonsus Cassel) in 1982 and later, in 1987, as a cover version by American artist, David Johansen. The song has become an unofficial anthem for the Carnival celebrations today, at least with those visiting the islands. Natives to Trinidad and Tobago, as well as surrounding islands, are more interested in modern artists, such as Destra Garcia and Bunji Garlin, who have more modest international appeal. Though soca dominates the Carnival soundscape today, calypso still maintains local interest with popular artists, such as David Rudder, as well as many older generation calypsonians, such as Mighty Sparrow. Chutney-soca is also a popular local music, leaning more heavily on Indian popular music influences with artists such as Rikki Jai.

Olivia Ahyoung

I consider myself fortunate to have been born in the country of Guyana (the former British Guiana) a land of six ethnic races each with its own interesting cultural background, co-existing and blending with each other to make a uniquely Guyanese culture. Being the only English-speaking country on the South American continent, Guyana shares cultural similarities with the English-speaking Caribbean rather than those of Latin America, and it was in this atmosphere that my appreciation and love of Caribbean music with its infectious rhythms grew and flourished.

Growing up in a musical household, at an early age I was exposed to classical music through private piano and string lessons, competitions at music festivals and annual examinations. Yet I had always been captivated by the performances of folk songs and dances by local groups and the fascinating array of drumming rhythms I heard in local African, Indian and Chinese ceremonies. But it was the sweet sound of pan emanating from the "pan yards" as the all-male steel bands played intricate melodies and arrangements without music that intrigued me the most.

In Guyana during my tenure teaching music at a boys' high school, I got the opportunity to learn more about the instrument by visiting pan yards to talk and learn from the players, and subsequently taught pan, and wrote arrangements of folk and other local music for the school's steel band. I was helped in this process by the shift in emphasis from classical to indigenous music that came about after the country's independence, and working with the pan alongside other classical instruments was a very rewarding experience for me and the students.

Some years later here in the USA, I again got the opportunity to teach and lead a college steel band that was started by

Olivia Ahyoung

my late husband, an ethnomusicology student who hailed from Trinidad. It was a fun and challenging experience introducing die hard classically trained musicians on the path to a music degree, to the infectious beat of Caribbean music and a different concept of rhythm. Challenge turned into excitement as the repertoire grew to include many styles of music including classical, even as the band spawned other groups.

It has been decades since I first heard and fell in love with the steel pan, and since playing the pan was not socially acceptable for females when first introduced in Guyana from Trinidad, I was delighted to find that my musical journey led me to it both at home and in the United States. As the twentieth century's only new instrument, I use every opportunity to talk to music teachers, students and other interested persons about the role pan has played in my musical life and my rich cultural heritage in general.

Mia Gormandy

I was born in 1988 in Port of Spain, Trinidad, a bustling city known as the capital of the Republic of Trinidad and Tobago. My father at the time was a fire officer and my mother worked for the Mayor's office for the City of Port of Spain. She also maintained a hairdressing business and pursued events management on the side. When I was five years old, my parents

bought a steelpan, our national musical instrument, for my older brother, Oni. When Oni was a few months old, his lungs had collapsed and he was rushed to the hospital. This episode resulted in brain damage, and he was given five years to live. Surprisingly, my older brother was fourteen years old when I was born. Though he had just started speaking at that age, my parents noticed his keen hearing and ability to sing popular calypso music heard on the radio. Therefore, they purchased a steelpan and hired a music teacher to harness his musical ability. However, he became more interested in the piano than pan. Instead, at five years old, I began reaching over my head attempting to play the pan. So, lessons that were initially intended for my older brother became lessons for me.

My parents enrolled me in formal lessons at the age of six, and I entered my first competition just a few months later. I performed a solo version of "Somewhere Over the Rainbow." To my parents' surprise, I won the competition where I competed against children who were more than twice my age. As I grew, I continued playing the steelpan as a soloist and entered many competitions. Different competitions called for different styles of music. At times I played classical pieces, and other times I performed popular calypsos or even popular American tunes. At nine years old, I joined the Trinidad All Stars Steel Orchestra (TASSO), one of the oldest living steelbands in Trinidad and Tobago. I performed on their stageside, a smaller group of 30–50 musicians that performed year round at local events. We rehearsed evenings during the week and performed mostly on the weekends. At that time, I was the youngest member of the stageside. Most members ranged from 18 to 80 years old. During the Panorama season (the largest steelband competition in the world held annually in Trinidad), which took place during Carnival, the orchestra grew to over 150 players and many young people joined at that time. At the age of twelve, I met my now husband who walked into the panyard (our rehearsal space) hoping to join at the age of thirteen years old. As a teenager, I maintained a very active lifestyle as I tried to keep up with my school work, performed with TASSO several times each weekend, and maintained my solo career where I entered competitions and performed around Trinidad and Tobago.

At fifteen years old, I attained a full scholarship to attend Northern Illinois University (NIU) to study under steelpan pioneer Cliff Alexis, and steelpan virtuoso Liam Teague. At NIU, I gained opportunities to perform around the United States, Europe, and islands throughout the Caribbean. I later attained my Bachelor of Music degree (2009) and Master of Music degree (2011) in steelpan performance. However, while pursuing my Master's degree, I realized that there weren't many books and articles written about the steelpan. The ones that existed were written by non-Trinidadians. So, I was unable to

Mia Gormandy

find materials published by locals for a research project I was working on. When I complained to my lecturer at NIU, she introduced me to the field of ethnomusicology, which I immediately knew I wanted to pursue. Once I graduated from NIU in 2011, I attended Florida State University where I attained a second Master of Music degree (2013) and later a Doctor of Philosophy degree (Ph.D.) in ethnomusicology (2017). Though I was initially interested in pursuing research on steelpan culture in Trinidad and Tobago, I was even more interested in the steelpan scene in Japan. Therefore, I conducted my dissertation research on "Pan in Japan." I spent several months in different parts of Japan familiarizing myself with many Japanese pannists and understanding their unique pan culture. Once I completed my fieldwork in Japan, I moved back to Trinidad to write my dissertation. While in the process, I was offered a position as Assistant Professor of Steelpan at the University of Trinidad and Tobago (UTT). Currently, I teach pan and ethnomusicology courses at UTT. I am working on several ethnomusicological projects where I hope to bring more steelpan history and cultural information to the forefront, and I serve as television and radio commentator for the Panorama competition each year. I perform less and less but I do maintain international performances mostly for school steelbands in the United States. With so many talented performers in Trinidad and Tobago, I aim to fill a gap in our culture, which includes the documentation and preservation of our national instrument, the steelpan.

MARACAS
A pair of small Caribbean gourd rattles with interior beads.

Aural Analysis. All but the rhythm instruments of the steel band began life as 55-gallon oil drums. A steel band ensemble consists of multiple steel drums, called pan (pronounced like "pahn"), plus a rhythm section known as the "engine room," which comprises a conventional drum set, conga drum, automobile brake drums, and possibly other kinds of percussion such as ***maracas*** (rattles), *claves* (sticks beaten together), the *güiro* (scraped gourd), and the cowbell (an echo of the African iron bell). There is no fixed number of pan, nor are their names used consistently. The higher-pitched pan are cut from the full drum, leaving a short "skirt" (side of the drum), whereas the lowest pans use the full skirt. Notes of definite pitch are produced by striking tuned dents that have been carefully hammered into the head of each pan; the higher-pitched instruments are capable of producing many more pitches than lower-pitched ones, because the area required for a high pitch is small and for a bass pitch large. Some pitch ranges require multiple pan, because bass pans often can produce only four pitches each. The leading melodic pan are known variously as the *tenor*, *ping-pong*, *lead*, *soprano*, and *melody* pan. Those creating harmony or "strumming" effects in imitation of guitars are called variously *guitar*, *double second*, *double guitar*, *quadraphonic*, *triple guitar*, and *cello*. The bass line is provided by the *bass* pan. Because the tuning process is most critical, and the ensemble's overall sound depends on good tuning, skilled tuners are highly sought after.

The title of our example, "Jump Up," refers to the kind of dancing also known as "breakaway," performed in the streets during Trinidad's Carnival. This is the joyful, outdoor kind of music that really epitomizes Carnival: fast, rhythmic, full of syncopation. Because performances are typically extended and because players have to learn all compositions by memory, repetition is naturally a part of most pieces. "Jump Up" is no exception. Listen carefully and you'll be able to follow its progression.

The piece begins with an eight-measure introduction with much syncopation, played four times. Then follows the main tune, also eight measures in length, which is played twice. Following this, a third section of eight measures, perhaps best called an interlude, is played four times, after which the melody is repeated twice and the interlude four more times. The main melody then returns before fading out in our excerpted example.

Steelbands arrive for the National Small and Medium Preliminaries competition at Victoria Square, Port of Spain (Sean Drakes / LatinContent/ Getty Images)

Full steelband with bass pans in front

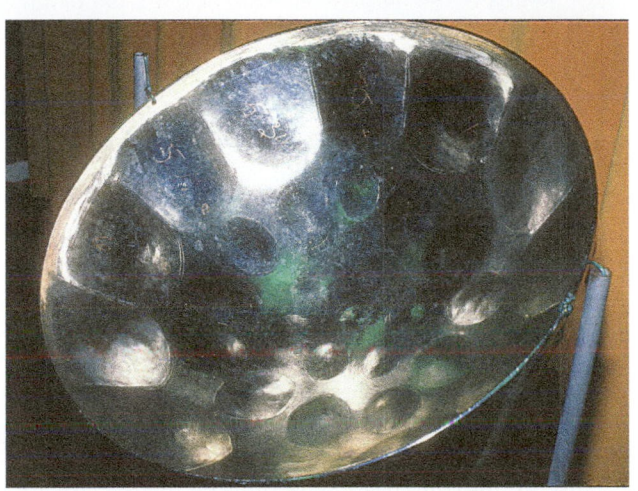

A lead or melody pan showing many sunken "note areas," each representing a pitch

LISTENING GUIDE
11.4 (2'02")

Site 11.4
Trinidad: Steel Band

Instruments: Steel drums (melodic idiophones), electric bass, drum set (membranophones and cymbals), brake drum (idiophone)

TIME	LISTENING FOCUS
0'00"	Listen for the drum set introduction, and the following introductory melodic section. Note the consistent rhythmic pattern of the idiophone and frequent use of syncopation in the melody and snare drums in particular.

0'07"	Listen for the contrasting descending melodic contour of the lower-ranged steel drums which sound to close the melodic phrase.
0'08"	Introductory melody repeats, and repeats again at 0'15" and 0'23."
0'30"	Listen for the short pause and drum accent that initiate the first melodic section.
0'39"	First melodic section repeats.
0'47"	Listen for new melodic material.
1'01"	First melodic section returns.
1'18"	Second melodic section returns.
1'32"	Listen for an ascending melodic contour in the main melody.
1'40"	First melodic section repeats. Listen for the addition of a secondary contrasting melody in the upper-range steel drums.
1'55"	Example fades.

Source: "Jump Up," performed by the Miami (Ohio) University Steel Band; from the recording entitled *One More Soca*. Ramajay Records. Used by permission.

MUSICAL MARKERS: Timbre/Medium—Metallic "pinging" quality of steel drums. Driving "Engine" room with drum set and brake drum. **Phonic Structure**—Harmony supporting a tuneful melody. **Rhythm**—Steady duple meter.
Other—Strongly associated with general "Caribbean" sound featured in tourism media.
ETHNO-CHALLENGE: Using a cookie tin or some other shapeable "steel drum," make your own pan by creating various pitches.

Cultural Considerations. The steel band, locally called pan, is doubtless the best-known and most widely distributed kind of ensemble invented in the New World. Pan were originally made from the thousands of oil drums left behind in Trinidad, first by the British, then during World War II by Americans, who had built a forward base west of Port of Spain for flights to Africa. Like the *tamboo bamboo* instruments, their invention was due to the British ban on drum playing during Carnival. In the 1930s revelers began picking up various discarded metal cans such as "biscuit tins" and beating rhythms on them; these groups became known as "dustbin bands." Creative Trinidadians soon discovered that by pounding (or "sinking") circles into the tops of oil drums abandoned as junk, it was possible to produce multiple pitches on a single surface. Obviously, these instruments were not portable like the dustbin instruments. Over the next few years, however, the makers developed *pan* of various sizes to allow for a full range of pitches and to enable performers to produce full chords. Little did the British or Americans know that their refuse would be recycled into the voice of a nation: in 1992 *pan* became the official national instrument of Trinidad.

In its early years, however, *pan* was not so respectable, for, like the *tamboo bamboo* and dustbin bands, it was associated with the shantytowns in the hills above Port of Spain and with gang violence. As with calypso, the authorities gradually tamed pan by integrating it into the country's social fabric, especially by arranging competitions. The earlier "Pan Is Beautiful" competition has given way to the current "Panorama" competitions. These are held near the end of Carnival, when dozens of bands, both amateur and near professional, compete by playing three currently required numbers: a Western classical composition of their choice, a mandatory test piece specific to that year, and a calypso of their choice.

Most players are amateurs who learn their parts by rote. Important to the process, then, is an arranger who creates the piece (more often than not in notation) and painstakingly teaches it one measure at a time to the ensemble. Many bands can play (from memory) extended and

A "panyard" where steel bands in Trinidad assemble to practice (M.Tyler Rounds)

sophisticated European compositions as long as symphony and concerto movements, and some now play entirely original compositions in a relatively modern style.

Steel bands have spread throughout the Caribbean, and some other islands, such as Antigua, have had them since the late 1940s. The use of a single tenor (melody) pan as part of an unrelated ensemble is now common too, sometimes just to invoke the idea of the "West Indies." Steel bands also flourish wherever West Indians have settled, especially in New York, Toronto, and London. Additionally, in recent years ensembles directed by non-West Indians and featuring non-West Indian players have sprung up in high schools, colleges, and universities throughout the United States. Steel bands are becoming prevalent in Europe as well, especially Sweden and Switzerland, and they have also been seen on the streets of Paris. Japan also has a growing community of pan performers and enthusiasts.

Arrival: Puerto Rico

Although the Caribbean island of Puerto Rico is a Commonwealth territory of the United States, and all Puerto Ricans are automatically American citizens, for non-Hispanic North Americans, this sunny island of 3.5 million people still seems foreign. For starters, the official language is Spanish, though most educated islanders also speak English and people in the large metropolitan area of San Juan, the capital, know enough of the language to communicate with tourists. Though Puerto Rico, as compared with Cuba, received a modest number of African slaves starting in the early sixteenth century, modern scholars are debating the extent of the African contribution to Puerto Rican culture. Arguably, due to sociological, political, and historical factors, the African aspect of the island's culture has been viewed as "hegemonized" by a socially stronger white class until social and political interest towards multiculturalism in the United States brought about a focus on the African roots of American culture. Ethnically, 75 percent of the population considers itself "white." Of the remainder, only 12 percent identify as Afro-Puerto Rican, yet there are African elements in some of the island's most distinctive music genres. Concurrently, Puerto Rican diaspora of Afro-Puerto Rican or black origin tend to identify themselves along cultural–national

Members of Los Pleneros de la 21, a Puerto Rican music group headquartered in New York's Spanish Harlem perform on stage in New York City. (Jack Vartoogian/Front Row Photos)

lines rather than by race. They do not consider themselves "Afro-Puerto Ricans" but "Puerto Ricans", a fact that may be puzzling for African Americans and Americans in general.

The pre-Columbian population was primarily the Taíno, a people who migrated from South America as long ago as 4000 years. Following the arrival of Christopher Columbus on November 19, 1493, the newly arrived Spanish settlers enslaved the Taíno, working them so harshly and transmitting to them European diseases, for which the Taíno had no immunity, that most died. No written record was left of their music, but historians have described a type of ceremonial dance called *areyto* or *areito*, in which the natives accompanied their movements and recitations with idiophones (percussion). By the time the Spanish softened their policies, the Taíno were nearly extinct, and today only 0.5 percent of the population identifies as "Amerindian." Until the early nineteenth century, there were only a modest number of slaves and Spanish settlers, mostly in and around what became the capital, San Juan on the northeastern coast. Puerto Rico came under American control following an invasion in July, 1898, and was ceded by Spain to the United States under the Treaty of Paris (when the United States also gained the Philippines and Guam). Puerto Ricans have been U.S. citizens since 1917, but efforts to attain statehood have not yet met with success. While political parties defending the various status options interpret this situation differently, Puerto Ricans remain fervently attached to their culture and traditions, and have yet to issue a strong mandate for their political future.

Site 5: Puerto Rican *Plena*

First Impressions. A seemingly simple and catchy song repeated with variations. A chorus singing in harmony answers the vocal soloist to create a call and response pattern. A guitar-like sounding instrument provides accompaniment, though its range and unique timbre qualities suggest it is something different. A small collection of percussion instruments accompany the vocalists and lute musician, adding a steady rhythmic flow that makes the music energetic, even in its seeming simplicity.

Aural Analysis. Among the vocal genres of Puerto Rico, the *plena* appears to be among the youngest, but because it absorbed so many elements of Puerto Rico's music and culture in general, it is also quintessentially Puerto Rican. Various scholars have offered differing origins, but all agree the elements that came to define the *plena* coalesced in Ponce, a city in the southwest of the island, considered an artistic and cultural center in the second decade of the twentieth century. The barrio or community from which it emerged (*San Antón*), was racially mixed, but considered mostly black.

"Carmelina" (or "Carmelia") is a light hearted song praising an attractive woman of that name who is said to live in Ponce, many of the stanzas beginning with "Tell me pretty girl, why are you so beautiful?" The singer praises her dancing and encourages her to perform with "traditional" *pleneros.* The chorus mostly repeats lines sung by the soloist, in call and response style. A 10-string guitar, known as *cuatro*, is the only melodic instrument, accompanied by a variety of percussion, including *panderetas* (small frame drums), *güiro* (a scraped gourd), and *barriles* (barrel drums).

The latest scholarly research on the *cuatro* (a Puerto Rican traditional lute-instrument), mentions the same activity included at the end of a famous *cuatro* festival celebrated in the United Sates. (Such displays take an artistic license to ignore the political reality that in Puerto Rico, both the Puerto Rican and the American flags must be displayed together as dictated by a law in 1952.) Plucked lutes are common throughout the world, but seemingly those of the Iberian Peninsula (Spain and Portugal) had a widespread influence not just in the Americas but also in Asia (especially the Philippines) and even in Hawaii on the ukulele. Since most Caribbean islands and much of Latin America were first dominated by Spain and Portugal, not surprisingly, the Spanish-Portuguese guitar and closely related *vihuela*, both being inexpensive and portable, came with the colonialists. Puerto Rico received the *vihuela* in 1512 and the guitar in 1516 according to scholars. Over time, these were modified into distinctive local chordophones throughout the area. Those of Puerto Rico are of three types, the smallest being the *tiple* with five

A player of the Puerto Rican *cuatro,* the island's most important instrument

single strings, the *cuatro*, in various sizes with five double strings and being the most usual one, and the *bordonúa*, also with five double strings. All have fretted necks.

The *cuatro* has become Puerto Rico's national instrument, its shape being more violin-like than Venezuela's *cuatro*, which more resembles a small guitar. The Puerto Rican instrument is 90 centimeters long, including the body, which measures 50 centimeters in width. Traditionally, the *cuatro*'s function is to play an improvisational melody above the foundation provided by the *bordonúa*. Within the context of traditional *jíbaro* music (the Puerto Rican peasant who inhabited the mountainous region of the island and worked the coffee plantations or haciendas), it can also accompany a solo singer. The rhythmic accompaniment of the *cuatro* is usually the *güiro* (a rasp idiophone made of a dried, hollow gourd with parallel notches carved in one side and played with a metal scraper), and a single-headed frame drum without jingles called *requinto de pandereta*. The latter is the highest pitched of two hand drums of the *pandereta* family. The two *panderetas* or *panderos* were originally used in earlier forms of the *plena*.

Cultural Considerations. *Plenas* are topical songs whose subjects can include everything one encounters in life, especially working people: current events, historical memories, philosophy, religion, crime, protest, and gradually across time, issues of cultural and national identity. Thus, some refer to *plena* as "sung newspapers." During the 1950s, the *plena* was arranged for popular music orchestra by local musicians and became a "popular" dance performed by the best pop music orchestras on the island. Known composers wrote the lyrics and music for new *plenas* that, together with the traditional *plena* repertoire, became standard dances in even the most exclusive social clubs. As such, the *plena* is only loosely described by some as "folkloric." In fact, modern scholars tend not to use the term in reference to this Puerto Rican song-dance form.

Within Puerto Rico's unique political status, the *plena*'s lyrics have also become a voice for the reaffirmation of cultural identity for islanders as well as the diaspora. The translation of a well-known modern *plena* states, "He who lives far away and claims to be a *Borinqueño* (derived from the island's indigenous name *Borikén*), must be willing to verify it by dancing well a *plena*." In the traditional "Que Bonita Bandera," the lyrics describe the beauty of the Puerto Rican flag. This *plena* is frequently choreographed as a stage dance that includes the final display by the dancers of an enormous Puerto Rican flag that occupies the whole stage, always to an exuberant audience.

According to scholars, Puerto Rico's traditional music favors singing and dancing over instrumental music. However, music for *cuatro,* considered Puerto Rico's national instrument, has been highly developed by both traditional and modern day "*cuatristas.*" Since the European-derived population vastly outnumbered those of African origin, Puerto Rico did not develop the variety of African religions, singing, and drumming found elsewhere, especially Cuba, Haiti, and Jamaica. Nonetheless, the *bomba* circle dance, accompanied by drums, reflects Africa, even when performed in conjunction with Christian festivals. Because this dance is only performed by specialists, it has not become "popular" among the general population of Puerto Ricans like the *plena* has. Other genres reflect greater European influence, especially numerous song types (e.g., *décimas, seis,* and *aguinaldo*) accompanied by an ensemble that may include *cuatro,* accordion, guitar, drums, and *güiro* (a scraped gourd of African origin). This is collectively known as *música jíbara* and constitutes most of what is considered "folk music" in Puerto Rico.

Because Puerto Rico is Roman Catholic, and Roman Catholicism allows for colorful public festivals that include dancing and music, much of the island's "folkloric" music is also associated with such celebrations. Some of the practices seen in these events reflect retentions from age-old practices brought from Spain, such as the singing of *aguinaldos,* performed at Christmas during early morning masses, and traditionally, by groups of children wandering through the streets. The *aguinaldo* also constitutes part of the main repertoire of the *trovadores,* the specialized singers of *jíbaro* music during Christmas time. The typical *parranda,* which consists of a group of friends (adults and children) singing with or without instrumental accompaniment, goes from house to house during the Christmas season singing *aguinaldos, plenas,* and *villancicos*, the latter being another form of Christmas religious music of Spanish origin. Puerto Rico also has music that is both reflective of Puerto Rican traditions but influenced by European classical music, especially the *danza*, dance-based music that could both accompany actual dance or be performed as concert music. In addition Puerto Rican composers produced light operas based on Spanish models.

Great numbers of Puerto Ricans migrated to New York City during the twentieth century, taking much of their music with them. Most song genres, including *plena* and particularly *cuatro* music, were performed in New York where facilities and opportunities to record were available. Puerto Rican musicians worked side by side with Cuban and other Caribbean musicians creating and developing popular forms that, although Cuban in origin, became the pop music idioms of most of what we know as "Latin America." In 1957 the Broadway Oscar winning musical *West Side Story*, a collaboration of Leonard Bernstein (music), Stephen Sondheim (lyrics), and Jerome Robbins (dance) inspired by Shakespeare's *Romeo and Juliet*, portrayed ethnic conflict between a Puerto Rican gang, the Sharks, against a white American gang, the Jets, and the frustrated love story between Tony, who is American, with Maria, who is Puerto Rican. *West Side Story* represents Bernstein's intention of fusing the Broadway musical with features from the classical opera. Rather than music idioms from Puerto Rican folk or traditional music, he used musical techniques present in opera and stylized versions of rhythms found in Hispanic America.

LISTENING GUIDE 11.5 (3'38")

Site 11.5
Puerto Rico: *Plena*

Voices: Male vocal lead with mixed chorus. Instruments: *cuatro* (plucked chordophone), *panderetas* (frame drums), *güiro* (scraped idiophone), *barriles* (barrel drum)

TIME	LISTENING FOCUS
0'00"	*Cuatro* enters with improvisatory introduction in free rhythm. Note that the instrument plays a single melodic line, rather than harmonic chords.
0'13"	Listen for the "Carmelina" motive and subsequent variation.
0'23"	Introduction ends, followed by a brief pause.
0'26"	*Cuatro* plays the main melody in rhythm, following a duple meter of four pulses to each phrase. The *güiro* and *panderetas* provide rhythmic accompaniment.
0'33"	Lead vocalist enters with the "Carmelina" melody.
0'40"	"Response" choir enters, along with the *barriles*.
0'48"	Lead vocalist returns with lyric variation.
0'56"	Group response.
1'03"	Lead vocal returns.
1'10"	Group response. Notice that the *cuatro* plays less rhythmically dense throughout the vocal sections, providing an unobtrusive harmonic accompaniment through short melodic lines and occasional chords.
1'17"	Lead vocal returns.
1'24"	Group response.
1'32"	*Cuatro* solo begins. Vocalist (presumably lead) spontaneously speaks during the solo.
1'44"	Note the brief chords heard in the *cuatro* solo.
1'53"	Listen for the harmonic shift to a minor key.
2'07"	The *cuatro* returns to the main melody, signaling that the extended solo has ended.

2'14"	The choir initiates the vocal section with the familiar "Carmelina" refrain. Note the percussion shifts to syncopated "punches" for rhythmic accompaniment.
2'21"	Lead vocal returns. Note the percussion returns to its original rhythmic pattern.
2'28"	Group vocal response.
2'35"	Lead vocal call. Listen for the lyric reference to "Bomba la Plena."
2'42"	Group response. Listen for this "Call and Response" form through the remainder of the performance.
3'32"	Note the group response is performed a second time to conclude the performance (3'38").

Source: "Carmelina," *plena tradicional*, performed by Los Pleneros de la 21, 2005, from the recording entitled *Los Pleneros de la 21: Para Todos Ustedes*, SFW 40519, provided courtesy of Smithsonian Folkways Recordings. © 2005. Used by permission.

MUSICAL MARKERS: Timbre/Medium—Scraped idiophone with hand-struck drums (barriles). Lead chordophone (cuatro) has a bright timbre. Lead vocal and group response. **Rhythm**—Heavy syncopation with steady "scraping" rhythm. **Melody**—Short memorable tune and repeated choral refrain. **Phonic Structure**—Call and response vocals. Chordophone plays supporting harmony during vocal sections; improvises solos at opening and during breaks.
ETHNO-CHALLENGE: Try performing along with the percussion instruments, or join the choir in their group vocal response.

Arrival: Cuba

Only some 90 miles from Florida, Cuba has been a difficult destination for Americans since 1961, but with the resumption of normal relations in 2015, Americans can now join those who have been coming from Europe and elsewhere for years. Before the revolution in 1959, when Fidel Castro swept away the American-backed dictatorship of Fulgencio Batista, Cuba was a playground for rich North Americans wishing to dodge the restrictions on alcohol consumption imposed during Prohibition. Havana, wide open to liquor, prostitution, and gambling, was one of the most enticing cities in the Western hemisphere, with its grand hotels, homes, and casinos. One of Cuba's great attractions today is its "time capsule" atmosphere: colonial architecture, classic American cars, and an abundance of old-time Cuban music, the latter made famous by a 1990s recording and movie titled *The Buena Vista Social Club* featuring surviving musicians from an actual members-only club in Havana whose heyday was the 1940s.

An island slightly larger than Indiana or Greece with a population of eleven million, Cuba was first "discovered" by Christopher Columbus in late 1492 but largely ignored by the Spaniards, who found Hispaniola to the east more rewarding. At that time Cuba's inhabitants were the native Tainos and Arawak, but after the beginning of colonialization in 1511, when the Spaniards forced the native people to work the gold mines, rebellions, disease, and starvation reduced that population to only 5,000 survivors by 1550. The first African slaves arrived in 1522 to work the new sugar plantations, and while treatment was harsh, the Spanish permitted the slaves to maintain tribal groups and therefore a semblance of their original culture. In addition to sugar, the Spaniards began cultivating tobacco and raising cattle, but with little supervision, Cuba (and the Caribbean generally) succumbed to the chaos brought about by pirates, especially the British. Friction between Spain and the United States over Cuba led finally to the Spanish-American War of 1898, triggered by the explosion of the U.S. battleship *Maine* in Havana harbor early that year and made famous by Teddy Roosevelt's charge up San Juan Hill with his Rough Riders. Following direct American control until 1902, Cuba achieved independence but remained under heavy American influence. A series of harsh and corrupt regimes, culminating in that of Batista, led to the Cuban Revolution in 1959, instigated by Fidel Castro and the now iconic Che Guevara, followed by the ill-fated "Bay of Pigs Invasion" of 1961 and the Cuban Missile Crisis of 1962. Relations between the United States and Cuba, long severed, have now been restored under Fidel's brother, Raul Castro. Whatever else we might say about its government, post-1959 Cuba has shown generous support for the traditional arts, particularly music, and now travelers to Cuba can enjoy performances by vintage musicians of the highest professional level.

What makes Cuba's music distinctive is its successful blending of European and African musical traditions. This mixing can be heard in a range of styles, from the mostly African **Santeria**, a syncretistic religion combining traditional African/Yoruba practices with Roman Catholicism, to genres such as *son* and *guaracha*, which mix African rhythms with European melodies and harmony, to mostly European genres such as *danzón*. It was the middle ground combining Europe and Africa that gave rise to what came to be called the "Latin styles," a plethora of types and artists which spread widely from their original Cuban roots. This led to a musical "rage" for Latin-styled music, a trend that continues today, and was particularly reinforced by the rising popularity of "Latin" ballroom dance.

Site 6: Cuban *Son*

First Impressions. Easygoing from the outset, this danceable piece of music starts with a guitar or related instrument, quickly joined by others including a trumpet and a variety of percussion instruments, including a prominent one with a sharp clap, another with a gentle scraping sound, and also some hollow-sounding drums. At first a group of men sing, but later a solo voice alternates with the group. Is it any wonder that Cuba attracts visitors, not just for its relaxed way of life and friendly people, but its music?

Aural Analysis. Field recorded around 1980 in Santiago, Cuba, in Oriente province where *son* was first created at the end of the nineteenth century, the group's instrumentation is much expanded from the original *son* groups, which consisted of just three instruments: *tres*, a

SANTERIA
An African-derived animistic belief system found primarily in Cuba and the United States.

GUARACHA
(pronounced *gwah-rah-cha*)
A Latin American ballroom dance, as well as a song type emphasizing call-and-response vocal organization.

Havana, Cuba, street musicians play music for tips from the many non-American tourists visiting Cuba each year. (Left to right) *claves*, *tres cubano*, guitar, (front) *bongos*, (right) *marimbala* (bass lamellophone) (Shutterstock)

Two street musicians in Trinidad, Cuba, declared a World Heritage Site in 1988. Claves (left), *maracas* (right) (Shutterstock)

Rumba clave, the patterns used for son as played by the *claves* (a pair of wooden sticks)

		1	-	2	-	3	-	4	-	5	-	6	-	7	-	8	-
Rumba Clave (3+2)		X "1"	-	-	X "2"	-	-	-	X "3"	-	-	X "1"	-	X "2"	-	-	-
"Reverse" (2+3)		-	-	X "1"	-	X "2"	-	-	-	X "1"	-	-	X "2"	-	-	-	X "3"

CLAVES
An instrument consisting of two sticks beaten together.

guitar-like instrument with three courses of two strings each, ***claves***, a pair of hardwood sticks struck together, and *maracas*, a pair of small gourds whose seeds create a "sheh-sheh" sound when shaken. After migrating to Havana early in the new century, *son* groups began adding more instruments, some African derived, such as the *marimbula* or *botija*, a wooden box with large metal lamellae plucked to provide bass pitches, and *bongos*, a pair of small single-headed drums, along with European derived ones, such as *timbales*, metal-framed drums of the military snare family, and trumpets or cornets. Additional instruments were gradually added, including the *güiro*, a gourd with ridges cut into the side which are scraped, the guitar itself, African-derived

A *güiro*, originally a scraped gourd—now often of wood—common throughout the Caribbean, including Cuba (Shutterstock)

conga drums, and later, as *son* was transformed into an urban, big band form, piano and other jazz instruments as well.

The *son*, occupying a point that balanced African and European musical traits, became the progenitor of most music now labeled "Latin." The typical form, heard here, consists of an introduction sung in chorus by the players, followed by a section called the *montuno*, where a soloist alternates with the group. Following this, the instrumentalists begin a free interplay that probably reflects more of a jazz influence than the traditions of Oriente province. Many scholars consider the *montuno* section to be the feature that was most influential on the many *son*-derived styles.

Titled "Soneros Son" and recorded by the song's creator, Pedro Fernandez of the group Estudiantina Invasora in Santiago de Cuba in 1978–1979 by ethnomusicologist Verna Gillis, the lyrics constitute an expression of pride by the author that "his songs" are known worldwide:

Eso es mi Son, bailalo bién
Es todo Cubano, gózalo mi hermano
Ha paseado el mundo, mi Son Cubano

This is my Son, dance it well
It is purely Cuban, enjoy it my brother
My Cuban Son has traveled around the world
This is my Cuban Son

Although non-Latin musicians hear this song in duple or 2/4 meter, Cuban/Latin musicians hear it in "son clave." The *claves*, a pair of hardwood sticks creating the sharp rap so prominent in the recording, are actually articulating a cyclic pattern of five clicks, this being the typical "clave" for *son*. Almost certainly derived from an African iron bell pattern, the *son clave* emphasizes the subordinate beats more than the main ones. Using both your ear and the clave rhythms chart (see above) as a guide, count "one and two and three and four" while clapping at the correct points.

LISTENING GUIDE

11.6 (4'42")

Site 11.6
Cuba: *Son*

Vocals: Three male vocalists (lead and two background)
Instruments: *tres* guitar, guitar, acoustic bass, maracas, claves, trumpet, timbales, cow bell

TIME	LISTENING FOCUS
0'00"	*Tres* guitar begins the performance.
0'06"	Timbales roll signals entrance of other instruments. Trumpet plays the main theme.
0'30"	Vocalists enter with polyphonic singing on the main theme. Note the reverse clave (also known as *son clave*) rhythm of the claves.
0'49"	Brief timbales fill.
0'52"	Trumpet returns.
1'15"	Voices return with repeat of lyrics.
1'33"	*Montuno* section begins. Note the "Eso es mi son cubano" repeated refrain. Listen for the improvisatory style of the trumpet.
1'36"	Note the appearance of cow bell with a complementary rhythm to the reverse clave pattern.
1'55"	Lead vocal sings in improvisatory style between the vocal duet's repeated refrain.
2'28"	Voices and cow bell drop out as the *tres* guitar takes lead melodic role in improvisatory style.
3'42"	*Tres* guitar plays repeated pattern to signal transition to trumpet melodic lead at 3'58".
4'00"	Voices return on *montuno* refrain. Trumpet plays lead improvisatory melody.
4'21"	Lead vocal returns to improvisatory style.
4'32"	Closing phrase.

Source: "Soneros Son" by Estudiantina Invasora from the recording entitled *Music of Cuba*. Recorded by Verna Gillis in Cuba 1978–1979, Folkways Records FW 04064, © 1985. Used by permission.

MUSICAL MARKERS: Timbre/Medium—Timbales (high-pitched drum pair) and Clave ("click," wood sticks) with additional percussion. Reverberant guitar and "brass" trumpet. Pair of vocalists in harmony. **Rhythm**—2+3 "Reverse" clave rhythmic pattern common. Timbales add syncopation and accented rhythm. **Form**—Begins with varied lyrical content and shifts to "montuno" section with repeated melodic refrain and improvised solos. **Other**—Cultural references common in lyrics (Spanish language), e.g., "Cubano."
ETHNO-CHALLENGE: Clap the reverse clave rhythm throughout the performance. Perform some vocal or instrumental improvisation during the *montuno* section, or sing along with the vocal refrain.

Cultural Considerations. The development of Cuban music is inextricably tied to dance, and while the various forms of Latin jazz, pop, and rock can stand on their own simply as music, their success is continuously reinforced by the prevalence of ballroom dance generally as well as programs such as *The Ohio Star Ball* and *Dancing with the Stars*. Modern ballroom dancers would rarely encounter old, genuine Cuban music like this track, but none would have difficulty in dancing the *rumba* (sometimes spelled rhumba) to it. Of all the Cuban-derived dances—including *bolero*, *cha cha chá*, and *mambo*—rumba is the most basic and easiest. But the terminology is confusing in that *rumba* (meaning "party") originally denoted a secular form of local dance music played primarily by African-derived percussion with singing. The misnamed "rumba craze" of the 1930s was set off by the popularity of a song called "The Peanut Vendor" (*El Manisero*) created from street vendors' cries by Moises Simons and first recorded by Rita Montaner for Columbia in 1927. Mislabeled "rumba" (actually it was a *son*), "The Peanut Vendor" led to innumerable imitations, some faster, some slower, all called "*rumba*." *Rumba* dance, however, only made use of the slower *bolero-son*.

The ballroom steps were only created later by Pierre Zurcher-Margolle and his partner, Doris Lavelle, then living in London, Zurcher-Margolle having observed local dancing in Havana during trips in 1947, 1951, and 1953. The basic "international" step pattern "breaks" (begins) on beat 2, as - 2 3 4 hold 2 3 4 hold, etc., whereas the American rumba patterns break on 1 (1 2 3 hold or 1 hold 3 4) in a box pattern.

While the *son*, with its *montuno* section, was the foundation for developments that led ultimately to *salsa* music (see Chapter 13, Site 9, *salsa*), two other types of music also associated with ballroom dances—the *cha cha chá* and *mambo*—must be considered. These arise from the European-derived *danzón*, a genre popular among Euro-Cubans that gave rise to numerous musical offspring. Derived from old French *contredanse*, both the dance and its music reflected European harmonic and melodic traditions almost exclusively, but over time Cuban musicians increasingly made it their own, especially by infusing African-derived rhythms.

First, the *mambo*. In 1938 Cuban musicians Orestes and Cachao López created a *danzón* song titled "Mambo," which gave rise to many imitations, all termed informally "*danzón-mambo.*" Cuban dancer Perez Prado became closely associated with this type of music in 1943, and after moving his group from Havana's La Tropicana to Mexico City in 1948, he and his musicians began recording many new "mambo" songs, and Prado evolved a dance style that came to be identified as "mambo." After success in Mexico, Prado and his followers brought the style to the United States where, during the 1950s, a "mambo craze" blossomed, centered at the Palladium Ballroom (the "Temple of Mambo") in New York City but also prominent in Los Angeles among Mexican Americans. American dance teachers, however, found Prado's choreography too difficult for social dancing and evolved named step patterns within reach of amateur dancers. Even so, mambo dancing was challenging, requiring dancers to break on beat 2 and also emphasize beat 4 in a complex syncopated pattern. The music for mambo had by then also absorbed characteristics of *son*.

Cuban *rhumba* (or *rumba*) dancer Zulema performs with a band at the Zombie Club in pre-revolutionary Havana, Cuba, in 1946 (Hulton Archive/Getty Images)

Second, the *cha cha chá*. Zurcher-Margolle, who also created the *rumba*, observed during his 1952 visit a variant of mambo music that subdivided the fourth beat, and dancers moved their feet close to the floor, creating what was heard as a "cha cha cha" sound. Cuban composer Enrique Jorrin came to be closely identified with this type of music. Zurcher-Margolle and partner Lavelle then created named step patterns for a new ballroom dance that was easier than mambo, because it was danced as 2 3 4 and 1 (with the "cha cha cha" on beats 4 and 1), though American teachers came to view it as beginning on beat 1 (the "prep step" for international dancers). Quickly the new *cha cha chá* caught on and, like *mambo* and *rumba*, was adopted into the fixed curricula of ballroom dance studios. What happened after that awaits the discussion for Chapter 13, Site 9, *salsa*.

Dance: Caribbean—Trinidad, Haiti, Latin America

by Janine Tiffe

There are many varying dance traditions throughout the Caribbean. With a history of diverse populations, Trinidad embraces forms of West African, Indian, Chinese, Amerindian, and Syrian dance as its own. Indeed in each case, the style has undergone a moderate change to reflect its new homeland and diverse population. Still, there are a few dance styles that appear to be unique to Trinidad. The limbo dates back to the mid- to late-1800s and may derive its name from either the term "limber," referring to much needed flexibility to perform the dance, or "limbo," referring to an intermediate or unresolved state. In fact, the dance may allude to moving from life into the afterlife, or symbolize the victory of life over death. Performing the limbo consists of walking underneath a vertical bar while keeping one's back facing the floor. After each pass under the bar, it is continually lowered until no one can pass beneath it without falling. The limbo gained a global popularity in the mid-twentieth century.

Other forms of popular dance commonly seen during Trinidadian carnival season include chipping and wining. Chipping is a simple type of foot shuffling motion that is performed to the beat of the music; it is a way to slowly parade during carnival or travel while dancing. The term chipping is an onomatopoeia referencing the scuffling sound that occurs as the bottom of your shoe scrapes the surface of the pavement. Wining, or winding your waist, refers to numerous variants of sensual hip and pelvic girdle gyrations that often involve a partner.

Dance and movements that accompany Haitian *Vodou* are intended to make a connection between the living and the spirit world. While the term *Vodou* often receives an undue negative connotation in the United States, these music and dance traditions stem from religious practices from West Africa and are related to other syncretic religious practices in the

Revelers dance and celebrate during Carnival in Trinidad

western hemisphere including Candomblé in Brazil, Santería in Cuba, Shango in Trinidad, and Lucumí in the United States. Dances are determined by which *lwa*, or spirit, one is attempting to entice; moreover, dances are organized according to *nanchons*, or nations that correspond with the concepts they represent. For example, the dances *Nago* and *Mayi* are dances typically performed together and relate to power, warriors, and leaders and are associated with iron, steel, fire, and black-smiths. By using Ogun's, the Yoruba god, machete, dancers embody him and defeat their enemies. *Mayi*'s dance features displays of tactical maneuvers, strength, and military imagery. By contrast, *Gède* is a *nanchon* of *Iwas* that represent eroti-cism and death. In other words, they control the complete life cycle. Movements are often sexually suggestive and center on the hips and pelvic girdle. Dancers embodying *Gède* typi-cally make use of the colors black, white, and purple, and may also utilize imagery that relates to cemeteries.

Salsa, *merengue*, and *bachata* are three popular partner danc-es, each with roots in Latin American locales. During an even-ing at a night club, dancers are able to decipher which move-ments to execute based on tempi, fundamental rhythms (e.g., *son clave*, or a syncopated verses a straight bass line), and instrumentation. For example, the *merengue* and *bachata* are both from the Dominican Republic but have very different sen-sibilities. The merengue tends to be a bit faster, have a greater sense of urgency, and emphasize the regular "1, 2, 1, 2" feel in the bass line. That even pulse corresponds to the consistent

and alternating *merengue* foot pattern, which is almost like an in-place march with a highly emphasized, side-to-side hip mo-tion that stems from a noticeable weight shift when moving from foot to foot. By contrast, *bachata* is somewhat slower in tempo, smoother in feel, and has a four-count beat. This dance is performed by moving sideways with your partner for the first three counts, and is punctuated on beat four by popping one's hip in the direction from which she or he just traveled.

Salsa is a dance that arose from a conglomeration of styles when individuals from countries including Cuba and Puerto Rico immigrated to New York City and other locations in the United States, merging their traditional dances and music styles. Dances including the *cha-cha-chá*, *mambo*, *rumba*, and *son-montuno* from Cuba, and the *bomba* and *plena* from Puerto Rico combined to become *salsa*. While *salsa* dancing may include a vast array of complicated steps and flourishes, the basic step can be thought of as an even, eight-count cycle and can be accomplished in the following manner: step back, front, together, pause, front, back, together, pause. A shifting of weight in the hips makes dancers look fluid rather than rigid.

Arrival: The Dominican Republic

The island of Hispaniola is divided into two countries: French-speaking Haiti in the west and the Spanish-speaking Dominican Republic in the east. Whereas an African-descended populace dominates Haiti, the Dominican Republic's population is largely a mix of Spanish and African heritages. While African cultural influence is strong throughout the Dominican Republic, Do-minicans prefer to emphasize their European roots and associate themselves with Hispanic cul-ture, largely due to the cultural policies promoted by the former dictator Rafael Leonidas Trujillo Molina (r. 1930–1961). These policies instilled a fear of anything Haitian, especially anything associated with the widespread practice of *Vodou*. Trujillo's influence is still felt today, though many youth are embracing their African roots.

Site 7: *Merengue*

First Impressions. **Merengue** is fast-paced. The "scraping" sound of the **güira** (a metal version of the guiro) is the primary timekeeper and perhaps the genre's most distinctive feature. The ac-companying drum (called a *tambora*) plays in "bursts," with a thudding fundamental sound and interlacing slaps. The repetitive melodic line moves at a frenetic pace, pausing only when the voices enter. As with much Caribbean music, *merengue* is highly danceable.

Aural Analysis. The identifying feature of *merengue* is the pairing of the *güira* and *tambora*. The *güira* is a rasp idiophone, typically a bulbous gourd with rings cut into the surface. The "scraping" sound is produced when a piece of wood or metal is rubbed along the coarse outside face of the instrument. The *güira* provides the fundamental tempo and typically emphasizes the offbeats with a long "scrape." The *tambora* is a small barrel drum made with two thick

MERENGUE
A Latin American/ Caribbean dance and music genre, originally from the Dominican Republic.

GÜIRA
(pronounced gwee-rah) A scraped metal idiophone commonly used in *merengue*. (Note: a *güiro* is a similar scraped idiophone made of gourd.)

Dancing to *merengue music* by a *merengue tipico moderno* group led by accordionist Adolfo Diaz (Paul Austerlitz)

leather faces and is held in the lap. Deep tones are produced by playing one face with a stick, while striking the other face with the hand creates slapping sounds. The "bursts" typical of the instrument are played with the stick and are followed by hand-slap punctuation. In rural performances, the *güira* and *tambora* not only provide the fundamental rhythm but are also frequently featured in improvisatory passages. Ballroom dance *merengue* styles do not generally include such vibrant improvisation on these instruments, however.

The melodic content in our recorded example is provided by a button-box accordion, as well as by the voices. The melody is rhythmically dense and contributes to the fast-paced feel of the music. The voices follow a call-and-response format, which is imitated by the accordion at the conclusion of its solo sections. The quickly repeated tone imitates the call, while the subsequent harmonic chords correspond to the group's response. Other styles of *merengue* may use guitars or saxophones as the primary melodic instruments.

Merengue songs are typically divided into three sections: *paseo*, *merengue*, and *jaleo*. These equate to an introduction, verse, and chorus. The *paseo*, or "walking" section, emphasizes the melodic instruments and often begins at a slower tempo, sometimes in free rhythm. This quickly leads to the *merengue* section, which is established by the *güira-tambora* rhythms. Vocalists sing different verses in this section followed by a refrain, the *jaleo*, which is repeated throughout the piece. The accordion (or saxophone) improvises its own *merengue* section and follows with a *jaleo* refrain before the voices return. This alternation between *merengue* and *jaleo*, which may be performed either by vocalists or instrumentalists, can continue indefinitely. The concluding *jaleo* often quickens in tempo as a sign that the performance is about to finish.

Cultural Considerations. While there are several styles of *merengue*, they are all generally categorized as either "folk" or "ballroom." A large orchestra, often backing a crooning vocalist, and

A group of *merengue* musicians: (left to right) accordion, *marimba* (bass lamellophone, sometimes called rumba box), *tambora*, and *güira* (scraped metal tube) (Paul Austerlitz)

Francisco Ulloa, one of *merengue's* most innovative and prominent accordionists

LISTENING GUIDE
11.7 (2'03")

Site 11.7

Dominican Republic: *Merengue*

Voices: Single male lead with supporting male ensemble
Instruments: Button-box accordion, *tambora* (barrel drum), *güira* (scraped metal idiophone)

TIME	LISTENING FOCUS
0'00"	The button-box accordion begins the performance.
0'02"	The *güira* enters, followed by the *tambora*. Listen for the contrasting timbres of the drum as one side is played with a stick (lower tone) and the other with the hand (higher "slap" sound).
0'12"	Listen for the *güira* briefly matching the rhythmic density of the button-box.
0'29"	Vocalist enters.
0'34"	Vocal ensemble responds. Listen for the transition to a quick call-and-response between the lead vocalist and vocal group. Note that the button-box is quieter and only sounds along with the group response.
0'47"	The button-box returns as the aural focus as the voices drop out. Listen for variations in the rhythmic pattern of the *tambora*.

0'58"	Listen for variations in the rhythmic pattern of the *güira*.
1'15"	Lead vocalist returns, followed by quick call-and-response section at 1'21".
1'29"	Listen for the button-box solo without the use of harmony.
1'38"	Listen for variations in the rhythmic pattern of the *güira*.
1'46"	Listen for the subtle return of harmony in the button-box part.
1'49"	Listen for the extended "scraping" of the *güira*.
1'57"	Example fades.

Source: "Apágame la Vela (Put Out my Candle)" performed by Nicolá Gutierres, Porfirio Rosario and Santo Pea, recorded by Verna Gillis with Ramon Daniel Perez Martinez, 1976, from the recording entitled *Raíces Latinas: Smithsonian Folkways Latino Roots Collection*, SF 40470, provided courtesy of Smithsonian Folkways Recordings. © 2002. Used by permission.

MUSICAL MARKERS: Timbre/Medium—Bright button-box accordion, scraped idiophone, two-tone "thuddy" drum (tambora), group vocals. **Form**—Call and response vocals with button-box responding as well. **Melody**—Short repetitive melody. **Rhythm**—Quick walking tempo.
ETHNO-CHALLENGE: Construct a scraper to imitate the sound of the *güira* and perform along with the example.

a consistent *güira-tambora* rhythm, characterizes ballroom *merengue*. The ballroom form still follows the *paseo-merengue-jaleo* pattern but has less improvisational freedom. Ballroom *merengue* was strongly promoted during the Trujillo years as a "national" dance in order to help establish a unique Dominican identity. Today, long after the end of Trujillo's rule, *merengue* remains the most popular music in the country.

As with many Caribbean music genres, *merengue* also refers to a dance. Outside the Dominican Republic *merengue* dance experienced a short-lived "craze" during the 1990s but remains one of the highly codified dances of the American ballroom curriculum, though not commonly played at dance events. The dance is a simple side-step in which the leg that follows drags on the ground. The modern form of the dance requires exaggerated hip movement from side to side, generally called "Latin (or Cuban) motion" by dancers. It is often danced in pairs, with the dancers' upper bodies poised in a standard ballroom dance position with one hand on the hip and the other held out at shoulder height. The dancers move to the left in a circle around the floor but may rotate in a single spot, which allows for numerous couples in a small space.

The origin of *merengue* and its associated dance is not entirely agreed upon, but many believe that the dance is a combination of West African circle dances and European salon dances. The side-step shuffle seems to evoke a time when slaves' feet were chained together while working in the sugarcane fields. The upper body movements mimic the dance positions of a French minuet. One of the step patterns in ballroom *merengue* is called the *ibo*, a term that, interestingly, refers to the Igbo ethnic group of West Africa. The music is also a blend of African and European elements. The *tambora* is believed to derive from similar West African instruments. The *güira* is thought by some to be a Dominican creation, while others consider it an innovation based on scraped gourd idiophones found in West Africa. The call-and-response vocal organization is reminiscent of West African vocal performance. On the other hand, the inclusion of the button-box accordion and the use of the guitar and saxophones as primary melodic instruments reveal musical connections with Europe.

Questions to Consider

1. Where do "African survivals" appear in music of the Caribbean? What makes them African?

2. How did differences in colonial rule affect the course of musical development in the Caribbean?

3. What role does music play in spirit possession in religions such as *Vodou* and *Santeria*?

4. Which Caribbean musics best exemplify the idea that music can express discontent and challenge authority? How are the examples chosen different in content and attitude?

5. How can you account for the fact that the most prominent music types in the Caribbean are popular in nature?

6. How has modern ballroom dance been influenced by music of the Caribbean? What ballroom dances derive from "Latin" music?

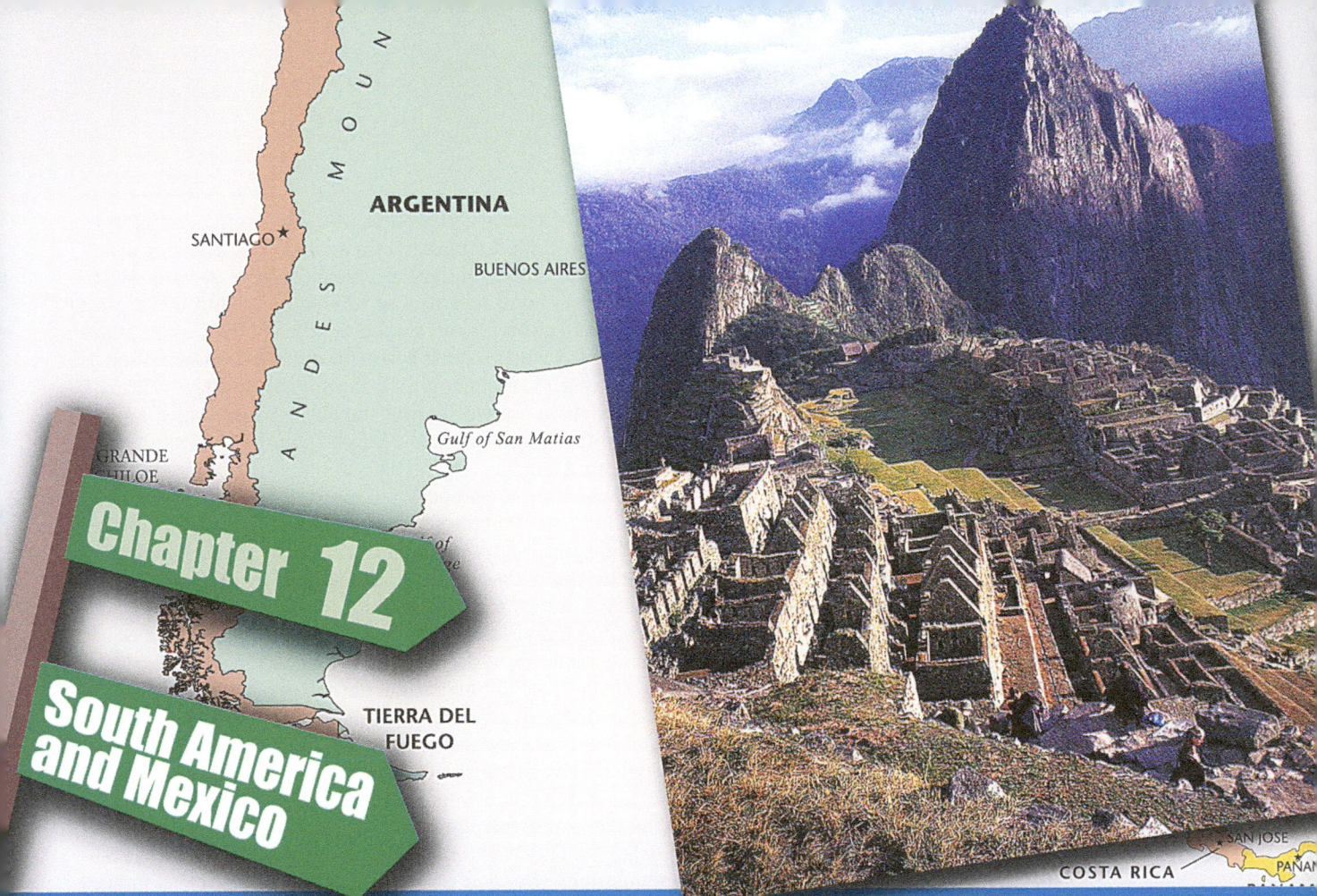

Chapter 12

South America and Mexico

The Amazon Rainforest, Peru, Argentina, Brazil, Mexico

Established by the ancient Incas in Peru at least by the thirteenth century, Machu Picchu, a ruined city at 9,000 feet/2740 meters in the Andes Mountains, was forgotten following the Spanish conquest in the early sixteenth century and only rediscovered in 1911 (M. Tyler Rounds)

Background Preparation

In the Western hemisphere, Central and South America, as well as Mexico, are frequently overshadowed by the global attention given to the United States. While tourism is increasing steadily, most travelers choose the United States or islands of the Caribbean for their vacation destinations. Many areas south of the U.S. border are still regarded as "developing," but many great cities in these areas are quite cosmopolitan and as highly developed as cities in the United States and Europe. The region also boasts some of the world's most beautiful natural wonders, such as the Amazon—the largest river in the world—and its surrounding rainforests (mostly in Brazil); Angel Falls (Venezuela), the highest waterfall in the world; and the Andes Mountains, second only to the Himalayas in peak height and the longest system of high mountains in the world, running all along the western coast of South America.

While the generally accepted theory is that the indigenous populations of the Americas crossed from Asia, recent archaeological evidence indicates that there were people living in modern Brazil some 30,000 to 50,000 years ago and in Chile and Venezuela roughly 13,000 years ago. Though little can be said for certain regarding the activities of these earliest inhabitants, the ancient empires of the Western hemisphere, namely the Maya, Aztec, and Inca empires, are better known and continue to influence the cultural identity of the present populations of Mexico, Central, and South America. Remnants of these ancient civilizations are visited by thousands of tourists every year, and archaeologists work tirelessly to uncover clues to the cultural activities of these early indigenous peoples. Evidence of advanced knowledge in astronomy, mathematics, and agriculture, as well as of highly structured political and religious systems, dates to as early as 200 B.C.E. and suggests that at their peak each empire may have rivaled those of ancient China or Rome.

Spanish conquerors, however, put an end to the development of these civilizations soon after Christopher Columbus arrived in the Western hemisphere in 1492 C.E. Coupled with the military conquests of the Spanish conquistadors, Old World diseases—such as smallpox and measles—decimated many indigenous populations who had no biological resistance to the foreign diseases. Throughout the region, Roman Catholic missionaries found fertile ground in which to establish new churches. By the end of the eighteenth century, the Spaniards had settled in far-reaching areas of North, Central, and South America that have since grown into some of today's largest cities, such as San Francisco, Los Angeles, Mexico City, Lima, and Buenos Aires.

In addition to subjugating native peoples, Spanish and Portuguese colonialists also brought many African slaves to the Americas to work in gold and silver mines, to raise cattle, and to farm

Perhaps Mexico's most famous Mayan ruin, the pyramid at Chichen Itza was begun about 900 c.e. and testifies to the advanced technological development of this early civilization (Andrew Shahriari)

In Cusco, Peru, the Iglesia de la Compania de Jesus in the Plaza de Armas was built in the late 1570s and rebuilt later after an earthquake. Its large plaza is where festivals including music and dance occur frequently (Max T. Miller)

plantations growing crops such as tobacco and sugarcane. Other European colonialists followed suit, and brought with them laborers from other colonized countries such as India and Indonesia, while the French transferred many prisoners to the region. Because of this, many areas of South America today, Guyana, Suriname, and French Guiana in particular, reveal strong cultural connections with non-European peoples. Eastern coastal areas, especially in Brazil, are densely populated with peoples of mixed African and Iberian ancestry, while Central America and much of the interior of South America comprise mainly indigenous populations, many of whom also have Spanish ancestry (those of mixed ancestry are known as *mestizos*). The rainforests of Brazil remained largely immune to the influx of foreigners until the late nineteenth and early twentieth centuries. Rapid deforestation in the 1980s led to increased interest in the protection of wildlife and the preservation of the traditional lifeways of the many indigenous Amazonian tribes.

The musical activities of the diverse peoples of Central and South America reflect these historical interactions. Indigenous populations in the rainforests and in rural areas of the Andes preserve musical traditions believed to predate the arrival of Columbus. Music found in urban areas reveals influences from Europe, specifically Spain and Portugal, as well as West Africa.

Planning the Itinerary

The music of Central and South America, and of Mexico (geographically part of North America), comprises three major ingredients: Indigenous traditions, European-derived music, and African-inspired musical activity. The music of the Amazonian tribes and Andean rural communities dates to pre-Columbian times and has presumably remained little changed for centuries. Spanish influence is felt in numerous music traditions, especially those found in urban areas. African influence can be seen in the survival of African secular and religious practices, the creation of new instruments modeled after African ones, and in the use of musical traits, such as polyrhythm, commonly associated with various ethnic groups from Africa.

Our introduction to the music of this region begins with a discussion of the Kayapó-Xikrin, an Amazonian indigenous tribe found in the rainforests of Brazil. Next we travel to the upper reaches of the Andes Mountains, where descendants of the ancient Inca civilization continue to

Martin Pereira Algarita

AN INSIDE LOOK

We created the ensemble "Impromptus" in 1985 while we were students at the Universidad Pedagogica Nacional de Bogota in the capital city of Colombia. Students from different academic disciplines began meeting at the campus to practice different styles of Latin American popular music just because we enjoyed it. We named ourselves after the Romantic musical form called Impromptus, meaning "spontaneous."

Through constant practice and exchanging musical experiences, including those from traditional styles, plus the creative urge of the group members, we found a common purpose, that of exploring new vocal and instrumental sonorities in search of a voice that would speak to the younger generations. As with all new tendencies, our group had both admirers and detractors. The fact that our director, Mauricio Rangel Valderrama, is the son and nephew, respectively, of Oton Rangel and Oriol Rangel, both considered among the best interpreters of Colombia's traditional music, did not make the evolutionary trajectory of this group any easier. Other members of the ensemble had also been nurtured by tradition and yet, by listening to groups from other countries, particularly elsewhere in Latin America and the Caribbean, and focusing more on vocal styles, particularly the immensely popular ballads of the 1980s, we developed a style that we call "New Colombian Music." This could be appreciated

Impromptus

from our first recorded work introduced in 1991. By then the ensemble had gained recognition and followers who continued the evolutionary path that "Impromptus" had started and expanded to reach a national audience. National competitions and festivals of this new music now take place in Colombia. Unfortunately, new media and means of communication seem to ignore the new styles. Moreover, the different genres of Colombian music, which are numerous due to the country's geographical location and diversity, are not equally appreciated. Andean-derived styles like ours do not seem to have the popular demand that the more popular *salsa*-like Caribbean styles have. Nonetheless, we will continue to assert our own voices.

play the *siku* (panpipes), which are believed to date from at least the thirteenth century. Moving to urban areas, we discuss the Spanish-influenced music of *mestizo* populations throughout Mexico and South America by examining the Argentinean *tango* and the Mexican *mariachi*. Finally, we turn to the coastline of Brazil, which is home to two of the clearest examples of African influence in South America: the unique martial arts dance form known as *capoeira* and the celebratory music of Carnival known as *samba*.

Arrival: The Amazon Rainforest

The Amazonian rainforest of Brazil is one of the largest remaining tropical forests on the planet. It is home to thousands of wildlife species, such as jaguars, toucans, and macaws, and numerous nomadic and semi-nomadic hunter-gatherer human communities. During the latter decades of the twentieth century, the Amazon became a flashpoint for environmental activities concerned about the earth's deteriorating ecosystem. Logging companies were destroying (and continue to destroy) millions of acres of rainforests and have consequently displaced many Amazonian peoples. Some of these groups were forced to integrate into modern society, while others retreated further into the rainforest. Still others, such as the Kayapó Indians, managed to resist the encroachment of the modern world by actively protesting against the intruders and organizing events that drew international attention to the plight of their peoples. Today, many Amazonians have managed to straddle both worlds by educating themselves about modern society while maintaining their traditional way of life. The romantic vision of the Amazonian Indian as a bare-footed, spear-toting, loin-clothed hunter-gatherer is no longer a realistic portrayal of the native population, who can often be found in T-shirts, hunting with rifles, and sitting in classrooms learning to read and write. Still, ceremonial activities based on traditional belief systems remain at the heart of the community life of each individual group of Amazonians.

There are many distinct tribes of Amazonian peoples, and cultural traits, such as language, dress, belief system, kinship practices, and so on, vary widely from group to group. Many commonalities do exist, however, and thus some general cultural tendencies can be represented by individual groups. In our case, we focus on the Kayapó-Xikrin, who live in the southwestern area of the state of Para in central Brazil, to gain a better understanding of the music of Amazonian peoples.

Site 1: Amazonian Chant

First Impressions. Our example begins with an "eagle cry," followed by group chanting. The singing seems to be part of a community ceremony or shamanic ritual—which is usually the case. To a non-specialist, the vocal performances of Amazonian tribes may seem indistinguishable from those of North American native groups, and indeed there are some parallel musical traits.

Aural Analysis. A first listening to an Amazonian musical performance reveals several identifiable features typical of the majority of Amerindian tribes of the Brazilian rainforests. Unison group singing is most common and is often unaccompanied. The singing is in a style characterized as chant and uses only a few pitches. Unaccompanied unison (monophonic) group chanting is not unique to Amazonian Indians, but it is a recognizable trait of most tribes of the Brazilian rainforest. Men and women usually sing separately, and indeed our example includes only male voices.

Many songs have a descending melodic contour, while others consist of only one or two pitches. A melodic drop-off usually closes a vocal phrase. The text setting is most often syllabic. The dynamic level is usually consistent, though shouting sometimes occurs but not usually as a central feature of the performance. Vocal pulsation (a slight periodic volume amplification) is sometimes employed to add a rhythmic element to purely vocal performances. Rattles, flutes, or small drums sometimes accompany these performances, though none are heard in this example. Handclapping

Amazonian Indians (Kayapó-Xikrin) native to the Brazilian rainforest (Alamy)

387

and foot-stomping are also frequently employed to maintain a steady pulse during performance. Additionally, large sticks or hollow tree branches are sometimes pounded on the ground to add a rhythmic element. Though the music follows a steady pulse, metrical units are frequently irregular as they follow the phrasing of the text rather than being organized into a set number of pulses.

LISTENING GUIDE

12.1 (1'13")

Site 12.1
Brazil: Amazonian Chant

Voices: Male ensemble

TIME	LISTENING FOCUS
0'00"	Listen for the "Eagle's Cry" which starts the performance.
0'04"	Listen for the "drop-off" pitch (an extended descending melodic contour of a single syllable) that will occur throughout the performance.
0'08"	Chant begins with unison group performance. Listen for the regular pulsation and gradually descending melodic contour.
0'14"	Note that each phrase follows a consistent tempo, but a meter does not regulate the space between phrases.
0'21"	Listen for the subtle "drop-off" at the end of each phrase. Note that its length is shorter than the upcoming "drop-off" pitch at the end of the first section.
0'30"	Listen for the extended "drop-off" pitch that concludes the section.
0'34"	Note that the initial pitch level is higher than in the first section. Note also that the gradually descending melodic contour continues throughout the example.
1'03"	Listen for the concluding "drop-off" pitch that ends the example.

Source: "Nhiok: Okkaikrikti" recorded by Max Peter Baumann, 1988, from the recording entitled *Ritual Music of the Kayapó-Xikrin, Brazil,* SF 40433, provided courtesy of Smithsonian Folkways Recordings. © 1995. Used by permission.

MUSICAL MARKERS: Timbre/Medium—"Eagle Cry" opening (imitating nature). All-male vocal. **Phonic Structure**—Unison singing (monophonic). **Melodic Contour**—Emphasis on repeated pitch before "falling" at the end of a phrase. **Rhythm**—Regular pulsation, but with an irregular meter. Tempo fluctuates between phrases.
ETHNO-CHALLENGE: A common speculation is that all indigenous populations in the Americas originally come from the same source. Compare some examples of chant traditions from other indigenous groups in the Americas (North and South) and draw your own conclusions as to the validity of this hypothesis.

Cultural Considerations. The music of Amazonian peoples is integral to their ritual activities. Some familiarity with these rituals is useful for a better understanding of the meaning of musical performance. The recording we have selected is the concluding section of a Kayapó-Xikrin naming ritual. Known as *takak-nhiok*, this ritual occurs in five stages over a period of five years. Each stage enables the initiates to participate in and gain new knowledge of a growing number of activities practiced by elder members of the community, such as feather handicrafts and hunting. The status of the initiates increases, and they are given secret knowledge regarding the community's history and belief system in the form of myths, dances, song, body-painting, and featherwork.

The concluding chant of the naming ritual begins at sunset and continues until dawn. It is identified by the opening call, which imitates the screech of a Harpy Eagle. The name-recipients, in this case female, form a semicircle with their backs to the setting sun. The male vocalists complete the circle while a select group of "jaguar men," generally the elder community leaders, dance counter-clockwise around the interior of the circle, approaching each female in turn with a symbolic "clawing" gesture that completes their naming. The Harpy Eagle's chant translates as: "The claws of the Harpy Eagle will claw the Nhiok / Breathe and come through the path / Breathe and keep seeing hummingbird's feathers being born." The reference to the hummingbird is significant: The Kayapó-Xikrin believe that the hummingbird is "the jaguar remedy" (*Ritual Music of the Kayapó-Xikrin, Brazil*, SF 40433, Washington, DC: Smithsonian Folkways, 1995, p. 59). The hummingbird is considered unique; indeed, it is the only bird capable of flying backward. As such, it is quick and elusive. Hummingbird feathers are burnt and mixed with a plant to produce an ointment believed to protect an individual from jaguars. The Harpy Eagle call proclaims the final stage of the initiation ceremony, the completion of which signals that the newly named participants have acquired a higher status among the community.

For most Amazonian tribes, music is an important means of communicating with natural and spiritual forces. **Totems** are acknowledged and respected through music. Shamans often use music to communicate with or appease spirits of the rainforest. Indeed, some tribes believe that songs are taught to them by these spirits through dreams. Music, then, is central to the lives of Amazonians and integral to their cultural identity. The chants of the Kayapó are integrally bound up with issues common to the realm of anthropology, such as kinship systems, social organization, and gender and age classifications. Many cultural aspects of the Kayapó are reflected in their music, as they are with any group, not just in the Amazon, but around the globe.

TOTEM
A plant, animal, or natural object used as an emblem for a person or group of people.

Arrival: Peru

Peru's landscape varies widely. Urban areas are found on the western coast, while much of the eastern interior is taken up by the tropical rainforests of the Amazon. Between these two zones are the highlands, where descendants of the ancient Inca Empire still live in adobe huts among llamas and alpacas, surrounded by the snow-capped mountains of the Andes. Peru's native and mestizo peoples form the majority of the population. Both Spanish and Quechua, an indigenous language formerly associated with the Inca Empire, are recognized as official languages of Peru.

The Inca Empire dates to roughly the thirteenth century and reached its peak in the last decades of the 1400s. Important centers of power and culture included the city of Cusco in southeastern Peru near Lake Titicaca, and the stronghold of Machu Picchu some 50 miles to the northwest and nearly 9,000 feet above sea level. Spanish conquistadors began arriving in the early 1500s and quickly toppled the ruling powers of the Inca, beheading the last Inca Emperor, Túpac Amaru, in 1572.

Though Inca heritage is still a vital aspect of the cultural identity of the native population, the Spanish influence is also felt in many ways. Roman Catholicism is especially prominent throughout the region, though in a form that reveals many influences from pre-contact religious systems. The numerous religious holidays associated with both Roman Catholicism and the earlier traditions provide ample opportunities for small- and large-scale festivals in both urban and rural areas. Among the most popular are Easter celebrations, which incorporate a variety of musical activities.

Site 2: *Sikuri* (Panpipe) Ensemble

First Impressions. Aside from the pounding drum beat, the breathy sound of the melodic panpipes, called **siku**, is the most distinctive feature of this example. The short repetitive melody, with its "calliope-like" timbre, sounds joyfully out of tune and is reminiscent of a carousel ride spinning non-stop.

SIKU
Panpipes common among indigenous populations from Peru and throughout the Andes.

Aural Analysis. The *sikuri* panpipe ensemble is common to many Andean communities throughout Peru and elsewhere in Andean South America. *Sikuri* ensembles normally have around twenty *siku* players, though the group in our example is larger, consisting of fifty-two musicians. The *siku* is made of several cylindrical reeds of varying lengths tied together to form one or two rows of pipes—in this case two. The performer holds these vertically and blows across the tops of the open pipes to produce breathy pitches, just as you would with a soda bottle: the shorter the pipe, the higher the pitch. Thus, they are open-ended flutes in the aerophone family.

One *siku* is not typically capable of playing all the notes of a scale. Rather, a second *siku* must complement it. The two performers use an interlocking technique to produce the entire melody. If, for example, the first player sounds the odd-numbered pitches, say 1–3–5, while the second player sounds the even ones, 2–4–6, then the two musicians must alternate in order to play pitches 1 through 6 consecutively. The musicians try to overlap their pitches slightly so that no gaps are heard between pitches. The breathy sound of the *siku* makes it easier for performers to smoothly connect successive pitches.

Another common feature of Andean music is the use of parallel polyphony. Parallel polyphony occurs when two melodic lines follow the same melodic contour but start on different pitches, thus moving in parallel but with a polyphonic structure as well. The most commonly used intervals between the two parallel lines are the fourth and fifth. The interval used here, however, is a third, which is typical of the Conima style of which this music is an example. Intentional tuning variances often occur, sometimes as wide as a quartertone or more, giving the music a slightly dissonant quality. As is typical of native Andean music, the melodic line is short and repetitive and features only minor variations.

BOMBOS
A large drum used in *sikuri* performances from Peru.

In our example, a large bass drum (**bombos**) and a snare drum (*cajas*) provide a driving beat. Drums in Peru are often made with a llama- or alpaca-skin face and are struck with a wooden mallet. Different genres of *sikuri* performance use different types of drums; in fact, the bass and snare drum accompaniment heard here rarely occurs outside Easter celebrations. In most performances, occasional whistles are heard, most notably toward the end of the performance, to signal the musicians to increase their tempo.

Cultural Considerations. Evidence of *siku* and other types of flutes dates to pre-Columbian times, while the many chordophones and brass instruments found today arrived only after the 1530s with Spanish conquistadors and Roman Catholic missionaries. The *sikuri* ensemble is most

Descendants of the ancient Inca still live today in the Andes Mountains of Peru (Max T. Miller)

LISTENING GUIDE

Site 12.2
Peru: *Sikuri* (Panpipe) Ensemble

Instruments: *Siku* (end-blown flutes), *bombos* (large drum), *cajas* (small drum)

TIME	LISTENING FOCUS
0'00"	Listen for the whistle used to call the musicians to attention and the sound of a few performers blowing quietly into their *siku*.
0'03"	Listen for the *siku* initiating the performance. Note the use of a homophonic structure (with parallel polyphony) throughout the performance.
0'05"	Listen for the *bombos* playing a regular beat. Note the number of pulses between each pause in the rhythmic pattern. Though not consistent, this pattern features two phrases with a short number of pulses (usually seven), and then a longer phrase (usually seventeen) that concludes with the end of the melodic phrase.
0'07"	Listen for the *cajas* entrance contrasting with the lower drum.
0'15"	First melodic phrase concludes.
0'18"	Listen for the pause of the lower drum. Note that this does not occur simultaneously with the end of the melodic phrase.
0'30"	Listen for the pause of the lower drum. Note that it occurs at the end of the melodic phrase.
0'41"	Listen again for the pause of the lower drum in relation to the end of the melodic phrase. Continue to note this relationship throughout the performance.

Source: "Easter Music" by Qhantati Urui performed by the Conimeño Ensemble, recorded by Thomas Turino, Conima, Peru, 1985, from the recording entitled *Mountain Music of Peru: Volume 2*, SF 40406, provided courtesy of Smithsonian Folkways Recordings. © 1994. Used by permission.

MUSICAL MARKERS: Timbre/Medium—Group of breathy "merry-go-round" flutes (panpipes). Booming drum with "buzzy" smaller drum. **Phonic Structure**—Parallel polyphony. **Melody**—Interlocking pitches (hocket) produce overall melody.
ETHNO-CHALLENGE: Construct your own panpipe. Use the Internet to research how to do this.

common among the Aymara-speaking peoples surrounding Lake Titicaca, the largest lake on the continent and the highest navigable lake in the world (at 12,500 feet above sea level). Living and farming in these highland rural areas requires collective effort and social cooperation, and scholars consider the *sikuri* ensemble a reflection of this social structure.

Sikuri is most often performed during monthly festivals associated with indigenous ceremonial rites that frequently are combined with Roman Catholic holidays. Instrumental performance is considered a male activity, while women generally dance or sing. During a *sikuri* performance, any man from the village can participate, regardless of his musical ability or familiarity with the tune. The emphasis of the performance is on social interaction rather than on a strict adherence to musical accuracy. The interlocking parts of the *siku* express the Aymara ideal of "playing as one."

Inter-community festivals may feature several *sikuri* ensembles, each representing a different village. The performers dance in one or more circles around the drummers, who stand in the center. Friendly competitions often occur between the different ensembles as non-performers dance and cheer. The choice of a "winner" is based primarily on who has given the most energetic performance

An Andean panpipe and drum ensemble performs on stage at a university folk festival (Dale Olsen)

The panpipes (*siku*) are among the most common indigenous instruments of the Andes and on the general reaction of the crowd, rather than on strictly musical qualities. In short, the response of the community is the essential factor in determining a successful *sikuri* performance.

Arrival: Argentina

The pre-contact history of Argentina is sketchy. None of the ancient empires of the Americas held dominion over the territory, which was sparsely populated by hunters and gatherers and home to a few agricultural settlements. Spanish colonization of the region began in the early sixteenth century, with the first attempt at a permanent settlement, Buenos Aires, in 1536. Five years later the settlement was abandoned, due in part to conflicts with the indigenous populations. Eventually, the region was successfully colonized and Buenos Aires was resettled in 1580. In time, the growing city became an important port and gained a reputation as a haven for smugglers. By the middle of the eighteenth century its population had swelled to more than 20,000.

The British attacked the city in 1806 but were ousted only a few months later by a citizen army. Subsequent attempts by the British to overtake the city failed and indeed encouraged a strong patriotic sentiment among the city's inhabitants. However, in 1810 the people of Buenos Aires rebelled against the Spanish crown, and only a few years later they succeeded in gaining their independence. It is this spirit of rebellion that drives the **tango** in its purest form.

Site 3: *Tango*

First Impressions. *Tango,* both as a dance and as music, embodies passion. The original form of the dance it accompanies symbolically represents a battle between two men for the affections of a fickle woman. At one point in the dance, one of the male dancers lustfully looms over the helpless woman before she is torn away by the other jealous suitor. Even in its simplest form, the music evokes the predatory stares of the men and the indecisiveness of the woman through variations of dynamics, tempo, and phonic structure.

TANGO
A dance and associated music originating in Argentina.

Aural Analysis. *Tango* ensembles vary in size, and *tango* itself comes in a variety of styles. A distinctive feature of most *tango* orchestras is the inclusion of the *bandoneón,* a type of button-box accordion. The **bandoneón** was invented in Germany in the mid-nineteenth century by Heinrich Band and was brought to South America around 1890, initially in the hands of missionaries who found it a portable alternative to the organ. The instrument has two square wooden manuals (keyboards) separated by a bellows made of leather. Larger *bandoneón* have up to seventy-two buttons, but the distribution pattern does not follow the usual melody–chord dichotomy found on typical accordions. As the performer alternately compresses or draws out the bellows, air passes through a series of "free" metal reeds to produce the tones; thus, the *bandoneón* is a free-reed aerophone. Dynamic variations are produced by squeezing or drawing the air through the instrument more quickly for greater volume or more slowly for a quieter sound. In addition to the *bandoneón,* the violin, guitar, flute, and piano are frequently found in *tango* ensembles and a vocalist is often present as well.

BANDONEÓN
A type of button-box accordion.

Tango rhythms are frequently syncopated, meaning some accents fall between the regular beat. Our example employs a common *tango* rhythm by emphasizing the offbeats of the first and second pulses. In order to hear this, you must first find the regular pulsation to establish a meter, in this case a duple meter with four beats. The melodic line anticipates the first beat of each four-beat grouping; therefore, it is probably easier to find the first pulse by listening to the underlying chords. The tempo is rather quick and fluctuates frequently, as is typical of *tango.*

The syncopated *tango* rhythm falls within the four-beat grouping. Once you have established the meter by counting the four-beat grouping, divide this by saying "and" between each pulse, that is, 1&2&3&4&. The "and" division indicates the "offbeat." The *tango* rhythm, articulated by the underlying chords, displays a fairly constant pattern of 1&–&3–(4)–. The "2" beat is absent, as is the "4&." Most of the melodic phrases also begin on the "offbeat," typically the "and" of the third beat. This emphasis on syncopation creates an off-balance feel throughout the performance: the musicians constantly flirt with the regular beat, but never commit to it. Indeed, this aspect of *tango* music parallels the fickle affections of the female character in *tango* dance's symbolic courtship battle. Interestingly, in American-style ballroom *tango* dance steps begin right on beat 1, but in International style, many steps begin on the "&" following beat 1.

The indecisive seductions of the female *tango* dancer are also manifested through fluctuations in dynamics, tempo, phonic structure, and even key. Bursts of volume with strong chord accompaniment at a quick tempo contrast with soft, sultry, slow passages with only a single melodic line. Though *tango* music is dominated by minor keys, the performers will often slip in brighter passages that utilize major keys, again keeping the music off-balance. As the dancers embrace in a loving gaze characterized by a major key, they suddenly turn from each other as the music abruptly shifts back to minor. Such variations of mood are essential to the unique character of the *tango*.

Cultural Considerations. Buenos Aires, Argentina, is the birthplace of *tango*. Since its resettlement in 1580 by Spanish sailors, this city has been a port of call for sea sojourners navigating around South America. As a hub of maritime trade for more than four hundred years, the city has attracted a variety of immigrants, primarily Spanish, but also Italian. Trade with European cities boomed after Argentina was officially proclaimed independent from Spain in 1816. By 1880, when it emerged as the capital city of Argentina, Buenos Aires was one of the most important economic and cultural centers of Latin America.

As often happened with port cities during the nineteenth century, the transient lifestyle of seamen encouraged a seedy subculture characterized by taverns and bordellos where sailors could unwind before heading to their next port of call. Knife fights and bar brawls over women were common occurrences among the *porteños* (people of the port area), typically initiated by inebriated sailors vying for the affections of a single seductive strumpet. *Tango* dance reflects these possessive relationships, originally casting two men and a woman in a sensual choreography

The *bandoneón*, an accordion common in Argentina, is the most prominent instrument that accompanies the tango (Getty)

LISTENING GUIDE
12.3 (1'54")

Site 12.3
Argentina: *Tango*

Instruments: *Bandoneón* (reed aerophone, i.e., accordion)

TIME	LISTENING FOCUS
0'00"	Listen for the use of melody and accompanying harmony. Note the "tango" rhythmic pattern (1 & – & 3 – (4) –) articulated by the chord accompaniment.
0'09"	Listen for the slight *ritard* (slowing tempo) at this point. Note the variations in tempo throughout the example.
0'19"	Note that the "tango rhythm" briefly drops out.
0'26"	Listen for the contrasting melodic line of the lower harmony and the less-consistent use of the tango rhythm.
0'44"	Listen for the swell in volume. Note the varying use of dynamics throughout the example.
0'47"	Listen for the slowing tempo and decrease in volume.
0'51"	Listen for the high-pitched melodic trill and the absence of harmony.
0'53"	Listen for the contrasting harmonic pitch underneath the melodic line.
1'01"	Listen for the return of the tango rhythm in the harmonic accompaniment and the gradual increase in volume.
1'07"	Listen for the syncopated rhythmic patterns of the harmony.
1'15"	Listen for the swell in volume, slowing of the tempo, absence of the harmony, and loss of tango rhythm.
1'19"	Listen for the dramatic swell of the harmony and the contrasting solo melody that follows.
1'24"	Listen for the return of the tango rhythm in the supporting harmony.
1'44"	Listen for the final swell in volume, which signals the end of the performance.

Source: "El Choclo"(The Ear of Corn): *Tango Criollo* by René Marino Rivero, recorded by Tiago de Oliveiro Pinto, 1991, from the recording entitled *Raíces Latinas: Smithsonian-Folkways Latino Roots Collection,* SF 40470, provided courtesy of Smithsonian Folkways Recordings. © 2002. Used by permission.

MUSICAL MARKERS: Timbre/Medium—"Moody" accordion. **Rhythm**—Follows a 1&–&3–(4)–rhythmic pattern with many tempo fluctuations, creating an "off-balance" feel. **Phonic Structure**—Upper melody with supporting harmony emphasizing rhythm.
ETHNO-CHALLENGE: Find an instructor in your area and take a tango dance lesson. You might also research various appearances of tango performance in movies and compare each version of the dance and musical accompaniment.

with a distinctly predatory nature: the "vertical expression of horizontal desire," as it is often described. *Tango* music also suggests such seduction as the musicians thrust and parry through dynamic variations and tempo fluctuations, echoing the love triangle narrative of the dance.

Because of its lurid association with the vagabonds of the brothels, *tango* was disdained by aristocrats, who considered the music and its dance to be vulgar. Yet, the lure of bohemian nightlife attracted many, especially among the younger generation, who flocked to *tango* just as teenagers in the United States later flocked to rock 'n' roll. By the end of the nineteenth century, *tango* had captured the youthful passions of popular culture in Buenos Aires and quickly spread throughout Argentina and the urban centers of many South American countries (including Uruguay, from which our example derives).

The attraction to *tango* was not limited to South America. By 1910 *tango* was tantalizing the playboys and dilettantes of salons in Paris, France, and it soon made its screen debut together with Rudolph Valentino in *The Four Horsemen of the Apocalypse* (1926). Carlos Gardel (1887–1935) became an international superstar as *tango-canción* (*tango* song) was popularized on the radio and in the cinema. But in the United States, where puritan moralists have long considered dance to be sinful, Vernon and Irene Castle, who brought *tango* into the ballroom dance world, felt obligated to reassure readers of their *tango*-instructional booklets that this new and exceptionally sensual dance would not corrupt anyone's morals:

> The much-misunderstood Tango becomes an evolution of the eighteenth-century Minuet. There is in it no strenuous clasping of partners, no hideous gyrations of the limbs, no abnormal twistings, no vicious angles. Mr. Castle affirms that when the Tango degenerates into an acrobatic display or into salacious suggestion it is the fault of the dancers and not of the dance. The Castle Tango is courtly and artistic, and this is the only Tango taught by the Castle House instructors.
>
> (Castle, 1914, quoted in Elisabeth Marbury, p. 20)

The Castle version of tango codified the choreography of tango for ballroom dance contexts, which has become the foundation for its performance around the world today. What is now distinguished as the "Argentine Tango" in social contexts, however, maintains a more fluid and "salacious" style, particularly in Argentina where the dance originated, than in the international ballroom world.

By the 1940s *tango* had seduced every social class, but the Golden Age of *tango* was nearing its end. After World War II, rock 'n' roll pushed *tango* (as well as jazz) from the airwaves and dance clubs, although it still found an audience in Argentina and among many of the upper classes who had accepted it as the sultry side of ballroom dance. *Tango* never regained its former popularity, although composers such as Astor Piazzolla (1921–1992) helped to establish it as a

The Argentine tango, unlike the regularized ballroom form, requires rapid changes of emotion, from control to inflamed passion (Jack Vartoogian/ FrontRowPhotos)

music genre independent of the dance itself. Interest in *tango* briefly surged in the 1980s, and it has maintained its visibility to the present day, in part through the inclusion of tantalizing *tango* scenes in hit films such as *The Scent of a Woman* (1992), starring Al Pacino, and *Moulin Rouge!* (2001), starring Nicole Kidman and Ewan McGregor.

Arrival: Brazil

Brazil is the largest country in South America and home to roughly 186 million inhabitants. Our earlier visit to the Amazonian rainforests presented a stark contrast to the bustling activity of the urban centers that dot the eastern half of the country. Brazil's largest cities are mostly found along the coastline and include Rio de Janeiro, São Paulo, and Salvador. The country was colonized by the Portuguese, who began arriving in the region around 1500. They discovered a land rich in natural resources and with fertile soil. Within fifty years Portuguese colonialists began to import slaves from Africa to work on sugar, tobacco, and coffee plantations. Gold was discovered in the late 1600s, encouraging the enslavement of more Africans to work as miners. African populations were imported to Brazil for more than three hundred years, resulting today in the largest African Diaspora in the world.

Brazil became an independent nation in 1822. The government was then ruled by a succession of emperors descended from members of the Portuguese royal family. The abolition of slavery in 1888 was followed the next year by a revolution initiated by the military, which ousted the monarchy and created a federal republic in Brazil. The new government struggled to represent its diverse population equitably. Most of the political power resided with the wealthy landowners, invariably of European descent, while the vast majority of the population, either of mixed ancestry or of purely African descent, occupied the slum areas of the urban centers and had little or no political voice. By 1930 discontent among the masses had come to a head, while a collapse in the economy, brought on by the global depression that began in 1929, caused the landowning elite to lose confidence in their elected officials. A disgruntled military once again encouraged revolution, which was personified by the rise to power of a single man, Getúlio Vargas (1883–1954).

Vargas was a central figure in the revolution of 1930 and became president and ruled as an elected official until 1937. Rather than risk losing power, Vargas initiated a revolution of his own with the help of the military and with the support of the urban working and middle classes. He eliminated the congress and ruled by decree as a dictator for the next eight years. Vargas began many social and economic reforms that were, ironically, modeled after the policies of the Italian dictator Benito Mussolini, against whom the Brazilian military fought (in aid of the United States) during World War II. His *Estado Novo* (New State) encouraged a strong sense of a unified national identity among the masses and a feeling of pride in being Brazilian, no matter what a person's ethnic background or social class. His propaganda machine was instrumental in the promotion of *samba* as a music for all Brazilians.

Site 4: *Samba*

First Impressions. **Samba** is dance music. Its boisterous beat, wailing whistles, and shouting *sambistas* encourage the party atmosphere associated with its most notable context, Carnival (see below). The driving *samba* beat conjures up images of revelers parading through the streets of Rio de Janeiro in frenetic celebration. *Samba* music makes you move from the bottom of your feet to the top of your head.

SAMBA
A popular music and type of dance from Brazil.

Aural Analysis. *Samba* is strongly Afro-Brazilian, meaning that its musical characteristics are primarily drawn from African ingredients but have a unique Brazilian flavor. Polyrhythm underlies the instrumental organization; thus, the majority of instruments in *samba* are percussion.

AGOGO
A double-bell found in Western Africa and used in African-derived musics in the Western hemisphere.

RÊCO-RÊCO
A notched scraper idiophone found in Latin American music traditions.

African-derived double bells *(agogo)*, tambourines, scraping instruments *(rêco-rêco)*, and drums, large *(surdo* or *bombo)* and small *(caixa)*, are all instruments commonly found in a wide variety of *samba* styles. The most distinct *samba* instrument is the friction drum *(cuíca)*, which is a membranophone that has its face pierced in the center with a long, thin stick. When the stick is pushed, pulled, or twisted, it rubs against the membrane to produce a unique squeaking sound. Call-and-response vocals, usually in Portuguese, are standard, and are generally accompanied by a guitar.

A prominent "*samba* rhythm," usually played by the largest drum or an electrified bass guitar, is what most differentiates the music from other Latin American dance musics. The *samba* rhythm is based on a standard duple meter but emphasizes the third beat by inserting a short pause just before it. In a four-beat pattern (though *samba* moves so quickly, it is typically thought of as having only two beats), the *samba* rhythm would sound on the first beat, the "and" of the second, and the top of the third beat, that is, 1–&3–. The rhythm is infectious and seems to call out: "Mooove your feet! Mooove your feet!" Other instruments add several other more rhythmically dense patterns to this fundamental *samba* groove.

LISTENING GUIDE

12.4 (2'05")

Site 12.4

Brazil: *Samba*

Vocals: Lead mixed ensemble and single male soloist
Instruments: Guitar, *cavaco* (high-ranged guitar), electric bass, *surdo* (low-pitched drum), *cuíca* (friction drum), *pandeiro* (tambourine), shaker

TIME	LISTENING FOCUS
0'00"	Example fades in. Listen for the underlying polyrhythm of the percussion and the consistent samba rhythm (1– &3–) of the electric bass and *surdo* (low-pitched drum). Note the contrasting middle-ranged guitar and high-ranged *cavaco*.
0'03"	Listen for the spoken dialogue of the solo vocalist.
0'10"	Listen for the mixed vocal ensemble entrance on the word "samba."
0'24"	Listen for the "squeaking" timbre of the *cuíca* (friction drum).
0'45"	Listen for the solo vocalist adding exclamations to complement the choral melody.
1'24"	Return to opening melody and verse.
1'52"	Example fades.

Source: "Agoniza, Mas Nao Morre" ("It suffers but doesn't die"), performed by Nelson Sargento, from the recording entitled *Brazil Roots: Samba*, Rounder CD 5045, 1989. Used by permission.

MUSICAL MARKERS: Timbre/Medium—"Squeaky" friction drum. Various percussion and guitars. Lead with mixed vocal group. **Rhythm**—Consistent 1–&3– "samba" beat. "Squeaky" accents from cuíca drum. **Melody/Phonic Structure**—Singable melody with simple harmony. **Lyrics**—Often make reference to "samba" and "Carnival."
ETHNO-CHALLENGE: Research *samba*, then compare and contrast the varying styles of *samba* music.

Cultural Considerations. *Samba* traces its roots to Angola and the Congo in Africa. Its name is believed to be derived from the term *semba*, a Bantu word describing the distinctive "belly bump" found in some circle dances of the region. The navel is considered a spiritually significant body part, and contact between two navels symbolically links two dancers together. In Brazil, the *samba* folk dance begins with this gesture of bumping bellies as a dancer invites another dancer to enter the circle and dance together as one.

Initially, the ruling powers of Brazil viewed *samba* as a vulgar dance performed by slum-dwellers who lived in the *favelas* (slums) on the hills surrounding the city of Rio de Janeiro and in the *bairro*, a section of the city known as "Little Africa" due to the large number of African-descended inhabitants. The popularity of *samba* was especially visible during the Carnival season (see below), when music and celebration in the streets were more tolerated by government authorities. The driving rhythms of the music and the erotic appeal of the dance gradually attracted members of the rising middle class, many of whom were of mixed African-Iberian ancestry, so that by the mid-1920s composing *samba* had become a full-time occupation for many talented artists. Each year, neighborhood associations would parade through the streets during Carnival playing music and dancing to popular *samba* melodies, usually composed by one of their own members. By the end of the decade, these associations were referring to themselves as *escolas de samba* (*samba* schools).

After taking power in 1930, Getúlio Vargas actively encouraged *samba* as part of his *Estado Novo* campaign to promote a unified Brazilian national identity. In 1934 he made Carnival an official national event and decreed that only *samba* schools legally registered with the government could perform in parades. He further encouraged *samba* and its association with Carnival by offering public funds to support the registered *samba* schools, which were strongly encouraged to create costumes and compose music that stimulated national pride by glorifying national heroes and promoting patriotic symbols. Though such overt nationalism has fallen out of fashion, public support of the *samba* schools and a focus on Carnival as the hallmark event of the Brazilian calendar year have remained.

Today, *samba* is nearly synonymous with Brazilian popular music. The term covers a variety of styles in much the same way the term *jazz* is used to describe a broad range of styles in the United States. The best-known styles, namely *samba-carnavalesco* (carnival *samba*), *samba-baiana* (Bahian *samba*), and *samba-enredo* (theme *samba*), are still associated with Carnival. Also popular is *samba-canção* (song *samba*), which is a staple of Brazilian nightclubs and the origin of *bossa nova*, a particularly popular style for ballroom dance. Since the 1990s *samba-reggae*, the Brazilian version of Jamaican *reggae*, has become widely known as well.

Members of a *Gongada* from Minas Geraes perform during Carnival celebrations in Brazil (Welson Tremura)

At Rio de Janeiro's Carnival, the largest in the world, a gigantic float passes through the *Sambadrome Marquês de Sapucaí*, an indoor arena for Carnival parades (Shutterstock)

Costumed drummers march in the Carnival parade of Montevideo, Uruguay (Shutterstock)

Explore More

Carnival

Carnival is a pre-Lenten festival associated in the Americas with countries where Roman Catholicism was the primary religious tradition of the colonizers. The tradition originated in Europe but has come to be most associated with the grand parades and intense revelry of places such as Rio de Janeiro (Brazil), Port of Spain (Trinidad), and New Orleans (USA, where it is known as *Mardi Gras*).

Traditionally, Carnival celebrations were considered the last "party" before the forty days of Lent, during which Roman Catholics are supposed to renew themselves spiritually by abstaining from activities such as drinking alcohol, eating meat, dancing, and playing music. Weddings and other celebratory events were also forbidden during the Lenten season. The elite social classes held masked balls to indulge themselves before the commencement of Lent. Among the "common folk," outdoor festivals were held, which typically included a variety of "Carnival" games, jugglers, comedians, storytellers, and so on, much like the Renaissance Fairs of today. Among those to encourage the Carnival celebration were Gypsies (see Chapter 9), many of whom made their living by performing as entertainers and musicians.

The Carnival season, which typically lasted four or five days, was considered a time to "forgive and forget" any animosity between individuals, and the authorities also tended to be more lenient during the celebrations. This carefree attitude was transferred to the New World. The European colonialists maintained their tradition of masked balls and indoor revelry in many cities throughout the Caribbean, while the lower classes, most of whom were of African descent, were usually allowed to celebrate with outdoor activities. A common feature of these outdoor activities was the street parade, which has since become the highlight of nearly every Carnival celebration around the world.

The Brazilian Carnival celebrations are considered by many to be the pinnacle of the festivals held the world over. Thousands of people travel to Rio de Janeiro to participate in the non-stop partying that characterizes the Carnival Season (between February and March, depending on the date of Ash Wednesday). Body paint, confetti and streamers, lots of alcohol, and continuous dancing to the *samba* beat mark the annual activities, which are capped with a parade through the city center featuring the most extravagant costumes and floats found in any festival the world over. *Sambistas* dance through the city streets followed by batteries of deafening percussion. *Samba* schools compete for prizes based on their music performance, dance choreography, and costumes. Each school's performance is organized around a specific theme, typically one that promotes Brazilian identity and revolves around national, historical, or political figures and events.

Site 5: *Capoeira* Music

First Impressions. **Capoeira** is music with a groove. Whereas the *samba* music of Carnival pushes the body to a frenetic extreme, *capoeira* music embodies the laid-back attitude Brazilians often take during the rest of the year. The music constantly bobs and weaves as if the listener is relaxing on a small fishing boat along the Brazilian coastline. The waves bring him closer and closer to shore, gradually picking up momentum as he casually steers himself onto the beach. Fluid motion is the general feel, but there is also a constant awareness that the waves can tip the boat at any moment.

Aural Analysis. Among the key features of *capoeira* music are the call-and-response organization of the vocal performers and the subtle polyrhythmic organization of the African-derived instruments. These instruments include the **pandeiros** (tambourines), *agogo* (double bell), *rêco-rêco* (notched scraper), and **atabaque** (drum), as well as the most distinctive instrument of the *capoeira* ensemble, the **berimbau** (musical bow). All of these instruments were recreated in Brazil by African slaves taken in particular from areas now comprising the modern Central African nations of Angola and the Democratic Republic of the Congo (formerly Zaire).

In our example, which is the *Capoeira Angola* style, three *berimbau* are played, to provide low, middle, and high parts. The *berimbau* is made from a wooden bow with a steel string. A piece of twine is looped around the base of the bow to attach a gourd resonator, which is pressed

CAPOEIRA
A dance that developed from a style of martial arts created by runaway slaves in Brazil.

PANDEIROS
A hand-held frame drum with attached cymbals (i.e., a tambourine), used in *capoeira* music.

ATABAQUE
A drum of West African origin used in *capoeira* music as well as *candomblé* rituals.

BERIMBAU
A musical bow used in *capoeira* music.

against the body to change the timbre and pitch of the instrument's sound. The smallest finger of one hand, usually the left for a right-handed player, balances the instrument on this loop during performance. A large coin or stone is held between the thumb and forefinger and is pressed against the string in order to change the acoustic length of the string and consequently alter the pitch. This coin is sometimes only lightly pressed against the string, so as to produce a buzzing timbre.

The other hand strikes the string with a small stick several inches long. This hand also holds a small wicker basket that encloses a handful of either pebbles or small seashells. The performer simultaneously shakes this rattle as he strikes the string of the bow with the stick. The timbre of the *berimbau* is much like the "boing" sound of a large spring. The use of the coin, rattle, and open string, along with the varied resonances produced by the gourd, allows the *berimbau* to provide a great variety of simultaneous timbres.

Though the vocalists carry the primary melody, the unique "springy" timbre of the *berimbau* is the focus of the dancing that this music typically accompanies. In the *Capoeira Angola* style, the lowest-pitched *berimbau* plays the basic pattern, while the middle *berimbau* plays a complementary rhythm. The highest *berimbau* ornaments these basic patterns with improvisation, paying close attention to the movements of the dancers.

The steady groove of the music is provided by the other instruments. The fundamental rhythm, 1–&3–4–, is set by the drum with three low tones and a "slap" on the fourth beat. This rhythm is common to most *capoeira* music as it corresponds to the basic **ginga** movement of

GINGA
(Also, JENGA)
A back-and-forth motion used as the basis for *capoeira* dancing.

The Brazilian *berimbau* (musical bow) on stage. (Jack Vartoogian/ FrontRowPhotos)

The Brazilian berimbau (musical bow in background) played during an outdoor capoeira performance in Salvador, Brazil.

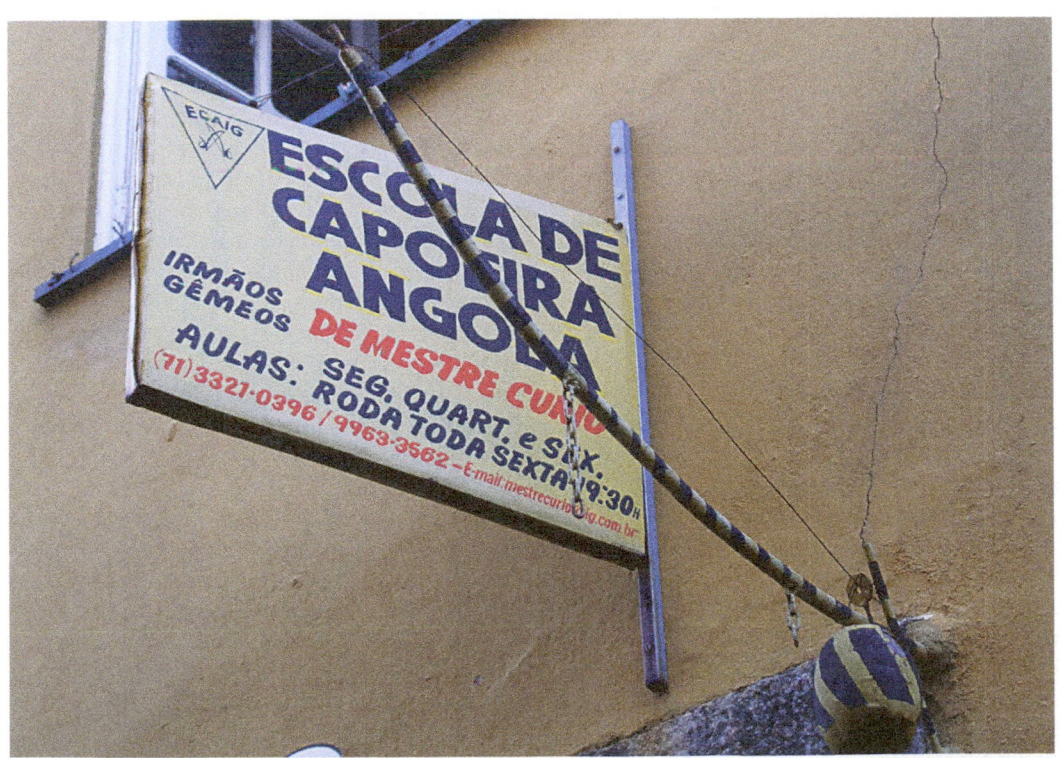

A sign outside the *Escola Capoeira Angola* in Salvador, Brazil, that offers instruction in the martial art

At the great tourist market in Salvador, Brazil, tourists are invited to purchase souvenir *berimbau*

the dancers (see below). The other instruments follow their own rhythms, being careful not to overshadow the fundamental beat or the sound of the *berimbau* trio.

As the music progresses, the tempo often gradually increases. The *berimbau* pattern will subtly shift throughout, urging the dancers to heighten their performance. The basic *ginga* pattern of the drum does not change, but the other instruments may shift their patterns, creating denser rhythms to correspond with the increased intensity of the music. The dynamic level typically remains constant, though the *berimbau* may increase its volume as the dancers "play" harder.

The vocal organization remains in call-and-response form throughout a performance. The text setting is primarily syllabic and has a descending melodic contour. The melody will change as the music progresses but generally keeps the same phrase length. The lyrics are generally sung in Portuguese, the national language of Brazil, and tend to focus on the dancers, the musicians, or other aspects of *capoeira* performance. Oftentimes the singers use symbolic language, such as describing a large dancer as a tall immobile tree, to prod the dancers to better or faster movements.

Cultural Considerations. *Capoeira* is a unique form of dance that developed from a distinctive style of martial arts created by runaway slaves in Brazil. Before abolition, many slaves who escaped the oppression of the sugar and coffee plantations would take refuge in the mountains near the country's coastline. Not having guns or swords, they developed a martial arts system that drew upon various fighting styles from Africa. The system that was created, which is known as *compé*, emphasizes the use of the feet during combat. The movements are characterized by cartwheels, handstands, flips, and spinning motions.

After slavery was abolished in Brazil, many of the *capoeira* artists continued to utilize their skills as bodyguards for Brazil's social elite. Many others formed gangs, which led to *capoeira* being associated with street fighting and vandalism. The authorities, of course, frowned on such

LISTENING GUIDE
12.5 (1'29")

Site 12.5
Brazil: *Capoeira* Music

Vocals: Single male lead and supporting male ensemble
Instruments: *Berimbau* (musical bow), *pandeiros* (tambourine), *atabaque* (drum), *rêco-rêco* (scraped idiophone), *agogo* (double bell)

TIME	LISTENING FOCUS
0'00"	Listen for the lead vocal "call" as the example fades in. Note the underlying polyrhythm along with the steady rhythmic pattern (1–& 3–4–) provided by the drum. Also, listen for the distinct two-pitch timbre of the *berimbau*.
0'06"	Listen for the group vocal response.
0'10"	Listen for the lead vocal "call" and subsequent group response. Note that this structure occurs throughout the performance.
0'21"	Listen for the change in melodic rhythm of the lead *berimbau* and subsequent emphasis on syncopated rhythms and divergence from emphasizing the basic pulse of the underlying polyrhythmic percussion.
0'50"	Listen for the lead *berimbau* returning to the basic pulse established by the underlying polyrhythmic percussion.
0'58"	Listen for the lead *berimbau* again emphasizing syncopated rhythmic activity.
1'08"	Listen for the return of the melodic rhythm of the lead *berimbau* heard at 0'21," and subsequent rhythmic improvisations.
1'19"	Example fades.

Source: "Saia do Mar Marinheiro" by Grupo de Capoeira Anglo Pelurinho, from the recording entitled *Capoeira Angola from Salvador, Brazil*, SF 40465, provided courtesy of Smithsonian Folkways Recordings. © 1996. Used by permission.

MUSICAL MARKERS: Timbre/Medium—"Bouncy" musical bow (berimbau). Scraped idiophone, various drums and other percussion. Vocal lead with group response. **Rhythm**—"Bob & Weave" groove, emphasizing 1–&3–4–rhythmic pattern. Instruments organized polyrhythmically. **Melody/Form**—Short sung phrases in call and response form. Berimbau produces just two pitches at a narrow interval (one whole step).
ETHNO-CHALLENGE: Construct a *berimbau*. Alternatively, provide the drum rhythm throughout the example. If possible, find a *capoeira* club in your local area and observe a practice session or performance.

disturbances, so the gangs attempted to disguise their practice sessions and street fights by simultaneously performing music. Because the music and fighting styles were African-based, the European-descended officials were fooled into accepting the *capoeira* movements as an unusual dance style rather than a combat technique. Eventually, the inclusion of music in the performance of *capoeira* became standard practice, so that today the genre is often regarded as more of a dance style than a martial arts system.

A *capoeira* performance takes place in a *roda*, a large circle approximately 18 feet (5.48 meters) in diameter that is outlined by the *capoeira* musicians and other participants standing in observation of the dancers. The two dancers typically begin the performance by "bowing" to the *berimbau*, typically the lowest sounding one, which is usually played by the senior *mestre* (master) of the group. The dancers then perform opening movements intended to assess the abilities of their opponent. This initial section is described as "cooperative," because the opponents do not attempt to strike their partner but rather work together to execute interesting moves, such as back flips and back-to-back body rolls. Throughout the performance, only the hands, feet, and head of the *capoeira* artist are allowed to touch the ground.

As the performance progresses, the dancers slow their movements in conjunction with a shift in the music. This "control" section is intended to develop the strength and balance of the performers as they slowly move through cartwheels and handstands, still making little attempt to strike their opponent. Finally, the music urges the performers to move to the "confrontational" section of the dance, in which the *capoeira* artists execute their movements with full force. The objective during this section is to knock the opponent off-balance and send him to the mat or into the ring of observers.

The basic beat of the music, which is articulated as 1–&3–4–, corresponds to the dance movement known as *ginga*. This movement requires the performer to cross one leg behind the other and lean back before springing forward to repeat the same movement with legs crossed in the opposite direction. The *ginga* is the starting position for all strikes, because it allows the performer to keep in constant motion and attain more momentum from the back position as he strikes forward.

The music is intended to encourage the performers, and the vocalists prod the dancers to higher feats of skill and comment on the action. If, for example, a smaller opponent topples a larger one, the lead vocalist may sing about the "falling of a tree" to tease the defeated foe. The *mestre* may shift the music to bring a performance "down" if he feels the dancers' performance is becoming too competitive and is threatening to turn into genuine fighting. While novice dancers focus on the *ginga* rhythm, advanced performers focus on the sound of the *berimbau* to spur themselves to perform more intense choreography. The sound of the *berimbau* bobs in and out of the basic rhythm in much the same way the performers weave in and out of reach of each other's strikes.

Capoeira has achieved an international reputation in the past decade as a unique martial art worthy of inclusion in competitions around the world. *Capoeira* clubs are increasingly popular in the United States and throughout the Western hemisphere. Though there is no direct relationship, the similarities between some of the *capoeira* moves and break-dancing, popular in the United States in the 1980s and experiencing a resurgence of interest in the early twenty-first century, have helped bring the *capoeira* tradition to the attention of many young Americans, especially because *capoeira* artists sometimes integrate their moves into dance club performances.

Arrival: Mexico

Mexico is the fourth largest country in the Western hemisphere and has a population of 129 million. Mexico City, one of the largest urban areas in the world today, with more than 8.8 million people, is built on the ruins of Tenochtitlán, the center of trade and military activity of the Aztec empire, which dominated the region for nearly one hundred years. The Aztec era (1427–1521) remains an important source of cultural pride for much of the population, many of whom are direct descendants of the Aztec.

While the native heritage of the Mexican population is important, the influence of Spanish culture is also quite prevalent. Many of the soldiers of the Spanish explorer Hernán Cortés, who conquered the Aztec, intermarried with the native populations, as did the Spanish colonialists who followed in their wake. As a result, more than 80 percent of Mexico's present population is *mestizo,* that is, a mix of Spanish and native ethnic heritage. The influence of the *mestizo*'s Spanish ancestry is visible in many aspects of Mexican culture. The architecture of Mexico's churches, the fact that Spanish is the national language (though many indigenous languages continue to flourish, including Nahuatl, the language of the Aztecs, spoken today by more than a million people), and, certainly, Mexico's music are all indicative of strong Spanish roots.

Gilbert Velez

I was raised in South Tucson, a small one-square-mile Hispanic and Native American city within the city of Tucson, Arizona. Although I understood Spanish, it was not until I started to sing *mariachi* songs at fourteen years of age that I finally learned to speak the language. In 1962 a children's group traveling in an old bus from an orphanage in Monterrey, Mexico, headed by a priest performed a concert at our church, and that's when I fell in love with *mariachi* music. Children as young as six years old dressed in their traditional "*charro*" uniforms performed to raise money for their orphanage. Using this concept a few of us along with a priest started a teenage *mariachi* group in 1963 that later became named "Los Changuitos Feos." This group still exists today, entering its thirteenth generation of children musicians. We also innovated by a scholarship fund for the graduating members to further their education.

Gilbert Velez

The instrumentation is violin, trumpet, guitar, and two essential original instruments modified from the Spanish Conquistadores, the guitarron and vihuela. Guitarra de golpe, flute, and harp add another dimension of sophistication. Modern *mariachi* does not use drums or percussion instruments; the guitarron and vihuela carry the rhythm.

In 2012, Mexico formally accepted the designation that *mariachi* music is a precious cultural legacy, a world patrimony, which must be preserved and promoted. UNESCO, the cultural and educational arm of the United Nations, last year declared *mariachi* music as an Intangible Cultural Heritage of Humanity.

The opinion in the 1960s, however, was that two or three Mexicans playing the guitar constituted a *mariachi* group. Our new eleven-piece *mariachi* ensemble grew in popularity and was soon performing across the nation in El Paso, Santa Fe, Chicago, Washington, DC, New York, Phoenix, Disney studios, Universal Studios and auditioning for the Ed Sullivan show in Manhattan, Mexico City, Guadalajara, and many other cities in México. The audience experienced well-trained children performing with dignity, precision, pride, exposing a Hispanic culture not yet seen across the nation. More than this, it gave parents an idea of what their own children could experience if they also learned the music.

Mariachi music has come to represent the true soul of the Mexican spirit in the United States. From a humble beginning and an idea from a Catholic priest and the hard work of some young teens, a cultural movement started over fifty years ago that has exploded throughout the United States. *Mariachi* music was not written down. It was traditionally taught aurally and orally. As it became more popular in the Southwest, many parents wanted it to be taught in the schools. In the 1980s a movement started in Arizona to create pedagogical materials for *mariachi* music, including lesson plans, goals, curriculum, etc. It was presented to school boards and accepted. There is still experimentation so that the true meaning of the music does not get lost in the technical translation. There are now thousands of arrangements of songs available as part of the official MENC (National Association for Music Education) curriculum for choir, band, jazz, and string orchestras. Two thousand K–12 schools now have some type of mariachi music program and so do many universities across the nation from Harvard, Boston College, UCLA, and the University of California, Berkeley. The Las Vegas School Districts have 5,000 students in their elementary, middle and high school programs playing *mariachi*.

Mariachi conferences have also spread across the nation with as many as 1,000 participants attending and taught by master teachers. Hispanic students have found a new path to fellowship and comradery in relation to their heritage. The culture of mariachi music is woven throughout the life of Tucson, Arizona. There are performances at parties, weddings, traditional *serenatas*, and also at conventions, political events, funerals, parades, and concerts.

One of my greatest accomplishments from forming that group fifty years ago is that we not only trained musicians but these students learned discipline and a love of their culture and heritage that continues in their lives. Many became doctors, lawyers, university Ph.D.s, senators, superintendents of school districts, educators, and had many other successful endeavors.

A mariachi group can include a choir, strings, and brass, and is highly organized, choreographed, structured, and the music has to be memorized. Praise and acknowledgement in a performance are immediate. The music makes one feel happy, passionate, exciting, soulful, loving, searching, historic, purposeful and exotic. The audience responds, admires, respects, and appreciates the effort of the performers.

Site 6: *Mariachi*

MARIACHI
An entertainment music associated with festivals and celebratory events in Mexico.

VIHUELA
A small, fretted plucked lute from Mexico, similar to a guitar but with a convex resonator.

GUITARRÓN
A large fretted plucked lute from Mexico, similar to a guitar but with a convex resonator.

First Impressions. **Mariachi** is often a festive music. While sad and romantic songs are common to the genre, contagiously peppy performances, such as the audio example, are the more common conception of mariachi music. A single listen to this celebratory style can conjure images of confetti and firecrackers with revelers holding their margarita glasses high and singing along with sombrero-topped musicians.

Aural Analysis. *Mariachi* is heavily imbued with European musical characteristics. This is shown most obviously by its instrumentation, which incorporates such familiar instruments as the violin, the trumpet, and the guitar. Guitars appear in a number of forms, including the **vihuela** (small guitar) and **guitarrón** (large guitar), both of which have convex resonators. Frequent changes in instrumentation are characteristic of *mariachi* music as different instrumental sections are highlighted to produce contrasting textures. Melodic passages are exchanged between the violins and the trumpets, with the guitars as a constant rhythmic and harmonic accompaniment. Few percussion instruments are heard in *mariachi*, because the percussive sound of the guitarists as well as the handclapping and foot-stomping of the dancers (absent from the recording) usually provide enough rhythm.

Vocalists use a full, often operatic voice, complemented by the occasional yells and laughter of fellow band members, who chime in to help make the music more festive. During vocal sections, the violins and trumpets generally play a secondary role to avoid overshadowing the singer. Song texts often have romantic themes, but they may also be about work, as with our example, *Los Arrieros* (The Muleteers). Lyrics with political or religious references are less common. Due to the Iberian descent of mestizo musicians, Spanish is the language of the *mariachi* singer.

Another key feature of *mariachi* is the use of clear, often memorable melodic lines, such as the melody of "La Cucaracha" (The Cockroach), a well-known Spanish folk tune that became popular in Mexico during the early twentieth century. Modern *mariachi* bands typically use trumpets and/or violins to play the main melody. Shifts in tempo corresponding to variations in instrumentation are also common; for example, if performance of the main melody switches from violins to trumpet. These changes in tempo typically correspond with changes in the movements of dancers and are reminiscent of the frequent tempo changes found in Spanish flamenco music. *Mariachi* music may follow a variety of meters, which are usually clear-cut and in duple or triple meter, occasionally shifting along with changes in tempo. Our example is a song style known as *son jalisciense*, which tends to be more rhythmically active than most *mariachi* music, with its frequent subtle shifts of meter and tempo.

STROPHIC
In song lyrics, the use of distinct units (strophes) that have the same number of lines, rhyme scheme, and meter.

Mariachi music is most often in a major key, which is characteristic of "happy" music in European-related music traditions. Dynamic variations result from changes in instrumentation, as the trumpet-highlighted sections are louder than those sections emphasizing the violins or vocalist. The form of our example includes many distinctive sections, essentially **strophic**, meaning that the music repeats with each new verse sung by the vocalist.

A Mexican *mariachi* group performs at a North American wedding. (From left to right) violin, *guitarrón*, *vihuela*, guitar, and trumpets (Getty)

The bass range *guitarrón*

Cultural Considerations. While Mexican music is much more varied than merely *mariachi*, it is the decorative *charro* suits, wide-brimmed sombreros, and dramatic serenades of the *son* singers that have come to characterize Mexico and Mexican music to the outside world.

The origin of the term *mariachi* is unknown. One popular theory is that the term is a corruption of the French term *mariage* (meaning marriage), because the music was frequently found at weddings and other festive events. Others believe the name comes from an indigenous word referring to a type of social event that features dancers stomping on a wooden platform. Whatever the etymology of its name, *mariachi* first appeared in the southwestern state of Jalisco.

Various instruments found in *mariachi*, such as the violin, harp, and guitar, were originally brought by Spanish missionaries for use in church services but soon became common in secular musical activities as well. The early *mariachi* bands were primarily string bands, with the violin as the dominant melodic instrument. The harp was originally a principal instrument accompanying the violin, but with the addition of trumpets to the ensemble, the *vihuela, guitarrón*, and other guitars became the instruments of choice in part because they could be played with greater volume. The inclusion of the trumpet also encouraged the use of several violins in an ensemble, so that today it is common to see *mariachi* orchestras that include a dozen or more performers.

Early *mariachi* groups played primarily for festive events and in restaurants and taverns. These contexts are still common places in which to find *mariachi* music, as well as for private functions. Musicians serenade their patrons with the expectation that they will be paid for each song they perform. During the 1940s–1950s, *mariachi* reached its peak of popularity, as it was the featured music in a number of Hollywood films set in Mexico, as well as films from Mexico itself. As a result, the elaborately decorated *charro* suits and sombreros presented in these films have become the standard dress for *mariachi* musicians throughout the country. In addition, *mariachi*-like music was made popular in the 1960s by an American-born band leader who performed as Herb Alpert and the Tijuana Brass. Along with these secular functions, *mariachi* has become common in many religious settings, including masses, communions, weddings, and even funerals. From about 1959 *mariachi* masses became prominent, especially at the Cathedral of Cuernavaca, a center for Liberation Theology.

Audiences in the United States temporarily lost interest in the music of Latin America following the appearance of rock 'n' roll, and thus *mariachi*, like *tango*, mostly slipped off the radar

LISTENING GUIDE

Site 12.6
Mexico: *Mariachi*

Vocals: Single male lead with supporting male ensemble
Instruments: Violins, trumpets, mid-range guitar, *vihuela* (high-range guitar), *guitarrón* (low-range guitar)

TIME	LISTENING FOCUS
0'00"	Listen for the freely rhythmic melodic introduction of violins and trumpets in harmony.
0'03"	Listen for the entrance of the guitar trio accompaniment, followed by an increased rhythmic density in the melody.
0'05"	Listen for the declamations of the lead vocalist.
0'08"	Listen for the decreased rhythmic density and freer rhythm. Note the subsequent return of a rhythmically dense passage with a regular beat.
0'15"	Listen for the descending melodic contour and steady triple meter.
0'28"	Listen for the repeat of the descending melodic contour in triple meter.
0'41"	Lead vocalist begins first verse. Listen for the shift to duple meter and increased tempo.
0'44"	Listen for the violins and trumpets closing the phrase with a thick rhythmic density and syncopated accents that contrast with the beat of the vocalist and guitars.
0'47"	Melodic phrase repeats.
0'55"	Listen for new melodic material from the vocalist and supporting guitars.
1'03"	Listen for the syncopated rhythmic activity of the supporting guitars.
1'06"	Listen for the violins closing the melodic phrase and the subsequent repetition of the vocal line by the supporting vocal ensemble.
1'15"	Listen for the syncopated rhythmic activity of the supporting guitars.
1'19"	Listen for the trumpets closing the melodic phrase.
1'20"	Listen for the shift to the trumpets and violins as the opening melodic material returns. Also, note the vocal declamations of the lead vocalist. Compare this material with that at the beginning of the performance.
2'00"	Vocalist begins second verse.
2'24"	Example fades.

Source: "Los Arrieros" ("The Muleteers"), performed by Mariachi Los Camperos de Naticano, from the recording entitled *Raíces Latinas: Smithsonian Folkways Latino Roots Collection,* SF 40470, provided courtesy of Smithsonian Folkways Recordings. © 2002. Used by permission.

MUSICAL MARKERS: Timbre/Medium—Guitars with violins and trumpets. "Operatic" lead vocal with vocal group. "Celebratory" vocal exclamations. **Rhythm**—Meter may shift from duple to triple. **Form**—"Sectional solos" emphasizing different instruments and vocals. **Phonic Structure**—Simple harmony, often in a major "festive" key.
ETHNO-CHALLENGE: If possible, attend a performance of a *mariachi* ensemble in your local area. Also, examine the portrayal of *mariachi* musicians in film history.

A *mariachi* (note instruments in background) mass at the Roman Catholic cathedral in Cuernavaca, Mexico

screen as far as North Americans were concerned. The most prominent North American pop star to promote *mariachi* in recent years has been Linda Ronstadt, whose album *Canciones de Mi Padre* (1987) includes many *ranchera* songs, *ranchera* being a style of *mariachi* that emphasizes vocal performance.

Questions to Consider

1. To what extent do each of the musics in this chapter reflect pre-Columbian, European, or African musical traits?

2. How does *siku* performance reflect community cohesion among Andean populations?

3. How does *tango* music reflect the essence of tango dance?

4. Is *capoeira* a dance or a martial art? Why might it be considered both?

5. How does *mariachi* affirm or challenge American stereotypes of Mexican culture?

6. How is the survival of indigenous music and culture related to the challenges of modernization and environmental degradation?

ARCTIC OCEAN

ALASKA

YUKON TERRITORY

NORTHWEST TERRITORIES

NUNAVUT TERRITORY

C A N A D A

Hudson Strait

Ungava Bay

BRITISH COLUMBIA

ALBERTA

SASKATCHEWAN

MANITOBA

ONTARIO

QUEBEC

Hudson Bay

NEWFOUNDLAND AND LABRADOR

UNITED STATES OF AMERICA

Gulf of St. Lawrence

Site 1

PRINCE EDWARD ISLAND

CAPE BRETON

NEW BRUNSWICK

NOVA SCOTIA

WASHINGTON

MONTANA

N. DAKOTA

MINNESOTA

MICHIGAN

VERMONT

MAINE

OREGON

IDAHO

WYOMING

S. DAKOTA

WISCONSIN

OTTAWA ★

NEW HAMPSHIRE

MASSACHUSETTS

Rocky Mountains

Great Plains

Mississippi River

NEW YORK

Site 11

NEVADA

NEBRASKA

IOWA

NYC

RHODE ISLAND

CONNECTICUT

Site 2

CALIFORNIA

UTAH

COLORADO

KANSAS

ILLINOIS

INDIANA

OHIO

PENNSYLVANIA

NEW JERSEY

DELAWARE

Site 9

Pueblo

MISSOURI

KENTUCKY

MARYLAND

DIST. OF COLUMBIA

WASHINGTON D. C.

Sites 3, 6 &

ARIZONA

NEW MEXICO

OKLAHOMA

ARKANSAS

TENNESSEE

Appalachian Mountains

N. CAROLINA

VIRGINIA

W. VIRGINIA

Site 12

TEXAS

LOUISIANA

MISSISSIPPI

ALABAMA

GEORGIA

S. CAROLINA

ATLANTIC OCEAN

Golfo de California

MEXICO

FLORIDA

Gulf of Mexico

Site 5

PACIFIC OCEAN

MEXICO CITY ★

Gulf of Tehuantepec

BELIZE

HONDURAS

GUATEMALA

EL SALVADOR

NICARAGUA

Site 10

Site 8

Site 4

Bering Strait

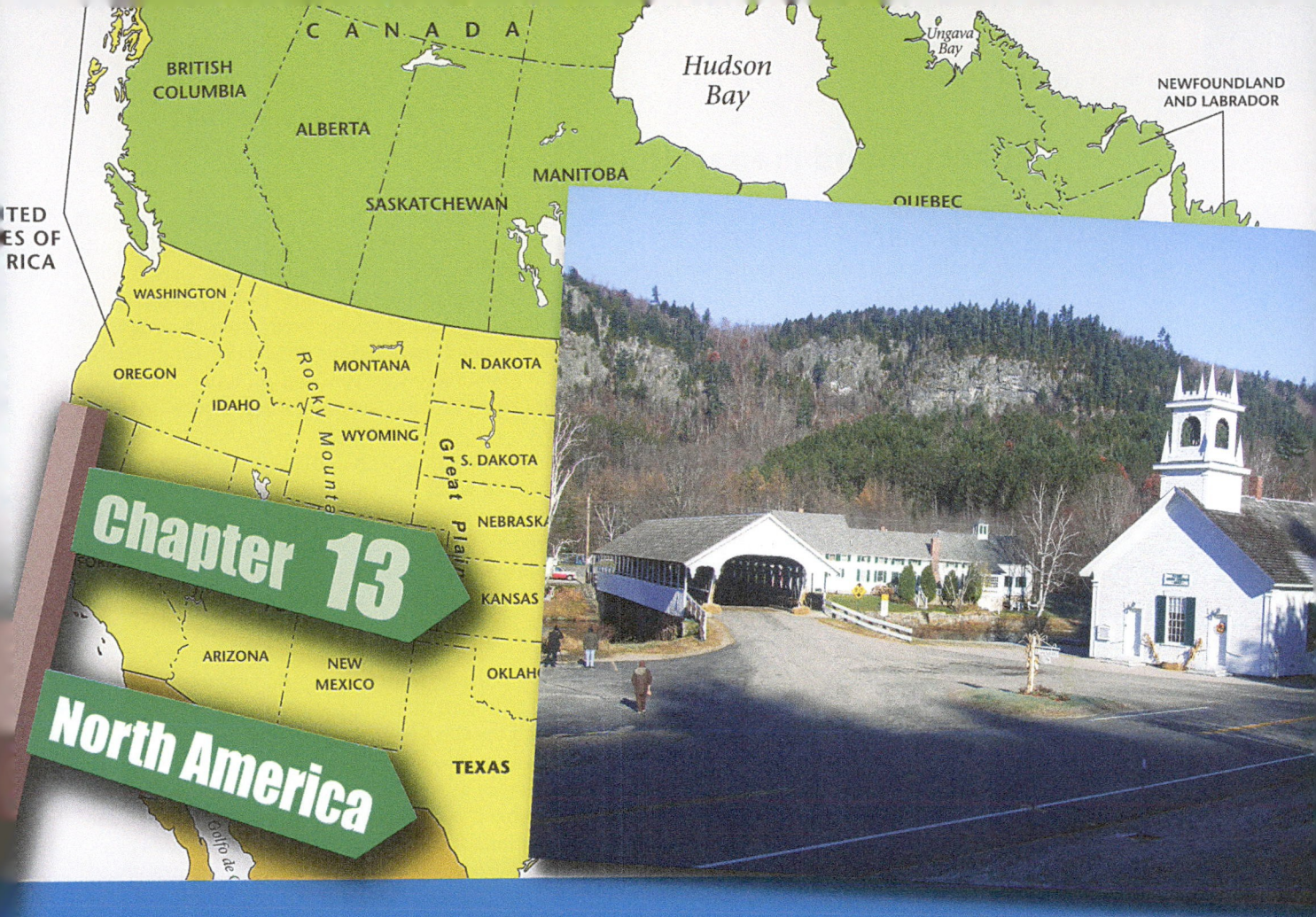

Canada and the United States

The village of Stark, New Hampshire, with its iconic covered bridge over the Upper Ammonoosuc River and white wooden church, typifies the ideal of a "small town in New England," and appears regularly on calendars, candy boxes, and dish towels

Background Preparation

For many of our readers this chapter covers what is essentially "home," the United States of America and Canada. Though Mexico is geologically part of North America, it is culturally part of South and Central America and thus was covered in the previous chapter. Formerly it was believed that the earliest people to inhabit North America, those who came to be called Native Americans, crossed the Bering Strait about 11,500 years ago, but recent excavations throughout the Americas have called this belief into question. Indeed, excavations at Meadowcroft, Pennsylvania, 30 miles/50 km south of Pittsburgh, have uncovered evidence of human civilization dating back to between 12,000 and 15,000 years. It is now thought that migrations from Northeast Asia could have begun 30,000 to 50,000 years ago.

By the end of the fifteenth century, Europeans—starting with Italian-born, but Spanish-backed Christopher Columbus—had found their way to what was called the New World, though there is evidence of earlier arrivals by Scandinavians in the late tenth century. From the early sixteenth century onward Spanish, Portuguese, French, Dutch, and English colonists came in increasing numbers. By the 1600s, England, France, and Spain had become the dominant powers in North America and the Caribbean. With the development of sugarcane and tobacco plantations, a need developed for large numbers of laborers. Because the number of colonists was still small, Europeans attempted to force Native Americans into slave labor. When this attempt failed, because Native American slaves resisted or died in the process, Europeans started importing slaves from Africa. The slave trade was at its peak from 1701 to 1810, though during that time the vast majority of Africans were sent to South America and the Caribbean rather than North America.

Eventually people from all over the world began immigrating into North America, making the United States and Canada two of the world's most diversely populated countries. Indeed, it can be said that in North America everyone's roots are somewhere else (except perhaps for Native Americans). The experience of starting a better life in a "new world" imbued many immigrants to North America with a spirit of energetic optimism. Many brought and preserved musical traditions from their homelands, some of which can be observed to this day. But it is also true that what is truly "American" (in the broadest sense) is the result of a mixing of peoples and traditions, a hybridization process that created new forms of musical expression. Indeed, America's musical culture has long been one of its most attractive, influential, and lucrative exports.

Ohio fiddler and fiddle maker Cliff Hardesty leads two friends playing guitar (center) and mandolin (left) in playing an old string band tune

North America's musical prominence is not borne of an immense population or size; the continent accounts for only about 13 percent of the earth's land surface and is home to only around 340 million people, a mere quarter of China's population, though the addition of Mexico's 111 million would change this somewhat. While Canada is the second-largest country in the world, its population of around thirty-five million is quite modest, about a quarter of Japan's population. Even the population of the United States, around 315 million, is small in comparison not only to that of China but also to that of India as well.

Both Canada and the United States began as colonies of Great Britain, though parts of each were earlier under French control, and the southwestern United States was under Spanish control. Unlike much of the Caribbean and most of Central and South America, where the colonial powers were mostly Roman Catholic, North America was largely Protestant. The dominance of Protestantism had at least two results: first, a greater tendency to suppress the religious traditions of both Native peoples and African slaves, and second, the flowering of an incredible number of highly diverse religious groups, many of which developed unusual or innovative musical traditions.

Planning the Itinerary

What *is* traditional North American music? Until recently, it would have been exclusively thought of as music from the British Isles, such as ballads and folk songs, fiddling and dance music, and some kinds of religious music. A broader view, however, must include Native American music, various African-American forms, and any number of other hybrid genres incorporating influences from Europe, Africa, Latin America, the Middle East, and Asia.

Despite this need for a broader perspective, it is of course still true that no tour of American "traditional" music would be complete without including the Anglo genres, even though many represent survivals more than they do American innovations. We will look at four such examples from the United States: a ballad, an archaic lined-out hymn, a singing school shape-note song, and a bluegrass song. While all of these typify the heart of Anglo-American culture, the traditions they represent remain little known to the general population. Sadly, it is possible to earn one or more degrees in music in most American institutions without being exposed to any (or more than a little) "traditional" American music. A foreigner arriving in the United States would be hard-pressed to locate any traditional styles, except perhaps bluegrass. Even that is mostly restricted to aficionados.

Canada's traditional music remains little known in the lower "48." What makes Canadian music distinctive is its abundance of Native American traditions. In addition, one finds various traditions associated with the *métis* (i.e., people of mixed Native American and European ancestry). There is also, of course, much music that derives from the British Isles. The primary influence is Scottish, as seen in the relatively familiar fiddling and piping traditions, but there are also pockets of Gaelic culture. French traditions remain strong as well, more obviously in Quebec, but also in Nova Scotia. Canada is here represented with an example of Scottish-rooted fiddling from the Cape Breton area of Nova Scotia.

Among America's greatest musical treasures are the contributions of people of African descent. Indeed, most of the musics that have come to represent America's energy and innovation have been African American in origin. Because so many of these musics have been absorbed into "white" culture, it would not be too outlandish to describe the United States as an "Africanized" culture in which people of all races participate in and appreciate African-American forms such as jazz, blues, and gospel, and in which much commercial music has "black" roots, e.g., rock and roll. While this entire book could be dedicated to just jazz or rock music and its roots, we have chosen to save those discussions for authors of other books. In this chapter, African-American music is represented by an old-time spiritual, a modern gospel choral song, and an old Delta blues.

People of Hispanic descent now constitute America's largest minority, as their population has recently surpassed the African-American population. Hispanics number at least thirty-three

Picturesque Peggy's Cove near Halifax, Nova Scotia, Canada, attracts numerous visitors to its peaceful fishing village atmosphere during the summer

million and constitute some 12 percent of the population of the United States. They come from many places, though those from Mexico, Puerto Rico, and Cuba constitute the vast majority. Hispanics are dispersed throughout the United States, with major concentrations in California, Florida, New York, and of course in all states bordering Mexico. Their influence on American music is pronounced. For example, a great deal of Anglo-American ballroom dance music is of Cuban, Puerto Rican, Brazilian, Dominican, and Argentine origin. *Salsa* music, an energetic style that developed in New York among Puerto Rican musicians but based on Afro-Cuban music, along with dancing, has become widely popular. The French-speaking Acadians in Louisiana—though originally from Canada—have also developed a distinctive music, known as *Cajun*, as well as its later offshoots, including *Zydeco*.

Because so many of the ancestors of today's Native Americans were forcibly moved from their ancestral lands, and because their religious rituals and cultural activities were suppressed by zealous Christian missionaries and government bureaucrats, much traditional Native musical culture has been lost. Nonetheless, numerous kinds of Native American music can still be found throughout the United States and Canada. In recent decades interest in Native music has increased, as Native American flute playing and drum circles, both based on Native traditions but innovations nonetheless, have come to be associated with "New Age" spirituality. We have chosen two examples to bring about a discussion of traditional Native American music: a pow-wow performance in the Plains style and a performance of Zuni flute music from the Pueblo region of the southwestern United States. We also highlight the highly unusual "throat-singing" of the Inuit peoples from Canada and Alaska.

Arrival: Canada

Although larger than its neighbor to the south, Canada is in many ways not well known by Americans. As similar as Canada's heritage and lifestyle are to those of the United States, Canadians proudly maintain a distinct identity. Like the United States, Canada is a nation that has attracted immigrants from around the world, and is home to many Native American peoples (called First Nations by Canadians). Because Canada's population is small, the relative significance of non-European

Natalie Macmaster

AN INSIDE LOOK

My name is Natalie MacMaster. I am a fiddler from Cape Breton Island, Canada. My music originated in Scotland, but the culture and the life it is a part of were nurtured here in Cape Breton.

We are a proud clan. For many of us on this island, the music has shaped who we are. It gets right to your core and gives you a lift, a joy. I even think it makes babies cuter and chocolate sweeter! What a gift it is to all those who were raised on it.

For me, what started as a genetically driven talent passed-down and played at home in the kitchen or at the community hall just down the road, has become a full-blown, thirty-year career spanning the globe with over 5,000 shows from Antarctica to Japan, New Zealand to Ireland. It is all I have ever done and it came about very naturally. I believe that timing had a lot to do with this success. I was a fresh face to an old tradition. Technology was advancing in the 1980s, and I produced my first cassette in 1989 at age sixteen. Making this a career was never my intention because I never saw it as an option. Most of the Cape Breton fiddlers whose music I admired so much had other jobs because playing local music could not be a full-time job. Even my uncle Buddy MacMaster, arguably the busiest of them all, worked at the railway station for over forty years. So I decided to go to teachers'

Natalie MacMaster

college as I loved children and would have my weekends, evenings, and summers free to play music. I did finish my degree but never set foot in the classroom. The music took over. Ironically, now I homeschool our children, and they travel with us and play their fiddles on stage even. I call myself a stay at home mom on the road!

Luckily for me, this music continues as my career and as my hobby. It fills me up now more than ever. As one gets older, you develop a deep appreciation for what you have been given, and you find more beauty in the simple. Cape Breton music is simple and honest. It is an important part of who I am and who I hope to be. I am grateful for this rich musical life that I now share with my husband and our six children.

immigrants and First Nations people is much greater than in the United States. Also important is French Canadian culture, which, while centered in Quebec, is found elsewhere as well, such as in Nova Scotia. Canada's culturally modern and ethnically diverse urban areas contrast with rural areas, where more culturally uniform populations continue to maintain long-practiced traditions. Our example of Canadian music originates in one such rural area, Cape Breton Island in Nova Scotia.

Site 1: Cape Breton Fiddling

First Impressions. This familiar-sounding dance-like music, which hardly seems exotic at all, features a violinist (known colloquially as a *fiddler*) performing with piano and guitar accompaniment. This music may sound vaguely "Celtic," though this term usually points toward Irish music. If you feel the urge to dance, you wouldn't be alone, for the sounds of dancing feet would normally accompany such playing.

Aural Analysis. The late Buddy MacMaster, one of Canada's best-known and most-loved fiddlers, plays a jig in our excerpted example: "The Golden Keyboard." Jigs are associated with a dance form (also called jig) known for its vigorous rising and falling movements. Along with other types of Scottish dance music—such as hornpipes, strathspeys, and reels—jigs came to North America

Map of Nova Scotia

with immigrants who settled in Nova Scotia ("New-Scotland"), one of Canada's eastern maritime provinces. Jigs are metrically organized in 6/8 time, with each of the two main beats having three sub-beats (**1** 2 3 / **2** 2 3). A given jig tune might be known by several different names depending on locale, while two jigs of the same name can also be musically distinct.

This jig is in the key of E minor. Its range is limited to less than two octaves because most folk fiddlers only play in "first position," meaning that they do not slide their left hand toward the instrument's body to play a higher range of pitches. In spite of their length in performance, most jigs consist of just two or three short sections, each of which is eight measures long. To keep the piece going, fiddlers repeat or alternate these sections. This jig performance can be charted as A A B B A A B B A A, though some of the repetitions incorporate variations.

Violins, in spite of their association with European classical music, have also been domestic instruments for centuries. While it is true that famous violinists use instruments valued in the millions of dollars, "folk" musicians usually play locally made instruments or ones bought by mail order at a modest price. Because the violin (called the *fiddle* in folk music contexts) was so often used for indoor dancing, and because families with "properly furnished parlors" usually had a piano, it became customary for fiddlers to be accompanied by a pianist who improvised a simple chordal or figured part. When the parlors were large enough, friends and neighbors could dance as well as listen.

Buddy MacMaster (1924–2014), Canada's best-known fiddler, lived on Cape Breton, Nova Scotia, in maritime Canada and played primarily music of Scottish origin (Buddy MacMaster)

LISTENING GUIDE

Site 13.1

Canada: Cape Breton Fiddling

Instruments: Fiddle (violin), guitar, piano

TIME	LISTENING FOCUS
0'00"	Listen for the three different instruments: violin, guitar, and piano. Note the main melody in this opening section (A) and listen for its return throughout the performance.
0'09"	Melody (A) repeats. Listen for the steady compound meter (six pulses divided into two groups of three) in the melodic line.
0'17"	Listen for new melodic material (B).
0'24"	Melody (B) repeats.
0'32"	Listen for the return of the opening melody (A). Listen for the steady low-range pitches of the piano contrasting with the syncopated rhythms of the upper range chords and guitar.
0'39"	Melody (A) repeats.
0'48"	Listen for the return of the second melody (B).
0'55"	Melody (B) repeats.
1'03"	Listen for the return of the opening melody (A). Note the subtle addition of grace notes and a more aggressive bowing technique.
1'11"	Melody (A) repeats.
1'19"	Listen for the return of the second melody (B). Note that the violin plays with "double-stops" (playing two strings at once) to add a harmony pitch to the melody.
1'26"	Melody (B) repeats and example fades.

Source: "E Minor Jigs," performed by Buddy MacMaster, fiddle, and Mac Morin, piano, from the recording entitled *Buddy MacMaster: The Judique Flyer*. Stephen MacDonald Productions, Atlantic Artists SMPCD 1012, n.d. Used by permission.

MUSICAL MARKERS: Timbre/Medium—Lead "fiddle" and supporting instruments (guitar, piano). Minimal percussion. **Rhythm**—Steady "Celtic jig-like" rhythm in a compound meter: underlying "duple" meter while melodic line follows denser "triplets." **Phonic Structure**—Clear melodic line (fiddle) with supporting harmony (guitar/piano).
ETHNO-CHALLENGE: Find a "fiddle" and learn to play a few simple melodies.

Cultural Considerations. Atlantic Canada includes four eastern provinces: New Brunswick, Nova Scotia, Prince Edward Island, and Newfoundland. The population is relatively diverse, as it includes First Nations, particularly the Mi'kmaq and Maliseet, as well as French Acadians and a small community of African-descended people. The majority, however, are of British (especially Scottish) extraction. Many among this latter group are (or were) Gaelic speakers, and have maintained Gaelic song traditions to the best of their abilities. The traditional context for their music-making was the *cèilidh* (pronounced "kaylee"), a kind of house party. Along with singing, fiddle music was especially popular. Several kinds of dance, including solo Scottish step dance, were enjoyed at these parties, accompanied by fiddle if possible. If no instrumentalists were available, someone could sing these dance tunes using nonsense syllables, called *peurt a beul* (pronounced approximately "porsht a boy") in Gaelic; some call this "mouth music."

PEURT A BEUL (pronounced *porsht a boy*) An unaccompanied dance song with nonsense syllables used to substitute for fiddling.

Cape Breton, from which our example originates, is an island separated from the mainland by the narrow Strait of Canso. Although Gaelic Scottish culture once flourished throughout Atlantic Canada, Cape Breton has come to be most closely identified with it. A revival in the Gaelic arts—part of an international Celtic revival—has made music and dance the primary markers of Scottish identity there. Today there is an active "Gaelic College"—actually a summer school for the arts—at St. Anne just north of Baddeck in central Cape Breton.

The fiddling tradition in Cape Breton consists primarily of Scottish dance music, particularly waltzes, reels, jigs, polkas, square dance tunes, and schottisches. Fiddle music found in Cape Breton is not purely Scottish in origin, however. There has been cross-pollination between the French Acadian and Scottish styles, and in recent years there have also been a number of innovative younger players who draw on a variety of traditions. Fiddling was in rapid decline by the 1960s, but the Glendale Festival of 1973 stimulated a broad revival. In addition, Rounder Records of Boston has released a great number of albums of Cape Breton fiddling, which helped bring the music to the attention of the wider public. Today Natalie MacMaster, Buddy's niece, has achieved an international reputation for playing updated Cape Breton fiddle tunes along with innovative compositions.

Arrival: The United States of America

Because the United States is a country of immigrants superimposed on the original culture of Native Americans, American culture is of necessity highly complex. Beneath the appearance of a generic American culture—primarily its popular, mass culture—there are uncounted sub-cultures comprising people who identify with a particular language, religion, racial stock, or other factor. Within these communities, whose diversity continues to expand to include such formerly little known groups as Karen and Mon from Burma and Nepalese expelled from Bhutan, are groups of people so completely insulated from mainstream culture that they live their original culture and never use English as well as groups that have become totally assimilated into American society, and every possibility between. This raises a challenge relative to what can represent the United States musically. Any answer is inevitably a compromise. Choosing to explore music unchanged from its foreign source (e.g., Persian music in the U.S.) makes for interesting reading but fails to enlighten on what "American music" means. Limiting ourselves to music that arises from the unique circumstances of the United States, that is, a music that could only result from the unique mixing here, creates a different set of dilemmas. "Jazz," for example, is considered distinctly American, but covers such a multitude of styles, both contemporary and historical, that no one audio example could capture its essence. A visitor to the United States seeking to know its music will have to make tough choices, and that includes us in considering the music for this book.

By size the United States, including Alaska, is equal to China, three times that of India, and only a little more than half of Russia. Their populations, however, are dramatically different, China having more than four times the population in the same space, India having more than 3.5 times the population in one-third of the space, while Russia has half the U.S. population in nearly twice the space. In terms of birthrates, China and India struggle to keep the populations from growing, Russia suffers from a flat growth rate, but much of the growth in the United States is from immigration, a factor that continues to increase its diversity, and consequently its definitions of what is "American music" as opposed to "music in the United States."

Of the immigrant cultures, the first to establish themselves were the English and Germans. Though German was seriously considered as the national language of the new nation, English was chosen instead. Two areas of the United States have preserved traditional Anglo music more than others: New England and the Southern **Appalachians**. Much of the traditional culture of both areas is disappearing, however, as once isolated and relatively economically disadvantaged communities have increasingly been incorporated into "modern" American life. Nonetheless, a good deal of collecting of ballads, songs, and dance music over the last one hundred or so years has preserved important examples of the music that once was common but distinctive throughout these regions.

APPALACHIA
A geographic region of the eastern United States along the Appalachian Mountains, which extend from New England to the southeast in Georgia.

Site 2: Ballad-Singing

First Impressions. This track may strike you as rather plain and unexciting. It features an unaccompanied vocalist, who sings with little ornamentation or rhythm, and whose words are perhaps hard to understand. Nonetheless, it is an example of an old-time traditional ballad-singing field recorded in the 1950s, the influence of which is still felt in popular music today.

Aural Analysis. A **ballad** is a song that tells a story. Though sung by one person, it may incorporate both dialogue among two or more individuals and a narrator who comments on the story. The ballad we have chosen was recorded in Rhode Island sometime around 1950 by a Miss E. Price, who claimed to have learned the song from a friend living in Massachusetts. With the passing of her generation and a breakdown in the transmission patterns, most ballad singers today have to learn their songs from recordings and are better called "revivalists."

Listen carefully to our example and you will notice that the unaccompanied singer makes use of only five pitches—that is, a pentatonic scale. Some might hear this scale as sounding "minor" because the three notes A, C, and E outline a minor triad (three-note chord), but in fact pentatonic scales are neither major nor minor.

The text is a poem organized in stanzas of four lines each, but because the fourth line is repeated, the song actually has strophes with five lines. Though the basic meter is duple (divisible by two or four), sometimes there are extra words that seem to disrupt this flow. Ballad texts and tunes were all orally transmitted. Over time the words were sometimes changed, either when a singer sought to localize a song by changing place names or by bringing the story up to date, or when a singer made inadvertent changes based on misunderstandings or forgot something. One such misunderstanding occurred with a ballad called "The Burley Banks of Barbry-O": the song was originally about a low-class "rank [coarse] robber," but in America the "rank robber" became a "bank robber."

Many ballads concern stories that are depressing, even violent, and the ballad we have chosen is no exception. The recording's original liner notes summarize the story:

> A mother sees blood on her son's clothing and asks him "How it came?" At first the son avoids giving a truthful answer but finally [he] confesses the murder of his father, brother, or, in this New England version, brother-in-law. Then follow a number of questions, each one bringing out a new fact.

> (*Eight Traditional British-American Ballads*, 1951)

Cultural Considerations. The ballad is one of Europe's most important song types, and its roots go back to medieval times. Ballads in continental Europe and the British Isles were primarily an orally transmitted folk form. With the rise of the Romantic Movement in the late eighteenth century, however, poets both major and minor began writing ballads. Among them were two of the greatest poets of the time: Johann Wolfgang von Goethe (1749–1832) and Johann Christoph Friedrich von Schiller (1759–1805). Some of these literary ballads were then set to music, most famously by Franz Schubert (1797–1828). Anyone who has taken a Western classical music appreciation class has no doubt encountered Schubert's ballad "Die Erlkönig" (1815). As with the traditional ballad, a single singer performs all the voices: a narrator, the father, the son, and the spirit of the Elf King.

British ballads were brought to the attention of British and American scholars by Francis James Child (1825–1896), Harvard University's first Professor of English. Between 1882 and 1898 Child published a five-volume collection, *The English and Scottish Popular Ballads*. Child compiled the verses (but not the music) of more than 1,000 ballads, mostly collected from printed and manuscript sources and not from living singers. "Edward," the example used here, is number 13 in the collection, and thus it is labeled "Child 13."

Though American students pored over the Child collection, none seemed to recognize that these very same ballads were part of a living American oral tradition and that singers throughout the United States (and Canada) were still singing them at home for friends and

BALLAD
A song that tells a story, usually performed by a solo voice but representing different "speakers."

LISTENING GUIDE

Site 13.2

United States of America: Ballad-Singing

Vocals: Single female

TIME	LISTENING FOCUS
0'00"	Verse 1 begins. Listen for the higher concluding pitch (D) at the end of this "question" line.
	Line 1: *How came this blood on your shirt sleeve? Oh dear Lord, tell me . . . me . . . me.*
0'12"	Listen for the lower concluding pitch (G) at the end of this "answer" line.
	Line 2: *It is the blood of my old gray hound that traced that fox for me . . . me . . . me . . . that traced that fox for me.*
0'27"	Verse 2 begins.
	Line 1: *It does look too pale for the old gray hound. Oh dear Lord, tell me . . . me . . . me.*
0'39"	Line 2: *It does look too pale for the old gray hound, that traced that fox for thee . . . thee . . . thee . . . that traced that fox for thee.*
0'57"	Verse 3 begins. Listen for the change from "hound" to "mare" in the lyrics.
	Line 1: *How came this blood on your shirt sleeve? Oh dear Lord, tell me . . . me . . . me.*
1'10"	Line 2: *It is the blood of my old gray mare that ploughed that field for me . . . me . . . me . . . that ploughed that field for me.*

Source: "Edward," performed by Edith B. Price, from the recording entitled *Eight Traditional British-American Ballads from [the] Helen Hartness Flanders Collection*, Middlebury College, 1953. Used by permission.

MUSICAL MARKERS: Timbre/Medium—Unaccompanied single vocal (though some performances include accompanying plucked lute, e.g., guitar or lap dulcimer). **Melody**—New "story" lyrics with each repetition. **Rhythm**—Tempo fluctuations common. **Lyrics**—Tell a story, often sad or longing.
ETHNO-CHALLENGE: Use numeral or staff notation to transcribe this example. Also, seek out unaccompanied ballads (lullabies, nursery songs, etc.) known by members of your own family and compile a transcription collection of them.

relatives. It took an English folk song collector, Cecil J. Sharp (1859–1924), to reveal this living tradition to Americans. Sharp's first visit to the United States took place during World War I and was followed by three more visits, during which he collected folk songs and ballads from singers in the Appalachian region. His publications, especially *English Folk-Songs from the Southern Appalachians* (1917), precipitated a gold rush in ballad and folk song collection throughout the United States. Most of the collectors, however, were professors of English, not ethnomusicologists, and because their goal was to collect texts, they usually paid little attention to the tunes. One important collector in New England was Helen Hartness Flanders, whose collection is housed at Middlebury College in Vermont and from which comes the present example, "Edward," collected in Rhode Island. It can be said that Sharp was especially responsible for this surge in collecting, which brought the new and little-known field of Folklore to prominence.

The golden age of collecting ended around 1950, and while there are still singers who know Child ballads, it is the progenitors of these ballads who were important in the development of American music, both in a generalized sense and especially in the popular realm. More recent

Cecil J. Sharp and assistant Maud Karpeles noting down songs from Mrs. Lucindy Pratt of Hindman, Knott County, Kentucky, September 1917 (Courtesy of the English Folk Dance and Song Society, London)

performers, such as Jean Ritchie, a Kentucky-born singer living in New York who was important in the "folk revival" movement, have continued to sing Child ballads, but usually accompanied by instruments, especially the Appalachian lap "dulcimer," a three-stringed fretted zither played flat on the lap or a table.

Site 3: Old Regular Baptist Lined Hymn

First Impressions. Some first-time hearers of Old Regular Baptist lined hymns are puzzled or even put off by these seemingly tuneless and meterless sounds. As with the previous track, you hear only unaccompanied singing but now by a group that seems unable to come together either melodically or beat-wise. This "smudge" of moving sound is occasionally interrupted by a male soloist who seems to be chanting rather than singing. However confusing it may be on first hearing, this track, which was recorded by Kentuckians living in Ohio, represents one of the most archaic kinds of music still heard in the United States: a form of religious song with roots going back at least as far as the seventeenth century.

Aural Analysis. "And Must This Body Die?" is an eighteenth-century hymn by the eminent English poet Sir Isaac Watts (1674–1748) and is sung here by members of Pleasant View Old Regular Baptist Church near Medina, Ohio, led by their Moderator (leader). The Moderator simply begins singing, without announcing the hymn, since only he has a copy of the hymnal, a small paperback book without musical notation. Members join in as they recognize the hymn. At the end of the first line, the Moderator "gives out" or "lines out" the next line of text—but uses a melodic formula to do this, *not* the tune. Because of differences in timing and degree of ornamentation, the singers produce simultaneous variants of the same tune (i.e., heterophony). The singing is quite slow, and therefore the music has little sense of beat or meter. Performers simply sing from memory, without even knowing the name or origin of the tune, which has been passed down through generations.

425

Elders and other members of Valley Home Memorial Old Regular Baptist Church in Kurtz, Indiana, sing a hymn during a service in 1971. The second man from the left "lines out" the hymn from a words-only songbook

The words of this hymn are both elegant and sobering, expressing the conviction that while the body is temporary, the spirit is timeless:

(Verse 1) And must this body die?
This mortal frame decay?
And must these active limbs of mine
Lie moldering in the clay?

(Verse 2) Corruption, earth, and worms, [audio example ends here]
Shall but refine this flesh,
Till my triumphant spirit comes
To put it on afresh.

Cultural Considerations. Martin Luther's attempt to reform the Roman Catholic Church was not the only cause of the Reformation. French theologian John Calvin (1509–1564) had ideas far more radical than those of Luther. He objected to most everything that was distinctively Roman Catholic, including vestments, stained glass, most Catholic rites, and everything sensual, such as incense, bells, and full-bodied music, especially with instruments. He asserted that only the **Psalms** of the Old Testament, being the "inspired word of God," could be sung in church. These, being prose, had to be put into regular poetic verse ("versified") to allow for singing. Calvin's influence on the continent was great, but his influence in the British Isles was greater.

In England momentous changes had already taken place. King Henry VIII, desiring a divorce from one of his many consecutive wives and being denied one by the Roman Catholic Church, broke from Rome in 1534 and created the Church of England. As Calvin's influence spread, England underwent a Reformation as well, which resulted in the founding of the "presbyterian-structured" Church of Scotland and a reform of the Church of England in conformity to Calvinist ideals. The "Presbyterian" form, which came out of an attempt to make the church less hierarchical, is a bottom-up system in which representatives are selected at four levels, from local to general: session, presbytery, synod, and general assembly. While these changes were occurring, the radical Protestant and anti-monarchist Oliver Cromwell took power in England. Cromwell executed King

PSALMS
A book of the Bible's Old Testament comprising texts praising God, used as the exclusive source for songs in strictly Calvinist churches.

LISTENING GUIDE

Site 13.3

United States of America: Old Regular Baptist Lined Hymn

Vocals: Single male lead and mixed male/female congregation

TIME	LISTENING FOCUS
0'00"	Listen for the single male lead initiating the verse in free rhythm. Note the melismatic text setting. Line 1: *And must this body die?*
0'10"	Listen for some members of the congregation joining the lead vocalist at the end of the first line.
0'13"	Listen for the lead vocal "lining out" the upcoming lyrics. Line 2: *This mortal frame decay?*
0'17"	Listen for the congregation joining the lead vocalist to sing the second line. Note the heterophonic structure.
0'32"	Listen for the lead vocal "lining out" the upcoming lyrics. Line 3: *And must these active limbs of mine.*
0'36"	Listen for the congregation joining the lead vocalist to sing the third line.
0'57"	Listen for the lead vocal "lining out" the upcoming lyrics. Line 4: *Lie moldering in the clay?*
1'00"	Listen for the congregation joining the lead vocalist to sing the fourth line.
1'15"	Listen for the lead vocal "lining out" the upcoming lyrics. Line 5: *Corruption, earth, and worms.*
1'18"	Listen for the congregation joining the lead vocalist to sing the fifth line.
1'28"	Example fades.

Source: "And Must This Body Die?" performed by a congregation led by Elder Larry Newsome, from the recording entitled *Grace 'Tis a Charming Sound: Pleasant View Old Regular Baptist Church in Worship*, privately issued on CD by Terry E. Miller and members of the Advanced Field and Lab Methods in Ethnomusicology Class, Kent State University, Spring, 2000. Used by permission.

MUSICAL MARKERS: Timbre/Medium—Nasal "chant-like" lead vocal with following group. No instruments. **Phonic Structure**—Group sings with a "smudged" heterophonic vocal line. **Rhythm**—Free rhythm with brief pauses between phrases. **Text Setting**—Lead is largely syllabic followed by slow moving repetition that includes some melisma. **ETHNO-CHALLENGE:** Sing along as if you were a member of the congregation.

Charles I in 1649 and began attacking Catholicism throughout the British Isles, including Ireland. Eventually, Cromwell's reforms were overturned in England, and in 1660 the crown was restored, but Calvinism nonetheless continued to develop deep roots in Scotland's rocky soil.

It was in Scotland that a tradition of psalm-singing that is one of the roots of Old Regular Baptist singing in America first flourished. Cromwell had organized the Westminster Assembly of Divines, a conference to reform the Church of England toward Calvinism, which ran from 1643 to 1648. In 1645 this conference published the *Directory for Publick Worship*, which prescribed how religious services were to be conducted. This book is not the first to document the performance practice of "lining out" a Psalm, but it was the first to sanction it. Because many church members lacked books or were unable to read, the writers of the *Directory* recommended that the "clerk" (pronounced "clark") or minister "read" the Psalm passage before it was sung.

This led to a performance practice in which a leader (called *precentor* in Scotland and *clerk* in England) gave out the line of text in a chant-like manner just before the congregation sang the line to the tune. In the United States this came to be called "lining out," because a leader "lines out" the words, one line at a time. Furthermore, when the Scottish congregation sang, they sang without accompaniment. Whereas Reformed churches on the continent allowed musical instruments, most of those in Scotland forbade them. Because their singing was unaccompanied and without harmony, it was quite slow and had no recognizable beat. Further, some singers fell behind, some added ornamentation, some thought the melody went up when others thought it went down. The result was a "sonic smudge" of simultaneous variants of the tune, or in technical terms, "heterophony."

These practices came to the American colonies almost immediately. Over time, and with the founding of various Baptist churches—a history far too long and complex to describe here—there was also a change from singing psalms to singing hymns, the difference being that psalms come from the "divinely inspired" Book of Psalms in the Bible's Old Testament, whereas hymns are poems of human creation and may reference the New Testament. Over a long period and as people migrated to the South and West after the Revolutionary War (1775–1782), isolated groups of Baptists found themselves in remote parts of Appalachia. The Old Regular Baptists were officially founded in 1870 out of earlier Baptist groups in eastern Kentucky. There they continue to worship in a manner they believe was true of the first-century Christians, without instruments and observing most of Calvin's ideas on austerity and theology. They also baptize by immersion, preferably in moving water.

If this denomination originated in eastern Kentucky, why was the track recorded in Ohio? After World War II as the troops returned from Europe and the Pacific, jobs were hard to come by in Appalachia. There was little more than coal mining in Appalachia, but the burgeoning auto plants in Indiana, Ohio, and Michigan offered jobs and could be reached by car. Many people from the "hollows" of eastern Kentucky drove north and found manufacturing jobs in places

Clearly the architecture of Scottish and English churches was carried over to New England, as seen in the Old North Church in Bennington, Vermont

Interior of a Free Church of Scotland near Uig on the Isle of Skye has enclosed family pews. The three-tiered front area reserves the highest position for the minister, then for the elders, then the precentor, the latter being a male who "gives out the line" of the sung Psalms

Old Regular Baptist elders at Pleasant View Church near Medina, Ohio, prepare to baptize a new member after having broken six-inch-thick ice

such as the Detroit area, northern and central Indiana, and the Cleveland area. When enough Old Regulars settled in a new area, they founded a congregation, preferring to meet in a small building in the countryside even if they lived in nearby cities. That is true of Pleasant View Church, located amidst cornfields west of Medina, Ohio.

Hugh McGraw (1931–2017)

N.B. While all other Inside Looks were written by living exponents of their art, we were unaware of Hugh McGraw's passing until recently. There being no time to find a substitute and McGraw having been a towering figure in the shape-note tradition, we have chosen to include this account written by Dr. David Warren Steel of the University of Mississippi and a specialist on shape-note music.

Hugh Winfred McGraw (February 20, 1931–May 17, 2017) was an important singer, teacher, composer, and promoter of Sacred Harp singing. Born near Centralhatchee, Georgia, and raised in Villa Rica, he was the son of railroad worker John Wesley McGraw and seamstress Lillie Mae Ashley. He worked as manager of a clothing factory in Bremen, Georgia. He married Donnie Mert Todd; they had two daughters.

Although he was exposed to Sacred Harp singing as a child, he never showed much interest in the tradition until, as an adult in 1952, he attended a singing in Mt. Zion, Georgia, that moved him strongly. He sought out instruction from H. N. McGraw (a cousin) and A. M. Cagle, both accomplished teachers and composers. He made rapid progress as a singer and composer and was recognized for his strong skills as a businessman and as an interpreter of the Sacred Harp to the world at large. In 1958 he became executive secretary of the Sacred Harp Publishing Company, the non-profit firm that publishes the most-used edition of *The Sacred Harp*. While fulfilling orders for the songbook, he noticed a growing interest in the book and its music by musicians and scholars throughout the United States and the world at large, and made it his mission to encourage this interest, and foster its traditional character.

As an ambassador of Sacred Harp singing, he pioneered in spreading the tradition beyond the South and beyond the United States. He presented lectures and workshops to academic, religious, and other organizations and taught singing schools and sold songbooks throughout the United States. He arranged for traditional singers to attend nascent conventions in New England, Illinois, and elsewhere, always insisting on four essential practices that define traditional

Hugh McGraw, Sacred Harp shape-note song teacher and singer, Bremen, Georgia

Sacred Harp singing: the hollow square seating arrangement, rotation of leaders, singing the *fasola* syllables before the words, and public prayers to begin and end the singing. All these, along with potluck dinner on the grounds, have become standard practice at singings around the world. As executive secretary of the Sacred Harp Publishing Company, he chaired the revision committees that produced the 1966, 1971, and 1991 editions of the songbook, which included many of his compositions; he also led the company in creating studio recordings by experienced traditional singers. He chaired many singings and conventions in the South, and in 1980 founded the National Sacred Harp Convention, which brought together singers from diverse regions, countries, and local traditions, including African American singers.

He appeared in *The Long Riders* (1980) and *Lawless* (2012), as well as in documentaries including Bill Moyers' *Amazing Grace* (1990) and *Awake My Soul: The Story of the Sacred Harp* (2006). The National Endowment for the Arts recognized his contributions to American traditional arts by awarding him a National Heritage Fellowship in 1982, the first year it was offered.

David Warren Steel, 2020

Site 4: Singing School Shape-Note Music

First Impressions. Arriving at a small wooden country church in rural Alabama near the town of Cullman on a hot June morning in 1971, I (TM) could hear the singing some distance away, because all the windows were wide open. Hopewell Primitive Baptist Church was surrounded on two sides by a cemetery, the likes of which I had never seen before. All the grass had been scraped away, leaving the ground bare. This practice, typical of the rural South, may be an

African-derived custom also adopted by the white population. The singing I heard is also typical of the South, particularly northern Florida, Georgia, Alabama, Mississippi, and east Texas. People refer to it as *Sacred Harp singing* or *fasola singing*, terms that will be explained presently. Others may refer to it as "an all-day singing with dinner on the ground."

This track once again features unaccompanied vocalists, though this time their singing has an easily detectable beat. The first time through the song, they seem to be singing syllables, not words. Their tone of voice is quite nasal and strident, and the pronunciation has a Southern twang. After all sing a line together, each part comes in one after another and all four sing together to the end. One senses a certain enthusiasm not heard in the previous two tracks.

Aural Analysis. Among the many songs recorded that day was "Exhortation," a "fuging tune" composed by Eliakim Doolittle in 1800, using a hymn text written in 1709 by English poet Sir Isaac Watts, the same poet who wrote the Old Regular Baptist hymn. The title, "Exhortation," actually refers to the tune or musical composition, rather than the text; tunes are named separately because the same text may be used with more than one tune. The singers are arranged in a square, and each holds a thick, oblong book entitled *The "Original" Sacred Harp, Denson Revision*. A male singer first intones the three pitches of the triad that defines the key, which is written as A minor, though the pitch level is set for the comfort of the voices, as there are no instruments in the building to sound a standard pitch.

"Exhortation" is an example of one of the most interesting song types in this tradition, called a *fuging tune*. Although fuging tunes have a slight resemblance to a "round" (e.g., "Row, row, row your boat"), they are closer to the fugue, an instrumental genre of the Baroque period (*c*.1600–1750). Fugues begin with a single part called the "subject" that is then imitated by the second part, then the third, then the fourth, and so on (depending on how many voices the fugue has). Fuging tunes

SINGING SCHOOL
A tradition of teaching four-part harmony techniques, earlier found in New England's towns and later in rural areas throughout the United States.

Hopewell Primitive Baptist Church near Cullman, Alabama, and its "scraped" (grassless) cemetery, site of an annual *"Original" Sacred Harp* sing

A male singer (standing) leads a song from *The "Original" Sacred Harp, Denson Revision* at an all-day singing at Hopewell Primitive Baptist Church near Cullman, Alabama

are not fugues, but after a first section in which all four parts sing together in harmony, a single voice part begins what sounds like a simple fugue. Usually this is the bass, which is followed by the tenors, then either of the upper two parts (called *counter* (alto) and *treble* (often pronounced "tribble")). The actual "melody" line (tune) is found in the tenor part, with the counter and treble providing harmonic parts; this was typical of virtually all singing school music. Fuging tunes first developed in England but became a favorite of the early New England singing schools.

In this example, all four parts begin singing simultaneously, but they use syllables, not words. The first time through the tune it is customary to sing these syllables, which are based on the syllables "fa, sol, la, fa, sol, la, mi" rather than the better known "do, re, mi, fa, sol, la, ti" used today. The singers then begin the first line of text, "Now, in the heat of youthful blood, Remember your Creator God." After these lines, the basses enter alone with the next phrase, "Behold the months come hast'ning on"; they are quickly followed by the tenors, then the altos, and finally the trebles, each "imitating" the original bass phrase. After all four parts have gotten back together, they continue to the end with the words "When you shall say, My joys are gone." The section with staggered entries, which resembles the beginning of a fugue, is customarily repeated.

While the music seems to be in a minor key, in fact it is in the Aeolian mode, one of the so-called "church modes" that preceded the development of the major–minor tonal system. The seven degrees of the scale are A, B, C, D, E, F, G, A. In A minor, the G would be sharp, but here it is natural, giving the scale an archaic sound. If you listen to the first and last chords, you will note that only two different pitches are sounded, A and E; the C that normally would be added to make the chord sound full is missing. Sometimes in the song you also hear nothing but the interval of a fifth, which gives the music a hollow sound. The way the vocal lines move melodically sometimes produces dissonance, caused by the clashing of neighboring pitches.

Cultural Considerations. Many of the early colonists in New England were members of "dissenting" churches—that is, denominations other than the Church of England. Most of these denominations were Calvinist, and some were far more radical than John Calvin himself had been. The "Pilgrims" who came to Plymouth in 1620—in whose memory Americans celebrate Thanksgiving—were dissenters, believing in congregational independence and sharing Calvin's austere views. Consequently, they and their brethren sang only the versified psalms, normally

LISTENING GUIDE

Site 13.4

United States of America: Singing School Shape–Note Music

Vocals: Mixed male/female ensemble

TIME	LISTENING FOCUS
0'00"	Listen for the opening voice establishing a tuning pitch (A) with the *solfège* syllable "La," followed by other voices.
0'03"	Listen for the full ensemble beginning the melodic line using *solfège* syllables. Note the use of *solfège* syllables throughout the opening verse, the homophonic structure, and the consistent use of duple meter.
0'14"	Listen for the entrance of the low-range male voices (*bass*), followed by, respectively, the high-range male voices (*tenors*), low-range female voices (*counters*), and high-range female voices (*trebles*). Each "fuging" entrance follows on the second pulse after the preceding voice.
0'28"	Listen for the "fuging" entrances of each vocal range, heard in ascending order.
0'44"	Listen for the change to lyrics (not *solfège*) and the repetition of melodic/harmonic content.
0'57"	Listen for the "fuging" entrances of each vocal range, heard in ascending order.
1'11"	Listen for the "fuging" entrances of each vocal range, heard in ascending order.

Source: "Exhortation," performed by Sacred Harp singers at Hopewell Primitive Baptist Church near Cullman, Alabama, 1971. Recorded by Terry E. Miller. Used by permission.

MUSICAL MARKERS: Timbre/Medium—Nasal or "strident" vocal choir. No instruments. **Rhythm**—"Regular" duple meter. **Phonic Structure**—Four-part harmony. Main melody heard in the upper male voice. "Fuging Tunes" feature sections where each part enters in succession, like a round (e.g., Row, Row your Boat). **Form**—Solfege syllables sung first, then performed with lyrics.
ETHNO-CHALLENGE: Sing a familiar tune using fa-sol-la *solfège* syllables. If possible, participate in a shape-note "sing" in your local area.

lined-out and sung heterophonically in a fashion similar to the performance of the lined-out hymn in Site 3 (see above).

By the end of the seventeenth century, learned voices in metropolitan areas such as Boston were raised against this practice, known then as the "Old Way of Singing." Ministers urged a turn away from what they felt was a moribund practice toward "Regular Singing," by which they meant singing by note, in parts, and in meter. In order for this change to be accomplished, however, a number of elements had to fall into place first. There needed to be a system of musical notation, a set of compositions, singing books, and people to teach the congregations Regular Singing. These elements, which came into being during the first half of the eighteenth century, are still in existence today in the form of the "singing school."

The old singing schools were taught by "singing masters"—though admittedly some had mastered very little. During the last third of the eighteenth century, however, a number of singing masters appeared who were also composers, and some published their four-voice compositions in oblong-shaped tunebooks that became normal for singing-school music.

"Exhortation" from *The "Original" Sacred Harp, Denson Revision* composed in 1800 by Eliakim Doolittle notated in fa-sol-la shape notes

Chart from the singing tutor of *The "Original" Sacred Harp, Denson Revision* showing the succession of pitches and shapes in three clefs, from bottom to top: C clef, G clef, and F clef

Each book began with a substantial singing tutorial that offered instruction on notation and singing. From the earliest times singers in New England used the syllables—what is called *solfège*—customarily used in England. Instead of the series of seven syllables known today (do, re, mi, fa, sol, la, ti, do), they used only four (fa, sol, la, fa, sol, la, mi, fa). In the singing schools it was customary to sing the syllables the first time the song was sung, before singing the verses.

After the Revolutionary War, many people migrated out of New England, and singing masters followed them. During the nineteenth century, singing schools were popular social events on the frontiers in the Midwest and the South. Around 1802 two clever singing masters, William Smith and William Little, authors of *The Easy Instructor*, created "shape notes," in which each of the four syllables of the "fasola" system had its own shape. *Fa* is a triangle, *sol* is round, *la* is rectangular, and *mi* is a diamond.

After that, most singing schoolbooks were published in **shape notes**, a notation style that continues to be used to this day. Of the many collections published, the most prominent and successful was *The Sacred Harp*, compiled in Georgia by Benjamin Franklin White and Elisha J. King and published in Philadelphia in 1844. During the rest of the nineteenth century and through the twentieth, new editions were published. It became the custom to have annual "conventions" during which singers assembled to sing from *The Sacred Harp* at an "all-day singing with dinner on the ground" (i.e., a potluck meal sometimes served outdoors). This lively tradition continues into the twenty-first century throughout Georgia, Alabama, Mississippi, and parts of Florida, Tennessee, and Texas.

SHAPE NOTES
A music notation system that uses differently shaped "note" heads to indicate pitch.

Singers still gather once a year at Cabe's Cove Missionary Baptist Church in Tennessee's Great Smokey Mountain National Park to sing from M. L. Swan's *The New Harp of Columbia*, a seven-shape book from 1867

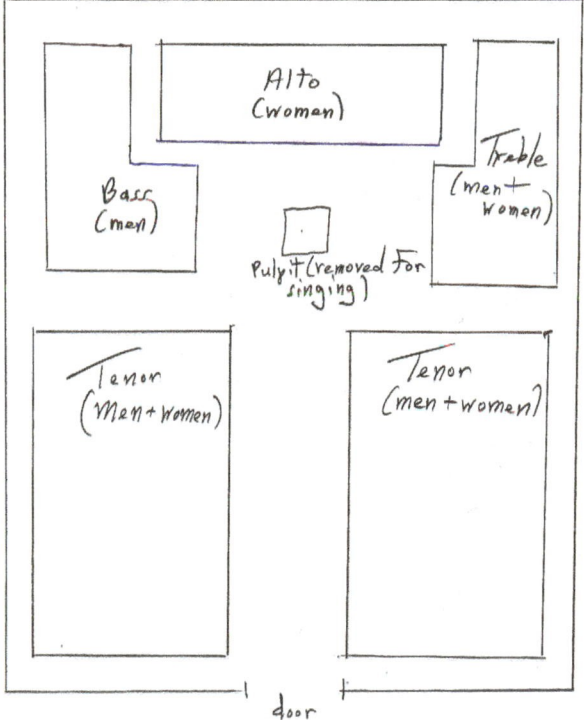

Typical seating plan for a *Sacred Harp* singing in a country church

Sacred Harp singings are often held in rural Baptist churches, and because these only meet one weekend a month, the church is open for one-, two-, and three-day singings on the other weekends. The arrangement of the church pews, with the pulpit in the center, creates a square. With the pulpit moved away, there is seating for each of the four parts. Anyone who wishes to do so is offered a chance to come up front and lead two songs. When lunchtime comes, everyone

Dance: American Folk & Square Dance by Janine Tiffe

The roots of American square dance stretch back to Europe. Mid-seventeenth century England saw an escalated interest in peasant dances among high society, and "English dances" became popular across Europe and the United States. In France, the term "country-dance" became "contre-danse," and eventually traveled back to England as "contra-dance." The French contributed the actual "square" influence in the dance forms, at times going by the term *cotillon*, or the Anglicized cotillion, referring to a peasant girl's petticoat. Quadrilles were another European dance style that influenced American square dancing, which consisted of pre-determined, memorized figures.

Western Square Dance Group. The women are wearing traditional layered net crinoline petticoats. (Wikimedia Commons)

Early country dancing in the American colonies was also comprised of pre-determined, memorized dance steps and the announcement of the song was ample information for dancers. Many of the distinct styles of country-dance in the United States influenced each other musically and choreographically. After the War of 1812, with increased contempt for the English and any of their cultural influences, greater support for French squares prevailed. The *contredanse française*, or *cotillon*, of the early nineteenth century required participants to bow to each other and their corners during the first eight bars of each set, and commonly perform balance and chain movements, all of which are typical movements for country dances in the United States. Circling, do-se-do, swing, forward, back, promenade, and aleman are other recurrent movement calls. Particular moves generally take a certain amount of time to execute. For example, circling the ring usually takes approximately eight counts as does executing an aleman left.

Possibly the most significant dance movement to arise in the United States has been swinging. Around 1870, social dances with roots in European traditions became less refined and more physically demanding. At this time, "swing" came to mean the practice of revolving in a circle with your partner, by each person anchoring his or her inside foot and quickly pivoting around them, creating significant momentum. Up until this time, swinging meant joining hands with your partner and revolving only once.

In the twentieth century regional differences in square dancing developed. The Eastern style, generally associated with New England and Appalachia, is the more traditional, slower style of dancing and sometimes alternates with contra-dances. The Western style, also referred to as the Modern Western square dance, is generally associated with the western United States. "Divide (or Split) the Ring," "Old Arkansaw (Gal From Arkansaw)," "Bird(ie) in the Cage," "The Girl I Left Behind Me (The Gal I Left Behind)," and "Virginia Reel" were common early twentieth-century square dances.

In the early nineteenth century, the tradition of "calling" developed. Instead of utilizing memorization, dancers listened for verbal calls to dictate the sequence of movements. Calling is comparable to the American tradition of lining-out; the caller provides a brief prompt or reminder to the dancers of the next movement or sequence. Song melodies were commonly borrowed from European sources, particularly Irish jigs and reels, as well as British and Scottish folk tunes, and the music for square dancing can be placed within the larger framework of Irish, British, and Scottish immigration in and around the Appalachian Mountains.

Toward the end of the nineteenth century, the singing of calls also became common. Instead of merely announcing the movements to dancers, callers began rhythmically singing calls, and including *chatter*. Chatter refers to the use of extra words and/or vocables by the caller to fill in the musical time during which dance moves are being executed. For example, if a move requires eight counts to complete, but only one for the caller to say "swing," the caller may fill in the other seven counts with chatter. Chatter can take the form of a simple story line, or other thread of prose to connect the entire dance to a larger theme. Chatter allows the dancer to enjoy clever humor and an amusing story line while simultaneously receiving instruction for the dance steps.

Square dancing has provided a sense of community and socialization for its participants. Through the execution of similar movements and by working as a unit, dancers, callers, and musicians form a sense of togetherness. In the twentieth century, square dance and other forms of related folk dance such as round dances, contra-dances, line dances, and clogging have been used for therapeutic and medical purposes. Square dance is unique to the United States and is so bonded with American culture that a bill known as the *Promenade Act* was submitted to the United States Congress in 2003 to make square dancing the official national folk dance.

spreads his or her food on long tables outside. Afterward, they continue singing until late afternoon. Similar "revival" singings have become popular elsewhere in the United States since the 1980s, providing "northerners" a chance to sing this style of music.

Site 5: Bluegrass

First Impressions. **Bluegrass** music is characterized by what is called the "high-lonesome sound": a high tenor harmony part over a baritone vocal melody, accompanied by a variety of stringed instruments. A bluegrass concert, typically a mix of "old-timey" tunes, "driving" instrumental solos, and the occasional gospel tune, is "down-home," a refuge from the hectic modern way of

BLUEGRASS
A style of American folk music characterized by virtuosic instrumental performance and the "high lonesome" vocal style, in which a harmony line is sung above the main melody.

A banjo player picks a tune during an outdoor wedding celebration in Nelson County, Virginia life. Perhaps you can picture the band in our recording set up under a gazebo in a town square on a sunny Sunday afternoon, surrounded by families on picnic mats.

Aural Analysis. Bluegrass music has clear melodic lines, simple harmonies, and a steady beat. Acoustic (non-electric) chordophones, namely the fiddle (violin), mandolin, banjo, guitar, and string bass, form the standard ensemble. Percussion instruments are rarely heard; the underlying rhythm is provided instead by the plodding bass line of a stringed bass or by the low strings of the guitar.

Each instrument has a unique timbre and different range. The bowed fiddle provides smooth melodies and countermelodies with frequent double-stops (the playing of two strings simultaneously) and sliding ornamentations. The other instruments are plucked, either with the fingers or with a plectrum. The five-stringed banjo has a "twangy" tone quality that contrasts with the mellow timbre of the six-string guitar. The banjo's unique timbre is due to the cowhide membrane used for the face of the resonator; this material brings out more high overtones than would be true of wood.

The bright timbre of the mandolin, the smallest instrument in the group, is primarily due to the high tension on the strings and the short neck, both of which contribute to the production of high, piercing pitches. The instrument has eight strings in four courses; this doubling of strings amplifies the mandolin's sound, allowing it to compete with the volume of the other instruments.

In vocal bluegrass music, the instruments play a secondary role, by supporting the voices with strummed harmony, "fills" (short melodic phrases played during pauses in the singing), and countermelodies (contrasting melodies played simultaneously with the vocalist at a lower volume). The string bass keeps the rhythm steady by playing on every first and third beat. The other plucked instruments often contribute to the rhythmic element by strumming on the up-beats (the second and fourth pulses), playing ornamented versions of the melody, or providing countermelodies.

Brought from Italy, the mandolin became popular in the United States early in the twentieth century, later becoming a mainstay of bluegrass music

LISTENING GUIDE

13.5 (2'36")

Site 13.5

United States of America: Bluegrass

Vocals: Two males
Instruments: Fiddle (violin), mandolin, guitar, banjo, string bass

TIME	LISTENING FOCUS
0'00"	Listen for the violin lead playing "double-stops" (two-pitches simultaneously), followed by guitar, string bass, and banjo accompaniment.
0'19"	Voices enter with a homophonic structure. Listen for the main melody in the lower voice and the "harmony" in the upper voice.
0'38"	The aural focus shifts to the banjo. Note that the main melody is played in the lower pitches, while the upper pitches supply harmonic support.
0'55"	Listen for the audience applause.
0'56"	The aural focus returns to the vocal duet for the second verse.
1'15"	The aural focus shifts to the mandolin.
1'32"	The aural focus returns to the vocal duet for the third verse.

1'50"	The aural focus shifts to the violin.
2'09"	The aural focus returns to the vocal duet for the fourth verse.
2'22"	Listen for the decrease in tempo.
2'25"	Instruments pause for final vocal line and then conclude the performance.
2'29"	Listen for the audience applause.

Source: "True Life Blues" performed by Bill Monroe and the Bluegrass Boys, from the recording entitled *Off the Record, Vol. 1: Live Recordings 1956–1969,* SF 40063, provided courtesy of Smithsonian Folkways Recordings. © 1993. Used by permission.

MUSICAL MARKERS: Timbre/Medium—"High Lonesome Sound" of vocal pair. Acoustic "string band" includes banjo, guitar, mandolin, fiddle. Minimal or no percussion. **Phonic Structure**—High vocal harmony over lower main melody. Instruments play harmonic accompaniment. Fiddle often includes "double-stops" (two notes in harmony). **Form**—Sung verses followed by instrumental solo breaks. **Rhythmic Density**—Often virtuosic rhythmically dense solos. **Lyrics**—Tend towards "nostalgic" themes. **ETHNO-CHALLENGE:** Watch some video recordings of the Grand Ol' Opry that feature Bill Monroe and the Bluegrass Boys. If possible, attend a local folk festival.

Bluegrass musicians are expected to be highly skilled performers and often play extremely virtuosic melodic passages. Each instrumentalist (except the bassist) is given the opportunity to perform a solo during sections without vocals, in which they play their own version of the melody at a greater volume than the other instruments. This alternation of the voice with instrumental solo breaks provides a clear example of a strophic form.

In our example, each verse has eight pulses. The fiddle opens the performance, anticipating very closely the main melody sung by the vocalists in the next verse. The banjo takes the next solo break and is followed by a second vocal verse. The **mandolin** is next and is followed by the third vocal verse; the fiddle then returns, this time with a bit more improvisation. A fourth verse concludes the performance.

MANDOLIN
A high-ranged fretted lute of Italian origin commonly used in bluegrass music.

The vocal timbre of bluegrass music tends to be nasal, even pinched. This is characteristic of Appalachian vocal music in general, but the "high lonesome" tenor voice enhances this strained quality, as the vocalist intentionally sings in the upper reaches of his voice. The main melody is carried by the lower voice, while the harmony is usually a third or fifth interval above, moving in parallel motion. The texts usually focus on male–female relationships or on the difficulties of having to "leave home" or family in, for example, their beloved state of Kentucky. Our example, "True Life Blues," performed by Bill Monroe and the Bluegrass Boys, focuses on the hardships of married life—interestingly, from the woman's perspective, even though the vocalist is male.

Cultural Considerations. Bluegrass music is truly an American music. Its elements are drawn from a wide variety of American music traditions, including the "old timey" tunes of Southern Appalachia, gospel, blues, jazz, and even mainstream pop. Bluegrass was inspired by nineteenth-century American roots music but was created during the booming economic era of the post-World War II years. Radio and television were integral to bluegrass's early success, but they have since mostly shunned its presentation. Bluegrass musicians generally prefer being ignored by the mass media and pop culture, which represent the hectic lifestyle of the urbanite. For them, the perfect environment is an outdoor performance in which technology is kept to a minimum and the music, rather than the presentation, is the focus.

The main figure of the bluegrass tradition was Bill Monroe (1911–1996). Indeed, even the term *bluegrass* itself is derived from the name of Monroe's group, "Bill Monroe and the Bluegrass Boys," after their home state, Kentucky being the "bluegrass state." Many of the most famous bluegrass musicians, such as Earl Scruggs and Lester Flatt, were members of the Bluegrass Boys at one time, and all bluegrass musicians, from Doc Watson to Alison Krauss, acknowledge Bill Monroe as the standard for the style.

Bill Monroe was born and raised in Kentucky. His older brothers, Charlie and Birch, already played fiddle and guitar, so Bill learned the mandolin as his major instrument. As is typical of most bluegrass musicians, Monroe acquired his musical skills informally. His mother and uncle were his primary influences—indeed, Monroe always credited his unique "shuffle" sound to his Uncle Pen (Pendleton Vandiver), who played fiddle for local dances. Having grown up in Appalachia, Monroe was inspired by a variety of musical traditions associated with the region.

Bill Monroe (Courtesy of BenCar Archives)

Shape-note singing strongly influenced Monroe's "high lonesome sound," with its upper-voiced harmony and nasal timbre. Gospel tunes became a standard part of his repertory. The instruments common to Appalachian string bands formed the basis for his own band. Monroe even claimed to have been inspired by the Scottish bagpipes, which, while not normally associated with Appalachia, were indeed known in the region due to the large number of inhabitants with Scottish ancestry.

The music traditions from which Monroe drew were associated with the white working-class rural populations of southern Appalachia. Beginning in the 1920s, large numbers of these Appalachians began migrating from rural areas to urban areas in search of work in factories. "Hillbilly" music, as the rural Appalachian music was then called, represented the life they had left behind. By mid-century, nostalgia for "country living" led to the popularity of radio and television broadcasts of this rural music, sung by groups such as the Carter family and later dubbed "country." The most important radio station in the South for country music was WSM in Nashville, which produced a program called "The Grand Ole Opry," because it followed a program of classical "Grand Opera" each week. Bill Monroe and his Bluegrass Boys became a prominent feature of this program, as well as of the subsequent television version. Monroe also released recordings of numerous songs, many of which, such as "Blue Moon of Kentucky," have become standards of the bluegrass repertory.

Discarding the "hillbilly" uniform of rustic overalls and worn-out shoes, Monroe dressed himself and his band in smart-looking suits and ties and donned clean, wide-brimmed cowboy hats. This polished stage presentation reflected the professional performances of the musicians in his band. Bluegrass, as the style was dubbed in 1956, was not "sing-along" music; it was concert music. The quick tempos and driving instrumental solos demanded exceptional virtuosity on the part of performers and serious attention from the listener. The solo breaks were infused with a competitive spirit, as performers vied to take the music to uncharted territory during each performance, an approach Monroe borrowed from jazz. Bluegrass had come to represent rural America, but with a sense of urban urgency.

Though overshadowed by the popularity of rock and roll, bluegrass acquired a large following during the 1950s and early 1960s. Interest in "folk music" surged in the mid-1950s with bands such as the Kingston Trio. The banjo became especially popular due to the success of folksinger Pete Seeger. Bluegrass became well known during this period, and musicians in particular gravitated toward its sound. Whereas the audiences for folk music performances were mostly made up of non-musicians, bluegrass concerts attracted musician-heavy audiences, who appreciated the high technical skills of the performers.

In 1965 the First Annual Bluegrass Festival was held in Fincastle, Virginia. At this event, Bill Monroe was deservedly dubbed the "father of bluegrass." Since then, bluegrass festivals and folk festivals in general have been the primary venues for the performance of bluegrass music. When the Coen Brothers' film *O Brother, Where Art Thou?* was released in 2000, many reconnected with Gospel bluegrass because one track on the film's soundtrack album featured veteran singer Ralph Stanley, originally one of The Stanley Brothers, a pair that was contemporary with Bill Monroe. Though a few somewhat bluegrass-based musicians have achieved success in the mainstream music industry, such as the Dixie Chicks and Alison Krauss, the majority of bluegrass musicians remain unknown to the general public. While "traditional" bluegrass continues to dominate the scene even today, since the 1950s there have been counter currents, collectively known as *newgrass*, associated with such groups as the Seldom Scene and the New Grass Revival.

Site 6: African-American Spiritual

First Impressions. This track, which sounds similar to the Old Regular Baptist track (Site 3), once again features unaccompanied vocalists. Their singing is rhythmically rather free and without any clearly articulated meter, and the pitches they employ do not always sound "in tune." There is an almost improvisatory character to this performance. While it is religious in nature, it does not really sound like regular congregational church song.

BLUE NOTE
A pitch not standard to the Euro-American tradition, believed to derive from West African tuning systems.

Aural Analysis. This widely sung spiritual makes use of only five pitches within the narrow range of an interval of a sixth, rising a third from the central pitch and falling a fourth below it. The upper third, however, wavers between being major or minor and is closer to what is called a "neutral" third. These pitches, which are characteristic of African-American singing in general, are commonly known as **blue notes**. It is this ambiguity between major and minor that gives spirituals and many other forms of African-American singing one of their distinct flavors.

LISTENING GUIDE

13.6 (2'30")

Site 13.6
United States of America: African–American Spiritual

Vocals: Single male lead with mixed male/female congregation

TIME	LISTENING FOCUS
0'00"	Listen for the lead vocalist initiating the first verse. Note the use of a duple meter with slightly varying tempo.
	Verse 1: *Come and go to that land* (repeats three times)
	Where I'm bound.
0'03"	Listen for the congregation joining the lead vocalist to finish the line. Note variations of the melody sung by individuals at the beginning and ending of each line throughout the performance.
0'22"	Verse 1 repeats.
0'38"	Listen for the melody line concluding the first verse sung by some of the congregation, while others repeat the "Where I'm bound" line a second time before concluding the melody.
0'43"	Verse 1 repeats.

1'01"	Listen for the lead vocalist overlapping the start of the second verse as some members of the congregation conclude the first verse.
	Verse 2: *I have a savior in that land* (repeats three times)
	Where I'm bound.
1'21"	Verse 2 repeats.
1'39"	Listen for the lead vocalist initiating the third verse, followed by the congregation.
	Verse 3: *Peace and happiness in that land* (repeats three times)
	Where I'm bound.
1'59"	Verse 3 repeats.
2'17"	Listen for the lead vocalist beginning to recite the Lord's Prayer as the congregation continues to hum the melody of the song.

Source: "Come and go to that land," recorded by Terry E. Miller at Gethsemene Baptist Church. Cleveland, Ohio, 1986. Used by permission.

MUSICAL MARKERS: Timbre/Medium—Congregational singing. **Text Setting/Melodic Contour**—Melismatic "moans" follow melodic contour. **Phonic Structure**—Prominent main melody with some individual improvisation (heterophony). **Melody**—Short repeated melodic phrases and lyrical content. **Rhythm**—"Freer" meter with slight tempo fluctuations. **Lyrics**—Often focus on "future" freedom/happiness. Frequent Old Testament biblical references.
ETHNO-CHALLENGE: Sing along as if you were a member of the congregation. If possible, attend a predominantly African-American "gospel music" church in your area.

A formal photo of the Fisk Jubilee Singers from Fisk University, Nashville, Tennessee, who began touring in 1871 to raise money for the struggling university. Their arrangements of "Negro spirituals" made the genre famous (from J. B. T. Marsh, *The Story of the Jubilee Singers*, London, 1885)

As is typical of spirituals, the words are simple, because they must be remembered. They also follow a structure in which stanzas are repeated with only a few words changed. Spirituals can have an unfixed number of stanzas, and these stanzas can appear in many different orders. This performance has three stanzas. The first line, "Come and go to that land," is sung three times, then completed with the phrase "where I'm bound." The second stanza substitutes "I have a savior in that land" for the first part of the first line, but finishes again with "where I'm bound." The final stanza begins with the phrase "Peace and happiness in that land."

Spirituals incorporate freely interpolated comments here and there, such as "woe." Inserting these extra sounds allows individuals to express themselves while remaining part of a group. These spontaneous interpolations also reflect the African-American attitude toward performance, which is not thought of as an exercise in lockstep precision but as a community event in which a certain amount of freedom is encouraged.

Cultural Considerations. While the term *spiritual* is usually associated with African Americans, it has also been used to denote a variety of Anglo pentatonic "folk hymns." But it was the African-American spiritual that caught the ears of travelers through America's South in the early nineteenth century, because its sound was so un-European. Although several scholars claimed these songs could not really be notated because of their free rhythms and non-European pitch intonations, several collections of transcribed spirituals were nonetheless printed during the nineteenth century. These notations, however, cannot capture the rhythmic and tonal subtleties of roots-style spirituals.

The spirituals constitute what is perhaps the oldest extant form of black singing in America. Because Protestant Christians almost always suppressed any Africanisms, particularly religious ones, slaves had to express themselves in a form acceptable to their masters. This meant singing something that resembled European melody, with a text in English, usually taken from the Bible. Most spiritual texts were sorrowful and looked forward to a release from earthly cares in Heaven. Some, however, were joyful, such as "Blow your trumpet, Gabriel"; this latter type of spiritual was often referred to as a *jubilee*. Many scholars have suggested that the texts of spirituals contained double meanings. For example, the words "Didn't my Lord deliver Daniel?" or "Steal Away" were perhaps coded expressions of the desire to escape from slavery.

Ironically, as spirituals declined in popularity in African-American culture toward the end of the nineteenth century, more and more outsiders came to appreciate them. During the twentieth century, "Negro spirituals" in many guises became a mainstay of American music; in arranged versions, they were sung by high school choirs and great black soloists such as Mahalia Jackson and Paul Robeson, and were played by bands and orchestras everywhere. Even classical vocal soloists often sang such spirituals in their programs, especially as an "encore."

The old-time spiritual, however, has not disappeared, as is attested to by our recording. In African-American churches, particularly Baptist ones, many different kinds of music representing different historical and style periods co-exist. One can encounter the old "Dr. Watts" or "long-meter" lined-out hymns that go back to the eighteenth century, the timeless spiritual, standard hymns from the nineteenth and twentieth centuries, and gospel songs of all sorts in numerous guises within a single service. The old-style spiritual is most likely to be heard during "Devotions," a brief period of preparation led by the deacons before or just after the main service begins. In a few churches these songs may also be accompanied by organ and piano.

Site 7: African-American Gospel Choir

First Impressions. On this track a full and enthusiastic-sounding choir accompanied by an electric organ sings a rhythmically active religious song, during a church service. Because it is so upbeat and joyful, this performance may not sound like typical American religious music to you. In fact, it may even remind you of "popular" music because of its strong rhythms and the style of the accompaniment.

Aural Analysis. Back in the days of record stores, the bins marked "gospel" included two kinds of music, "white gospel" and "black gospel." The latter has had the wider appeal to audiences both inside and outside African-American churches. Indeed, there are now gospel choirs, especially on college campuses, whose members come from many backgrounds. African-American gospel has become, like jazz, everyone's music. The present example was recorded at New Hope

The Convent Avenue Baptist Church Inspirational Ensemble directed by Dr. Gregory Hopkins at the piano in "A Special Concert in Harlem" at the Convent Avenue Baptist Church, Harlem, New York City (Jack Vartoogian/ FrontRowPhotos)

Baptist Church in Akron, Ohio, a typical urban, northern, African-American church. "God is Good All the Time," composed by Paul Smith, a local musician, has been the church's theme song for some years and is sung every Sunday.

The choir, made up of approximately thirty adult members, is accompanied by a Hammond C-3 electric organ. The old Hammond organ sound is still the preferred sound in African-American churches even though their electromagnetic tone-wheel technology dates to 1935 and was superseded by solid-state electronics in the 1970s. Combined with ordinary speakers or those with rotating drums made by Leslie, an acoustic piano, and oftentimes a drum set, the Hammond organ (B-3 club model or C-3 church model) provides accompaniments that range from straight "pipe organ" to nightclub stylings frequently played with much vibrato. Adding to the sound is the choir's clapping on beats two and four.

"God is Good All the Time" is a purely choral composition—that is, without a soloist—consisting of a main section lasting half the song, a middle section based around the word "Hallelujah," and a closing section that partly restates the main theme. Many other gospel compositions, however, feature a solo vocalist who alternates with the choir. Both kinds are heard during a typical service at New Hope Baptist Church. "God is Good all the Time" also exemplifies the predominantly joyful side of gospel. Other compositions may be much more subdued—at least at the beginning, though they usually become more animated and emotional by the end.

For choir members, gospel is an aural tradition, transmitted by the director to the singers through demonstration. While some directors write fairly complete scores mostly for their own use, others write only skeletal "charts" and some use no notes whatsoever. Singers rarely use any kind of score. Directors typically use their own arrangements, which are often derived from recordings. Accompaniments are provided either by the director or by a separate person and are mostly improvised from memory or based on an incomplete chart. Many directors also compose their own songs or create gospel-style arrangements of well-known hymns and "Negro spirituals." Stylistically, there is no attempt to distinguish gospel from the contemporary popular genres heard outside the church, for the secular and sacred sides of African-American music have long influenced each other.

13 WORLD MUSIC: A GLOBAL JOURNEY

LISTENING GUIDE
13.7 (2'01")

Site 13.7

United States of America: African–American Gospel Choir

Vocals: Female ensemble
Instruments: Electric organ, piano

TIME	LISTENING FOCUS
0'00"	Listen for the electric organ as it plays once through the melodic content. Note the use of a duple meter with a steady tempo.
0'12"	Listen for the piano adding occasional melodic embellishments throughout the performance.
0'22"	Listen for the choir singing the refrain with a homophonic structure.
	Refrain: *God is good all the time, all the time.*
	God is good all the time.
	When I look and see, all He's done for me
	There's no cause to complain, I can truly say.
	God is good all the time.
	GOD IS GOOD ALL THE TIME.
0'45"	Refrain repeats.
1'09"	Listen for the choir singing the first verse.
	Verse 1: *Let's give him some praise.*
	Clap your hands, Clap your hands.
	Let's give him some praise.
	RAISE YOUR VOICE, RAISE YOUR VOICE.
1'12"	Listen for the choir and congregation clapping their hands on the second and fourth pulses of the meter.
1'25"	Refrain repeats. Note that the handclaps continue.
1'48"	Listen for the change in musical content.
	Verse 2: *Hallelujah, Praise the Lord*
	For He is good, all the time.
1'55"	Verse 2 repeats as the example fades.

Source: "God is Good All the Time," performed by New Hope Baptist Choir, from the recording titled *God is Good: The Total Musical Experience at New Hope Missionary Baptist Church, Akron, Ohio*, privately issued on CD by Terry E. Miller and members of the Advanced Field and Lab Methods in Ethnomusicology Class, Kent State University, Spring, 1998.

MUSICAL MARKERS: Timbre/Medium—Warbly electric organ (popular music band common as well). Handclaps. Jubilant choir (can include soloist). **Rhythm**—Steady duple meter. **Melody**—Short memorable repeated melodic phrases. **Lyrics**—Repetitive and easy to remember. Frequent references to New Testament and "praise/celebratory" themes. **Phonic Structure**—Emphasizes simple harmony, major "happy" keys. **Form**—Verses with memorable refrain. **ETHNO-CHALLENGE:** Sing along as if you were a member of the choir. If possible, attend a predominantly African-American "gospel music" church in your area.

Cultural Considerations. The term *gospel*, besides referring to the first four books of the New Testament of the Christian Bible, refers to a complex of musical types running the gamut from simple, unadorned hymns sung dispassionately to elaborate, passionately sung compositions/arrangements involving a soloist and choir and multiple instrumentalists. "Gospel" music has a single root that, over time, split into separate histories for Anglo-Americans and African-Americans. Although "white gospel" remains a major musical force in the United States, "black gospel" has not only attracted greater attention, but it has also become one of the prominent forms of American "popular" music. It has also been exported, as thriving gospel traditions found in the Caribbean, the United Kingdom, and Africa demonstrate.

As a musical term, *gospel* originally referred to the hymns and songs associated with American evangelism from the mid-nineteenth century onward. Gospel songs developed out of three sources during the first half of the nineteenth century: the simple but "correct" or "scientific" harmonies found in the hymns of white New Englanders such as Lowell Mason ("My Faith Looks Up to Thee") and Thomas Hastings ("Rock of Ages"), Civil War-era Sunday School songs (such as William Bradbury's "Jesus Loves Me"), and the songs used in evangelistic services from the Civil War onward, such as "What a Friend We Have in Jesus," "Softly and Tenderly Jesus is Calling," and "Jesus, Keep Me Near the Cross." The term *gospel* **hymn** (or *gospel song*) was coined in the early 1870s by Ira D. Sankey, the musical associate of evangelist Dwight L. Moody. Gospel hymns are always in a major key and are characterized by the presence of a verse–chorus structure, the use of mostly simple chords (though some have complex, chromatic chords), and by the use of *afterbeats*—that is, echo-like repetitions of short text phrases—heard while one part holds a long note. Perhaps the best-known gospel hymn is "The Old Rugged Cross" (music and verses by the Rev. George Bennard, 1913).

Gospel hymns have been spread worldwide by evangelists, but in the South they were taken into the shape-note singing school tradition in the late nineteenth century. But it was their absorption into the Pentecostal movement, founded in Los Angeles in 1906, that caused them to flourish among African Americans. Some of the standard gospel hymns were composed by African Americans, but these songs in their written versions were indistinguishable from white songs. One man, though, Charles A. Tindley, composer of "We'll Understand It Better By and By" (1905), brought black gospel hymns into the limelight. During this same period black street preachers began singing gospel hymns as part of their sermonizing, accompanying themselves on guitar. Among the best known of these preachers were Blind Willie Johnson and the Rev. Gary Davis, first active in the 1930s.

HYMN
A "humanly composed" religious verse set to music.

With its pastor, the Rev. Benny Williams, singing solo, the Gospel Choir of New Hope Missionary Baptist Church, Akron, Ohio, is directed by Mr. Robert Nation during the Sunday service (Daniel Ledingham)

Standard gospel hymns, now treated as the starting point for increasingly free performances, developed into other new forms from the 1920s on, especially the vocal "quartet" (called "quartets" even though some groups had more than four singers). The most prominent black composer of the time was Thomas A. Dorsey (1899–1993), formerly a barrelhouse pianist known as "Georgia Tom." His gospel hymn "Precious Lord, Take My Hand" remains the virtual anthem of black religious music today. Solo gospel singers, the most famous of them including Mahalia Jackson, Clara Ward, and Marion Williams, brought gospel to the concert stage. Gospel performances involving choirs, often combined with one or more soloists, became increasingly prominent in the 1950s. During the 1960s vocalist James Cleveland brought choral gospel to prominence not just within the African-American community but for the outside world as well. Gospel music was increasingly influenced *by* and influential *on* popular genres. Indeed, much of black popular music, especially *soul*, derives ultimately from the old lined hymns and gospel performances of the churches.

Today "black gospel" mainly means choral music, with or without soloists. While it was originally associated with rough and ready street evangelists and "storefront" churches (small churches started in rented storefronts in the inner cities), over time it has been accepted by the mainstream denominations, including Baptists, Methodists, Roman Catholics, and even black Lutherans, Presbyterians, and Episcopalians. Gospel music remains one of the most exciting and creative of America's many musical expressions, and it is less and less restricted to the domain of black churches. Each year more and more colleges and universities add "gospel choir" to their list of official ensembles, and these attract students of every ethnic background. Gospel, like jazz earlier, has become an American music rather than a specifically African-American music.

Site 8: Country Blues

BLUES
A secular folk tradition originating within the African-American community in the southern United States with lyrics commenting on life.

First Impressions. **Blues** music is raw. Though vocal prowess and musicianship are valued, the essence of blues music is emotion. Through his music and words, the blues musician reveals his innermost feelings, whether of sorrow, anger, joy, or lust. Even the first-time listener to real rural blues may recognize features, such as harmony and scale, that are the foundation of much rock and popular music around the world today.

Aural Analysis. Country or folk blues features a solo voice, typically male, and an accompanying instrument, usually a guitar but sometimes a harmonica. The vocal timbre is often gritty, and the singing is declamatory and interspersed with melismatic moans. The lyrics are primarily sung in the first person. The vocalist expresses his emotions frankly and often deals with serious subject matter.

The guitar acts as a second voice, responding to the vocal phrases with "riffs" that affirm the proclamations of the singer. Though based on European equal-tempered tuning, blues is characterized by the use of one or more "blue" notes, which fall between those pitches normally used in the Western tradition. These "blue" notes make the music neither major nor minor—yet suggestive of both—and create tension and an "edgy" sound that reflects the unsettled mood of the music. Though much of the more familiar "urban" blues music of today is quite polished, folk blues was always rough around the edges.

Most blues music uses a minor-sounding key, because minor keys are perceived to indicate sadness. The typical blues song, however, usually uses only five or six tones, with the second and/or sixth pitches of the scale being omitted. The "blues" notes are generally found between the fourth and fifth scale degrees or the sixth and seventh scale degrees. Pianists will use the "augmented" (raised) fourth and a flatted seventh to play these "blue" notes, because the pitches of the piano cannot be altered. The harmonic progression of most (but not all) blues follows a standard "12-bar blues" stanza form. Each "bar" comprises four beats. The first four bars correspond to the first vocal phrase. The phrase is typically repeated in the second four bars, while the poetic response is sung in the last four bars. The harmonic structure of the blues utilizes the I–IV–V chords (roman numerals are used to represent harmonic scale degree) in the following form:

    Line 1 I - - - | I - - - |I - - - |I - - - |
    Line 2 IV- - -|IV- - - |I - - - |I - - - |
    Line 3 V - - -|IV- - - |I - - - |I - - - | (repeated for
each succeeding stanza)

This structure is often modified, especially in the last four bars, frequently as V–V–I–I or by having the last bar be V, which acts as a "turn around" that leads into the next 12-bar stanza. The non-musician can think of these chord symbols as representing tension and release. I is home, the most relaxed and comfortable chord. IV increases that tension, but then returns home. V increases the tension even more before returning to the I chord. Listen for this release of tension in the closing phrase (V–IV–I–I) of the first verse, in which the vocalist proclaims, "Back to the land of California (V), to my sweet home, Chicago (IV–I)." The guitar arpeggios complete the verse on the home chord with a "turn around" shift to V leading to the next verse.

While the 12-bar blues is the standard model for performance, blues musicians frequently take liberties with various aspects of the form. Rhythmic flexibility is an essential feature—bars can be added or excluded and the tempo can be changed—and even the chord structure can be modified. In our selection, the tempo is roughly 92 beats per min-

LISTENING GUIDE 13.8 (3'02")

Site 13.8
United States of America: Country Blues

Vocal: Single male (Robert Johnson)
Instruments: Guitar

TIME	LISTENING FOCUS
0'00"	Guitar introduction.
0'06"	Vocalist enters as 12-bar blues progression begins (I). Following four-beat measures, the chord progression is

First Line:	I	IV	I	I
Second Line:	IV	IV	I	I
Third Line:	V	IV	I	I (with V "turn-around" change)

TIME	LISTENING FOCUS
0'17"	First lyric is repeated. Listen for the harmony chord change of second line (IV).
0'26"	Response lyric, "Back to the . . ." leads into third harmonic line (V). Note the vocal line implies the shift to IV harmony as guitar riff sounds. This is followed by a resolution (I) and "turn-around" chord change to V leading into the next verse.

449

0'36"	Repeat of the first verse.
1'05"	New verse, "Now, one and one . . ."
1'34"	New verse, "Now, two and two . . ."
2'02"	New verse, "Now, six and two . . ."
2'30"	New verse, "I'm going to California . . ."
2'54"	Closing phrase on guitar.

Source: "Sweet Home Chicago" from *The Complete Recordings*. Sony/BMG, 2008. Used by permission.

MUSICAL MARKERS: Timbre/Medium—Lead vocal with acoustic guitar "conversation" most typical of country blues. **Form/Phonic Structure**—Follows 12-bar blues harmonic progression. **Lyrics**—"Troubled Life" themes. **Melody**—Typically minor key with "blues" notes.
ETHNO-CHALLENGE: Note the track times for the harmonic changes after the first verse. Listen for the 12-bar blues progression in the music of various blues artists, such as Robert Johnson, Son House, B.B. King, and Muddy Waters. In addition, you might research cover recordings by various artists of "Sweet Home Chicago," which is a blues standard.

ute as the performance starts, but by the end it has increased to more than 104 beats per minute. Such fluid musical elements add tension and enhance the unsettled mood of much blues music.

Cultural Considerations. An appreciation of the blues requires only that the listener have empathy for the hurts, joys, desires, and frustrations the singer expresses through his music. Though the country blues originate from the experience of being an African American in a racist and unjust world, the music's heartfelt and realistic perspective on the fundamental emotions of all human beings have given it broad appeal around the world.

The roots of much African-American music can be traced to the field hollers and work songs of slaves who labored under the broiling sun in the South, especially Mississippi, Alabama, Georgia, Tennessee, the Carolinas, and Virginia, as well as Louisiana and Texas. Singing was commonplace among slaves, who were forced to work long, hot days on plantations and elsewhere. The singing, especially the work songs, provided distraction from the tediousness of the work, while the music's regular beat often helped organize whatever physical activity the slaves were engaged in, be it pounding rocks or tamping railroad ties. The vocal style and melodic and rhythmic freedom of these work songs and field hollers, as well as many of the songs themselves, became the basis for early blues, spirituals, and gospel songs among African Americans after Emancipation in 1865.

By the 1890s, the blues form had appeared in many places throughout the Deep South. The most famous blues came from the Yazoo River delta in northern Mississippi and are called the "delta blues." While the instrumentation and harmonic progression of the music were inspired by the folk ballad traditions of Europe, the three-line form and use of an instrumental accompaniment as a "second voice" were African-American innovations. The characteristic "blue" notes are believed to derive from African conceptions of tuning. Even the itinerant lifestyle of the "bluesman" is thought to have its roots in the West African *griot* (jali) tradition (see Chapter 10, Site 7).

The "troubled" life of the bluesman provided a major resource for the lyrical content of blues music. Lost loves, promiscuity, alcohol and drugs, the bluesman's nomadic existence, racism, and death are all common themes in the country blues. Many of the early blues artists were blind, such as Blind Willie McTell, Blind Lemon Jefferson, and Blind Blake. Being blind made life difficult for a black man in the Deep South, as finding work was nearly impossible. Many other early blues artists chose the lifestyle as preferable to hard labor that paid little. A weekend's music performance at a picnic or other event could earn them as much or more than a week's wages farming on plantations or building levees. For the country bluesman, the burdens

African Americans dance at a "Juke Joint" social venue. Notice the police observer (Photo by Wolcott, Marion Post, pub. 1939, courtesy of Library of Congress)

of a nomadic life were preferable to the struggle to maintain a sedentary existence. Sleeping in railroad cars, shacking up with a female admirer for a weekend or two, and avoiding the law or racist thugs all became fodder for the bluesman's songs.

Many possible venues for blues performances existed in the early years of the twentieth century. Traveling tent and medicine shows often hired blues musicians to accompany them to attract audiences—particularly black populations, as the vendors themselves were generally white. Bluesmen frequently found work at house parties or in *juke joints*, the latter being the term for social clubs with a primarily black clientele. Brothels also commonly hired blues musicians to entertain and were one of the earliest contexts for blues pianists.

An important activity for the blues artist was playing in what are called *cuttin' heads* contests. These contests pitted musicians against each other in a kind of duel judged by the audience, which determined who was the better player. Competitions were a necessary way for a musician to demonstrate his skills and gain a reputation in order to find work. However, if a musician was "cut" (i.e., if he lost), he generally had to hand over his guitar to the winner. Losing meant a musician would have to earn, borrow, or steal enough money to buy back his guitar from the local pawnshop. For obvious reasons, these contests were a great incentive for musicians to develop their skills and expand their repertory.

The popularity of the blues was recognized by the budding music industry of the 1920s and 1930s, which released a slew of recordings by country blues artists. These recordings were a staple of the "race record" industry, which featured primarily black artists, whose recordings were sold to black customers. As the industry grew, blues musicians saw it as an opportunity to make some quick cash (musicians were paid a one-time fee for their services) and maybe gain some notoriety through a successful record.

When the Great Depression of the 1930s hit the Deep South, many rural workers moved to distant cities to seek employment. Northern cities, such as Detroit, Cleveland, New York, and especially Chicago, offered the greatest opportunities for work in factories and mills. As the black population left the South, the bluesman found that his audience was disappearing. Consequently, he followed his patrons to the city where he adapted his music to his new situation. Our audio example, performed by country blues legend, Robert Johnson, reflects this "gold rush" to the big city, that is, Chicago, in its lyrical content. Artists such as Muddy Waters, Howlin' Wolf, and Elmore James gave the urban blues a jolt of energy, literally, by adding electric guitars and forming combo groups that included less portable instruments, such as drums and piano.

Creative use of the microphone gave great harmonica players, such as Little Walter and James Cotton, a new sound and a prominent role as soloists in many blues bands. Later this updated form of the blues came to be known as *rhythm and blues*. These innovations led to the development of a new genre in the 1950s, namely *rock and roll*. Early American popular artists, such as Elvis Presley, Jerry Lee Lewis, Chuck Berry, and Little Richard, based much of their repertoire on the blues forms, as did later successful rock bands from overseas, such as the Rolling Stones, Cream, and Led Zeppelin. Not only rock was influenced by the blues, however: much early jazz was played in 12-bar blues form, and the distinctive piano style called *boogie-woogie* was essentially piano blues.

Blues was perhaps one of the most influential musics of the twentieth century and today is still a prominent feature of America's musical landscape. Many contemporary blues artists, despite usually traveling with a band, maintain the rural roots of the music by performing solo pieces drawn from recordings made in the early years of the twentieth century. Older artists such as Robert Johnson, Charlie Patton, and Blind Willie Johnson are still revered as the models for performance and are legends of the genre.

Site 9: "Nuyorican" *Salsa*

First Impressions. This recording is perhaps more rhythmically complex than any of our other examples of music from the Americas. As danceable as it is listenable, it offers both African-derived polyrhythmic patterns and European- and jazz-inspired harmonies, played in a crisp fashion with everything from brass "punches" to a florid, jazz-inspired flute solo.

Aural Analysis. Because the Caribbean is known for its cultural fusions, it comes as no surprise to hear European brass and the piano combined with a *slit-gong* wood block. Other instruments, such as the cowbell, are perhaps African in origin, but the clarinet, trumpet, trombone, string bass, and

New York's Spanish Harlem around 1970 s howing the area's many small shops (H. Armstrong Roberts/Retrofile/ Getty Images)

A local salsa band plays on the stage of the Eastman School of Music in Rochester, New York

Celia Cruz (left) and Tito Puente (right), two of the most famous artists associated with *salsa* (Jack Vartoogian/ FrontRowPhotos)

flute are European. This mixing of instruments representing different cultures (European, African, and Amerindian) is typical of the music we know as *salsa*, a term that otherwise denotes a colorful, pungent sauce much associated with salty corn chips. Our example also includes a solo male voice that works in a kind of call-and-response pattern with the melodic instruments and a small chorus.

While the melody and harmony are Euro-American, with a clear influence from jazz, the whole metrical/rhythmic structure is from another source: Africa. True, the music is ostensibly in duple meter—4/4 time—but this is no march, with a heavy, obvious downbeat. Here and there beat 1 is easy to find, perhaps by focusing on the melody, but in other passages it is obscure. Accented sounds are heard on the offbeats, giving the music a highly syncopated feel. This is because the underlying organization is closer to African timeline patterns than to European meter based on units of four beats each (i.e., measures). The basic organizational unit in this music is a two-measure pattern called the *son clave*, which consists of either 3 + 2 or 2 + 3 beats played in a syncopated fashion (see Chapter 11, Site 6, Cuban *Son*). Other percussion instruments play their particular patterns in opposition to the *clave*, giving the rhythm section a changeable complexity that is as difficult to sort out as it is to ignore. Indeed, in many compositions, beat 1 is de-emphasized or even omitted, requiring the listener to feel the missing pulse in order to know where the measures begin.

Our example begins with a melody played twice by piano and string bass, underpinned by the *clave* pattern (2 + 3) played on a wood block (called a *slit-gong* because the block has a deep slit cut in it near one edge). As the piano-bass pattern is played twice more, a tall barrel-shaped, single-headed drum called *tumbadora* or *conga* enters, playing its own *tumbao* pattern accompanied by the *maracas* (rattles). When the brass instruments begin playing melody, the *timbales* also enter, these being a pair of metal-framed drums of European military origin. The pattern that the *timbales* play, called *cascará*, is categorized as a *palito* because it is struck on the side of the drum. After this, the solo voice alternates with brass "punches" and flute. Finally, a section begins in which the voice alternates with a chorus comprising several singers, while the *timbale* player adds a bell pattern.

Entitled "Quítate de la vía Perico," the song is a mock lament for someone nicknamed Perico (meaning "parakeet"). *Perico*, perhaps a local odd fellow, was sucking sugarcane while walking on the railroad tracks and, not hearing the train, was killed. After an opening that sounds like a

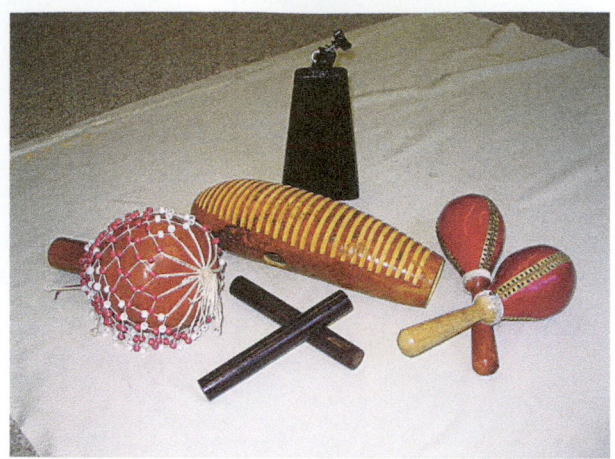

Left photo: (front) a pair of *tumbador* or *conga* drums, (right rear) a pair of *timbales* or *pailas* drums with metal bell attached, (left rear) a pair of *bongo* drums

Right photo: (from top clockwise) *concerro* cow bell, *maracas* (shakers), *claves* (wood sticks), *shekere* (gourd shaker), and *güiro* scraper (Andrew Shahriari)

train whistle, someone calls out "And here comes Perico again; let's have fun once more! And what a machine [locomotive], man." The vocalists then warn Perico in a sung "call": "Move away from the train track, Perico; the train is coming. . . . Later you may not say that you were not warned." In the response section the group sings, "If I had known that Perico was deaf, I would have stopped the train." The rest of the song more or less repeats these ideas, though we will spare you certain grisly details. This song was originally recorded by Puerto Rican musicians, including singer Ismael Rivera and band leader Rafael Cortijo Verdejo, but its text includes phrases associated with Cuba, not Puerto Rico. It is classified as a *guaracha*, a type of dance music derived from the *son*, and maintains the *son*'s *montuno* call-and-response section.

LISTENING GUIDE
13.9 (2'43")

Site 13.9

Nuyorican (New York City): *Salsa*

Voices: Single male lead with mixed male/female supporting ensemble
Instruments: Trumpets, trombone, piano, electric bass, bongo and *conga* drums, *timbales* (membranophone), flute, shaker, *slit-gong* (wood idiophone), cowbell

TIME	LISTENING FOCUS
0'00"	Brass instruments open with a "train whistle" imitation.
0'04"	Listen for the piano and electric bass establishing an underlying melodic rhythm used throughout the main sections of the performance. Also, note the entrance of the *clave son* (2 + 3) rhythm on the *slit-gong*.
0'08"	Brass instruments imitate "train whistle" again. Also, listen for the *conga* drum briefly improvising in the background.

0'13"	Listen for the *timbales* accent just before the *conga* drum and shaker enter with a regular rhythm. Also, note a single strike on the cowbell.
0'22"	Listen again for the *timbales* accent just before the melodic instruments enter.
0'25"	Vocalist enters with extemporaneous spoken dialogue. Listen for references to "Perico," the subject of the lyrics.
0'42"	First verse begins. Listen for the piano and rhythm instruments accompanying the vocalist, while the remaining instruments punctuate the end of the lyric's phrases.
1'12"	Listen for a short instrumental break.
1'17"	Listen for the appearance of the backing vocals as the music moves to the *montuno* section.
1'21"	Lead vocalist improvises while the backing vocals provide a consistent "response" refrain.
2'11"	Listen for the new instrumental melodic material, which emerges as backing vocals sing a new refrain, "Perico!"
2'30"	Listen for the flute improvising in a new *montuno* section with melodic rhythmic support from the piano and percussion as the example fades.

Source: "Quítate de la vía Perico," performed by Tolú, from the recording entitled *Bongo de Van Gogh, Tonga* Productions TNGCD 8405, 2002. Used by permission.

MUSICAL MARKERS: Timbre/Medium—"Jazz" instrumentation (Brass, saxophone, piano, various percussion). Flute often a featured soloist. Timbales accents also characteristic. Lead vocal with backing group singers. **Phonic Structure**—Vocal group and instruments in harmony. Lead vocal improvisations followed by choral responses. **Rhythm**—2+3 Clave pattern over polyrhythmic instruments. **Melody**—"Montuno" piano, i.e., short-repeated melodic pattern. Instrumental punctuations between phrases. **ETHNO-CHALLENGE:** Keep the *clave* rhythm going throughout the performance. Additionally, visit a *salsa* club in your local area or take some *salsa* dance lessons.

Cultural Considerations. The road that led to *salsa* started in Cuba, continued on to New York City, and then spread throughout the Americas, if not the world. Numerous factors account for its creation, and sorting them out properly requires understanding practically the entire history of Latin music in North America. First, we emphasize Cuba as the primary source for virtually all the styles of Latin music that developed elsewhere. In addition to influencing Americans visiting Havana before 1959, numerous Cuban musicians and band leaders either toured or moved to the United States to take advantage from the rapidly growing taste for Latin "pop," Cuban music that was adapted to the tastes of American popular culture. Among those exponents was Xavier Cougat, a Spanish-born immigrant to Cuba whose family moved to New York City in 1915. A band leader who first flourished during the "tango craze" of the 1920s, Cougat followed the changing tastes, and by the later 1940s and 1950s emphasized what some would call "watered down" Cuban music. Another impetus to the spread of Latin music was Desi Arnaz, a Cuban-born musician and actor whose family fled to Miami in 1933. Long after marrying actress Lucille Ball in 1940, Arnaz, formerly a guitarist in Cougat's band and later a band leader in his own right, joined his wife for the long-running television series "I Love Lucy," in which he played Enrique "Ricky" Ricardo, a Latin band leader. Cougat and Arnaz, then, helped create the space for Latin music's popularity in the 1950s.

A more direct factor was the development of Latin jazz. This began in the 1940s when Cuban conga drum players began coming to New York, bringing with them the timeline patterns of Cuban *Santeria*, an African-derived religion that had syncretized with Roman Catholicism. Among them was Chano Pozo, a feisty Cuban drummer who teamed with jazz trumpeter Dizzy Gillespie, along with Machito (Frank Raul Grillo) and trombonist Juan Tizol to begin the evolution of Latin jazz, a history too extensive and complex for inclusion here. Although Pozo died only one year later (in a car accident), Latin jazz continued to develop parallel to the new crazes for rumba, mambo, and cha cha chá, both the dances and the music associated with them. By 1959, when Fidel Castro's Cuban Revolution ended tourism to Cuba as well as the migration of Cuban musicians north, the nation's attention was drawn from things Latin to the new craze for the idols of the "British Invasion," especially the Beatles. Yet Latin music in the United States continued to develop and flourish, though to more specialized audiences.

In the absence of new Cuban blood, the Latin music scene began a series of changes that lead directly to the emergence of *salsa* music. One major factor was the growing population of "Latinos" in New York City, the majority having come from Puerto Rico. This population began producing most of the upcoming Latin artists as well as provided a ready market for both concerts and recordings of Latin music. Responding to this need, Dominican band leader Johnny Pacheco and Italian-American lawyer Jerry Masucci founded Fania Records in 1964. Besides producing most of the successful Latin albums until the company's demise in 2005, the Fania All Stars, a group of the label's best musicians, toured widely, launching some of Latin music's greatest new artists such as Celia Cruz (Cuban born, died 2003), Willie Colon (New York born of Puerto Rican descent), Hector Lavoe (Puerto Rican born, died 1993), and Rubén Blades (Panamanian born). A third factor was the emergence of Santana, a Mexican-born rock guitarist who later pioneered the development of *salsa* and Latin fusion. Santana's 1971 concert before 40,000 people in Yankee Stadium was also a key reminder for the broader public of Latin music's continuing vigor.

The musical term *salsa*—otherwise a spicy, tomato-based sauce—was gradually applied to the Latin music that emerged in New York in the 1970s out of Cuban-derived *mambo*, *cha cha chá*, and Latin jazz. Although he rejected the term, preferring to call himself an exponent of Latin Jazz, many people consider *salsa*'s most famous exponent was Tito Puente (1923–2000), a "nuyorican" ("New York-born Puerto Rican") classically trained at Julliard but later known as "The Mambo King" and the "King of the Timbales" for his work in most of the styles leading to and including *salsa*. Featured in films, known for live performances worldwide, and honored by institutions such as the Smithsonian, Puente became synonymous with *salsa*. Puente's music is among the most rhythmically complex Latin music ever recorded.

Finally, *salsa* continues its popularity today under a great variety of younger artists, both well known and obscure. Because *salsa* music is generally faster than *mambo* and much faster than *cha cha chá*, the ballroom steps associated with those dances are difficult to execute to this music. *Salsa* dance, while taught in most ballroom studios, remains outside the ballroom canon, but the steps are generally the easier ones borrowed or derived from *mambo*, but unlike *mambo*, where dance steps break on beat 2, in *salsa* they break on beat 1. Nonetheless, because of the rhythmic/metrical complexity of *salsa*, articulated by the *clave* pattern rather than European meter, even finding beat 1 can be challenging.

Dance: Ballroom Dance

Stimulated by the success of such TV shows as *Dancing with the Stars* and *So You Think You Can Dance*, ballroom dance has recently achieved greater prominence than it has had since the days of movies starring Fred Astaire and Ginger Rogers in the 1930s. But the kind of ballroom dance seen on these shows along with that of the Ohio Star Ball does not reflect "normal" social-style ballroom dance, a form of dancing enjoyed by people of all ages, including some into their nineties. In recent years there has been a worldwide push to add ballroom dance to the Olympics by renaming it as "Dancesport," but thus far this has not become a reality.

Ballroom includes any kind of couple dance performed in social situations, on dance floors large and small, elegant and rough, accompanied by either recorded or live music. "Ballroom" strictly speaking, however, only includes a closed canon of named dances codified and supervised by certain dance organizations. Standard ballroom dance originated in

Dancers at a formal European ball perform the waltz, known as "Viennese waltz" in the ballroom world. (Corbis)

England in the early twentieth century and remains under the direction of the Imperial Society of Teachers of Dancing (ISTD) headquartered in London. Their codification of ten dances, with named steps at three levels of difficulty (bronze, silver, gold), is observed by ballroom dancers worldwide. Because of this standardization, a trained dancer from South Africa can walk into a Chinese ballroom and dance with any other trained dancer: they both know the same steps. ISTD divides dances into two groups: International Standard (waltz, Viennese waltz, foxtrot, quickstep, and jive) and International Latin (tango, rumba, cha cha chá, samba, and pasodoble). Books describe in utter detail each step differentiated between male and female.

Although American dance instructors usually know the "international" curriculum, there is no single American standard, though most teach the same set of thirteen dances. Rather, dancers might learn steps codified by one of the national organizations such as the National Dance Council of America (NDCA) or Dance Vision International (a.k.a. DVIDA), or in a franchise studio under the Fred Astaire or Arthur Murray names. The American curricula are divided into American Smooth (foxtrot, waltz, tango, Viennese waltz) and American Rhythm/Latin (rumba, mambo, merengue, bolero, pasodoble, cha cha, East Coast swing, West Coast swing, and samba). Social dance parties held in studios or in commercial ballrooms may also offer additional dances that are not part of the canon; these include polka, peabody, hustle, nightclub two-step, Texas two-step, salsa, and a variety of "line dances."

Whatever their roots, ballroom dance types are not "folk" or "traditional" in the same way that Hawaiian hula or Thai classical are. Each dance has a separate history, some having European roots (such as waltz, Viennese waltz, and

bolero), some American (such as foxtrot and both East and West Coast swing), and many of them Caribbean and Latin American roots (such as rumba, cha cha, and mambo from Cuba, merengue from the Dominican Republic, tango from Argentina, and samba from Brazil). Whatever their origin or their continuing status as a "traditional" dance in the country of origin, ballroom versions have undergone a thorough process of being "tamed" and codified by British or American professional dancers. This was especially true of tango, which was converted by the Castles, Vernon and Irene, from what many considered a lascivious display of passion to a restrained dance fit even for father and daughter (see Chapter 12, Site 3). Historical and cultural stereotypes may come into play. Professional dancers who specialize in Latin dances, though they may come from Canada, Russia, or China, may use skin creams to darken themselves and wear exotic and skimpy costumes so to look "latino." Professional and showcase dancers may don fancy evening attire, including tailcoats, when dancing foxtrot, so to imitate the high society of the past which sponsored private soirees in their own personal ballrooms (usually the third floor of the mansion).

The relationships between male and female dancers are fixed: men lead, women follow, though it is the man's duty to make his partner "look good." Thus men favor black clothing that de-emphasizes them while females wear excessively colorful costumes with plenty of jewelry and makeup when performing Showcases. Dance positions are highly formalized, and consequently, it is customary for men to dance with as many different partners as he wishes at a given social ballroom event.

Dance may be accompanied by either a live dance band performing mainly "standards" in defined dance tempos, with or without a vocalist, or by a DJ through a sound system. Many commercial recordings, though appropriate for particular dances, are incon-

Amateur ballroom social dancers enjoy a dinner-dance sponsored by USA Dance.

sistent in tempo, sometimes slowing down or speeding up, but dance organizations have also recorded "strict tempo" recordings of the same standards, carefully adhering to the specified tempos required in all competitions. A common problem with live bands is that none of the members themselves dance, and thus they do not understand how critical tempo can be. A foxtrot played a few beats too fast or too slow is undanceable.

Ballroom dance has long been a worldwide phenomenon, and, as noted earlier, dance steps/figures are uniform across borders. Ballroom was often seen as a sign of international/Western/modern sophistication in tradition-bound countries, where, for example, men and women were prohibited from touching, let alone embracing, in public; ballroom dance was an acceptable way to break the "taboo." Thus, the high society of many Asian, African, and Middle Eastern societies embraced ballroom dance. China's Mao Zedong, Vietnam's Ho Chi Minh, Cambodia's King Norodom Silhanouk, and Thailand's Queen Sirikit danced ballroom. In 1996 the Japanese film *Shall We Dance?* parodied both ballroom and Japanese society and inspired imitations in the West. The popular musics of many countries, particularly those of East, Central, and Southeast Asia, derived from imported ballroom dance music in the 1940s and 1950s, sometimes brought by Filipino or Malaysian dance bands performing on cruise ships. Some countries have developed additional ballroom dances reflecting their own traditions, for example, Thailand's *ramwong* and *jangwa talung* and Malaysia's *ronggeng*.

Thus, ballroom dance is open to anyone of whatever age or level of skill in virtually any country of the world. Besides private studios, many public recreation centers offer group instruction at a modest cost, and many universities sponsor dance clubs for students. Only one American university offers a major in ballroom dance, however: Brigham Young University in Provo, Utah.

Site 10: Cajun Music

First Impressions. This is relatively simple music with an infectious beat and much forward drive, which places the accordion at the center. The singing is in French, though it sounds like French with a southern twang. Cajun music, like Cajun food, has attracted a growing number of followers and, like the spiciness of the alleged "Cajun sauces" served in many American restaurants, has a certain spiciness of its own. This is music that practically pushes you out of your seat onto the dance floor.

Aural Analysis. Besides the voices, only two melodic instruments are heard, the accordion and fiddle, but if you listen closely you will also hear the high, clear tones of a metal triangle. The accordion has just one row of melody buttons. Like the way the basic and inexpensive accordions usually mail-ordered from "up north" are used, the harmonies of Cajun music are simple—basically I and V (tonic and dominant). The melodic range is just one octave, rising a fifth above the tonic and descending a fourth below. Because such an accordion can be played in only one key, an instrument must match the singer's range. But much Cajun singing, as this example shows, is sung in the singer's upper range. The accordionist gives the vocal melody greater energy by repeating most notes.

A favorite Cajun expression is *laissez les bons temps rouler*, meaning, "let the good times roll"—but this sentiment masks the hard realities of life in southwestern Louisiana and seems contradicted by the sometimes distressing words to Cajun songs. Cajun musicians frequently quickly invent new songs to comment on local events and community scandals. Our example, entitled "The Blackberry Bush," deals with more general human foibles, as it concerns the misbehavior of a young woman who goes into the blackberry bushes with her boyfriend. They become lost in the briars—perhaps a metaphor for being lost in a broader sense.

Cultural Considerations. The term *Cajun* is a shortened colloquial form of *Acadian*, a word referring to the French settlers who first migrated to Atlantic Canada in 1605. Caught in the wrangling between the French and English during the seventeenth and eighteenth centuries, they were

LISTENING GUIDE 13.10 (1'50")

13.10
United States of America: Cajun Music

Vocals: Single male lead
Instruments: Fiddle (violin), accordion (reed aerophone), metal triangle (idiophone)

TIME	LISTENING FOCUS
0'00"	Listen for the spoken introduction.
0'01"	Listen for each instrument in the opening musical material. Note the foot-stomping of the performers, which articulates the steady duple meter.
0'11"	Opening musical phrase repeats.
0'20"	Vocalist enters with the first verse. Listen for the violin imitating the melodic contour of the singer. Note that the accordion plays with a quieter volume whenever the vocalist sings.
0'30"	Listen for the aural focus returning to the instruments.
0'38"	Listen for new melodic harmonic material.
0'48"	Listen for the return of the vocalist for the second verse and the shift back to the "home" harmony.
0'58"	Listen for the aural focus returning to the instruments.
1'06"	Listen for the return of the secondary melodic harmonic material.
1'17"	Listen for the return of the vocalist for the third verse and the shift back to the "home" harmony.
1'26"	Listen for the aural focus returning to the instruments.
1'34"	Listen for the return of the secondary melodic harmonic material.

Source: "La talle des ronces," performed by Adam and Cyprien Landreneau and Dewey Balfa, from the recording entitled *Louisiana Cajun from the Southwest Prairies. Recorded 1964–1967, Volume 2*, Rounder 6002, 1989. Used by permission.

MUSICAL MARKERS: Timbre/Medium—Button-box accordion, fiddle, and driving metal triangle (washboard sometimes included as well). Vocalist considered a complement to the instruments, rather than central focus. **Melody/Phonic Structure**—Short repetitive melodic phrases with supporting harmony. **Rhythm**—Steady "two-step" dance beat with rhythmically dense triangle pattern. **Other**—"Cajun" language lyrics.
ETHNO-CHALLENGE: Play the triangle's rhythmic pattern throughout the performance.

forcibly deported, starting in 1755, and scattered south to various places, including Louisiana, which was then still a French colony. Although many of the French returned to Canada during the later eighteenth century, several thousand who had gone to Louisiana remained there. Louisiana was also home to French-speaking peoples of African or mixed ancestry who came from the French islands of the Caribbean. Today the latter are called **Creoles**, though the term once referred to all French speakers. The Cajun community is concentrated in southwestern Louisiana from Lafayette westward to the Texas border.

The older and more traditional context for Cajun music and dancing was the home, where parties called *bals de maison* (house dances) were held. Visitors to Cajun country are now more likely to encounter the music on Saturday nights in public dancehalls. These dancehalls are called *do-do*, which means "go to sleep"—something parents probably said to their children

CREOLE
A term referring to populations of French descent that are found in the southern United States, primarily Louisiana.

459

Louisiana Cajun music played at a National Folk Festival

Cajun button-box accordion and player from Louisiana (Jack Vartoogian/ FrontRow)

Cajun accordion
(Shutterstock)

before going to the dance. There, ordinary folks danced a great variety of styles, at least in the past—today, waltzes and two-steps predominate.

In the early days, long before accordions were available and before people could afford fiddles, Cajuns sometimes danced to wordless vocal melodies called *reels à bouche*, similar to the *peurt a beul* of the Gaelic Scottish of Cape Breton, Nova Scotia. Eventually, the presence of one or two fiddles became usual. After contact with German settlers, Cajuns absorbed the diatonic, single-row button box accordion, now the signature Cajun instrument. Contemporary Cajun music has also added electrical amplification, guitar, bass, and drums. At the same time, old-fashioned acoustic Cajun music has enjoyed a revival, because of tourism and the rise of folk festivals in the 1960s.

The Creoles had much in common with the white Cajuns, and their music was sometimes indistinguishable from that of the Acadian French. But over time they blended elements from the Caribbean, of both African and Spanish origin, into their music. Since their parties were called *la la* or **zydeco**, the latter term came to denote the music of Creole Cajuns. Today's *zydeco* also shows influence from blues and even rock. While they use the same instruments as their white brethren, Creoles are more likely to add a metal washboard, called *frottoir*, which is played with thimbles, bottle openers, or other kitchen utensils.

ZYDECO
Creole dance music that blends African-American styles with *Cajun* styles from the southern United States, primarily Louisiana.

Arrival: Native American Reservations

Many Americans would be surprised to learn that Native American (also, American Indian) reservations are found in more than half of the states of the U.S. Though the best-known reservations are found in southwestern states, primarily Arizona and New Mexico, there are significant reservations throughout the country, including the east and southeast. While many Native Americans choose to live on these reservations, more than two-thirds of the roughly nine million Native Americans in North America live elsewhere. Indeed, because of intermarriage with Anglo Americans and African Americans, many Native Americans are actually of mixed ancestry, have

Anglo names, and live as the mainstream population does. The stereotypes of the old "Western" films resemble in no way modern Native American life.

The Native American population is the most diverse ethnic "group" in North America. Though unified by their Native American ethnicity, their cultural practices vary greatly. Distinctions in Native American dress, subsistence patterns, spiritual beliefs, marriage customs, language, kinship systems, and so on, have intrigued anthropologists and linguists since the start of their respective disciplines. The earliest ethnomusicologists (1890–1930s) in the United States focused much of their attention on Native American musical traditions. With more than three hundred different tribes throughout North America, the research produced in the last one hundred years, while extensive, is still far from complete.

Scholars generally identify nine primary culture areas among the Native Americans of the United States, Canada, and northern Mexico: Southeast, Southwest, Plains, Plateau and Basin, California, Northwest Coast, Subarctic, Arctic, and Northeast.

Though a great variety of musical activity occurs throughout these regions, there are several qualified generalizations that can be made about most Native American music traditions. The foremost characteristic of Native American music is the use of the voice as the primary focus of performance. While instrumental traditions exist, vocal solos and group singing are most frequent in both spiritual and secular contexts. The use of *vocables* or non-lexical (untranslatable) syllables, such as *yaa, heh, daa, weh,* and so on, is common in many traditions. Vocables are often believed to hold a secret meaning that enables the performer to communicate with the spirit world. Drums and rattles are the most common instruments used to accompany the voice.

VOCABLES
Words considered only with regards to sound, not in terms of meaning.

Musical performance, even in secular contexts, usually has a spiritual or symbolic significance for the musicians. Many songs are believed to have been taught by spirits and animals through dreams and by other means. Nature is often an inspiration for songs, and many songs are intended to honor and respect the environment. Other songs relate the history of a community or great deeds of warriors from the past. The myths and legends of a tribe are passed on through song, and frequently music plays an important role in male–female relationships and courting rituals. Practically all traditional music is passed on orally from generation to generation.

Though Native American musical practices are quite diverse, we will focus on two distinct styles of performance. Both styles have become quite visible to the general public in the past few decades. First, the Plains Indian style is typical of singing practices originating among American Indian populations of the Midwest. It is the source for many of the musical traditions presented at Native American powwows, now the most common pan-tribal event found throughout the United States. The second style is represented by a courting song performed on the Native American flute by a Zuni musician from the Taos Pueblo region of the southwestern United States. This music has recently become closely associated with the "New Age" movement that has flourished since the 1980s.

Site 11: Plains Indian Dance Song

First Impressions. The drum is the spiritual center of this performance. Pulsating like a heartbeat, the pounding rhythm becomes hypnotic as the listener closes his eyes to imagine the scene. Dancers dressed in feather-adorned regalia form a circle as they move around the drummer and vocalists, whose singing style produces a tense warble characteristic of this style of Native American performance.

Aural Analysis. As with most Native American music, the voice is the focus of Plains Indian music performance. The singing style is chant-like, with a distinctive "cascading" or "terraced" melodic contour, which starts high and remains primarily on one pitch before falling to successively lower pitch levels. The range between the starting pitch of a phrase and the closing pitch is wide in the Plains style. Vocal pulsation, in which a periodic slight increase in volume is used to create rhythmic accents, is common, especially when vocables are sung. This pulsation

Located in northern Arizona, "Montezuma's Castle" is the best preserved cliff dwelling in America. Consisting of twenty rooms, it was built by the Sinagua Indians around 1,000 years ago

creates a warbling sound on a single pitch but is not considered melisma, because melisma requires more than one pitch per syllable.

Vocal timbre varies among performers, but a strained sound is often desirable in the Plains singing style. Some practitioners will gently press on their throat to tighten the vocal cords in order to produce the preferred sound. This tense timbre is most strongly associated with the vocable sections, when the clear articulation is less important. During the translatable sections of performance, a tense voice and vocal pulsation is less noticeable as the extended vowels are fewer and the emphasis is on the text itself rather than the singing style. Group performances in the Plains style usually feature a leader who begins a vocal phrase and is followed shortly thereafter by the other voices, who either enter at the end of the leader's initial call or overlap the lead voice to complete the phrase. Group singing is most prominent during vocable sections, while the leader may either sing the translatable sections as solos or with the group.

A large double-sided frame drum is the most common instrument found in Plains group performances. The instrument can be round or edged, even sometimes square or octagonal. The drum is placed on a stand with one face upward. The drummers sit around the drum and strike the face with padded mallets. The beat is steady, often with an unequal (short–long) rhythm that imitates the sound of a heartbeat, symbolic of Mother Earth. The accents of the vocal pulsation and of the drum do not necessarily correspond, creating a polyrhythmic interaction.

Cultural Considerations. The Native American group activity most open to the general public is the **powwow**. The modern powwow is a pan-tribal event central to maintaining the cultural identity of American Indians throughout North America. Public powwows are much like outdoor fairs. While music and dance performances are the central activity, there are also vendors selling jewelry, crafts, instruments, clothes, books, food, and so on. For non-Native Americans, powwows are the most available opportunity to experience Native American culture.

The powwow was created by several Plains Indian tribes in the mid-1800s. During this period, the influx of white settlers into the Midwest was contributing to the decline of traditional

POWWOW
A pan-tribal American Indian event celebrating Native American identity and culture, generally also open to non-Native Americans.

LISTENING GUIDE

Site 13.11

United States of America: Plains Indian Dance Song

Vocals: Male ensemble
Instruments: Double-sided frame drum (membranophone)

TIME	LISTENING FOCUS
0'00"	Listen for a single male beginning the performance with non-lexical lyrical content. Note the consistent "heartbeat" rhythm of the drum and the high range of the vocalist focusing on a single pitch (F).
0'04"	Listen for the descending pitch range of the lead vocalist, emphasizing two middle pitches (C, then B). Note that other vocalists join the lead performer.
0'10"	Listen for the descending pitch range of the lead vocalist, focusing on a low-range pitch (F).
0'19"	Listen for the single accent on the drum as the vocalists shift to singing lexical text beginning in a middle range and descending to a lower range. Note that the drum quiets its volume during the sung text.
0'27"	Listen for the drum's increase in volume.
0'33"	Listen for the return of non-lexical text and the melodic contour's return to the high range of pitches.
0'53"	Listen for the single accent on the drum as the vocalists again shift to singing lexical text.
1'00"	Listen for the drum's increase in volume.
1'06"	Listen for the return of non-lexical text and the melodic contour's return to the high range of pitches.
1'24"	Listen for the vocalists again shifting to singing lexical text as the example fades.

Source: "Rock Dance Song" performed by The Pembina Chippewa Singers. Recorded by Nicholas Curchin Peterson Vrooman, Turtle Mountain, North Dakota, 1984, from the recording entitled *Plains Chippewa/Metis Music from Turtle Mountain,* SF 40411, provided courtesy of Smithsonian Folkways Recordings. © 1992. Used by permission.

MUSICAL MARKERS: Timbre/Medium—Single deep drum. "Warbling" vocal group singing. **Rhythm**—Characteristic "heartbeat" rhythmic pattern on drum. **Melodic Contour**—"Cascading" descending contour, typically following upper–middle–low range progression. **Melody/Text Setting**—Unison "pulse" singing, often including extended melismatic "non-lexical" syllables.

ETHNO-CHALLENGE: Diagram the melodic contour of the example. If possible, attend a powwow event in your local area.

Native spiritual, social, political, and economic practices. At the same time, intertribal warfare had become greatly curtailed, because all tribes were threatened equally by the American military. As Native American populations dwindled, many groups were forced to resettle among other culturally distinct tribes.

The powwow events were created in response to these developments. They became a means of reinforcing the unity and strength of Native American culture in order to ensure its survival. The many social differences among tribes were acknowledged but were made secondary to the Native American identity shared by all. The events have changed over the years, but since the 1950s they have functioned primarily as a means of honoring and expressing Native American identity within and outside the American Indian community. Powwows usually last between one and four days. The public events can be held outdoors or indoors, in parks, on college

A typical inter-tribal powwow. The drum circle in the foreground provides the accompaniment for the dancers behind them

Typical of a powwow, dancers representing many tribes join together to celebrate their Native American heritage (Andrew Shahriari)

campuses, in gymnasiums, or in conference centers. Most are minimally advertised, and, as public events, are often free. Though variations in the proceedings occur, a powwow typically begins with a "Grand Entry" parade led by flag-bearers representing the participating tribes. These marchers are then followed by dancers, respected elders and tribal chiefs, and children.

Music and dance are the main focus of powwow events. Each tribe displays its unique traditions through regalia and performance. Intertribal dances are also common, usually using a basic toe-to-heel dance step that corresponds to the beat of the drum. The Plains style of singing is the most common musical accompaniment for these dances. Non-natives are sometimes encouraged to participate in these dances as well.

Other group dances also encourage intertribal participation. Social dances are common, such as the Round Dance, which is performed in a circle and based on a basic side-step motion. In Rabbit Dances, male and female dancers hold hands or interlock their arms as they dance to a love song and the beat of the drum. Contest dancing is a more specialized but important activity in which dancers competing for prizes and prestige dress in elaborate regalia with sophisticated symbolic meanings. The most successful of these dancers often perform outside the powwow context to earn a living, doing concerts and workshops around the United States and internationally.

Site 12: Native American Flute

First Impressions. If the sound of the Plains Indian drum is symbolic of Mother Earth, then the sound of the Native American flute represents the wind. This is the sound of sublime solitude, an escape from the hectic life of the city into a peaceful unity with nature.

A musician plays the contemporary Native American flute (courtesy of Canyon Records; photo by John Running)

Aural Analysis. Native American flute performance is one of the few solo instrumental traditions found among Native American peoples. Vertically blown flutes are more common than side-blown or transverse flutes and are made from soft woods such as cedar or other geographically available woods and materials such as bone, reed, clay, and metal.

While each flute is considered unique, the contemporary "Native American flute," a term that was coined in the early 1980s to describe a newly created instrument, was modeled after the handmade traditional courting flutes used by Plains peoples. Presently, the traditional courting flute is often referred to as the North American indigenous flute as a means to delineate it from the contemporary Native American flute. The indigenous courting flute is still being crafted and played within the culture. Many of the traditional flute songs have their foundation in the vocal songs of the culture. Both indigenous and contemporary flutes have five or six fingerstops or fingerholes that, when opened and closed, produce a melody. This flute is distinctive for its "bird," "block," or "saddle" ornament, which is tied firmly on to the sound-producing mechanism located just below the mouthpiece or blow-hole. This ornament is vital to the sound production as it channels the air flow across an edge to create the sound vibrations.

Today, there are many genres of music incorporating the contemporary Native American flute, from solo works, to ambient, to classical, to jazz, to world fusion musical styles, as well as so-called "New Age," a marketing label applied to many modernized indigenous music traditions from around the world. Solo recordings frequently make use of nature sounds and "canyon" sound effects to emulate how the Native American flute may have sounded in its traditional context, although not all flute traditions come from areas that have canyons within their geography. The effect creates a "distant," transcendent sound as if the music were echoing through a great canyon.

While the music does not always follow an articulated steady beat, clear melodic phrases are the norm. Both indigenous and contemporary Native American flute music in a solo context often exhibit an indirect beat that may be felt rather than heard. Melodic ornamentation

LISTENING GUIDE

13.12 (0'52")

Site 13.12

United States of America: Native American Flute

Vocals: Male ensemble
Instruments: End-blown flute (aerophone)

TIME	LISTENING FOCUS
0'00"	Listen for the "breathy" timbre and "distant" reverberation of the flute. Note that the performance is in free rhythm, with each melodic phrase following its own sense of timing.
0'22"	Listen for a return to emphasis on the initial pitch (A). Note that the return to this "musical thought" is followed by entirely new melodic material.
0'47"	Listen for the closing pitch and the extended reverberation that follows.

Source: "Courting Song" performed by John Rainer, Jr., from the recording entitled *Music of New Mexico: Native American Traditions*, SF 40408, provided courtesy of Smithsonian Folkways Recordings. © 1992. Used by permission.

MUSICAL MARKERS: Timbre/Medium—"Breathy" flute with "distant" reverberation (often a faint echo). **Melody**—lyrical with strong tonal center. Some "sliding" into pitches and occasional "flutters" between two pitches. Mild vibrato on extended pitches. **Rhythm**—Free rhythm common.
ETHNO-CHALLENGE: Transcribe this performance using numeral or staff notation.

or embellishment techniques are varied among flute performers and are often dependent upon whether the music is traditional or contemporary in nature, as well as the cultural, social, and song-type contexts. A few of the ornamental techniques that may be heard within both indigenous and contemporary Native American flute music include trills, mordants, pitch bending, flutter tonguing, and the characteristic "pop" (quick ascending pitch) that is used to indicate the conclusion of a phrase, a sub-phrase, or the song itself. Vibrato (wavering of the pitch) is often heard on sustained tones. Most compositions use a scale of between five and seven pitches, with a range of little more than an octave. Overtones are not commonly used, though special effects are sometimes employed to imitate the sounds of birds or natural elements, such as the wind. Often, Native American flute music is quiet, with little dynamic variation.

Cultural Considerations. The indigenous flute is the most widespread melodic instrument found in Native American culture. In the early 1980s, flute maker and performer Michael Graham Allen (Coyote Oldman) created a contemporary scale based upon notes from the shakuhachi, which gave rise to the contemporary Native American flute that was able to play more modern, mainstream music. This revised Plains Indian vertically-held flute type became most popular in the modern era, but is only one of many types. The vertically held flute made of wood is the most common, since the resurgence of interest in American Indian flute traditions that began in the 1970s.

The renaissance of the Native American flute was brought about in particular by two people: Dr. Richard W. Payne, a physician from Oklahoma, and Doc Tate Nevaquaya (1932–1996), a Comanche visual artist, flute maker, and flute player. Throughout his life, Payne encouraged the playing and making of the flute among the Native American peoples, including Nevaquaya. Among the notable Native American flutists who play or played music in the traditional style, such as John Rainer, Jr.'s "Taos Pueblo Courting Song," include: Doc Tate Nevaquaya (Comanche), Belo Cozad (Kiowa), Kevin Locke (Lakota/Anishnabe), Dan Red Buffalo (Lakota), Richard Fool Bull (Lakota), Woodrow Haney (Seminole), Bryan Akipa (Sisseton Wahpeton Oyate), and Tom Mauchahty-Ware (Kiowa-Comanche). Especially important in the renewed interest in flute making and playing was R. Carlos Nakai, who brought the contemporary Native American flute into the mainstream with his pivitol recording, *Canyon Trilogy*. Of Navajo-Ute heritage, and considered the premier performer of the contemporary Native American flute, Nakai is credited with creating a significant surge of worldwide interest in the contemporary Native American flute with his profound solo flute creations and his innovative cross-cultural, cross-genre musical collaborations with some of the world's finest musical artists.

This revival of interest has spurred much debate within Native American communities, as many who now play the contemporary flute are not of Native American ancestry. Flute circles, organizations, and social clubs dedicated to the contemporary Native American flute are

Detail showing "bird block" on a Native American flute (courtesy of Canyon Records; photo by John Running)

increasingly popular and open to anyone. Many people within the flute community take the attitude that the instrument and its music are not the exclusive property of Native Americans but are to be shared with everyone. Others take an opposing stance, asserting that the music has a sacred dimension and cultural value and thus is only appropriately performed by Native Americans.

Traditionally, among the Plains people, the flute was primarily used in courting rituals and is associated with the Elk Dreamer Society. Love songs were performed on the flute, which substituted for the voice. This usage dwindled to near non-existence by the end of the nineteenth century, although traditionalist scholars like Lakota flutist Kevin Locke are striving to educate Indian youth in the traditional arts and ways like flute making/playing and dance. Another important context was storytelling. Often an elder would tell a story that ended with a moral,

Explore More

Inuit Throat-Singing

One of the more interesting vocal traditions to surface in recent decades is Inuit throat-singing. The Inuit, often referred to as Eskimos, live in several arctic areas of North America. Though modernization has considerably changed the Inuit lifestyle, hunting and fishing are still the primary means of subsistence as they have been for centuries. In the past, hunting expeditions would often last for more than a month. Throat-singing developed among the women of the Inuit communities as a means of entertainment during the long absences of the men.

Throat-singing among the Inuit (in contrast to the "two-tone" throat-singing found in Mongolia and elsewhere) is characterized by its deep, breathy sounds and rhythmically dense performance technique. Two women (sometimes four) face each other at a close distance, typically holding each other's arms. One woman leads while the other follows. The lead voice establishes a short, fast-paced rhythmic phrase, and the second voice is expected to interlock with this phrase in the gaps between the sounds. The performance is considered a kind of game. The first person who runs out of breath or who cannot keep pace with the other loses. Good performers will subtly change the rhythm of their phrases.

Many variations of the throat-singing style are found throughout Canada, the most commonly known type being *katajjaq* (pronounced "kawta-jock") from northern Quebec. In this style, the performers frequently imitate the sounds of nature and everyday life, such as the barking of dogs, the whistling of wind, or the buzzing of insects. For many years this tradition was strongly discouraged by Christian missionaries,

By Rudolf H. Boettcher (Wikimedia Commons)

but it is again finding popularity among the Inuit youth, who consider throat-singing an important means by which to express their cultural identity.

much like Aesop's fables in the Western tradition. When the story was finished, the storyteller would play the flute while the listeners reflected on the meaning of the story.

The main characters of these stories are often animals or natural elements, reflecting the importance that the environment plays in the cultural, social and spiritual lives of the Native American people. Native Americans believe that humans can learn much from their surroundings if they only pay attention. The "bird" ornament on the top of the flute is an example of the symbiotic relationship between people and nature, since Plains mythology states that the woodpecker is responsible for giving/gifting the flute to the people. Today, the contemporary Native American flute is frequently sold at powwow events, flute gatherings/festivals, and on the Internet, and it has become broadly representative of Native American musical identity.

Questions to Consider

1. What is "American" music and what differentiates it from European or African music?

2. How does music from the British Isles underlie music surviving today in the United States and Canada?

3. Compare and contrast the performance of "lined" hymns and "shape-note" singing. What makes these types of music especially archaic?

4. How have Protestant Christian values influenced music in the United States?

5. Compare and contrast African-American spirituals and gospel music. What elements of each might reflect the African heritage of their creators?

6. How does blues music express the social conditions of African Americans in the United States?

7. Discuss the relationships and differences between the Cuban *son* (see Chapter 11, Site 6) and North American *salsa*.

8. How have the powwow and the Native American flute shaped the outsider's view of Native American culture?

Glossary

Authors' Note: As some of the transliterated words below are difficult to pronounce or have no English equivalent, we have included pronunciation approximations in parentheses following a number of the glossary terms.

A

A-AK: A Confucian ritual ensemble from Korea. (Chapter 7)

ABAKWA: An animistic belief system found primarily in Cuba. (Chapter 11)

ABORIGINES: A generic term for an indigenous population, often used to describe native peoples of Australia. (Chapter 4)

ACCENT: An emphasized beat. (Chapter 2)

ACCORDION: A bellows-driven free-reed *aerophone* with buttons or keys that enable a performer to play melody and harmony simultaneously. (Chapter 9)

ACOUSTIC: Term used for non-electric instruments. (Chapter 13)

ADHAN (Also, AZAN): The Islamic call to prayer. (Chapter 8)

AEROPHONE: Ethnomusicological classification referring to instruments that require air to produce sound; namely, flutes, reeds, trumpets, and bellows-driven instruments. (Chapter 2)

AFIRIKYIWA: An iron clapper-bell from Ghana. (Chapter 10)

AFRIKANER: A South African of Dutch descent. (Chapter 10)

AGOGO: A double-bell found in western Africa and used in African-derived musics in the Western hemisphere. (Chapter 12)

AKADINDA: A large, heavy log *xylophone* from sub-Saharan Africa, associated with the former kingdom of Buganda. (Chapter 10)

ALAP (Also, ALAPANA): The opening, freely rhythmic period of improvisation of *raga* performance in Indian classical music. (Chapter 5)

AL-'UD: See UD.

AMADINDA: A log *xylophone* similar to the *akadinda*, but with fewer pitches; from sub-Saharan Africa. (Chapter 10)

ANTHEM: A category of shape-note song that is *through composed*, meaning it has different music from beginning to end. (Chapter 13)

ANTHROPOLOGY: The study of all aspects of human culture, including music. (Chapter 1)

ANUDRUTAM: The first element of the *tala* in Indian classical music. (Chapter 5)

ANUPALLAVI: The second section of a *kriti* vocal performance from South India. (Chapter 5)

APARTHEID: The official South African policy of racial segregation, abolished in 1992. (Chapter 10)

APPALACHIA: A geographic region marked by the Appalachian Mountains, which extend throughout the eastern part of the United States. (Chapter 13)

APREMPRENSEMMA: A low-ranged *lamellophone* from Ghana. (Chapter 10)

ARABIAN PENINSULA: A geographic region in the Middle East that includes Saudi Arabia, Yemen, Oman, and the various smaller nations on the Persian Gulf. (Chapter 8)

ARADHANA: A South Indian festival. (Chapter 5)

ARAWAK: A pre-Columbian indigenous population of the Caribbean. (Chapter 11)

ATABAQUES: A drum of West African origin used in *capoeira* music as well as *candomblé* rituals from Brazil. (Chapter 12)

ATUMPAN: A pair of goblet-shaped drums often used as a speech surrogate by several ethnic groups from Ghana. (Chapter 10)

AULOS: A double-reed *aerophone* from Ancient Greece. (Chapter 3)

AVAZ: The improvised, non-metrical section of a performance in the Persian classical tradition. (Chapter 8)

AYATOLLAH: A high-rank clergyman in Islam. (Chapter 8)

AZAN: See ADHAN.

AZTEC: A pre-Columbian indigenous population found in central and southern Mexico. (Chapter 12)

B

BAĞLAMA: A round-bodied lute from Turkey. (Chapter 3)

BAGPIPES: A reed *aerophone* consisting of an airbag, *chanter* (melody pipe), and drone pipes. (Chapter 9)

BAIRRO: A poor housing area found in the city of Rio de Janeiro, Brazil. (Chapter 12)

BALAFON: A *xylophone* from West Africa often played by oral historians. (Chapter 10)

BALALAIKA: A triangle-shaped, fretted plucked lute from Russia. (Chapter 9)

BALLAD: A song that tells a story, usually performed by a solo voice and commonly associated with music from the Appalachian region of the United States. (Chapter 13)

BALS DE MAISON: A house party that typically has *Cajun* music as entertainment, found in the southern United States, primarily Louisiana. (Chapter 13)

BANDIR: A frame drum common to Turkish and Arabic music. (Chapter 8)

BANDONEON: A type of button-box accordion. (Chapter 12)

BANJO: A fretted, plucked lute from the United States, the resonator of which has a membrane face. (Chapter 13)

BANSRI (Also, BANSURI): A transverse flute from North India. (Chapter 5)

BANTU: An African linguistic category. (Chapter 10)

BAR MITZVAH: A Jewish "coming-of-age" ceremony. (Chapter 8)

BASHRAF: An Arabic musical form. (Chapter 8)

BASSER: The lowest vocal part in a *rhyming spiritual* performance from the Bahamas. (Chapter 11)

BATA: Ritual drums used in *Santeria* ceremonies. (Chapter 11)

BATUQUE: An animistic belief system found primarily in Brazil. (Chapter 11)

BAULS: A group of itinerant musicians from India, especially noted for their poetry. (Chapter 5)

BAYA: A small bowl-shaped drum that is one of the pair of North Indian drums known as *tabla*. (Chapter 5)

BAYIN: The Chinese organological system. (Chapter 7)

BEAT: A regular pulsation. (Chapter 2)

BELLOWS: An apparatus for producing a strong current of air; used with the Irish bagpipes, as well as the pump organ and other *aerophones*. (Chapter 9)

BERIMBAU: A musical bow used in *capoeira* music from Brazil. (Chapter 12)

BHAJAN: Devotional songs from India. (Chapter 5)

BHANGRA: A folk dance from the Punjabi region of north India/south Pakistan that is also the basis of a popular music style of the same name that developed in London, England. (Chapter 5)

BIBLE: The sacred text of Christianity. (Chapter 13)

BIN: A fretted plucked lute considered the origin of other popular lutes in India, such as the *sitar*. (Chapter 5)

BINO: A sitting dance typical of traditional music and dance performances from Kiribati. (Chapter 4)

BIRA: A spirit possession ceremony of the Shona ethnic group from Zimbabwe. (Chapter 10)

BIRIMINTINGO: The instrumental solo sections of a *jali* performance from West Africa. (Chapter 10)

BIWA: A fretted, pear-shaped plucked lute from Japan. (Chapter 7)

BLUEGRASS: A style of American folk music characterized by virtuosic instrumental performance and the so-called "high lonesome" vocal style, in which a harmony pitch is sung above the main melody. (Chapter 13)

BLUES: A secular folk music tradition originating within the African-American community of the southern United States. (Chapter 13)

BODHRAN: A frame drum from Ireland, played with a beater. (Chapter 9)

BOLERO: A Latin American dance and music. (Chapter 11)

BOLLYWOOD: An informal name for India's film industry derived from a combination of the words "Bombay" and "Hollywood." (Chapter 5)

BOLS: Mnemonic syllables corresponding to drum strokes in Indian drumming traditions. (Chapter 5)

BOMBARDE: A double-reed *aerophone* from France. (Chapter 3)

BOMBOS: A large drum used in *sikuri* performances from Peru. (Chapter 12)

BON: Festive dancing from Japan. (Chapter 7)

BONANG: A rack gong found in *gamelan* ensembles from Indonesia. (Chapter 6)

BONES: A small pair of wooden slats struck together to create rhythm. Common to folk music in the United States as well as Great Britain. (Chapter 9)

BOSSED GONG: A gong with a bump-like protuberance. (Chapter 6)

BOUZOUKI: A round-bodied lute from Greece. (Chapter 3)

BUGAKU: A Confucian ritual ensemble from Japan that incorporates dance. (Chapter 7)

BUNRAKU: A popular form of puppet theater from Japan. (Chapter 7)

BUZUK (Also, BUZUQ): A round-bodied lute from Turkey. (Chapter 3)

BYZANTINE CHANT: A chant style associated with the Greek Orthodox Church, centered on a complex system of *modes*. (Chapter 9)

C

CAIXA ("x" pronounced *sh*): A small drum from Brazil found in *samba* performances. (Chapter 12)

CAJAS: A small drum from Peru used in *sikuri* performances. (Chapter 12)

CAJUN: A term describing the cultural traditions, including music, of French-speaking Louisiana, USA. (Chapter 13)

CALL AND RESPONSE: A style of vocal organization characterized by having a leader who "calls" and a group that "responds." (Chapters 10 and 13)

CALYPSO: A popular music form from Trinidad characterized by improvised lyrics on topical and broadly humorous subject matter. (Chapter 11)

CANCIÓN: A general term for "song" in Mexico. (Chapter 12)

CANDOMBLÉ: A belief system combining animism and syncretized Roman Catholicism, found primarily in Brazil. (Chapter 10)

CANTAORA: A vocalist in Spanish flamenco music. (Chapter 9)

CANTE: A traditional Spanish style of singing incorporating a strained timbre and heavy use of *melisma*. (Chapter 9)

CANTINA: A social venue for drinking and dancing found in the Texas-Mexico borderland region of the United States. (Chapter 13)

CANTON: The term used for the states of the Swiss Federation. (Chapter 13)

CAPOEIRA: A form of dance that developed from a distinctive style of martial arts created by runaway slaves in Brazil. (Chapter 12)

CARANAM: The final section of a *kriti* vocal performance from India. (Chapter 5)

CARIB: A pre-Columbian indigenous population of the Caribbean. (Chapter 11)

CARNATIC (Also, KARNATAK): A term referring to the cultural traditions of South India. (Chapter 5)

CARNIVAL: A pre-Lent festival celebrated primarily in Europe and the Caribbean. Known as Mardi Gras in the United States. (Chapter 12)

CASCARÁ: A rhythmic pattern played on the *timbales* in *salsa* music. (Chapter 11)

CASTE SYSTEM: A system of social organization based on hereditary status found in India. (Chapter 5)

CÉILI: An Irish band that performs in a public house (pub) for entertainment and dancing. (Chapter 9)

CÉILIDH (pronounced *kay-lee*): A kind of "house party" associated with fiddling traditions in Canada, Ireland, and Scotland. (Chapter 13)

CELTIC: A subfamily of the Indo-European language family that is associated with the Scottish and Irish peoples of Great Britain. (Chapter 9)

CHA-CHA: A Latin American ballroom dance. (Chapter 11)

CHAHAR-MEZRAB: A metered piece in the Persian classical music tradition. (Chapter 8)

CHANTER: The melody pipe found on various bagpipes. (Chapter 9)

CHARRO: A style of suit worn by *mariachi* performers from Mexico. (Chapter 12)

CHASTUSHKI: A category of songs from Russia considered "playful." (Chapter 9)

CHÉQUERES (Also, SHEKERE): A gourd rattle with external beaded netting. (Chapter 11)

CHING: A pair of cup-shaped cymbals from Thailand. (Chapter 6)

CHIZ: The composed section of vocal performance in Indian classical music. (Chapter 5)

CHOBO: The narrator and accompanying shamisen performers of the Kabuki theater in Japan. (Chapter 7)

CHORD: The simultaneous soundings of three or more pitches. (Chapter 2)

CHORDOPHONE: Ethnomusicological classification referring collectively to the four types of stringed instruments: lutes, zithers, harps, lyres. (Chapter 2)

CHOU: The comic role-type in Beijing Opera from China. (Chapter 7)

CHUIDA: An outdoor "wind and percussion" ensemble from China that includes suona (double-reed aerophone) and loud percussion. (Chapter 7)

CH'UN HYANG KA: The name of one of five stories performed in Korean *p'ansori*. (Chapter 7)

CIMARRONS: A term for escaped slaves from the Spanish-colonized regions in the Caribbean and Americas. (Chapter 11)

CIMBALOM: A hammered zither from Eastern Europe, commonly associated with Rom (gypsy) music. Also, the national instrument of Hungary. (Chapter 9)

CIRCULAR BREATHING: A technique used to maintain a continuous air flow in *aerophone* performance. (Chapter 4)

CITERA: A small zither from Hungary. (Chapter 9)

CLAVES: A pair of hand-held wooden bars used as percussion instruments in many African and Latin American music traditions. (Chapters 10 and 11)

CLERK (pronounced *clark*): A religious leader in Calvinist churches in the United States and Scotland. (Chapter 13)

COBZA: A pear-shaped lute from Romania. (Chapter 3)

COLOTOMIC STRUCTURE: The organizational system of *gamelan* music from Indonesia. (Chapter 6)

COMPARSA: A Latin American dance music. (Chapter 11)

COMPÉ: A martial arts style from Brazil that emphasizes striking "with the foot." (Chapter 12)

CONCERTINA: A small hexagonal accordion with bellows and buttons for keys. (Chapter 9)

CONGA (Also, TUMBADORA): A tall, barrel-shaped, single-headed drum used often in Latin American music. (Chapter 11)

CONJUNTO: A popular dance music found along the Texas-Mexico border in North America. (Chapter 13)

CONTRADANZA: A Cuban dance form. (Chapter 11)

CORROBOREE: A nighttime ritual performed by Australian aborigines. (Chapter 4)

CREOLE: A term referring to populations of French or mixed African and French descent that are found in the southern United States, primarily Louisiana. (Chapter 13)

CRESCENDO: A gradual increase in volume. (Chapter 2)

CROSS-RHYTHM: A "two-against-three" rhythmic pattern often found in polyrhythmic performance in sub-Saharan Africa and Latin America. (Chapters 10 and 11)

CUATRO: A plucked lute with five sets of double-strings commonly used in *plena* music. (Chapter 11)

CUÍCA (pronounced *kwi-kha*): A small friction drum used in *samba* music. (Chapter 12)

CULTURAL REVOLUTION: A ten-year period (1966–1976) in China's history marked by severe social and political upheaval. (Chapter 7)

CUMINA: An animistic belief system found primarily in Jamaica. (Chapter 11)

CUTTIN' HEADS: A music contest found in African-American communities, typically involving blues musicians. (Chapter 13)

CZARDAS: A popular dance from Hungary. (Chapter 9)

D

DAN (pronounced *dahn*): The female hero role-type in Beijing opera from China. (Chapter 7)

DAN CO: A fiddle from Vietnam. (Chapter 6)

DAN KIM: A fretted plucked lute from Vietnam. (Chapter 6)

DAN TRANH: A plucked zither from Vietnam. (Chapter 6)

DAN TYBA (pronounced *dahn tee-bah*): A pear-shaped lute from Vietnam. (Chapter 6)

DANCEHALL: See DUB.

DANZA (Also, DANZON and DANZONETE): A Cuban dance form. (Chapter 11)

DARABUKA: A goblet-shaped hand drum common to various Turkish music traditions. (Chapter 8)

DARAMAD: The freely rhythmic opening and conclusion of a *dastgah* performance in the Persian classical music tradition. (Chapter 8)

DASTGAH: A *mode* or system of rules and expectations for composition and improvisation in Persian classical music. (Chapter 8)

DECRESCENDO: A gradual decrease in volume. (Chapter 2)

DEFINITE PITCH: A sound with a dominating frequency level. (Chapter 2)

DENSITY REFERENT: A reference pattern heard in polyrhythmic music, usually articulated by a bell, rattle, or woodblock. (Chapter 10)

DERVISH: Turkish word literally meaning "beggar," but often used to refer to Sufi Muslims. (Chapter 8)

DHIKR (Also, ZIKR): A ritual commonly performed by Sufi Muslims in which believers chant the names of Allah with the goal of entering a spiritually ecstatic state. (Chapter 8)

DHRUPAD: A category of vocal music from India. (Chapter 5)

DIAO: The *key* used in a music performance from China. (Chapter 7)

DIDJERIDU: A long trumpet made from a hollowed tree branch played by aborigines from Australia. (Chapter 4)

DILRUBA: A bowed lute from India. (Chapter 5)

DIZI: A transverse flute from China. (Chapter 7)

DOMBAK: A goblet-shaped hand drum used in Arabic music traditions. (Chapter 8)

DOMRA: A round-shaped fretted plucked lute from Russia. (Chapter 9)

DONDO (Also, DONNO): An hourglass-shaped pressure drum from Ghana. (Chapter 10)

DOUBLE-STOPS: The practice of playing two strings simultaneously on bowed lutes such as the violin. (Chapter 13)

DOULCEMELLE: A hammered dulcimer from France. (Chapter 3)

DR. WATTS: An informal term for a *lined hymn* employed in some African-American communities. (Chapter 13)

DREAMTIME: A term describing the Australian aboriginal spiritual belief system and concept of creation. (Chapter 4)

DRONE: A continuous sound. (Chapter 2)

DRUTAM: The second element of the *tala* in Indian classical music. (Chapter 5)

DUB (Also, DANCEHALL): Recorded music that emphasizes the bass and rhythm tracks so that a DJ can talk over the music through a microphone. (Chapter 11)

DUDA: Bagpipes from Hungary. (Chapter 9)

DUENDE: A Spanish word meaning "passion," which refers to an emotional quality considered essential in performances by Spanish flamenco singers. (Chapter 9)

DUFF: A small, single-headed drum, sometimes having snares, common to Turkish and Arabic music traditions. (Chapter 8)

DULAB: A compositional form found in Turkish and Arabic music. (Chapter 8)

DUNG CHEN: A long metal trumpet from Tibet. (Chapter 7)

DUNG KAR: A conch-shell trumpet from Tibet. (Chapter 7)

DYNAMICS: The volume of a musical sound. (Chapter 2)

E

ECHOS (pl. ECHOI): *Mode* used for Byzantine Chant. (Chapter 9)

EKÓN: An iron bell used in *Santeria* rituals. (Chapter 11)

EKTARA: See GOPIYANTRA.

ELECTROPHONE: Ethnomusicological classification that refers to instruments that require electricity to produce sound, such as the synthesizer. (Chapter 2)

EMIC: A term borrowed from linguistics, used by anthropologists and ethnomusicologists to describe the perspective of a cultural insider. (Chapter 3)

ERHU: A fiddle from China. (Chapter 7)

ESCOLAS DE SAMBA: Samba schools of Brazil. (Chapter 12)

ETHNOCENTRISM: The unconscious assumption that one's own cultural background is "normal," while that of others is "strange" or "exotic." (Chapter 1)

ETHNOMUSICOLOGY: The scholarly study of any music within its contemporary context. (Chapter 1)

ETIC: A term borrowed from linguistics, used by anthropologists and ethnomusicologists to describe the perspective of a cultural outsider. (Chapter 3)

F

FAIS-DO-DO (pronounced *fai-doh-doh*): Literally meaning "go to sleep," this term refers to a public dancehall that hosts performances of Cajun dance music. (Chapter 13)

FASOLA SINGING: A singing style that uses shape-note notation. (Chapter 13)

FAVELA: Poor housing areas in the hills around Rio de Janeiro, Brazil. (Chapter 12)

FIDDLE: A generic term used to describe a bowed lute. (Chapter 2) Also, a slang term for a violin. (Chapters 9 & 13)

FIESTA: A festival or celebration in Spain or Latin America. (Chapter 9)

FILMI (Also, FILMI GIT): Popular music taken from films in India. (Chapter 5)

FIRQA (pronounced *feer-kah*): Large orchestral ensembles consisting of traditional Arabic instruments from the Middle East. (Chapter 8)

FLAMENCO: A Spanish musical tradition featuring vocals with guitar accompaniment, characterized by passionate singing and vibrant rhythm. (Chapter 9)

FLUTE: A type of *aerophone* that splits a column of air on an edge to produce sound. (Chapter 2)

FOLKLORE: The study of orally transmitted folk knowledge and culture. (Chapter 1)

FORM: Underlying structure of a musical performance. (Chapter 2)

FREE RHYTHM: Music with no regular pulsation. (Chapter 2)

FRET: A bar or ridge found on the fingerboard of chordophones that enables performers to produce different melodic pitches with consistent frequency levels. (Chapter 2)

FRICTION DRUM: A type of drum with a membrane that is "rubbed" rather than struck. (Chapter 9)

FROTTOIR (pronounced *fwaht-twah*): A metal washboard used in Cajun-Zydeco music. (Chapter 13)

FUGING TUNE (pronounced *fyu-ging*): A category of shape-note song in which individual voices enter one after the other. (Chapter 13)

G

GADULKA: A spiked fiddle from Bulgaria. (Chapter 3)

GAELIC (pronounced *gaa-lik*): The indigenous language of Scotland. (Chapter 9)

GAGAKU: A Confucian-derived ritual ensemble from Japan. (Chapter 7)

GAIDA: Bagpipes from Bulgaria. (Chapter 9)

GAMELAN: An ensemble from Indonesia comprised primarily of *metallophones*. (Chapter 6)

GAMELAN GONG KEBYAR: An ensemble type from Bali, Indonesia, comprised primarily of *metallophones* and characterized by rhythmically dense performance technique. (Chapter 6)

GANJA: A Rastafarian word for marijuana, borrowed from the Hindi term for "herb." (Chapter 11)

GARAMUT: A slit drum from Papua New Guinea. (Chapter 4)

GARDON: A struck lute from Hungary. (Chapter 9)

GAT (pronounced *gaht*): The composed section of instrumental performance in Indian classical music. (Chapter 5)

GEISHA: A Japanese girl or woman trained to provide entertainment, including musical entertainment. (Chapter 7)

GHAWAZI: Term in Arabic cultures for female dancers who specialize in very rapid hip-shaking movements. (Chapter 8)

GHUNUR: A string of bells worn around the ankle, commonly associated with the Bauls of South Asia. (Chapter 5)

GIG: A slang term referring to a musical job or performance-for-hire. (Chapter 9)

GINGA (Also, JENGA): A back-and-forth motion used as the basis for *capoeira* dancing. (Chapter 12)

GONG AGENG: The largest gong of an Indonesian *gamelan* ensemble. (Chapter 6)

GOOMBAY: A type of folk music ensemble from the Bahamas. (Chapter 11)

GOPIYANTRO (Also, EKTARA): A single-stringed *chordophone* with a membrane base found in India and often associated with the Bauls. (Chapter 5)

GOSPEL: An American religious music tradition associated with Christian evangelism. (Chapter 13)

GRIOT (pronounced *gree-oh*): The French term for a wandering minstrel, often used to describe the West African *jali.* (Chapter 10)

GUARACHA (pronounced *gwah-rah-cha*): A Latin American ballroom dance, as well as a song type emphasizing call-and-response vocal organization. (Chapter 11)

GUIRO (pronounced *gwee-roh*): A scraped gourd *idiophone.* (Chapter 11)

GUITAR: A fretted plucked lute common to American folk and popular music, as well as Spanish flamenco and various other traditions. (Chapter 13)

GUITARRÓN: A large fretted plucked lute from Mexico, similar to a guitar but with a convex resonator. (Chapter 12)

GUQIN (pronounced *goo-chin*): See QIN.

GURU: A teacher or spiritual guide, primarily associated with Hindu traditions from India. (Chapter 5)

GUSHEH: Short composed melodic phrases found in Persian classical music. (Chapter 8)

GYPSY: See ROM.

H

HACKBRETT: A hammered zither from Germany. (Chapter 3)

HAILE SELASSIE I: An Ethiopian emperor considered by Jamaican Rastafarians to be a black incarnation of Jesus Christ. (Chapter 11)

HAJJ: The Islamic pilgrimage to Mecca, Saudi Arabia. (Chapter 8)

HALILE: A pair of cymbals found in Sufi Muslim music performance. (Chapter 8)

HANUMAN: The "monkey-hero" in the Indian epic, *Ramayana.* (Chapter 5)

HARHIRAA: A type of throat-singing from Mongolia. (Chapter 7)

HARMONICA: A free-reed *aerophone* common to folk music from the United States. (Chapter 13)

HARMONIC: An *overtone* produced by lightly touching a string at a vibrating node. (Chapter 7)

HARMONIUM: A free-reed pump organ. (Chapter 5)

HARMONY: The simultaneous combination of three or more pitches in the Euro-American music tradition. (Chapter 2)

HAWAIIAN STEEL GUITAR: A guitar style of performance characterized by sliding tones (portamento) and wide vibrato. (Chapter 4)

HETEROPHONY: Multiple performers playing simultaneous variations of the same line of music. (Chapter 2)

HICHIRIKI: A double-reed *aerophone* used in *gagaku* music from Japan. (Chapter 7)

HIGHLAND PIPES: Bagpipes from Scotland. (Chapter 9)

HIGHLIFE: A generic term describing urban popular music traditions found throughout sub-Saharan Africa. (Chapter 10)

HINDUSTANI: A term referring to the cultural traditions of northern India. (Chapter 5)

HOCKET: A performance technique in which performers trade pitches back and forth to create a complete melody. (Chapter 12)

HOMOPHONY: Multiple lines of music expressing the same musical idea. (Chapter 2)

HOSHO: A gourd rattle from Zimbabwe. (Chapter 10)

HOSSZÚ FURULYA: A long end-blown flute from Hungary. (Chapter 9)

HULA PAHU: Hawaiian dance songs using drum accompaniment. (Chapter 4)

HURDY GURDY (Also Tekerölant): A *chordophone* common in France and Hungary that uses a wheel turned by a crank to vibrate the strings. (Chapter 9)

HYMN: A "humanly composed" religious work. (Chapter 13)

I

IDIOPHONE: Ethnomusicological classification encompassing instruments that themselves vibrate to produce sound, such as rattles, bells, and various other kinds of percussion. (Chapter 2)

ILAHI: A Sufi Muslim hymn. (Chapter 8)

IMPROVISATION: An instrumental or vocal performance or composition created spontaneously without preparation. (Chapters 4–13, especially Chapter 5)

INCA: A pre-Columbian indigenous people from the Andes region of South America. (Chapter 12)

INDEFINITE PITCH: A sound with no single dominating frequency level. (Chapter 2)

INDEPENDENT POLYPHONY: Multiple lines of music expressing independent musical ideas as a cohesive whole. (Chapter 2)

INTERVAL: The distance between two pitches. (Chapter 2)

INUIT: The term for specific Native American populations that live primarily in Canada and Alaska; often referred to as "Eskimos." (Chapter 13)

IQ'A (pronounced *eek-ah*): Rhythmic *modes* used in Arabic music. (Chapter 8)

ISAN (pronounced *ee-sahn*): A term referring to Northeast Thailand and its regional culture, including music. (Chapter 6)

ISICATHAMIYA (pronounced *isi-"click"ah-tah-mee-yah*): A term meaning, "to walk like a cat," that is, stealthily, which describes a soft style of *mbube* all-male vocal performance from South Africa. (Chapter 10)

IST: The central or "home" pitch of a Persian classical music performance. (Chapter 8)

J

JALEO: Clapping and shouts of encouragement associated with a *juerga* ("happening") in Spanish flamenco music. (Chapter 9) Also, refers to the closing section of a *meringue* performance from the Dominican Republic. (Chapter 11)

JALI (Also, JELI; pl. JALOLU): Term for a Mandinka poet/praise singer and oral historian from Senegal–Gambia. (Chapter 10)

JALTARANG: An instrument from India, consisting of a series of small china bowls each filled/tuned with a different level of water and struck with a small beater. (Chapter 5)

JAMACA (pronounced *yah-mah-kah*): In Islam, word used for an important *mosque*. (Chapter 8)

JANIZARY (pronounced *ye-nis-air-ee*); (Also, JANISSARY or YENICERI): A corps of elite troops commanded by the Ottoman caliphs from the late fourteenth century until their destruction in 1826. (Chapter 8)

JATI: The final section of the *tala* in Indian classical music in which the number of beats in the cycle varies. (Chapter 5)

JHALA: Refers to a set of drone strings on Indian *chordophones*. Also, a reference to the climactic end of the *alap* section of *raga* performance in India. (Chapter 5)

JIG: A musical form in 6/8 time, popular both in British and in North American fiddle traditions (Chapters 9 & 13).

JING: The warrior role-type in the Beijing Opera from China. (Chapter 7)

JINGHU: The lead fiddle of the Beijing Opera's instrumental ensemble. (Chapter 7)

JINGJU (Also, JINGXI): Beijing Opera from China. (Chapter 7)

JOR: A regularizing of the beat in the opening section of *raga* performance in Indian classical music. (Chapter 5)

JUERGA (pronounced *hwair-ga*): An informal event associated with Spanish flamenco music in which the separation between musicians and audience is blurred. (Chapter 9)

JUJU: A popular music style from Nigeria. (Chapter 10)

JUKE JOINT: An African-American social venue serving alcohol and hosting dance music, typically *blues*. (Chapter 13)

K

KABUKI: Popular music theater form from Japan. (Chapter 7)

KAHUNA: A Hawaiian term for a ritual specialist. (Chapter 4)

KALIMBA: A *lamellophone* from sub-Saharan Africa. (Chapter 10)

KANG DUNG: A trumpet from Tibet made from a human thighbone. (Chapter 7)

KANUN: See QANUN.

KAPU: Strict taboo system from precolonial Hawaii. (Chapter 4)

KARNATAK: See CARNATIC.

KARTAL: Indian percussion instrument consisting of a steel rod struck by a horseshoe-shaped beater. (Chapter 5)

KASIDE: Freely rhythmic melismatic passages performed by a vocal soloist in a Sufi Muslim ritual. (Chapter 8)

KATAJJAQ (pronounced *kah-tah-jahk*): An Inuit throat-singing style from northern Quebec, Canada. (Chapter 13)

KATHAKALI: A classical dance drama from South India. (Chapter 5)

KAYAGUM: A plucked zither from Korea. (Chapter 7)

KECAK: A Balinese theatrical performance of the *Ramayana*. (Chapter 6)

KEMENCE (Also, KEMANCHEH or KEMANJA): A spiked fiddle common to Turkish and Arabic music traditions. (Chapter 8)

KERESHMEH: A type of metered piece in the Persian classical music tradition. (Chapter 8)

KEY: A tonal system consisting of several pitches in fixed relationship to a fundamental pitch. (Chapter 7)

KHAEN: A bamboo mouth organ from Northeast Thailand. (Chapter 6)

KHANEGAH: A type of Sufi Muslim monastery. (Chapter 8)

KHAWNG WONG LEK/KHAWNG WONG YAI: Respectively, the higher- and lower-ranged gong circles found in classical ensembles from Thailand. (Chapter 6)

KHON: A classical masked drama based on the Thai version of the *Ramayana*. (Chapter 6)

KHÖÖMEI: Throat-singing tradition from Mongolia. (Chapter 7)

KHRU: A Thai teacher; the term is linguistically associated with the word *guru* found in Hinduism. (Chapter 6)

KHRUANG SAI: A classical Thai ensemble characterized by stringed instruments and rhythmic percussion. (Chapter 6)

KHYAL: A category of vocal music from India. (Chapter 5)

KILT: A knee-length skirt made of wool associated with Scottish Highlanders. (Chapter 9)

KILU: A small drum from Hawaii, usually made from a coconut shell with a fish-skin face. (Chapter 4)

KISAENG: A professional entertainer from Korea. (Chapter 7)

KLEZMER: A European-derived dance music commonly associated with Jewish celebrations, influenced by jazz and other non-Jewish styles. (Chapter 8)

KOMUSO: Lay-priest associated with Zen Buddism from Japan who performed the *shakuhachi*. (Chapter 7)

KONI: A plucked lute from West Africa. (Chapter 10)

KORA: A harp-lute or bridge-harp performed on by *jalolu* from Senegal-Gambia. (Chapter 10)

KORAN (Also, QUR'AN): The sacred text of Islam. (Chapter 8)

KOTO: A plucked zither from Japan. (Chapter 7)

KO-TUZUMI: A small, hourglass-shaped drum from Japan that is held on the shoulder. (Chapter 7)

KRITI: A genre of devotional Hindu poetry from South India. (Chapter 5)

KUDUM: A type of kettle drum common to Turkish and Arabic music. (Chapter 8)

KUMBENGO: The sung sections of a *jali* performance from West Africa. (Chapter 10)

KUNDU: An hourglass-shaped drum from Papua New Guinea. (Chapter 4)

KUSHAURA: The "leading" rhythmic pattern of *mbira dza vadzimu* performance from Zimbabwe. (Chapter 10)

KUTSINHIRA: The "following" rhythmic pattern of *mbira dza vadzimu* performance from Zimbabwe. (Chapter 10)

L

LA LA: A Creole dance party. (Chapter 13)

LADYSMITH BLACK MAMBAZO: A popular vocal group in the mbube/isicathamiya style from South Africa. (Chapter 10)

LAGHU: The final element of the *tala* in Indian classical music. (Chapter 5)

LAM KLAWN (pronounced *lum glawn*): Vocal repartee with *khaen* accompaniment from Northeast Thailand. (Chapter 6)

LAM SING (pronounced *lum sing*): A popular music form from Northeast Thailand. (Chapter 6)

LAMELLOPHONE: A type of *idiophone* that uses vibrating "lamellae" or strips of material, usually metal, to produce sound. (Chapter 2)

LANGAJ: A ceremonial language found in the *vodou* (voodoo) tradition from Haiti. (Chapter 11)

LATA MANGESHKAR: Famous *filmi* singer from India. (Chapter 5)

LAUTO: A pear-shaped lute from Greece. (Chapter 3)

LAYALI: A vocal improvisational form in Arabic music traditions. (Chapter 8)

LIKEMBE: A *lamellophone* from sub-Saharan Africa. (Chapter 10)

LINED HYMN: An archaic form of singing found in Scotland and the United States, in which a leader "lines" out a verse and the congregation repeats it heterophonically. (Chapter 13)

LONG-METER SONG: An informal term for a *lined hymn*. (Chapter 13)

LUTE: A type of chordophone with a resonating body and a neck with a fingerboard that enables individual strings to sound different pitches. (Chapter 2)

LWA (Also, LOA): A category of deities in Haitian vodou (voodoo). (Chapter 11)

LYRA: A spiked fiddle from Greece. (Chapter 3)

M

MAGHRIB: A geographic region in North Africa that includes Morocco, Algeria, Tunisia, and Libya. (Chapter 8)

MAHORI: A classical ensemble from Thailand characterized by melodic and rhythmic percussion, stringed instruments, and a fipple flute. (Chapter 6)

MAKAM (Also, MAQAM): A *mode* or system of rules and expectations for composition and improvisation in Arabic classical music. (Chapter 8)

MAMBO: A Latin American dance and music form. (Chapter 11)

MANA: Term for spiritual power in the Hawaiian belief system. (Chapter 4)

MANDOLIN: A high-ranged fretted lute commonly used in bluegrass music from the United States. (Chapter 13) Also, the term for a medieval round-bodied lute. (Chapter 3)

MANEABA: Term for a communal meetinghouse in Kiribati. (Chapter 4)

MARACAS: A pair of small Caribbean gourd rattles with interior beads. (Chapter 11).

MARIACHI: An entertainment music associated with festivals and celebratory events in Mexico. (Chapter 12)

MAROONS: Anglicized term for *cimarrons*. (Chapter 11)

MASHRIQ (pronounced *mah-shrik*): A geographic region in the Middle East that includes Egypt, Israel, Jordan, Lebanon, Syria, and Iraq. (Chapter 8)

MASJID: Term for a local *mosque* in Islam. (Chapter 8)

MAWLAM (pronounced *maw-lum*): A professional *lam klawn* singer from Northeast Thailand. (Chapter 6)

MAWWAL: A vocal improvisational form in Arabic music traditions. (Chapter 8)

MAYA: A pre-Columbian indigenous group from Central America, primarily Mexico and Guatemala. (Chapter 12)

MBIRA: A general reference to lamellophones found throughout Africa. (Chapter 10)

MBIRA DZA VADZIMU: A *lamellophone* from Zimbabwe. (Chapter 10)

MBUBE: A choral style of all-male vocal groups from South Africa. (Chapter 10)

MEDIUM: The source of a sound, be it instrumental or vocal. (Chapter 2) Also, the term for a person in a possessed or trance state. (Chapter 10)

MEHTER: Ceremonial music of the Turkish *Janizary*. (Chapter 8)

MELANESIA: A collection of islands in the Pacific Ocean. The term is derived from Greek, meaning "black islands," a reference to the darker skin pigmentation of the majority population. (Chapter 4)

MELE (pronounced *meh-leh*): Poetic texts used in Hawaiian drum dance chant. (Chapter 4)

MELE HULA (pronounced *meh-leh hoo-lah*): Unaccompanied Hawaiian songs specifically associated with dance. (Chapter 4)

MELISMA: Term for a text-setting style in which more than one pitch is sung per syllable. (Chapter 2)

MELODEON: A small reed organ. (Chapter 9)

MELODIC CONTOUR: The general direction and shape of a melody. (Chapter 2)

MELODY: An organized succession of pitches forming a musical idea. (Chapter 2)

MEMBRANOPHONE: Ethnomusicological classification referring to instruments such as drums that use a vibrating stretched membrane as the principle means of sound production. (Chapter 2)

MENTO: A creolized form of ballroom dance music considered a predecessor to *reggae*. (Chapter 11)

MERENGUE: A Latin American dance and music form, originally from the Dominican Republic. Also, the term for the middle section of a *merengue* performance. (Chapter 11)

MESTIZO: A person of mixed Native-American and Spanish descent. (Chapter 12)

MESTRE: A Brazilian term for a senior *capoeira* artist considered a master of the tradition. (Chapter 12)

METALLOPHONE: An *idiophone* consisting of several metal bars graduated in length to produce different pitches. (Chapter 6)

METER: A division of music beats into regular groupings. (Chapter 2)

MICRONESIA: A collection of islands in the Pacific Ocean. The term, meaning "tiny islands," is derived from Greek. (Chapter 4)

MIHRAB: A small "niche" or focal point found in a *mosque*, used to orient Islamic worshippers in the direction of Mecca, Saudi Arabia. (Chapter 8)

MINARET: The tall tower of a *mosque*, used for the Islamic call to prayer. (Chapter 8)

MIXOLYDIAN: A medieval church *mode* that predates the "equal tempered" tuning system used today as the basis of Western music. (Chapter 9)

MODE: A set of rules or guidelines used to compose or improvise music in a particular tradition. (Chapter 5)

MODERNISM: In an academic context, a term for scholarship that emphasizes objective "truth" and objective description in favor of subjective interpretation. (Chapter 1)

MONOPHONY: Music with a single melodic line. (Chapter 2)

MORIN HUUR: A fiddle from Mongolia with a distinctive horse head ornament. (Chapter 7)

MOSQUE (pronounced *mosk*): A house of worship for Islamic believers. (Chapter 8)

MRIDANGAM: A barrel-shaped drum from India. (Chapter 5)

MUEZZIN: A person who calls Islamic believers to worship five times a day. (Chapter 8)

MUHAMMAD: Muslim prophet and Arab leader who during his lifetime (570–632 C.E.) spread the religion of Islam and unified a great deal of the Arabian Peninsula. (Chapter 8)

MULLAH: A low-ranking clergyman in Islam. (Chapter 8)

MUMMER: A type of street theater actor, usually in performances staged during the Christmas season. (Chapter 11)

N

NAGASVARAM: A double-reed *aerophone* from India. (Chapter 5)

NEY (Also, NAY): A vertical flute found in Turkish and Arabic music traditions. (Chapter 8)

NGA BOM: A double-faced drum from Tibet. (Chapter 7)

NODE: A point of minimum amplitude on a vibrating string. (Chapter 7)

NOH: Classical drama form from Japan. (Chapter 7)

NOKAN: A transverse flute from Japan. (Chapter 7)

NONGAK: Style of folk music from Korea associated with farmers. (Chapter 7)

O

ORGANOLOGY: The study of musical instruments. (Chapter 3)

ORISHA: A category of deity in the animistic spiritual belief system of *Santeria* and in other African-derived religious traditions. (Chapter 11)

ORNAMENTATION: An embellishment or decoration of a melody. (Chapter 2)

ORUS: A rhythmic pattern associated with an *orisha* in the *Santeria* religious tradition. (Chapter 11)

OSSIAN: Legendary Gaelic hero and bard of the third century C.E. (Chapter 9)

OTTOMAN EMPIRE: An empire centered in what is now Turkey that spread throughout West Asia, eastern Europe, and northern Africa from the fourteenth to the nineteenth century. (Chapter 8)

O-TUZUMI: A small, hourglass-shaped drum from Japan that is held at the hip. (Chapter 7)

OVERTONE: A tone that is heard above a fundamental pitch, and that is one of the ascending group of tones that form the harmonic series derived from the fundamental pitch. (Chapter 7)

P

PAHU: A single-headed cylindrical *membranophone* from Hawaii that stands vertically on a carved footed base. (Chapter 4)

PALILLOS (pronounced *pah-lee-yohs*) (Also, PITOS): A type of finger-snapping commonly found in Spanish flamenco music. (Chapter 9)

PALITO: The term for a rhythmic pattern played on the side of a drum in *salsa* music. (Chapter 11)

PALLAVI: The first section of a *kriti* vocal performance from India. (Chapter 5)

PALM WINE GUITAR: A popular music style from sub-Saharan Africa. (Chapter 10)

PALMAS: The term for the hand-clapping commonly found in Spanish flamenco music. (Chapter 9)

PAN: A musical instrument from Trinidad made out of a steel oil drum. (Chapter 11)

PANDEIROS: A hand-held frame drum with attached cymbals (i.e., a tambourine), used in *capoeira* music from Brazil. (Chapter 12)

PANORAMA: A steel drum orchestra competition held at the end of the Carnival festival in Trinidad. (Chapter 11)

P'ANSORI: Narrative vocal performance style from Korea. (Chapter 7)

PARANG: A Portuguese-derived music sung during Christmas season. (Chapter 11)

PARLANDO RUBATO: A term meaning "speech-rhythm," indicating a fluctuating tempo. (Chapter 9)

PASEO: The opening section of a *merengue* performance. (Chapter 11)

PENTATEUCH: See TORAH.

PENTATONIC SCALE: A scale consisting of only five pitches. (Chapter 2)

PEURT A BEUL (pronounced *porsht a boy*): Unaccompanied dance song with nonsense syllables used to substitute for fiddling. (Chapter 13)

PHIN (pronounced *pin*): A fretted plucked lute from Northeast Thailand. (Chapter 6)

PHLENG LUK THUNG (pronounced *pleng look toong*): A popular music form from Thailand. (Chapter 6)

PHONIC STRUCTURE: The relationship between different sounds in a given piece; this relationship can be either m*onophony* or some form of *polyphony*. (Chapter 2)

PI (pronounced *bee*): A double-reed *aerophone* found in the *piphat* classical ensemble of Thailand. (Chapter 6)

PIBROCH (pronounced *pee-brahk*): A form of Scottish bagpipe music with an elaborate theme-and-variations structure. (Chapter 9)

PIPA: A pear-shaped lute from China. (Chapter 7)

PIPHAT (pronounced *bee-paht*): A type of classical ensemble from Thailand characterized by the use of melodic and rhythmic percussion and a double-reed *aerophone.* (Chapter 6)

PITCH: A tone's specific frequency level, measured in Hertz (Hz). (Chapter 2)

PITOS: See PALILLOS.

PLENA: A topical song from Puerto Rico. (Chapter 11)

POIETIC: The process of creating the meaning of a symbol. (Chapter 1)

POLYNESIA: A collection of islands in the Pacific Ocean. The term is derived from Greek, and means "many islands." (Chapter 4)

POLYPHONY: The juxtaposition or overlapping of multiple lines of music; the three types of polyphony are *homophony, independent polyphony*, and *heterophony.* (Chapter 2)

POLYRHYTHM: A term meaning "multiple rhythms"; the organizational basis for most sub-Saharan African music traditions. (Chapter 10)

PORTAMENTO: A smooth, uninterrupted glide from one pitch to another. (Chapter 4)

PORTEÑOS: A term for residents of the port area of Buenos Aires, Argentina. (Chapter 12)

POSTMODERNISM: A general term applied to numerous scholarly approaches that reject "modernism," with its emphases on objective "truth" and objective description, in favor of subjective interpretations. (Chapter 1)

POWWOW: A pan-tribal American Indian event celebrating Native American identity and culture, generally also open to non-Native Americans. (Chapter 13)

PRECENTOR: A song leader who recites the "line" of a *lined hymn* in Calvinist churches in the United States. (Chapter 13)

PROGRAMMATIC MUSIC: Music that has a "program"—that is, tells a story, depicts a scene, or creates an image (Chapter 3).

PSALMS: A book of the Christian Bible used as the source for many songs in Calvinist churches in the United States. (Chapter 13)

PUK: Drum used to accompany Korean *p'ansori* performance. (Chapter 7)

PYGMIES: A generic term applied to a diverse population of forest-dwellers in Central Africa. (Chapter 10)

Q

QANUN (Also, KANUN): A plucked zither used in Turkish and Arabic music traditions. (Chapter 8)

QAWWALI (Also, KAWWALI): Sufi Muslim devotional songs. (Chapter 5)

QIN (pronounced *chin*; also, GUQIN): A bridgeless plucked zither from China, the playing of which is characterized by the frequent use of overtones. (Chapter 7)

QUR'AN: See KORAN.

R

RADA: Ritual drums used in *vodou* (*voodoo*) ceremonies from Haiti. (Chapter 11)

RADIF: A collection of *gusheh* for each *dastgah* in Persian classical music. (Chapter 8)

RAGA: A mode or system of rules and expectations for composition and improvisation in Indian classical music. (Chapter 5)

RAKE AND SCRAPE: A folk music from the Bahamas. (Chapter 11)

RAMA: The central figure of the Hindu Indian epic *Ramayana*. (Chapter 5)

RAMAYANA: An Indian mythological epic about the Hindu god Rama found throughout South and Southeast Asia. (Chapter 6)

RANAT EK (pronounced *rah-nahd ek*): The lead *xylophone* of classical ensembles from Thailand. (Chapter 6)

RANAT THUM (pronounced *rah-nahd toom*): The supporting *xylophone* of classical ensembles from Thailand. (Chapter 6)

RANCHERA: A style of "country" *mariachi* from Mexico that emphasizes vocal performance. (Chapter 12)

RANGE: All the pitches that a voice or instrument can potentially produce. (Chapter 2)

RAQS SHARQI (pronounced *rocks shar-kee*): Middle Eastern dance form characterized as "belly dance" by outsiders to the region. (Chapter 8)

RASA: The mood or sentiment of an artistic expression in India. (Chapter 5)

RASTA: A believer in *Rastafarianism*. (Chapter 11)

RASTAFARIANISM: A religious belief system centered in Jamaica, which purports that the second coming of Jesus Christ has already occurred in the form of Haile Selassie, an Ethiopian king. (Chapter 11)

RAVANA: The villain in the Indian epic *Ramayana*. (Chapter 5)

RAVI SHANKAR: A famous musician and composer from India. (Chapter 5)

REBAB: A fiddle commonly found in gamelan ensembles from Indonesia. (Chapter 6)

REBEC: A spiked fiddle from France. (Chapter 3)

RÊCO-RÊCO: A notched scraper *idiophone* found in Latin American music traditions. (Chapter 12)

REEDS: A type of *aerophone* that uses a vibrating reed to produce sound. (Chapter 2)

REELS: A type of dance music found in Scottish and Appalachian music. (Chapter 13)

REELS À BOUCHE: An unaccompanied song used for dance music in the Cajun region of Louisiana in the United States. (Chapter 13)

REGGAE: A popular music form from Jamaica characterized by a rhythmic emphasis on the offbeat and by politically and socially conscious lyrics. (Chapter 11)

REGULATORS: The metal keys that "regulate" the drone pipes on the Irish bagpipes to produce different pitches. (Chapter 10)

RENAISSANCE LUTE: A pear-shaped plucked lute from Europe. (Chapter 3)

RHYMER: The lead vocalist in a *rhyming spiritual* performance from the Bahamas. (Chapter 11)

RHYMING SPIRITUAL: A vocal genre from the Bahamas. (Chapter 11)

RHYTHM: The lengths, or durations, of sounds as patterns in time. (Chapter 2)

RHYTHMIC DENSITY: The quantity of notes between periodic accents or over a specific unit of time. (Chapter 2)

RHYTHMIC MELODY: The complete musical idea of polyrhythmic music. (Chapter 10)

RIQQ (pronounced *rik*): A small, single-headed drum with pairs of small cymbals inserted into its frame (i.e., a tambourine), common to Turkish and Arabic music traditions. (Chapter 8)

RITARD: A musical term for slowing the tempo, normally at the end of a piece. (Chapter 2)

ROCK STEADY: A popular music form from Jamaica considered a precursor to *reggae.* (Chapter 11)

RODA: A circular area used for the dancers in *capoeira* performances. (Chapter 12)

ROM (Also, ROMANI or GYPSIES): An ethnic group originating in India characterized by a semi-nomadic lifestyle; popularly known as *gypsies.* (Chapter 9) *Rom* is also the term used for large paired cymbals from Tibet. (Chapter 7)

RUMBA (Also, RHUMBA): A Latin American dance and music form. (Chapter 11)

RYUTEKI: A transverse flute from Japan. (Chapter 7)

S

SACRED HARP: The most popular collection of *shape-note* songs. (Chapter 13)

SACHS–HORNBOSTEL SYSTEM: Standard classification system for musical instruments created by Curt Sachs and Erik M. von Hornbostel, which divides musical instruments into four categories: *aerophones*, *chordophones*, *idiophones*, and *membranophones.* (Chapter 2)

SALSA: A Latin American dance music form. (Chapter 11)

SAMBA: A popular music form from Brazil. (Chapter 12)

SAMBA-BAIANA: "Bahian samba" from Brazil. (Chapter 12)

SAMBA-CANÇÃO (pronounced *samba kahn-syao*): "Song samba" from Brazil. (Chapter 12)

SAMBA-CARNAVALESCO: "Carnival samba" from Brazil. (Chapter 12)

SAMBA-ENREDO: "Theme samba" from Brazil. (Chapter 12)

SAMBA-REGGAE: "Reggae samba" from Brazil. (Chapter 12)

SAMBISTAS: Dancers in the *samba schools* that parade during Carnival in Brazil. (Chapter 12)

SAMUL-NORI: A type of folk music from Korea. (Chapter 7)

SANDOURI: A hammered zither from Greece. (Chapter 3)

SANJO: An instrumental form from Korea. (Chapter 7)

SANKYOKU: A classical ensemble type from Japan, consisting of *koto*, *shakuhachi*, and *shamisen.* (Chapter 7)

SANTERIA: A belief system combining animism and syncretized Roman Catholicism, found primarily in Cuba and the United States. (Chapter 10)

SANTUR: A hammered zither from the Persian classical tradition. Often cited as the origin of hammered zithers found throughout Asia, northern Africa, Europe, and the Western hemisphere. (Chapter 3)

SARANGI: A bowed lute from India. (Chapter 5)

SAROD: A fretless plucked lute from India. (Chapter 5)

SAW U (pronounced *saw oo*): A Thai fiddle with a coconut resonator. (Chapter 6)

SAZ: A fretted plucked lute from Turkey. (Chapter 8)

SCALE: The pitches used in a particular performance arranged in ascending order. (Chapter 2)

SCHALMEI: A medieval double-reed *aerophone* from Europe. (Chapter 3)

SCHEITHOLT: A spiked fiddle from Germany. (Chapter 3)

SEMIOTICS: The study of "signs" and systems of signs, including music. (Chapter 1)

SHAH: The title formerly given to hereditary monarchs in Iran. (Chapter 8)

SHAKA ZULU (1787–1828): Leader of the Zulu ethnic group from South Africa. (Chapter 10)

SHAKUHACHI: A vertical flute from Japan. (Chapter 7)

SHAM'IDAN: A Middle Eastern dance in which the dancer performs with a large, heavy candelabrum with lighted candles balanced on the head. (Chapter 8)

SHAMISEN: A fretless plucked lute from Japan with a membrane resonator face. (Chapter 7)

SHANGO: An animistic belief system found primarily in Trinidad. (Chapter 11)

SHAPE NOTES: A music notation system from the United States that uses differently shaped "note" heads to indicate pitch. (Chapter 13)

SHAWM: A medieval double-reed *aerophone* from Europe. (Chapter 3)

SHENG: A mouth organ from China. Also the term for the male hero role-type in Beijing Opera from China. (Chapter 7)

SHIA: The fundamentalist branch of Islam. (Chapter 8)

SHO: A mouth organ from Japan. (Chapter 7)

SHOFAR: A Jewish ritual trumpet made of a ram's horn. (Chapter 8)

SIKU: Panpipes common among indigenous populations from Peru and throughout the Andes. (Chapter 12)

SIKURI: A type of ensemble from Peru, consisting of *siku* performers with accompanying drummers. (Chapter 12)

SINGSINGS: A cultural festival common to Papua New Guinea that comprises several ethnic groups performing indigenous music and dance traditions. (Chapter 4)

SINGING SCHOOL: A tradition of teaching four-part harmony techniques, found in rural areas throughout the United States. (Chapter 13)

SITA (pronounced *see-tah*): The wife of the Hindu God *Rama* in the Indian epic *Ramayana*. (Chapter 5)

SITAR: A fretted plucked lute from India. (Chapter 5)

SIZHU (pronounced *sih-joo*): An ensemble comprising "silk and bamboo" instruments from China. (Chapter 7)

SKA: A popular music form from Jamaica considered a precursor to *reggae.* (Chapter 11)

SOCA: A popular music style related to calypso music from Trinidad. (Chapter 11)

SOCIOLOGY: The study of human social behavior, emphasizing its origins, organization, institutions, and development. (Chapter 1)

SOLFÈGE: Mnemonic syllables corresponding to individual pitches in a scale. (Chapter 5)

SON: An Afro-Cuban music genre from Latin America. (Chapter 11)

SONG LANG: A clapper *idiophone* from Vietnam. (Chapter 6)

SON JALISCIENSE: A category of *mariachi* that features frequent subtle shifts of meter and tempo, making it more rhythmically active than most *mariachi* music. (Chapter 12)

SPIRITUAL: A term for religious folk music. (Chapter 13)

SPOONS: A pair of spoons struck together to play rhythm. (Chapter 9)

STEEL DRUM: A musical instrument from Trinidad made from steel oil drums. (Chapter 11)

STRING BASS: A large fretless plucked lute heard in many music traditions from the United States. (Chapter 13)

STROPHIC: A song form in which the music repeats with each new poetic verse. (Chapter 13)

SUFI (pronounced *soo-fee*): The mystical branch of Islam. (Chapter 8)

SUNNI (pronounced *soo-nee*): The mainstream branch of Islam. (Chapter 8)

SUONA (pronounced *swoh-nah*): A double-reed *aerophone* from China. (Chapter 7)

SURDO: A large drum used in Samba music in Brazil. (Chapter 12)

SUSAP: A mouth harp (lamellophone) from Papua New Guinea. (Chapter 4)

SYLLABIC: A text setting in which only one pitch is sung per syllable. (Chapter 2)

SYMPATHETIC STRINGS: A set of strings, most commonly found on Hindustani Indian chordophones, that vibrate "in sympathy" with the vibrations of other strings on the instrument. (Chapter 5)

SYMPHONIA: A medieval European instrument similar to the *hurdy gurdy*. (Chapter 9)

SYNAGOGUE: A Jewish house of worship. (Chapter 8)

SYNCOPATION: The accenting of a normally weak beat. (Chapter 2)

T

TABLA: A pair of drums found in Hindustani music from India. (Chapter 5) Also, a goblet-shaped hand drum found in Arabic music. (Chapter 8)

TAHMALA: A compositional form found in Turkish and Arabic music. (Chapter 8)

TAHRIR: A freely rhythmic section emphasizing melismatic performance found in Persian classical music. (Chapter 8)

TAI THU (pronounced *tai tuh*): A type of chamber music ensemble from Vietnam. (Chapter 6)

TAIKO: Generic term for *drum* in Japan. (Chapter 7)

TAKHT: A type of instrumental ensemble found in Arabic music traditions. (Chapter 8)

TALA: Rhythmic framework found in *raga* performance in India. (Chapter 5)

TAMBOO-BAMBOO: A type of ensemble developed after drums were banned in Trinidad, which used cane and bamboo tubes that were beaten with sticks and stamped on the ground. (Chapter 11)

TAMBORA: A small barrel-drum made with a thick leather face, commonly used in *merengue* from the Dominican Republic. (Chapter 11)

TAMBURA: A round-bodied lute used to provide the "drone" element in Indian classical music. (Chapter 5) Also, a term used to describe round-bodied lutes from Bulgaria, Croatia, and Serbia in Southeastern Europe. (Chapter 3)

TANBUR: A fretted plucked lute common to Turkish and Arabic music. (Chapter 8)

TANGO: A dance and associated music originating in Argentina, but now commonly associated with ballroom dance. (Chapter 12)

TAQSIM (pronounced *tahk-seem*): An instrumental improvisational form in Turkish and Arabic music traditions. (Chapter 8)

TARAB: Arabic word for a state of emotional transformation or ecstasy achieved through music. (Chapter 8)

TASLAM: A compositional form found in Turkish and Arabic music. (Chapter 8)

TAVIL: A pair of drums from India, often used to accompany the *nagasvaram*. (Chapter 5)

TEJANO (pronounced *teh-hah-noh*): Term referring to populations and cultural activities from the Texas-Mexico borderlands in North America. (Chapter 13)

TEJAS (pronounced *teh-hahs*): Native American name for what is now Texas in the United States. (Chapter 13)

TEKEROLANT: See Hurdy Gurdy.

TEKKE: A type of Sufi Muslim monastery. (Chapter 8)

TEMPO: The relative rate of speed of a beat. (Chapter 2)

TEMPO GIUSTO: A regular or "precise" metered rhythm following an unmetered section. (Chapter 9)

TEXT SETTING: The rhythmic relationship of words to melody; can be *syllabic* (one pitch per syllable) or *melismatic* (more than one pitch per syllable). (Chapter 2)

THEKA (pronounced *teh-kah*): The entire pattern or set of words (*bols*) for a given *tala* in classical Indian music. (Chapter 5)

TIMBALES: A pair of metal-framed drums of European military origin used often in *salsa* music. (Chapter 11)

TIMBER FLUTE: A wooden transverse flute from Ireland. (Chapter 9)

TIMBILA: A log *xylophone* from Mozambique. (Chapter 10)

TIMBRE: The tone quality or "color" of a musical sound. (Chapter 2)

TIN WHISTLE: A metal vertical flute from Ireland. (Chapter 9)

TOMTOM: A pair of tall, single-headed hand drums from Ghana. (Chapter 10)

TORAH (Also, PENTATEUCH, pronounced *pent-a-toik*): In Judaism, the first five books of the Bible, or more generally, all sacred literature. (Chapter 8)

TOTEM: An animal, plant, or other natural object used as the emblem of a group or individual, and strongly associated with an ancestral relationship. (Chapter 13)

TRUMPET: A type of *aerophone* that requires the performer to vibrate his or her lips to produce sound. (Chapter 2)

TUMBADORA (Also, CONGA): A tall barrel-shaped single-headed drum used in *salsa* music. (Chapter 11)

TUMBAO: A rhythmic pattern played on the *conga* in *salsa* music. (Chapter 11)

TUNING SYSTEM: The pitches common to a musical tradition. (Chapter 2)

U

UD (Also, AL'UD): A fretless, plucked pear-shaped lute found in Arabic music traditions. (Chapter 8)

UILLEANN PIPES (pronounced *il-en*; Also, UNION PIPES): Bagpipes from Ireland, called *uilleann* (meaning "elbow") because the performer uses an elbow to pump the bellows. (Chapter 9)

UKELELE: A high-ranged plucked lute from Hawaii. (Chapter 4)

UMBANDA: A belief system combining animism and syncretized Roman Catholicism, found primarily in Brazil. (Chapter 11)

URTYN DUU: A Mongolian vocal form described as "long song"; performers are accompanied by the *morin huur*. (Chapter 7)

V

VENU: A transverse flute from South India. (Chapter 5)

VIHUELA: A small, fretted plucked lute from Mexico, similar to a guitar but with a convex resonator. (Chapter 12)

VINA: A plucked lute from South India, often associated with the Hindu goddess Saraswati. (Chapter 5)

VODOU (Also, VOODOO): An animistic belief system found primarily in Haiti. (Chapter 10)

W

WAI KHRU: A teacher-honoring ceremony from Thailand. (Chapter 6)

WAULKING SONG: Work songs from Scotland performed while working with wool. (Chapter 9)

X

XYLOPHONE: An idiophone consisting of several wooden bars graduated in length to produce different pitches. (Chapter 10)

Y

YANGQIN (pronounced *yang chin*): A hammered zither from China. (Chapter 7)

YENICERI: See JANIZARY.

YUE QIN (pronounced *yweh chin*): A plucked lute from China. (Chapter 7)

Z

ZAKIRLER: A specialist group of male vocalists who perform metered hymns in unison during a Sufi ritual. (Chapter 8)

ZARB: A goblet-shaped hand drum used in Persian classical music traditions from Iran. (Chapter 8)

ZHENG (pronounced *jeng*): A plucked zither from China. (Chapter 7)

ZIKR: See DHIKR

ZITHER: A type of chordophone in which the strings stretch across the length of the resonating body. (Chapter 2)

ZOUK: Popular music form from the French Lesser Antilles in the Caribbean. (Chapter 11)

ZURNA (Also, ZOURNA): A double-reed aerophone from Turkey and Greece. (Chapter 3)

ZYDECO: Creole dance music from the southern United States, primarily Louisiana. (Chapter 13)

Resources for Further Study

As comprehensive as this book seeks to be, there is no way to include enough material to cover all possible questions. Further, we have suggested that both teachers and students will supplement our Sites by constructing their own. Thirty years ago, when ethnomusicology was still young in American institutions and resources were severely limited, it was difficult to find information on many world music traditions. Today, with the explosion of available information and new technologies for delivering it, anyone can obtain further information on virtually any topic. Not all libraries will have a broad selection of print, audio, or video publications available, but anyone with access to the Internet will find it profitable to at least visit any of the better, more professional websites devoted to virtually any musical type or style in the world. The following, also found in part at the end of Chapter 1, is a guide to some of the available resources that will lead you to further explore the world's musics.

We have arranged these resources into four categories: (1) print materials; (2) visual materials; (3) audio materials; and (4) additional resources. Our inclusion of an item does not necessarily imply our complete approval of its contents, but does mean we feel it offers something of value. Our exclusion of an item does not signal our disapproval; we are attempting to deal with limitations of space and the limits of our own knowledge. We have also limited ourselves to materials in English.

Lastly, a word of caution about using the Internet as a research tool. While the Internet is quite a valuable resource, articles found on it are generally not "refereed" to ensure accuracy of content, so do not rely on the Internet alone. Nevertheless, using a search engine, such as Google, to get started on a topic of interest can save you a lot of time digging through hard copy bibliographies for more information.

Print Materials

Encyclopedias and Dictionaries

Randall, Don Michael, ed. *The Harvard Dictionary of Music*, 4th ed. Cambridge, MA: Belknap Press of Harvard University Press, 2003.

Originally a slender book written entirely by one man, musicologist Willi Apel, this dictionary first appeared in 1944 and has undergone many revisions. The present volume supercedes the previous edition, called *The New Harvard Dictionary of Music*. This resource provides lengthy but broad articles, such as "East Asia," "Folk Music," and "American Indian Music," but there are also short entries for particular instruments (e.g., "sitar"), ensembles (e.g., "gamelan"), and genres (e.g., "reggae"), though there are none on individuals.

Sadie, Stanley, and John Tyrrell, eds. *The New Grove Dictionary of Music and Musicians*, 2nd ed. 29 vols. London: Macmillan, 2001.

Originally a small encyclopedia published by Englishman Sir George Grove in the 1870s, the "Grove" (as it is known familiarly) was long biased toward England in particular and Europe in general. The advent of the twenty-volume first edition of the *New Grove* in 1980 was a milestone in the study of world musics, for the encyclopedia now included substantial entries by recognized scholars on most countries of the world. The second edition of 2001 incorporates those articles plus everything that had appeared in the earlier *New Grove American* and the *New Grove Dictionary of Musical Instruments*. Thus, the Grove now includes articles at the level of continent (or subcontinent), nation, genre, ensemble, instrument, and individual performer/composer/ innovator.

The Garland Encyclopedia of World Music. 10 vols. New York and London: Routledge, 1998–2002.

This monumental encyclopedia, each volume having from 900 to 1,200 pages, is the first such work devoted entirely to the world's musics. Each volume has three sections: The first is an introduction that includes overview articles; the second, called "Issues and Processes," includes articles on specific questions or approaches;

and the third is devoted to individual nations, cultures, or genres. Volume 10, entitled *The World's Music: General Perspectives and Reference Tools,* includes articles by individual scholars under the heading "Ethnomusicologists at Work," and a section called "Resources and Research Tools" that combines the bibliographies, discographies, and videographies of volumes 1 through 9, each of which is devoted to a single continent or subcontinent (e.g., South Asia). Each volume, save for volume 10, is liberally illustrated with photos, charts, and notations and includes a compact disc. The appropriate volumes will be cited under each of our chapters.

The Bloomsbury Encyclopedia of Popular Music of the World. 10 vols. New York: Bloomsbury, 2003–2015.
  From the publisher's website: The ten EPMOW Genre volumes contain entries on the genres of music that have been or currently are popular in countries and communities all over the world. Included are discussions on cultural, historical and geographic origins; technical musical characteristics; instrumentation and use of voice; lyrics and language; typical features of performance and presentation; historical development and paths and modes of dissemination; influence of technology, the music industry and political and economic circumstances; changing stylistic features; notable and influential performers; and relationships to other genres and sub-genres.

Books and Journals

World Music: The Rough Guide. 2 vols. (vol. 1: Africa, Europe, and the Middle East; vol. 2: Latin and North America, the Caribbean, India, Asia, and the Pacific). London: Rough Guides, Inc., Third edition, 2009.
  While a few of the articles were written by known scholars and discuss traditional kinds of music, the bulk are devoted to contemporary forms, especially popular, revivalist, and innovative forms, with special attention to groups and individuals who make recordings. With its extensive illustrations, the two-volume set is nonetheless valuable for understanding at least certain aspects of each country's music scene. The Rough Guide also produced a growing series of recordings, mostly presenting popular and "worldbeat" forms that complement this literary source. Although these books are no longer in print, it is worth searching for them for a handy reference resource.

Oxford University Press Global Music Series. 26 vols. Oxford: Oxford University Press, 2004–2018.
  This series of short books, intended for a non-specialist audience, provides in-depth discussion of specific cultural areas as well as an accompanying CD of common musical types. The volumes have a strong "music education" approach, as one of the series editors, Patricia Shehan Campbell, is well known as a music educator specializing in world musics. Some of the volumes are mentioned below, but there are a growing number of areas covered, such as: East Africa, Central Java, Trinidad, Bali, Ireland, the Middle East, Brazil, America (United States), Bulgaria, North India, West Africa, South India, Japan, China, and more specifically *mariachi* music in the United States.
Oxford University Handbooks. Oxford: Oxford University Press, 2012–2015.
  The Oxford Handbook Series includes a wide array of music-related studies, from computer music to the American musical to the philosophy of music education, music psychology, and even mobile music studies. Three volumes are particularly relevant to ethnomusicology, *The Oxford Handbook of Medical Ethnomusicology, The Oxford Handbook of Applied Ethnomusicology* and *The Oxford Handbook of Children's Musical Cultures.*

Shahriari, Andrew. *Popular World Music,* 2nd ed. New York: Routledge, 2018.
  After writing the first edition of *World Music: A Global Journey*, we realized how much more there was to say about popular music genres around the world. Given the size and scope of this text already, we could not offer such study here. Andrew, consequently, took up the challenge of writing a more complete review of popular world music with an emphasis on musical style and genre history. If some of our introductions to popular music, such as reggae and salsa, piqued your interest, consider further investigation with this complementary publication.

We would be remiss if we did not include a few texts specific to various world music traditions discussed herein. We have intentionally limited the list to just a handful of resources as some areas have a wealth of associated material, some of which the serious student will no doubt easily discover on his or her own. The sources listed below, however, are a useful starting point. We have organized them according to chapters in the current book.

Chapter 1 Before the Trip Begins: Fundamental Issues

Blacking, John. *How Musical Is Man?* Seattle: University of Washington Press, 1973.
Hood, Mantle. *The Ethnomusicologist.* Kent, OH: Kent State University Press, 1982 (New York: McGraw-Hill, 1971).
Nettl, Bruno. *The Study of Ethnomusicology.* Urbana: University of Illinois Press, 1983.
Myers, Helen, ed. *Ethnomusicology: An Introduction.* New York: Norton, 1992.

Chapter 2 Aural Analysis: Listening to the World's Musics

Kamien, Roger. *Music: An Appreciation*, 4th brief ed. New York: McGraw-Hill, 2002 (1990). The opening sections of any number of "introductory" Euro-American art music texts, such as Kamien's, are useful for understanding basic music terminology. The above-mentioned dictionaries also provide detailed discussion.

Kartomi, Margaret J. *On Concepts and Classifications of Musical Instruments*. Chicago: University of Chicago Press, 1990.

Sachs, Curt. *The History of Musical Instruments*. New York: Norton, 1940.

Chapter 3 Cultural Considerations: Beyond the Sounds Themselves

Barz, Gregory F., and Timothy J. Cooley. *Shadows in the Field: New Perspectives for Fieldwork in Ethnomusicology*. New York: Oxford University Press, 1997.

Clayton, Martin, Trevor Herbert, and Richard Middleton, eds. *The Cultural Study of Music: A Critical Introduction*. New York: Routledge, 2003.

Merriam, Alan P. *The Anthropology of Music*. Evanston, IL: Northwestern University Press, 1964. This text is particularly important to the "anthropology" branch of ethnomusicology and is considered fundamental to the field.

Stobart, Henry, ed. *The New (Ethno)musicologies*. Lanham, MD: Scarecrow Press, Inc., 2008. Comprised of mostly European authors, this text prompted more serious research in several areas of ethnomusicology that have become significant sub-disciplines within the field.

Chapter 4 Oceania: Australia, Papua New Guinea, Hawai'i, Kiribati

Chenoweth, Vida. *A Music Primer for the North Solomons Province*. Ukarumpa, Papua New Guinea: Summer Institute of Linguistics, 1984.

Feld, Steven. *Sound and Sentiment: Birds, Weeping, Poetics, and Song in Kaluli Expression*, 2nd ed. Philadelphia: University of Pennsylvania Press, 1990.

Malm, William P. *Music Cultures of the Pacific, the Near East, and Asia*, 3rd ed. Englewood Cliffs, NJ: Prentice Hall, 1996 (1967).

Moyle, Alice M. *Songs from the Northern Territory*. Canberra, Australia: Australian Institute of Aboriginal Studies, 1974 (1967).

Moyle, Richard M. *Traditional Samoan Music*. Auckland, New Zealand: Auckland University Press, 1988.

Chapter 5 South Asia: India, Pakistan

Capwell, Charles. *The Music of the Bauls of Bengal*. Kent, OH: Kent State University Press, 1986.

Clayton, Martin. *Time in Indian Music: Rhythm, Metre, and Form in North Indian Rag Performance*. Oxford: Oxford University Press, 2000.

Kaufmann, Walter. *The Ragas of North India*. Bloomington: Indiana University Press, 1968.

_____. *The Ragas of South India*. Bloomington: Indiana University Press, 1976.

_____. *Sai Devotional Songs*. Tustin, CA: Sathya Sai Book Center of America, n.d.

Wade, Bonnie C. *Music in India: The Classical Traditions*. Englewood Cliffs, NJ: Prentice Hall, 1979.

Chapter 6 Southeast Asia: Vietnam, Thailand, Laos and Northeast Thailand, Indonesia (Java and Bali)

Becker, Judith. *Traditional Music in Modern Java: Gamelan in a Changing Society*. Honolulu: University of Hawaii Press, 1980.

Miller, Terry E. *Traditional Music of the Lao*. Westport, CT: Greenwood Press, 1985.

Morton, David. *The Traditional Music of Thailand*. Berkeley: University of California Press, 1976.

Nguyen, Thuyet Phong, ed. *New Perspectives in Vietnamese Music*. New Haven, CT: Department of International and Area Studies, Yale University, 1990.

Shahriari, Andrew. *Khon Muang Music and Dance Traditions of North Thailand*. Bangkok: White Lotus Press, 2005.

Spiller, Henry. *Gamelan: The Traditional Sounds of Indonesia*. Santa Barbara, CA: ABC-CLIO World Music Series, 2004.

Tenzer, Michael. *Gamelan Gong Kebyar: The Art of Twentieth-Century Balinese Music*. Chicago: University of Chicago Press, 2000.

Chapter 7 East Asia: China, Mongolia, Korea, Japan, Tibet

Garfias, Robert. *Music of a Thousand Autumns: The Togaku Style of Japanese Court Music*. Berkeley: University of California Press, 1975.

Heyman, Alan C. *Korean Musical Instruments*. New York: Oxford University Press, 1995.

Jones, Stephen. *Folk Music of China: Living Instrumental Tradition.* Oxford: Clarendon Press, 1992.
Liang, Mingyue. *Music of the Billion: An Introduction to Chinese Musical Culture.* New York: Heinrichshofen, 1985.
Mackerras, Colin. *The Rise of the Peking Opera, 1770–1870.* Oxford: Clarendon Press, 1972.
Malm, William P. *Japanese Music and Musical Instruments.* Tokyo: Tuttle, 1968 (1959).
Park, Chan E. *Voices from the Straw Mat: Toward an Ethnography of Korean Story Singing.* Honolulu: University of Hawaii Press, 2003.
Wichmann, Elizabeth. *Listening to Theatre: The Aural Dimension of Beijing Opera.* Honolulu: Hawaii University Press, 1998.

Chapter 8 The Middle East: Islam and the Arab World, Iran, Egypt, Turkey, Israel

During, Jean. *The Art of Persian Music.* Washington, DC: Mage Publishers, 1991.
Nettl, Bruno. *The Radif of Persian Music: Studies in Structure and Cultural Context.* Champaign, IL: Elephant & Cat, 1987.
Picken, Laurence. *Folk Music Instruments of Turkey.* London: Oxford University Press, 1975.
Shiloah, Amnon. *Jewish Musical Traditions.* Detroit, MI: Wayne State University Press, 1992.
_____. *Music in the World of Islam: A Socio-Cultural Study.* Detroit, MI: Wayne State University Press, 2003 (1995).
Touma, Habib Hassan. *The Music of the Arabs.* Portland, OR: Amadeus Press, 1996.

Chapter 9 Europe: Greece, Spain, Russia, Scotland, Ireland, Hungary, Bulgaria

Bohlman, Philip V. *The Study of Folk Music in the Modern World.* Bloomington: Indiana University Press, 1988.
_____. *The Music of European Nationalism: Cultural Identity and Modern History.* Santa Barbara, CA: ABC-CLIO World Music Series, 2004.
Chuse, Loren. *The Cantaoras: Music, Gender, and Identity in Flamenco Song.* New York: Routledge, 2003.
Nettl, Bruno. *Folk and Traditional Music of the Western Continents,* 3rd ed. Englewood Cliffs, NJ: Prentice Hall, 1990 (1965).
Rice, Timothy. *May It Fill Your Soul: Experiencing Bulgarian Music.* Chicago: University of Chicago Press, 1994.
Slobin, Mark, ed. *Retuning Culture: Musical Changes in Central and Eastern Europe.* Durham, NC: Duke University Press, 1996.
Totton, Robin. *Song of the Outcasts: An Introduction to Flamenco.* Portland, OR: Amadeus Press, 2003.

Chapter 10 Sub-Saharan Africa: Ghana, Nigeria, Central Africa, Zimbabwe, Uganda, Senegal, South Africa

Berliner, Paul F. *The Soul of Mbira.* Chicago: University of Chicago Press, 1993 (1981).
Charry, Eric. *Mande Music: Traditional and Modern Music of the Maninka and Mandinka of Western Africa.* Chicago: University of Chicago Press, 2000.
Chernoff, John Miller. *African Rhythm and Sensibility.* Chicago: University of Chicago Press, 1979.
Erlmann, Veit. *Nightsong: Performance, Power, and Practice in South Africa.* Chicago: University of Chicago Press, 1996.
Kisliuk, Michelle. *Seize the Dance! BaAka Musical Life and the Ethnography of Performance.* New York: Oxford University Press, 1998.
Locke, David. *Drum Gahu: An Introduction to African Rhythm.* Tempe, AZ: White Cliffs Media, 1998.
Nketia, J.H. Kwabena. *The Music of Africa.* New York: Norton, 1974.

Chapter 11 The Caribbean: Haiti, Jamaica, Trinidad and Tobago, Puerto Rico, Cuba, The Dominican Republic

Béhague, Gerard H., ed. *Music and Black Ethnicity: The Caribbean and South America.* London: Transaction Publishers, 1994.
Hill, Donald R. *Calypso Calaloo: Early Carnival Music in Trinidad.* Gainesville: University Press of Florida, 1993
Johnson, Howard, and Jim Pines. *Reggae: Deep Roots Music.* London: Proteus Books, 1982.
Manuel, Peter. *Popular Musics of the Non-Western World.* New York: Oxford University Press, 1988.
Stuempfle, Stephen. *The Steelband Movement: The Forging of a National Art in Trinidad and Tobago.* Philadelphia: University of Pennsylvania Press, 1995.

Waxer, Lise. *Situating Salsa: Global Markets and Local Meaning in Latin Popular Music.* New York: Routledge, 2002.

Wilcken, Lois. *The Drums of Vodou.* Tempe, AZ: White Cliffs Media, 1992.

Chapter 12 South America and Mexico: The Amazon Rainforest, Peru, Argentina, Brazil, Mexico

Almeida, Bira. *Capoeira: A Brazilian Art Form.* Berkeley, CA: North Atlantic Books, 1986.

Clark, Walter Aaron, ed. *From Tejano to Tango.* New York: Routledge, 2002.

Marbury, Elisabeth. *"Introduction." In Vernon and Irene Castle's Modern Dancing.* New York: World Syndicate, 1914.

Perrone, Charles A., and Christopher Dunn. *Brazilian Popular Music and Globalization.* New York: Routledge, 2002 (2001).

Seeger, Anthony. *Why Suyá Sing: A Musical Anthropology of an Amazonian People.* Cambridge, U.K.: Cambridge University Press, 1987.

Sheehy, Daniel. *Mariachi Music in America: Experiencing Music, Expressing Culture.* Oxford: Oxford University Press, 2005.

Stevenson, Robert. *Music in Mexico: A Historical Survey.* New York: Thomas Y. Crowell, 1952.

Turino, Thomas. *Moving Away from Silence: Music of the Peruvian Altiplano and the Experience of Urban Migration.* Chicago: University of Chicago Press, 1993.

Chapter 13 Canada and the United States

Cantwell, Robert. *Bluegrass Breakdown: The Making of the Old Southern Sound.* Urbana: University of Illinois Press, 1984.

Cobb, Buell E., Jr. *The Sacred Harp: A Tradition and Its Music.* Athens: University of Georgia Press, 1989 (1978).

Crawford, Richard. *The American Musical Landscape.* Berkeley: University of California Press, 1993.

Flanders, Helen Hartness. *Eight Traditional British-American Ballads.* Middlebury, VT: Middlebury College, 1951.

Herndon, Marcia. *Native American Music.* Hatboro, PA: Norwood, 1980.

Koskoff, Ellen, ed. *Music Cultures in the United States: An Introduction.* New York: Routledge, 2005.

Nettl, Bruno. *Blackfoot Musical Thought: Comparative Perspectives.* Kent, OH: Kent State University Press, 1989.

Oliver, Paul. *Songsters and Saints: Vocal Traditions on Race Records.* Cambridge, U.K.: Cambridge University Press, 1984.

Peña, Manuel. *The Texas-Mexican Conjunto: History of a Working-Class Music.* Austin: University of Texas Press, 1985.

Periodicals

There are several periodicals devoted to the study of world music. Among the most prominent are: *Ethnomusicology: Journal of the Society for Ethnomusicology* (www.ethnomusicology.org/), *Ethnomusicology Forum* (www.bfe.shef.ac.uk/), *Asian Music* (asianmusic.skidmore.edu/academics/asianmusic), and *The World of Music* (www.uni-bamberg.de/~ba2fm3/wom.htm). Two invaluable websites, *The Scholarly Journal Archive* (www.jstor.org) and *Project MUSE* (muse.jhu.edu), provide online access to many scholarly journals.

The journals mentioned above are varied in content, but all often include reviews of books, recordings, and video documentaries. Membership to the organizations that publish these journals is usually less than $100US and cheaper for students. Membership provides access to electronic forums and contact lists that will allow you to network with ethnomusicologists around the globe.

Visual Materials

Video Collections

The JVC Video Anthology of World Music and Dance. 30 vols. (1990)

The original series of thirty videotapes and nine books was produced in Japan by JVC, and offered clips of five hundred performances from one hundred countries. While this collection is quite valuable, it is also heavily oriented toward dance and does not include some important kinds of music—for example, Javanese gamelan. With fifteen volumes on Asia and two on the Americas, the collection is obviously weighted away from the Western hemisphere. Furthermore, certain features, such as the section "Soviet Union," date the collection. The volumes are arranged as follows: East Asia, 1–5; Southeast Asia, 6–10; South Asia, 11–15; the Middle East and Africa, 16–19; Europe, 20–22; Soviet Union, 23–26; the Americas, 27–28; Oceania, 29–30.

The JVC Smithsonian Folkways Video Anthology of World Music and Dance of the Americas. 6 vols. (1995)
Produced in the mid-1990s, this set of six videos and booklets offers 158 performances, making up for the paucity of clips from the Americas in the earlier set.

The JVC Smithsonian Folkways Video Anthology of World Music and Dance of Africa. 3 vols. (1995)
This set of three videos and booklets was produced in the mid-1990s and offers seventy-two performances from eleven countries in Africa.

The JVC Smithsonian Folkways Video Anthology of World Music and Dance of Europe. 2 vols. (1996)
Also produced in the mid-1990s, this set includes fifty-nine performances to supplement those in the original set.
Multicultural Media (www.multiculturalmedia.com) has produced a series of ten video documentaries on various topics. In conjunction with Lyrichord, Multicultural Media has also re-released a series of documentary films by Deben Battacharya.
Shanachie Entertainment Corporation (www.shanachie.com) has released numerous videos and DVDs, including Jeremy Marre's documentary series *Beats of the Heart.*
Certainly, any investigation of video resources today should begin with searches on the Internet, as a platform such as YouTube will likely provide much more current and higher quality video. The above resources are still useful for their "historical" value, if nothing else.

Audio Materials

It is not possible to list all the companies that produce world music audio materials. The following is a sampler of the best-known companies:

- ARCMusic (www.arcmusic.co.uk)
- Arhoolie (www.arhoolie.com)
- Auvidis (www.auvidis.com)
- Hugo Records (Hong Kong) (www.hugocd.com)
- King Records (World Music Library series) (www.kingrecords.co.jp)
- Multicultural Media (www.multiculturalmedia.com)
- Naxos Records (including the Marco Polo series) (www.naxos.com)
- PAN Records (Leiden, The Netherlands) Playa Sound Records (including the Air Mail Music series) (www.playasound.com)
- Rounder Records (www.rounder.com)
- Shanachie Entertainment Corp (including Yazoo Records) (www.shanachie.com)
- Smithsonian Folkways (www.folkways.si.edu)

Additional Resources

We have prepared a website to accompany this book: **www.routledge.com/cw/miller5e**. It includes additional listening examples and articles, plus photos and web links, among other features. The "On Your Own Time" sections originally in the third edition of this book are now on the website and intended as starting points for further explanation of world music and culture.
There are several institutions around the country with ethnomusicology programs for those that are interested in turning their interest in world music into a career. Most prominent among these is the program at UCLA in Los Angeles, California (www.ethnomusic. ucla.edu), though many others exist, including the MA program at Kent State University where the authors of this book are found.
A complete list of programs can be found on the SEM website (www.ethnomusicology. org) under Resources (webdb.iu.edu/sem/scripts/guidetoprograms/guidelist.cfm).
Archives are also a source of much useful information. Notable among these are the UCLA Ethnomusicology Archive (www.ethnomusic.ucla.edu/Archive/) and the Ethnomusicology Institute at Indiana University (www.indiana.edu/~folklore/ethnomusicologyinstitute.htm). Again, check the SEM website for a more complete list.

Index

Page numbers in **bold** refer to figures, page numbers in *italic* refer to tables.

Audio Examples

All examples can be found on the companion website: www.routledge.com/cw/miller5e

Chapter 4

Site 4.1 Australia: Aboriginal song. "Bushfire" by Alan Maralung with Peter Manaberu, from the recording entitled *The World's Musical Traditions, Vol. 4: Bunggridj-Bunggridj: Wangga Songs: Northern Australia* recorded by Allan Marett and Linda Barwick, SFW40430, courtesy of Smithsonian Folkways Recordings. ℗ © 1993. Used by permission.

Site 4.2 Papua New Guinea: *Susap*. "Badra Song from Buzi" ("Sounds of a *Susap*") performed by Amadu, recorded by Wolfgang Laade, Buki, Western Province, Papua New Guinea, 1964, by Amadu, Guiga, and Yabba, from the recording entitled *Music from South New Guinea*, Folkways 04216, courtesy of Smithsonian Folkways Recordings. ℗ © 1971. Used by permission.

Site 4.3 Hawai'i: Drum-dance chant. "Kau ka hali'a I ka manawa / Kaulīlua I ke anu Wai'ale'ale" (medley) by Noenoelani Zuttermeister Lewis and Hau'olionalani Lewis, from the recording entitled *Hawaiian Drum Dance Chants: Sounds of Power in Time*, SF 40015, provided courtesy of Smithsonian Folkways Recordings. ℗ © 1989. Used by permission.

Site 4.4 Kiribati: Group Song for bino. "Kai e titirou e matie," sung with clapping by men and women of Ititin Rotorua Dance Troupe, Betio Village, Tarawa Island, Kiribati; recorded by Mary Lawson Burke, 1981. Used by permission.

Chapter 5

Site 5.1 North India: Hindustani (Instrumental) Raga. "Khamaj" by Shamim Ahmed, from the recording entitled *India's Great Shamim Ahmed: Three Ragas*, MON00489, courtesy of Smithsonian Folkways Recordings. © 1967. Used by permission.

Site 5.2 South India: Carnatic Classical (Vocal) Kriti: "Manasā! Etulörttunë" Raga Malayamārutam, Rūpakam Tala, composed by Sri Tyāgarāja and performed by Sri V. Ramachandran, vocal; Sri S. Varadharajan, violin; Ramnad Sri Raghavan, mrdangam; Sri R. Balasubramaniam, kanjira; recorded at the 2002 St. Thyagaraja Festival by the Thyagaraja Aradhana Committee, Cleveland, Ohio, 2002. Used by permission.

Site 5.3 India: Hindu Bhajan devotional song. "Parvati Nandana Gajanana," recorded by Terry E. Miller at the Sai Baba Temple, Longdenville, Trinidad, 1985. Used by permission.

Site 5.4 Pakistan: Qawwali (Sufi devotional song). "Jamale kibriya main hoon" performed by the Sabri Brothers, from the recording entitled *Musiciens Kawwali du Pakistan/Les Fréres Sabri/Musique Soufli*, Vol. 3, Arion ARN 64147, 1991. Used by permission.

Chapter 6

Site 6.1 Vietnam: Upland bronze gong ensemble. Gong ensemble of the Jarai, Pleiku City, Pleiku province, recorded by Terry E. Miller and Phong Nguyen, from the recording entitled *Vietnam: Mother Mountain and Father Sea*, White Cliffs Media WCM 9991 (6 CDs and 47 pp. book), 2003. Used by permission.

Site 6.2   Vietnam: Tai tu amateur chamber music. "Xuan tinh (Spring Love)" performed by Nam Vinh, *dan kim*, Sau Xiu, *dan tranh*, and Muoi Phu, *dan co*, recorded by Terry E. Miller and Phong Nguyen, from the recording entitled *Vietnam: Mother Mountain and Father Sea*, White Cliffs Media WCM 1991 (6 CDs and 47 pp. book), 2003. Used by permission.

Site 6.3   Central Thailand: Classical piphat music. "Sathukan" and "Sathukan klawng," from the recording entitled *Wai Khru/The Traditional Music of Siam*, produced by The Committee of the College of Music Project, Mahidol University, Saliya, Thailand, 1994.

Site 6.4   Northeast Thailand: Lam klawn repartee singing. "Lam thang san" (excerpts) sung by Saman Hongsa (male) and Ubon Hongsa (female), and accompanied by Thawi Sidamni, khaen, recorded by Terry E. Miller in Mahasarakham, Thailand, 1988.

Site 6.5   Northeast Thailand: Phleng Luk thung popular song. "Sao Jan Kang Kop" sung by Phawnsak Sawng-saeng, from the recording entitled *Sao Jan Kang Kop*, JKC Marketing Co., Ltd, JKC-CD 157, n.d. Used by permission.

Site 6.6   Indonesia: Javanese court gamelan. "Udan Mas" ("Golden Rain"), from the recording entitled *Music of the Venerable Dark Cloud: The Javanese Gamelan Khjai Mendung*, Institute of Ethnomusicology, UCLA, IER 7501, 1973. Used by permission.

Site 6.7   Indonesia: Balinese gamelan gong kebyar. "Hudjan Mas," recorded in south Bali by a gamelan gong kebjar ensemble, from the recording entitled *Gamelan Music of Bali*, Lyrichord CD 7179, n.d. Used by permission, Multicultural Media Inc.

Chapter 7

Site 7.1   China: The guqin (seven-string zither). "Yangguang sandie" performed and recorded by Bell Yung, Pittsburgh, PA, 2002. Used by permission.

Site 7.2   China: *Sizhu* "Silk and bamboo" ensemble. "Huan Le Ge," recorded in Shanghai, People's Republic of China, 2007, by Terry E. Miller.

Site 7.3   China: Beijing opera (jingju). "Tao Ma Tan" (role), aria from Mu Ko Chai (opera), from the recording entitled *The Chinese Opera: Arias from Eight Peking Opera*, Lyrichord LLST 7212, n.d. Used by permission; Licensed from Multicultural Media Inc.

Site 7.4   China: *Chuida* "Wind and percussion" ensemble. "Taizi you" from the recording entitled *China: Chuida Wind and Percussive Instrumental Ensembles,* AUVIDIS-UNESCO D8209, 1992. Used with permission; Licensed from Multicultural Media Inc.

Site 7.5   Mongolia: Long song with "throat" singing. "Urtïn duu: Sünder Mountain," from the recording entitled *Mongolia: Living Music of the Steppes/Instrumental Music and Song of Mongolia*. Multicultural Media, MCM 3001, 1997. Used by permission.

Site 7.6   South Korea: P'ansori. "P'ansori, Ch'un-Hyang-Ka, Song of Spring Fragrance" sung by Mme. Pak Chowol with drum accompaniment by Han Ilsup, recorded by John Levy, from the recording entitled *Korean Social and Folk Music*, Lyrichord LLST 7211, n.d. Used by permission; Licensed from Multicultural Media Inc.

Site 7.7   Japan: *Gagaku*. "Entenraku," performed by the Kyoto Imperial Court Music Orchestra, from the recording entitled *Gagaku: The Imperial Court Music of Japan*, Lyrichord LYRCD 7126, n.d. Used by permission; Licensed from Multicultural Media Inc.

Site 7.8   Japan: Kabuki theater. Excerpt from "Dozyozi [Dojoji]" performed by the Kyoto Kabuki Orchestra, recorded by Jacob Feuerring, from the recording entitled *Japanese Kabuki Nagauta Music*. Lyrichord LLST 7134, n.d. Used by permission; Licensed from Multicultural Media Inc.

Site 7.9   Tibet: Buddhist ritual. "Genyen gi topa (In praise of Ge-nyen)," performed by the monks of Thimphu and nuns of Punakha, recorded by John Levy, from the recording entitled *Tibetan Buddhist Rites from the Monasteries of Bhutan, Volume 1: Rituals of the Drukpa Order*, Lyrichord LYRCD 7255, n.d. Used by permission, Multicultural Media Inc.

Chapter 8

Site 8.1   Islamic Call to Prayer: "Azan" by Saifullajan Musaev, from the recording entitled *Bukhara: Musical Crossroads of Asia*, SFW40050, courtesy of Smithsonian Folkways Recordings. ℗ © 1991. Used with permission.

Site 8.2   Arabic Taqsim for Ud and Buzuq. "Maqam Kurd" performed by Ali Jihad Racy, *buzuq*, and Simon Shaheen, *ud*, from the recording entitled *Taqasim: Improvisation in Arab Music*, Lyrichord LYRCD 7374., n.d. Used by permission; Licensed from Multicultural Media Inc.

Site 8.3   Iran: "Dastgah of Shour" by Khatereh Parvaneh, performed by Mohamed Heydari, *santour*, and Khatereh Parvaneh, voice, from the recording entitled *Classical Music of Iran: The Dastgah Systems*, SF 40039, provided courtesy of Smithsonian Folkways Recordings. ℗ © 1966. Used by permission.

Site 8.4   Egypt: *Takht* instrumental ensemble suite, recorded by the Middle Eastern Ensemble of the University of California, Santa Barbara, directed by Dr. Scott Marcus, 2011. Used by permission.

Site 8.5   Turkey: Sufi Dhikr ceremony. "Sufi Hymn", performed by Jarrahi Dervishes. Recorded by J. During, Konya, Turkey, 1982, from the recording entitled *The Silk Road: A Musical Caravan*, SF 40438, provided courtesy of Smithsonian Folkways Recordings. ℗ © 2002. Used by permission.

Site 8.6   Israel: Jewish shofar blowing and liturgical cantillation. "Cycle of 10 Calls During Additional Service" by David Hausdorff, from the recording entitled *Kol Ha'shofar* (Call of the Shofar), FW08922, courtesy of Smithsonian Folkways Recordings. ℗ © 1957. Used by permission. "L'dor vador" sung by Dr. Peter Laki, recorded by Terry E. Miller, Kent, Ohio, 2005. Used by permission.

Chapter 9

Site 9.1   Greece: Byzantine chant. "Come, Faithful," from the recording entitled *Byzantine Hymns of Christmas*, Society for the Dissemination of National Music, SDNM 101, n.d. Used by permission.

Site 9.2   Spain: Flamenco. "Alegrias" performed by Carlos Lomas and Pepe De Malaga, from the recording entitled *Andalusian Flamenco Song and Dance*, Lyrichord LYRCD 7388, n.d. Used by permission; Licensed from Multicultural Media Inc.

Site 9.3   Russia: Balalaika. "Yablochka," from the recording entitled *Eastern European Folk Heritage Concert: St. Nicholas Balalaika Orchestra*, Private issue, 2003. Courtesy of St. Nicholas Balalaika Orchestra.

Site 9.4   Scotland: Highland bagpipes by the City of Glasgow Police Pipe Band. "The Royal Scots Polka" and "The Black Watch Polka," from the recording entitled *All the Best from Scotland/ 35 Great Favorites*, Vol. 2, CLUC CD 77, n.d.

Site 9.5   Ireland: Uilleann bagpipes ("Piob Uilleann"). "The Lilies of the Field" and "The Fairhaired Boy," private studio recording by Eliot Grasso, 2011. Used by permission

Site 9.6   Hungary: Hurdy gurdy. Medley of traditional tunes performed by Sean Folson, Ft. Bragg, CA, 2003 (private studio recording). Used by permission.

Site 9.7   Georgia: Georgian choral singing. "Makruli" by Georgian Voices, from the recording entitled *Songs of Survival: Traditional Music of Georgia*, TSCD935D, courtesy of Topic Records, Ltd., ℗ © 2007. Used by permission.

Chapter 10

Site 10.1   Ghana: Polyrhythmic ensemble. "Vocal Band" by Odo ye few korye kuw Vocal Band (Love is Beautiful Unity Vocal Band), recorded by Roger Vetter, Abura Tuakwa, Ghana, 1984, from the recording entitled *Rhythms of Life, Songs of Wisdom: Akan Music from Ghana*, SFW40463, provided courtesy of Smithsonian Folkways Recordings. ℗ © 1996. Used by permission.

Site 10.2   Ghana: Talking drums. "Talking Drum" by Elizabeth Kumi and Joseph Manu, from the recording entitled *Rhythms of Life, Songs of Wisdom: Akan Music from Ghana*, SFW40463, courtesy of Smithsonian Folkways Recordings. ℗ © 1996. Used by permission.

Site 10.3   Nigeria: Jùjú popular music. "Oro Yi Bale," from the recording entitled *Bábá mo Túndé*, composed and arranged by King Sunny Adé and his African Beats. ℗ © 2010 Mesa/Blue Moon Recordings/ IndigeDisc. Used by permission.

Site 10.4   Central Africa: Pygmy song from the Democratic Republic of the Congo. "Elephant Song" performed by Mbuti Pygmies, from the recording entitled *Music of the Rain Forest Pygmies: The Historic Recordings Made by Colin M. Turnbull*, Lyrichord LYRCD 7157 (original recording, 1961). Used by permission; Licensed from Multicultural Media Inc.

Site 10.5   Zimbabwe: *Mbira dza vadzimu* Shona ancestral spirit song. "Nyama musango," performed by Elias Kunaka and Kidwell Mudzimirema (Mharadzirwa), recorded by John E. Kaemmer, Jirira, Zimbabwe, 1973. Used by permission.

Site 10.6   Uganda: Akadinda (xylophone) Baganda akadinda song. "Gganga aluwa" ("Gganga escaped with his life") performed by Sheikh Burukan Kiwuuwa and his group of royal akadinda musicians, recorded by Peter Cooke, Kidinda Village, Mpigi, Buganda, Uganda, 1987. Used by permission.

Site 10.7   Senegal: Jali with kora. "Kuruntu Kallafa" performed by Salieu Suso (kora), from the recording entitled *Griot: Salieu Suso*, Lyrichord LYRCD 7418, n.d. Used by permission; Licensed from Multicultural Media Inc.

Site 10.8   South Africa: Mbube vocal choir. "Phesheya Mama (Mama, they are overseas)" sung by the Utrecht Zulu Singing Competition, recorded by Gary Gardner and Helen Kivnick, 1984, from the recording entitled *Let Their Voices Be Heard: Traditional Singing in South Africa*. Rounder 5024, 1987. Used by permission of Concord Music Group, Inc.

Bonus Track South Africa: Ladysmith Black Mambazo, "Because I Love You," from the recording entitled *Wenyukela*, © Gallo Record Company, 2003, Courtesy of Gallo Record Company. Published by Gallo Music Publishers.

Chapter 11

Site 11.1 Haiti: Vodou ritual. Excerpts from "Bosou Djo Eya (Mayi rhythm)" performed by Sociètè Jour M'alongè Fòc Nan Point Dieu Devant, recorded by David Yih, Carrefour, Haiti, 1987, and "Guantanamo Song (Rara Rhythm, Southern Style)," recorded by Elizabeth McAlister, Port-au-Prince Haiti, 1993. From the recording entitled *Rhythms of Rapture: Sacred Musics of Haitian Vodou*. SF 40464, courtesy of Smithsonian Folkways Recordings. ℗© 1995. Used by permission.

Site 11.2 Jamaica: Reggae. "Torchbearer," composed by Carlos Jones and performed by Carlos Jones and the Plus Band, from the recording entitled *Roots with Culture*, Little Fish Records LF02912, 2004. Used by permission of Cross Track Music, Inc.

Site 11.3 Trinidad: Calypso. "Money is King" performed by Growling Tiger and the Trans-Caribbean All-Star Orchestra, from the recording entitled *Growling Tiger: High Priest of Mi Minor—Knockdown Calypsos*, Rounder 5006, 1979. Used by permission of Concord Music Group, Inc.

Site 11.4 Trinidad: Steel band. "Jump Up," performed by the Miami [Ohio] University Steel Band, from the recording entitled *One More Soca*, Ramajay Records. Used by permission.

Site 11.5 Puerto Rico: *Plena*. "Carmelina" by Los Pleneros de la 21, from the recording entitled *Para Todos Ustedes*, SFW40519, courtesy of Smithsonian Folkways Recordings. ℗© 2005. Used by permission.

Site 11.6 Cuba: Afro-Cuban Son. "Soneros Son" by Estudiantina Invasora, from the recording entitled *Music of Cuba*, FW04064, courtesy of Smithsonian Folkways Recordings. ℗© 1985. Used by permission.

Site 11.7 The Dominican Republic: Merengue. "Apágame la Vela (Put Out my Candle)" performed by Nicolá Gutierres, Porfirio Rosario and Santo Pea, recorded by Verna Gillis with Ramon Daniel Perez Martinez, 1976, from the recording entitled *Raíces Latinas: Smithsonian Folkways Latino Roots Collection*, SF 40470, provided courtesy of Smithsonian Folkways Recordings. ℗ © 2002. Used by permission.

Chapter 12

Site 12.1 Brazil: Amazonian Indian chant. "Nhiok: Okkaikrikti", performed by a group of Xikrin men, recorded by Max Peter Baumann, from the recording entitled *Traditional Music of the World, Vol. 7: Ritual Music of the Kayapó-Xikrin, Brazil*, SFW40433, courtesy of Smithsonian Folkways Recordings. ℗© 1995. Used by permission.

Site 12.2 Peru: Sikuri ensemble. "Qhantati Ururi: Easter Music" by n/a, from the recording entitled *Mountain Music of Peru*, Vol. 2, SFW40406, courtesy of Smithsonian Folkways Recordings. ℗© 1994. Used by permission.

Site 12.3 Argentina: Tango. "El choclo" ["The Ear of Corn"]: *Tango Criollo,* by René Marino, recorded by Tiago de Oliveiro Pinto, 1991, from the recording entitled *Traditional Music of the World, Vol. 5: Bandoneon Pure: Dances of Uruguay*, SFW40431, courtesy of Smithsonian Folkways Recordings. ℗© 1993. Used by permission.

Site 12.4 Brazil: Samba. "Agoniza, Mas Nao Morre (It Suffers But Doesn't Die)" performed by Nelson Sargento, Kuarup Records, from the recording entitled *Brazil Roots: Samba.* Rounder CD 5045, 1969. Used by permission.

Site 12.5 Brazil: Capoeira. "Rei Zumbi dos Palmares: Saia do Mar, Marinheiro" by Grupo de Capoeira Angola Pelourinho, from the recording entitled *Capoeira Angola from Salvador, Brazil*, SF 40465, provided courtesy of Smithsonian Folkways Recordings. ℗© 1996. Used by permission.

Site 12.6 Mexico: Mariachi. "Los Arrieros" by Nati Cano's Mariachi Los Camperos, from the recording entitled *¡Viva el Mariachi!: Nati Cano's Mariachi Los Camperos*, SFW40459, courtesy of Smithsonian Folkways Recordings. ℗© 2002. Used by permission.

Chapter 13

Site 13.1 Canada: Cape Breton fiddling. "E Minor Jigs" performed by Buddy MacMaster, fiddle, and Mac Morin, piano, from the recording entitled *Buddy MacMaster: The Judique Flyer*, Stephen MacDonald Productions, Atlantic Artists SMPCD 1012, n.d. Used by permission.

Site 13.2 USA: Ballad singing. "Edward" performed by Edith B. Price, from the recording entitled *Eight Traditional British-American Ballads from the Helen Hartness Flanders Collection*, Middlebury College, 1953. Used by permission.

Site 13.3 USA: Old Regular Baptist lined hymn. "And Must This Body Die," performed by congregation led by Elder Larry Newsome, from the recording entitled *Grace 'Tis a Charming Sound: Pleasant View Old Regular Baptist Church in Worship*. Privately issued CD by Terry E. Miller and members of the Advanced Field and Lab Methods in Ethnomusicology Class, Kent State University, Spring, 2000. Used by permission.

Site 13.4 USA: Singing school shape-note music. "Exhortation" performed by Sacred Harp singers at Hopewell Primitive Baptist Church near Cullman, Alabama, 1971. Recorded by Terry E. Miller. Used by permission.

Site 13.5   USA: Bluegrass. "True Life Blues" by Bill Monroe & The Blue Grass Boys, from the recording entitled *Live Recordings 1956-1969: Off the Record*, Vol. 1, SFW40063, courtesy of Smithsonian Folkways Recordings. ℗© 1993. Used by permission.

Site 13.6   USA: African-American spiritual. "Come and Go to That Land" recorded by Terry E. Miller at Gethsemene Baptist Church, Cleveland, Ohio, 1986. Used by permission.

Site 13.7   USA: African-American gospel choir. "God is Good All the Time" performed by New Hope Baptist Choir, from the recording titled *God is Good: The Total Musical Experience at New Hope Missionary Baptist Church, Akron, Ohio*. Privately issued CD by Terry E. Miller and members of the Advanced Field and Lab Methods in Ethnomusicology Class, Kent State University, Spring, 1998.

Site 13.8   USA: Country Blues, "Sweet Home Chicago" by Robert Johnson, from the recording entitled *The Complete Recordings*, Sony/BMG, 2008. Used by permission of Sony Music Entertainment.

Site 13.9   USA: Salsa. "Quitate de la Via Perico," performed by Tolú, from the recording entitled *Bongó de VanGogh*, Tonga Productions TNGCD 8405, 2002. Used by permission.

Site 13.10   USA: Cajun music. "La talle des ronces" performed by Adam and Cyprien Landreneau and Dewey Balfa, from the recording entitled *Lousiana Cajun from the Southwest Prairies*, recorded 1964–1967, Vol. 2, Rounder 6002, 1989. Used by permission of Concord Music Group, Inc.

Site 13.11   USA: Plains Chippewa song. "Rock Dance Song" performed by The Pembina Chippewa Singers, recorded by Nicholas Curchin Peterson Vrooman, Turtle Mountain, North Dakota, 1984, from the recording entitled *Plains Chippewa/Metis Music from Turtle Mountain*, SF 40411, courtesy of Smithsonian Folkways Recordings. ℗© 1992. Used by permission.

Site 13.12   USA: Native American flute. "Courting Song" by John Rainer, Jr., from the recording entitled *Music of New Mexico: Native American Traditions*, SFW40408, courtesy of Smithsonian Folkways Recordings. ℗© 1992. Used by permission.